Anthropology

Anthropology

WHAT DOES IT MEAN TO BE HUMAN?

SECOND EDITION

Robert H. Lavenda
St. Cloud State University

Emily A. Schultz
St. Cloud State University

New York   Oxford
OXFORD UNIVERSITY PRESS

Oxford University Press, Inc., publishes works that further Oxford University's
objective of excellence in research, scholarship, and education.

Oxford   New York
Auckland   Cape Town   Dar es Salaam   Hong Kong   Karachi
Kuala Lumpur   Madrid   Melbourne   Mexico City   Nairobi
New Delhi   Shanghai   Taipei   Toronto

With offices in
Argentina   Austria   Brazil   Chile   Czech Republic   France   Greece
Guatemala   Hungary   Italy   Japan   Poland   Portugal   Singapore
South Korea   Switzerland   Thailand   Turkey   Ukraine   Vietnam

For titles covered by Section 112 of the US Higher Education
Opportunity Act, please visit www.oup.com/us/he for the latest
information about pricing and alternate formats.

Published by Oxford University Press, Inc.
198 Madison Avenue, New York, New York 10016
http://www.oup.com

Library of Congress Cataloging-in-Publication Data

Lavenda, Robert H.
    Anthropology: what does it mean to be human? / Robert H. Lavenda, Emily A. Schultz.—
2nd ed.
       p. cm.
    Includes bibliographical references and index. ISBN: 978-0-19-539287-6
    1. Anthropology. I. Schultz, Emily A. (Emily Ann), 1949– II. Title.
    GN25.L38 2013
    301—dc23

                                                                    2011041708
Printing Number: 9 8 7 6 5 4

Printed in the United States of America
on acid-free paper

*To Beatrice G. Schultz and in memory of
Violet H. Lavenda, George Lavenda,
and Henry W. Schultz*

Contents in Brief

Contents

Chapter 3   What Can Evolutionary Theory Tell Us about Human Variation?   56

Chapter 6   How Do We Know about the Human Past?   152

Chapter 9   Why Is Understanding Human Language Important?   244

Chapter 10 How Do We Make Meaning?   282

Chapter 11 Why Do Anthropologists Study Economic Relations?   314

Chapter 12 How Do Anthropologists Study Political Relations?   338

Chapter 13 Where Do Our Relatives Come From and Why Do They Matter?   362

Chapter 14 What Can Anthropology Tell Us about Social Inequality?　404

Chapter 15 What Can Anthropology Tell Us about Globalization?   436

Boxes

Preface

This book emerged out of our increasing dissatisfaction with all the available general anthropology texts. We found that they either overwhelmed beginning students with detail and the sheer volume of material or else provided overly brief introductions that failed to convey the richness of the field. We therefore set out to write a book that introduces this broad field concisely yet thoroughly, providing diverse perspectives and examples to foster not only an appreciation of anthropology but also a deeper engagement with it—one that helps students better understand themselves and the world around them. We (and our students) needed a general anthropology text that struck the right balance, fit into a 15-week semester, and came with a complete package of ancillary materials including quizzes, exams, suggested videos, and supplemental readings.

Throughout the process of writing the first edition and revising for this second edition, two central questions have guided our decisions on what material to include. First, what is the essential material that a balanced introduction to four-field anthropology must cover? Second, how much detail on any particular topic could we include without overwhelming beginning students? Most general anthropology textbooks are essentially cultural anthropology textbooks that have bulked up, but we decided to start anew and build a general anthropology text chapter by chapter. We address the central issues of the discipline, highlighting the controversies and commitments that shape contemporary anthropology and that make it interesting and exciting.

Approach

This book may be concise, but we cover the field effectively and in a way that is intellectually honest. **We take a question-oriented approach that illuminates major concepts for students and shows them the relevance of anthropology in today's world.** Structuring each chapter around an important question and its subquestions, we explore what it means to be human, incorporating answers from all four major subfields of anthropology—biological anthropology, archaeology, linguistic anthropology, and cultural anthropology—as well as from applied anthropology. We have made every effort to provide a balanced perspective, both in the level of detail we present and in our coverage of the major subfields.

The questioning approach not only sparks curiosity but orients students' reading and comprehension of each chapter, highlighting the concepts every student should take away from a general anthropology course. For example, students need to know about evolutionary theory, human variation, and the biological, social, and cultural critique of the concept of race, since knowledge in these areas is one of the great achievements of the discipline of anthropology. No other discipline (and possibly no other course) will teach about these matters the way anthropologists do. Students need to know about the fossil evidence for the evolution of *Homo sapiens*, which they are not likely to learn about elsewhere. Students need to know what archaeology can tell us about the human past, as well as what ethnography can teach us about social complexity and inequality. They need to know that culture isn't just the Festival of Nations and unusual foods and interesting traditional costumes. They need to know about language and cognition and the central role of learning in human development. They need to understand the wellsprings of human creativity and imagination. It is valuable for them to see the panoply of forms of human relatedness, and how people organize themselves. They need to know about globalization from the bottom up and not just the top down. They need to see how all the subfields of anthropology together can provide important, unique insights into all these topics, and how anthropology can provide a vital foundation for their university education.

The world we face as anthropologists has changed dramatically in the last quarter century, and anthropology has changed, too. We have always felt it necessary to present students with a view of what contemporary anthropologists are doing; we therefore address the most current issues in the field and have thoroughly updated the text accordingly for this edition. Your students will take away from the book an appreciation of how these areas of specialization have developed over time, and how they contribute to our understanding of the world in the twenty-first century.

Organization

Divided into 15 chapters and 4 modules, this book is the ideal length for one semester. After Chapter 1, which introduces the entire field, 6 chapters are devoted to biological anthropology and archaeology: evolutionary theory (Chapter 2); human variation (Chapter 3); the primates (Chapter 4); the fossil record and human origins (Chapter 5); the human past (Chapter 6); and the first farmers, cities, and states (Chapter 7). Topics in cultural and linguistic anthropology are covered in chapters on culture (Chapter 8); language and cognition (Chapter 9); symbolic practices (Chapter 10, covering play, art, myth, ritual, and religion); economics (Chapter 11); politics (Chapter 12); kinship, marriage, and sexuality (Chapter 13); social inequality (Chapter 14, covering gender, class, caste, race, ethnicity, and nationalism); and globalization (Chapter 15). In addition, brief methodological modules after Chapters 1, 3, 8, and 9 discuss anthropology, science, and storytelling; dating methods for paleoanthropology and archaeology; ethnographic methods; and the components of language. Throughout the book, we incorporate discussions of gender and pay special attention to issues of power and inequality in the contemporary world.

Key Features

- **We take an explicitly global approach.** In addition to the substantially revised chapter on globalization, we systematically point out the extent to which the current sociocultural situation of particular peoples has been shaped by their particular histories of contact with capitalism, and we highlight ways that the post–Cold War global spread of capitalism has drastically reshaped the local contexts in which people everywhere live their lives.

- **We incorporate current anthropological approaches to power and inequality throughout the text.** We explore how power is manifested in different human societies, how it permeates all aspects of social life, and how it is deployed, resisted, and transformed. We discuss issues of trauma, social suffering, and human rights.

- **Material on gender and feminist anthropology is featured throughout the text.** In addition to the discussion of gender inequality in Chapter 14, the topic of gender is tightly woven into the fabric of the book, and includes (for example) material on gender and feminist archaeology, controversies over female genital cutting, supernumerary sexes and genders, varieties of human sexual practices, language and gender, women and electoral politics, gay marriage, women and colonialism, and contemporary forms of social inequality.

- **"In Their Own Words."** New voices, including those of indigenous peoples, anthropologists, and nonanthropologists, are presented in the text in commentaries called "In Their Own Words." These short commentaries provide alternative perspectives—always readable and sometimes controversial—on topics featured in the chapter where they appear.

- **"EthnoProfiles."** These text inserts provide a consistent, brief information summary for each society discussed at length in the text. They emerged from our desire as teachers to supply our students with basic geographical, demographic, and political information about the peoples anthropologists have worked with. Each EthnoProfile also contains a map of the area in which the society is found. They are not intended to be a substitute for reading ethnographies, nor are they intended to reify or essentialize the "people" or "culture" in question. Their main purpose is simply to provide a consistent orientation for readers, though of course it is becoming more and more difficult to attach peoples to particular territories in an era of globalization. How does one calculate population numbers or draw a simple map to locate a global diaspora? How does one construct an EthnoProfile for overseas Chinese or transborder Haitians? We don't know how to answer these questions, which is why EthnoProfiles for those groups are not included in the textbook.

- **"Anthropology in Everyday Life."** Following the suggestions of reviewers, we have provided selections on anthropology in practice throughout the text; topics include agricultural development, archaeology and community engagement, doing business in Japan, Human Terrain Teams, and forensic anthropology and human rights, among others.

- **Additional learning aids.** Key terms are boldfaced in the text and defined in a running glossary on the page where they appear, in addition to in a glossary at the back of the text. Each chapter ends with a list of the key terms in alphabetical order with page references, a numbered chapter summary, review questions, and annotated suggested readings. Maps are featured extensively throughout the text.

- **Use of citations and quotations.** In our discussions, we have tried to avoid being omniscient narrators by making use of citations and quotations in order to indicate where anthropological ideas come from. In our view, even first-year students need to know that an academic discipline like anthropology is constructed by the work of many people; no one, especially not textbook authors, should attempt to impose a single voice on the field. We have avoided, as much as we could, predigested statements that students must take on faith. We try to give them the information that they need to see where particular conclusions come from. In our experience, students appreciate being taken seriously.

- **Supplemental chapter materials provide flexibility for instructors.** As we considered how to create a new book for this course, we realized we would have to omit material that you may want your students to know about or that might interest them. To offer you flexibility, we decided to include some of that material on the Instructor's CD and on the Companion Website (www.oup.com/us/lavenda). Each entry ranges in length from one or two paragraphs to about three pages and can easily be used either for lecture topics or as handouts. For example, if you'd like to stress the different routes that led to the rise of civilization, you could assign the reading about the rise of civilization in Mesopotamia to supplement the textbook's discussion of the rise of civilization in the Andes. If you're looking for more examples to illustrate ritual and cultural patterns in the United States, you could assign the selection on children's birthday parties in the United States. The bulk of the supplemental chapter material on the Instructor's CD and website is linked to the cultural chapters, and many entries are additional ethnographic examples.

What's New in the Second Edition?

Taking into account our own experience using the first edition in our introductory classes, as well as the very helpful reviews commissioned by Oxford University Press, we have done a significant amount of revision for this edition. The entire book has undergone a close review for readability. We have carefully rethought and updated the content, honing it for effectiveness in a one-semester course that covers all aspects of what it means to be human.

Revision Highlights

- We include new discussions of gender and archaeology (Chapter 6), domestication (Chapter 7), social organization (Chapter 11), nutritional anthropology (Chapter 11), and aboriginality (Chapter 14).

- We have significantly updated the discussions of genetics and race (Chapters 2 and 3) and human origins (Chapter 5). We also made some complex discussions in these sections more readable and accessible, presenting concepts more concretely. The primatology and paleoanthropology chapters (4 and 5), which emphasize the broad outlines of human origins and evolution, have been brought up to date to include new fossils and interpretations, including Neandertal and Denisovan DNA studies. Our goal was to keep the level of detail manageable for students in a class that can devote only a few weeks of the semester to these areas of specialization.

- We expanded the discussions of economic and political relations and put them in separate chapters (11 and 12).

- Particularly in Chapter 6, we have significantly expanded our coverage of archaeology.

- We created "Anthropology in Everyday Life" boxes to continually show students the applicability of anthropology (e.g., forensic anthropology and human rights, Human Terrain Teams, and anthropological ethics). Rather than saving this discussion for the end of the book, as we did in the first edition, we now point out throughout the book the many ways anthropology can be used in the world.

- We include new "In Their Own Words" commentaries on DNA testing, reforming the Crow constitution, the fight over opening Peru's Amazon, gay marriage, attacks on Hungary's gypsies (Roma), Japan's Burakumin minority, and slum tourism.

- We now include a glossary at the back of the text in addition to the running glossary.

- In response to reviewer comments, we added a module on the components of language.

- We have worked the key elements of ethnographic fieldwork into Module 3, bringing the book's overall treatment of methods-oriented material into better balance.

- We have drawn attention to new ways that anthropologists address questions of inequality and struggles over meaning in our coverage of phenomena such as global flows of people, wealth, objects, images, and ideologies, including new discussions of transborder identities and struggles over human rights.

- Throughout, we have thoroughly updated the references and the annotated suggested readings.

- We have added "For Review" sections at the end of each chapter, which include discussion questions and prompts that connect chapters and support hands-on learning.

- We also now offer a series of higher-order critical-thinking questions, available online at **www.oup .com/us/lavenda**.

Chapter-by-Chapter Improvements

- *Chapter 1 What Is Anthropology?* We have streamlined this chapter but added material on sex and gender in discussing explanations for differences in human behavior. This chapter also now includes the "In Their Own Words" box "What Can You Learn from an Anthropology Major?"

- *Module 1: Anthropology, Science, and Storytelling.* We have brought the *Homo floresiensis* controversy up to date both in this module and later in the book.

- *Chapter 2: Why Is Evolution Important to Anthropologists?* This chapter continues to illustrate the innovative power of evolutionary theory by comparing it to the explanations that preceded it and provided the context within which it emerged. We have added an "Anthropology in Everyday Life" feature on forensic work by the Argentine Forensic Anthropology Team in identifying the "disappeared" in Argentina.

- *Chapter 3: What Can Evolutionary Theory Tell Us about Human Variation?* We have added a new section on the molecularization of race, as well as a new "In Their Own Words" selection on race and DNA testing. Also new is a brief segment that looks at how disease organisms have put selection pressures on human beings.

- *Module 2: Dating Methods in Paleoanthropology and Archaeology.* We have updated the discussions of dating methods.

- *Chapter 4: What Can the Study of Primates Tell Us about Human Beings?* All nomenclature and fossil information have been brought up to date. The

major goal of the chapter remains to give students an idea of the richness and variety of primate ways of life, and to provide a context for the discussion of human evolution in Chapter 5.

- *Chapter 5: What Can the Fossil Record Tell Us about Human Origins?* Chapter 5 has seen a lot of changes. We have updated all fossil references, revised nomenclature in light of the latest research, and added further material on "Ardi," *Ardipithecus ramidus.* The latest material on the status of *Homo floresiensis* is discussed in this chapter, as are recent studies about the evolution and significance of endurance running, the importance of fire in human evolution and digestive processes, and debates concerning Neandertal cannibalism. We introduce the "Mostly-Out-of-Africa" hypothesis for the spread of *Homo sapiens* and discuss the latest research on DNA studies of Neandertals and Denisovans, asking what it might mean to be 1–4 percent Neandertal. Finally, we discuss pre-Clovis tools found in Texas. We have also edited the chapter to be as clear and concise as possible in presenting what paleoanthropologists know best about the 6–7 million years of hominin evolution. The overall goal of the chapter remains to acquaint students with the best attested key features of the paleoanthropological story of human origins.

- *Chapter 6: How Do We Know about the Human Past?* We have significantly expanded our coverage of archaeology. This chapter includes a revised and expanded section on archaeology and gender, a revised and expanded discussion of collaborative approaches to studying the past, and a new "Anthropology in Everyday Life" section on archaeology as a tool of civic engagement. There is also a new, cutting-edge discussion of cosmopolitan archaeologies. This chapter maintains a substantial section called *Interpreting the Past,* which covers the way archaeologists use cultural anthropological work on subsistence strategies and social organizational types to interpret archaeological remains; we discuss both the advantages and disadvantages of this approach. Also continuing into this edition is a section called *Whose Past Is It?* that discusses NAGPRA and comparable legislation in Australia, followed by an update on the conflict over "Kennewick Man." A section called *Plundering the Past* addresses the looting of archaeological sites, and we also discuss the development of CRM archaeology in the United States and the commitment to stewardship that is coming to characterize the contemporary practice of archaeology.

- *Chapter 7: Why Did Humans Settle Down, Build Cities, and Establish States?* This chapter has a new discussion of niche construction and the rise of domestication.

- *Chapter 8: Why Is the Concept of Culture Important?* This chapter has been extensively revised. Sections that were more appropriately found in a cultural anthropology class have been eliminated, and the entire chapter has been tightened. The section on holism has been revised, and there is a new discussion of genital cutting and cultural relativism. The section "Does Culture Explain Everything?" has also been extensively revised.

- *Module 3: On Ethnographic Methods.* This module has been completely rethought and expanded with key sections taken from the first edition's chapter on ethnographic research. This revision brings the book's overall treatment of methods-oriented material into better balance. Key elements of contemporary ethnographic methodology and theory are still covered, but the level of detail has been reduced and streamlined. Our goal here is to emphasize that this is a four-field anthropology text, not a cultural book with a few additional chapters.

- *Chapter 9: Why Is Understanding Human Language Important?* This chapter now has a new introduction, new material on call systems and the evolution of language, and new material on the Whorfian question. There have been major revisions in the section on cognitive anthropology, including the elimination on an extended discussion of metaphor.

- *Module 4: Components of Language.* Based on reviewer requests, we have incorporated a module on the formal components of linguistics—phonology, morphology, syntax, and semantics. This is a lightly edited version of material that was online in the first edition. Each major subfield now has a module dedicated to methodological building blocks.

- *Chapter 10: How Do We Make Meaning?* We have renamed this chapter to better highlight what the chapter is about, and we have revised the section on myth. Overall, we have streamlined the chapter, though we have expanded the discussion of shamanism. Additional, related ethnographic examples from our cultural text, such as our discussion of sport, are available on the Companion Website at **www.oup.com/us/lavenda** and on the Instructor's Resource CD.

- *Chapter 11: Why Do Anthropologists Study Economic Relations?* As noted before, we have split the first edition's chapter on politics and economics into two chapters. This decision was based not only on our experience using the book but also on reviewers' recommendations. In addition to the materials on economic anthropology from the first edition, the chapter has a new introduction and a new section on the anthropology of food and nutrition. We have also added a new "In Their Own Words" feature based on material from *Questioning Collapse*, the anthropological critique of Jared Diamond's work.

- *Chapter 12: How Do Anthropologists Study Political Relations?* We have significantly revised the section on coercion, updated the Sri Lanka example with the defeat of the Tamil Tigers, and substantially revised the sections on governmentality and the power of the imagination. There is a new section on matrilineality and electoral politics in northern Thailand. We have made significant changes to the section on multiculturalism in Europe, and we have added to it a discussion of Islamic marriage in France, drawn from the work of John Bowen. We have added an "In Their Own Words" box on the Crow Indian constitution, and one on protestors in the Peruvian Amazon, and included "Anthropology in Everyday Life" segments on doing business in Japan and on Human Terrain Teams.

- *Chapter 13: Where Do Our Relatives Come From, and Why Do They Matter?* This chapter has been lightly edited and also now includes an "In Their Own Words" selection from Roger Lancaster, "Two Cheers for Gay Marriage."

- *Chapter 14: What Can Anthropology Tell Us about Social Inequality?* This chapter has been edited and continues to cover gender, class, caste, race, ethnicity, and nationalism.

- *Chapter 15: What Can Anthropology Tell Us about Globalization?* This chapter has been significantly edited and contains a new introduction. We have added a new section on Anna Tsing's *Friction* that deals with logging in Indonesia. We have also added a new "In Their Own Words" feature on slum tourism.

Supplements

- A free **Companion Website** at **www.oup.com/us/lavenda** features (1) **Instructor Resources**, including guest editorials (brief essays by anthropologists written specifically for our text), PowerPoint-based slides for lectures, an image bank containing digital versions of all of the images from the text, a sample syllabus, assignments, in-class activities, film suggestions and related questions by chapter, critical-thinking questions, suggestions for class discussion, and helpful links; (2) **Student Resources**, including a study skills guide (filled with hints and suggestions on improving study skills, organizing information, writing essay exams, and taking multiple-choice exams), self-quizzes, interactive exercises, video exercises, flashcards, chapter outlines, detailed annotated lists of suggestions for further reading (beyond the lists provided in the text), and helpful links; and (3) **Supplemental Chapter Materials**, which are materials we could not include in the text due to space constraints, but which you may wish to assign.

- Further Instructor Resources include a free **Computerized Test Bank and Instructor's Manual on CD** and free **Cartridges for Course Management Systems**, available from your Oxford University Press sales representative.

Acknowledgments

Our thanks to our new editor at Oxford, Sherith Pankratz, as well as development editors Thom Holmes and Lauren Mine. It has been a pleasure to work with them, as well as with production editor Barbara Mathieu. Editorial assistant Cari Heicklen has been wonderful in keeping track of and organizing all the details involved with a project of this magnitude. Finally, our thanks and gratitude to Jan Beatty, our editor since Mayfield days, for her support, her insight, and her friendship.

Once again, we are amazed at how much time and effort reviewers put into their task. The many reviewers and survey respondents for this project have contributed significantly to both the shape and the details of the book. We hope they can see where we have taken their advice, and we would like them to know that we carefully thought through every suggestion, even the ones we decided we could not follow. So, our thanks to the reviewers for this edition:

Jason Antrosio, Hartwick College
Mary Theresa Bonhage-Freund, Alma College
James L. Boone, University of New Mexico
Charles Ewen, East Carolina University
Vance Geiger, University of Central Florida
Rosalyn Howard, University of Central Florida
Ron Kephart, University of North Florida

Scott Lacy, Emory University
Scott S. Legge, Macalester College
Ian Lindsay, Purdue University
Bernard K. Means, Virginia Commonwealth University
Kathryn Molohon, Laurentian University
Ken Nystrom, SUNY New Paltz
Faidra Papavasiliou, Georgia State University
Geoff Pope, William Paterson University
Eleanora A. Reber, University of North Carolina at Wilmington
Charles Riggs, Fort Lewis College
John F. Scarry, University of North Carolina at Chapel Hill
Imanni Sheppard, University of Houston
Kristrina Shuler, Auburn University
Susan Kirkpatrick Smith, Kennesaw State University
William Walker, New Mexico State University
Frank Williams, Georgia State University

Our sincere thanks also to our supplement authors, who created high-quality additional resources specifically for this text:

Kelly Branam, St. Cloud State University (project assignments)
Bernard K. Means, Virginia Commonwealth University (detailed annotated further reading, PowerPoint presentations, sample syllabus)
Ken Nystrom, SUNY New Paltz (critical-thinking questions, in-class activities, self-quizzes, relevant links)
Cory Schneider, Oxford University Press contributor (interactive exercises)
Imanni Sheppard, University of Houston (film suggestions and film questions)

This book is dedicated to our parents, both living and in memory. Relatedness remains important in human societies, and as we grow older, we better understand why. So we also recognize our children, Daniel and Rachel, whose lives have been bound up with our books in so many ways, not the least of which are our hopes that they and their generation will find something of value in the anthropological approach.

Anthropology

What Is Anthropology?

1

This chapter introduces the field of anthropology. We look at what anthropology is and explore its different subfields. We touch on anthropology's key concept—culture—as well as its key research method—fieldwork. We conclude with a discussion of the ways anthropological insights are relevant in everyday life.

Chapter Outline

◀ *Children gathered in school playground with Maasai instructor.*

In early 1976, the authors of this book traveled to northern Cameroon, in western Africa, to study social relations in the town of Guider, where we rented a small house. In the first weeks we lived there, we enjoyed spending the warm evenings of the dry season reading and writing in the glow of the house's brightest electric fixture, which illuminated a large, unscreened veranda. After a short time, however, the rains began, and with them appeared swarms of winged termites. These slow-moving insects with fat, two-inch abdomens were attracted to the light on the veranda, and we soon found ourselves spending more time swatting at them than reading or writing. One evening, in a fit of desperation, we rolled up old copies of the international edition of *Newsweek* and began an all-out assault, determined to rid the veranda of every single termite.

The rent we paid for this house included the services of a night watchman. As we launched our attack on the termites, the night watchman suddenly appeared beside the veranda carrying an empty powdered milk tin. When he asked if he could have the insects we had been killing, we were a bit taken aback but warmly invited him to help himself. He moved onto the veranda, quickly collected the corpses of fallen insects, and then joined us in going after those termites that were still airborne. Although we became skilled at thwacking the insects with our rolled-up magazines, our skills paled beside those of the night watchman, who simply snatched the termites out of the air with his hand, squeezed them gently, and dropped them into his rapidly filling tin can. The three of us managed to clear the air of insects—and fill his tin—in about 10 minutes. The night watchman thanked us and returned to his post, and we returned to our books.

The following evening, soon after we took up our usual places on the veranda, the watchman appeared at the steps bearing a tray with two covered dishes. He explained that his wife had prepared the food for us in exchange for our help in collecting termites. We accepted the food and carefully lifted the lids. One dish contained *nyiri*, a stiff paste made of red sorghum, a staple of the local diet. The other dish contained another pasty substance with a speckled, salt-and-pepper appearance, which we realized was termite paste prepared from the insects we had all killed the previous night.

The night watchman waited at the foot of the veranda steps, an expectant smile on his face. Clearly, he did not intend to leave until we tasted the food his wife had prepared. We looked at each other. We had never eaten insects before or considered them edible in the North American, middle-class diet we were used to. To be sure, "delicacies" like chocolate-covered ants exist, but such items are considered by most North Americans to be food fit only for eccentrics. However, we understood the importance of not insulting the night watchman and his wife, who were being so generous to us. We knew that insects were a favored food in many human societies and that eating them brought no ill effects (Figure 1.1). So we reached into the dish of *nyiri*, pulling off a small amount. We then used the ball of *nyiri* to scoop up a small portion of termite paste, brought the mixture to our mouths, ate, chewed, and swallowed. The watchman beamed, bid us goodnight, and returned to his post.

We looked at each other in wonder. The sorghum paste had a grainy tang that was rather pleasant. The termite paste tasted mild, like chicken, not unpleasant at

Figure 1.1 Many people around the world eat insects. Here, a restaurant worker in Bangkok, Thailand, prepares grubs for cooking.

all. We later wrote to our families about this experience. When they wrote back, they described how they had told friends about our experience. Most of their friends had strong negative reactions. But one friend, a home economist, was not shocked at all. She simply commented that termites are a good source of clean protein.

What Is Anthropology?

This anecdote is not just about us, but also illustrates some of the central elements of the anthropological experience. Anthropologists want to learn about as many different human ways of life as they can. The people they come to know are members of their own society or live on a different continent, in cities or in rural areas. Their ways of life may involve patterns of regular movement across international borders, or they may make permanent homes in the borderlands themselves. Archaeologists reconstruct ancient ways of life from traces left behind in the earth that are hundreds or thousands of years old; anthropologists who strive to reconstruct the origin of the human species itself make use of fossil remains that reach back millions of years into the past. Whatever the case may be, anthropologists are sometimes exposed to practices that startle them. However, as they take the risk of getting to know such ways of life better, they are often treated to the sweet discovery of familiarity. This shock of the unfamiliar becoming familiar—as well as the familiar becoming unfamiliar—is something anthropologists come to expect and is one of the real pleasures of the field. In this book, we share aspects of the anthropological experience in the hope that you, too, will come to find pleasure, insight, and self-recognition from an involvement with the unfamiliar.

Anthropology can be defined as the study of human nature, human society, and the human past (Greenwood and Stini 1977). It is a scholarly discipline that aims to describe in the broadest possible sense what it means to be human. Anthropologists are not alone in focusing their attention on human beings and their creations. Human biology, literature, art, history, linguistics, sociology, political science, economics—all these scholarly disciplines and many more—concentrate on one or another aspect of human life. Anthropologists are convinced, however, that explanations of human activities will be superficial unless they acknowledge that human lives are always entangled in complex patterns of work and family, power and meaning.

What is distinctive about the way anthropologists study human life? As we shall see, **anthropology is holistic, comparative, field based, and evolutionary.** First, anthropology emphasizes that all the aspects of human life intersect with one another in complex ways. They shape one another and become integrated with one another over time. Anthropology is thus the integrated, or *holistic*, study of human nature, human society, and the human past. This **holism** draws together anthropologists whose specializations might otherwise divide them. At the most inclusive level, we may thus think of anthropology as the integrated (or holistic) study of human nature, human society, and the human past. Holism has long been central to the anthropological perspective and remains the feature that draws together anthropologists whose specializations might otherwise divide them.

Second, in addition to being holistic, anthropology is a discipline interested in **comparison**. To generalize about human nature, human society, and the human past requires evidence from the widest possible range of human societies. It is not enough, for example, to observe only our own social group, discover that we do not eat insects, and conclude that human beings as a species do not eat insects. When we compare human diets in different societies, we discover that insect eating is quite common and that our North American aversion to eating insects is nothing more than a dietary practice specific to our own society.

Third, anthropology is also a field-based discipline. That is, for almost all anthropologists, the actual practice of anthropology—its data collection—takes place away from the office and in direct contact with the people, the sites, or the animals that are of interest. Whether they are biological anthropologists studying chimpanzees in Tanzania, archaeologists excavating a site high in the Peruvian Andes, linguistic anthropologists learning an unwritten language in New Guinea, or cultural anthropologists studying ethnic identity in West Africa or small-town festivals in Minnesota, anthropologists are in direct contact with the sources of their data. For most anthropologists, the richness and complexity of this immersion in other patterns of life is one of our discipline's most distinctive features. Field research connects anthropologists directly with the lived experience of other people or other primates or to the material evidence of that experience that they have left behind. Academic anthropologists try

---

anthropology The study of human nature, human society, and the human past.

holism A characteristic of the anthropological perspective that describes, at the highest and most inclusive level, how anthropology tries to integrate all that is known about human beings and their activities.

comparison A characteristic of the anthropological perspective that requires anthropologists to consider similarities and differences in as wide a range of human societies as possible before generalizing about human nature, human society, or the human past.

to intersperse field research with the other tasks they perform as university professors. Other anthropologists—applied anthropologists—regularly spend most or all of their time carrying out field research. All anthropology begins with a specific group of people (or primates) and always comes back to them as well.

Finally, anthropologists try to come up with generalizations about what it means to be human that are valid across space and over time. Because anthropologists are interested in documenting and explaining change over time in the human past, **evolution** is at the core of the anthropological perspective. Anthropologists examine the *biological evolution* of the human species, which documents change over time in the physical features and life processes of human beings and their ancestors. Topics of interest include both human origins and genetic variation and inheritance in living human populations. If evolution is understood broadly as change over time, then human societies and cultures may also be understood to have evolved from prehistoric times to the present.

Anthropologists have long been interested in *cultural evolution*, which concerns change over time in beliefs, behaviors, and material objects that shape human development and social life. As we will see in Chapter 4, early discussions of cultural evolution in anthropology emphasized a series of universal stages. However, this approach has been rejected by contemporary anthropologists who talk about cultural evolution, like William Durham (1991) and Robert Boyd (e.g., Richerson and Boyd 2006). Theoretical debates about culture change and about whether it ought to be called "cultural evolution" or not are very lively right now, not only in anthropology but in related fields like evolutionary biology and developmental psychology. In the midst of this debate, one of anthropology's most important contributions to the study of human evolution remains the demonstration that biological evolution is not the same thing as cultural evolution. Distinction between the two remains important as a way of demonstrating the fallacies and incoherence of arguments claiming that everything people do or think can be explained biologically, for example, in terms of "genes" or "race" or "sex."

---

evolution A characteristic of the anthropological perspective that requires anthropologists to place their observations about human nature, human society, or the human past in a temporal framework that takes into consideration change over time.

culture Sets of learned behavior and ideas that human beings acquire as members of society. Human beings use culture to adapt to and to transform the world in which they live.

biocultural organisms Organisms (in this case, human beings) whose defining features are codetermined by biological and cultural factors.

What Is the Concept of Culture?

A consequence of human evolution that had the most profound impact on human nature and human society was the emergence of **culture**, which can be defined as sets of learned behavior and ideas that human beings acquire as members of society. Human beings use culture to adapt to and transform the world in which we live.

Culture makes us unique among living creatures. Human beings are more dependent than any other species on learning for survival because we have no instincts that automatically protect us and help us find food and shelter. Instead, we have come to use our large and complex brains to learn from other members of society what we need to know to survive. Learning is a primary focus of childhood, which is longer for humans than for any other species.

From the anthropological perspective, the concept of *culture* is central to explanations of why human beings are what they are and why they do what they do. Anthropologists are frequently able to show that members of a particular social group behave in a particular way *not* because the behavior was programmed by their genes, but because they observed other people and copied what they did. For example, North Americans typically do not eat insects, but this behavior is not the result of genetic programming. Rather, North Americans have been told as children that eating insects is disgusting, have never seen any of their friends or family eat insects, and do not eat insects themselves. As we discovered personally, however, insects can be eaten by North Americans with no ill effects. This difference in dietary behavior can be explained in terms of culture rather than biology.

However, to understand the power of culture, anthropologists must also know about human biology. Anthropologists in North America traditionally have been trained in both areas so that they can understand how living organisms work and become acquainted with comparative information about a wide range of human societies. As a result, they can better evaluate how biology and culture contribute to different forms of human behavior. Indeed, most anthropologists reject explanations of human behavior that force them to choose either biology or culture as the unique cause. Instead, they emphasize that human beings are **biocultural organisms**. Our biological makeup—our brain, nervous system, and anatomy—is the outcome of developmental processes to which our genes and cellular chemistry contribute in fundamental ways. It also makes us organisms capable of creating and using culture. Without these biological endowments, human culture as we know it would not exist. At the same time, our survival as biological organisms depends on learned ways of thinking and acting that help us find food, shelter, and mates and that teach us how to rear our children. Our biological endowment, rich as it is, does not provide us with instincts that would automatically take care of these survival needs. Human biology makes culture possible; human culture makes human biological survival possible.

What Makes Anthropology a Cross-Disciplinary Discipline?

Because of its diversity, anthropology does not easily fit into any of the standard academic classifications. The discipline is usually listed as a social science, but it spans the natural sciences and the humanities as well. What it is *not*, as we will see, is the study of the "exotic," the "primitive," or the "savage," terms that anthropologists reject. Figure 1.2 brings some order to the variety of interests found under the anthropological umbrella.

Traditionally, North American anthropology has been divided into four subfields: *biological anthropology, cultural anthropology, linguistic anthropology*, and *archaeology*. Because of their commitment to holism, many anthropology departments try to represent most or all of the subfields in their academic programs. However, universities in other parts of the world, such as Europe, usually do not bring all these specialties together. Many North American anthropologists, however, associate holistic four-field North American anthropology with the successful repudiation of nineteenth-century scientific racism by Franz Boas and other early twentieth-century anthropologists. They also value four-field anthropology as a protected "trading zone" within which anthropologists are encouraged to bring together fresh concepts and knowledge from a variety of research traditions. North American anthropologist Rena Lederman, for example, has stressed that four-field anthropology does not insist on a single way of bringing the subfields together (2005).

Anthropological holism is attractive even to those who were not trained in North America. British anthropologist Tim Ingold, for example, argues, "The best anthropological writing is distinguished by its receptiveness to ideas springing from work in subjects far beyond its conventional boundaries, and by its ability to connect these ideas in ways that would not have occurred to their originators, who may be more enclosed in their particular disciplinary frameworks" (1994, xvii). We share the views of Lederman and Ingold: trained in holistic, four-field anthropology, we continue to value the unique perspective it brings to the study of human nature, human society, and the human past. Indeed, as the organizers of a recent anthropological conference observed, "Even those who were the least persuaded that the traditional four-field organization of American anthropology was

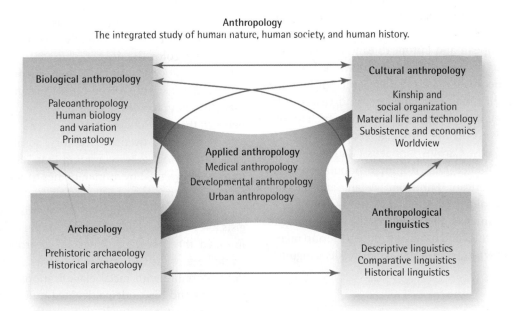

Anthropology
The integrated study of human nature, human society, and human history.

Biological anthropology
Paleoanthropology
Human biology and variation
Primatology

Cultural anthropology
Kinship and social organization
Material life and technology
Subsistence and economics
Worldview

Applied anthropology
Medical anthropology
Developmental anthropology
Urban anthropology

Archaeology
Prehistoric archaeology
Historical archaeology

Anthropological linguistics
Descriptive linguistics
Comparative linguistics
Historical linguistics

Figure 1.2 In the United States, anthropology is traditionally divided into four specialties: biological anthropology, cultural anthropology, anthropological linguistics, and archaeology. Applied anthropology draws on information provided by the other four specialties.

still viable (if it ever was) came away with a strong sense that the subfields had a great deal to say to one another and indeed needed one another" (McKinnon and Silverman 2005; viii).

Biological Anthropology

Since the nineteenth century, when anthropology was developing as an academic field, anthropologists have studied human beings as living organisms in order to discover what makes us different from or similar to other animals. Early interest in these matters was a by-product of centuries of exploration. Western Europeans had found tremendous variation in the physical appearance of peoples around the world and had long tried to make sense of these differences. Some researchers developed a series of elaborate techniques to measure different observable features of human populations, including skin color, hair type, body type, and so forth, hoping to find scientific evidence that would allow them to classify all the peoples of the world into a set of unambiguous categories based on distinct sets of biological attributes. Such categories were called **races**, and many scientists were convinced that clear-cut criteria for racial classification would be discovered if careful measurements were made on enough people from a range of different populations.

European scientists first applied racial categories to the peoples of Europe itself, but their classifications soon included non-European peoples, who were coming under increasing political and economic domination by expanding European and European American capitalist societies. These peoples differed from "white" Europeans not only because of their darker skin color but also because of their unfamiliar languages and customs. In most cases, their technologies were also no match for the might of the West. In the early eighteenth century, the European biologist Carolus Linnaeus (Carl von Linné, 1707–1778) classified known human populations into four races (American, European, Asian, and Negro) based on skin color (reddish, white, yellow, and black, respectively). Linnaeus also connected racial membership with the mental and moral attributes of group members. Thus, he wrote, Europeans were "fickle, sanguine,

blue-eyed, gentle, and governed by laws," whereas Negros were "choleric, obstinate, contented, and regulated by custom" and Asians were "grave, avaricious, dignified, and ruled by opinion" (Molnar 2001, 5–6).

In the nineteenth century, influential natural scientists such as Louis Agassiz, Samuel George Morton, Francis Galton, and Paul Broca built on this idea of race, ranking different populations of the world in terms of brain size; they found the brains of "white" Europeans and North Americans to be larger and saw the other "races" as representing varying grades of inferiority, with Africans ranked at the bottom (Gould 1996). These findings were used to justify the social practice of **racism**: the systematic oppression of members of one or more socially defined "races" by another socially defined "race" that is justified in terms of the supposed inherent biological superiority of the rulers and the supposed inherent biological inferiority of those they rule.

Biological or physical anthropology as a separate discipline had its origins in the work of scholars like these, whose training was in some other discipline, often medicine. Johann Blumenbach (1752–1840), for example, whom some have called the "father of physical anthropology," was trained as a physician. Blumenbach identified five different races (Caucasoid, Mongoloid, American, Ethiopian, and Malayan), and his classification was influential in the later nineteenth and twentieth centuries (Molnar 2001, 6). He and his contemporaries assumed that the races of "mankind" (as they would have said) were fixed and unchanging subdivisions of humanity.

However, as scientists learned more about biological variation in human populations, some of them came to realize that traits traditionally used to identify races, such as skin color, did not correlate well with other physical and biological traits, let alone mental and moral traits. Indeed, scientists could not even agree about how many human races there were or where the boundaries between them should be drawn.

By the early twentieth century, some anthropologists and biologists were arguing that "race" was a cultural label invented by human beings to sort people into groups and that races with distinct and unique sets of biological attributes simply did not exist. Anthropologists like Franz Boas, for example, who in the early 1900s founded the first department of anthropology in the United States, at Columbia University, had long been uncomfortable with racial classifications in anthropology. Boas and his students devoted much energy to debunking racist stereotypes, using both their knowledge of biology and their understanding of culture. As the discipline of anthropology developed in the United States, students were trained in both human biology and human culture to provide them with the tools to fight racial

races Social groupings that allegedly reflect biological differences.

racism The systematic oppression of one or more socially defined "races" by another socially defined "race" that is justified in terms of the supposed inherent biological superiority of the rulers and the supposed inherent biological inferiority of those they rule.

In Their Own Words

Anthropology as a Vocation

Listening to Voices

James W. Fernandez (Ph.D., Northwestern University) is a professor of anthropology at the University of Chicago. He has worked among the Fang of Gabon and among cattle keepers and miners of Asturias, Spain. This is an excerpt from an essay about the anthropological vocation.

For me, the anthropological calling has fundamentally to do with the inclination to hear voices. An important part of our vocation is "listening to voices," and our methods are the procedures that best enable us to hear voices, to represent voices, to translate voices.

By listening carefully to others' voices and by trying to give voice to these voices, we act to widen the horizons of human conviviality. If we had not achieved some fellow feeling by being there, by listening carefully and by negotiating in good faith, it would be the more difficult to give voice in a way that would widen the horizons of human conviviality. Be that as it may, the calling to widen horizons and increase human conviviality seems a worthy calling—full of a very human optimism and good sense. Who would resist the proposition that more fellow feeling in the world is better than less, and that to extend the interlocutive in the world is better than to diminish it?

At the same time, there is a paradox here, one that demands of us a sense of proportion. Although the anthropologist is called to bring diverse people into intercommunication, he or she is also called to resist the homogenization that lies in mass communication. We are called by our very experience to celebrate the great variety of voices in the human chorus. The paradox is that we at once work to amplify the scale of intercommunication—and in effect contribute to homogenization—while at the same time we work to insist on the great variety of voices in communication. We must maintain here too a sense of proportion. We must recognize the point at which wider and wider cultural intercommunication can lead to dominant voices hidden in the homogenizing process. Human intercommunication has its uses and abuses.

Source: Fernandez 1990, 14–15.

---

stereotyping. After World War II, this position gained increasing strength in North American anthropology, under the forceful leadership of anthropologist Sherwood Washburn. The "new" physical anthropology Washburn developed at the University of California, Berkeley, repudiated racial classification and shifted attention to patterns of variation and adaptation within the human species as a whole. This shift in emphasis led many of Washburn's followers to define their specialty as **biological anthropology**, a move that highlighted their differences with the older "physical anthropology" devoted to racial classification.

Some biological anthropologists work in the fields of **primatology** (the study of the closest living relatives of human beings, the nonhuman primates), **paleoanthropology** (the study of fossilized bones and teeth of our earliest ancestors), and human skeletal biology (measuring and comparing the shapes and sizes—or morphology—of bones and teeth using skeletal remains from different human populations) (Figure 1.3). Newer specialties focus on human adaptability in different ecological settings, on human growth and development, or on the connections between a population's evolutionary history and its susceptibility to disease. Forensic anthropologists use their knowledge of human skeletal anatomy to aid law enforcement and human rights investigators. Molecular anthropologists trace chemical similarities and differences in the immune system, an interest that has led to active research on the virus that causes HIV/AIDS. Moreover, new analytic techniques, such as biostatistics, three-dimensional imaging, and electronic communication and publishing, have revolutionized the field. In all these ways, biological anthropologists can illuminate what makes human beings similar to and different from one another, other primates, and other forms of life (Boaz and Wolfe 1995; Weinker 1995).

---

biological anthropology (or physical anthropology) The specialty of anthropology that looks at human beings as biological organisms and tries to discover what characteristics make them different from other organisms and what characteristics they share.

primatology The study of nonhuman primates, the closest living relatives of human beings.

paleoanthropology The search for fossilized remains of humanity's earliest ancestors.

Figure 1.3 Some biological anthropologists are primatologists, such as Jane Goodall (*a*). Other biological anthropologists are paleoanthropologists, such as Matthew Tornow, who studies ancient primate ancestors (*b*).

Whether they study human biology, primates, or the fossils of our ancestors, biological anthropologists clearly share many methods and theories used in the natural sciences—primarily biology, ecology, chemistry, and geology. What tends to set biological anthropologists apart from their nonanthropological colleagues is the holistic, comparative, and evolutionary perspective that has been part of their anthropological training. That perspective reminds them always to consider their work as only part of the overall study of human nature, human society, and the human past.

Cultural Anthropology

The second specialty within anthropology is **cultural anthropology**, which is sometimes called *sociocultural anthropology*, *social anthropology*, or *ethnology*. By the early twentieth century, anthropologists realized that racial biology could not be used to explain why everyone in the world did not dress the same, speak the same language,

pray to the same god, or eat insects for dinner. About the same time, anthropologists such as Margaret Mead were showing that the biology of sexual difference could not be used to predict how men and women might behave or what tasks they would perform in any given society. Anthropologists concluded that something other than biology had to be responsible for these variations. They suggested that this "something else" was culture.

Many anthropologists did significant research throughout the twentieth century to separate human biological variation from human cultural practices, showing that these practices could not be reduced to "racial" difference. By the latter part of the twentieth century, anthropologists also regularly distinguished between the biological **sex** of an individual and the culturally shaped **gender** roles considered appropriate for each sex in a given society. As we shall see throughout the text, attention to gender has become an integral part of all anthropological work. Because people everywhere use culture to adapt to and transform everything in the wider world in which they live, the field of cultural anthropology is vast.

Cultural anthropologists tend to specialize in one or another domain of human cultural activity (Figure 1.4). Some study the ways particular groups of human beings organize themselves to carry out collective tasks, whether economic, political, or spiritual. This focus within cultural anthropology bears the closest resemblance to the discipline of sociology, and from it has come the identification of anthropology as one of the social sciences.

Sociology and anthropology developed during the same period and share similar interests in social

---

cultural anthropology The specialty of anthropology that shows how variation in the beliefs and behaviors of members of different human groups is shaped by sets of learned behaviors and ideas that human beings acquire as members of society—that is, by culture.

sex Observable physical characteristics that distinguish two kinds of humans, females and males, needed for biological reproduction.

gender The cultural construction of beliefs and behaviors considered appropriate for each sex.

organization. What differentiated anthropology from sociology was the anthropological interest in comparing different forms of human social life. In the racist framework of nineteenth- and early-twentieth-century European and North American societies, some people viewed sociology as the study of "civilized" industrial societies and labeled anthropology as the study of all other societies, lumped together as "primitive." Today, by contrast, anthropologists are concerned with studying *all* human societies, and they reject the labels *civilized* and *primitive* for the same reason they reject the term *race*. Contemporary anthropologists do research in urban and rural settings around the world and among members of all societies, including their own.

Anthropologists discovered that people in many non-Western societies do not organize bureaucracies or churches or schools, yet they still manage to carry out successfully the full range of human activity because they developed institutions of relatedness that enabled them to organize social groups through which they could live their lives. One form of relatedness, called *kinship*, links people to one another on the basis of birth, marriage, and nurturance. The study of kinship has become highly developed in anthropology and remains a focus of interest today. In addition, anthropologists have described a variety of forms of social groups organized according to different principles, such as secret societies, age sets, and numerous forms of complex political organization, including states. In recent years, cultural anthropologists have studied contemporary issues of gender and sexuality, transnational labor migration, urbanization, globalization, the post–Cold War resurgence of ethnicity and nationalism around the globe, and debates about human rights.

Cultural anthropologists have investigated the patterns of material life found in different human groups. Among the most striking are worldwide variations in clothing, housing, tools, and techniques for getting food and making material goods. Some anthropologists specialize in the study of technologies in different societies or in the evolution of technology over time. Those interested in material life also describe the natural setting for which technologies have been developed and analyze the way technologies and environments shape each other. Others have investigated the way non-Western people have responded to the political and economic challenges of colonialism and the capitalist industrial technology that accompanied it.

People everywhere are increasingly making use of material goods and technologies produced outside their own societies. Anthropologists have been able to show that, contrary to many expectations, non-Western people do not slavishly imitate Western ways. Instead, they make use of Western technologies in ways that are creative and

Figure 1.4 Cultural anthropologist Robert Laughlin with members of the Sna Jtz'ibajom group puppet theater in San Cristóbal de las Casas, Mexico. Cultural anthropologists talk to many people, observe their actions, and participate as fully as possible in a group's way of life.

often unanticipated but that make sense in their own local cultural context. For example, some anthropologists are currently tracing the various ways in which populations both inside and outside the West make use of cybertechnology for their own social and cultural purposes.

As cultural anthropologists have become increasingly aware of the sociocultural influences that stretch across space to affect local communities, they have also become sensitive to those that stretch over time. As a result, many contemporary cultural anthropologists make serious efforts to place their cultural analyses in detailed historical context. Cultural anthropologists who do comparative studies of language, music, dance, art, poetry, philosophy, religion, or ritual often share many of the interests of specialists in the disciplines of fine arts and humanities.

Cultural anthropologists, no matter what their area of specialization, ordinarily collect their data during an extended period of close involvement with the people in whose language or way of life they are interested. This period of research, called **fieldwork**, has as its central feature the anthropologists' involvement in the everyday routine of those among whom they live. People who share information about their culture and language with anthropologists have traditionally been called **informants**; however, anthropologists use this term less today

---

fieldwork An extended period of close involvement with the people in whose language or way of life anthropologists are interested, during which anthropologists ordinarily collect most of their data.

informants People in a particular culture who work with anthropologists and provide them with insights about their way of life. Also called *respondents, teachers,* or *friends.*

and some prefer to describe these individuals as *respondents*, *collaborators*, *teachers*, or simply as *"the people I work with"* because these terms emphasize a relationship of equality and reciprocity. Fieldworkers gain insight into another culture by participating with members in social activities and by observing those activities as outsiders. This research method, known as *participant-observation*, is central to cultural anthropology.

Cultural anthropologists write about what they have learned in scholarly articles or books and sometimes document the lives of the people they work with on film or video. An **ethnography** is a description of "the customary social behaviors of an identifiable group of people" (Wolcott 1999, 252–3); **ethnology** is the comparative study of two or more such groups. Thus, cultural anthropologists who write ethnographies are sometimes called *ethnographers*, and anthropologists who compare ethnographic information on many different cultural practices are sometimes called *ethnologists*. But not all anthropological writing is ethnographic. Some anthropologists specialize in reconstructing the history of our discipline, tracing, for example, how anthropologists' fieldwork practices have changed over time and how these changes may be related to wider political, economic, and social changes within the societies from which they came and within which they did their research.

Linguistic Anthropology

Perhaps the most striking cultural feature of our species is **language**: the system of arbitrary vocal symbols we use to encode our experience of the world and of one another. People use language to talk about all areas of their lives, from material to spiritual. **Linguistic anthropology** therefore studies language, not only as a form of symbolic communication, but also as a major carrier of important cultural information. Many early anthropologists were the first people to transcribe non-Western languages and to produce grammars and dictionaries of those languages (Figure 1.5). Contemporary

Figure 1.5 Linguist Alan Rumsey listens to a warrior from highland New Guinea.

linguistic anthropologists and their counterparts in sociology (called *sociolinguists*) study the way language differences correlate with differences in gender, race, class, or ethnic identity. Some have specialized in studying what happens when speakers are fluent in more than one language and must choose which language to use under what circumstances. Others have written about what happens when speakers of unrelated languages are forced to communicate with one another, producing languages called *pidgins*. Some linguistic anthropologists study sign languages. Others look at the ways children learn language or the styles and strategies followed by fluent speakers engaged in conversation. More recently, linguistic anthropologists have paid attention to the way political ideas in a society contribute to people's ideas of what may or may not be said and the strategies speakers devise to escape these forms of censorship. Some take part in policy discussions about literacy and language standardization and address the challenges faced by speakers of languages that are being displaced by international languages of commerce and technology such as English.

In all these cases, linguistic anthropologists try to understand language in relation to the broader cultural, historical, or biological contexts that make it possible. Because highly specialized training in linguistics as well as anthropology is required for people who practice it, linguistic anthropology has long been recognized as a separate subfield of anthropology. Contemporary linguistic anthropologists continue to be trained in this way, and many cultural anthropologists also receive linguistics training as part of their professional preparation.

---

ethnography An anthropologist's written or filmed description of a particular culture.

ethnology The comparative study of two or more cultures.

language The system of arbitrary vocal symbols used to encode one's experience of the world and of others.

linguistic anthropology The specialty of anthropology concerned with the study of human languages.

Figure 1.6 Members of the Argentine Forensic Anthropologists Team work on the biggest dictatorship-era mass grave to date, where around 40 suspected victims of the 1976–1983 military junta were buried in a local cemetery in Córdoba, 800 km (500 miles) northwest of Buenos Aires.

Archaeology

Archaeology, another major specialty within anthropology, is a cultural anthropology of the human past involving the analysis of material remains. Through archaeology, anthropologists discover much about human history, particularly *prehistory*, the long stretch of time before the development of writing. Archaeologists look for evidence of past human cultural activity, such as postholes, garbage heaps, and settlement patterns. Depending on the locations and ages of sites they are digging, archaeologists may also have to be experts on stone-tool manufacture, metallurgy, or ancient pottery. Because archaeological excavations frequently uncover remains such as bones or plant pollen, archaeologists often work in teams with other scientists who specialize in the analysis of these remains.

Archaeologists' findings complement those of paleoanthropologists. For example, archaeological information about successive stone-tool traditions in a particular region may correlate with fossil evidence of prehistoric occupation of that region by ancient human populations. Archaeologists can use dating techniques to establish ages of *artifacts*, portable objects modified by human beings. They can create distribution maps of cultural artifacts that allow them to make hypotheses about the ages, territorial ranges, and patterns of sociocultural change in ancient societies. Tracing the spread of cultural inventions over time from one site to another allows them to hypothesize about the nature and

degree of social contact between different peoples in the past. The human past that they investigate may be quite recent: Some contemporary archaeologists dig through layers of garbage deposited by human beings within the last two or three decades, often uncovering surprising information about contemporary consumption patterns.

Applied Anthropology

Applied anthropology is the subfield of anthropology in which anthropologists use information gathered from the other anthropological specialties to propose solutions to practical problems (Figure 1.6). Some may use a particular group of people's ideas about illness and health to introduce new public health practices in a way that makes sense to and will be accepted by members of the group. Other applied anthropologists may use knowledge of traditional social organization to ease the problems of refugees trying to settle in a new land. Still others may use their knowledge of traditional and Western methods of cultivation to help farmers increase their

archaeology A cultural anthropology of the human past involving the analysis of material remains left behind by earlier societies.

applied anthropologists Specialists who use information gathered from the other anthropological specialties to solve practical cross-cultural problems.

crop yields. Given the growing concern throughout the world with the effects of different technologies on the environment, this kind of applied anthropology holds promise as a way of bringing together Western knowledge and non-Western knowledge in order to create sustainable technologies that minimize pollution and environmental degradation. Some applied anthropologists have become management consultants or carry out market research, and their findings may contribute to the design of new products.

In recent years, some anthropologists have become involved in policy issues, participating actively in social processes that attempt to shape the future of those among whom they work (Moore 2005, 3), and this has involved a change in their understanding of what applied anthropology is. Les W. Field, for example, has addressed the history of applied anthropology on Native American reservations—"Indian Country"—in the United States. He observes that by the end of the twentieth century, a major transformation had occurred, "from applied anthropology in Indian Country to applications of anthropological tools in Indian country to accomplish tribal goals" (2004, 472). This often draws anthropologists into work in the legal arena, as when, for example, they have lent their expertise to arguments in favor of legislation mandating the repatriation of culturally significant artifacts and tribal lands in North America or to efforts by tribal groups to reclaim official government-recognized status (Field 2004), or to defending indigenous land rights in Latin America (Stocks 2005).

Although many anthropologists believe that applied work can be done within any of the traditional four fields of anthropology, increasing numbers in recent years have come to view applied anthropology as a separate field of professional specialization (see Figure 1.2). More and more universities in the United States have begun to develop courses and programs in a variety of forms of applied anthropology. Anthropologists who work for government agencies or nonprofit organizations or in other nonuniversity settings often describe what they do as the *anthropology of practice*. In the twenty-first century, it has been predicted that more than half of all new Ph.D.s in anthroplogy will become practicing anthropologists rather than take up positions as faculty in university departments of anthropology.

---

medical anthropology The specialty of anthropology that concerns itself with human health—the factors that contribute to disease or illness and the ways that human populations deal with disease or illness.

Medical Anthropology

Medical anthropology is one of the most rapidly growing branches of anthropology. Beginning half a century ago as a form of applied anthropology, it has developed into an important anthropological specialty that has offered new ways to link biological and cultural anthropology. Medical anthropology concerns itself with human health—the factors that contribute to disease or illness and the ways that human populations deal with disease or illness (Baer et al. 2003, 3). Medical anthropologists may consider the physiological variables that are involved with human health and disease, the environmental features that affect human well-being, and the way the human body adapts to various environments. Contemporary medical anthropologists engage in work that directly addresses the anthropological proposition that human beings must be understood as biocultural organisms (Figure 1.7).

Particularly significant has been the development of *critical medical anthropology*, which links questions of human health and illness in local settings to social, economic, and political processes operating on a national or global scale. Indeed, critical medical anthropologists have been among the most vocal in pointing out how various forms of suffering and disease cannot be explained only by the presence of microbes in a diseased body, but may depend on—or be made worse by—the presence of social inequality and a lack of access to health care. According to anthropologist Merrill Singer, critical medical anthropology "is committed to the 'making social' and the 'making political' of health and medicine" (1998, 195). Thus, critical medical anthropologists pay attention to the way social divisions based on class, "race," gender, and ethnicity can block access to medical attention or make people more vulnerable to disease and suffering. They draw attention to the way traditional Western biomedicine "encourages people to fight disease rather than to make the changes necessary to prevent it," for example, by linking low birth weight in newborn babies to poor nutrition, but failing to note that poor nutrition "may be a major health factor among impoverished social classes and oppressed ethnic groups in developed countries despite an abundance of food in society generally" (Singer 1998, 106, 109).

One of the most important insights of critical medical anthropologists has been to point out that "various practices that bioculturalist anthropologists have traditionally called 'adaptations' might better be analyzed as social adjustments to the consequences of oppressive sociopolitical relationships" (M. Singer 1998, 115). Gavin

Figure 1.7 Medical anthropologist Andrea Wiley is shown here in a high–altitude setting in the Himalayas of Ladakh (India), where she studied maternal and child health.

Smith and R. Brooke Thomas, for example, draw attention to situations where "social relations compromise people's options" for attaining biological well-being and cultural satisfaction but where people do not passively accept this situation and choose instead to "try to escape or change these relations"; Smith and Thomas call these practices "adaptations of resistance" (G. Smith and Thomas 1998, 466). In later chapters we cite case studies by medical anthropologists that illustrate the complex and nuanced views they are able to bring to the explanation and treatment of human suffering.

The Uses of Anthropology

Why take a course in anthropology? An immediate answer might be that human fossils or broken bits of ancient pots or the customs of faraway peoples inspire a fascination that is its own reward. But the experience of being dazzled by seemingly exotic places and peoples carries with it a risk. As you become increasingly aware of the range of anthropological data, including the many options that exist for living a satisfying human life, you may find yourself wondering about the life you are living. Contact with the unfamiliar can be liberating, but it can also be threatening if it undermines your confidence in the absolute truth and universal rightness of your previous understanding of the way the world works.

The contemporary world is increasingly interconnected. As people from different cultural backgrounds come into contact with one another, learning to cope with cultural differences becomes crucial. Anthropologists experience both the rewards and the risks of getting to know how other people live, and their work has helped to dispel many harmful stereotypes that sometimes make cross-cultural contact dangerous or impossible. Studying anthropology may help prepare you for some of the shocks you will encounter in dealing with people who look different from you, speak a different language, or do not agree that the world works exactly the way you think it does.

Anthropology involves learning about the kinds of living organisms we human beings are, the various ways we live our lives, and how we make sense of our experiences. Studying anthropology can equip you to deal with people with different cultural backgrounds in a less threatened, more tolerant manner. You may never be called on to eat termite paste. Still, you may one day encounter a situation in which none of the old rules seem to apply. As you struggle to make sense of what is happening, what you learned in anthropology class may help you relax and dare to try something totally new to you. If you do so, perhaps you too will discover the rewards of an encounter with the unfamiliar that is at the same time unaccountably familiar. We hope you will savor the experience.

In Their Own Words

What Can You Learn from an Anthropology Major?

The Career Development Center at SUNY Plattsburgh developed a document that highlights what students typically learn from a major in anthropology.

1. **Social agility**

   In an unfamiliar social or career-related setting, you learn to quickly size up the rules of the game. You can become accepted more quickly than you could without this anthropological skill.

2. **Observation**

   You must often learn about a culture from within it, so you learn how to interview and observe as a participant.

3. **Analysis and planning**

   You learn how to find patterns in the behavior of a cultural group. This awareness of patterns allows you to generalize about the group's behavior and predict what they might do in a given situation.

4. **Social sensitivity**

   Although other people's ways of doing things may be different from your own, you learn the importance of events and conditions that have contributed to this difference. You also recognize that other cultures view your ways as strange. You learn the value of behaving toward others with appropriate preparation, care, and understanding.

5. **Accuracy in interpreting behavior**

   You become familiar with the range of behavior in different cultures. You learn how to look at cultural causes of behavior before assigning causes yourself.

6. **Ability to appropriately challenge conclusions**

   You learn that analyses of human behavior are open to challenge. You learn how to use new knowledge to test past conclusions.

7. **Insightful interpretation of information**

   You learn how to use data collected by others, reorganizing or interpreting the data to reach original conclusions.

8. **Simplification of information**

   Because anthropology is conducted among publics as well as about them, you learn how to simplify technical information for communication to nontechnical people.

9. **Contextualization**

   Although attention to details is a trait of anthropology, you learn that any given detail might not be as important as its context and can even be misleading when the context is ignored.

10. **Problem solving**

    Because you often function within a cultural group or act on culturally sensitive issues, you learn to approach problems with care. Before acting, you identify the problem, set your goals, decide on the actions you will take, and calculate possible effects on other people.

11. **Persuasive writing**

    Anthropologists strive to represent the behavior of one group to another group and continually need to engage in interpretation. You learn the value of bringing someone else to share—or at least understand—your view through written argument.

12. **Assumption of a social perspective**

    You learn how to perceive the acts of individuals and local groups as both shaping and being shaped by larger sociocultural systems. The perception enables you to "act locally and think globally."

Source: Omohundro 2000.

Chapter Summary

1. Anthropology aims to describe in the broadest sense what it means to be human. The anthropological perspective is holistic, comparative, and evolutionary and has relied on the concept of culture to explain the diversity of human ways of life. Human beings depend on cultural learning for successful biological survival and reproduction, which is why anthropologists consider human beings to be biocultural organisms. Anthropology is also a field-based discipline. In the United States today, anthropology is considered to have five major subfields: biological anthropology, archaeology, cultural anthropology, linguistic anthropology, and applied anthropology.

2. Biological anthropology began as an attempt to classify all the world's populations into different races. By the early twentieth century, however, most anthropologists had rejected racial classifications as scientifically unjustifiable and objected to the ways in which racial classifications were used to justify the social practice of racism. Contemporary anthropologists who are interested in human biology include biological anthropologists, primatologists, and paleoanthropologists.

3. Cultural anthropologists study cultural diversity in all living human societies, including their own. Linguistic anthropologists approach cultural diversity by relating varied forms of language to their cultural contexts. Both gather information through fieldwork, by participating with their informants in social activities, and by observing those activities as outsiders. They publish accounts of their research in ethnographies. Archaeology is a cultural anthropology of the human past, with interests ranging from the earliest stone tools to twenty-first-century garbage dumps. Applied anthropologists use information from the other anthropological specialties to solve practical cross-cultural problems. Medical anthropology overlaps biological anthropology, cultural anthropology, and applied anthropology and concerns itself with human health and illness, suffering, and well-being.

For Review

1. What is anthropology, as defined in the text?
2. What are the four distinctive approaches anthropologists take to the study of human life?
3. How do anthropologists define culture?
4. What makes anthropology a cross-disciplinary discipline?
5. Describe the main subfields of modern anthropology.
6. What are some of the main topics of interest in biological anthropology?
7. What are some of the main topics of interest in cultural anthropology?
8. Summarize the difference between ethnography and ethnology.
9. What do linguistic anthropologists try to learn about human languages?
10. What are some of the things archaeologists study?
11. How is applied anthropology connected to the other branches of anthropology?
12. What is critical medical anthropology?

Key Terms

anthropology   5
applied anthropology   13
archaeology   13
biocultural organisms   6
biological anthropology
    (or physical
    anthropology)   9

comparison   5
cultural anthropology   10
culture   6
ethnography   12
ethnology   12
evolution   6
fieldwork   11

gender   10
holism   5
informants   11
language   12
linguistic
    anthropology   12
medical anthropology   14

paleoanthropology   9
primatology   9
races   8
racism   8
sex   10

Suggested Readings

Ashmore, Wendy, and Robert J. Sharer. 2009. *Discovering our past: A brief introduction to archaeology*, 5th ed. New York: McGraw-Hill. *An engaging introduction to the techniques, assumptions, interests, and findings of modern archaeology.*

Besteman, Catherine, and Hugh Gusterson (eds). 2005. *Why America's top pundits are wrong: Anthropologists talk back.* Berkeley: University of California Press. *According to the editors, "pundits" are media personalities—conservative and liberal—who lack authoritative knowledge on important issues but whose confident, authoritative, and entertaining pronouncements attract large audiences, especially when they defend simplified views of issues that reinforce rather than challenge popular prejudices. Twelve anthropologists offer critical assessments of the writings of pundits Samuel Huntington, Robert Kaplan, Thomas Friedman, and Dinesh D'Sousa and also explore questionable popular accounts of the origins of racial inequality and sexual violence.*

Feder, Kenneth L. 2011. *Frauds, myths and mysteries: Science and pseudoscience in archaeology*, 7th ed. New York: McGraw-Hill. *An entertaining and informative exploration of fascinating frauds and genuine archaeological mysteries that also explains the scientific method.*

Kidder, Tracy. 2004. *Mountains beyond mountains: The quest of Dr. Paul Farmer, a man who would cure the world.* New York, Random House. *Kidder follows Dr. Farmer, an anthropologist and physician, relating his efforts to enlist powerful funders, the World Health Organization, and ordinary people in neglected communities in a quest to bring the best modern medicine to those who need it most.*

Relethford, John. 2009. *The human species: An introduction to biological anthropology*, 8th ed. New York: McGraw-Hill. *An excellent, clear introduction to biological anthropology.*

Strang, Veronica. 2009. *What anthropologists do.* Oxford: Berg. Written for students, this book provides illustrations of many ways anthropology is being used in everyday life.

Module 1: Anthropology, Science, and Storytelling

"Things are similar: this makes science possible. Things are different: this makes science necessary" (Levins and Lewontin 1985, 141). Many anthropologists claim that their attempts to explain human nature, human society, and the human past are scientific. A scientific approach is what distinguishes the ethnographer from the tourist, the archaeologist from the treasure hunter. But scientists are clearly not the only people who offer explanations for the intriguing and often contradictory features of our world. People in all societies tell stories about why we are the way we are and why we live the way we do. What makes these nonscientific explanations different from the scientific explanations of an anthropologist?

Scientific and Nonscientific Explanations

In some respects, scientific and nonscientific explanations of the way the world works have much in common. For one thing, scientists today are more aware than ever before of the fact that scientific theorizing is a form of storytelling (Landau 1984). Like the tales collected by anthropologists from peoples all over the world, scientific theories offer narrative accounts of how things got to be the way they are.

Consider the following two extracts taken from longer narratives. The first is from the Amazon and is part of the creation story of the Desana (Tukano) people (Figure M1.1):

> The sun created the Universe and for this reason he is called Sun Father (*pagé abé*). He is the father of all the Desana. The Sun created the Universe with the power of his yellow light and gave it life and stability. From his dwelling place, bathed in yellow reflections, the Sun made the earth, with its forests and rivers, with its animals and plants. The Sun planned his creation very well, and it was perfect.
>
> The world we live in has the shape of a large disk, an immense round plate. It is the world of men and animals, the world of life. While the dwelling place of the Sun has a yellow color, the color of the power of the Sun, the dwelling place of men and animals is of a red color, the color of fecundity and of the blood of living beings. Our earth is *maria turí*, and is called the "upper level" (*vekámaha turí*) because below is another world, the "lower level" (*dohkámaha turí*). The world below is called *Ahpikondia*, Paradise. Its color is green, and the souls of those who were good Desana throughout their life go there. . . . Seen from below, from Ahpikondia, our earth looks like a large cobweb. It is transparent, and the Sun shines light through it. The threads of this web are like the rules that men should live by, and they are guided by these threads, seeking to live well, and the Sun sees them. . . .

Figure M1.1   Desana (Tukano) man playing panpipes.

> The Sun created the animals and the plants. To each one he assigned the place he should live. He made all of the animals at once, except the fish and the snakes; these he made afterward. Also, together with the animals, the Sun made the spirits and the demons of the forest and the waters.
>
> The Sun created all of this when he had the yellow intention—when he caused the power of his yellow light to penetrate, in order to form the world from it. (Reichel-Dolmatoff 1971, 24–25)

The second extract comes from an American work on modern physics:

> At the start of the lepton era the universe is one ten-thousandth of a second old, the temperature is 1 trillion Kelvin (10^{12} K) and each cubic centimeter of the cosmic quantum soup weighs about a thousand tons. The universe consists of a mixture of approximately equal numbers of photons, electrons, electron

neutrinos, muons, muon neutrinos, some other particles like pions . . . and their antiparticles, plus a relatively small "contamination" of equal numbers of protons and neutrons which are no longer in equilibrium with the other particles. . . .

As the temperature falls from its value at the beginning of the lepton era, the production threshold for the muons is crossed. All the muons and antimuons now annihilate into electrons, positrons and muon and electron neutrinos. Any excess charge of the muons can be passed on to the electrons. . . . For this reason no muons survive the muon slaughter. . . .

At the end of the lepton era all the heavy leptons, muons and tauons have disappeared, while hordes of neutrinos flood the universe but no longer interact with anything. Photons, electrons and antielectrons are still in equilibria, creating and destroying one another. When the temperature falls below the production threshold to create electron–positron pairs, most of the pairs annihilate into photons. This temperature threshold marks the beginning of the photon era. . . .

At the first second (which marks the beginning of the photon era, which goes on to last for 300,000 years), the temperature of the photons was 10 billion Kelvin and the density of the radiation about 100 kilograms (about 220 pounds) per cubic centimeter—a very thick viscous fluid of light. . . . (Pagels 1985, 250–53)

Both the Desana story and the scientific story might be called **myths**—as long as we use this term the way anthropologists use it. For anthropologists, myths are stories that recount how various aspects of the world came to be the way they are. The power of myths comes from their ability to make life meaningful for those who accept them. The truth of myths seems self-evident because they effectively integrate personal experiences with a wider set of assumptions about the way society, or the world in general, operates. In everyday speech, by contrast, the term *myth* is used to refer to a story that is false. To be sure, origin myths like the Desana tale contain marvelous and fantastic elements that stretch the credulity of ordinary sensible

---

myths Stories that recount how various aspects of the world came to be the way they are. The power of myths comes from their ability to make life meaningful for those who accept them. The truth of myths seems self-evident because they effectively integrate personal experiences with a wider set of assumptions about the way society, or the world in general, must operate.

science The invention of explanations about what things are, how they work, and how they came to be that can be tested against evidence in the world itself.

---

folk. Still, the anthropological understanding of myth does not assume that myths are necessarily false. Stories that survive to become myths usually connect in important ways with everyday human experiences in a particular society. But what about stories that recount events that we could never experience personally, such as the origin of the universe? If we study a variety of origin myths from different cultural traditions, we learn that many of these stories differ substantially from one another. Since nobody alive today was around when the world began or when our ancestors first walked its surface, how could we ever find out what actually happened?

For increasing numbers of people over the past few centuries, the answer to this question has lain with science. The growth of modern science in western Europe and its spread throughout the world are largely a result of scientists' belief that the answers to the history of the world could be found in the world itself if only people looked at the world in a new way. **Science** was a new worldview claiming that "the world of phenomena is a consequence of the regular operation of repeatable causes and their repeatable effects, operating roughly along the lines of known physical law" (Lewontin 1983, xxvi). Scientists believed that remarkable new insights about the universe, the objects in it, and even ourselves could be gained if we carried out observations according to a new set of rules.

These rules were first set on a firm foundation by Isaac Newton (Figure MI.2). A pious Christian, Newton did not doubt that God had created the universe, yet he believed that the universe God had created was orderly, that the movements of objects within it were constrained by laws discoverable by human reason, and that those laws could be precisely described using the language of mathematics. Newton's approach gained followers because it was extremely successful at describing and predicting, exactly as it had promised. Moreover, different observers could independently test the descriptions and predictions, and scientific knowledge could grow as the verified predictions were retained and the unverified predictions were discarded. Most fatefully, the new, scientifically verified knowledge about nature's laws could be put to work to transform nature in unprecedented ways. It appeared that human desires could be satisfied through scientific mastery of the material world. For many people, the practical application of scientific discoveries in astronomy, navigation, and industry became the clinching proof of scientific superiority.

Niles Eldredge and Ian Tattersall, two prominent evolutionary biologists, have written that science is "storytelling, albeit of a special kind. Science is the invention of explanations about what things are, how they work, and how they came to be. There are rules, to be sure: for a statement to be scientific, we must be able to go to nature and assess how

Figure M1.2 One of the founders of the new worldview of science, Sir Isaac Newton (1642–1727), made major contributions to mathematics, optics, and experimental investigation.

well it actually fits our observations of the universe" (1982, 1). Indeed, these rules give science its particular dynamic, for science is firmly and explicitly committed to open-ended self-correction. If ideas about the way the world works can be shown not to fit our observations of the universe, then the scientist must reject those ideas, regardless of the consequences, and invent better ones.

Scientists believe that the answers to questions about how the world works can be found by going to the world itself. Put another way, science is *empirical*, based on concrete experience and observation. Scientists have never been content to observe the world without getting their hands dirty. Scientific theories must build on and be tested against direct physical contact with real objects in the world. Of course, scientists did not invent trial-and-error experimentation with the material world; that activity lies behind the technical achievements of all human societies. Nevertheless, scientific research has taken experimentation to a new level of complexity. Using elaborate tools that are themselves the

product of previous scientific work, scientists have engaged in increasingly refined experimental manipulation of material objects and processes in the world. One result of this activity has been the production of more sophisticated stories about the way the world works. The success and persuasive power of evolutionary biology, for example, are due in no small measure to the fact that scientists have been able to generate new evidence about the living world, reinterpret old evidence, and produce a new story that remains richer, more comprehensive, and more fruitful than any of its rivals.

Some Key Scientific Concepts

The first step in understanding scientific stories is to master a few key concepts that are part of every scientist's vocabulary. In this section, we introduce some terms you will encounter frequently as you read this book. Special attention must be paid to the way scientists define these terms because they are also often used in everyday speech with rather different meanings. Six terms are particularly important: assumptions, evidence, hypotheses, testability, theories, and objectivity.

Assumptions   **Assumptions** are basic, unquestioned understandings about the way the world works. Under ordinary circumstances, most human beings do not question whether the sun will come up in the morning; it is taken for granted. The sun has always risen in the morning as far back as anyone can remember. If you want to go birdwatching tomorrow, you might be concerned about how cold it will be or whether it will rain; but you need not worry whether the sun will rise.

Everybody, scientist or not, operates on the basis of assumptions. If we did not take certain basic things about the world for granted, we would never be able to get anything done. Scientists are particularly concerned about the assumptions they bring to their observations of the natural world because the significance of what they see and measure is never obvious. If their observations are guided by incorrect assumptions about the way the world works, their measurements will be meaningless and the conclusions they draw from those measurements will be misleading.

Evidence   In science, **evidence** refers to what we can see when we examine a particular part of the world with great care. The structures and processes of living cells as revealed

---

assumptions Basic, unquestioned understandings about the way the world works.

evidence What is seen when a particular part of the world is examined with great care. Scientists use two different kinds of evidence: material and inferred.

under the microscope, the systematic distribution of related species of birds in neighboring geographical regions, the different kinds of bones found together again and again in the same geological strata—these are examples of the kinds of evidence scientists use to support theories of biological evolution. There are two different kinds of evidence: material and inferred.

Material evidence consists of things—material objects—themselves, information recorded about them, or scientific measurements made of them. In the study of human origins, for example, bones and stones are the most conspicuous forms of material evidence (Figure M1.3a) but so are careful records (including photographs) of other material objects recovered from the site of an excavation. The precise geological layering at a site is an important form of material evidence but so are objects at a site (e.g., certain kinds of rocks or baked clay) that can be subjected to forms of laboratory analysis that yield reliable information about the dates when they formed. For cultural anthropologists, ritual performances observed and transcribed in the field constitute material evidence (Figure M1.3b). Material evidence is ordinarily what scientists mean when they refer to "the facts" or "the data."

Material evidence has two striking attributes. First, "the facts" can be inspected by anyone who wants to examine them. Like cowpats in a pasture, the facts exist in their own

right, and their existence, shape, and position cannot be ignored by people who wish to walk through the particular field and keep their shoes clean. Second, the facts cannot speak for themselves. That a particular accumulation of bones and stones was found at a certain place in an archaeological site and that certain people perform a particular ritual are material facts verifiable by inspection. How or why the bones and stones got there or what the ritual means may be far from obvious. This leads to the second kind of evidence used by scientists: the interpretation put on material evidence.

Inferred evidence is material evidence plus interpretation. As one paleoanthropologist observes, "We can all see a bone and know it is a bone, but what it is 'evidence' for depends upon one's interpretation" (Clarke 1985, 176–77). Interpretation begins with the simple description of individual objects or events and is followed by the description of patterns of distribution of similar objects and events. The final stage of interpretation consists of elaborate explanatory frameworks that link many different objects or events to one another by drawing on findings from many different fields of knowledge. The connection between material evidence and inferred evidence is an intimate one. Several scientists examining the same material evidence frequently emphasize different descriptions and construct different explanations of what it is and how it got there. Rather than the facts speaking for

Figure M1.3 That particular material features, such as this pot (*a*) are found in an archaeological site and that the people of Bali perform a certain dance (*b*) are material facts, verifiable by inspection. How or why the pot came to be here and what it was used for or what this dance means may be far from obvious and must be inferred.

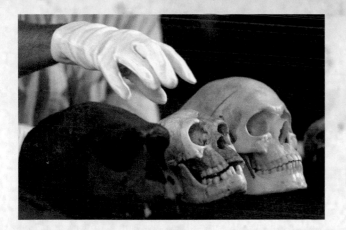

Figure M1.4 Ancient hominin bones from the Indonesian island of Flores (the skull is pictured above, between a *Homo erectus* skull on the left and a modern human skull on the right) have been the subject of much debate among paleontologists.

themselves, the observers speak to one another about the facts in an attempt to make sense of them.

The discovery of ancient hominin bones on the Indonesian island of Flores in 2003 has sparked much debate among paleontologists (Figure M1.4). The bones are tens of thousands of years old and look human but are unusually small. Some paleontologists have argued that the bones belonged to modern humans who suffered from a disease that reduced their stature. Other paleontologists insist that the bones show no morphological signs of such disease and that they most likely represent a previously undiscovered species of *Homo*. Further, they argue that this species evolved to have a small stature in response to selective pressures associated with living on an island, a phenomenon known as *insular dwarfing*. Others prefer to withhold judgment until more fossil evidence is available.

As you will see, scientific debate about evolution has long involved just this sort of interpretive dialogue. But it is important to remember that the debates about interpretation would be pointless without something to interpret. Science is more than just "the data," but it can never get too far away from the data before it is not science anymore. The data are the pretext and the context for debate among observers. The data, in their stubborn materiality, set limits to the kinds of interpretation that are scientifically plausible.

Hypotheses   Scientists state their interpretations of data in the form of **hypotheses**, which are statements that assert a particular connection between fact and interpretation, such as "The bones found at the Hadar site in Ethiopia belonged to an extinct form of primate that appears ancestral to modern

human beings." Hypotheses are also predictions about future data based on data already in hand. On the basis of the Hadar findings, paleoanthropologists might hypothesize as follows: "Bones similar to those found at Hadar are likely to be found in geological strata of the same age elsewhere in eastern Africa." Indeed, hypotheses of the latter kind have guided paleoanthropologists in their search for fossils of human ancestors. The impressive collections of fossils of all kinds that have been amassed over the past couple of centuries show just how successful such hypotheses have been in guiding scientific discovery.

Testability   **Testability** is the scientific requirement that a hypothesis must be matched against nature to see whether it is confirmed or refuted. That is, our assertion about the connection between fact and interpretation must be subject to testability if it is to be regarded as a scientific hypothesis.

How might we test the hypothesis about the bones from the Hadar site? The first step would be to make sure the bones were not simply those of a modern primate that had recently died. If examination of the bones revealed them to be permeated by mineral deposits, making them hard and stonelike, we would be justified in concluding that they were very old because such a process takes a long time. The next step might be to compare the fossil bones with the bones of living primates, human and nonhuman, to see how they matched. If the bones from Hadar appeared more similar to the bones of humans than to the bones of monkeys or apes, we would be justified in concluding that we had found the bones of an organism ancestral to modern humans. Our confidence in the correctness of the original hypothesis would increase, especially if a number of experts in primate anatomy agreed.

Why would the experts not simply claim, however, that the fossils from Hadar belonged to a human being just like ourselves who happened to have lived and died millions of years ago? What would lead them to conclude that these fossils belonged to a primate ancestral to modern human beings? The answer to this question depends on just how similar to modern human bones the Hadar fossils appeared to be. Paleoanthropologists would be justified in assigning the bones from Hadar to an ancestor of modern humans if the bones, though clearly humanlike, nevertheless differed in some significant respect from the bones of modern

---

hypotheses Statements that assert a particular connection between fact and interpretation.

testability The ability of scientific hypotheses to be matched against nature to see whether they are confirmed or refuted.

human beings. If the bones were significantly smaller than those of modern human beings, if the teeth were significantly larger in proportion to the jaw, if the skull were significantly smaller, if the arm bones were relatively longer in proportion to the leg bones, if the finger and toe bones appeared curved—all these traits would suggest strongly that the bones from Hadar, though humanlike, did not belong to a modern human being.

In addition, if the same geological strata yielding the Hadar bones produced the fossils of other organisms that were equally unlike the bones of living animals, we might well conclude that we had discovered the remains of more than one extinct animal species. The plausibility of our original hypothesis about the bones from the Hadar site would be further strengthened.

Some hypotheses, however, may not be subject to testability. That is, there may be no way, even in principle, to find evidence in nature that could show a hypothesis to be false. As a result, even if such a hypothesis were correct, it could not be considered a scientific hypothesis. Suppose someone were to hypothesize that all of the fossils from the Hadar site (together with all the objects in every geological layer on the surface of the earth) had been placed in the ground 10,000 years ago by aliens from another planet. These aliens had the desire and the skill to trick us about the history of life on earth. Is such a hypothesis testable? What sort of evidence could nature give us that would either confirm or refute such a hypothesis?

Certainly, if we found the remains of sophisticated technological devices alongside the fossil bones, we would instantly suspect that the site was very odd. Our suspicion might be confirmed if laboratory analysis reported that these devices were constructed using materials and engineering principles unknown on earth. Our suspicion would deepen if the remains of similar devices began to appear regularly in paleontological digs, and it would become more than suspicion if datable remains from every site, analyzed by a variety of laboratory techniques, consistently turned out to be around 10,000 years old! But what if no such material evidence were ever found? What if nothing in any archaeological site suggested the presence of high technology, alien or otherwise? What if the objects recovered from digs turned out to vary in age in a manner consistent with the geological layers in which they were found? What if only a few sites could be reliably dated to 10,000 years ago and

many more could be reliably dated to either older or more recent times?

Perhaps die-hard supporters of the alien story might offer a new hypothesis. They might claim that the aliens were so amazingly skilled that they were able to arrange the pattern of burial so as to trick us into thinking we were observing a series of deposits laid down over time. The aliens were so fiendishly clever that they were able to chemically treat the objects they buried in a way that would make them yield misleading dates—a pattern of misleading dates—whenever they were subjected to laboratory analysis!

We now have a new alien hypothesis to consider, but this time we cannot call it a scientific hypothesis. The first version of the alien hypothesis was not confirmed: it was tested against nature and did not match. But there is no way of testing the new hypothesis that aliens carried out this massive task of rearranging the layers in the earth's crust and tampering with its contents. If scientists objected that the bones and stones in their laboratories showed no evidence of chemical tampering, a defender of the new hypothesis could reply that this demonstrated how adept the aliens were at covering their tracks. Indeed, any evidence offered by a scientist to refute the new hypothesis would simply be interpreted by supporters as another part of the alien scheme to deceive earthlings.

In the absence of any evidence to support it and the presence of overwhelming evidence against it (all the patterned geological deposits with older or younger dates, cross-checked by more than one dating method), the new alien hypothesis holds no scientific interest. This does not mean that scientists have proved beyond question that aliens never visited our planet or buried fake fossils in our soil; it does mean, however, that the alien hypothesis need not be taken seriously by scientists. Under these circumstances, to continue to support the alien hypothesis would be to leave the realm of science and enter the realm of science fiction.

Theories In everyday speech, we frequently use the word *theory* to refer to an explanation that is as likely to be false as it is to be true. Indeed, we tend to invent "theories" in the absence of evidence. This is why we often plead "It's just a theory" in order to defend ourselves against critics who demand that we produce evidence to back up our claims. In science, the contrary is true. Scientists speak of a **scientific theory** only when they are able to link up a series of testable hypotheses in a coherent manner in order to explain a body of material evidence. Scientific theories are the combined result of sifting data, testing hypotheses, and imagining how all the resulting information might be put together in an

---

scientific theory A coherently organized series of testable hypotheses used to explain a body of material evidence.

enlightening way. Scientific theories are taken seriously because they account for a wide range of material evidence in a coherent, persuasive manner even though their hypotheses remain open to testing and possible falsification. The most powerful theories in science, such as the theory of relativity or the theory of evolution, are valued not just because they explain more of the material evidence than their competitors but also because their central hypotheses are open to testing and potential falsification—and yet, after repeated tests, they have never been disconfirmed.

It is often the case that the same body of material evidence, interpreted in different ways, gives rise to rival theories. Scientists have long been involved in a lively dialogue with one another about the meaning of material evidence, as well as about what should count as material evidence in the first place. This scientific give-and-take helps refine and strengthen some theories over time while exposing the weaknesses of others. Areas in which scientists agree at one period, however, may be reopened for debate at a later time, when new material evidence or a new hypothesis, or both, arises. As scientists compare their theories not only with nature but also with the theories of their rivals, their understanding is deepened and their theories are revised.

Objectivity   One reason scientific findings are highly respected is that they are considered objective. But what do we mean when we speak of "objectivity"? The meaning of this concept in Western thought has varied over time, but by the nineteenth century **objectivity** had acquired the meaning many people associate with it today: a judgment about some feature of the world that is free of individual idiosyncrasies (Daston 1999, 111). Western science has traditionally emphasized the demands that objectivity places on individual scientists. From this point of view, objectivity can be defined as "the separation of observation and reporting from the researcher's wishes" (Levins and Lewontin 1985, 225). Because theories are rooted in material evidence, new material evidence can tip the balance in favor of one theory over its alternatives or expose all current theories as inadequate. Scientific researchers who faithfully report results even when these results undermine their own pet hypotheses would be viewed as objective in this individual sense.

But scientific objectivity may also be understood as an attribute of communities of scientists, not just of individual researchers. Most historians and philosophers of science recognize that science as it developed in western Europe has always been a social activity. The testability of scientific hypotheses, for example, makes sense only when we understand that an individual's work is carried out in a scientific community whose members share their work, in the form of public presentations or articles in professional journals. Members of the same scientific community scrutinize each other's stories about nature, testing to see if they are confirmed or disconfirmed, in a process called "peer review." Public evaluation of scientists' work ideally appeals to the same standards for everyone, and members of the community are expected to be responsive to the observations of all knowledgeable critics (Figure M1.5). As philosopher of science Helen Longino emphasizes, responsiveness to other members of a scientific community "does not require that individuals whose data and assumptions are criticized recant. . . . What is required is that community members pay attention to the critical discussion taking place and that the assumptions that govern their group activity remain logically sensitive to it" (1990, 78).

Longino adds that criticism cannot go on indefinitely if scientific research is to achieve its goals. Scientists become impatient if their detractors repeat the same criticisms over and over but never develop an alternative research program of their own that produces rich new evidence in support of their own views (1990, 79). In part, this is because scientists are often unwilling to give up on even an inadequate research program until they find an alternative that somehow works better than what they already have. This unsatisfactory state of affairs regularly provokes the development of new approaches in science that produce new evidence, thus allowing critics to do more than merely point out the deficiencies of other scientists' work. The history of paleoanthropology is full of lively debates that have produced new theories, new evidence, and new research techniques (such as those associated with dating ancient fossils and artifacts) that have enormously increased our understanding of the complex evolutionary history of our species and our closest relatives.

Alternative stories about the natural world may seem confusing to a layperson. How can you be sure you support the right one? Or, if certainty is impossible, why not simply decide to support the story you like best, regardless of the evidence? In recent years, scholars in many different academic disciplines, as well as ordinary citizens from a variety of backgrounds, have claimed that there is no such thing as "scientific objectivity." Many argue that it is impossible for researchers to separate observation and reporting from their wish to defend the interests of their own social groups, be these groups defined in terms of race, religion, national

---

objectivity   The separation of observation and reporting from the researcher's wishes.

Module 1: Anthropology, Science, and Storytelling (continued)

M1.5 There is an important social aspect to science. It is not just that scientists work in teams, but they also meet regularly to discuss and debate their research, informally as conference goers seek food (*a*) or formally as bioanthropologist Jonathan Marks presents his research (*b*).

origin, gender, or sexual orientation. Some would even suggest that communities of scientists can be as biased as any other social group in defense of their own interests. If total objectivity is impossible, why should individuals not choose, if not the story they like best, at least the story that best furthers their political interests?

Science, like all human activities, does not take place in a cultural vacuum. Although scientific theories have always been influenced by wider currents of social and political thought and experience, they need not be hopelessly biased or incapable of revealing truth. Scientific theories are bound to be partial, highlighting some dimensions of reality and downplaying or ignoring other dimensions. Recognizing this, we may be able to move, as philosopher of science Philip Kitcher urges, "beyond the simple opposition of proof and faith [or, we might add, proof and political expediency]. Between these extremes lies the vast field of cases in which we believe something on the basis of good—even excellent—but inconclusive evidence" (1982, 34).

In order to evaluate the scientific stories told about human origins, people need to become more knowledgeable about the kinds of material evidence and the interpretations of that evidence that scientists use. This book deals with both matters. The next two chapters provide an overview of the basic elements of modern evolutionary

theory and the evidence that evolutionary biologists have collected to support their hypotheses. Subsequent chapters will discuss, step by step, the way scientific inquiry into the biology of living primates, the analysis of fossils, the interpretation of archaeological remains, and the study of a wide range of contemporary human societies has provided a vast body of evidence in support of an evolutionary story about human origins, the origin of culture, and the development of human cultural diversity.

Module Summary

1. Anthropologists regularly claim that their attempts to explain human nature, human society, and the human past are scientific. Scientists are not the only people to tell stories about the way the world works. But scientific stories are different from other stories because they must be open to testing that will confirm or refute them. Stories about the material world that are not open to this kind of testing cannot be considered scientific.

2. Scientists use the term *theory* in a way that is different from everyday, nonscientific usage. Well-confirmed scientific theories are taken very seriously by scientists because they account for a wide range of

material evidence in a coherent, persuasive manner, even though they remain open to testing and possible refutation. The most powerful scientific theories are those whose key hypotheses have been tested repeatedly and have never been disconfirmed.

For Review

1. According to the text, what is science?
2. How does science differ from myth?
3. Why must scientists be particularly concerned about the assumptions they bring to their observations of the natural world?
4. Explain the difference between material and inferred evidence.
5. Why does a hypothesis need to be testable in order to be considered scientific?
6. What are scientific theories, and why are they taken seriously even when their hypotheses remain open to testing?
7. What is objectivity?
8. Summarize the discussion in the text about scientific communities.

Key Terms

assumptions 21	objectivity 25
evidence 21	science 20
hypotheses 23	scientific theory 24
myths 20	testability 23

Why Is Evolution Important to Anthropologists?

2

This question is fundamental to contemporary anthropology and is a topic of great significance in wider scientific discussions. In this chapter, we will look at how the living world was understood before the nineteenth century, where Darwin's ideas came from, how they have been further elaborated since his time, and why evolutionary theory continues to be our most powerful tool for understanding biological processes today.

Chapter Outline

◀ *Small ground finch* (Geospiza fuliginosa), *one of Darwin's finches, in the Galápagos Islands, Ecuador.*

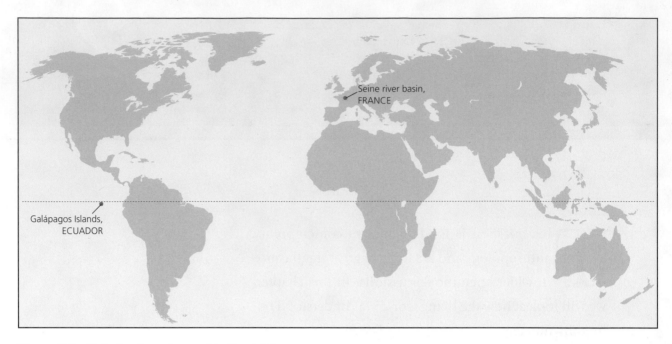

Figure 2.1   Major locations discussed in Chapter 2.

Philosopher of science Philip Kitcher (1982) has suggested that successful scientific theories are testable, unified, and fruitful. A theory is testable when its hypotheses can be independently matched up against nature. A theory is unified when it offers just one or a few basic problem-solving strategies that make sense of a wide range of material evidence. And a theory is fruitful when its central principles suggest new and promising possibilities for further research. The modern theory of biological evolution possesses all three characteristics. Evolutionary hypotheses are highly testable in a number of ways. As we shall see, material evidence from widely diverse sources has consistently fit evolutionary predictions. Because it is based on a few central concepts and assumptions, the evolutionary research program is also highly unified. Charles Darwin's *On the Origin of Species by Means of Natural Selection* appeared in 1859. As Kitcher (1982, 48) puts it, Darwin "gave structure to our ignorance." After that date, biologists could borrow Darwin's methods to guide them in new and promising directions. The study of life has not been the same since. As we begin our study of human evolution, you may be surprised at the number of terms and concepts that you are learning from biology, genetics, and ecology. The theory of evolution has engaged the

efforts of many scientists for nearly a century. Their work has produced a still-developing, powerful, multistranded theory. In order to understand the arguments made by modern evolutionary biologists, we have to learn the language of evolution. The payoff will be a nuanced view of what the theory of evolution is really about and how powerful it really is.

What Is Evolutionary Theory?

Evolutionary theory claims that living species can change over time and give rise to new kinds of species, with the result that all organisms ultimately share a common ancestry. Because of this common ancestry, information about biological variation in finches or genetic transmission in fruit flies can help us understand the roles of biological variation and genetics in human evolution.

Eldredge and Tattersall observe that evolution "is as highly verified a thesis as can be found in science. Subjected to close scrutiny from all angles for over a century now, evolution emerges as the only naturalistic explanation we have of the twin patterns of similarity and diversity that pervade all life" (1982, 2). Steven Stanley, another evolutionary biologist, states that "the theory of evolution is not just getting older, it is getting better. Like any scientific concept that has long withstood the test of time, this one has suffered setbacks, but, time

---

evolutionary theory The set of testable hypotheses that assert that living organisms can change over time and give rise to new kinds of organisms, with the result that all organisms ultimately share a common ancestry.

and again, has rebounded to become richer and stronger" (1981, xv). Evolutionary thinkers are convinced that the story they propose to tell about the history of life on earth is more persuasive than any of its rivals. To what do they owe this sense of confidence?

What Material Evidence Is There for Evolution?

Two kinds of material evidence have been particularly important in the development of evolutionary theory: material evidence of change over time and material evidence of change across space. Geological research led to the discovery of the fossil record—the remains of lifeforms that had been preserved in the earth for a long time. When scientists compared these fossils with each other and with living organisms, they noted that the living organisms were quite different from the fossilized organisms. This was material evidence of change over time, or **evolution**, in the kinds of organisms that have lived on the earth. Any persuasive biological theory would have to find a way to explain this material evidence.

Equally important material evidence for the development of evolutionary theory came from the study of living organisms. Darwin himself was most interested in explaining the pattern of distribution of living species of organisms. In one of his best-known studies, Darwin noted that neighboring geographic areas on the islands of the Galápagos Archipelago were inhabited by species of finch different from the finch species found on the Ecuadorian mainland. At the same time, the various Galápagos species resembled one another closely and resembled mainland finch species (Figure 2.2). Species distribution patterns of this kind suggested change over space, which, again, any persuasive biological theory would have to explain.

In the centuries before Darwin, however, the fossil record was mostly unknown, and many of those concerned with biology did not see the pattern of distribution of living species as evidence for past change. To understand why Darwin's ideas had such a powerful impact requires an understanding of pre-Darwinian views of the natural world (Table 2.1).

Pre-Darwinian Views of the Natural World

In the Western societies of antiquity, the Greeks thought the world had been, and would be, around forever; in the Judeo-Christian tradition, it was thought that the world was young and would end soon. Both traditions saw the world as fixed and unchanging.

Essentialism

If the world does not change, then the various forms of life that are part of that world also do not change. We can trace this view back to the ancient Greek philosopher Plato. A central element of Plato's philosophy was a belief in an ideal world of perfect, eternal, unchanging forms that exist apart from the imperfect, changeable, physical world of living things. Plato believed that these two worlds—ideal and material—were linked and that every ideal form—the ideal form of "cowness," for instance—was represented in the physical, material world by a number of imperfect but recognizable real cows of varying sizes, colors, temperaments, and so on. When observers looked at real cows and saw their similarities despite all this variation, Plato believed that what they were really seeing was the ideal form, or essence, of "cowness" that each individual cow incarnated.

According to Plato, all living things that share the same essence belong to the same "natural kind," and

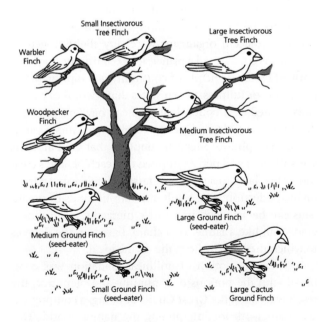

Figure 2.2 Charles Darwin and Alfred Russel Wallace explained the pattern of distribution of living species of organisms (such as the various species of finches living on the Galápagos Islands) by arguing that all the variants had evolved from a single ancestral species.

---

evolution The process of change over time.

TABLE 2.1 Pre-Darwinian Views of the Natural World	
VIEW	KEY FEATURES
Essentialism	Each "natural kind" of living thing is characterized by an unchanging core of features and separated from all other natural kinds by a sharp break.
Great Chain of Being	Based on three principles: 1. *Continuity:* Attributes of one kind of organism always overlap to some extent with the attributes of organisms closest to it in the classification. 2. *Plentitude:* A world of organisms created by a benevolent God can have no gaps but must include all logically conceivable organisms. 3. *Unilinear gradation:* All organisms can be arranged in a single hierarchy based on various degrees to which they depart from divine perfection.
Catastrophism	The notion that natural disasters, such as floods, are responsible for the extinction of species, which are then replaced by new species.
Uniformitarianism	The belief that the same gradual processes of erosion and uplift that change the earth's surface today had been at work in the past. Thus, we can use our understanding of current processes to reconstruct the history of the earth.
Transformational evolution	Assuming essentialist species and a uniformly changing environment, Lamarck argued that individual members of a species transform themselves in identical ways in order to adapt to commonly experienced changes in the environment. To explain why, Lamarck invoked (1) the law of use and disuse and (2) the inheritance of acquired characters.

there are many natural kinds in the world, each of which is the result of the imperfect incarnation in the physical world of one or another eternal form or ideal ("cowness," "humanness," "ratness," and the like). This view is called **essentialism**. For essentialists, as Ernst Mayr explains, "each species is characterized by its unchanging essence . . . and separated from all other species by a sharp discontinuity. Essentialism assumes that the diversity of inanimate as well as of organic nature is the reflection of a limited number of unchanging universals. . . . All those objects belong to the same species that share the same essence" (1982, 256). That essence is what made every individual cow a cow and not, say, a deer.

The Great Chain of Being

Greek ideas were adopted and adapted by thinkers in the Judeo-Christian religious tradition. By the Middle Ages, many scholars thought they could describe the organizing

---

essentialism The belief, derived from Plato, in fixed ideas, or "forms," that exist perfect and unchanging in eternity. Actual objects in the temporal world, such as cows or horses, are seen as imperfect material realizations of the ideal form that defines their kind.

Great Chain of Being A comprehensive framework for interpreting the world, based on Aristotelian principles and elaborated during the Middle Ages, in which every kind of living organism was linked to every other kind in an enormous, divinely created chain. An organism differed from the kinds immediately above it and below it on the chain by the least possible degree.

---

principles responsible for harmony in nature. According to Arthur Lovejoy ([1936] 1960), they reasoned as follows: the ancient Greek philosopher Aristotle suggested that kinds of organisms could be arranged in a single line from most primitive to most advanced. He further argued that the attributes of one kind of organism always overlap to some extent with the attributes of organisms closest to it in the classification so that the differences between adjacent organisms were very slight. Together, these ideas constituted a principle of continuity. Logically implied by the principle of continuity is the principle of plenitude, or fullness, which states that a world of organisms created by a benevolent God can have no gaps but must include all logically conceivable organisms. Finally, the ancient philosophers' assumption that God alone is self-sufficient and perfect implied that each of God's creatures must lack, to a greater or lesser degree, some part of divine perfection. As a result, the various kinds of organisms can be arranged in a single hierarchy, or unilinear gradation, like a ladder or a chain, based on the degrees to which they depart from the divine ideal.

When the notion of unilinear gradation was combined with the notions of continuity and plenitude, the result was called the **Great Chain of Being**, a comprehensive framework for interpreting the natural world. This framework suggested that the entire cosmos was composed "of an immense, or of an infinite, number of links . . . every one of them differing from that immediately above and that immediately below it by the 'least possible' degree of difference" (Lovejoy [1936] 1960, 59). Degrees of difference were understood in theological terms to be degrees of excellence. Creatures farthest away from divine perfection were lowest in the hierarchy, whereas creatures most like God (such as the angels) ranked highest. Human beings occupied a unique position in the chain. Their material bodies linked them to other material beings; but unlike other material creatures, they also possessed souls and were thereby linked to the spiritual realm by a God who had created them in his image.

For several hundred years—from the Middle Ages through the eighteenth century—the Great Chain of Being was the framework in the Western world within which all discussions of living organisms were set. As late as the mid-eighteenth century, Carolus Linnaeus (1707–1778), the father of modern biological **taxonomy** (or classification), operated within this framework. Linnaeus was committed to an essentialist definition of natural kinds. He focused on what modern taxonomists call the **genus** (plural *genera*) (Figure 2.3) and used the morphology of reproductive organs to define the "essence" of a genus (Mayr 1982, 178). (The term **species**, which modern biologists assign to subpopulations of the same genus who share certain specific attributes, was used more loosely in the past, by essentialists and by nonessentialists.) Essentialists like Linnaeus knew that individuals sometimes differ markedly from what is considered "normal" for others of their kind. But these deviations were still thought of as accidents, or "degradations," that could not affect the unity of the natural kind.

Catastrophism and Uniformitarianism

The unprecedented social and scientific changes brought about by the eighteenth-century Enlightenment in Europe gradually raised doubts about the Great Chain of Being. The principle of continuity was criticized by the French scientist Georges Cuvier (1769–1832), a pioneer in modern anatomy who also carried out some of the first important excavations of fossils in the Seine River basin near Paris. He was a firm believer in the essentialist definition of natural kinds, but his anatomical studies convinced him that there were only four natural categories of living things. Each category was excellently adapted to its way of life but had no connection to any of the others. Cuvier's studies of the fossil record convinced him that, over time, some species had been abruptly wiped out and replaced, equally abruptly, by new species from somewhere else. He called these abrupt transitions "revolutions," although this term was translated into English as "catastrophe." Hence, the term **catastrophism** came to refer to the notion that natural disasters, such as floods, are responsible for the extinction of some natural kinds, which are later replaced by new natural kinds.

In some ways, Cuvier's ideas were perfectly traditional: he did not reject the essentialist understanding of species and never suggested that new species were simply old species that had changed. Yet, his idea that some species might disappear in mass extinctions was quite radical because, according to Judeo-Christian theology, God had created all possible forms of life only once. In the same way, Cuvier's assertion in 1812 that there were no connections whatsoever among the four basic categories of living things seriously undermined the principle of unilinear gradation. That is, if the four categories had nothing in common with one another, then they could not be arranged in a simple chain of natural kinds, each precisely placed between the one slightly less advanced and the one slightly more advanced. Ernst Mayr concluded that this argument dealt the Great Chain of Being its death blow (1982, 201).

But the Great Chain of Being did not die gently, for its principles had become inextricably intertwined with Judeo-Christian beliefs about the natural world. By the late eighteenth and early nineteenth centuries, one result of this process of amalgamation was the development of an approach arguing that the perfection of each organism's adaptation could only be due to intentional design by a benevolent creator. One group of thinkers, known as "catastrophists," modified Cuvier's theory and argued that the new species that replaced old ones had been specially created by God. Others subscribed to a position known as **uniformitarianism**, which stressed nature's overall harmonious integration as evidence for God's handiwork. These "uniformitarians" criticized the ideas of Cuvier and the catastrophists. God might allow the world to change, they admitted, but a benevolent God's blueprint for creation could not include sharp breaks between different forms of life and the abrupt disappearance of species through extinction. The uniformitarian position gained powerful support from the book *Principles of Geology* by Charles Lyell (1797–1875),

---

taxonomy A classification; in biology, the classification of various kinds of organisms.

genus The level of the Linnaean taxonomy in which different species are grouped together on the basis of their similarities to one another.

species (1) For Linnaeus, a Platonic "natural kind" defined in terms of its essence. (2) For modern biologists, a reproductive community of populations (reproductively isolated from others) that occupies a specific niche in nature.

catastrophism The notion that natural disasters, such as floods, are responsible for the extinction of species, which are then replaced by new species.

uniformitarianism The notion that an understanding of current processes can be used to reconstruct the past history of the earth, based on the assumption that the same gradual processes of erosion and uplift that change the earth's surface today had also been at work in the past.

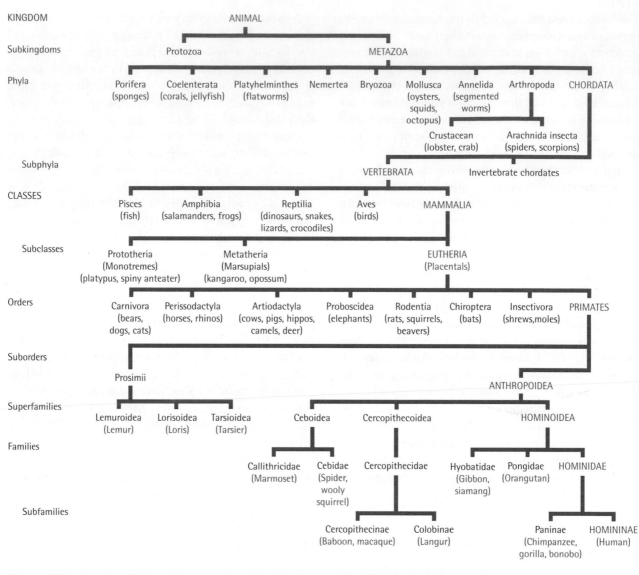

Figure 2.3 A modern biological taxonomy based on the Linnaean classification (popular names are in parentheses). Organisms sharing structural similarities are still grouped together, but their similarities are understood to be the result of common ancestry, indicated by the horizontal line connecting them. Thus, Paninae (chimpanzees, gorillas, and bonobos) and Homininae (human beings) all share a recent common ancestor.

published between 1830 and 1833. Lyell argued that the same gradual processes of erosion and uplift that change the earth's surface today had also been at work in the past. Assuming the uniformity of these processes, he contended that our understanding of current processes could be used to reconstruct the past history of the earth.

The quarrel between catastrophists and uniformitarians has often been portrayed as a conflict between narrow-minded dogmatism (identified with the catastrophists) and open-minded, empirical science (identified with the uniformitarians). But, as Stephen Jay Gould (1987) demonstrated, this portrayal misrepresents the nature of their disagreement. Both Cuvier

and Lyell were empirical scientists: the former, a leading anatomist and excavator of fossils; the latter, a field-working geologist. Both confronted much of the same material evidence; however, as Gould points out, they interpreted that evidence in very different ways. Catastrophists were willing to accept a view of earth's history that permitted ruptures of harmony in order to preserve their belief that history, guided by divine intervention, was going somewhere. By contrast, the harmonious, nondirectional view of the uniformitarians was rooted in their belief that time was cyclic, like the changing seasons. Uniformitarians promoted the view that God's creation was the "incarnation of rationality"—that is, that God's creation unfolded in accordance with God's laws, without requiring subsequent divine intervention or a fixed historical trajectory.

Transformational Evolution

Thus, by the early years of the nineteenth century, traditional ideas about the natural world had been challenged by new material evidence and conflicting interpretations of that evidence. In the ferment of this period, the French naturalist Jean-Baptiste de Monet de Lamarck (1744–1829) grappled with the inconsistencies described above, dealing the first serious blow against essentialism (Figure 2.4). Lamarck wanted to preserve the traditional view of a harmonious living world. One of the most serious challenges to that view was the problem of extinction. How could perfectly adapted creatures suddenly be wiped out, and where did their replacements come from? Some suggested that the extinctions were the result of Noah's flood, but this could not explain how aquatic animals had become extinct. Others suggested that extinctions were the result of human hunting, possibly explaining why mastodons no longer roamed the earth. Some hoped that natural kinds believed to be extinct might yet be found inhabiting an unexplored area of the globe.

Lamarck suggested an original interpretation of the material evidence that had been used to argue in favor of extinction. Noticing that many fossil species bore a close resemblance to living species, he suggested in 1809 that perhaps fossil forms were the ancestors of living forms. Fossil forms looked different from their descendants, he believed, because ancestral features had been modified over time to suit their descendants to changing climate and geography. Such a process would prove that nature was harmonious after all—that, although the world was a changing world, living organisms possessed the capacity to change along with it.

Many elements of the Great Chain of Being could be made to fit with Lamarck's scheme. Lamarck believed that once a natural kind had come into existence, it had the capacity to evolve over time into increasingly complex (or "perfect") forms. This could happen, Lamarck suggested, because all organisms have two attributes: (1) the ability to change physically in response to environmental demands and (2) the capacity to activate this ability whenever environmental change makes the organism's previous response obsolete. Otherwise, the resulting lack of fit between organisms and environment would create disharmony in nature. Lamarck never suggested that a species might adapt to change by splitting into two or more new species; rather, every member of every species is engaged in its own individual adaptive transformation over time. This is why

Figure 2.4 Jean-Baptiste de Monet de Lamarck. Lamarck wanted to preserve the traditional view of a harmonious living world, but his interpretation of the evidence of fossils eventually undermined exactly the view he was trying to defend.

Lamarckian evolution has also been called **transformational evolution**.

Lamarck proposed two "laws" to explain how such transformation occurs. First, he said, an organ is strengthened by use and weakened by disuse (an early statement of "use it or lose it"). If environmental changes cause members of a species to rely more heavily on some organs than on others, the former will become enhanced and the latter reduced. But the law of use and disuse had evolutionary consequences, Lamarck argued, because the physical result of use or disuse could be passed from one generation to the next. This was the law of inheritance of acquired characteristics.

Consider the following example: modern pandas possess an oversized, elongated wristbone that aids them

---

transformational evolution Also called *Lamarckian evolution*, it assumes essentialist species and a uniform environment. Each individual member of a species transforms itself to meet the challenges of a changed environment through the laws of use and disuse and the inheritance of acquired characters.

complex organs and attains, over many generations, increasingly higher levels of "perfection."

Because transformational evolution works through the efforts of individual members of a species, what would prevent different individuals from transforming themselves in different directions? Part of the answer is that Lamarck expected a changing environment to affect all individuals of the same species in the same way, leading to identical responses in terms of use and disuse. But the rest of the answer lies with the fact that Lamarck still accepted the view that every individual member of a species was identical in essence to every other member. Only if this were so could all members of the same species respond in the same ways to the same environmental pressures and retain their species identity over time.

Lamarck's transformational theory of biological evolution was rejected by biologists in the early twentieth century, when geneticists were able to demonstrate that neither the law of use and disuse nor the law of inheritance of acquired characters applied to genes. In the early nineteenth century, however, Lamarck's speculations opened the door for Darwin.

What Is Natural Selection?

Lamarck had argued that a species could vary over time. Contemporaries of Lamarck, observing living organisms in the wild in Europe, the Americas, Africa, and Asia, had demonstrated that species could vary over space as well. Where did all this mutually coexisting but previously unknown living variation come from?

The mystery of geographical variation in living organisms was particularly vexing to Charles Darwin (1809–1882, Figure 2.6) and Alfred Russel Wallace (1823–1913), whose field observations made it impossible to ignore. Wallace reasoned that the relationship between similar but distinct species in the wild could be explained if all the similar species were related to one another biologically—that is, if they were considered daughter (or sibling) species of some other parental species. Darwin, comparing the finches on the Galápagos Islands with finches on the Ecuadorian mainland, reasoned that the similarities linking the finches could be explained if all of them had descended from a single parental finch population. Both men concluded independently that similar species must descend from a common ancestor, meaning that any species might split into a number of new species given enough time. But how much time? In the 1650s, James Ussher, the Anglican archbishop of Ireland, used information in the Bible to calculate that God created the earth on October 23,

Figure 2.5 Lamarckian transformational evolution and Darwinian variational evolution offer two different explanations for how the panda got its "thumb." The pandas' "thumb" is actually an elongated wristbone that aids them in stripping bamboo leaves, their favorite food, from bamboo stalks.

in stripping bamboo leaves, their favorite food, from bamboo stalks (Figure 2.5). This bone has been called the panda's "thumb," although pandas retain all five digits on each paw. Had Lamarck known about the panda's thumb, he might have explained its origin as follows: suppose that pandas originally had wristbones like other bears. Then the environment changed, obliging pandas to become dependent on bamboo for food. Pandas, unable to survive on bamboo unless they found an efficient way to strip the leaves off the stalk, were forced to use their forepaws more intensively (the law of use and disuse) in order to remove enough bamboo leaves to satisfy their appetite. Continual exercise of their wrists caused the wristbone to enlarge and lengthen into a shape resembling a thumb. After acquiring "thumbs" through strenuous activity, pandas gave birth to offspring with elongated wristbones (the law of inheritance of acquired characters). Thus, Lamarck's laws could explain how each species builds up new, more

Figure 2.6 Charles Darwin (1809–1882).

for over a century and remains the best explanation we have today for the diversity of life on earth.

Charles Darwin's theory of evolution was possible only because he was able to think about species in a new way. Although Lamarck had begun to do this when he suggested that species could change, Darwin completed the job. If organisms could change, then they did not have a fixed essence. This, in turn, meant that variation—or differences—among individual members of a species might be extremely important.

Thus, Darwin turned the essentialist definition of *species* on its head. He argued that the important thing about individual members of a species is not what they have in common but how they are different. The Darwinian theory of evolution by natural selection argued that variation, not a unitary essence, is the ground condition of life. This is why it is called **variational evolution**, in contrast to the transformational evolution of Lamarck (see, e.g., Lewontin 1982). The idea of variational evolution depends on what Ernst Mayr (1982) calls "population thinking"—that is, seeing the populations that make up a species as composed of biological individuals whose differences from one another are genuine and important.

Population Thinking

Darwin combined this new view of species with other observations about the natural world. Consider, for example, frogs in a pond. Nobody would deny that new frogs hatch from hundreds of eggs laid by mature females every breeding season, yet the size of the population of adult frogs in a given pond rarely changes much from one season to the next. Clearly, the great potential fertility represented by all those eggs is never realized or the pond would shortly be overrun by frogs. Something must keep all those eggs from maturing into adults. Darwin (following Thomas Malthus) attributed this to the limited food supply in the pond, which means that the hatchlings are forced to struggle with one another for

4004 B.C., a date that was still widely accepted. Charles Lyell and other geologists, however, claimed that the earth was much more than 6000 years old (indeed, it is about 4.5 billion years old). If the geologists were right, there had been ample time for what Darwin called "descent with modification" to have produced the high degree of species diversity we find in the world today.

Darwin had refrained from publishing his work on evolution for years but was moved to action when Lyell warned him that Wallace was ready to publish his ideas. As a result, Darwin and Wallace first published their views in a scientific paper carrying both their names. Darwin became better known than Wallace in later years, in part because of the mass of material evidence he collected in support of his theory together with his refined theoretical interpretations of that evidence.

The theory of **common origin**—"the first Darwinian revolution" (Mayr 1982, 116)—was in itself scandalous, for it went far beyond Lamarck's modest suggestion that species can change without losing their essential integrity. Not only did Darwin propose that similar species can be traced to a common ancestor, but he also offered a straightforward, mechanistic explanation of how such descent with modification takes place. His explanation, the theory of **natural selection**, was "the second Darwinian revolution." That natural selection remains central to modern evolutionary theory is testimony to the power of Darwin's insight, for it has been tested and reformulated

common origin Darwin's claim that similar living species must all have had a common ancestor.

natural selection A two-step, mechanistic explanation of how descent with modification takes place: (1) every generation, variant individuals are generated within a species due to genetic mutation, and (2) those variant individuals best suited to the current environment survive and produce more offspring than other variants.

variational evolution The Darwinian theory of evolution, which assumes that variant members of a species respond differently to environmental challenges. Those variants that are more successful ("fitter") survive and reproduce more offspring, who inherit the traits that made their parents fit.

food and that the losers do not survive to reproduce. Darwin wondered what factors determined which competitors win and which lose. Pointing to the variation among all individuals of the species, he argued that those individuals whose variant traits better equip them to compete in the struggle for existence are more likely to survive and reproduce than those who lack such traits. Individuals who leave greater numbers of offspring are said to have superior **fitness**.

Such an argument makes no sense, of course, unless species are understood in variational terms. For an essentialist, the individual members of a species are identical to one another because they share the same essence; it makes no difference which or how many of them survive and reproduce. From an essentialist point of view, therefore, competition can only occur between different species because only the differences between entire species (not between a species' individual members) matter. Once we think of a species in variational terms, however, the notion that competition for resources "is 'dog eat dog' rather than 'dog eat cat'" begins to make sense (Depew and Weber 1989, 257).

When Darwin interpreted his observations, he came up with the following explanation of how biological evolution occurs. Levins and Lewontin (1985, 31ff.) summarize his theory in three principles and one driving force that sets the process in motion:

1. The principle of variation. No two individuals in a species are identical in all respects; they vary in such features as size, color, intelligence, and so on.

2. The principle of heredity. Offspring tend to resemble their parents.

3. The principle of natural selection. Different variants leave different numbers of offspring.

The driving force, Darwin suggested, was the struggle for existence. In a later edition of *On the Origin of Species*, he borrowed a phrase coined by sociologist Herbert Spencer and described the outcome of the struggle for existence as "survival of the fittest."

---

fitness A measure of an organism's ability to compete in the struggle for existence. Those individuals whose variant traits better equip them to compete with other members of their species for limited resources are more likely to survive and reproduce than individuals who lack such traits.

aptation The shaping of any useful feature of an organism, regardless of its origin.

adaptation The shaping of useful features of an organism by natural selection for the function they now perform.

exaptation The shaping of a useful feature of an organism by natural selection to perform one function and the later reshaping of it by different selection pressures to perform a new function.

Natural Selection in Action

To illustrate the operation of natural selection, let us return to the problem of how pandas got their "thumbs." Lamarck would explain this phenomenon by arguing that individual pandas all used their wrists intensively to obtain enough bamboo leaves to survive, causing their wristbones to lengthen, a trait they passed on to their offspring. Darwin, by contrast, would explain this phenomenon by focusing attention, not on individual pandas, but on a *population* of pandas and the ways in which members of that population differed from one another. He would argue that originally there must have been a population of pandas with wristbones of different lengths (the principle of variation). Because offspring tend to resemble their parents, pandas with long wristbones gave birth to offspring with long wristbones and pandas with short wristbones gave birth to offspring with short wristbones (the principle of heredity). When the climate changed such that pandas became dependent upon bamboo leaves for food, pandas with wristbones of different lengths had to compete with one another to get enough leaves to survive (the struggle for existence). Note that, in this example, "the struggle for existence" does not imply that the pandas were necessarily *fighting* with one another over access to bamboo. The pandas with long wristbones functioning as "thumbs" for stripping bamboo stalks were simply more successful than pandas who lacked such a "thumb"; that is, in this new environment, their elongated wristbones made them fitter than pandas with short wristbones. Thus, pandas with "thumbs" survived and left more offspring than did those without "thumbs." As a result, the proportion of pandas with elongated wristbones in the next generation was larger than it had been in the previous generation and the proportion of pandas with short wristbones was smaller. If these selective pressures were severe enough, pandas with short wristbones might not leave any offspring at all, resulting at some point in a population made up entirely of pandas with "thumbs."

In Darwinian terms, adaptation has been traditionally understood as the process by which an organism "is engineered to be in harmony with the natural environment" as a result of natural selection (Little 1995, 123). However, this concept contains ambiguities that can confuse the *process* of adaptation with its *outcomes* (also often called "adaptations"). In 1982, paleontologists Stephen Jay Gould and Elisabeth Vrba helped to resolve this confusion by distinguishing among aptation, adaptation, and exaptation. An **aptation** refers to any useful feature of an organism, regardless of its origin. An **adaptation** refers to a useful feature of an organism that was shaped by natural selection for the function it now performs. An **exaptation**, by contrast, refers to a useful feature of an organism that was originally shaped by natural selection to perform one function but later reshaped by different selection pressures to perform a new function.

The distinction between adaptation and exaptation is important because mistaking one for the other can lead to evolutionary misinterpretations. For example, it has been standard practice to explain an organism's current form (e.g., an insect's wing shape) as an adaptation for the function it currently carries out (i.e., flight). This kind of explanation, however, raises problems. If insect wings evolved gradually via natural selection, then the first modest appendages on which selection would operate could not have looked like—or worked like—the wings of living insects. As a result, those early appendages could not have been used for flying. But what adaptive advantage could something that was not yet a wing confer on insect ancestors? Gould and Vrba showed that appendages that were not yet wings could have been adaptive for reasons having nothing to do with flying. For example, the original adaptive function of insect appendages was body cooling, but these appendages were later exapted for the function of flying, once they had reached a certain size or shape (Figure 2.7). Specialists in human evolution like Ian Tattersall (1998, 108) use the concepts of aptation, adaptation, and exaptation to explain some of the twists and turns in human evolutionary history.

Darwin's theory of evolution by natural selection is elegant and dramatic. As generations of biologists have tested its components in their own research, they have come to examine it critically. For example, much debate has been generated about the concept of fitness. Some people have assumed that the biggest, strongest, toughest individuals must be, by definition, fitter than the smaller, weaker, gentler members of their species. Strictly speaking, however, Darwinian, or biological, fitness is nothing more (and nothing less) than an individual's ability to survive and leave offspring. There is no such thing as "absolute" fitness. In a given environment, those who leave more offspring behind are fitter than those who leave fewer offspring behind. But any organism that manages to reproduce in that environment is fit. As geneticist Richard Lewontin puts it, "In evolutionary terms, an Olympic athlete who never has any children has a fitness of zero, whereas J. S. Bach, who was sedentary and very much overweight, had an unusually high Darwinian fitness by virtue of his having been the father of twenty children" (1982, 150).

Clearly, Darwinian theory has been challenged to show that biological heredity operates to produce ever-renewing variation and to explain how such variation is generated and passed on from parents to offspring. Darwin's original formulation of the theory of evolution by natural selection was virtually silent about these matters. Darwin was convinced on the basis of considerable evidence that heritable variation must exist, but he and his colleagues were completely ignorant about the sources of variation. Not until the beginning of the twentieth century did knowledge about these matters begin to accumulate, and not until the 1930s did a new evolutionary synthesis of Darwinian principles and genetics become established.

Unlocking the Secrets of Heredity

Offspring tend to look like their parents, which suggests that something unchanging is passed on from one generation to the next. At the same time, offspring are not identical to their parents, which raises the possibility that whatever the parents pass on may be modified by environmental forces. Whether biological inheritance was stable or modifiable, or both, challenged Darwin and his contemporaries.

In the absence of scientific knowledge about heredity, Darwin and many of his contemporaries adopted a theory of heredity that had roots in antiquity: the theory of pangenesis. **Pangenesis** was a theory of inheritance in which multiple particles from both parents blended

Figure 2.7 How did wings evolve for flight? Gould and Vrba (1982) suggest that appendages on early insects were for body cooling but later exapted for flying once they had reached a certain size or shape.

pangenesis A theory of heredity suggesting that an organism's physical traits are passed on from one generation to the next in the form of multiple distinct particles given off by all parts of the organism, different proportions of which get passed on to offspring via sperm or egg.

Figure 2.8 Mendel crossbred peas with red flowers and peas with white flowers (the parental, or P$_I$, generation). This produced a generation (F$_1$) of only red flowers. When Mendel crossed red-flowered peas from the F$_1$ generation, they produced the F$_2$ generation of peas, in which there were approximately three red-flowered plants for every one plant with white flowers. This 3:1 ratio of red to white flowers, together with the reappearance of white flowers, could be explained if each plant had two genetic factors and the factor for red flowers was dominant. Only a plant with two factors for white flowers would produce white flowers, whereas red flowers would appear in every plant that had at least one factor for red.

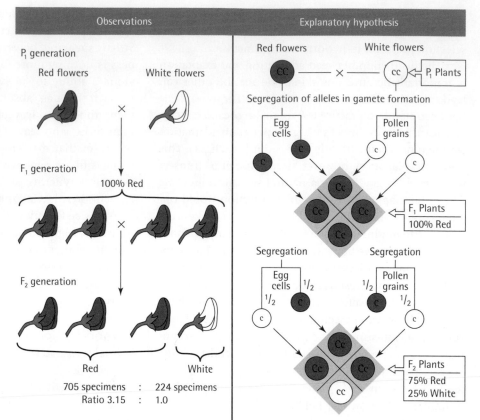

in their offspring. That is, it claimed that an organism's physical traits are passed on from one generation to the next in the form of distinct particles. Supporters of pangenesis argued that all the organs of both mother and father gave off multiple particles that were somehow transmitted, in different proportions, to each of their offspring. For example, suppose that a child resembled her father more than her mother in a particular trait (say, hair color). Pangenesis explained this by arguing that the child had received more "hair color particles" from her father than from her mother. The particles inherited from both parents were believed to blend in their offspring. Thus, the child's hair color would be closer to her father's shade than to her mother's.

Mendel's Experiments

The notion of particulate inheritance was already common in the middle of the nineteenth century when the Austrian monk Gregor Mendel (1822–1884) began conducting plant-breeding experiments in the

Mendelian inheritance The view that heredity is based on nonblending, single-particle genetic inheritance.

garden of his monastery. His great contribution was to provide evidence in favor of nonblending, single-particle inheritance, called **Mendelian inheritance**. When Mendel crossed peas with strikingly different traits, some of those traits did not appear in offspring of the first (F$_1$) generation (Figure 2.8). They did, however, reappear in their original form in the next (F$_2$) generation. Had the particles blended, all the offspring of plants with red flowers and plants with white flowers should have been some shade of pink; but this did not happen, providing strong evidence that the particles responsible for the trait did not blend in offspring but remained discrete.

When Mendel carefully counted the number of offspring in the F$_2$ generation that showed each trait, he consistently came up with a 3:1 ratio of one form to the other, a factor nobody before him had noticed. This ratio recurred whenever Mendel repeated his experiments. If pangenesis were correct, no such ratios would have occurred because each individual would have inherited an unpredictable number of particles from each parent. However, the 3:1 ratio made excellent sense if, as Mendel assumed, each individual inherited only one particle from each parent (Mayr 1982, 721).

The results of his breeding experiments suggested to Mendel something else as well—that the particle responsible for one form of a particular trait (flower color, e.g.) could be present in an organism but go unexpressed. Those particles whose traits are expressed in an organism are said to be *dominant*; those whose traits are not expressed are said to be *recessive*. (We now know that sometimes both traits can be expressed, in which case they are said to be *codominant*.) Mendel thus concluded that the particles responsible for a particular trait, such as the pea's flower color, occur in pairs. An individual gets one particle for each trait (i.e., one-half of the pair) from each parent. This is the **principle of segregation**. Mendel further argued that each pair of particles separates independently of every other pair when what he called "germ cells" (egg and sperm) are formed. This is the **principle of independent assortment**. As a result, each sperm and ovum is virtually guaranteed to be different from all others produced by an individual because the collection of particles that each contains will be distinct. Moreover, the pairs of particles that come together in any individual offspring are random, depending on which egg and which sperm happened to unite to form that individual.

The Emergence of Genetics

Mendel's insights were ignored for nearly 35 years until three biologists rediscovered them at the beginning of the twentieth century, resulting in an explosion of research and vast growth of scientific knowledge about heredity. The British scientist William Bateson coined the term **genetics** in 1908 to describe the new science being built on Mendelian principles. He invented the term **homozygous** to describe a fertilized egg that receives the same particle from both parents for a particular trait and the term **heterozygous** to describe a fertilized egg that receives a different particle from each parent for the same trait. In 1909, the Danish geneticist W. L. Johannsen suggested the term **gene** to refer to the particle itself. Although genes occur in pairs in any individual, geneticists discovered that there might be many more than two forms of a given gene. Bateson used the term **alleles** to refer to all the different forms that a particular gene might take.

At first, nobody knew what physical structures corresponded to the genes and alleles they had been describing. However, advances in cell biology led some scientists to suggest that the **chromosomes** in the cell nucleus might play an important role. These sets of paired bodies were easy to see under the microscope because they accepted a colored stain very well (hence their name, from Greek, meaning "colored bodies"). Animals of different species have different numbers of chromosomes

(humans have 46), but all chromosomes are found in pairs (humans have 23 pairs).

What Are the Basics of Contemporary Genetics?

Biologists learned that living cells undergo two different kinds of division. The first kind, **mitosis**, is simply the way cells make copies of themselves (Figure 2.9a).

The process is different, however, when the sex cells (sperm and eggs) are formed. This process is **meiosis**, or reduction division (Figure 2.9b).

The behavior of the chromosomes during meiosis intrigued geneticists. Slides of cells made at different stages in the process showed that chromosomes obey the principles of segregation and independent assortment, just like Mendelian genes. This fact led geneticists, early in the twentieth century, to hypothesize that genes and chromosomes are connected. The first real test of this hypothesis came when a number of geneticists looked at the ratio of males to females among the offspring of sexually reproducing species. They found that this 1:1 ratio is the same as "the ratio resulting from the cross of a heterozygote (*Aa*) and a homozygous recessive (*aa*). Mendel himself had already suggested this possibility" (Mayr 1982, 750).

---

principle of segregation A principle of Mendelian inheritance in which an individual gets one particle (gene) for each trait (i.e., one-half of the required pair) from each parent.

principle of independent assortment A principle of Mendelian inheritance in which each pair of particles (genes) separates independently of every other pair when germ cells (egg and sperm) are formed.

genetics The scientific study of biological heredity.

homozygous Describes a fertilized egg that receives the same particle (or allele) from each parent for a particular trait.

heterozygous Describes a fertilized egg that receives a different particle (or allele) from each parent for the same trait.

gene Portion or portions of the DNA molecule that code for proteins that shape phenotypic traits.

alleles All the different forms that a particular gene might take.

chromosomes Sets of paired bodies in the nucleus of cells that are made of DNA and contain the hereditary genetic information that organisms pass on to their offspring.

mitosis The way body cells make copies of themselves. The pairs of chromosomes in the nucleus of the cell duplicate and line up along the center of the cell. The cell then divides, each daughter cell taking one full set of paired chromosomes.

meiosis The way sex cells make copies of themselves, which begins like mitosis, with chromosome duplication and the formation of two daughter cells. However, each daughter cell then divides again without chromosome duplication and, as a result, contains only a single set of chromosomes rather than the paired set typical of body cells.

Figure 2.9 Cells divide in two different ways. (*a*) In mitosis, ordinary body cells double the number of chromosomes they contain before dividing so that each daughter cell carries a full copy of the genetic information in the mother cell. (*b*) Meiosis occurs only when sex cells (sperm or eggs) are produced. In meiosis, each daughter cell retains only half the genetic material of the mother cell; the other half will be supplied when sperm and egg join in fertilization.

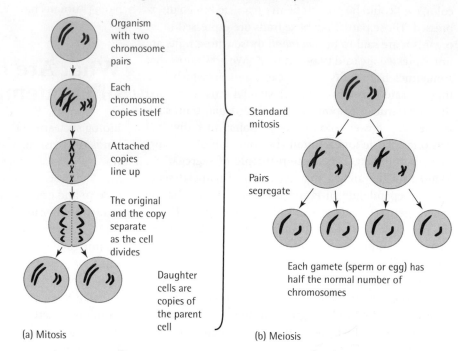

Organism with two chromosome pairs

Organism with two chromosome pairs

Each chromosome copies itself

Attached copies line up

The original and the copy separate as the cell divides

Daughter cells are copies of the parent cell

(a) Mitosis

Standard mitosis

Pairs segregate

Each gamete (sperm or egg) has half the normal number of chromosomes

(b) Meiosis

A gene was understood as a unit occupying a particular position, or **locus** (plural, *loci*), on the chromosome. Early geneticists discovered that frequently one trait appears in an organism only when another trait is also present. This discovery suggested that the genes responsible for those traits must, for some reason, always be passed on together, a phenomenon called **linkage**. We now know that linkage occurs when genes for different traits occur on the same chromosome (Figure 2.10a). However, in some cases, the expected linkages do not occur. Geneticists eventually discovered that part of a chromosome can break off and reattach itself to a different chromosome during meiosis, a phenomenon known as **crossing over**, or incomplete linkage (Figure 2.10b).

Genes and Traits

Geneticists originally thought (and many nonscientists still believe) that one gene equals one trait. Sometimes a single allele does appear to govern a single physical trait. This may be true of many physical traits that show **discontinuous variation**, that is, sharp breaks from one individual to the next. Recall that the flowers on Mendel's pea plants were either red or white; they did not come in various shades of pink. This observation led Mendel to conclude that a single dominant particle (or two identical recessive particles) determines flower color.

Early research, however, showed that one gene–one trait was too simplistic an explanation for many hereditary traits. Sometimes many genes are responsible for producing a single trait, such as skin color (Figure 2.11); such traits are thus said to be the result of **polygeny**. Traits like skin color in human beings are different from traits like flower color in Mendel's peas because they show **continuous variation**. That is, the expression of the trait grades imperceptibly from one individual to another, without sharp breaks. The discovery of polygenic inheritance showed that Mendelian concepts could be used to explain discontinuous and continuous variation alike.

Perhaps even more surprising than polygenic activity was the discovery that a single gene may affect more than

locus A portion of the DNA strand responsible for encoding specific parts of an organism's biological makeup.

linkage An inheritance pattern in which unrelated phenotypic traits regularly occur together because the genes responsible for those co-occurring traits are passed on together on the same chromosome.

crossing over The phenomenon that occurs when part of one chromosome breaks off and reattaches itself to a different chromosome during meiosis; also called *incomplete linkage*.

discontinuous variation A pattern of phenotypic variation in which the phenotype (e.g., flower color) exhibits sharp breaks from one member of the population to the next.

polygeny The phenomenon whereby many genes are responsible for producing a phenotypic trait, such as skin color.

continuous variation A pattern of variation involving polygeny in which phenotypic traits grade imperceptibly from one member of the population to another without sharp breaks.

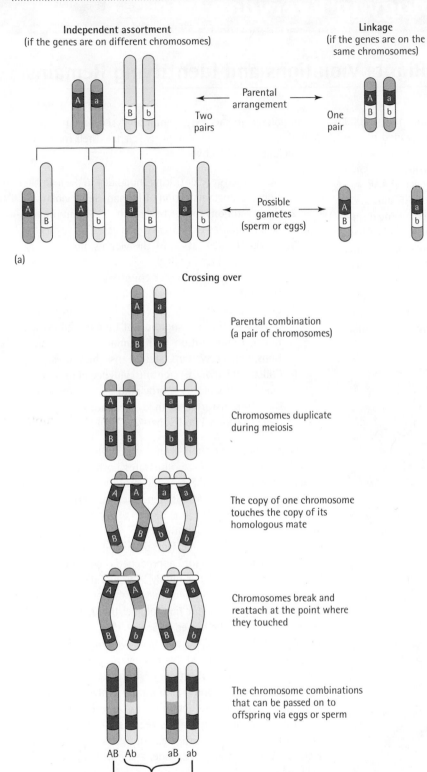

Independent assortment
(if the genes are on different chromosomes)

Linkage
(if the genes are on the same chromosomes)

Parental arrangement

Two pairs

One pair

Possible gametes (sperm or eggs)

(a)

Crossing over

Parental combination
(a pair of chromosomes)

Chromosomes duplicate during meiosis

The copy of one chromosome touches the copy of its homologous mate

Chromosomes break and reattach at the point where they touched

The chromosome combinations that can be passed on to offspring via eggs or sperm

AB   Ab   aB   ab

Old   New   Old

(b)

Figure 2.10 The principle of independent assortment predicts that genetic factors on different chromosomes will not be passed on together; each will be passed on to a different sex cell during meiosis. (*a*) Linkage predicts that genetic factors on the same chromosome will tend to be passed on together because it is the chromosomes that separate during meiosis, not individual genes. (*b*) The predictions about independent assortment and linkage do not hold if chromosomes cross over prior to meiosis. When this occurs, chromosomes break and reattach to their mates, leading to new combinations of genes on each chromosome that can then be passed on to offspring.

Investigating Human-Rights Violations and Identifying Remains

In Argentina between 1976 and 1983, more than 10,000 people disappeared during the "dirty war" waged by the Argentine military government against supposed subversives. A not-for-profit nongovernmental organization called the *Equipo Argentino de Antropología Forense* (EAAF, Argentine Forensic Anthropology Team; Figures 1.5 and 2.12) was established in 1984 to investigate the cases of the disappeared. This organization, which notable anthropologist Clyde Snow helped found, has gone on to investigate human-rights violations in more than forty countries, from Bolivia, Bosnia, and Brazil to Guatemala, Venezuela, Kosovo, and Zimbabwe. They have also trained similar forensic teams in Chile, Guatemala, Peru, and elsewhere. The EAAF takes a multidisciplinary approach to its work, drawing on both forensic and cultural anthropology, archaeology, dental analysis, human genetics, pathology, ballistics, and computer science. Their formal mission includes six objectives:

1. Apply forensic scientific methodology to the investigation and documentation of human-rights violations.
2. Give testimony of our findings in trials and other judicial inquiries in human-rights cases.
3. Provide identification of the victims, providing closure for victims' families.
4. Train new teams in other countries where investigations into human-rights violations are necessary.
5. Conduct seminars on the applications of forensic science to the investigation of human-rights violations in cooperation with human-rights organizations, judicial systems, and forensic institutes.
6. Collect and analyze scientific evidence of massive human-rights violations, providing data to reconstruct the often distorted or hidden histories of repressive regimes (Doretti and Snow 2009, 306).

One example of their work, which Doretti and Snow (2009) call the Manfil Case, illustrates both the multidisciplinary skills of the EAAF and the profound human drama that human-rights violations generate. In 1991, the EAAF team was working in Sector 134, a small, walled-off area inside a huge municipal cemetery in Avellaneda, a suburb of Buenos Aires, Argentina. One day, an eighteen-year-old woman named Karina Manfil approached them and informed them of her search for her family, who had disappeared fifteen years earlier during a death-squad raid on their home on October 27, 1976. Someone had told her that her parents and little brother might be buried in Sector 134.

At that time, the EAAF had been working in Sector 134 for 3 years using their regular four-step approach: (1) historical research, (2) collection of antemortem (predeath) data, (3) archaeology, and (4) laboratory analysis (Doretti and Snow 2009, 308). In conducting historical research, they collected information from written records and through interviews with witnesses toward the goal of answering questions such as "Why was the grave made, and how long was it used to bury bodies? Who made the grave? How was it made? How many people may be buried there?" (308). The researchers discovered that the death squads who operated during the dirty war had created a network of clandestine detention centers (CDCs) throughout the country and that CDCs tended to use the same cemetery for disposing of the remains of their victims. This meant that the remains of people who were swept up together in raids (members of the same political party, student group, union, or occupation) at times ended up in

Figure 2.11 Members of the Argentine Forensic Anthropology Team excavating in the Avellaneda cemetery, sector 134, where Karina's family were secretly buried.

the same cemetery, sometimes in the same grave. This pattern also applied to families who were arrested together.

Once the historical investigation gave some sense of who might be buried in the Avellaneda cemetery, the team collected antemortem data—such as age at death, sex, height, handedness, dental work, and any old injuries—through interviews with family members, doctors, and dentists. As DNA testing became more sophisticated, they also took DNA samples from relatives. They could then apply these data to the analysis of skeletal material recovered.

Third, the team used archaeological techniques to excavate the cemetery. In Sector 134, they found nineteen mass graves, eleven single burials, and more than 300 bullets. In the mass graves, the number of skeletons ranged from ten to twenty-eight. Nearly all had been buried without clothing or jewelry. Laboratory analysis, the fourth step in EAAF's approach, indicated the remains of 324 individuals—104 more than cemetery records indicated. About three-quarters of the skeletons were male, about a third elderly, but most of the female skeletons were of women who were between the ages of 21 and 35 at the time of death. The elderly seemed to have died of natural causes. Almost all of the much larger group of younger individuals (male and female) had died of gunshot wounds.

Through their work, the EAAF team who took on Karina's quest were able to reconstruct what had happened on the night of October 27. A joint police-army death squad had broken into the Manfil family's third-floor apartment, where most of the family members were asleep: 35-year-old Carlos Manfil, a politically active member of the party that had been overthrown by the military; his 28-year old wife, Angélica; and three of their four children—Carlitos, age 9; Karina herself, age 4; and 6-month-old Cristian. Also asleep in the apartment were guests of the Manfils, Rosario Ramírez, her husband José Vega, and their two children. As the attack began, 9-year-old Carlitos leaned out the window to see what was happening and was shot in the forehead. The other children hid under the bed and were wounded when the attackers sprayed the room with bullets.

The EAAF team determined that Karina's mother, Angélica, was killed inside the apartment. The other three adults tried to escape by climbing down the drainpipes. Carlos Manfil and Rosario Ramírez fell, fracturing their legs, and were shot and killed on the spot. Karina, her infant sibling Cristian, and the two Vega children, apparently overlooked by the death squad, were the only survivors. José Vega escaped but was caught about a year later and disappeared. The bodies of Carlos and Angélica, their son Carlitos, and Rosario Ramírez were not returned to their families, and the families were not even informed of their deaths. Some family members heard rumors that they were buried in Sector 134. The team interviewed family members about the antemortem details of the people who had disappeared and

searched the official records, where they discovered the death certificates that showed that the bodies had, in fact, been buried in Sector 134.

The only skeleton of a young boy recovered from this sector had a gunshot entrance wound in the frontal bone of the skull. The archaeological records showed that this particular skeleton came from a mass grave containing several adult skeletons, including three that matched the sex, age, height, and dental information that family members had provided about Carlos, Angélica, and Rosario. The male and one of the females had perimortem (meaning from around or at the time of death) fractures of the long bones of the legs. In 1991, the EAAF group found a file on the Manfil case from a military court that included an autopsy report, which described gunshot wounds and leg fractures corresponding to those of the skeletons.

The EAAF team felt that they could provisionally identify the skeletons but were not yet able to make a positive identification. So they sent bone samples to a lab at Oxford University, where nuclear DNA was extracted, and they sent teeth from each skull, along with blood samples from family members, to a lab at the University of California Berkeley for mitochondrial DNA (mtDNA) testing. By August 1992, the geneticists had connected the DNA of two of the skeletons—those of Carlitos and his mother, Angélica. Furthermore, the mtDNA testing of a tooth from the skeleton believed to be Angélica's matched the mtDNA from the blood of her daughter Karina, and the mtDNA of the male presumed to be Carlos Manfil matched mtDNA from the blood of his mother. The genetic analyses confirmed the historical and anthropological results, and the Argentine Federal Court of Appeals accepted the EAAF report on the Manfil case, releasing the remains to the family. This case marked the first time that the court had accepted DNA evidence for skeletal identification. It took several more years to locate relatives of Rosario Ramírez, but once found, DNA analysis established a positive identification of the remaining skeleton. "In December 1992, Karina's sixteen-year quest finally ended when she was able to inter the long-lost bones of her father, mother, and little brother Carlitos in a modest family crypt. Ironically, it stands in the cemetery of Avellaneda, not far from Sector 134" (Doretti and Snow 2009, 311).

Despite the difficulty in resolving such cases, the EAAF continues its work. They point out that their work benefits from the four-field anthropological approach: their skills as biological anthropologists are complemented by their training in archaeology, which allows them to excavate properly and to interpret the burials they find, and their training in cultural anthropology, which provides them "with some insight and sensitivity in dealing with families and communities oppressed by the violence" (329). The EAAF's website is www.eaaf.org.

Figure 2.12 Skin color in human populations shows continuous variation, that is; different skin shades grade imperceptibly into one another without sharp breaks. Geneticists have shown that such continuous variation is produced by polygeny, the interaction of many genes to produce a single, observable trait.

one trait, a phenomenon called **pleiotropy**. For example, the *S* allele that gives human red blood cells increased resistance to malarial parasites also reduces the amount of oxygen these cells can carry (Rothwell 1977, 18). Similarly, the allele that causes the feathers of chickens to be white also works to slow down their body growth (Lerner and Libby 1976). The discovery of pleiotropy showed that genes do not produce traits in isolation. Many geneticists came to focus attention on what the Russian geneticist Sergei Chetverikov called the "genetic milieu," investigating the effects that different genes could have on one another (Figure 2.13). For example, Theodosius Dobzhansky was able to demonstrate that "certain genes or chromosomes could convey superior fitness in some combinations, and be lethal in combination with other chromosomes" (Mayr 1982, 580).

Mutation

Early in the twentieth century, geneticists discovered that very occasionally a new allele can result when the old form of a gene suddenly changes (or undergoes a **mutation**) but that, otherwise, genes are stable. Mutation thus explains how genetic inheritance can be unchanging and still produce the variation that makes evolutionary change possible (Mayr 1982, 755). Being part of a process of stable inheritance means, however, that the occurrence of genetic mutations is random with respect to the adaptive challenges facing the organism in which

it occurs: mutations do not occur because the organism "needs" them. Thus, modern geneticists rejected Lamarckian transformational evolution because it assumes a theory of modifiable inheritance. That is, to put it in modern terms, Lamarck assumed that information about the adaptive needs of an organism can somehow be fed back directly into the eggs or sperm cells of that organism, reshaping the information they contain, thereby allowing an adaptation to be passed on to offspring.

Modern genetics, by contrast, assumes that, apart from mutation, genes are inherited unchanged from parent organisms and that it is impossible for an organism's experiences or "needs" to feed back and reshape the genetic information in the sex cells. Natural selection can act only on randomly produced variation, which makes evolution by natural selection a two-step process. First, random genetic variation is produced. Second, those organisms whose variant traits better equip them to meet environmental challenges survive and produce more offspring than those whose traits equip them less well.

It is important to emphasize that, from a Darwinian point of view, *individual organisms* do not evolve genetically. Barring mutations (or the interventions of genetic engineering), individual organisms are stuck with the genes they are born with. However, the *populations* to which individuals belong *can evolve* as each generation contributes different numbers of offspring to the generation that comes after it. Put another way, from a Darwinian perspective, the only *biological* effect an individual can have on its population's evolution is in terms of the *number of offspring* that it bequeaths to the next generation. More (or fewer) offspring mean more (or fewer) copies of parental genes in the next generation. This is why Darwinian population biologists traditionally track evolutionary change by measuring changes in gene frequencies over time.

---

pleiotropy The phenomenon whereby a single gene may affect more than one phenotypic trait.

mutation The creation of a new allele for a gene when the portion of the DNA molecule to which it corresponds is suddenly altered.

Gene effects

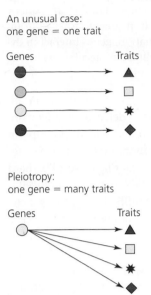

An unusual case:
one gene = one trait

Polygeny trait:
many genes = a single trait

The most usual case, a
combination of polygeny
and pleiotropy:
many genes = many traits

Pleiotropy:
one gene = many traits

Figure 2.13 Only rarely is a single physical trait the result of the action of a single gene. Many traits are the result of gene interaction, involving polygeny, or pleiotropy or, as is usually the case, both.

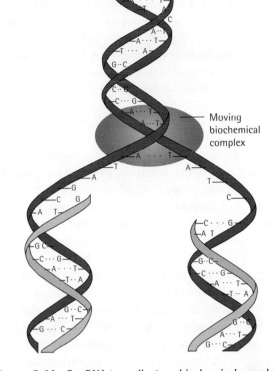

Moving biochemical complex

Figure 2.14 For DNA to replicate, a biochemical complex moves along the molecule and "unzips" the double helix, and two complete copies are rebuilt from appropriate molecules floating in the nucleus. Adenine (A) always attracts thymine (T), and cytosine (C) always attracts guanine (G).

DNA and the Genome

The discovery in the early 1950s of the structure of chromosomes greatly expanded our understanding of genetic mutation. We now know that chromosomes are made up largely of long molecules of deoxyribonucleic acid, or **DNA**, parts of which are used by living cells as templates for the construction, or *synthesis*, of proteins that make up most of the tissues and organs of any living organism. The DNA molecule, assembled in the shape of a double helix, resembles a twisted ladder, the rungs of which are made up of chemical components called "bases." Although there are many bases, DNA ordinarily makes use of only four: guanine, cytosine, adenine, and thymine. Each rung of the DNA ladder is made up of two of these bases: guanine always links to cytosine, and adenine always links to thymine. Faithful copies of DNA molecules are made when chromosomes are copied prior to mitosis or meiosis. The biochemical machinery of the cell breaks the chemical bonds holding the bases together and the DNA ladder splits apart, like a zipper unzipping (Figure 2.14). The absent half of each separated strand of DNA is then rebuilt from appropriate complementary bases that float freely within the nucleus of a cell. When this process is complete, two identical copies of the same DNA molecule are produced. The sum total of all the genetic material in the cell nucleus is called the **genome**.

Discovery of the structure and operation of DNA solidified the rejection of Lamarckian views by geneticists.

Simply put, no matter how useful or valuable a particular adaptation might be to an organism, genetic inheritance provides no mechanism whereby such information could be directly transmitted through that organism's tissues and cells in order to restructure the organism's DNA in a more "adaptive" form. At the same time, knowledge of DNA explained what mutations were: changes in the structure of the DNA molecule. Cosmic radiation, heat, and chemicals can all alter the structure of DNA; and when these alterations occur in the sex cells, they can be passed on to offspring.

Mutations can be harmful or helpful, but they may also have no effect at all. Mutations that neither help nor harm an organism are called "neutral" mutations. Molecular biologists have found an enormous amount of variation in those portions of the DNA molecule involved in protein synthesis, much of which appears to

---

DNA (deoxyribonucleic acid) The structure that carries the genetic heritage of an organism as a kind of blueprint for the organism's construction and development.

genome The sum total of all the genetic information about an organism, carried on the chromosomes in the cell nucleus.

be neutral, although this is controversial. We remain ignorant of the functions played by many portions of the human genome. Especially mysterious are those DNA sequences that apparently remain inactive, or "silent." One such sequence in humans, known as Alu, has 300 base pairs, "copies of which are periodically generated and integrated into the genome at apparently random places" (Marks 1995, 140).

When segments of the DNA molecule are required for particular cellular processes, parts of the cellular machinery enter the cell nucleus, unwind the relevant portion of a chromosome, and make copies of (or *transcribe*) relevant portions of the DNA molecule. These transcriptions are then transported into the cytoplasm of the cell and used to construct proteins, molecules that are basic to an organism's life processes (Figure 2.15). But this process is far from simple. Ironically perhaps, the more molecular biologists have learned about the way DNA functions in cells, the more difficult it has become for them to provide an unambiguous definition of what a "gene" is and what it does. As biologist Henry Plotkin observes, until the 1950s, geneticists assumed that genes occupied discrete positions on chromosomes, "like beads on a string."

This image has had to be radically revised. Genes, it turns out, are structurally complex, almost messy. They are smeared across chromosomes, with large reaches of DNA not coding for anything as far as currently known. Genes also form complex families of spatially widespread units. . . . Far from being rather dull, inert, passive stores of information, genes interact in dynamic ways with other cellular molecules, including their own products. (2003, 38)

Many popular accounts of genes portray DNA as an all-powerful "master molecule" that determines an organism's physical appearance, with the added assumption that unless genes mutate, new physical traits will never appear. This is incorrect. Biologist Mary Jane West-Eberhard points out that most of the genetic variation in multicellular organisms comes from the shuffling of *existing* genetic sequences at different stages of the developmental process, rather than from mutation (2003, 334). Moreover, when more and more *different* developmental events become dependent on the *same* DNA sequences, these sequences become more resistant to evolutionary change, a phenomenon known as *generative entrenchment* (West-Eberhard 2003, 326; Wimsatt and Schank 1988). For these reasons, many biologists argue that an exclusive focus on the role of DNA in evolution must give way to a more complex view that situates genes as one component in the biological processes of living cells, playing different roles at different stages in the life cycles of developing organisms and in the evolutionary histories of living species.

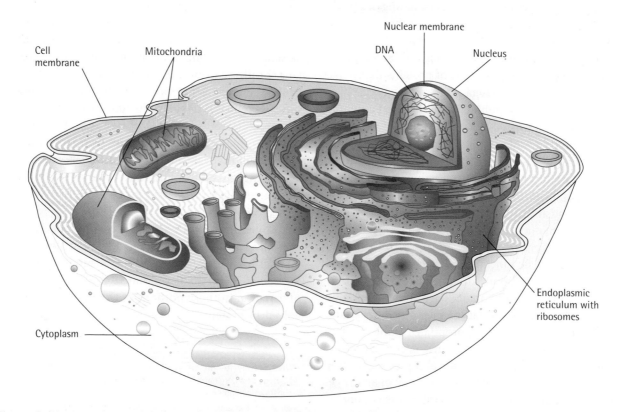

Figure 2.15   A nucleated cell is a complex system involving many components. DNA replication and protein synthesis are cellular processes that both involve and affect many cellular components.

Our experiences do not affect our genes, however: evolutionary biologists have rejected the Lamarckian notion of genetic transmission of experience. Further, "the history of a species' biological evolution is stored nowhere in the individual members of the species. Their present state is, indeed, a consequence of their history, but the genes currently possessed by the species are all that matter for its evolutionary future, irrespective of how it acquired those genes" (Lewontin 1982, 148).

"There Is No 'Race Memory' in Biology, Only in Books"

"Genetic inheritance is unchanging inheritance," which means that a Lamarckian inheritance of acquired characteristics is impossible via genetic mechanisms. Because of the overwhelming evidence we now possess to support this statement, evolutionary biologists have rejected the notion that something experienced by individuals in one generation can be genetically transmitted to their offspring and become a permanent part of their genetic heritage, a notion sometimes referred to as "race memory." Science fiction writers often use the concept of race memory in their plots, but they are not alone. We still encounter popular explanations of human behavior that appeal to race memory. One well-known example is the following: our ancestors killed animals for food, and this habit somehow sent a message to their genes to produce descendants who were born with an instinctive appetite for murder.

As you can see, genetic race memory is scientific nonsense. There is no biological mechanism that transforms an organism's experiences into messages that penetrate the eggs and sperm and restructure the genes inside them. Evolutionary history can only be inferred on the basis of information about the way a species, or its ancestors, lived at particular times in its past. None of that information is genetic; it is behavioral, ecological, and—in the human case—cultural. As Lewontin puts it, "There is no 'race memory' in biology, only in books" (1982, 148).

Genotype, Phenotype, and the Norm of Reaction

Geneticists realized long ago that the molecular structure of genes (or **genotype**) had to be distinguished from the observable, measurable overt characteristics of an organism which genes help to produce (its **phenotype**). For example, the sequences of bases on a stretch of DNA (genotypes) are used by living cells to assemble strings of amino acids that bond to form proteins (phenotypes), but bases are not the same thing as protein molecules. How does a genotype get realized in a phenotype? The question is not idle because fertilized eggs do not turn into organisms in a vacuum. Living organisms grow in a physical environment that provides them with nourishment, protection, and other vital resources to support their development over time until they are mature and able to reproduce their own offspring. Without the raw materials for protein synthesis supplied by the ovum, and later by food, genotypes can do nothing. At the same time, just as one gene does not equal one trait, different genotypes may be associated with the same phenotype. Mendel first showed this when he was able to demonstrate the existence of recessive genes. That is, red flowers could be produced by homozygous dominant parents (i.e., both red) as well as by heterozygous parents (i.e., one red and one white); but only one in every four offspring of heterozygous parents would have the chance of producing white flowers (i.e., if it received a recessive white gene from each parent). Nevertheless, individuals with the same genotype—twins, for example, or cuttings from a single plant or cloned animals—may also develop a range of different phenotypes.

To understand how we get from an organism's genotype to its phenotype, we must consider both genotype and phenotype in relation to the environment in which that organism developed. Biologists compare the phenotypic outcomes of organisms with the same genotype in different environments and with different genotypes in the same environment, and they plot these outcomes on what is called a **norm of reaction**. Levins and Lewontin define the norm of reaction as "a table or graph of correspondence between the phenotypic outcome of development and the environment in which the development took place. Each genotype has its own norm of reaction, specifying how the developing organism will respond to various environments. In general, a genotype cannot be characterized by a unique phenotype" (1985, 90–91).

Figure 2.16 shows the norms of reaction for three different genotypes for a particular trait in *Drosophila*, the fruit fly. The genotype in question controls the number of ommatidia, or light-receptor cells, that a particular individual will have in its compound eye. Flies carrying the Wild genotype usually have about 1,000 ommatidia in

---

genotype The genetic information about particular biological traits encoded in an organism's DNA.

phenotype The observable, measurable overt characteristics of an organism.

norm of reaction A table or graph that displays the possible range of phenotypic outcomes for a given genotype in different environments.

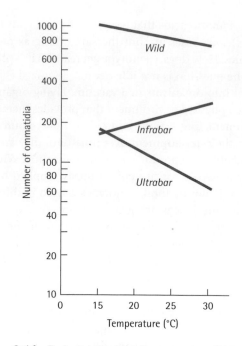

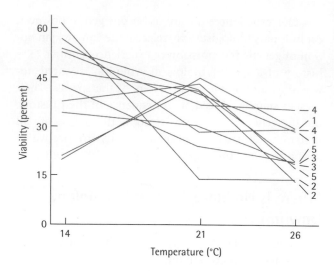

Figure 2.16 Each genotype has its own norm of reaction, specifying how the developing organism will respond to various environments. How many eye cells (*ommatidia*) a fruit fly develops depends both on that fly's genotype and the environmental temperature at which development takes place. Not only does the same genotype produce different phenotypes at different temperatures, but different genotypes may produce the same phenotype at the same temperatures (Levins and Lewontin 1985, 91).

Figure 2.17 Comparison of norms of reaction for variant fruit fly genotypes in variant environments shows two things: (1) some genotypes always do better than others at any temperature and (2) no single genotype does better than all the rest at every temperature. Such evidence argues against the concept of a single, ideal genotype that is supposed to be produced deterministically by the genes (Levins and Lewontin 1985, 92).

their eyes, whereas those with the Ultrabar and Infrabar genotypes have far fewer. However, as the graph shows, the number of ommatidia a fly develops depends not only on that fly's genotype but also on the environment (in this case, the temperature) at which development takes place—that is, the same genotype produces different phenotypes at different temperatures.

Figure 2.16 demonstrates yet another surprising fact about the relationship of genes to the environment: at about 15°C, both Ultrabar and Infrabar genotypes develop about the same number of ommatidia! In other words, different genotypes may also produce the same phenotype in a particular environment. This fact illustrates what Levins and Lewontin call the "many-to-many relationship between gene and organism" (1985, 94) and shows that the fitness of a particular genotype can vary depending on the environment. Figure 2.17 displays norms of reaction for the survival at different temperatures of immature fruit flies with different genotypes, all of which were taken from natural populations. As the graph illustrates, some genotypes always do better than others at any given temperature, but there is no single genotype that does better than all the rest at every temperature. The complexity of the relationship between

genes, organism, and environment does not mean "that the organism is infinitely plastic, or that any genotype can correspond to any phenotype. Norms of reaction for different genotypes are different, but it is the norms of reaction that are the proper object of study for developmental biologists rather than some ideal organism that is supposed to be produced deterministically by the genes" (Levins and Lewontin 1985, 94).

The principles apply to humans as well. Different genotypes can produce the same phenotype in some environments, and the same genotype can produce different phenotypes in different environments. Despite very different genotypes, the eyes of newborn babies all tend to be the same color, as does hair color as we age. Indeed, the phenotype of a single individual can vary markedly from one environment to the next. As Lewontin points out, "People who 'tend to be fat' on 5,500 calories a day 'tend to be thin' on 2,000. Families with both 'tendencies' will be found living in the same towns in Northeastern Brazil, where two thirds of the families live on less than what is considered a minimum subsistence diet by the World Health Organization" (1982, 20).

Increasing numbers of biologists are addressing not only the ways in which the organism's phenotype is shaped by the environment in which it develops, but also how organisms shape the environments in which they develop. For example, in their book *Niche Construction*, F. John Odling-Smee, Kevin Laland, and Marcus

In Their Own Words

How Living Organisms Construct Their Environments

Geneticist Richard Lewontin rejects the notion that living organisms are passively molded by the "environment," thereby challenging us to rethink exactly what an environment is.

We must replace the adaptationist view of life with a constructionist one. It is not that organisms find environments and either adapt themselves to the environments or die. They actually *construct* their environment out of bits and pieces. In this sense, the environment of organisms is coded in their DNA and we find ourselves in a kind of reverse Lamarckian position. Whereas Lamarck supposed that changes in the external world would cause changes in the internal structures, we see that the reverse is true. An organism's genes, to the extent that they influence what that organism does in its behavior, physiology, and morphology, are at the same time helping to construct an environment. So, if genes change in evolution, the environment of the organism will change, too.

Consider the immediate environment of a human being. If one takes motion pictures of a person, using schlieren optics that detect differences in the refractive index of the air, one can see that a layer of warm, moist air completely surrounds each one of us and is slowly rising from our legs and bodies and going off the top of our heads. In fact, every living organism including trees has this boundary layer of warm air that is created by the organism's metabolism. The result is that we are encapsulated in a little atmosphere created by our own metabolic activities. One consequence is what is called the wind-chill factor. The reason that it gets much colder when the wind blows across us is because the wind is blowing away the boundary layer and our skins are then exposed to a different set of temperatures and humidities. Consider a mosquito feeding on the surface of the human body. That mosquito is completely immersed in the boundary layer that we have constructed. It is living in a warm, moist world. Yet one of the most common evolutionary changes for all organisms is a change in size, and over and over again organisms have evolved to be larger. If the mosquito species begins to evolve to a larger size, it may in fact find itself with its back in the "stratosphere" and only up to its knees in the warm, moist boundary layer while it is feeding. The consequence will be that the mosquito's evolution has put

it into an entirely different world. Moreover, as human beings early in their evolution lost hair and the distribution of sweat glands over their bodies changed, the thickness of the boundary layer changed and so changed the microworld that they carry with them, making it rather less hospitable for fleas, mosquitoes, and other parasites that live on hairy animals. The first rule of the real relation between organisms and environment is that environments do not exist in the absence of organisms but are constructed by them out of bits and pieces of the external world.

The second rule is that the environment of organisms is constantly being remade during the life of those living beings. When plants send down roots, they change the physical nature of the soil, breaking it up and aerating it. They exude organic molecules, humic acids, that change the soil's chemical nature as well. They make it possible for various beneficial fungi to live together with them and penetrate their root systems. They change the height of the water table by removing water. They alter the humidity in their immediate neighborhood, and the upper leaves of a plant change the amount of light that is available to the lower leaves. When the Canadian Department of Agriculture takes weather records for agricultural purposes, they do not set up a weather station in an open field or on the roof of a building. They take measurements of temperature and humidity at various levels above the ground in a field of growing plants because the plants are constantly changing the physical conditions that are relevant to agriculture. Moles burrow in the soil. Earthworms through their castings completely change the local topology. Beavers have had at least as important an effect on the landscape in North America as humans did until the beginning of the last century. Every breath you take removes oxygen and adds carbon dioxide to the world. Mort Sahl once said, "Remember, no matter how cruel and nasty and evil you may be, every time you take a breath you make a flower happy."

Source: Lewontin 1991, 112–14.

Feldman argue that organisms play two roles in evolution, carrying genes and interacting with environments.

> Specifically, organisms interact with environments, take energy and resources from environments, make micro- and macrohabitat choices with respect to environments, construct artifacts, emit detritus and die in environments, and by doing all these things, modify at least some of the natural selection pressures in their own and in each other's local environments. This second role for phenotypes in evolution is not well described or understood by evolutionary biologists and has not been subject to a great deal of investigation. We call it "niche construction." . . . (2003, 1)

Niche construction is understood to occur either when an organism actively perturbs the environment or when it actively moves into a different environment (Odling-Smee et al. 2003, 41). If the physical, environmental consequences of niche construction are erased between generations, this process can have no long-term effects on evolution. But if these consequences endure, they feed back into the evolutionary process, *modifying the selection pressures* experienced by subsequent generations of organisms (Figure 2.18). Odling-Smee et al. provide numerous examples taken from all taxonomic groups of living organisms, including blue-green algae, earthworms, dam-building beavers, burrowing rodents, and nest-building birds (2003, 50–115). Their most controversial proposal is that niche construction be incorporated into evolutionary theory as an additional adaptive process alongside natural selection and that nongenetic "legacies of modified natural selection pressures" be recognized in addition to the genetic legacies passed on in the egg and sperm. In their view, a suitably extended evolutionary theory would recognize both niche construction and natural selection as evolutionary processes contributing together to the dynamic adaptive match between organisms and environments (2003, 2–3).

Taking niche construction into account encourages biologists to look at organisms in a new way. Rather than picturing them as passively staying in place, subject to selection pressures they cannot affect, organisms are now seen as sometimes capable of actively intervening in their evolutionary fate by *modifying the environment:* Odling-Smee et al. predict that "those members of the population that are least fit relative to the imposed selective regime will be the individuals that exhibit the strongest evidence for niche

Figure 2.18   Many species, including beavers, construct key features of their own ecological niches. Beaver dams modify selection pressures experienced by beavers, but they also alter selection pressures experienced by neighboring species whose own niches are altered by the presence of the beaver dam in their habitats.

construction" (2003, 298). Alternatively, organisms that *move into a new environment* with different selection pressures can no longer be automatically identified as the unquestionable losers in evolutionary competition in their former environment. Niche construction portrays all organisms (not just human organisms) as active agents living in environments that are vulnerable to the consequences of their activities, contributing in potentially significant ways to the evolutionary histories of their own and other species.

According to Odling-Smee et al., acknowledging niche construction as an adaptive process offers a way to link evolutionary theory and ecosystem ecology, and it also alters the relationship between evolutionary theory and the human sciences (2003, 3). Odling-Smee and colleagues regard human beings as "virtuoso niche constructors" (2003, 367), and their arguments should be of great interest to anthropologists, especially cultural

---

niche construction   When an organism actively perturbs the environment or when it actively moves into a different environment.

anthropologists who insist that any explanation of social and culture change must make room for **human agency**: the way people struggle, often against great odds, to exercise some control over their lives. The agency of organisms as niche constructors matters in evolution "because it introduces feedback into the evolutionary dynamic [which] significantly modifies the selection pressures [on organisms]" (Odling-Smee et al. 2003, 2; see also Deacon 2003). As we will see in later chapters, we as humans are never free to do exactly as we please but always have options for action. And the actions we choose to undertake can sometimes reshape the selective pressures we experience, exactly as niche construction theorists would predict.

What Does Evolution Mean?

Ever since Darwin, evolutionary theory has been subjected to repeated testing. Although the results of those tests have led to modifications of the theory in certain respects, none of them has ever called the concept of evolution itself into question. Indeed, the power of evolutionary theory is illustrated by how the work of Linnaeus, Darwin, and Mendel meshes together so beautifully, even though each of them worked independently. Modern biologists agree that no process other than evolution can explain nearly as much about the history of life on earth.

The study of evolution in contemporary biology is very lively. New evidence and new ways of interpreting evidence have led many evolutionists to question the adequacy of their old ways of understanding and to develop different perspectives on the evolutionary process. They are keenly aware that a phenomenon as complex as evolution requires theoretical pluralism—that is, the recognition that a variety of processes operating at different levels work together to produce the similarities and differences that characterize the living world. As evolutionary theorists Peter Richerson, Robert Boyd, and Joseph Henrich remind us, "Evolutionary theory prescribes a method, not an answer, and a wide range of hypotheses can be cast in an evolutionary framework. . . . Darwinism as a method is not at all committed to any particular picture of how evolution works or what it produces. Any sentence that starts with 'evolutionary theory predicts' should be regarded with caution" (2003, 366).

Life has a comprehensible history for modern evolutionists. How it is likely to change next, however, cannot be predicted with any certainty because random

factors continue to play an important evolutionary role. Human biologists have been forced to rethink the place of their own species in the web of life. Unquestionably, the result has been to dislodge human beings from the center. Most contemporary evolutionists would probably agree with Steven Stanley that "not all paths lead toward *Homo sapiens*, and possibly no persistent path led directly toward him" (1981, 151). Indeed, the very notion that organisms are "going somewhere" along a linear evolutionary "path" has been questioned. Stephen Jay Gould has argued that apparent directional trends in evolution such as increasing body size are "really random evolution away from small size, not directed evolution toward large size" (1996, 162). He suggests that a more appropriate way to think of the history of life is in terms of expansion or contraction over time in the total range of variation in living forms (i.e., life's "full house"). To do so is to recognize that bacteria have always been the most common form of life on this planet. Organisms of extreme complexity (such as human beings) were bound to appear as the range of variation expanded, but the kind of organisms they turned out to be "is utterly unpredictable, partly random, and entirely contingent—not at all foreordained by the mechanisms of evolution. . . . Humans are here by the luck of the draw, not the inevitability of life's direction or evolution's mechanism" (Gould 1996, 174–75).

Moreover, once we consider our own species alongside other species whose comings and goings have been so well documented in the fossil record, we cannot avoid grappling with the following well-known facts:

> The only certainty about the future of our species is that it is limited. Of all the species that have ever existed 99.999% are extinct. The average lifetime of a carnivore genus is only 10 million years, and the average lifetime of a species is much shorter. Indeed, life on earth is nearly half over: Fossil evidence shows that life began about 3 billion years ago, and the sun is due to become a red giant about 4 billion years from now, consuming life (and eventually the whole earth) in its fire. (Lewontin 1982, 169)

Our species' story is far from over. Who knows? Perhaps we will find a way to spread beyond our solar system, and our descendants may escape the grim fate that awaits our planet in 4 billion years. In the meantime, we remain on earth, searching for answers about who we are and how we are to live our lives.

human agency The way people struggle, often against great odds, to exercise some control over their lives.

Chapter Summary

1. Evolutionary theory is a testable, unified, and fruitful scientific theory. Material evidence of evolutionary change over time can be found in the fossil record and in the pattern of distribution of living species of organisms.

2. Before Darwin, European thinkers divided living things into natural kinds, each of which was thought to have its own unchanging essence. The Great Chain of Being was understood as God's creation, naturally harmonious and without gaps, and it inspired Linnaeus's important eighteenth-century taxonomy of living organisms.

3. In the nineteenth century, catastrophism and uniformitarianism undermined the Great Chain of Being. Catastrophism was based on the ideas of Georges Cuvier, who argued that some species had become extinct in massive natural disasters, after which new species were introduced from elsewhere. Uniformitarianism was promoted by geologist Charles Lyell, who argued that the same processes of erosion and uplift that can be observed to change the earth's surface today had been at work in the past. Uniformitarianism implied that changes in life-forms were as gradual and reversible as changes in the earth's surface.

4. Lamarck tried to preserve the view of a harmonious Great Chain of Being by claiming that fossil species had not become extinct. Lamarck argued that individual members of a species are all able to transform themselves in the same way when facing the same environmental pressures. Lamarckian transformational evolution has been rejected by contemporary evolutionary researchers. In contrast to Lamarck, Darwin and Wallace concluded that the similarities shared by distinct living species could be explained if all such species had descended from a single parental species that had lived in the past. In addition, Darwin proposed that such "descent with modification" could occur as a result of the straightforward, mechanistic process of natural selection.

5. Darwin's theory of evolution by natural selection (or variational evolution) was based on the principle of variation, the principle of heredity, and the principle of natural selection. Variational evolution was driven by what Darwin called the "struggle for existence" between individuals of the same species to survive and reproduce. In a given environment, those variant individuals who survive and leave greater numbers of offspring are said to have greater fitness than other members of their species who leave fewer offspring. There is no such thing as "absolute" fitness. Today, evolutionists recognize four evolutionary processes, including natural selection, that can determine which variant individuals in a population will leave greater numbers of offspring than others.

6. Evolutionary theorists use the concept of adaptation to refer both to a process of mutual adjustment between organisms and their environments and to the phenotypic features of organisms that are produced by this process. Reconstructing accurate evolutionary histories of organisms requires distinguishing adaptations from exaptations.

7. Darwin did not know why offspring tend to resemble their parents, nor did he understand how variation was introduced into populations. Answers to these questions were developed in the field of genetics. Genes are associated with particular portions of the DNA molecules located on the chromosomes in the cell nucleus. The machinery of the cell uses DNA to synthesize proteins necessary for life processes and makes it possible for chromosomes to be copied before cells divide. Gene interaction helps explain how continuous traits, such as skin color or hair color, are the result of unchanging inheritance. Different genotypes may produce the same phenotype, and the same genotype may produce different phenotypes, depending on the kinds of environments in which organisms possessing these genotypes live and grow. That is, each genotype has its own norm of reaction.

8. The study of evolution in contemporary biology is very lively. Modern biologists agree that life on earth has evolved, but they have different views about how evolutionary processes work. Many evolutionary thinkers are increasingly convinced that a phenomenon as complex as biological evolution requires theoretical pluralism.

For Review

1. Define evolution.
2. Explain the kinds of material evidence that have been important in the development of evolutionary theory.
3. Define essentialism and the Great Chain of Being.
4. Explain the difference between transformational (Lamarckian) evolution and variational (Darwinian) evolution.

5. Describe the basic principles and driving force of natural selection.
6. Distinguish among aptation, adaptation, and exaptation.
7. Why is variation so important in evolutionary theory?
8. Explain nonblending, single-particle inheritance (Mendelian inheritance).
9. What is the difference between discontinuous and continuous variation?
10. Explain how, from a Darwinian perspective, it is populations (not individual organisms) that can evolve.
11. Explain what Richard Lewontin meant when he wrote "There is no 'race memory' in biology, only in books."
12. What are the differences between genotype and phenotype, and why are they important?
13. What is a norm of reaction? Explain its significance for the evolution of human populations.
14. Summarize the main components of niche construction.

Key Terms

adaptation 38
alleles 41
aptation 38
catastrophism 33
chromosomes 41
common origin 37
continuous variation 42
crossing over 42
discontinuous
  variation 42
DNA 47
essentialism 32
evolution 31

evolutionary theory 30
exaptation 38
fitness 38
gene 41
genetics 41
genome 47
genotype 49
genus 33
Great Chain of Being 32
heterozygous 41
homozygous 41
human agency 53

linkage 42
locus 42
meiosis 41
Mendelian
  inheritance 40
mitosis 41
mutation 46
natural selection 37
niche construction 52
norm of reaction 49
pangenesis 39
phenotype 49

pleiotropy 46
polygeny 42
principle of independent
  assortment 41
principle of
  segregation 41
species 33
taxonomy 33
transformational
  evolution 35
uniformitarianism 33
variational evolution 37

Suggested Readings

Gould, Stephen Jay. 1987. *Time's arrow, time's cycle: Myth and metaphor in the discovery of geological time.* Cambridge, MA: Harvard University Press. *A fascinating account of the historical and cultural context out of which catastrophism and uniformitarianism were forged in the nineteenth century.*

———. 1996. *Full house: The spread of excellence from Plato to Darwin.* New York: Harmony Books. *An eloquent and entertaining defense of the view that human beings were not the end point of biological evolution and that bacteria are more properly regarded as the dominant life-forms on earth.*

Kevles, Daniel J., and Leroy Hood. 1992. *The code of codes: Scientific and social issues in the Human Genome Project.* Cambridge, MA: Harvard University Press. *This edited collection contains a wide range of articles by geneticists, molecular biologists, biochemists, historians of science, and social scientists who examine the prospects and consequences of mapping all the genes in the human body. The book offers a range of opinions on how fully we will know what it means to be human if we learn one day all there is to know about our genes.*

Lewontin, Richard. 1991. *Biology as ideology: The doctrine of DNA.* New York: Harper Perennial. *The text of this book began as a series of radio broadcasts for the Canadian Broadcasting Company and is supplemented with an article Lewontin published in the* New York Review of Books. *Lewontin's accessible and hard-hitting essay addresses excessive claims that are sometimes made in the name of human genetics and offers incisive criticism of current efforts by geneticists to map all the genes in the human body.*

———. 2001. *The triple helix: Gene, organism, and environment.* Cambridge, MA: Harvard University Press. *Lewontin reminds biologists not to forget the role of organisms and environment in discussions of evolution; these are often ignored in discussions that attribute everything to genes.*

Lovejoy, Arthur O. [1936] 1960. *The Great Chain of Being.* New York: Harper Torchbooks. *Originally published in 1936, this classic is as fresh and relevant as anything being written about evolution today. A marvelously clear and detailed account of pre-Darwinian thinking about life on earth.*

Marks, Jonathan. 1995. *Human biodiversity.* New York: Aldine. *Marks is a biological anthropologist with a strong commitment to a biocultural approach to human nature. This book is an excellent introduction to biological anthropology.*

What Can Evolutionary Theory Tell Us about Human Variation?

Not everyone looks the same. Why is that? Does it make a difference? Do the differences cluster together? In this chapter, we will look at the way evolutionary theory explains patterns of human biological variation. In particular, we will show why anthropologists have concluded that these patterns cannot be explained by the concept of biological "race."

Chapter Outline

◀ *San mother and daughter. Recent research shows that the San are the most genetically diverse people on earth.*

Chapter 2 presented some of the central concepts of modern evolutionary theory. This chapter looks at how biologists have used evolutionary theory in their research, especially research on human evolution. Evolutionary studies can be divided into two major subfields. **Microevolution** devotes attention to short-term evolutionary changes that occur within a given species over relatively few generations. It involves what is sometimes called "ecological time," or the pace of time as experienced by organisms living in and adapting to their ecological settings. **Macroevolution**, by contrast, focuses on long-term evolutionary changes, especially the origins of new species and their diversification across space and over millions of years. Macroevolutionary events, which span many generations and the growth and decay of many different ecological settings, are measured in geological time.

What Is Microevolution?

The Modern Evolutionary Synthesis and Its Legacy

In the 1930s and 1940s, biologists and geneticists worked to formulate a new way of thinking about evolution that combined Darwinian natural selection and Mendelian ideas about heredity. Until recently, this approach (called the "modern evolutionary synthesis" or "neo-Darwinism") dominated research and thinking in biology. As we saw in the last chapter, contemporary evolutionary theorists have challenged, expanded, and enriched this neo-Darwinian research program, much the way the formulators of the modern synthesis had earlier challenged, expanded, and enriched the contributions made by Darwin, Mendel, and other early evolutionary thinkers. But some achievements of the modern synthesis remain fundamental to our understandings of living organisms. In anthropology, perhaps the most significant contribution of neo-Darwinism was the way it undermined the nineteenth-century anthropological concept of "biological race," refocusing attention on a new understanding of biological species. After World War II, anthropologists like Sherwood Washburn rejected the old, race-based physical anthropology of the nineteenth and early twentieth centuries and replaced it with a "new physical anthropology" or "biological anthropology." Research in biological anthropology took for granted the common membership of all human beings in a single species and addressed human variation using concepts and methods drawn from neo-Darwinism (Strum et al. 1999).

Neo-Darwinians defined a **species** as "a reproductive community of populations (reproductively isolated from others) that occupies a specific niche in nature" (Mayr 1982, 273). This definition is based on several attributes of species. Species normally are subdivided into populations that are more or less separated from one another, although the separation is not complete. For example, prior to the rise of the great ancient civilizations, the human species was made up of widely scattered populations. Those populations living in North America had been separated from populations in Europe for thousands of years, until the European explorations of the Americas began in the fifteenth century. However, when Europeans and the native peoples of North America did come into contact, they were able to interbreed and produce viable, fertile offspring. From the biologist's perspective, this ability to interbreed and produce fertile offspring indicates that members of these different populations belong to the same reproductive community and, hence, the same species.

By contrast, members of one species are reproductively isolated from other species when interbreeding is impossible or when the offspring produced from such mating are not fertile. Horses and donkeys can interbreed to produce mules, but mules are infertile; hence, horses and donkeys do not belong to the same reproductive community.

Neo-Darwinians were also concerned about the genetic makeup of species. They introduced the concept of the **gene pool**, which includes all of the genes in the bodies of all members of a given species (or a population of a species). Using mathematical models, evolutionary theorists can estimate the **gene frequency** of particular genes—that is, the frequency of occurrence of gene variants or alleles within a particular gene pool. Measuring the stability or change of gene frequencies in populations over time allowed geneticists to trace short-term evolutionary change, in a new field called **population genetics**. Once population geneticists had identified a

---

microevolution A subfield of evolutionary studies that devotes attention to short-term evolutionary changes that occur within a given species over relatively few generations of ecological time.

macroevolution A subfield of evolutionary studies that focuses on long-term evolutionary changes, especially the origins of new species and their diversification across space and over millions of years of geological time.

species A reproductive community of populations (reproductively isolated from others) that occupies a specific niche in nature.

gene pool All the genes in the bodies of all members of a given species (or a population of a species).

gene frequency The frequency of occurrence of the variants of particular genes (i.e., of alleles) within the gene pool.

population genetics A field that uses statistical analysis to study short-term evolutionary change in large populations.

TABLE 3.1 Example of Allele Frequency Computation

Imagine you have just collected information on *MN* blood group genotypes for 250 humans in a given population. Your data are:
Number of *MM* genotype = 40
Number of *MN* genotype = 120
Number of *NN* genotype = 90
The allele frequencies are computed as follows:

GENOTYPE	NUMBER OF PEOPLE	TOTAL NUMBER OF ALLELES	NUMBER OF *M* ALLELES	NUMBER OF *N* ALLELES
MM	40	80	80	0
MN	120	240	120	120
NN	90	180	0	180
Total	250	500	200	300

The relative frequency of the *M* allele is computed as the number of *M* alleles divided by the total number of alleles: 200/500 = 0.4.
The relative frequency of the *N* allele is computed as the number of *N* alleles divided by the total number of alleles: 300/500 = 0.6.
As a check, note that the relative frequencies of the alleles must add up to 1.0 (0.4 + 0.6 = 1.0).

Source: Relethford 1996, 66.

target population, they analyzed its gene pool by calculating the frequencies of various alleles within that gene pool and trying to figure out what would happen to those frequencies if the carriers of the various alleles were subjected to particular selection pressures (Table 3.1). Some evolutionary geneticists tested these predictions on such organisms as fruit flies, but others concentrated on human beings.

The ability of human beings from anywhere in the world to interbreed successfully is one measure of membership in a single species. Comparing our genotypes provides additional evidence of our biological closeness. As we have seen, most alleles come in a range of different forms (i.e., are **polymorphous**), and known polymorphous variants fall into one of two groups. The first group, *polymorphic alleles*, accounts for most genetic variation across populations. Populations differ not because they have mutually exclusive sets of alleles but because they possess different *proportions* of the same set of alleles. An example is the ABO blood groups: the polymorphic alleles *A*, *B*, and *O* are found in all human populations, but the frequency of each allele differs from population to population. The second group, *private polymorphisms*, includes alleles that are found in the genotypes of some, but usually not all, members of a particular population. One example is a genetically determined blood cell antigen known as the "Diego antigen." The Diego antigen occurs only in Asian and African populations, but 60 percent to 90 percent of the members of the populations where it is found do not have it (Marks 1995, 165). This work leads to the inescapable conclusion that the traditional Western concept of "race" is biologically

meaningless. Racial thinking is essentialistic. As we have seen, however, modern biologists, who think in population terms, have demonstrated that "humankind . . . is not divided into a series of genetically distinct units" (Jones 1986, 324). It also means that the boundaries said to define human "races" have been culturally imposed on shifting and unstable clusters of alleles (Marks 1995, 117).

Because genetic variation in human populations is mostly a matter of differences in the relative proportions of the same sets of alleles, the distribution of particular phenotypes shifts gradually from place to place across populations as the frequencies of some alleles increase while those of others decrease or stay the same. Moreover, the distributions of some traits (like skin color) do not match the distributions of other traits (like hair type). The pattern of gradually shifting geographic frequency of a phenotypic trait across human populations is called a **cline**. Clines can be represented on maps like Figure 3.4, which shows the gradually shifting distribution of differences in human skin color from the equator to the poles.

Phenotypic contrasts are greatest when people from very different places are brought together and compared, while ignoring the populations that connect

polymorphous Describes alleles that come in a range of different forms.
cline The gradual intergradation of genetic variation from population to population.

them (Marks 1995, 161). This is what happened when Europeans arrived in the New World, conquered the indigenous peoples, and imported slaves from Africa to work on their plantations. But if you were to walk from Stockholm, Sweden, to Cape Town, South Africa (or from Singapore to Beijing, China), you would perceive gradual changes in average skin color as you moved from north to south (or vice versa). Evolutionary biologists argue that skin pigmentation is distributed in this way as a consequence of natural selection: individuals in tropical populations with darker skin pigmentation had a selective advantage in equatorial habitats over individuals with light pigmentation. By contrast, populations farther away from the equator faced less intense selection pressure for darkly pigmented skin and perhaps even selective pressures in favor of lighter skins. But *different* selection pressures would have been at work on other traits, such as stature or hair type, within the same population, which is why the geographical distributions of these traits do *not* match up neatly with the distribution of skin pigmentation. To make things even more complex, different genes may be involved in the production of similar phenotypic traits in different populations: for example, although different ancestral populations of humans living near the equator have dark skin, the identity and the number of alleles involved in the production of this phenotypic trait may be different in different populations.

Evidence of intergradation in human phenotypes led biological anthropologist Frank Livingstone to declare over 40 years ago that "There are no races, there are only clines" (1964, 279). Clinal variation explains why people searching for "races" have never been able to agree on how many there are or how they can be identified. *Clines are not groups.* The only group involved in clinal mapping is the entire human species. Each cline is a map of the distribution of a *single* trait. Biologists might compare the clinal maps of trait A and trait B to see if they overlap and, if so, by how much. But the more clines they superimpose, the more obvious it becomes that the trait distributions they map *do not coincide* in ways that neatly subdivide into distinct human subpopulations. Since the biological concept of "race" predicts exactly such overlap, it cannot be correct. In other words, *clinal analysis tests the biological concept of "race" and finds nothing in nature to match it.* And if biological races cannot be found, then the so-called races identified over the years can only be symbolic constructs, based on cultural elaboration of a few superficial phenotypic differences— skin color, hair type and quantity, skin folds, lip shape, and the like. In short, early race theorists "weren't extracting races from their set of data, they were imposing races upon it" (Marks 1995, 132).

The Molecularization of Race?

During the 1960s and 1970s, anthropologists and others explained that there was no biological basis for race; in other words, all humans are part of a single species. Although there is internal variation within the species, it does not easily fall into the cultural categories of "race" as they had developed in the United States. In the past 30 years, however, we have witnessed in the United States and elsewhere a resurgence of attempts to explain group differences in terms of race. Sometimes it is the powerful who engage in such practices, in controversial books such as *The Bell Curve* (Herrnstein and Murray 1994). Sometimes, however, it is members of politically and economically marginalized groups who do so, as a calculated move in political struggles with those who dominate them.

Perhaps no more complicated set of questions has been raised about race in the twenty-first century than those that have emerged following the completion of the Human Genome Project (HGP) in 2003. The goals of the project were as follows:

- to identify all the approximately 20,000–25,000 genes in human DNA
- to determine the sequences of the 3 billion chemical base pairs that make up human DNA
- to store this information in databases
- to improve tools for data analysis
- to transfer related technologies to the private sector
- to address the ethical, legal, and social issues that may arise from the project (http://www.ornl.gov/sci/techresources/Human_Genome/home.shtml).

As anthropologist Nadia Abu El-Haj has shown (2007), some molecular biologists quickly mobilized the information produced by the HGP to develop *biomedicine*, a form of medical treatment based on the identification of genes associated with particular diseases. Some formed private biomedical research companies that promised to help create a future of *personalized medicine*: therapies based on knowledge of individuals' genomes that were precisely tailored to a particular individual's degree of genetic risk for a particular disease.

Sequencing individual genomes is expensive, however, which is the reason that researchers have used genetic data from other members of populations to which individuals belong as a surrogate for an individual's particular genome. For example, if your mother's brother suffers from a particular disease with a genetic component, researchers may conclude that you and other biological relatives have an increased risk for that disease. That is, your biological family becomes a surrogate, or stand-in, for genetic risk factors that potentially are faced by individual family members. As Abu El-Haj explains, some biomedical researchers in the United States use "racial" groups as surrogates for individuals who consider themselves to be members of such groups. The thinking is that if a disease marker shows up in the genomes of some people said to be members of a particular "race," then this may be an indication that other people classified in the same "race" might also be at risk for the disease.

As Abu El-Haj shows, it is incorrect to conclude that medical researchers who use "race" in this pragmatic fashion are also committed to the doctrines associated with scientific racism. Rather, their main motivation is to discover whether "race"-based research techniques produce useful biomedical information. Nevertheless, some observers suspect that this kind of research will only give the older racial classifications a new lease on life (see In Their Own Words, page 64). Abu El-Haj agrees that the growth of biomedicine has indeed revived a concept of "race," but she asks, "Is this 'race' the same scientific object or concept as that produced at the turn of the twentieth century?" (Abu El-Haj 2007, 284). And her answer is "no."

First, the old race concept focused on the classification of *phenotypes*, whereas the new race concept classifies *genotypes*. The transition from a phenotypic to a genotypic view of race came about, she says, as a consequence of changing historical understandings of sickle-cell disease in the United States. In the first part of the twentieth century, sickle-cell anemia was identified as a disease of "black" people—of African Americans. But later, after the development of population genetics, its cause was traced to molecular genes: the presence of an abnormal "sickling" hemoglobin allele at a particular locus on a chromosome. "At the meeting point between these two definitions of the disease . . . the commitment to race as a molecular attribute took form," leading over time to "the correlation of disease risk and racial difference" (Abu El-Haj 2007, 287).

Second, nineteenth-century race science aimed to discover how many races existed and to assign all individuals to their "true race." The commercial technologies used by biomedical researchers do distinguish human populations in terms of the continents from which their ancestors presumably came. But all these technologies assume that everyone has a mixed ancestry of some kind; the goal is to measure how much of which ancestry markers are present in each population, thereby determining the degree of risk that members of that population face for genetic diseases associated with particular

ancestries. As Abu El-Haj says, ancestry markers "are not used to discover one's 'true' race . . . . Instead, ancestry markers are used, for example, to understand the Puerto Rican population's risk for asthma" (Abu El-Haj 2007, 288). That is, if genome analysis determined that some ancestral population contributed genes to contemporary Puerto Rican populations that enhanced their risk for developing asthma, this information would be crucial in devising personalized drugs precisely keyed to individuals with different risks for asthma.

The best known example of a biomedical treatment designed to treat members of a particular "race" is probably BiDil. On its BiDil website, NitroMed, the manufacturer of BiDil, describes this drug as "a fixed-dose combination medicine consisting of isosorbide dinitrate and hydralazine hydrochloride. It is approved by the FDA for the treatment of heart failure in self-identified African American patients when added to standard heart failure medicines" (http://www.bidil.com/pnt/questions .php#1). FDA approval, the site reports, was based on results of the African-American Heart Failure Trial (or A-HeFT), which "studied 1,050 self-identified African American patients with heart failure: It is the largest number of African American patients ever studied in a major heart failure trial . . . . A-HeFT was started on May 29, 2001, and the study was halted early in July 2004 due to a significant survival benefit seen with BiDil as compared to standard therapy alone" (http://www.bidil .com/pnt/questions.php#2).

The BiDil website lists a series of "common questions" people ask about BiDil, including the following: "What about claims that BiDil is a 'race drug'?" The site's answer includes the following excerpt from a 2007 article by the FDA doctors who approved the drug:

> Only African American patients were studied in A-HeFT, so the FDA approval for BiDil is for 'self-identified African American patients with heart failure' only. There is insufficient clinical trial data to draw any conclusions about the effects of BiDil in other populations . . . .
>
> Not understanding the reasons for the difference in treatment effect by race did not justify withholding the treatment from those who could benefit from it. . . . Race or ethnicity is clearly a highly imperfect description of the genomic and other physiologic characteristics that cause people to differ, but it can be a useful proxy for those characteristics until the pathophysiologic bases for observed racial differences are better understood. (http://www.bidil.com/pnt/questions.php#9)

As these excerpts show, neither NitroMed nor the FDA endorses nineteenth-century American racial categories. They emphasize that the drug trial showing the effectiveness of BiDil involved only "self-identified" African

American subjects, which the FDA agrees is a "highly imperfect" but "useful proxy" for whatever factors are responsible for the observed "racial differences." The FDA admits that other populations besides self-identified African Americans might well benefit from BiDil, but this was not demonstrated by the A-HeFT drug trial, because its participants were only African Americans.

Abu El-Haj points out that many African Americans view drug trials such as A-HeFT as nothing less than a form of long-overdue biomedical justice. After all, African Americans' past participation in drug trials included the notorious Tuskegee Study of Untreated Syphilis in the Negro Male, conducted between 1932 and 1972. According to the website for the Centers for Disease Control and Prevention (http://www.cdc.gov/tuskegee/timeline.htm), a review panel set up in 1972 found that participants in this study

> had agreed freely to be examined and treated. However, there was no evidence that researchers had informed them of the study or its real purpose. In fact, the men had been misled and had not been given all the facts required to provide informed consent.
>
> The men were never given adequate treatment for their disease. Even when penicillin became the drug of choice for syphilis in 1947, researchers did not offer it to the subjects. The advisory panel found nothing to show that subjects were ever given the choice of quitting the study, even when this new, highly effective treatment became widely used.

But biomedical justice is not the only matter at issue. Abu El-Haj notes that the successful production and marketing of drugs such as BiDil have transformed race into "a potentially profitable commodity" (Abu El-Haj 2007, 293). Moreover, "giving federal recognition to a drug like BiDil implies recognizing the biological reality of race" (Abu El-Haj 2007, 293). The current situation is perplexing, to say the least: such notions as "race" and "biology" are still with us, but their meanings appear to have changed, producing consequences that seem to be both positive and negative. Abu El-Haj concludes that, "Nature, too . . . has a history," and that history "may well differ not just across time but between the various disciplines. . . . The same of course is true of race" (Abu El-Haj 2007, 294).

Biological evidence alone cannot dismantle oppressive sociopolitical structures, but it can provide an important component in the struggle to eliminate racist practices from our societies. Anthropologists need to be vigilant, emphasizing in no uncertain terms the lack of biological justification for the racial categories promoted by scientific racists. As Jonathan Marks reminds us, it was the recognition that human variation did not come in neat divisions called "races" that "began to convert racial studies into studies of human microevolution" (1995, 117).

The Four Evolutionary Processes

What controls the patterns of gene frequencies that characterize a given population? As we have seen, **natural selection** among variant traits is responsible for evolutionary changes in organisms, and **mutation** is the ultimate (and constant) source of new variation. These two important evolutionary processes shape the histories of living organisms; however, they are not the only processes in the natural world that can alter gene frequencies.

Most genetic variation results from mixing already existing alleles into new combinations. This variation is the natural result of chromosomal recombination in sexually reproducing species. However, gene frequencies can be drastically altered if a given population experiences a sudden expansion due to the in-migration of outsiders from another population of the species, which is called **gene flow**. A population that is unaffected by mutation or gene flow can still undergo **genetic drift**—random changes in gene frequencies from one generation to the next. Genetic drift may have little effect on the gene frequencies of large, stable populations, but it can have a dramatic impact on populations that are suddenly reduced in size by disease or disaster (the *bottleneck effect*) or on small subgroups that establish themselves apart from a larger population (the *founder effect*). Both of these effects accidentally eliminate large numbers of alleles.

Therefore, modern evolutionists recognize four evolutionary processes: mutation, natural selection, gene flow, and genetic drift. Chance plays a role in each. The occurrence of a mutation is random, and there is no guarantee that a useful mutation will occur when it is needed; many mutations are neutral, neither helping nor harming the organisms in which they occur. Nor is there any way to predict the factors that make population migrations

---

natural selection A two-step, mechanistic explanation of how descent with modification takes place: (1) every generation, variant individuals are generated within a species due to genetic mutation, and (2) those variant individuals best suited to the current environment survive and produce more offspring than other variants.

mutation The creation of a new allele for a gene when the portion of the DNA molecule to which it corresponds is suddenly altered.

gene flow The exchange of genes that occurs when a given population experiences a sudden expansion due to in-migration of outsiders from another population of the species.

genetic drift Random changes in gene frequencies from one generation to the next due to a sudden reduction in population size as a result of disaster, disease, or the out-migration of a small subgroup from a larger population.

In Their Own Words

DNA Tests Find Branches but Few Roots

*The ambiguities surrounding the molecularization of race in biomedicine also show up
in some genetics researchers' efforts to use DNA testing to trace "racial" ancestry. In 2007,
journalist Ron Nixon reported in the* New York Times *about the growth of private companies
that will trace genetic ancestry for their clients, sometimes for a hefty fee.*

Henry Louis Gates, Jr., whose PBS special *African American Lives* explores the ancestry of famous African Americans using DNA testing, has done more than anyone to help popularize such tests and companies that offer them. But recently this Harvard professor has become one of the industry's critics.

Mr. Gates says his concerns date back to 2000, when a company told him his maternal ancestry could most likely be traced back to Egypt, probably to the Nubian ethnic group. Five years later, however, a test by a second company startled him. It concluded that his maternal ancestors were not Nubian or even African, but most likely European.

Why the completely different results? Mr. Gates said that the first company never told him he had multiple genetic matches, most of them in Europe. "They told me what they thought I wanted to hear," Mr. Gates said.

An estimated 460,000 people have taken genetic tests to determine their ancestry or to expand their known family trees, according to *Science* magazine. Census records, birth and death certificates, ship manifests, slave narratives, and other documents have become easier to find through the Internet, making the hunt for family history less daunting than in years past.

Yet for many, the paper or digital trail eventually ends. And for those who have reached that point, genetic DNA tests may help to provide the final piece of the puzzle.

The expectations and reasons for taking the test vary. For some, the test allows them to reconnect with African ancestors after centuries of slavery wiped out links between African Americans and their forebears. Others want to see if they have links to historical figures like Genghis Khan or Marie Antoinette. For still others, it's an attempt to fill gaps in family histories and find distant cousins they might not otherwise have known.

The demand has spawned an industry. Almost two dozen companies now offer such services, up from just two or three only 6 years ago. The field is so hot that private equity investors have moved in: Spectrum Equity Investors recently bought Ancestry.com, an online genealogical site, for about $300 million shortly after the site added genetic testing as a service.

But as the number of test takers and companies has grown, so has the number of scientists or scholars like Mr. Gates who have questioned assertions that companies make about their tests. One of the most controversial issues is the ability of the tests to determine the country or the ethnic group of origin for African Americans or Native Americans.

Mr. Gates, director of the W. E. B. Dubois Institute for African and African American Research at Harvard, said his experience and similar stories from others have prompted him to enter the field.

Mr. Gates recently teamed up with Family Tree DNA, a DNA testing and genealogy firm in Houston, to provide genetic testing and genealogy work for African Americans. The new venture is called AfricanDNA.

"What we hope to do is combine this with genealogical and other records to try to help people discover their roots," he said. "The limitations of current genetic DNA tests mean you can't rely on this alone to tell you anything. We hope to bring a little order to the field."

In an editorial in *Science* magazine in October [2007], a number of scientists and scholars said companies might not be fully explaining the limitations of genetic testing, or what results actually mean.

The authors said that limited information in the databases used to compare DNA results might lead people to draw the wrong conclusions or to misinterpret results. The tests trace only a few of a customer's ancestors and cannot tell exactly where ancestors might have lived, or the specific ethnic group to which they might have belonged. And the databases of many companies are not only small—they're also proprietary, making it hard to verify results.

"My concern is that the marketing is coming before the science," said Troy Duster, a professor of sociology at New York University who was an advisor on the Human Genome Project and an author of the *Science* editorial.

"People are making life-changing decisions based on these tests and may not be aware of the limitations," he added. "While I don't think any of the companies are deliberately misleading customers, they may have a financial incentive to tell people what they want to hear."

Bennett Greenspan, founder and president of Family Tree DNA, said his company sometimes has to tell clients just the opposite. "We'll have people who may think that they have a certain type of ancestry and we'll tell them based on the test they are not," he said. "I can only tell them what the tests show, nothing more. And sometimes it's not what they want to hear."

(continued on next page)

In Their Own Words *(continued)*

DNA Tests Find Branches but Few Roots

Nixon explains that the tests can either analyze mitochondrial DNA, which is passed on only by females to their male and female offspring, or the Y chromosome, which is passed on only to males. He reviews the practices of several different companies and the mixed experiences of different customers. He then continues:

Even some early proponents of DNA testing for ancestry have doubts about how useful the tests are.

Bert Ely, a geneticist at the University of South Carolina, was a cofounder of the African American DNA Roots Project in 2000, hoping to use DNA tests as a way to find connections between African Americans and ethnic groups in Africa.

"I originally thought that the mitochondrial DNA test might be a good way for African Americans to trace their country of origin," Mr. Ely said. "Now I'm coming to the opposite conclusion."

[Mr. Ely] matched the DNA sequences of 170 African Americans against those of 3,725 people living in Africa. He found that most African Americans had genetic similarities to numerous ethnic groups in Africa, making it impossible to match African Americans with a single ethnic group, as some companies assert they can do.

Mr. Ely also published a paper in which he tried to determine whether the country of origin of native Africans could be found by using mitochondrial DNA tests. Several of the Africans in the study matched multiple ethnic groups. For example, DNA results for a person from Ghana provided genetic matches with people in 20 African countries . . . .

It's not that the tests are wrong, scientists say. Most companies use the same statistical methods and, in some cases, the same labs to extract DNA from samples. But even the largest databases have only a few thousand records in them, and some areas and populations are sampled more than others. Most companies get data from information published in publicly available research papers; few collect samples themselves. Scientists emphasize that much of this data was gathered for other purposes and was never intended to be used for personal genealogical testing.

For their part, testing companies say they continually update their databases to get a larger number of samples.

As part of the reporting for this article, I [Mr. Nixon] decided to submit my own samples for a mitochondrial DNA test. *Roots* had left an impression on me. . . . Like most African Americans, I longed to know where I came from. Could tests tell me? . . .

Six weeks after I submitted the first samples, the results started to roll in. Every company told me that my mother's female ancestors were all African. But after that things got murky.

African Ancestry said my DNA was a match with that of the Mende and Kru people from Liberia. Family Tree

At a 2007 reunion for descendants of slaves of James Madison, Dr. Bruce Jackson, director of the African American DNA Roots Project at the University of Massachusetts, collects a DNA sample from Dr. Gladys Marie Fry of Washington, DC.

In Their Own Words

DNA Tests Find Branches but Few Roots

DNA's database showed a match with one person who was Mende. But my DNA also matched that of several other groups, like the Songhai in Mali, and various ethnic groups in Mozambique and Angola. Other peoples cited were the Fula-Fula (also known as the Fulani), who live in eight African nations, and the Bambara, who are primarily in Mali.

Why so many? "We try to be brutally honest and give you everything the test results show," said Mr. Greenspan of Family Tree DNA. "If there are multiple matches, we're going to show you that."

Mr. Ely's African American DNA Roots Project, which examined DNA sequences that other companies provided to me, confirmed many matches from Family Tree DNA and African Ancestry, but added additional ethnic groups. DNA Tribes, whose test shows DNA results from a combination of genetic material from both parents, added even more ethnic matches.

I once thought that my ancestors, like those of most African Americans, would have come from West Africa. But some of the results showed links to regions that I had thought weren't engaged in the slave trade with the United States—like Mozambique. But then a search of the TransAtlantic Slave Trade database, which was compiled from slave ship records, showed that some Africans from Mozambique did indeed end up in the United States. So maybe the Mozambique results were possible.

The companies also offered technical support to understand the results, and I spent considerable time trying to make sense of them. I learned a lot about how they reached conclusions, but not much about where I or my ancestors ultimately came from.

"What this all means is that you can't take one of these tests and go off and say you're this and that," Mr. Gates said. "Somewhere down the road, the results could change and you might have another group of people who might also be your genetic cousins."

Sandra Jamison contributed reporting.

Source: New York Times, Sunday, November 25, 2007, BU 1,7.

possible or to foresee the natural accidents that diminish populations. Unpredictable changes in the environment can modify the selection pressures on a given population, affecting its genetic makeup. Moreover, as we saw in Chapter 2, *niche construction*—the enduring consequences of efforts organisms make to modify the environments in which they live—can sometimes alter the selection pressures they, their descendants, and other neighboring organisms experience in those environments. As we shall see, control of fire and the invention of clothing made it possible for early humans to colonize cold environments that were inaccessible to earlier ancestors, who lacked these cultural skills. Niche construction of this kind buffers us from experiencing some selection pressures, but it simultaneously exposes us to others.

Today, many biologists and anthropologists agree that the most intense selection pressures our species faces come from disease organisms that target our immune systems and from human-made environmental threats, such as pollution and the ozone hole (Leslie and Little 2003, Farmer 2003). Evidence that microorganisms are a major predatory danger to humans comes from research on the connection between infectious diseases and polymorphic blood groups (i.e., blood groups that have two or more genetic variants within a population). Biological anthropologists James Mielke, Lyle Konigsberg, and John Relethford (2011) point out, for example, that the diseases human beings have suffered from have not always been the same. When our ancestors were living in small foraging bands, they were susceptible to chronic parasitic infections, such as pinworms, or diseases transmitted from animals. After the domestication of plants and animals, however, human diets changed, settled life in towns and cities increased, and sanitation worsened. Populations expanded, individuals had more frequent contact with one another, and the stage was set for the rise and spread of *endemic* diseases (i.e., diseases particular to a population) that could persist in a population without repeated introduction from elsewhere. As a result,

the increase in endemic diseases started to apply selective pressures that were different from those exerted by chronic diseases. These diseases usually select individuals out of the population before they reach reproductive age. Differential mortality (natural selection) based on genetic variation in the blood types would be expected to influence genetic polymorphisms. Thus recurrent epidemics of diseases such as smallpox, cholera, plague, and measles, which swept through continents, undoubtedly contributed to the shaping of the genetic landscape. (Mielke et al. 2011, 105–06)

Several evolutionary processes may affect a population at the same time. For example, a rare, helpful allele (say, one that increased resistance to a disease like malaria) might appear in a population through mutation. If malaria were an environmental threat to that population, we would expect natural selection to increase the frequency of this new allele. But suppose a natural disaster like an earthquake struck the population and many people died. If the new allele were still very rare, it might be completely lost if its few carriers were among those who perished (genetic drift). Alternatively, the frequency of a harmful new allele might increase in subsequent generations if its carriers survived such a disaster and if they introduced the new allele into a larger population through inbreeding (gene flow). Niche construction could also be implicated if, for example, gene flow were enabled or intensified as a result of persisting, environment-modifying activities of the populations exchanging genes.

Measuring the interaction among these evolutionary processes allows population geneticists to predict the probable effects of inbreeding and outbreeding on a population's gene pool. Inbreeding tends to increase the proportion of homozygous combinations of alleles already present in a population. If some of these alleles are harmful in a double dose, inbreeding increases the probability that a double dose will occur in future generations and thus decrease fitness. If helpful combinations of alleles occur in an inbreeding population, their proportions can increase in a similar way.

At the same time, inbreeding over several generations tends to reduce genetic variation. Natural selection on genes has a better chance of shaping organisms to changed environments if it has a wider range of genetic variation to act on. Perhaps for this reason, mating with individuals from outgroups is widely observed in the animal kingdom. Monkeys and apes, for example, regularly transfer into a new social group before they begin to reproduce (Figure 3.1). Human beings ordinarily do the same thing, except that our reproductive practices are shaped by culture; people in different societies draw the boundaries around in-groups and out-groups differently. In one society, the children of brothers and sisters may be considered members of the same "family" and, thus, off limits for marriage; in another, they may be considered members of different "families" and, thus, ideal marriage partners. However, cultural rules forbidding *incest*, or sexual relations with close kin, do not always succeed in preventing such relations from occurring.

Table 3.2 summarizes the effects of the four standard evolutionary processes on gene frequencies within and between populations.

Microevolution and Patterns of Human Variation

Gene Flow As we have seen, phenotypic variation in different human populations does not require different alleles for different populations; rather, the variation we find mostly involves differences in the proportions of the same sets of alleles common to the human species as a whole. Therefore, genetic relationships between interbreeding human groups are best understood in terms of gene flow between superficially distinct populations whose gene pools already overlap considerably. For example, we know that individuals from European and

Figure 3.1 Monkeys and apes regularly transfer into a new social group before they reproduce.

TABLE 3.2 Effects of the Four Evolutionary Processes on Variation within and between Populations

EVOLUTIONARY PROCESS	VARIATION WITHIN POPULATIONS	VARIATION BETWEEN POPULATIONS
Mutation	Increases	Increases
Gene flow	Increases	Decreases
Genetic drift	Decreases	Increases
Natural selection	Increases *or* decreases	Increases *or* decreases

African populations have interbred considerably since Europeans brought the first Africans to the New World as slaves. Similar processes have mixed the genes of these and other in-migrating populations with the genes of indigenous American populations. These are examples of gene flow among populations of a single species that had experienced relative isolation in the past but that continued to exchange enough genes often enough with neighboring populations to prevent speciation.

Accidents of geography and history had allowed for relative isolation between these populations prior to the European voyages of exploration in the fifteenth century. From the fifteenth century on, similar chance factors brought them together. Moreover, the way in which reproductive isolation ended was powerfully shaped by the social and cultural forces that brought Europeans to the New World in the first place, structured their relationships with the indigenous peoples, and led them to enslave Africans. Similar cultural forces continue to affect the degree to which different human populations in the Americas remain reproductively isolated or exchange genes with other populations.

Genetic Drift One kind of genetic drift, the founder effect, occurs when a small subgroup of a larger population becomes isolated for some reason, taking with it unrepresentative proportions of the alleles from the larger population's gene pool. One of numerous examples of genetic drift that have occurred in human history began early in the nineteenth century when British soldiers occupied the island of Tristan da Cunha in the Atlantic Ocean. Eventually, the soldiers withdrew, leaving only a single married couple who were later joined by a few other settlers. Throughout the nineteenth century, the population of Tristan da Cunha never grew much beyond 100 individuals. This tiny population was later reduced even more, once in the late 1850s by the out-migration of 70 inhabitants and again in 1885 by the drowning of all but four adult males (only one of whom contributed genes to the next generation). Over the twentieth century, the population has grown to as many as 270 people, all of whom owe an enormous

proportion of their genes to a very few individuals. It was calculated that nearly a third of those living on the island in 1961 had genes contributed by just two members of the original founding population (Roberts 1968, Underwood 1979).

Mutation and Natural Selection Mutation is responsible for variant alleles that may be present at a single locus. Some of these mutant alleles are mobilized during development to help produce specific physical traits. When a trait proves helpful, evolutionary theory predicts that the frequency of the alleles involved in its production will be increased by natural selection. Perhaps the most famous instance of microevolution of such a trait by means of natural selection concerns a variant of hemoglobin, one of the proteins in red blood cells.

In many human populations, only one allele—hemoglobin A (*HbA*)—is present. In other populations, however, mutant forms of hemoglobin A may also be present. One such mutant allele, known as *HbS*, alters the structure of red blood cells, distorting them into a characteristic sickle shape and reducing their ability to carry oxygen (Figure 3.2). When individuals inherit the *HbS* allele from both parents, they develop sickle-cell anemia. About 85 percent of those with the *HbS/HbS* genotype do not survive to adulthood and, hence, do not reproduce. Although many people in the United States think that sickle-cell anemia affects only people with ancestors who came from Africa, in fact many people in India, Saudi Arabia, and Mediterranean countries such as Turkey, Greece, and Italy also suffer from the disease.

Because the *HbS* allele seems to be harmful, we would expect it to be eliminated through natural selection. But in some populations of the world, it has a frequency of up to 20 percent in the gene pool. Why should that be? Geneticists might have concluded that this high frequency was the result of genetic drift if it were not for the fact that the areas with a high frequency of *HbS* are also areas where the mosquito-borne malaria parasite is common. There is, in fact, a connection. People exposed to malaria have a better chance of resisting the parasite if their hemoglobin genotype is *HbA/HbS* rather

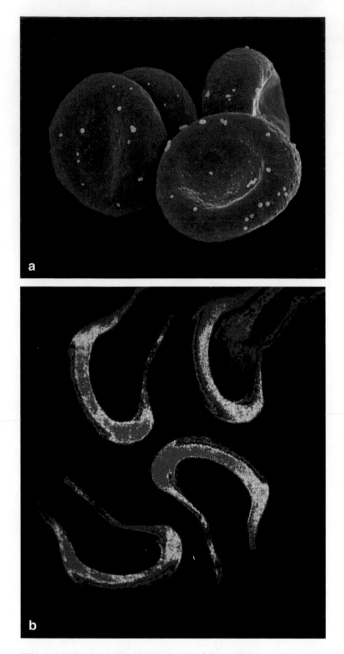

Figure 3.2 Normal red blood cells (*a*) are easily distinguished from the distorted, "sickled" red blood cells (*b*). Sickled red blood cells carry less oxygen than do normal red blood cells, but they resist malarial parasites more successfully.

than the normal *HbA/HbA*. This is an example of what geneticists call a "balanced polymorphism," in which the heterozygous genotype is fitter than either of the homozygous genotypes. In Mendelian terms, we would say that the *HbA* and *HbS* alleles are codominant, with the result that a single *HbS* allele changes the structure of red blood cells enough to inhibit malarial parasites but not enough to cause sickle-cell anemia.

The rise of malarial infection in human beings appears to have begun only a few thousand years ago

(Livingstone 1958). Before that time, the people who lived where malaria is now found gathered and hunted wild foods for a living. This way of life kept forests intact, leaving few open areas where water could collect and malaria-carrying mosquitoes could breed in large numbers. As these inhabitants began to cultivate plants for food, however, they needed to clear large tracts of forest for their fields, creating large open spaces where rainwater could collect in stagnant pools, providing ideal breeding conditions for mosquitoes. And as the population of cultivators grew, so grew the number of hosts for the malaria parasite.

If the *HbS* allele first appeared in the populations of gatherers and hunters, it probably had a low frequency. But once cultivation began, land was cleared, water accumulated in open spaces, and the number of malaria-infested mosquitoes increased, selection pressures changed. At that point, individuals with the *HbA/ HbS* genotype were fitter because they had a greater probability of surviving and reproducing than individuals with *HbA/HbA* or *HbS/HbS*. As a result, the frequency of *HbS* increased in the population, despite the fact that in a double dose it was generally lethal. This example also illustrates the way niche construction can reshape the selection pressures that a population experiences. In this case, a switch from one pattern of human food getting to another created new niches for humans, mosquitoes, and malaria parasites, simultaneously reshaping the selection pressures experienced by all three populations (Odling-Smee et al. 2003). Indeed, niche construction may also be implicated in discussions of gene flow and genetic drift since in both cases activities undertaken by particular human populations may alter their respective niches in persistent ways, thereby altering the selection pressures which each population subsequently experiences.

Adaptation and Human Variation

One of the breakthroughs of modern genetics was the discovery of *gene interaction*. That is, a single gene may contribute to the production of more than one phenotypic feature (*pleiotropy*), and many genes regularly combine forces (*polygeny*), helping to produce a single phenotypic feature. Pleiotropy and polygeny help explain how it is that genes, which are discrete, could influence phenotypic traits such as body size or skin color, which show continuous gradations. Traits that are the product of multiple genes offer multiple and varied opportunities for natural selection to shape phenotypic traits in ways that are adaptive for the organisms in which they are found.

In discussions of gene action, biologists commonly distinguish between genes of major effect and polygenes of intermediate or minor effect. A *gene of major effect* is a gene at one locus whose expression has a critical effect on the phenotype. The *HbS* allele that produces the sickling trait in red blood cells is an example of a gene of major effect. But phenotypic traits that depend on one or a few genes of major effect are rare. The evolution of a phenotypic trait may begin with selection on genes of major effect, but the products of such genes may be pleiotropic, producing adaptive as well as harmful consequences for the organism. Further selection on multiple *polygenes of intermediate or minor effect* that also affect the trait, however, may modify or eliminate those harmful consequences (West-Eberhard 2003, 101–4). Finally, because gene expression does not take place in an environmental vacuum, many phenotypic traits in organisms are even more finely tuned for their adaptive functions by inputs from environmental factors such as nutrients, temperature, humidity, altitude, or day length. Human phenotypic traits such as body size or skin color, for example, are the outcome of complex interactions among multiple gene products and environmental influences throughout the life cycle.

Many students of human genetics have devoted attention to the way natural selection may mold complex human phenotypic traits, better adapting human populations to their specific environments. More recently, developmental biologists have been able to show how the responsiveness of organisms to their environments also contributes to the abilities of those organisms to adapt to their environments. A fertilized human egg (or zygote) has its own phenotype, and the zygote's phenotype can respond to environmental influences—such as those encountered in a woman's uterus—*even before its own genes are active*. This responsiveness is called phenotypic **plasticity**: "the ability of an organism to react to an environmental input with a change in form, state, movement, or rate of activity" (West-Eberhard 2003, 35). Because all living organisms exhibit phenotypic plasticity, it is *incorrect* to assume that genes "direct" the development of organisms or "determine" the production of phenotypic traits. Indeed, much of the "action" that goes into producing adult organisms with distinctive phenotypes goes on during development (Figure 3.3).

It is important to stress that acknowledging the phenotypic plasticity of organisms has nothing to do with Lamarckian ideas of use and disuse and the inheritance of acquired characteristics, neither of which is accepted by modern evolutionary biologists. As West-Eberhard points out,

> There is no hint of direct (Lamarckian) influence of environment on genome in this scheme—it is entirely consistent with conventional genetics and inheritance. By the view adopted here, evolutionary change depends upon the genetic component of phenotypic

Figure 3.3 Changes in environment can have major effects on phenotype. Generational differences in height are often connected with changes in diet.

variation screened by selection, whether phenotypic variants are genetically or environmentally induced. It is the genetic *variation* in a response (to mutation or environment) that produces a response to selection and cross-generational, cumulative change in the gene pool. . . . (2003, 29)

Some of the most exciting work in evolutionary biology today involves linking new understandings about developmental influences on phenotypes with understandings of traditional evolutionary processes like mutation, gene flow, genetic drift, and natural selection (West-Eberhard 2003, Gould 2002, Oyama et al. 2001)

As we saw earlier, **adaptation** as a process refers to the mutual shaping of organisms and their environments.

plasticity Physiological flexibility that allows organisms to respond to environmental stresses, such as temperature changes.

adaptation (1) The mutual shaping of organisms and their environments. (2) The shaping of useful features of an organism by natural selection for the function they now perform (see Chapter 2).

However, the term *adaptation* can also be used to refer to the phenotypic traits that are the outcome of adaptive processes. Biological anthropologists traditionally distinguish three levels of phenotypic adaptation: genetic adaptations, short-term adaptations, and developmental adaptations. Each of these shows differing degrees of phenotypic plasticity. The sickling trait in hemoglobin described in the previous section is a classic example of a genetic adaptation since the form of the hemoglobin molecule is the phenotypic product of a single-locus gene of major effect. Most human phenotypic traits, however, are the product of pleiotropy, polygeny, and inputs from the environment.

Often the environmental input operates as a triggering mechanism for an adaptive response. This is the case for the shivering response, an adaptive physiological response in human beings sometimes called "short-term **acclimatization**." Human beings are warm-blooded organisms who need to maintain a constant internal body temperature to function properly. When the surrounding temperature drops, however, and threatens to cool our internal organs below this threshold temperature (roughly 98.6° Fahrenheit), this temperature drop triggers a twitching response in the muscles that surround our vital organs, as a way of generating heat. If we are able to increase our body temperature above the threshold—by going indoors, putting on clothes, or moving closer to the fire—the shivering stops.

Other forms of acclimatization are longer-lasting than the shivering response and take shape over the course of many months or years as human beings are born, grow up, or come to spend much of their lives in particular environments. The physiological or morphological changes they undergo are consequences of human phenotypic plasticity, not genetic variation. For example, some environments in which human populations live, such as the highlands of the Andes Mountains in South America, are characterized by *hypoxia*; that is, less oxygen is available to breathe than at lower altitudes. Studies have shown that people who grow up in high altitudes adapt to lower oxygen levels by developing greater chest dimensions and lung capacities than do people living at low attitudes. These changes—sometimes called "developmental acclimatization"—are a consequence of human phenotypic plasticity and occur when the human body is challenged by a low level of oxygen in the environment. Studies have shown that individuals who were not born in such an environment increased in chest

dimensions and lung capacity the longer they lived in such an environment and the younger they were when they moved there (Greska 1990).

Skin Color Skin color is a highly visible, complex, continuous phenotypic trait in human populations. Variation in skin color seems to be the product of a few genes of major effect, additional polygenes of intermediate or minor effect, and input from the environment. As Nina Jablonski writes, "determination of the relative roles of variant genes and varying environments has proven extremely challenging" (2004, 613), and it is not clear how many alleles are involved or whether identical genes are responsible for the dark skin of apparently unrelated human populations (Marks 1995, 167–68). Biological anthropologists agree that skin color is adaptive and related to the degree of ultraviolet radiation (UVR) that human populations have experienced in particular regions of the globe.

It is important to emphasize that "similar skin colors have evolved independently in human populations inhabiting similar environments," making skin color "useless as a marker for membership in a unique group or "'race'" (Jablonski 2004, 615). Indeed, some of the most striking features of human skin are clearly consequences of developmental and phenotypic plasticity: variations in skin thickness are a function of age and history of sun exposure; the outer layers of the skin in darkly pigmented or heavily tanned people have more, and more compact, cell layers, making the skin more effective as a barrier to sun damage. The overall intensity of skin color is thus determined by a combination of morphological, physiological, environmental, and developmental factors. When the intricate articulation of these factors is destabilized, the outcome can be anomalous skin conditions such as *albinism* (an absence of pigmentation), abnormally intense pigmentation, or a patchy spotting of light and dark skin (Jablonski 2004, 590).

Human skin color exhibits clinal variation, with average pigmentation growing gradually lighter in populations that live closer to the poles (Figure 3.4). The pigments in human skin (melanins) protect the skin against sunburn by absorbing and scattering UVR and by protecting DNA from damage that can lead to cancer (Jablonski 2004, 590). Of course, as humans we risk sun damage to the skin because we do not grow fur coats, like our closest primate relatives. Dark fur coats can actually protect primates from tropical heat by absorbing short-wave radiation (UVA) near the surface of the coat and reflecting much long-wave radiation (UVB) away before it reaches the skin. These advantages of fur, however, are reduced if the fur is wet with sweat, which can happen if the temperature rises or the organism's activity level

---

acclimatization A change in the way the body functions in response to physical stress.

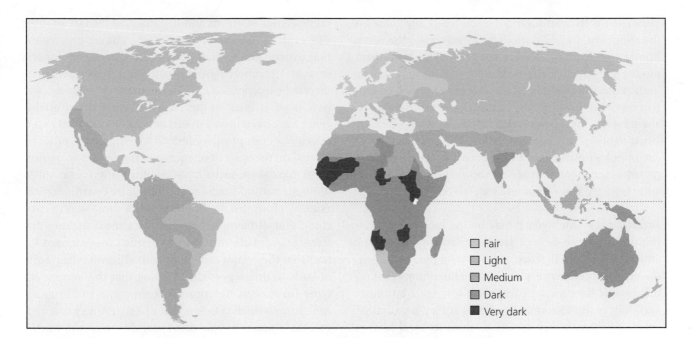

Figure 3.4 When the unexposed skin of indigenous peoples is measured and mapped according to the degree of pigmentation, skin shades tend to grow progressively lighter the farther one moves from the equator.

increases. Under these conditions, "thermal sweating as a method of cooling becomes more important" and it is "greatly facilitated by the loss of body hair" (Jablonski 2004, 599). It is now hypothesized that the last common ancestor of humans and chimpanzees probably had light skin covered with dark hair, like other Old World primates. However, the loss of hair created new selection pressures in favor of increasingly darker skin, such that by 1.2 million years ago (mya), early members of the genus *Homo* would have had darkly pigmented skin (Rogers et al. 2004). In addition, contemporary human populations all seem to show sexual dimorphism in skin color, "with females being consistently lighter than males in all populations studied" (Jablonski 2004, 601; Jablonski and Chaplin 2000).

Exposure of human skin to solar radiation has complex and contradictory consequences. Too much sunlight produces sunburn, and long-wavelength radiation (or UVB) destroys a B vitamin, folic acid, which is a crucial factor in healthy cell division. At the same time, solar radiation also has positive consequences: short-wavelength radiation (or UVA) stimulates the synthesis of vitamin D in human skin. Vitamin D is crucial for healthy bone development and other cellular processes. According to Jablonski and Chaplin (2000), these selective pressures have produced two opposing clines of skin pigmentation. The first cline grades from dark skin at the equator to light skin at the poles and is an adaptive protection against sun damage. The second cline grades from light

pigmentation at the poles to dark pigmentation at the equator and is an adaptive response favoring vitamin D production. In the middle of these two clines, they argue, natural selection favored populations with enhanced phenotypic plasticity who could tan more easily during hot, sunny seasons but easily lose their tans in seasons when temperature and sunlight levels decreased.

Jablonski concludes that "the longer wavelengths of UVR . . . have been the most important agents of natural selection in connection with the evolution of skin pigmentation" (2004, 604). At the same time, because people have always migrated, different populations vary in the numbers of generations exposed to the selective pressures of any single regime of solar radiation. Human cultural practices (wearing clothes, using sun block, staying indoors) have shaped the levels of pigmentation and levels of vitamin D production in particular individuals or populations. Gene flow following the interbreeding of human populations with different selective histories would further complicate the relationship between the skin colors of their offspring and selection pressures imposed by local levels of solar radiation.

Many of these factors may explain why the skin colors of the native people of South America are lighter than those of native populations in Asia or Europe who live at similar latitudes. Most anthropologists estimate these populations migrated from the Old World perhaps 10,000–15,000 years ago, which means they have had far less time to experience the selective pressures associated with local solar radiation levels anywhere on the continent. In addition, these migrants were modern humans with many cultural adaptations to help them modify the negative effects of solar radiation, including both protective clothing and a vitamin D–rich diet. Obtaining vitamin D from food rather than sunlight has thus altered selection pressures that otherwise would have favored lighter skin. Thus, the darker skin pigmentation of circumpolar peoples may be the consequence of selection pressures for darker skin as a protection against solar radiation reflected from snow and ice (Jablonski 2004, 612).

Intelligence Intelligence may be the most striking attribute of human beings. However, attempts to define and measure "intelligence" have a long history of controversy. Is intelligence a single, general, unitary "thing" that people have more or less of? If not, what attributes and skills ought to count? Psychologist Howard Gardner points out that "Every society features its ideal human being" (2000, 1). In his view, "the intelligent person" in modern Western societies has been exemplified by individuals who could do well at formal schooling and succeed in commerce. It is perhaps not surprising, then, that tests developed in Western societies purporting to measure individuals' intelligence quotient (IQ) traditionally have equated high scores on verbal and mathematical reasoning with high intelligence.

But these are not the only areas in which humans display differing levels of ability or skill. Gardner, for example, has long argued that in addition to linguistic and logicomathematical intelligence, human beings possess different types of intelligence, including bodily–kinesthetic intelligence (displayed by exceptional athletes and dancers), interpersonal or intrapersonal intelligence (displayed by individuals with exceptional understanding of social relations or their own psyches), musical intelligence, spatial intelligence, and naturalist intelligence (which attunes us to plants and animals in the world around us). In Gardner's view, these types of intelligence can probably be enhanced in all individuals, given the right kind of environmental support. Indeed, even linguistic intelligence and logicomathematical intelligence require the proper environmental support—long-term training and practice in rich cultural settings—to produce the highest levels of achievement.

Because the definition of *intelligence* is so controversial and because not all forms of intelligence are equally rewarded in the United States, great controversy results when attempts to measure intelligence are applied not only to individuals but also to entire social groups, defined on the basis of gender, class, or "race." The former president of Harvard University was subjected to strong criticism when he acknowledged that fewer women than men become scientists and suggested, in the face of massive evidence to the contrary, that perhaps this meant that women simply had less "intrinsic aptitude" for science and engineering than men (http://www.president.harvard.edu/speeches/2005/nber.html). Controversies have been as great or greater when ideas about intelligence have been linked to ideas about race. In the United States, for example, people tend to assign each other to "races" on the basis of phenotypic criteria like skin color. As we have seen, such "races" are then often regarded as different natural kinds, each sharing its own biological essence. From this assumption, it is a short step to conclude that differences between races must include differences in intelligence. Some scientists have devised IQ tests that they claim can measure intelligence, the results of such testing repeatedly showing that the average IQ score for African Americans is below that of European Americans, which is below that of Asian Americans.

Do IQ scores show that racial differences in intelligence are clear-cut and genetically determined? They do not. First, the idea that races are natural kinds assumes that racial boundaries are clear and that traits essential to racial identity (e.g., skin color) are discrete and nonoverlapping. However, as we noted above, skin color is a continuously varying phenotypic trait, both among members of the so-called racial groups as well as across the boundaries of those groups. Particular shades of skin color cannot be assigned exclusively to particular socially defined races, nor can they be used to infer any other so-called racial attribute, such as intelligence or athletic ability.

Second, it is far from clear that there is a single, accurately measurable substance called "intelligence" that some people have more of than others. Performing well on paper-and-pencil tests tells us nothing about problem-solving skills and creativity, which might equally deserve to be called "intelligence." Third, even if intelligence is such a measurable substance, we do not know that IQ tests actually measure it. People can score badly on an IQ test for many reasons that have nothing to do with intelligence: they may be hungry or ill or anxious, for example. When different social groups within a society consistently score differently as groups, however, we may suspect that the test itself is to blame. Arguing that IQ tests measure cultural knowledge, not intelligence, many critics contend that the vocabulary items used on most IQ tests reflect experiences typical of European American middle-class culture. People from different cultural backgrounds do poorly on the test because their experiences have not provided them with the knowledge being tested.

Many studies have shown that how an individual will do on an IQ test is more accurately predicted by social class and educational background than by "race." When African Americans and European Americans are matched in terms of these factors, the differences in average IQ scores disappear (Molnar 1992). Similarly, African American children adopted by middle-class European American parents scored an average of 12 points higher on IQ tests than did African American children who remained in the lower-income communities from which the adoptees had come (Woodward 1992). Studies like these demonstrate repeatedly that IQ scores are not phenotypic traits uniquely determined by genes but that they are powerfully affected by a range of environmental factors over the course of the human life cycle.

Phenotype, Environment, and Culture

In recent years, many evolutionary biologists and biological anthropologists have recognized that trying to attribute every phenotypic trait of an organism to adaptation is problematic. Sometimes an adaptive explanation seems transparently obvious, as with body shape in fish and whales or wing shape in bats and birds, which equips these animals for efficient movement through water and air. Other times, adaptive explanations are less obvious, or even contrived. As we saw in Chapter 2, the wings of contemporary insects are better understood as an exaptation, when appendages that evolved as an adaptation to one set of selective pressures began at some point to serve an entirely different function.

In other words, the trait an organism possesses today may not be the direct result of adaptation but, instead, may be the by-product of some other feature that was being shaped by natural selection. It may also be the consequence of random effects. Jonathan Marks has observed, for example, that anthropologists have tried, without notable success, to offer adaptive explanations for the large, protruding brow ridges found in populations of human ancestors. He suggests that brow ridges might well have appeared "for no reason at all—simply as a passive consequence of growing a fairly large face attached to a skull of a small frontal region" (1995, 190).

We must also remember that phenotypes are shaped by environment as well as by genes. For example, some have argued that slow growth in height, weight, and body composition and delayed onset of adolescence among Guatemalan Mayan children constitute a genetic adaptation to a harsh natural environment. However, by comparing measurements of these traits in populations of Mayans who migrated to the United States with those in Guatemala, Barry Bogin was able to disprove these claims, for "the United States–living Maya are significantly taller, heavier and carry more fat and muscle mass than Mayan children in Guatemala" (Bogin 1995, 65). Similarly, other biological anthropologists working in the Andean highlands have refuted the hypothesis that

hypoxia is responsible for poor growth among some indigenous populations (de Meer et al. 1993, Leonard et al. 1990). They point out that the genetic explanation fails to consider the effects on growth of poverty and political marginalization.

At the beginning of the twenty-first century, it has become fashionable for many writers, particularly in the popular media, to treat genes as the ultimate explanation for all features of the human phenotype. Given the great achievements by molecular biology that followed the discovery of the structure of the DNA molecule, this enthusiasm is perhaps understandable. But discussions of human adaptive patterns that invoke natural selection on genetic variation alone are extremely unsatisfactory. For one thing, they mischaracterize the role genes play in living organisms. Speaking as if there were a separate gene "for" each identifiable phenotypic trait ignores pleiotropy and polygeny, as well as phenotypic plasticity. It also ignores the contribution of the other classic evolutionary processes of genetic drift and gene flow, as well as the influences of historical and cultural factors on human development (as in the case of the Mayan migrants). Researchers in the Human Genome Project originally expected that, given our phenotypic complexity, the human genome would contain at least 100,000 genes; today, we know that the actual number is more like 30,000, only three times as many as the roundworm *Caenorhabditis elegans*, one of the simplest organisms that exists (http://www.genome.gov/11007952). Clearly, the number of genes possessed by an organism is not coupled in any straightforward way to its phenotypic complexity.

The gene-centered approach gained considerable influence in anthropology after 1975, due to the widespread theoretical impact of a school of evolutionary thought called "sociobiology." Sociobiology attracted some anthropologists who proposed explanations of human adaptations based on sociobiological principles. Other anthropologists have been highly critical of sociobiology. However, after 30 years, some proposals emerging from this debate have come a long way toward meeting the objections of sociobiology's original critics.

It is important to understand that much of this research is based on **formal models**. These models are "formal" because scientists use the tools of formal logic or mathematics to find answers to particular questions about the evolution of human behavior. For example, evolutionary psychologists typically assume that the psychological

---

formal models Mathematical formulas to predict outcomes of particular kinds of human interactions under different hypothesized conditions.

abilities possessed by modern human beings are adaptations that were shaped by specific environmental challenges early in our species' evolutionary history. They employ formal psychological tests on contemporary human subjects to demonstrate the presence of these abilities and then use logical deduction to "reverse engineer" from these contemporary abilities back to the hypothetical selective pressures that would have shaped these abilities. By contrast, scientists who study gene-culture coevolution, cultural group selection, or niche construction use mathematical formulas to predict outcomes of particular kinds of human interactions under different hypothesized conditions. Computers allow them to simulate, for example, what happens when certain behavioral patterns are repeated for many generations. The researchers then examine the reports of ethnographers or other social scientists to see if any of the outcomes produced by their mathematical calculations match the actual behavior patterns found in real human societies.

No beginning anthropology textbook can offer an in-depth introduction to formal modeling of human biological and cultural evolutionary processes (Table 3.3). But students should be aware of this dynamic and contentious field of research, in which anthropologists, biologists, ecologists, psychologists, and other scientists collaborate. Students should also be aware that many anthropologists—cultural anthropologists in particular—are highly critical of formal models, especially formal models of cultural evolution. They point out that formal modeling cannot work unless actual human interactions, which are messy and complex, are tidied up and simplified so that they can be represented by variables in mathematical equations. Reverse engineering has also been criticized for being overly reliant on logical deduction, rather than empirical evidence, in the generation of hypotheses about the human past. Critics argue that these approaches produce nothing more than cartoon versions of everyday life that often reveal systematic Western ethnocentric bias.

In our view, the perspective with the most promise is that of niche construction, which articulates in unusually clear language a point of view many anthropologists and others have held for a very long time. And they are not the only ones. As ecologist Richard Levins and biologist Richard Lewontin pointed out in 1985,

> [using] cultural mechanisms to control our own temperature has made it possible for our species to survive in almost all climates, but it has also created new kinds of vulnerability. Our body temperature now depends on the price of clothing or fuel, whether we control our own furnaces or have them set by landlords, whether we work indoors or outdoors or leave places with stressful temperature regimes. . . . Thus our temperature regime is not a simple consequence of thermal needs but rather a consequence of social and economic conditions. (1985, 259)

What Is Macroevolution?

Unlike microevolution, which studies changes within a single species over relatively short stretches of ecological time, macroevolution studies evolution at or above the species level over extremely long stretches of geological time and is concerned with tracing (and explaining) the extinction of old species and the origin of new species. Evidence for these processes comes from close study of fossils and of the comparative anatomy of living organisms. As we shall see, the way we understand macroevolution shapes our understanding of human evolution.

Until about 25 years ago, most evolutionary biologists were more or less convinced that the problems of macroevolution had been solved in a satisfactory manner by Darwin himself. Darwin claimed, and neo-Darwinians agreed, that macroevolution—the origin of new species—is simply what happens when microevolution continues over a long enough period of time (Table 3.4). Such a view seemed plausible because, as we have seen, all these evolutionary thinkers assumed that, over time, genetic and environmental changes are inevitable. Mutation (if unchecked by natural selection) inevitably changes a species' physical attributes over time in the same way that the natural environment, perpetually subject to uniformitarian processes of erosion and uplift, never remains constant. Evolution was thought to occur when independent processes of genetic change and environmental change intersect in the phenotypes of organisms living in a particular habitat.

In his final formulation of the theory of natural selection, Darwin argued that there is no such thing as a fixed species, precisely because evolution is gradual. And evolution is gradual because environments change slowly. Lamarck's concept of long-term evolutionary change was also gradualistic, except that he pictured *individual members* of a long-lived natural kind (and their offspring) tracking the changing environment over a long period of time. For Darwin, however, one species gradually transforms over time itself into a new species, a process called **anagenesis**, although the actual boundary between species can never be detected but only drawn

---

anagenesis The slow, gradual transformation of a single species over time.

TABLE 3.3 Formal Models in the Study of Human Biological and Cultural Evolution

THEORETICAL PERSPECTIVE	KEY FEATURES
Sociobiology	• Defined by E. O. Wilson, one of its founders, as "the systematic study of the biological basis of all social behavior" (1980, 322). Originally focused on explaining the evolution of *altruism*—the willingness to give up benefits for oneself in order to help someone else. Sociobiologists argued that altruism makes sense if we pay attention not to individuals but to the genes they carry. • Organisms share the most genes with their close relatives; therefore, sociobiologists hypothesize, natural selection will preserve altruistic behaviors if the altruists sacrifice themselves for close kin, a concept known as *kin selection*. Some anthropologists adopted the sociobiological approach to human societies, whereas others viewed sociobiology as a pernicious perspective that threatened to resurrect nineteenth-century racism.
Behavioral Ecology	• A school of thought based on sociobiological reasoning that accepts the importance of natural selection on human adaptations, but rejects sociobiology's genetic determinism. Behavioral ecologists accept the view that human adaptations depend on cultural learning rather than on genetic control, but they insist that the cultural behavior human beings develop is closely circumscribed by the selection pressures imposed upon us by the ecological features of the environments in which human populations have lived (see Cheverud 2004; Sussman and Garber 2004).
Evolutionary Psychology	• Like earlier sociobiologists, evolutionary psychologists insist that human adaptations are phenotypes under close genetic control. Unlike earlier sociobiologists, however, evolutionary psychologists do not invoke natural selection on genes to explain human behavior patterns as adaptations to present-day conditions. Rather, they argue that natural selection on human genes was most significant millions of years ago, in the environment in which our ancestors lived when they were first evolving away from the other African apes (called the "environment of evolutionary adaptedness" or EEA). • Evolutionary psychologists argue that natural selection in the EEA produced a human brain consisting of a set of sealed-off "mental modules," each of which was designed by natural selection to solve a different adaptive problem (see Barkow, Cosmides, and Tooby 1992).
Gene-Culture Coevolution	• An analysis of the origin and significance of culture in human evolution that is critical of standard Sociobiological accounts. The version developed by Robert Boyd and Peter Richerson argues that human behavior is shaped by two inheritance systems, one genetic and one cultural. Cultural traits are passed on by learning, not via the chromosomes; but since these traits vary, are passed on from individual to individual, and confer differential fitness on those who use them, they can undergo natural selection (1985, 76). • The two inheritance systems are interconnected: human biological evolution creates the possibility for cultural creativity and learning, while human cultural traditions created the environment that allows human biological processes to continue, even as culture creates selection pressures of its own that shape human biological evolution. This is why the process is called gene-culture *coevolution* (see also Durham, 1991; Cavalli-Sforza and Feldman 1981).
Cultural Group Selection	• Sociobiologists argue that group selection cannot occur as the outcome of natural selection operating on genes unless group members are biological kin who share genes (see *kin selection*, above). If group members do not share genes, the good of the individual and the good of the group no longer coincide; this means that individuals who sacrificed themselves for other group members would take their "group selection" genes with them to the grave. • But if behaviors are shaped by cultural inheritance rather than genetic inheritance (as in gene-culture coevolution) this argument may not hold. When the forces of cultural learning are powerful enough, the fitness of an individual may come to depend on the behaviors of other individuals in a local group. This is known as cultural group selection. Once the forces of cultural transmission take hold, it is usually easier and cheaper to behave the way the group dictates than it is to strike out on one's own (Richerson and Boyd 2005; D. S. Wilson 2002).
Niche Construction	• Odling-Smee, Laland, and Feldman argue that human evolution depends not just on our genetic heritage and our cultural heritage but also on an additional heritage of modified selection pressures which we pass on to our descendants in the form of a constructed niche (2003). They use the concept of "artifact" to represent these environmental modifications: artifacts include birds' nests and rodents' burrows as well as human artifacts like clothing and furnaces. Odling-Smee et al. argue that their "triple-inheritance" theory offers a more satisfactory explanation of the evolutionary histories of organisms than do accounts focusing on genes and culture alone.

TABLE 3.4 Models of Macroevolution

	PHYLETIC GRADUALISM	PUNCTUATED EQUILIBRIA
Macroevolution	A uniform process, the eventual outcome of microevolution, given enough time	*Different* from microevolution, not a uniform process
Motor of speciation	The result of *anagenesis*, the gradual transformation of one species into another species	The result of *cladogenesis*, the rapid production of multiple new species alongside parent species
Species boundary	Species boundaries are arbitrary	Species boundaries are real
Consequences	No sharp breaks in fossil record between old and new species	Speciation achieves the shifting of "genetic and morphological centers of gravity of parent and daughter species" such that "each species is now free to accumulate more variation and hence more potential species differences" (Tattersall 1998, 163)

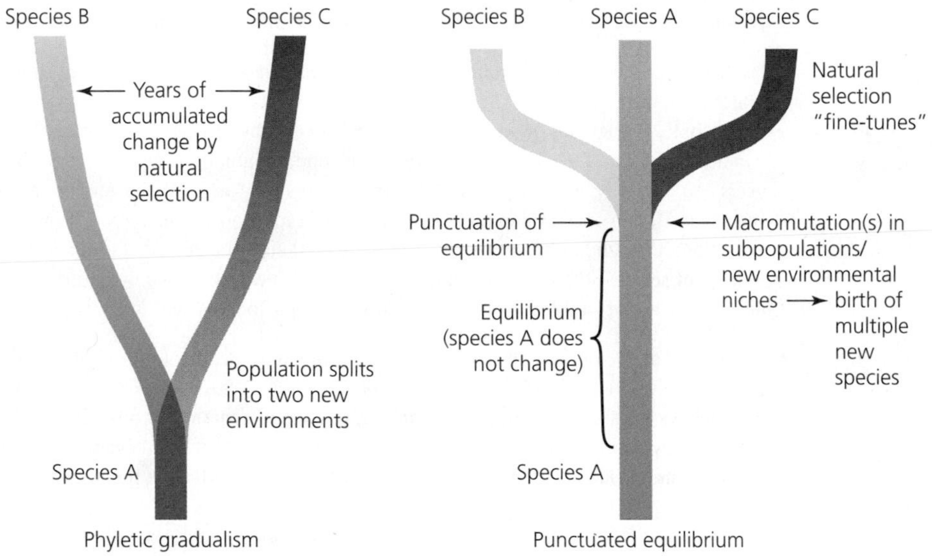

Figure 3.5   Research and theories about punctuated equilibria have challenged the common neo-Darwinian understanding of speciation by means of phyletic gradualism.

arbitrarily. Darwin's theory of the origin of new species is called **phyletic gradualism** (Figure 3.5).

Arguing for phyletic gradualism made a lot of sense in Darwin's day, given the kind of opposition he faced; and it has many defenders today. But some biologists have argued that phyletic gradualism does not explain a number of things that evolutionary theory must explain. In particular, it cannot explain the fact that a single fossil species often seems to have given birth to a number of

---

phyletic gradualism A theory arguing that one species gradually transforms itself into a new species over time, yet the actual boundary between species can never be detected and can only be drawn arbitrarily.
cladogenesis The birth of a variety of descendant species from a single ancestral species.

---

descendant species, a process called **cladogenesis**. What about those breaks in the fossil record that led Cuvier to argue that old species disappeared and new species appeared with what, from the point of view of geological time, was extreme rapidity? Is this just the result of poor preservation of intermediate forms, or do new species arise suddenly without having to go through any drawn-out intermediate stages? Or do the fossils that we thought represented intermediate stages in the anagenesis of a single species actually belong to several different species that resulted from the process of cladogenesis?

In the early 1970s, these problems led evolutionists Stephen Jay Gould and Niles Eldredge to propose that the rate and manner of evolutionary change may differ at the level of genes, of organisms, and of species. They argued that patterns in the fossil record (including the patterns Cuvier had recognized) suggest that phyletic

Figure 3.6 An individual may have high cultural fitness and no genetic fitness at all. Here, a religious teacher who is celibate (thereby reducing her genetic fitness to zero) passes cultural knowledge to a new generation of other people's offspring.

gradualism might not explain all cases of evolutionary change. Between the breaks in the fossil record, many fossil species show little—if any—change for millions of years. Moreover, it is often the case that new species appear in the fossil record alongside their unchanged ancestors (Eldredge and Tattersall 1982, 8). We observe this phenomenon when we compare ourselves to the other living primates (see Chapter 4). Gould and Eldredge contended that evolutionary change is not a uniform process but rather that most of evolutionary history has been characterized by relatively stable species coexisting in equilibrium (plural, *equilibria*). Occasionally, however, that equilibrium is punctuated by sudden bursts of speciation, when extinctions are widespread and many new species appear. This view is called the theory of **punctuated equilibrium** (see Figure 3.6). Gould and Eldredge claimed "that speciation is orders of magnitude more important than phyletic evolution as a mode of evolutionary change" (1977, 116).

But if phyletic gradualism is not the rule, where do new species come from? Gould and Eldredge argue that drastic changes in the natural environment trigger extinction and speciation by destroying habitats and breaking reproductive communities apart. When this happens, the populations that remain have both a radically modified gene pool and the opportunity to construct a new niche in a radically modified environment. When adaptive equilibria are punctuated this way, speciation is still thought to require thousands or hundreds of thousands of years to be completed. From the perspective of ecological time, the process still appears "gradual," but from the perspective of geological time, speciation appears "rapid" when compared to the long periods of stasis that precede and follow it.

Research and theorizing about punctuated equilibria have challenged the common neo-Darwinian understanding of speciation by means of anagenesis. Punctuationists view speciation as the outcome of cladogenesis, which had always been recognized as part of the neo-Darwinian synthesis but had never been given the important role that punctuationists assign it. Punctuationists also reject neo-Darwinian descriptions of speciation as the outcome of changing gene frequencies, insisting that speciation itself triggers adaptive change (Eldredge and Tattersall 1982, 62). Finally, punctuationists propose that natural selection may operate among variant, related species within a single genus, family, or order, a process called **species selection**. Just like natural selection among individuals of the same species, however, species selection is subject to random forces. Some species flourish simply because they tend to form new species at a high rate. Sometimes, however, none of the variant species is able to survive in the changed environment, and the entire group—genus, family, or order—may become extinct (Stanley 1981, 187–88). If speciation events occur rapidly in small, isolated populations, punctuationists predict that fossil evidence of intermediate forms between parent species and descendant species may not survive or may be hard to find, although occasionally paleontologists might get lucky (see also Eldredge 1985).

---

punctuated equilibrium A theory claiming that most of evolutionary history has been characterized by relatively stable species coexisting in an equilibrium that is occasionally punctuated by sudden bursts of speciation, when extinctions are widespread and many new species appear.

species selection A process in which natural selection is seen to operate among variant, related species within a single genus, family, or order.

Geneticists have not yet been able to pinpoint the genetic changes involved in speciation, but one hypothesis links speciation to mutations in genes involved in the timing of interrelated biological processes, which have major pleiotropic effects. Ernst Mayr argued, however, that only a few such mutations might be sufficient if the population undergoing speciation was small and isolated, involving few reproducing individuals and thus subject to the force of genetic drift (1982, 605–6). This is, in fact, the sort of speciation scenario the punctuationists also imagine, the setting in which cladogenesis has long been presumed to occur. As Steven Stanley observed, "It is estimated that 98 or 99 percent of the protein structures of humans and chimpanzees are the same! Clearly, evolution is reshaping animals in major ways without drastically remodeling the genetic code" (1981, 127).

Thinking about evolution in terms of punctuated equilibria fundamentally restructures our view of life. As Stanley explains, "the punctuational view implies, among other things, that evolution is often ineffective at perfecting the adaptations of animals and plants; that there is no real ecological balance of nature; that most large scale evolutionary trends are not produced by the gradual reshaping of established species, but are the net result of many rapid steps of evolution, not all of which have moved in the same direction" (1981, 5). He later observes that the theory of punctuated equilibrium "accentuates the unpredictability of large-scale evolution" and interprets speciation as "a kind of experimentation, but experimentation without a plan" (181).

Needless to say, these suggestions remain highly controversial. Many modern evolutionary biologists are convinced that phyletic gradualism is well supported by the fossil records of many species. As we will see in Chapter 5, punctuationists and gradualists have argued vehemently about whether our own species, *Homo sapiens*, is the product of phyletic gradualism or of a punctuated equilibrium. So far, the fossil information that might shed light on the debate is so fragmentary that supporters of both sides can use it to support their own interpretation. Nevertheless, the debate between gradualists and punctuationists has triggered a close reexamination of biological ideas about macroevolution that promises to increase our understanding in unanticipated ways.

Can We Predict the Future of Human Evolution?

Current arguments among evolutionary biologists illustrate their varied attempts to grasp the meaning of evolution. How we classify the natural world matters not only to scientists, who want to be sure their classifications match what they find when they go to nature, but also to nonscientists. How we make sense of evolution is important because people of all societies see a connection between the way they make sense of the natural world and the way they make sense of their own lives. Many people believe that human morality is, or ought to be, based on what is natural. For such people, evolutionary interpretations of nature can be threatening even if they portray a natural world that is orderly. If nature's order is dog-eat-dog and if human morality must be based on nature's order, then survival at any cost must be morally correct because it is "natural." This is clearly why many people find the more extreme claims of human sociobiology so repugnant. For those who want to root compassion and generosity in human nature, sociobiology offers a portrait of human nature in which such behavior has little or no value.

But perhaps the uncontrolled and uncontrollable pursuit of food and sex is no more natural in our species than sharing, compassion, and nonviolent resolution of differences. As we will see in Chapter 4, many primatologists have evidence to show that, most of the time, most apes and monkeys do not live by the "law of the jungle." Possibly, the law of the jungle is not a law after all.

Human beings, like all living organisms, are subject to evolutionary processes. Like other organisms, our species shares a gene pool whose different combinations, together with environmental input, create different human phenotypes that are able, within certain limits, to allow us a certain range of adaptive responses. But we are not like other organisms in all respects, and this is what makes the study of human nature, human society, and the human past necessary. In order to adapt to our environments—to make a living and replace ourselves—we have options that do not exist for other organisms: cultural adaptations that are passed on by learning, even when there is no biological reproduction (see Figure 3.6).

The rich heritage of human culture is the source of much wisdom to guide us in our moral dealings with one another. The more we learn about biology, however, the more we realize that neither genotypes nor phenotypes nor environmental pressures provide obvious answers to our questions about how to live. If anything, "nature" offers us mixed messages about what is, or is not, likely to promote survival and reproduction. And in any case, with the development of culture, for good or for ill, human beings have long been concerned not only with survival and reproduction but also with what it takes to lead a meaningful life. Physical life and a meaningful life usually, but not always, go together. This paradox has been part of the human condition for millennia and is likely to remain with us long after our contemporary scientific debates have become history.

Chapter Summary

1. The neo-Darwinian evolutionary synthesis of the 1930s and 1940s combined Darwinian natural selection with Mendelian ideas about heredity. Neo-Darwinians studied populations of reproductively isolated species, concentrating on the population's gene pool, estimating the frequency of occurrence of different alleles of a particular gene, and predicting how those gene frequencies might be affected by different selection pressures.

2. Human population genetics has shown that different human populations from all over the world share basically the same range of genotypic variation, no matter how different they may appear phenotypically, reinforcing the position that the concept of "race" is biologically meaningless.

3. Natural selection, mutation, gene flow, and genetic drift are four evolutionary processes that can affect change in gene frequencies in a population over time. Sometimes one evolutionary process may work to increase the frequency of a particular allele while a different process is working to decrease its frequency. Inbreeding over several generations can be harmful because it decreases genetic variation and increases the probability that any alleles for deleterious traits will be inherited in a double dose, one from each parent.

4. Natural selection seems to have molded many complex human phenotypic traits, better adapting human populations to their environments. Anthropologists have studied how variation in traits such as skin color appear to have been shaped by natural selection. Anthropologists have also shown how variations in IQ test scores reflect variations in social class and educational background rather than "race."

5. Many evolutionary biologists and biological anthropologists recognize that trying to attribute every phenotypic trait of an organism to adaptation is problematic. Some traits may not be the result of adaptation but the by-product of some other feature that was shaped by natural selection—or even the consequence of random effects.

6. Gene-centered explanations of human evolution gained considerable influence in anthropology after 1975, due to the widespread theoretical impact of a school of evolutionary thought called "sociobiology." Sociobiologists have used formal mathematical models borrowed from population genetics and game theory to back up some of their claims. However, critics have also used formal models to test sociobiological principles.

7. Anthropologists have been involved in the development of formal models critical of sociobiological models. The most influential critical models include those of gene–culture coevolution, cultural group selection, and niche construction. Anthropologists still face the challenge of deciding how to situate such critical formal models within broader anthropological discussions of human culture and history.

8. Until recently, most evolutionists were phyletic gradualists, who thought that microevolutionary anagenesis led to macroevolutionary speciation, given enough time. Gould and Eldredge, however, proposed that most of evolutionary history has consisted of relatively stable species coexisting in equilibrium. Macroevolution occurs, in their view, when this equilibrium is punctuated by a burst of speciation by cladogenesis. They further propose that species selection may operate among variant, related species. Debate between phyletic gradualists and punctuationists has been lively.

For Review

1. Distinguish between microevolution and macroevolution.
2. How is a species defined in your text?
3. Explain what a cline is and why it is important.
4. Explain what is meant by the "molecularization of race."
5. What are the four evolutionary processes discussed in the text?
6. Describe how natural selection explains why a high proportion of the sickling allele is maintained in certain human populations and not others.
7. What is phenotypic plasticity, and why is it important?
8. Explain the difference between short-term acclimatization and developmental acclimatization.

(continued on next page)

For Review *(continued)*

9. Summarize the discussion of skin color in the text.
10. Why do anthropologists and many other scholars insist that IQ is not determined by genes alone?
11. Explain why natural selection on genetic variation alone is not sufficient to explain the range of human adaptive patterns revealed by archaeology, ethnography, and history.

12. What are formal models?
13. Compare and contrast phyletic gradualism and punctuated equilibria.
14. Define cladogenesis and explain how evolutionary biologists use it to develop taxonomies of species.

Key Terms

acclimatization   70
adaptation   69
anagenesis   74
cladogenesis   76
cline   59
formal models   73

gene flow   62
gene frequency   58
gene pool   58
genetic drift   62
macroevolution   58
microevolution   58

mutation   62
natural selection   62
phyletic gradualism   76
plasticity   69
polymorphous   59
population genetics   58

punctuated
  equilibrium   77
species   58
species selection   77

Suggested Readings

Gould, Stephen Jay. 1989. *Wonderful life: The Burgess Shale and the nature of history.* New York: Norton. *In this now-classic account of the discovery and interpretation of an important paleontological site, Gould analyzes what it tells us about the nature of evolution and sciences that study history.*

Marks, Jonathan. 2011. *The alternative introduction to biological anthropology.* New York and Oxford: Oxford University Press. *An up-to-date introduction to the subfield, raising critical issues in the field that are often sidestepped in introductory textbooks. Especially strong on the value of the anthropology of science for biological and cultural anthropology.*

Mielke, James H., Lyle W. Konigsberg, and John H. Relethford. 2011. *Human biological variation,* 2nd ed. New York: Oxford University Press. *Provides a thorough and contemporary view of our biological diversity. Integrates real-world examples on interesting topics, including genetic testing, lactose intolerance, dyslexia, IQ, and homosexuality.*

Relethford, John H. 2004. *The human species: An introduction to biological anthropology,* 6th ed. New York: McGraw-Hill. *A fine introduction to modern biological anthropology, with up-to-date reviews of current research on human variation as well as chapters on primatology and human evolution. Comes with a related web page.*

Robins, A. H. 1991. *Biological perspectives on human pigmentation.* Cambridge: Cambridge University Press. *A concise survey of what is known about the biological factors responsible for human pigmentation as well as the possible evolutionary significance of variation in pigmentation in different human populations.*

Stanley, Steven. 1981. *The new evolutionary timetable.* New York: Basic Books. *A classic, accessible introduction (by a punctuationist) to the debate between phyletic gradualists and punctuationists.*

Module 2: Dating Methods in Paleoanthropology and Archaeology

The people who study the human and prehuman past—paleoanthropologists and archaeologists—are vitally concerned with accurately determining when the organisms whose fossils they find actually lived and at what point in time artifacts were made. Without firm dates, paleoanthropologists cannot accurately reconstruct the path of extinction and speciation that led to modern humans, and, as we will see in Chapters 5–7, archaeologists cannot accurately trace cultural development. Fortunately, a number of scientific procedures, developed over the past century or so, can aid paleoanthropologists and archaeologists in assigning dates to fossils and artifacts. The following discussion relies primarily on Richard Klein's discussion (2009, Chapter 2).

Relative dating methods identify a particular object as being older or younger in relation to some other object and arrange material evidence in a linear sequence so that we know what came before what (Klein 2009, 22–24). By themselves, however, relative dating methods cannot tell us how long ago a sequence began or how long each stage in the sequence lasted. For such information, we must turn to **numerical dating** methods, which use laboratory treatment or analysis of various items recovered from an excavation. These techniques can tell us how many years ago a rock layer was formed, a piece of clay was fired, or an animal died (Klein 2009, 33–54).

Numerical dates are sometimes called "absolute dates." Strictly speaking, this term is not accurate because numerical dates always have a margin of error (sometimes in hundreds or thousands of years) ordinarily expressed as plus or minus a certain number of years. The precision of a numerical date depends on the quality of the sample being analyzed and the method of analysis. Nevertheless, because the time frame within which scientists work ordinarily involves thousands or millions of years, the margins of error for most numerical dates are impressively small, explaining why most geologists, paleontologists, and archaeologists continue to call them "absolute" dates.

In any case, experienced paleontologists and archaeologists rarely rely on only one dating method. Professional practice demands using as many different dating methods, both relative and numerical, as can be applied to any recovered material. When the same materials are subjected to a series of independent analyses and the resulting dates reinforce one another, scholars are increasingly confident of the accuracy of the data.

Relative Dating Methods

Stratigraphic Superposition The oldest and most venerable of all dating techniques, stratigraphic superposition, interprets what we find when we dig deeply into the earth and look at a wall of the resulting hole, which tends to resemble a layer cake of rocks and soil of different color and composition (Figure M2.1). Geologists reason that, other things being equal, things on the bottom are older than things on the top. When applied to soil layers, or strata (singular **stratum**), this so-called **law of superposition** states that layers lower down must be older than the layers above them. If so, then objects embedded in lower layers must be older than those in upper layers, whether these objects are fossils or artifacts fashioned by human hands.

Superposed layers of rock rarely remain undisturbed forever. Sometimes old rocks are crosscut by other geological features, as when molten lava forces its way through fractures in several superposed layers on its way to the surface. The intruding features must be younger than the layers of rock they cut across, a deduction called the **law of crosscutting relationships**. In addition, periods of uplift and subsidence in the earth's crust have sometimes tilted or twisted large sections of layered rock from a horizontal to a vertical position (Figure M2.2). These rearranged rock layers (*unconformities*) may be exposed to erosion for a considerable period of time before new layers of sediment begin to collect and bury them again.

The pattern of stratigraphic superposition in a given rock column tends to be distinctive, something like a fingerprint. As a result, geologists are often able to correlate deposits at one site with those at another site when those deposits have the same distinctive pattern. This enables them to generalize about what was happening geologically over wider regions and longer periods of time.

Typological Sequences Classifying fossils or artifacts into a series of types on the basis of their similarities and differences is a time-honored and very useful form of relative dating. Those objects that look most alike are grouped together, compared to other objects of similar kinds (often recovered from other excavations), and ordered in a chronological or developmental sequence. If at least one end of the typological

---

relative dating Dating methods that arrange material evidence in a linear sequence, each object in the sequence being identified as older or younger than another object.

numerical dating Dating methods based on laboratory techniques that assign age in years to material evidence.

stratum Layer; in geological terms, a layer of rock and soil.

law of superposition A principle of geological interpretation stating that layers lower down in a sequence of strata must be older than the layers above them and, therefore, that objects embedded in lower layers must be older than objects embedded in upper layers.

law of crosscutting relationships A principle of geological interpretation stating that where old rocks are crosscut by other geological features, the intruding features must be younger than the layers of rock they cut across.

Module 2: Dating Methods in Paleoanthropology and Archaeology (continued)

Figure M2.1 Stratigraphic superposition is dramatically on display in the Grand Canyon, where layers of rock and soil, laid down sequentially over millions of years, have been exposed by erosion.

sequence can be anchored by a numerical date, the sequence then becomes a powerful tool for understanding evolutionary change, even in the absence of fossil evidence.

Certain kinds of fossil evidence can provide an extremely helpful framework for the relative dating of other fossils or of the artifacts associated with them. As we saw, scientific confidence in the law of superposition increased when geologists found that not only rock layers but also the fossils they contained could be systematically correlated. Two kinds of fossil species are most useful for relative dating: those that spread out quickly over a large area following the widespread extinction of their parent species and those that evolved so rapidly that a fossil representing any evolutionary stage is a good indicator of the relative age of other fossils found in association with it. Relative dating that relies on patterns of fossil distri-bution in different rock layers is called **biostratigraphic dating** (Klein 2009, 24–33).

For paleoanthropologists, the most useful biostratigraphic patterns deal with regions and periods of time in which human beings, or our ancestors, were evolving. Although biostratigraphy can establish only relative dates, its correlations are indispensable for cross-checking dates provided by numerical methods. For example, fossils of the

one-toed horse played an important role in the 1970s when paleoanthropologists were attempting to assign firm dates to important hominin fossil–bearing layers at the eastern African site of Koobi Fora. The potassium-argon dating method (see the section Isotopic Methods) yielded a date for the Koobi Fora site that would have made it over half a million years older than a site only 100 kilometers north, in the lower Omo River valley, yet the biostratigraphy of these two sites was identical. The paleoanthropologists reasoned that either the one-toed horse had appeared at Koobi Fora over half a million years earlier than it had in the Lower Omo or something was wrong with the potassium-argon dates. Eventually, they determined that the potassium-argon date for Koobi Fora was 700,000–600,000 years too early (Klein 2009, 38). This is exactly what can happen if paleoanthropologists give too much importance to a single, "absolute" date.

Archaeologists also use typological sequences based on collections of artifacts. Artifacts that look alike are assumed to have been made at the same time, which allows archaeologists to arrange them in a linear order, a technique called **seriation**. Seriation can only indicate patterns of change; some other source of information must be used to anchor one end of the series in time. *Contextual seriation*, based on changes in artifact styles, is most successfully applied to artifacts like pottery, whose stylistic features are visible and highly modifiable. At the end of the nineteenth century, archaeologist Sir Flinders Petrie used contextual seriation to analyze variations in the pottery recovered from predynastic burials at Diospolis Parva in Upper Egypt. Petrie had no method to assign firm dates to these burials, so he devised a relative chronology in

---

biostratigraphic dating A relative dating method that relies on patterns of fossil distribution in different rock layers.

seriation A relative dating method based on the assumption that artifacts that look alike must have been made at the same time.

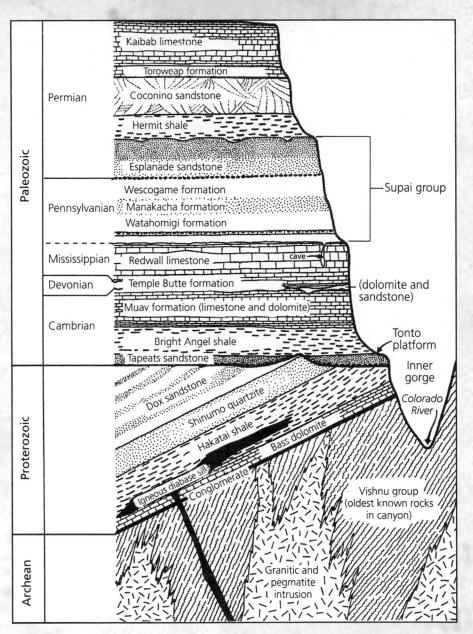

Figure M2.2 Geological analysis of one wall of the Grand Canyon yields evidence of superposition (e.g., Coconino sandstone lies atop Hermit shale and is thus younger), unconformities (e.g., the Paleozoic and Proterozoic strata), and cross-cutting relationships (e.g., granitic and pegmatitic intrusions into the Vishnu group).

the following way. All the contents of each grave were written on a separate sheet of paper. Then, Petrie moved the sheets around until he had a sequence in which as many similar artifacts as possible were arranged as closely as possible to one another. Then, he created a relative chronology based on stylistic changes in the artifacts they contained (Figure M2.3). Later research confirmed that Petrie's relative sequence was very close to the actual historical sequence.

Artifacts and structures from a particular time and place in a site are called an **assemblage**. *Frequency seriation* measures changes in artifact percentages from one undated

assemblage to another. Archaeologists assume that different proportions of artifact styles in an assemblage are a measure of popularity, that all styles gain and lose popularity over time, and that styles popular at one site should also be popular at contemporary sites nearby. When the frequencies of different artifacts from a series of assemblages are plotted

---

assemblage Artifacts and structures from a particular time and place in an archaeological site.

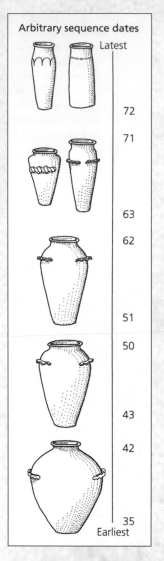

Arbitrary sequence dates

Latest

72
71
63
62
51
50
43
42
35
Earliest

Figure M2.3 Contextual seriation is a time-honored and very useful form of relative dating. The classic use of seriation in archaeology is attributed to Sir Flinders Petrie, who used it at the end of the nineteenth century to analyze variations in pottery recovered from predynastic burials in Egypt.

on a graph and sites containing the styles in similar frequencies are kept together, the result, once again, is a relative chronology of assemblages based on the rising and falling frequencies of the different styles. Frequency seriation has been used by archaeologists to arrange a number of undated

isotopic dating Dating methods based on scientific knowledge about the rate at which various radioactive isotopes of naturally occurring elements transform themselves into other elements by losing subatomic particles.

pottery assemblages into relative sequences that have been confirmed by stratigraphic sequences from excavations (Renfrew and Bahn 2004, 128).

Obsidian hydration is a relative dating method based on the principle that when obsidian (volcanic glass that can be made into extremely sharp tools) is fractured, it starts to absorb water along the newly exposed surface, forming a hydration layer. This hydration layer gets thicker over time and can be measured. Every time obsidian breaks, the hydration process begins anew on the freshly revealed surface. If the rate of hydration is constant, then it should be possible to tell how long it has been since the obsidian was fractured, either naturally or by someone making a tool out of it. Unfortunately, the hydration rate of obsidian is not uniform throughout the world—different kinds of obsidian have different hydration rates, and the atmospheric temperature at the time the obsidian surface is revealed also affects the hydration rate. However, correlation maps of climate and hydration rates have been prepared and several researchers are working on how to distinguish among different kinds of obsidian. But where these limitations can be controlled, obsidian hydration can be very helpful to archaeologists: it can be used for dates from 7.8 mya to the present, it is relatively inexpensive, and it can be used to trace the trade routes of obsidian in the past. The technique has been quite helpful in Mesoamerica, where Ann Corinne Freter and her colleagues, for example, were able to analyze an abundant collection of obsidian artifacts at Copán and to plot changing settlement patterns over time with great accuracy (Fagan and DeCorse 2005, 161).

Numerical Dating Methods

Numerical dating methods are valuable because they anchor a series of fossils dated by relative methods to a numbered date, a fixed point in time that can be used to estimate rates of evolution. Perhaps best known are **isotopic dating** methods, which are based on knowledge about the rate at which various radioactive isotopes of naturally occurring elements transform themselves into other elements by losing subatomic particles. This process is called *decay*, and the rate of decay of a given radioactive isotope is measured in terms of its *half-life*, or the time it takes for half of the original radioactive sample to decay into the nonradioactive end product. Rates of decay make useful atomic clocks because they are unaffected by other physical or chemical processes. Moreover, because each radioactive element has a unique half-life, we can cross-check dates obtained by one isotopic method with those obtained by another. As geologists Sheldon Judson and Marvin Kauffman conclude, "The fact that several clocks regularly agree indicates that radioactive dating is self-consistent and reassures us that we are measuring real ages" (1990, 146).

Geologists using isotopic dating methods to determine the ages of rocks generally agree that the earth is about 4.6 billion years old. Paleoanthropologists are most interested in only a tiny fraction of all that geological time, perhaps the last 65 million years, the period during which nonhuman primates and then human beings evolved. Archaeologists focus on an even narrower slice: the last 2.5 million years.

Isotopic Methods   Described below are several reliable isotopic dating methods. A more complete list of numerical dating methods, with the periods for which dates are the most accurate, appears in Figure M2.4.

Potassium-Argon Dating Potassium is one of the most commonly occurring elements in the earth's crust. One isotope of potassium that occurs in relatively small quantities is radioactive potassium 40, which decays at a known rate into argon 40. During volcanic activity, very nearly all of the argon 40 in molten lava escapes, resetting the atomic clock to zero. Potassium, however, does not escape. As lava cools and crystallizes, any argon 40 that collects in the rock can only have been produced by the decay of potassium 40. The date of the

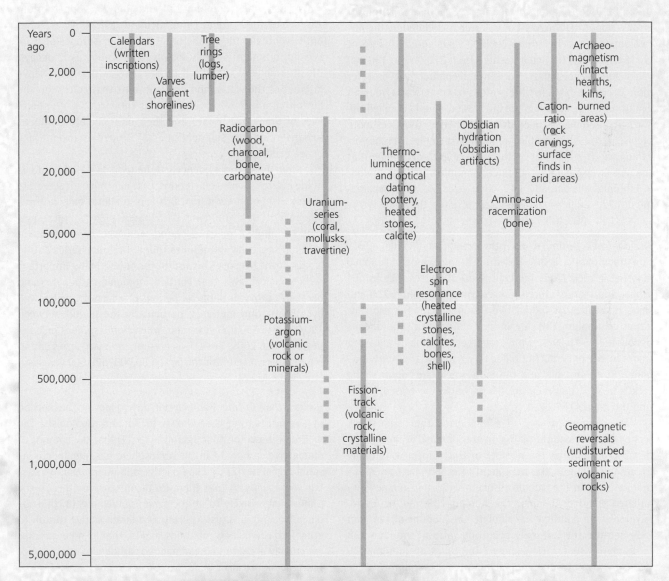

Figure M2.4 Chronometric dating methods can be used to anchor a series of fossils or artifacts dated by relative methods to a fixed point in time. This chart summarizes some of the most important chronometric methods, showing the spans of time and materials for which each is applicable. (Adapted from Renfrew and Bahn 2008, 133)

Module 2: Dating Methods in Paleoanthropology and Archaeology (continued)

formation of the volcanic rock can then be calculated, based on the half-life of potassium 40, which is 1.3 billion years.

The potassium-argon method is accurate for dates from the origin of the earth up to about 100,000 years ago. This method is valuable to paleoanthropologists because it can date volcanic rock formed early in the evolutionary history of nonhuman primates and human beings and thus any fossils found in or under volcanic rock layers themselves. Fortunately, volcanic activity was common during these periods in areas like eastern Africa, where many important fossils of early human ancestors have been found.

Potassium-argon dating has two main limitations. First, it can be used only on volcanic rock. Second, its margin of error is about ±10 percent. A volcanic rock dated by the potassium-argon technique to 200,000 years ago ±10 percent could have been formed anywhere from 220,000 to 180,000 years ago. Nevertheless, no other technique yet provides more accurate dates for the periods in which early hominin evolution occurred. Since the late 1980s, a variant called the $^{40}Ar/^{39}Ar$ method has been developed, which produces more precise dates using samples as small as a single grain of volcanic rock. The $^{40}Ar/^{39}Ar$ method was able to determine that the ash layer beneath the oldest hominin fossils at Aramis, in Ethiopia, was actually 4.4 million years old, after separating out 23.6 million-year-old volcanic grains that were intrusions (Klein 2009, 37).

Fission-Track Dating A recently developed technique, fission-track dating, is also based on the decay of radioactive material in rock. Many minerals, natural glasses such as obsidian, and manufactured glasses contain uranium 235 and small quantities of radioactive uranium 238. Occasionally, atoms of uranium 238 split in half. During this spontaneous fission, the two halves of the atom fly apart violently, leaving tracks in the mineral. The older the material, the more uranium 238 atoms split and the more tracks are found. If the rock is heated, however, the fission tracks are erased, resetting the radioactive clock to zero.

To calculate the age of a rock using the fission-track technique, two counts of fission tracks must be made. The first count identifies the number of tracks formed naturally by uranium 238. In the next step, to determine how much uranium was in the sample to begin with, the sample is irradiated to induce fission in the uranium 235, and the resulting tracks are counted to calculate the amount of uranium 235. Because the naturally occurring ratio of uranium 238 to uranium 235 in rock is known, the count of uranium 235 indirectly measures the original quantity of uranium 238. Because the fission rate of uranium 238 is also known, the date of the sample can now be calculated based on the ratio of uranium 238 tracks to the quantity of uranium 238 the sample is thought to have originally contained.

The range of dates from the fission-track technique overlaps the range from the potassium-argon method: from about 300,000 to some 2.5 billion years ago. Fission-track dating can be used where the potassium-argon method cannot be applied and can also provide a second opinion on materials already dated by the potassium-argon method. Paleontologists and archaeologists have applied fission-track dating to sites where volcanic rock layers lie above or below sediments containing hominin fossils, especially in eastern Africa (Klein 2009, 38).

Uranium-Series Dating This dating method is based on two facts. First, when uranium 238, uranium 235, and thorium 232 decay, they produce intermediate radioactive isotopes until eventually they transform into stable isotopes of lead. Second, uranium is easily dissolved in water; as it decays, the intermediate isotopes it produces tend to solidify, separate out of the water, and mix with salts that collect on the bottom of a lake or sea. Using their knowledge of the half-lives of uranium isotopes and their intermediate products, scientists can date soil deposits that formed in ancient lake or sea beds.

Uranium-series evidence can be used to date broad climatic events, such as glaciations, that may have affected the course of human evolution. But it also allows paleoanthropologists to date inorganic carbonates, such as limestones, that accumulate in cave, spring, and lake deposits where hominin fossils are sometimes found. Uranium-series dating is significant because it is useful for dating many important archaeological sites that contain inorganic carbonates and because it provides dates for periods of time not covered well by other dating methods, particularly the period between 150,000 and 350,000 years ago, when *Homo sapiens* first appeared (Klein 2009, 38–41). At present, uranium-series dating is particularly useful for the period 50,000–500,000 years ago (see Figure M2.4).

Radiocarbon Dating Radiocarbon dating may be the method of absolute dating best known to nonanthropologists. The method is based on four assumptions: (1) that the amount of radioactive carbon 14 in the atmosphere has remained constant over time, (2) that radioactive and nonradioactive carbon mix rapidly so that the ratio of one to the other in the atmosphere is likely to be the same everywhere, (3) that radioactive carbon is just as likely as nonradioactive carbon to enter into chemical compounds, and (4) that living organisms are equally likely to take radioactive carbon and nonradioactive carbon into their bodies.

If these assumptions hold, then we can deduce that equal amounts of radioactive and nonradioactive carbon are present in all living tissues. Once an organism dies, however, it stops taking carbon into its system and the radioactive carbon 14 in its remains begins to decay at a known rate. The half-life of carbon 14 is 5,730 years, making radiocarbon dating extremely useful for dating the remains of organisms that died as long ago as 30,000–40,000 years. Samples older than about 40,000 years usually contain too little carbon 14 for accurate measurement. However, a recent refinement in radiocarbon technology called accelerator mass spectrometry (or AMS) solves that problem in part for smaller samples. AMS counts the actual atoms of carbon 14 in a sample. Charcoal, for example, can be reliably dated to 55,000 years ago using AMS (Klein 2009, 46; Figure M2.5).

Radiocarbon dating is not flawless. Evidence shows that the amount of carbon 14 in the earth's atmosphere fluctuates periodically as a result of such factors as solar activity, changes in the strength of the earth's magnetic field, and changes in the amount of carbon dioxide dissolved in the world's oceans. Scientists are also concerned that an organism's tissues can become contaminated by carbon from outside sources either before or after death; this problem is particularly acute in very old samples analyzed by AMS. If undetected, any of these factors could yield inaccurate radiocarbon dates.

Scientists have discovered that radiocarbon dates for samples less than about 7,500 years old differ from their true ages anywhere from 1 to 10 percent. Fortunately, radiocarbon dates can be corrected by dendrochronology over roughly the same 7,000-year time span. Most archaeologists use radiocarbon dates corrected by dendrochronology to convert radiocarbon years into calendar years, assigning dates in "radiocarbon years" rather than in calendar solar years. Radiocarbon years are indicated when they are followed by the letters B. P., meaning "before present"; and for purposes of calibration, "present" was established as 1950. In addition, radiocarbon ages are always given with a plus-or-minus range, reflecting the statistical uncertainties of the method (e.g., 14,000 ± 120 years ago [Klein 2009, 45]).

Thermoluminescence If a natural substance is exposed to radiation emitted by naturally occurring radioactive isotopes of uranium, thorium, and potassium, the electrons released become trapped in the crystal structure of the irradiated substance. If the irradiated substance is subsequently heated, however, the trapped electrons will be released together with a quantity of light directly in proportion to their number. The light released in this process is called *thermoluminescence.*

If we know the amount of radiation our sample receives per year, heat it up, and measure the amount of thermoluminescence released, then we can calculate the number of years since the sample was last heated. This is a handy way of determining the date when ancient pottery fragments were last fired, when burnt-flint artifacts were last heated, or even when naturally occurring clays were heated accidentally by a fire burning above them. The accuracy of this method may be questioned if it can be determined either that trapped electrons sometimes escape without being heated or that radiation doses are not constant. Nevertheless, thermoluminescence is valuable because, like the uranium-series method, it uses an alternative set of materials to yield reliable dates for the troublesome gap between the upper limits of the radiocarbon method and the lower limits of the potassium-argon method—between 40,000 and 100,000–300,000 years ago (Fagan 1991, 64; Klein 2009, 35).

Electron Spin Resonance (ESR) This method is based on the fact that tooth enamel in a living organism is free of uranium but begins to absorb uranium after burial. Dates are determined by estimating background radioactivity, measuring the amount of uranium in the enamel of a fossilized tooth, and then determining the rate at which the uranium accumulated in the tooth after burial. ESR dates are often used to cross-check dates provided by thermoluminescence, but sometimes ESR dates do not match up very well. It may be that the process of uranium uptake is more complicated than previously understood and that a variety of factors can affect the level of uranium that actually accumulates in tooth enamel at a particular site. According to Klein, both luminescence dates and ESR dates are affected by site-specific factors that may interfere with their degree of accuracy. ESR dates, in particular, need to be evaluated with great care (Klein 2009, 47–48).

Figure M2.5 The University of Arizona accelerator mass spectrometry lab is a center for the dating of organic materials that are 50,000–80,000 years old.

Nonisotopic Methods Unlike isotopic techniques, **nonisotopic dating** methods do not use rates of nuclear decay to provide numerical dates of materials recovered from excavations.

Dendrochronology Dendrochronology yields numerical dates for trees and objects made of wood. A crosscut section of a mature tree exposes a series of concentric rings, which normally accumulate one per year over the tree's life. (Old trees do not need to be cut down to recover the tree-ring chronology they contain; instead, scientists bore long, thin holes into their trunks and remove samples that preserve the sequence.) Tree rings are thicker in wet years and thinner in dry years. The pattern of thick and thin rings is similar for all trees growing in the same habitat over many years. The older the tree, the more growth rings it has and the more complete is its record of the growth pattern for the locality. Clearly, only trees with seasonal growth patterns can be used successfully in dendrochronology—those that grow all year-round, such as those in tropical rain forests, do not produce variable ring patterns.

Tree rings are similar to rock layers because scientists can use their distinctive sequences to correlate different sites with one another. Figure M2.6 shows how the tree-ring sequences from three old trees cut down at different times can be cross-correlated to yield an uninterrupted chronology that covers 100 years. Scientists use this master chronology to match wood recovered from archaeological sites against the appropriate sequence to determine when a tree lived and when it was cut down. Tree-ring chronologies based on the California bristlecone pine extend more than 8,000 years into the past. In Europe, chronologies based on oak trees go back to about 6,000 years ago (Renfrew and Bahn 2008, 139).

Amino Acid Racemization (AAR) This method is based on the fact that amino acids in proteins can exist in two mirror-image forms, left-handed (L amino acids) and right-handed (D amino acids). Usually, only L amino acids are found in living organisms, but after the organism dies, they are converted into D amino acids. The rate of conversion is different for each amino acid and depends on a variety of factors, including the surrounding temperature, moisture and acidity level. If those levels can be determined since the time the specimen died, the ratio of D to L forms can be used to calculate how long ago death occurred. AAR has proved most accurate when dating fossilized shells (Klein 2009, 50.).

Paleomagnetism This dating method is based on the discovery that the earth's magnetic poles have not always been where they are today, perhaps because of shifting currents within the

earth's molten core. A magnet points north during some periods of earth history, south during others. Sometimes a past polarity shift lasted for a long period, called a *chron*; at other times, shifts alternated repeatedly for short intervals, called *subchrons*. Changes in polarity are preserved in volcanic rocks or rocks composed of fine-grained sediments that settled slowly. When volcanic rocks cool or sediments settle, their particles align themselves toward the current magnetic pole and retain this pattern. By examining geologic cores to map the positions and deduce the time of particular changes in polarity, geologists have been able to create a master chronology of paleomagnetic shifts that covers the past 5 million years.

Boundary dates between chrons are better established than boundary dates between subchrons, but because all paleomagnetic dates are less precise than other numerical dating methods, paleomagnetism looks more like a form of relative dating than a form of numerical dating. However, paleomagnetism is extremely valuable because, unlike other dating methods, it has the potential to provide a temporal framework within which geological, climatological, and evolutionary events can be related on a worldwide scale. It is particularly helpful to paleoanthropologists because the human line evolved during the last 5 million years. Paleomagnetic dates can be used to cross-check dates for important sites and to provide a general time frame for sites undatable by other means (Klein 2009, 51–54).

The Molecular Clock The concept of a molecular clock is based on the assumption that genetic mutations accumulate in DNA at a constant rate. This is most accurately measured in DNA that is unlikely to experience natural selection, such as mitochondrial DNA (mtDNA). Geneticists compare the genes of different living species (or the proteins produced by those genes), measure the degree of genetic (or protein) differences among them, and deduce the length of time since they all shared a common ancestor.

This dating method begins as a form of cladistic analysis. However, it can be converted into a numerical dating method if other numerical techniques tell us when the fossil ancestors of one of the living species being compared first appeared (Ruvolo and Pilbeam 1986, 157). For example, "if a fossil (geological) date of 25 mya for the divergence of Old World monkeys from apes is assumed, recently developed DNA hybridization data imply that the human and chimpanzee lines split about 5.5 mya and that the gorilla lineage became distinct about 7.7 mya, the gibbon lineage about 16.4 mya, the orangutan lineage about 12.2 mya, and (by definition) the line leading to Old World monkeys about 25 mya" (Klein 1989, 28). When this series of dates was first suggested, it contradicted dates for the divergence of primate species established on other grounds. However, new fossils and further research appear to vindicate the chronology suggested by the molecular clock.

---

nonisotopic dating Dating methods that assign age in years to material evidence but not by using rates of nuclear decay.

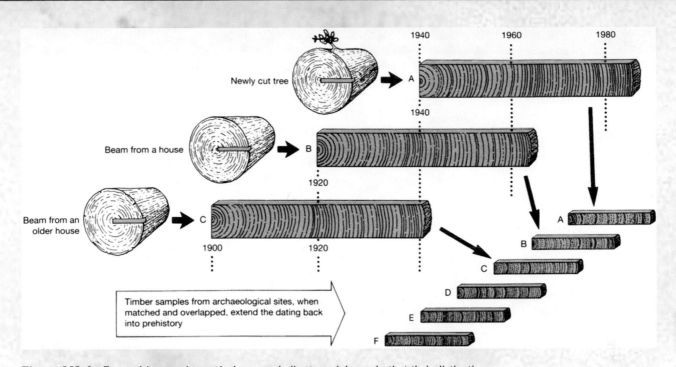

Figure M2.6 Trees with annual growth rings are similar to rock layers in that their distinctive sequences can be correlated across sites to yield an uninterrupted chronology that may go back hundreds or thousands of years. Researchers use this master chronology to assign chronometric dates to wood recovered from archaeological sites. *Acknowledgments:* Original drawn by Simon S. S. Driver, based on other sources (Renfrew and Bahn 2008, 139).

Not all paleoanthropologists accept the validity of this technique. Some question the key assumption that genetic mutations accumulate at a constant rate; others point out that the accuracy of the molecular clock depends on the accuracy of some other numerical method used to date the presumed fossil ancestors of one of the species being compared. If the original numerical date is wrong or if variation in a population's DNA has been affected by evolutionary forces other than mutation (genetic drift, e.g.), the molecular clock will provide a series of erroneous dates for later species' divergences (see, e.g., Templeton 1993, Thorne and Wolpoff 1992). Klein, however, observes that recent African fossil finds "now support the 8–5 Ma molecular estimate for African ape and human divergence, and few specialists now ignore the molecular clock" (2009, 94).

Modeling Prehistoric Climates

Much of the geological data that provide primate paleontologists with dates for their fossils and archaeologists with dates for their artifacts also provide information about the environment in which those fossil organisms and the artifacts' makers once lived (Table M2.1). In recent years, information about ancient climates and climate changes has

accumulated and aided primate paleontologists and archaeologists in better reconstructing the various selective pressures under which prehistoric nonhuman primate and human populations would have lived. Evidence for major fluctuations in ancient climates has been incorporated into the theory of punctuated equilibrium, discussed in Chapter 3.

A major source of information on past climate comes from the contents of cores drilled into the ocean floor or into glaciers (Figure M2.7). Deep sea sediments are especially reliable because their deposition shows fewer interruptions than do dry land deposits, and they rarely experience erosion (Klein 2009, 59). Ocean water contains two different isotopes of oxygen, the lighter ^{16}O and the heavier ^{18}O. The lighter isotopes are taken out of ocean water when glaciers form but return to it when glaciers melt. Furthermore, oxygen is incorporated into the skeletons of microscopic marine organisms called *foraminifera*. For millions of years, foraminifera have been settling on the ocean bottom after they die, which means that those collected in ocean cores can be analyzed to see which isotope of oxygen they contain. Foraminifera with ^{18}O in their skeletons must have lived and died when glaciers took up ^{16}O, whereas those with ^{16}O must have lived and died when glaciers were not present. Oxygen isotope curves can be plotted to trace climate changes over the past 2.3 million

Module 2: Dating Methods in Paleoanthropology and Archaeology *(continued)*

TABLE M2.1 The Major Divisions of Geological Time Relevant to Paleoanthropologists				
ERA	PERIOD	EPOCH	MILLION YEARS AGO (MYA)	IMPORTANT EVENTS
Cenozoic	Quaternary	Recent	.01	Modern genera of animals
		Pleistocene	2	Early humans and giant mammals now extinct
		Pliocene	5.1	Anthropoid radiation and culmination of mammalian speciation
	Tertiary	Miocene	25	
		Oligocene	38	
		Eocene	54	Expansion and differentiation of mammals
		Plaeocene	65	

Source: Price and Feinman 2001, 27.

a

b

Figure M2.7 Ice cores can provide information about the sequences of changing climate over extended periods of time. They are carefully extracted from glaciers (*a*) and stored in temperature-controlled rooms (*b*) until they can be analyzed.

years. Isotope sequences can be correlated with paleomagnetic reversals and the forams themselves can be dated by carbon 14. The result is a powerful worldwide chronology of climate change within which biological evolutionary events may be contextualized (Potts 1996, 50–51; Renfrew and Bahn 2004, 130).

Scientists do not fully understand the causes of climatic fluctuations but suspect that they are connected with such phenomena as changes in the shape and position of the continents, the tilt of the earth's axis, sunspot activity, the shape of the earth's orbit around the sun, and volcanic activity (Potts 1996). Debate continues about whether some of these fluctuations correlate with evolutionary events: the temperature drop around 15 mya seems to coincide with the diversification of hominoids in Africa and Asia, while the development of a drier, more seasonal climate between 10 and 5 mya may be connected with widespread hominoid extinctions and the appearance of the first human ancestors (Vrba et al. 1995). Data on climate also show that human prehistory for the last million years developed during periods of intense glaciation interrupted by periods of warmer climate. Different interpretations of these climatic fluctuations affect the way paleoanthropologists model the selective pressures that eventually gave rise to our own species some 200,000 years ago. They also affect explanations of major shifts in cultural adaptation (such as the domestication of plants and animals and the adoption of a sedentary life) that closely followed the retreat of the last glaciers some 12,000 years ago.

Module Summary

1. Scientific dating methods assist paleoanthropologists and archaeologists in their work. Relative dates indicate which objects are older or younger in a given sequence. Numerical dates identify how many years ago a rock layer was formed, a piece of clay was fired, or a living animal died. Paleoanthropologists and archaeologists ordinarily use as many dating methods as possible to assign reliable dates to the objects they recover.

2. Stratigraphic superposition underlies all relative and numerical dating methods. Scientists can cross-correlate strata from different locations to generalize about what was happening geologically over wider regions and longer periods of time. These correlations apply not only to the rock layers themselves but also to the fossils or artifacts they contain.

Biostratigraphic dating uses the fossils of widespread or rapidly evolving species to date the relative age of other fossils associated with them.

3. Numerical dating methods can anchor a series of fossils dated by relative methods to a fixed point in time. Isotopic dating methods are based on scientific knowledge about the rate at which various radioactive isotopes of naturally occurring elements transform themselves into other elements by losing subatomic particles. Nonisotopic dating methods that do not involve radioactive decay include paleomagnetism and the molecular clock.

4. Paleontologists have drawn upon climatic data to better reconstruct the various selective pressures under which prehistoric nonhuman primate and human populations would have lived. Between 1.6 mya and 12,000 years ago, temperatures plunged and ice sheets expanded and contracted during the Pleistocene. Some of these climatic fluctuations appear to correlate to evolutionary events and changes in human cultural adaptation.

For Review

1. What is the difference between relative dating methods and numerical dating methods?
2. Explain stratigraphic superposition and the law of crosscutting relationships.
3. What is seriation? What is the difference between contextual seriation and frequency seriation?
4. List the main forms of relative dating discussed in the text.
5. What are the isotopic methods of dating discussed in the text?
6. What are the nonisotopic methods of dating?
7. Why are climatic data useful to paleontologists?

Key Terms

assemblage 83	nonisotopic dating 88
biostratigraphic	numerical dating
dating 82	methods 81
isotopic dating 84	relative dating
law of crosscutting	methods 81
relationships 81	seriation 82
law of	stratum 81
superposition 81	

What Can the Study of Primates Tell Us about Human Beings?

Our closest animal relatives are the primates. This chapter introduces you to the richness and variety of primate ways of life, as well as providing an overview of primate evolution. Primates are fascinating in their own right but also can help us understand more about what it means to be human.

Chapter Outline

◄ *Dark and light gibbons grooming.*

Human beings are primates, and the evolution of human beings constitutes one strand of the broader evolutionary history of the primate order. Because knowledge of living primate species offers important clues to their evolutionary past, this chapter begins with an overview of what we know about living nonhuman primates. Because modern nonhuman primates have their own evolutionary history but also share an evolutionary history with human beings, we then turn to a brief look at their evolution.

What Are Primates?

Western Europeans first learned about African apes in the seventeenth century. Ever since, these animals have been used as a mirror to reflect on and speculate about human nature. But the results of this exercise have been contradictory. The physical characteristics that humans share with other primates have led many observers to assume that these primates also share our feelings and attitudes. This is called **anthropomorphism**, the attribution of human characteristics to nonhuman animals. In the twentieth century alone, Westerners vacillated between viewing primates as innocent and comical versions of themselves (Curious George) and as brutish and degraded versions of themselves (King Kong, Figure 4.1). When studying nonhuman primates, we must remain aware of how our own human interests can distort what we see (Haraway 1989). If you think humans are basically kind and generous, nonhuman primates will look kind and generous; if you think humans are basically nasty and selfish, nonhuman primates will look nasty and selfish. Primatologists have an obligation to avoid either romanticizing or demonizing primates if they are to understand these animals in their own right.

Approaches to Primate Taxonomy

The first step in understanding primates is to address the variety they exhibit. Primatologists, like other biologists, turn for assistance to modern biological **taxonomy**, the foundations of which were laid by Linnaeus in the eighteenth century. Today, taxonomists group organisms

Figure 4.1   In the West, nonhuman primates are often portrayed in ways that embody human fears and anxieties. In the 1930s, the giant ape in the original *King Kong* (*a*) embodied a racial threat to the power of white males and the sexual virtue of white females. Since that time, the popularization of Jane Goodall's chimpanzee research and Dian Fossey's gorilla research, as well as worries about the extinction of wild ape populations, seems to have reshaped the recent remake of *King Kong* (*b*), in which the white human heroine and the giant ape become allies in an effort to evade greedy, abusive, and exploitative white males.

together on the basis of morphological traits, behavioral traits, and geographical distribution (Mayr 1982, 192). Perhaps the most remarkable new tool for taxonomists has been the development of DNA hybridization, a laboratory technique that allows researchers to combine single strands of DNA from two species to see how closely they match. When human DNA is combined with the DNA of other primates, they all match very closely, with the closest match being between humans and chimpanzees.

Taxonomists classify organisms by assigning them to groups and arranging the groups in a hierarchy based

anthropomorphism The attribution of human characteristics to nonhuman animals.

taxonomy A biological classification of various kinds of organisms.

on the seven levels originally recognized by Linnaeus: kingdom, phylum, class, order, family, genus, and species. Biologists continue to assign Latin names to species (e.g., *Homo sapiens*). The species name consists of (1) a generic name (always capitalized) that refers to the genus in which the species is classified and (2) a specific name that identifies particular species (any distinguishing name will do, including the Latinized name of the person who first identified the species). Genus and species names are always italicized. The taxonomy recognized by modern biologists is an *inclusive hierarchy*. That is, related lower groups are combined to make higher groups: related species make up a genus, related genera make up a family, and so on. Each species—and each set of related species grouped at any level of the hierarchy—is called a **taxon** (plural, *taxa*). For example, *H. sapiens* is a taxon, as is Hominoidea (the superfamily to which humans and apes belong) and Mammalia (the class to which primates and all other mammals belong).

Contemporary taxonomies are designed to reflect the evolutionary relationships that modern biologists believe were responsible for similarities and differences among species, and taxonomists debate which kinds of similarities and differences they ought to emphasize. Traditional evolutionary taxonomies focused on the **morphology** of organisms—the shapes and sizes of their anatomical features—and related these to the adaptations the organisms had developed. Organisms that seemed to have developed similar adaptations at a similar level of complexity in similar environments were classified together in the same evolutionary *grade*. Primates are classified into four evolutionary grades: the least complex grade is represented by prosimians ("premonkeys") and includes lemurs, lorises, and tarsiers; anthropoids (monkeys, apes, and humans) represent a more advanced grade; followed by the hominoids (apes and humans); the most advanced grade is the hominins (humans). The lesser apes (gibbons and siamangs) are distinguished from the great apes (gorillas, chimpanzees, and orangutans) on the grounds that the great apes had achieved a more complex adaptation than the lesser apes. For the same reason, the great apes were grouped together on the grounds that their adaptations were more similar to one another than any of them were to human beings.

The traditional approach to taxonomy has much to recommend it—especially to paleontologists because fossils are often so few and so incomplete that any classification more precise than "grade" is likely to be misleading. However, paleontologists realize that adaptive morphological similarity by itself is not a foolproof indicator of evolutionary relatedness. This is because similarity can arise in one of two ways: either as the result of **homology** (inheritance due to common ancestry) or as the result of **analogy** (convergent, or parallel, evolution, as when two species with very different evolutionary histories develop similar physical features as a result of adapting to a similar environment). Examples of convergent evolution include wings in birds and in bats and long, hydrodynamic body shapes in fishes and in whales.

To avoid confusing homologous and analogous similarities, some twentieth-century taxonomists developed an alternative taxonomic method called *cladistics* that is based on evolutionary relatedness alone. Cladistics attempts to reconstruct the degrees of similarity and difference that result from *cladogenesis* (the formation of one or more new species from an older species). First, cladists must distinguish between homologous and analogous physical traits, focusing on homologous traits only. Then, they must determine which of the homologous traits shared by a group of organisms belonged to the ancestral population out of which they all evolved. These are called "primitive traits."

In order to trace later evolutionary developments, cladists identify phenotypic features shared by some, but not all, of the descendant organisms. A group of organisms possessing such a set of *shared, derived* features constitutes a natural group called a *clade* that must be recognized in the taxonomy. Finally, if cladists find derived features that are unique to a given group, this too requires taxonomic recognition. A group of organisms sharing a set of unique, derived features that sets them apart from other such groups within the same genus would qualify as a species (Figure 4.2). In recent years, cladistic methods have been widely adopted by primatologists and human paleontologists, and the following discussion uses cladistic categories.

The Living Primates

Nonhuman primates are found today in all the major rain forests of the world, except those in New Guinea and northeastern Australia. Some species, such as the Japanese macaque, have moved out of the tropics and

taxon Each species, as well as each group of related species, at any level in a taxonomic hierarchy.

morphology The physical shape and size of an organism or its body parts.

homology Genetic inheritance due to common ancestry.

analogy Convergent, or parallel, evolution, as when two species with very different evolutionary histories develop similar physical features as a result of adapting to a similar environment.

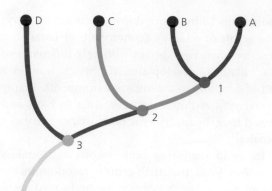

Figure 4.2 This cladogram shows the relationships among four hypothetical species. *A, B, C,* and *D* are assigned separate species status on the basis of unique, derived traits. *A* and *B* together possess shared, derived traits not found among *C* or *D*, indicating that *A* and *B* share a recent common ancestor *(1)*. *A, B,* and *C* together possess shared, derived traits that distinguish them from *D*, indicating that they, too, share a common—but more distant—ancestor *(2)*. *A, B, C,* and *D* are grouped together for analysis on the basis of shared, primitive traits common to them all or shared, derived traits that distinguish their common ancestor *(3)* from an out-group not shown in the cladogram.

into temperate climates. Primates are unusual, however, because, unlike most mammalian groups, their many and varied species are nearly all found in the tropics. Primates are studied in laboratories, in captive populations in zoos or research facilities, and in the wild. Primatologists must gather and compare information from all these settings to construct a picture of primate life that does justice to its richness and diversity.

And primate life is tremendously diverse. Different species live in different habitats, eat different kinds of food, organize themselves into different kinds of social configurations, and observe different patterns of mating and raising offspring. In light of all this diversity, most primatologists would probably caution against taking any single primate species as a model of early human social life (Cheney et al. 1987, 2). Alison Jolly points out that any species' way of life—what it eats and how it finds mates, raises its young, relates to companions, and protects itself from predators—defines that species' **ecological niche**. And, she adds, "With primates, much

ecological niche Any species' way of life: what it eats and how it finds mates, raises its young, relates to companions, and protects itself from predators.

dentition The sizes, shapes, and number of an animal's teeth.

prehensile The ability to grasp, with fingers, toes, or tail.

diurnal Describes animals that are active during the day.

of the interest lies in guessing how our ancestors evolved from narrow confinement in a particular niche into our present cosmopolitan state" (1985, 36).

Strepsirhines

Strepsirhini includes lemurs and lorises (see Figure 4.3), the prosimians that have a *rhinarium*, or upper lip, attached to the gums by a web of skin. Today, lemurs are native only to the island of Madagascar, off the east coast of Africa, where they were isolated from competition from later-evolving primate species on the African mainland (Figure 4.4). Lorises are found in Africa and Asia.

Haplorhines

Haplorhini includes tarsiers and anthropoids, primates whose upper lips are not attached to their gums.

Tarsiers Tarsiers are small nocturnal primates (Figure 4.5) that eat only animal food, such as insects, birds, bats, and snakes. Tarsiers used to be grouped with lemurs and lorises, but cladists have argued persuasively that they belong in the same clade as anthropoids. This is because they share a number of derived traits with the anthropoids, including dry noses, detached upper lips, a similarly structured placenta (and heavier infants), and a structure in their skulls called the "postorbital partition" (Bearder 1987, Aiello 1986).

Anthropoids Anthropoids include New World monkeys, Old World monkeys, apes, and humans. New World monkeys are called *platyrrhines*, a term referring to their broad, flat noses; Old World monkeys, apes, and humans are called *catarrhines* in reference to their downward-pointing nostrils (Figure 4.6). Platyrrhines also differ from catarrhines in **dentition** (the sizes, shapes, and number of their teeth): platyrrhines have three premolars, while catarrhines have two. Some platyrrhines have **prehensile**, or grasping, tails, whereas no catarrhines do. Finally, all platyrrhines are tree dwellers, whereas some catarrhine species live permanently on the ground.

Old World monkeys include two major groups: the colobines and the cercopithecines. *Colobines*, including the langurs of Asia (Figure 4.7) and the red colobus monkeys of Africa, are all **diurnal** (active during the day) and primarily adapted to arboreal life, although they have been observed to travel on the ground between tracts of forest. Colobines have four-chambered stomachs, presumably an adaptation to a heavy diet of leaves (Struhsaker and Leland 1987). *Cercopithecines* include some species adapted to live in the trees and others adapted to live on the ground. Those species living

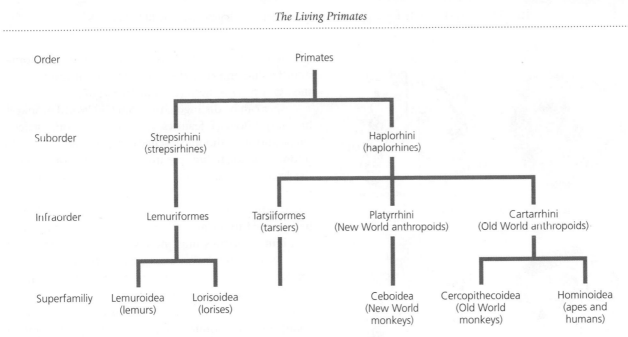

Figure 4.3 Cladistic taxonomy of the primates. (Relethford 1996, 175)

Figure 4.4 Lemurs are native only to the island of Madagascar, off the east coast of Africa. They managed to avoid competition from later-evolving monkeys and apes in Africa thanks to their geographical isolation.

Figure 4.5 Although tarsiers used to be grouped together with lemurs and lorises on phenetic grounds, cladists point out that tarsiers share a number of derived traits with the anthropoids.

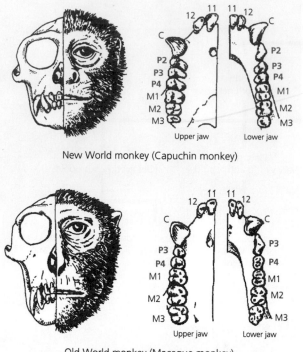

New World monkey (Capuchin monkey)

Old World monkey (Macaque monkey)

Figure 4.6 New World monkeys, such as the capuchin, have flat noses with nostrils pointing sideways and three premolars (P2, P3, and P4). By contrast, Old World anthropoids, including Old World monkeys such as the macaque, have noses with downward-pointing nostrils and only two premolars (P3 and P4).

in forests, such as African guenons, are often found in one-male breeding groups; females remain in the groups where they were born, while males ordinarily transfer out at puberty. Groups of more than one species are often found feeding and traveling together (Cords 1987).

Ground-dwelling cercopithecines include several species of baboons, perhaps the best known of all Old World monkeys. Hamadryas baboons (*Papio hamadryas*) and gelada baboons (*Theropithecus gelada*) are found in Africa (Figure 4.8). Although they belong to different genera, they both live in social groups that possess a single breeding male. However, this superficial similarity turns out to be the result of very different social processes. Hamadryas males build up their one-male units by enticing females away from other units or by "adopting" immature females and caring for them until they are ready to breed. They carefully police the females in their units, punishing those that stray with a ritualized neck bite. In addition, hamadryas males thought to be kin form bonds to create a higher-level social unit known as a "clan." Several one-male units, several clans, and some individual males congregate in a band to forage together; and three or four bands may sleep together at night in a troop. By contrast, gelada baboons construct their one-male units on a core of strongly bonded

female relatives that are closely influenced by the dominant female and that stay together even if the male of their group is removed (Stammbach 1987).

Apes can be distinguished from Old World monkeys by morphological features such as dentition, skeletal shape and size, and the absence of a tail. Traditional taxonomies divide living apes into three grades, or families: the lesser apes (gibbons and siamangs), the great apes (orangutans, gorillas, and chimpanzees), and the hominids (humans). In recent years, however, many cladists have argued that classification within the great ape and hominin categories must be revised. Biochemical tests and DNA hybridization results show that humans and the African apes (gorillas and chimpanzees) are far more closely related to one another than they are to orangutans (see Goodman 1986). Cladists disagree, however, about how taxonomies ought to be modified to reflect this information. The most radical cladists would place all the apes and humans in the family Hominidae. Less

Figure 4.7 Gray langurs are Old World colobine monkeys. Some primatologists have described events in which all-male langur groups "invade" one-male langur groups. Invading males have been reported to deliberately kill unweaned offspring of resident females. Whether this behavior should be interpreted as adaptive or maladaptive has been one of the great controversies of contemporary primatology.

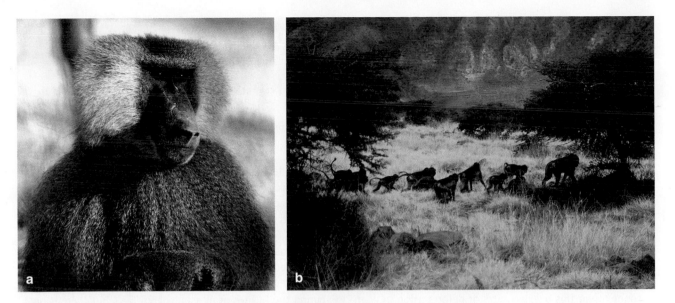

Figure 4.8 Both hamadryas baboons (*a*) and gelada baboons (*b*) are ground-dwelling Old World cercopithecine monkeys. Although both species live in social groups with a single breeding male, hamadryas groups are created when the male entices females away from other groups, whereas gelada groups construct their one-male units on a core of closely related females.

Figure 4.9 Gibbons are the smallest of the apes. Unlike most primate species, gibbons are monogamous, and male and female gibbons show no sexual dimorphism in size.

radical proposals place only chimpanzees (genus *Pan*) and humans in the family Hominidae; humans and their immediate ancestors are placed into a subfamily called Homininae and are called **hominins** (Bailey et al. 1991, Goodman et al. 1990. This usage, now adopted by many leading authorities (e.g., Klein 2009, 74–75; Stringer and Andrews 2005, 16), will be followed in this book.

Both traditionalists and cladists agree that gibbons (Figure 4.9) belong in their own family, Hylobatidae. Gibbons, smallest of the apes, are found in the tropical rain forests of southeastern Asia. Most primate species show **sexual dimorphism** in size; that is, individuals of one sex (usually the males) are larger than individuals of the other sex. Gibbons, however, show no sexual dimorphism in size, although in some species males and females have different coat colors. Gibbons are monogamous, neither male nor female is consistently dominant, and males contribute a great deal of care to their offspring. Gibbon groups usually comprise the mated pair and one or two offspring, all of whom spend comparatively little time in social interactions with one another. Gibbon pairs defend their joint territory, usually by vocalizing together to warn off intruders but occasionally with physical encounters. Establishing a territory appears to be difficult for newly mated pairs, and there is some evidence that parents may assist offspring in this effort. Evidence also suggests that

hominins Humans and their immediate ancestors.

sexual dimorphism The observable phenotypic differences between males and females of the same species.

In Their Own Words

The Future of Primate Biodiversity

In a recent collection presenting the latest research on primates, Karen Strier writes about one of the most critical concerns for all who work with primates: conservation.

Between the inevitable effects of global warming on the world's endangered ecosystems and the ongoing expansion of human populations in and around the world's biodiversity hotspots, it is difficult to foresee how the future of primates—and other animals—that are threatened with extinction can be protected. Global losses of biodiversity and ecosystem changes are predicted to occur by 2050, and major primate extinctions may occur even sooner than this because rates of deforestation in countries such as Indonesia and Madagascar are so high. . . .

There is no question that human pressures are accelerating the extinction risks for many primate taxa. Whether through direct actions, such as unsustainable hunting and habitat destruction, or indirect activities, such as the far-reaching effects of atmospheric pollution on global climate, the impact of humans on other primates today is much greater than it has been in the past. . . . Yet, despite the depressing forecast for primates, increased awareness about the status of the world's endangered primates has fueled intensified international conservation efforts. It is too soon to tell whether these efforts will ultimately succeed in securing the futures of all endangered taxa, but there is no doubt that they are helping gain essential time in what for many primates is now an urgent race against extinction.

Source: Strier 2007, 506.

Figure 4.10 Orangutans are an extremely solitary species that lives deep in the rain forests of Sumatra and Borneo.

some young male gibbons inherit the territory of their parents by pairing with their widowed mothers, although these pairs do not seem to breed (Leighton 1987).

Orangutans (Figure 4.10) are found today only in the rain forests of Sumatra and Borneo in southeastern Asia. Their dentition is different from that of chimpanzees and gorillas. Orangutans are an extremely solitary species whose way of life has made them difficult to study in the wild. Adult female orangutans and their offspring occupy overlapping ranges that also overlap the ranges of more than one male. Mating between males and females is promiscuous (Leighton 1987). Orangutans are the only nonhuman primates in which young males have been observed apparently forcing unwilling females to copulate.

There are five living subspecies of gorillas, all of which are found in Africa: the western lowland gorilla, the Cross River gorilla, Grauer's gorilla, the Bwindi gorilla, and the mountain gorilla. The rarest subspecies, the mountain gorilla, is probably the best known, thanks to the work of Dian Fossey (Figure 4.11), whose experiences have been popularized in books and film. Mountain gorillas eat mostly leaves. Like the New World howler monkeys, both male and female gorillas transfer out of the group in which they were born before they start breeding. The transfer, which does not appear forced, may occur more than once in a female's life. An adult female gorilla may produce three surviving offspring in her lifetime. Gorillas are highly sexually dimorphic, and the dominant male often determines group activity and

Figure 4.11 The mountain gorilla of central Africa is the rarest of the living species of gorilla found in Africa.

Figure 4.12 Chimpanzees are probably the most studied of all the apes.

the direction of travel. Immature gorillas are attracted to dominant males, who ordinarily treat them with tolerance and protect them in dangerous situations (Stewart and Harcourt 1987, Whitten 1987).

Chimpanzees (*Pan troglodytes*) are probably the most studied of all the apes (Figure 4.12). Jane Goodall and her associates in Gombe, Tanzania, have followed some chimpanzee groups for 50 years. Other long-term field research on chimpanzees has been carried out elsewhere in eastern and western Africa as well (Boesch-Ackermann and Boesch 1994). In recent years, a second species belonging to the genus *Pan, Pan paniscus*, known as the "pygmy chimpanzee" or bonobo (Figure 4.13), has received increasing attention, both in the wild and in captivity. Bonobos are found only in central Africa south of the Zaire River and may number fewer than 100,000; forest destruction, human predation, and capture for illegal sale all threaten their survival (de Waal 1989, 177). The two species differ morphologically: bonobos have less rugged builds, shorter upper limbs, and longer lower limbs than chimpanzees and sport a distinctive coiffure. Both species share a fluid social structure; that is, temporary smaller groups form within the framework of a larger community (de Waal 1989, 180; Nishida and Hiraiwa-Hasegawa 1987, 172). Their patterns of social interactions differ however. Bands of unrelated adult males are very common among chimpanzees but rare among bonobos. Bonds formed between unrelated females are relatively weak among chimpanzees but strong among bonobos. Bonds between the sexes are much stronger among bonobos as well. This means that female bonobos play a more central role in their society than female chimpanzees play in theirs (de Waal 1989, 180).

Chimpanzees and bonobos eat both plant and animal foods. Indeed, one of Goodall's famous early discoveries was that chimpanzees deliberately make tools to help them find food. They have been observed preparing

sticks to fish for insects in termite mounds or anthills, using leaf sponges to obtain water from tree hollows, and using rocks to smash open nuts. Indeed, patterns of tool use seem to vary regionally, suggesting the existence of separate cultural traditions in different chimpanzee groups. Male chimpanzees have been observed hunting for meat and sharing their kill with other members of the group; interestingly, forest-dwelling chimpanzees are more likely to hunt in groups, presumably because the foliage makes their prey harder to secure (Boesch-Ackermann and Boesch 1994).

Bonobos have never been observed using tools (Nishida and Hiraiwa-Hasegawa 1987, 166). However, the sexual life of chimpanzees cannot compare with the highly eroticized social interactions typical of bonobos. Bonobo females are able and willing to mate during much of their monthly cycle, but researchers have also observed a high degree of mounting behavior and sexual play between all members of bonobo groups, young and old, involving individuals of the same sex and of the opposite sexes. Studying a captive colony of bonobos in the San Diego Zoo, Frans de Waal and his assistants observed 600 mounts, fewer than 200 of which involved sexually mature individuals. Although this might be a function of life in captivity, it does not appear to be contradicted by data gathered in the wild. Nishida and Hiraiwa-Hasegawa, who refer to material gathered under both conditions, conclude that elaborate bonobo sexual behavior is "apparently used

Figure 4.13 Social interactions among bonobos are highly eroticized, apparently in order to manipulate social relationships rather than to increase reproductive rates. Female bonobos play a more central role in their society than female chimpanzees play in theirs.

to manipulate relationships rather than to increase reproductive rates" (1987, 173). de Waal agrees, suggesting that "conflict resolution is the more fundamental and pervasive function of bonobo sex" (1989, 212). Wolfe (1995) notes that same-sex mounting behavior has been observed in 11 different primate species.

Flexibility as the Hallmark of Primate Adaptations

When we try to summarize what makes primate life unique, we are struck by its flexibility, resilience, and creativity. Primates can get by under difficult circumstances, survive injuries, try out new foods or new social arrangements and take advantage of the random processes of history and demography to do what none has done before (Jolly 1985, 80–81, 242, 319). Simplistic models of primate behavior assuming that all primates are fundamentally alike, with few behavioral options, are no longer plausible. Mary Ellen Morbeck observes that "Most current models are inadequate when applied to the complex lives of large-bodied, long-lived, group-living mammals, primates, and humans with big brains and good memories" (1997, 14).

---

cranium The bones of the head, excluding the jaw.
mandible The lower jaw.
postcranial skeleton The bones of the body, excluding those of the head.

Primatologists have also become increasingly aware of just how deeply our approach to apes and monkeys has been affected by our approach to ourselves. In *Primate Visions* (1989), Donna Haraway shows how human ambivalence about race and gender has shaped much traditional Western scientific thinking about nonhuman primates. Increasing numbers of contemporary primatologists are concluding that field studies of primates need to be connected with conservation activities that take into consideration the welfare not just of the animals themselves but also of the ecosystems and human communities with which primates in the wild are inextricably interconnected (e.g., Strier 1997, Jolly 2004, SAGA 2005). These efforts may help us find ways to reverse some of the negative consequences of our own primate adaptation, making it possible for us and our nearest relatives to survive and thrive side by side for many generations to come.

Past Evolutionary Trends in Primates

How do we begin to trace evolutionary developments within the primate order? The first step is to create a framework for comparison. For example, to trace the evolution of the mammalian skeleton, paleontologists collect samples of fossil mammal bones that span a long stretch of geological time, and they distinguish the bones of the animal's head—the skull, or **cranium** (plural, *crania*), and lower jaw, or **mandible**—from the rest of the animal's bones, its **postcranial skeleton**. Homologous

In Their Own Words

Chimpanzee Tourism

Thirty years ago, the closest human neighbors of the Gombe chimpanzees were African villagers and Jane Goodall's research team. Today, human encroachment on chimpanzee territory is an everyday fact of life, with negative consequences.

Gombe National Park in Tanzania, the locus of most of Jane Goodall's studies, has been inundated by the most intrepid tourists who find their own way there, on foot or by water taxi, camp on the beach, and attempt to make their own arrangements with the underpaid park staff. This situation compromises the research program at Gombe and also endangers the chimpanzees, who are even more susceptible than gorillas to human diseases. In 1966, a polio epidemic that began among the human population in Kigoma district killed about 10–15% of the Gombe chimpanzee population in one year, and in 1988, an additional 14 animals died from an introduced respiratory infection. Bacteria, parasites, and other infectious organisms can be transmitted both by tourists and by resident staff.

In Burundi, Jane Goodall has been working to help set up a tourism program in a small vestige of forest that has been turned into a sanctuary for chimpanzees confiscated from poachers and dealers. Given the demand for chimpanzees as medical research subjects, the threat of illegal recapture is constant. One group of 30 vagabond animals is followed around full-time by ten armed guards. Goodall and others involved in this conservation effort hope that the greater visibility of the chimpanzees and daily contact with tourists when the program is well-established will help deter poachers.

One of the greatest problems with marketing chimpanzee tourism is delivering the chimpanzee experience on a predictable daily schedule. Chimpanzees are much more mobile than gorillas, and unlike gorillas, live in fluid social groupings whose membership is changing constantly. Not only do individuals move up to 25 km per day, but they often travel above ground level, leaving little or no trail for an earthbound tourist to follow.

Source: Brooks and Smith 1991, 14.

---

bones of different ages can then be compared for similarities and differences. The fossilized and living species grouped together in the primate order share no single attribute that sets all of them apart from other living creatures (Figure 4.14). What does distinguish primates, living and extinct, are three different sets of features: ancestral characteristics (often called "primitive characteristics"), past evolutionary trends, and unique features. In addition, primates are unusual because they are "distinguished mainly by a tendency to retain specific parts that other animals have lost during their evolution" (Klein 2009, 68). This is why primates are often described as *generalized* organisms.

Ancestral characteristics that primates inherited from earlier, nonprimate, mammalian ancestors appear in their generalized postcranial skeletons. These characteristics include the following:

- The presence of five digits on the hands and feet
- The presence of the clavicle, or collar bone, allowing for flexibility in the shoulder joint
- The use of the palms of the hand and foot (rather than the toes) for walking, called *plantigrade locomotion*

W. E. LeGros Clark (1963) identified four evolutionary trends that can be traced across the primate order since the first primates evolved away from their primitive mammalian ancestors:

1. An increase in brain size, relative to body size, and an increase in the complexity of the neocortex (or new brain)
2. A reduction of both the projection of the face and the reliance on the sense of smell
3. An increasing dependence on the sense of sight, resulting in the relocation of the eyes onto the same plane on the front of the face so that the visual field of each eye overlaps, producing depth perception (or **stereoscopic vision**) (Figure 4.15)
4. A reduction in the number of teeth

---

stereoscopic vision A form of vision in which the visual field of each eye of a two-eyed (binocular) animal overlaps with the other, producing depth perception.

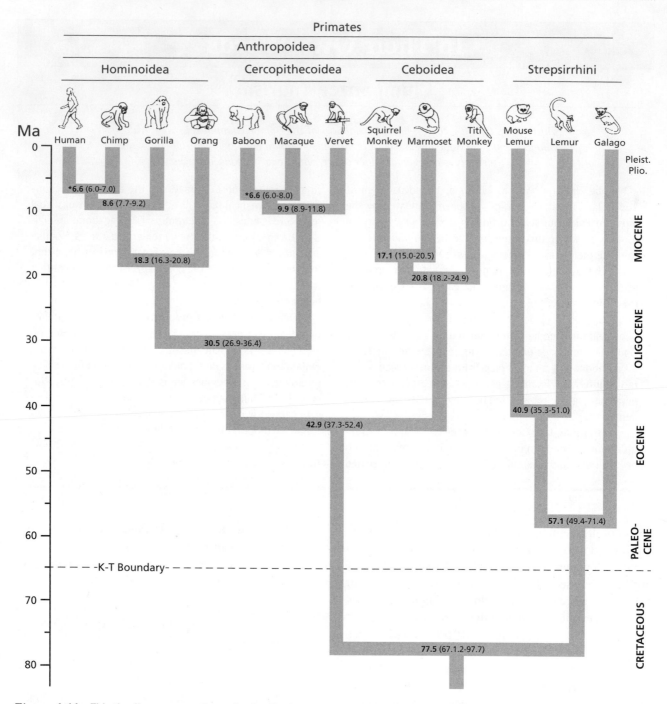

Figure 4.14 This timeline arranges the major fossil primate taxa by date and geological epoch and indicates estimated divergence dates in millions of years.

Some scholars have suggested two additional evolutionary trends: an increasing period of infant dependence and a greater dependence on learned behavior.

Finally, primates' unique prehensile morphological features include the following:

1. Opposable thumbs and great toes (i.e., the thumb is opposite the other fingers and can be "opposed to" the other fingers for grasping)

2. Nails rather than claws on at least some digits

3. Pads at the tips of fingers and toes that are rich in nerve endings

4. Dermal ridges, or friction skin, on the digits, soles, palms, and underside of prehensile tails

LeGros Clark (1963) argued that primate evolutionary trends and unique features were the outcome of an arboreal adaptation—that is, adaptation to life in

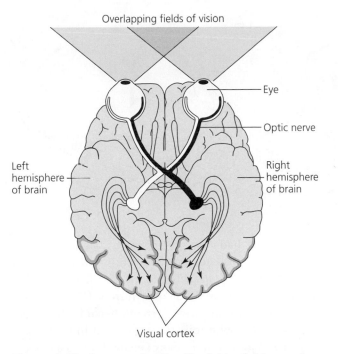

Figure 4.15 Stereoscopic vision. The fields of vision overlap, and the optic nerve from each eye travels to both hemispheres of the brain. The result is true depth perception.

the trees. In his view, creatures with excellent grasping abilities, acute binocular vision, and a superior brain are well suited to an arboreal habitat. However, many other organisms (e.g., squirrels) have adapted to life in the trees without having evolved such traits. Matt Cartmill (1972) offered the "visual predation hypothesis." He suggested that many of these traits derive from an ancestral adaptation to feeding on insects at the ends of tree branches in the lower levels of tropical forests. Selective pressure for improved vision resulted from the fact that these ancestral primates fed at night and relied on sight to locate their prey. More recently, Robert Sussman (1991) and Katherine Milton (1993) have argued that switching from insect predation to consumption of edible plant parts set the stage for future primate evolution leading to grasping hands, visual acuity (including color vision), larger brains, and increased behavioral flexibility.

It is important to remember that while past evolutionary trends apply to the primate order as a whole, all primate species were not affected by these trends in the same way. R. D. Martin (1986, 13) suggests that lessened reliance on smell probably only developed in primates that were diurnal rather than those that were **nocturnal** (active at night). Some living primates are still nocturnal and continue to rely heavily on a well-developed sense of smell.

Primate Evolution: The First 60 Million Years

The following survey of primate evolution is organized in terms of the five geological divisions, or epochs, recognized in the Tertiary period of the geological era called the Cenozoic. The Cenozoic began 65 mya, about the same time as the primates did.

Primates of the Paleocene

Very little is known about primates from this epoch, which lasted from about 65 to 55 mya. The best current candidate for the oldest probable primate is *Altiatlasius*, whose fragmentary fossils have been found in late Paleocene deposits in North Africa. Too little is known about *Altiatlasius*, however, to relate it clearly to later primate taxa; indeed, exactly where the first primates evolved is still unknown (Rose 1994).

Primates of the Eocene

The first undisputed primates appeared during the Eocene epoch, which lasted from about 55 to about 38 mya. Most of the fossils are jaws and teeth, but skulls, limb bones, and even some nearly complete skeletons have also been recovered. The best-known Eocene primates fall into two basic groups. The first group, *adapids*, looks a lot like living lemurs. However, a number of morphological features—dentition in particular—distinguish them from their modern counterparts. Eocene adapids had four premolars, whereas modern lemurs have only three; and their lower incisors and canines were generalized, whereas modern lemurs possess a specialized tooth comb. The second group, the *omomyids*, resembles living tarsiers (Figure 4.16). Most omomyids were much smaller than adapids. Adapted for climbing, clinging, and leaping, omomyids appear to have been nocturnal, feeding on insects, fruit, or gum (Rose 1994). Recent fossil discoveries suggest that members of a third primate group also appeared in the late Eocene, perhaps 44 to 40 mya (Fleagle 1995, R. D. Martin 1993, Simons and Rasmussen 1994). These are the earliest *anthropoideans*—primates ancestral to all later monkeys, apes, and humans. Exactly how and when anthropoideans originated is still a matter for debate (Klein 2009, 106; Fleagle 1995, 8).

nocturnal Describes animals that are active during the night.

Figure 4.16 The fossil omomyid *Necrolemur* (*left*) belongs to the superfamily Omomyoidea, thought to be ancestral to the modern tarsier (*right*).

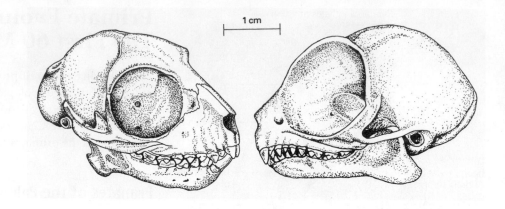

1 cm

Primates of the Oligocene

The Oligocene epoch lasted from about 38 to about 23 mya. Temperatures cooled and environments dried out. Those adapids whose ancestors made it to the island of Madagascar unwittingly found a safe refuge from evolutionary competition elsewhere and evolved into modern lemurs. Elsewhere, anthropoideans and their descendants flourished.

Oligocene layers at the Fayum, in Egypt, dating from between 35 and 31 mya have long been our richest source of information on anthropoidean evolution. During this part of the Oligocene, the region was a warm, tropical rain forest laced with rivers. All the anthropoideans were small, none were leaf eaters, and none lived on the ground. In this respect, they appear to resemble living New World monkeys.

Fossil anthropoideans from this period have been placed in two groups. One group, called the *parapithecids*, seems to have been much more primitive and may be ancestral to New World monkeys (Fleagle 1995, 4). We still do not know how the earliest platyrrhines reached the New World (R. D. Martin 1993). The other group is the *propliopithecids*, which appears to have given rise to all later Old World anthropoids, the catarrhines.

Propliopithecus (formerly *Aegyptopithecus*) *zeuxis*, the largest of the Oligocene anthropoideans, is well known from numerous fossilized teeth, skulls, and limb bones, and appears ancestral to later Old World anthropoids, or *catarrhines* (Figure 4.17). *P. zeuxis* lived 35 mya and looked very much like a primitive monkey (Simons 1985, 40). The bones of its lower jaw and upper cranium are fused along the midlines, and the eye orbits are closed off from the brain by a bony plate. Nevertheless, its limb bones show none of the features that allow modern apes to hang upright or swing from the branches of trees. Its cranium also shows some primitive characteristics: its brain was smaller, its snout projected more, its eye orbits did not face as fully to the front, and its ear was not as fully developed.

P. zeuxis had two premolars (a diagnostic catarrhine [Old World monkey] feature), and it also had Y-5 molars. A *Y-5 molar* is a tooth with five cusps that are separated by a "Y"-shaped furrow (Figure 4.18). Later Old World monkeys (cercopithecoids) have *bilophodont molars* with four cusps arranged in pairs, each of which is joined by a ridge of enamel called a "loph." Early Miocene fossils, 17–19 million years old, of undoubted cercopithecoid monkeys have molars with a fifth cusp and incomplete lophs. This suggests that the Y-5 pattern was primitive for all Old World anthropoids, making *P. zeuxis* and other Oligocene catarrhines likely ancestors of both Old World monkeys and hominoids (apes and humans) (Klein 2009, 108; Stringer and Andrews 2005, 84).

The earliest known hominoid fossils date to the late Oligocene (26 mya) and come from Kenya (Benefit and McCrossin 1995, 240). It was during the Miocene, however, that hominoid evolution took off.

Primates of the Miocene

The Miocene lasted from about 23 to about 5 mya. Between 18 and 17 mya, the continents finally arrived at their present positions, when the African plate (which includes the Arabian Peninsula) contacted the Eurasian plate. This helps explain why fossil hominoids from the early Miocene (about 23–16 mya) have been found only in Africa. More recent fossil hominoids have been found from western Europe to China, presumably because their ancestors used the new land bridge to cross from Africa into Eurasia. During the middle Miocene (about 16–10 mya), hominoid diversity declined. During the late Miocene (about 9–5 mya), cercopithecoid monkeys became very successful, many hominoid species became extinct, and the first members of a new lineage, the hominins, appeared.

In the early Miocene, eastern Africa was covered with tropical forest and woodland. One well-known

Figure 4.17 *Propliopithecus* (formerly *Aegyptopithecus*) *zeuxis* is the largest of the Oligocene fossil anthropoids and may be ancestral to all catarrhines (Old World monkeys, apes, and humans).

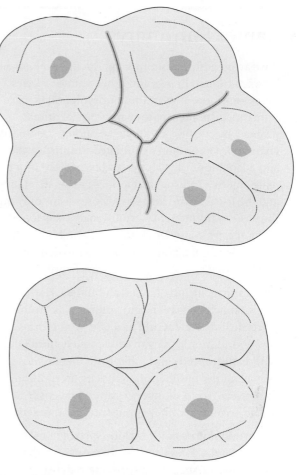

Figure 4.18 The upper molar shows the characteristic Y–5 pattern of apes and humans; the lower molar exhibits the bilophodont pattern of Old World cercopithecoid monkeys. Current evidence suggests that the Y–5 molar was primitive for all Old World anthropoids and that the bilophodont molar of the cercopithecoids developed later.

collection of early Miocene primate fossils has been assigned to the hominoid genus *Proconsul*. The best evidence, including a nearly complete skeleton, exists for the species *Proconsul heseloni* (formerly *P. africanus*) (Figure 4.19), which was about the size of a modern gibbon (Klein 2009, 117). *Proconsul heseloni* is very apelike in its cranium, teeth, and shoulder and elbow joints. However, its long trunk, arm, and hand resemble those of modern monkeys. It appears to have been a fruit-eating, tree-dwelling, four-footed (four-handed?) proto-ape that may have lacked a tail. Some argue that it is also generalized enough in its morphology to have been ancestral to later hominoids, including modern apes and human beings, although this is debated (Fleagle 1995). *Proconsul* and other early Miocene hominoids were confined to Africa and the Arabian Peninsula.

Most of the mid-Miocene (16–10 mya) fossils we have come from hominoids whose ancestors had crossed the land bridge connecting Africa to Eurasia. However, the Eurasian hominoid fossils are so morphologically diverse that experts have had a difficult time devising a taxonomy on which they can all agree. Unfortunately, very few African hominoid fossils of any kind date from the late Miocene or early Pliocene (roughly 11–5 mya) (Benefit and McCrossin 1995, 251). In the absence of hard data, attempts to identify either the last common ancestor of the African apes and human beings or the earliest ancestors of chimpanzees and gorillas must be based on educated speculation (Stringer and Andrews 2005, 114). Nevertheless, we know that it was during the late Miocene that the first ancestors in our own lineage appeared. Tracing their evolutionary history is the topic of the next chapter.

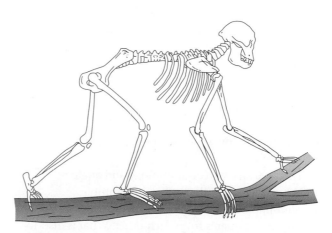

Figure 4.19 *Proconsul*, perhaps the best known of the earliest African hominoids. Some argue that *Proconsul* is generalized enough in its morphology to have been ancestral to later hominoids, including modern apes and human beings, although this is debated.

Chapter Summary

1. If we avoid anthropomorphism, careful comparison between human beings and other primate species offers enormous insight into our evolutionary past. Primatologists attempt to make sense of primate diversity by creating a primate taxonomy. Traditional taxonomies of primates compared the phenotypes and adaptations of primates and recognized four primate grades. Cladistic taxonomies ignore adaptation and the fossil record and classify organisms only on the basis of homologous evolutionary traits found in living species. Many primatologists combine features of both kinds of taxonomies in order to demonstrate relations of evolutionary relatedness between species.

2. Strepsirhines include lemurs and lorises. Haplorhines include tarsiers and anthropoids. Anthropoids include New World and Old World forms. New World monkeys evolved separately from Old World anthropoids and differ from them in nose shape and the number of premolars; in addition, some New World monkeys evolved prehensile tails. All New World monkey species are tree dwellers.

3. Old World anthropoids include species of monkeys and apes, as well as human beings: all share the same nose shape and the same number of premolars. Apes are distinguished from Old World monkeys by dentition, skeletal shape and size, and the absence of a tail. The African apes are far more closely related to one another than they are to gibbons or orangutans, and human beings are more closely related to chimpanzees than to any other ape species. Chimpanzees deliberately make simple tools to help them find food. Bonobos, or pygmy chimpanzees, are known for their highly eroticized social interactions and for the central role females play in their society.

4. Primates show at least six evolutionary trends of their own and four unique features associated with prehensility. These evolutionary trends have not affected all primate species in the same way.

5. Paleontologists assign primate fossils to various categories after examining and comparing cranial and postcranial skeletal material. They have concluded that the first undisputed primates appeared during the Eocene. The best-known Eocene primates are the adapids, which resemble living lemurs, and the omomyids, which resemble living tarsiers. Anthropoideans, ancestral to all later monkeys, apes, and humans, appeared in the late Eocene and are known from sites in northern Africa and Asia. Some Oligocene primate fossils look like possible ancestors to modern New World anthropoids; others, like *Propliopithecus zeuxis*, appear ancestral to all later Old World anthropoids.

6. The first hominoids that evolved in Africa during the early Miocene are very diverse. One of the best-known examples is *Proconsul*, which is generalized enough to have been ancestral to later apes and human beings. During the middle Miocene, hominoids rapidly spread and diversified, and their fossils are found from Europe to eastern Asia. In the late Miocene, many hominoid species became extinct. Paleoanthropologists agree that chimpanzees, gorillas, and human beings shared a common ancestor in the late Miocene.

For Review

1. Summarize the discussion of taxonomy at the beginning of the chapter.
2. Distinguish between homology and analogy.
3. What are clades? Illustrate with examples.
4. Summarize the features used to distinguish different kinds of primates from each other. What is distinctive about the anthropoids?
5. Discuss the differences and similarities of chimpanzees and bonobos.
6. What are primate ancestral characteristics? evolutionary trends? unique morphological features?
7. What adaptive explanations do paleoanthropologists give for the unique features of primates?
8. Prepare a table or chart that displays what is currently known about key developments in primate evolution, from the Paleocene to the Miocene.

Key Terms

Suggested Readings

Campbell, Christina, Agustín Fuentes, Katherine MacKinnon, Melissa Panger, and Simon Bearder. 2007. *Primates in prespective.* New York: Oxford University Press. *A comprehensive overview of the primates and what we know about them.*

de Waal, Frans. 2003. *My family album: Thirty years of primate photography.* Berkeley: University of California Press. *In addition to being an influential primatologist, de Waal is a superb photographer. These images are an excellent visual introduction to the various primate species he has studied.*

Fossey, Dian. 1983. *Gorillas in the mist.* Boston: Houghton Mifflin. *Dian Fossey's account of research among the mountain gorillas of Rwanda over a 13-year period; includes many color photographs. Fossey was murdered at her field station in 1985. This book inspired a major motion picture of the same name.*

Goodall, Jane. 1986. *The chimpanzees of Gombe: Patterns of behavior.* Cambridge, MA: Harvard University Press. *This volume presents the results of a quarter of a century of scientific research among chimpanzees in Gombe, Tanzania.*

———. 1999. *Jane Goodall: 40 years at Gombe.* New York: Stewart, Tabori and Chang. *After 1986, Jane Goodall shifted the emphasis of her work from scientific observation to rescuing and rehabilitating laboratory animals and working for environmental causes, as have many primatologists concerned about threats to the continued viability of the species they have studied.*

Haraway, Donna. 1989. *Primate visions.* New York: Routledge. *This volume, a major landmark in primate studies, contains a series of essays by a feminist historian of science who describes the way Western cultural assumptions about gender, race, and nature have shaped American primatology. Chapters discussing how collections were made for the American Museum of Natural History and the symbolic significance of white female primatologists should be of particular interest to beginning students.*

Smuts, Barbara, Dorothy Cheney, Robert Seyfarth, and Richard Wrangham, eds. 1987. *Primate societies.* Chicago: University of Chicago Press. *This volume is a classic, comprehensive survey of research on primates from all over the world, and includes articles by 46 contributors.*

Tudge, Colin, with Josh Young. 2009. *The link.* New York: Little, Brown. *This volume was written in connection with a film, The Link, broadcast in May 2009 on the History Channel in the USA and on several other television channels worldwide. Science writer Colin Tudge wrote chapters 3–8, plus the epilogue, and he provides a brief, solid, reader-friendly introduction to contemporary work in primate evolution. Josh Young, who wrote chapters 1, 2, and 9, describes how fossils have become valuable commodities in twenty-first-century antiquities markets. He also shows the high stakes facing scientists who introduce new primate fossils to a media-saturated world—in this case, "Ida," a remarkably complete 47-million-year-old fossil prosimian from Germany.*

What Can the Fossil Record Tell Us about Human Origins?

5

Anthropology has made major contributions to our understanding of human biological and cultural evolution. This chapter tells the story of what we have learned from fossils, stone tools, and other cultural remains and, from the appearance of our earliest known ancestors about 6 million years ago through the appearance of modern *Homo sapiens* about 200,000 years ago.

Chapter Outline

◀ *Measurement of the mandible of an* Australopithecus garhi *in the Laboratory of Paleontology in Addis-Ababa, Ethiopia.*

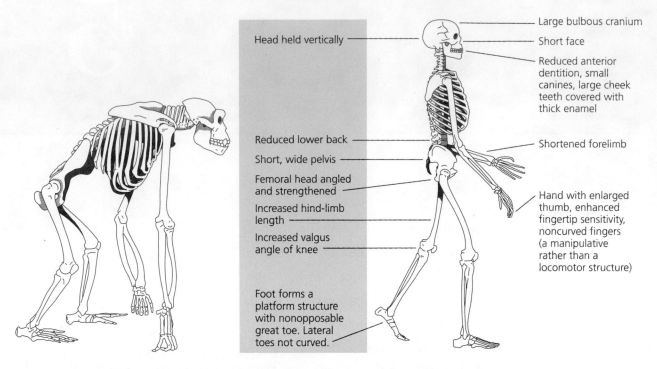

Head held vertically

Large bulbous cranium

Short face

Reduced anterior dentition, small canines, large cheek teeth covered with thick enamel

Reduced lower back

Short, wide pelvis

Femoral head angled and strengthened

Increased hind-limb length

Increased valgus angle of knee

Shortened forelimb

Hand with enlarged thumb, enhanced fingertip sensitivity, noncurved fingers (a manipulative rather than a locomotor structure)

Foot forms a platform structure with nonopposable great toe. Lateral toes not curved.

Figure 5.1 Apes (*left*) are adapted anatomically for a form of quadrupedal locomotion called knuckle walking, although they often stand upright and occasionally may even walk on their hind limbs for short distances. A human skeleton (*right*) shows the kinds of reshaping natural selection performed in order to produce the hominid anatomy, which is adapted to habitual bipedalism.

Hominin Evolution

About 10 mya, when the Miocene epoch was drawing to a close, grasslands increased at the expense of forests and many species of hominoids became extinct throughout Europe, Asia, and Africa. Some African hominoids seem to have adapted to the changed conditions by spending more time on the ground, a move that apparently exposed them to new selective pressures favoring **bipedalism**—walking on two feet rather than four. *Hominins* (bipedal hominoids) first appeared in Africa at the end of the Miocene or beginning of the Pliocene, between 10 and 5 mya.

As we saw in Chapter 4, contemporary taxonomists classify the African great apes and humans together as *hominids*; and within the hominid category, they separate out humans and their bipedal ancestors, who are classified together as *hominins*. Within the hominin category, a further distinction is also commonly made between recent hominin species assigned to the genus *Homo* and earlier hominin species assigned to such genera as *Ardipithecus*, *Australopithecus*, or *Paranthropus*. Several authorities informally refer to all the earlier hominins as "australopiths" (Tattersall 2009, 120; Klein 2009, 131), and that is what we will do here.

Fossil hominins are grouped together with living human beings because of a set of skeletal features that indicate habitual bipedalism, a feature that seems to be the first of our distinctive anatomical traits to have appeared (Figure 5.1). Hominin evolution has also been marked by additional evolutionary changes in dentition. Finally, some developed an expanded brain and ultimately came to depend on tools and language—that is, on culture—for their survival (Table 5.1). These developments did not occur all at once but were the result of **mosaic evolution** (different traits evolving at different rates). This is the reason anthropologists speak of human *origins* when describing the evolution of our species.

Who Were the First Hominins (6–3 mya)?

The Origin of Bipedalism

The skeletons of all primates allow upright posture when sitting or swinging from the branches of trees. Many primates often stand upright and occasionally walk on their hind limbs for short distances. Because bipedalism

---

bipedalism Walking on two feet rather than four.

mosaic evolution A phenotypic pattern that shows how different traits of an organism, responding to different selection pressures, may evolve at different rates.

TABLE 5.1 Four Major Trends in Hominin Evolution

TREND	DEVELOPMENT	DATES
Bipedalism	Evidence of bipedalism marks the appearance of the hominin line.	Between 10 and 5 mya
Distinctive dentition	The development of huge cheek teeth (molars) and much smaller front teeth was characteristic of the australopiths.	4 to 2 mya
Expanded brain	Brain expansion beyond 400 to 500 cm³ of the australopiths was characteristic of genus *Homo*.	Beginning 2.4 mya
Culture	Greater reliance on learned patterns of behavior and thought, on tools, and on language became important for *Homo*.	Beginning 2.5 mya

requires upright posture, primates have already, so to speak, taken a step in the right direction. Put another way, we could say that hominoid morphology for upright posture that evolved in an arboreal context was exapted for hominin bipedalism in a terrestrial context.

What sort of selective pressures might have favored bipedal locomotion in hominoids? To answer this question, paleoanthropologists examine the advantages bipedalism would have conferred. Moving easily on the ground might have improved hominoids' ability to exploit food resources outside the protective cover of the shrinking Miocene forests. Upright posture would have made it easier for them to spot potential predators in open country, and skillful bipedal locomotion would have made it easier for them to escape. Finally, walking upright simultaneously reduces the amount of skin surface exposed to the sun, allows greater distances to be covered (albeit at slow speeds), and is more energy-efficient (Day 1986, 189; R. Foley 1995, 143).

Michael Day suggests that this greater stamina may have permitted bipedal hominins to become "endurance hunters," slowly tracking game over long distances as they moved into the previously vacant ecological niche of daylight hunting (1986, 190). However, endurance walking would have been equally important in enabling the first hominins to cover long distances between widely scattered sources of plant food or water. Indeed, the teeth of these hominins suggest that they were probably **omnivorous**, not carnivorous; that is, they ate a wide range of plant and animal foods. Equipped with just a simple digging stick, their diet might have included "berries, fruits, nuts, buds, shoots, shallow-growing roots and tubers, fruiting bodies of fungi, most terrestrial and the smaller aquatic reptiles, eggs, nesting birds, some fish, mollusks, insects, and all small mammals, including the burrowing ones. This diverse diet . . . is very close to that of the Gombe National Park chimpanzees . . . and living gatherer/hunters" (Mann 1981, 34). As the forests retreated and stands of trees became smaller and more widely scattered,

groups of bipedal hominins appear to have ranged over a variety of environments (Isaac and Crader 1981, 89; see also Freeman 1981, Mann 1981). They would have been able to carry infants, food, and eventually tools in their newly freed hands (Lewin 1989, 67–68).

The oldest known hominins are the australopiths, and their fossils come from Africa (Figure 5.2), some dating back into the Miocene. The oldest remains are fragmentary, however, and their significance for later hominin evolution is still being debated. The most noteworthy of recent australopith finds are *Sahelanthropus tchadensis*, from Chad, in central Africa (6–7 million years old) (Brunet et al. 2002, 6); *Orrorin tugenensis* from Kenya (6 million years old) (Senut et al. 2001); and *Ardipithecus kadabba* (5.8–5.2 million years old) and *Ardipithecus ramidus* (5.8–4.4 million years old) (White et al. 2009, Haile Selassie et al. 2004, Haile Selassie 2001, T. D. White et al. 1994). After 15 years of reconstruction and analysis, Tim White and his colleagues formally announced the discovery of "Ardi," a relatively complete skeleton of *A. ramidus*, which apparently could walk bipedally on the ground, though in a manner different from later australopiths and members of the genus *Homo* (see Figure 5.3). *A. ramidus* is unusual because it lived in a forest. If this species is indeed a hominin, therefore, the selection pressures responsible for bipedalism will need to be reconsidered since most paleoanthropologists have traditionally viewed bipedal locomotion as an adaptation to life in open country. Other fossil fragments include two lower jaws and an arm bone from Kenya, ranging in age between 5.8–5.6 and 4.5 mya. Some fragmentary remains from Ethiopia and Kenya are between 4.5 and 3.8 million years old (Boaz 1995, 35; R. Foley 1995, 70).

The earliest direct evidence of hominin bipedalism is 3.6 million years old. It comes from a trail of footprints that extends over 70 feet, preserved in a layer of

---

omnivorous Eating a wide range of plant and animal foods.

Figure 5.2 Major sites in eastern and southern Africa from which fossils of australopiths and early *Homo* have been recovered.

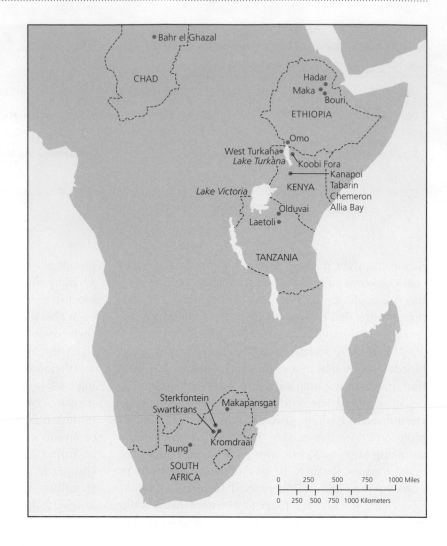

hardened volcanic ash laid down during the middle Pliocene at the site of Laetoli, Tanzania (Figure 5.4). When compared to footprints made by modern apes and human beings, experts agree that the Laetoli prints were definitely produced by hominin bipedal locomotion (Day 1985, 92; 1986, 191; Feibel et al. 1995/96).

Most early hominin fossils showing skeletal evidence of bipedalism have been placed in the genus *Australopithecus*. The oldest of these is *Australopithecus anamensis*, whose fossils come from Kanapoi and Allia Bay in Kenya. *A. anamensis* dates from 4.2 to 3.9 mya. *A. anamensis* shows that bipedality had evolved at least a few hundred thousand years before the previous date of 3.6 mya provided by the Laetoli footprints (Leakey et al. 1995).[1]

The remaining early hominin fossils have been assigned to the species *Australopithecus afarensis*. Fossils assigned to this taxon have also been found at Laetoli and in a region of Ethiopia known as the Afar Depression—hence the species name "afarensis" (see Figure 5.2). These fossils, which are quite numerous, range between 3.9 and 3.0 million years of age (Johanson and Edey 1981, Kimbel et al. 1994, T. D. White et al. 1993). The famous *A. afarensis* fossil Lucy (named after the Beatles song "Lucy in the Sky with Diamonds"; Figure 5.5) was found 40 percent intact and undisturbed where she had died, which allowed Donald Johanson and his colleagues to reconstruct her postcranial skeleton in great detail. The first fairly complete adult skull of *A. afarensis*, found in the early 1990s, confirmed its small-brained, apelike features. The 0.9 million-year age range of these Hadar fossils suggests a period of prolonged evolutionary stasis within *A. afarensis*.

Some features of the skeleton of *A. afarensis* reveal its adaptation to habitual bipedalism, especially when we compare it to the skeletons of modern humans and apes. The spinal column of a chimpanzee joins its head at the back of the skull, as is normally the case in quadrupedal animals. This is revealed by the position of a

---

[1]Leakey and colleagues (2001) have also described a 3.4 million-year-old eastern African fossil said to possess a series of derived features not found in other australopiths, thus justifying its being placed in a separate genus, *Kenyanthropus platyops*, although this interpretation is controversial.

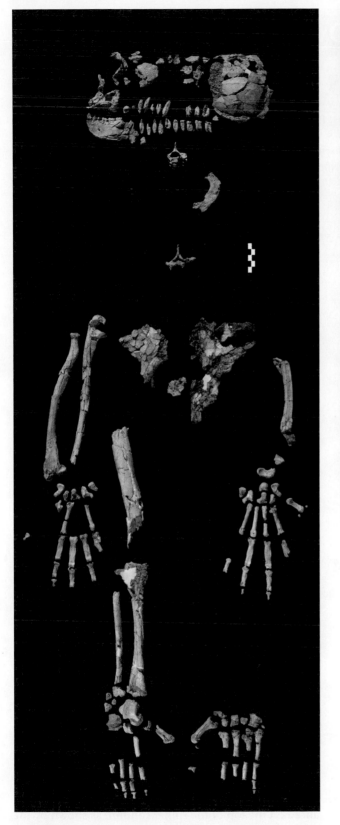

Figure 5.3   The fossils of *Ardipithecus ramidus*, pictured above, have been interpreted as belonging to a bipedal hominoid living in a forested environment, which challenges the traditional notion that bipedalism evolved in an open, savannah environment.

Figure 5.4   The earliest evidence of hominin bipedalism comes from the 3.6 million-year-old fossil footprints preserved in hardened volcanic ash at Laetoli, Tanzania.

large hole, the *foramen magnum*, through which the spinal cord passes on its way to the brain. The ape pelvis is long and broad, and the knee is almost directly in line with the femur (or thigh bone) and therefore ill-adapted to support the ape's center of gravity when it tries to move on its hind legs. As a result, when apes walk bipedally, they appear to waddle in an awkward attempt to stay upright. Finally, the great toe of the ape foot diverges like a thumb from the rest of the digits, a feature that allows apes to use their feet for grasping but inhibits their ability to use this toe for the "push-off" so important for effective bipedalism.

By contrast, the modern human head balances on the top of the spinal column. The foramen magnum in humans is located directly beneath the skull rather than at its back. The basin-shaped human pelvis is the body's center of gravity, supporting and balancing the torso above it. Finally, the bones of human legs have a

In Their Own Words

Finding Fossils

Searching for remains of the human past is not glamorous work. As he relates the experiences of Alemayehu, one of the most successful fossil hunters on his team, Donald Johanson reveals both the extraordinary discipline required for the search as well as the near delirium that ensues when the search is successful.

One day Alemayehu found a small piece of a lower jaw with a couple of molars in it. They were bigger than human molars, and he told me that he had a baboon jaw with funny big teeth.

"You think this is a baboon?" I asked him.

"Well, with unusually large molars."

"It's a hominid."

The knee joint of the year before had proved the existence of hominids at Hadar. Everyone had been sanguine about finding more of them in 1974. In fact, the French had been so eager that they had gone rushing out to survey on the very first day, leaving it to the Americans to put up the tents. But after weeks of searching without results, that ardor had dimmed somewhat. Now it flared again, but in no one more than Alemayehu himself.

It is impossible to describe what it feels like to find something like that. It fills you right up. That is what you are there for. You have been working and working, and suddenly you score. When I told Alemayehu that he had a hominid, his face lit up and his chest went way out. Energized to an extraordinary degree, and with nothing better to do in the late afternoons, Alemayehu formed the habit of poking quietly about for an hour or so before dark. He chose areas close to camp because, without the use of a Land-Rover, they were easy to get to. He refrained from saying—although I feel sure that this was a factor in his choice of places to survey—that he had begun to realize that he was a more thorough and more observant surveyor than some of the others who were doing that work.

The day after he found the hominid jaw, Alemayehu turned up a complete baboon skull. I had it on the table for a detailed description the next afternoon when Alemayehu burst into camp.

His eyes were popping. He said he had found another of those things. After having seen one, he was sure this was another human jaw. I dropped the baboon skull and ran after Alemayehu, forgetting that I was barefoot. I began to cut my feet so badly on the gravel that I was forced to limp back to my tent to put on shoes. Guillemot and Petter, who were with me, kept going. When I rejoined them, it was in a little depression just a few hundred yards beyond the Afar settlement. Guillemot and Petter were crouching down to look at a beautiful fossil jaw sticking out of the ground. Guillemot ruefully pointed out his own footprints, not ten feet away, where he had gone out surveying that first morning in camp and seen nothing.

A crowd of others arrived and began to hunt around feverishly. One of the French let out a yell—he had a jaw. It turned out to be a hyena, an excellent find because carnivores are always rare. But after that, interest dwindled. It began to get dark. The others drifted back to camp. I stopped surveying and was about to collect Alemayehu's jaw when I spotted Alemayehu struggling up a nearby slope, waving his arms, completely winded.

"I have another," Alemayehu gasped. "I think, two."

I raced over to him. The two turned out to be two halves. When I put them together, they fitted perfectly to make a complete palate (upper jaw) with every one of its teeth in position: a superb find. Within an hour Alemayehu had turned up two of the oldest and finest hominid jaws ever seen. With the addition of the partial jaw of a few days before, he has earned a listing in the *Guinness Book of World Records* as the finder of the most hominid fossils in the shortest time.

Source: Johanson and Edey 1981, 172–73.

knock-kneed appearance, with the femur pointing inward toward the knee joint at the *valgus angle*. As a result, humans can easily transfer their center of gravity directly over the stepping foot in the course of bipedal walking.

The skeleton of *A. afarensis* more closely resembles that of modern human beings than that of apes. As Figure 5.6 shows, the great toe does not diverge from the rest of the digits on the foot, the femur bends inward toward

the knee joint at the valgus angle, and the pelvis is short and basinlike. In addition, the skull of *A. afarensis* balanced on the top of the spinal column, as shown by the position of its foramen magnum. Nevertheless, elements of the postcranial skeleton of *A. afarensis* clearly recall its recent ape ancestry (Figure 5.7). It has longer arms, in proportion to its legs, than any other hominin. Also, the bones of its fingers and toes are slightly curved, and the

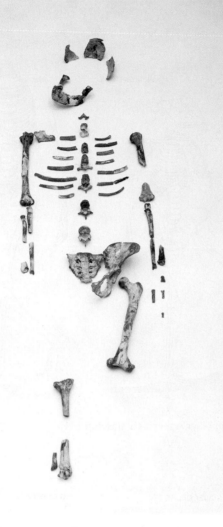

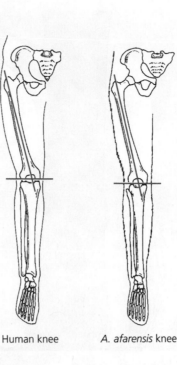

Human knee   *A. afarensis* knee   Ape knee

Figure 5.6 The bones of human legs have a somewhat knock–kneed appearance, with the femur pointing inward toward the knee joint at the valgus angle. This allows human beings to easily transfer the center of gravity directly over the foot in the course of bipedal walking. Ape femurs do not angle inward in this manner, so apes waddle when they try to walk bipedally. Because *A. afarensis* is humanlike in its valgus angle and in the shape of its pelvis, we conclude that, like us, it walked bipedally.

Figure 5.5 Forty percent of Lucy's bones were found undisturbed, and her remains included much of her postcranial skeleton.

toes are much longer, resembling the finger and toe bones of apes. Because these features are related to the typical tree-climbing adaptation of most hominoids, some paleoanthropologists have concluded that *A. afarensis* must have had significant tree-climbing ability along with bipedalism (Klein 1989, 143–47; Lewin 1989, 77; Susman et al. 1985). A 3.5 million-year-old australopith fossil found in Chad, in central Africa, is contemporaneous with *A. afarensis*. Called *Australopithecus bahrelghazali*, this specimen extends the range of australopiths far beyond southern and eastern Africa (Brunet et al. 1995).

Changes in Hominin Dentition

Once the first australopiths ventured regularly down from the trees and into a variety of new habitats, they presumably began to rely on new food sources. Their new diet appears to have created a set of selective pressures that led to important changes in hominin dentition, first evident in the teeth of *A. afarensis*. In order to assess the importance of these changes, it helps to compare the teeth of *A. afarensis* with those of modern apes and humans.

A striking feature of ape dentition is a "U"-shaped dental arch that is longer front to back than it is side to side. By contrast, the human dental arch is parabolic, or gently rounded in shape and narrower in front than in back. Apes have large, sexually dimorphic canine teeth that project beyond the tooth row. In addition, they possess a *diastema* (plural, *diastemata*), or space in the tooth row for each canine of the opposite jaw to fit into when the jaws are closed. Human canine teeth do not project beyond the tooth row and show little sexual dimorphism, and humans have no diastemata. Ape teeth show functional

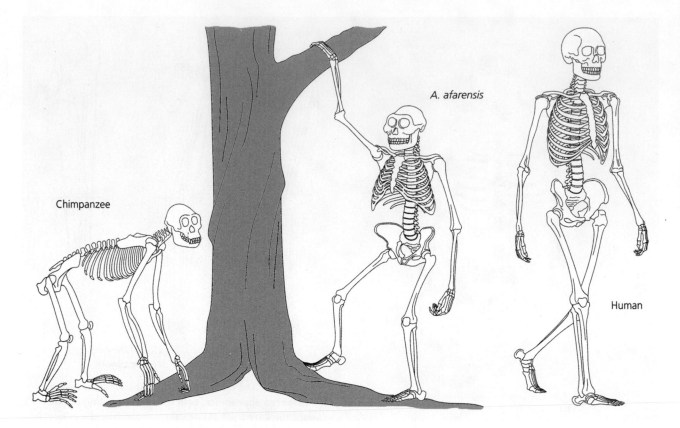

Chimpanzee

A. afarensis

Human

Figure 5.7 Although *A. afarensis* was humanlike in some respects, in other respects its skeleton retained adaptations to life in the trees.

Figure 5.8 The upper jaw of *A. afarensis* shows some apelike features, but its dentition shows signs of change in the direction of smaller front teeth and large cheek teeth that would appear fully developed in later australopith species.

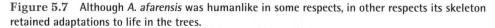

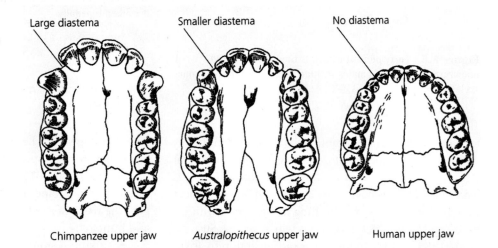

Large diastema   Smaller diastema   No diastema

Chimpanzee upper jaw   *Australopithecus* upper jaw   Human upper jaw

specialization, with biting incisors, shearing canines, and grinding molars. In addition, the incisors are about the same size as the molars, and the canines are the largest teeth of all. Functional specialization in human teeth is very different. Humans have canines and incisors that are similar in shape and much smaller than their molars.

How does *A. afarensis* compare? As Figure 5.8 shows, the *A. afarensis* dental arcade is "U"-shaped, like that of the apes. Its canines, though relatively smaller than those of apes, still project somewhat; and 45 percent of the *A. afarensis* specimens examined have diastemata (Lewin 1989, 70). Although *A. afarensis* canines were getting smaller, *A. afarensis* molars were getting larger, marking the beginning of an evolutionary trend toward smaller front teeth and enormous cheek teeth that appears, fully developed, among australopiths that

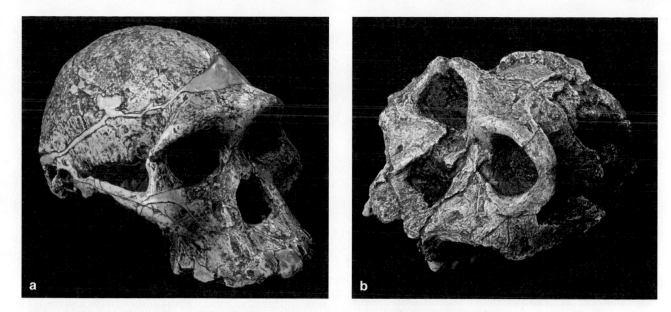

Figure 5.9 Two-million-year-old bipedal hominins with small front teeth and large cheek teeth fall into two major categories. (*a*) Gracile australopiths (such as this specimen of *A. africanus* from Sterkfontein, South Africa) have smaller, more lightly built faces. (*b*) Robust australopiths (such as this specimen from Swartkrans, South Africa) have more rugged jaws, flatter faces, truly enormous molars, and sagittal crests.

flourished a million years after *A. afarensis*. The increase in the size of later australopith molars is greater than would be expected if it were merely the result of a larger-bodied hominin having proportionately larger teeth. Thus, paleoanthropologists deduce that the enlarged molars were produced by natural selection (McHenry 1985, 179). Some experts argue that this dental pattern is an effective adaptation to grassland diets consisting of coarse vegetable foods. Because projecting canine teeth prevent the side-to-side jaw movement that grinding tough foods requires, natural selection may have favored australopiths whose canines did not project beyond the tooth row.

Who Were the Later Australopiths (3–1.5 mya)?

Fossils of 3 million-year-old australopiths with small front teeth and large cheek teeth were found first in southern Africa and later in eastern Africa, beginning in the 1920s and 1930s. Some of them possessed the typical late-australopith enlargement of the cheek teeth, but their faces were small and lightly built; they were classified together as *Australopithecus africanus* and came to be known as the "gracile australopiths" (Figure 5.9a). *A. africanus* lived between 3 and 2 mya. Other australopith fossils with more rugged jaws, flatter faces,

and enormous molars have been assigned to the species *Australopithecus* (or *Paranthropus*) *robustus*, and they are called the "robust australopiths" (Figure 5.9b). *A. robustus* lived between 2 and 1.5 mya.

Both gracile and robust australopith fossils show the same adaptation to bipedalism found in *A. afarensis*. The foramen magnum of both forms was directly underneath the skull, and the size of the braincase (or **cranial capacity**) in both forms ranged between 400 and 550 cubic centimeters. Despite such small brains, australopiths living at Swartkrans in present-day South Africa 1.5 mya apparently controlled fire and used it to cook meat (C. K. Brain and Sillen 1988). Whether they had hands capable of making stone tools is unclear (Lewin 1989, 83; McHenry and Berger 1998). Robust australopiths in southern Africa may have used fragments of bone and animal horn as digging tools. (Tattersall 1998, 125). Some research suggests that australopiths resemble apes in the timing of tooth eruption and the patterns of surface wear on teeth (Lewin 1989, 71, 73).

It turns out that the striking morphological differences between gracile and robust australopiths have to do almost exclusively with their chewing anatomy. To begin with, selection seems to have favored large molars to grind tough plant foods. But large molars are

---

cranial capacity The size of the braincase.

Figure 5.10 The "Zinjanthropus" skull, classified as *Australopithecus* (or *Paranthropus*) *boisei*. When the potassium–argon method was used in 1959 to date the volcanic rock lying above the sediment in which this fossil was found, the date of 1.75 million years stunned the scientific community.

ineffective without jaws massive enough to absorb the shock of grinding and muscles large enough to move the jaws. The robust australopiths had the flattest faces because their cheekbones had expanded the most, to accommodate huge jaw muscles that attached to bony crests along the midlines of their skulls.

All australopith fossils from southern Africa have been recovered from limestone quarries or limestone caves. Unfortunately, none of the deposits from which these fossils came can be dated by traditional numerical methods, but newer uranium-series and paleomagnetic techniques are more promising. Dating is much easier at eastern African sites like Olduvai Gorge, Tanzania, where volcanic rock layers can be dated using isotopic methods (Figure 5.10). Since 1959, eastern Africa has become the most important source of hominin fossils in the world.

How Many Species of Australopith Were There?

How many australopith species (and genera) ought to be recognized continues to be debated (see Table 5.2). It now appears that robust australopiths go back some 1.75 million years in southern Africa and perhaps 2.5 million years in eastern Africa, becoming extinct between 1.2 and 0.7 mya. Gracile australopiths apparently flourished between 3 and 2 mya, in both southern and eastern Africa, suggesting an early divergence between the robust and gracile australopith lineages. Because the earliest fossils assigned to the genus *Homo* are lightly built, robust australopiths are unlikely to have been ancestors of later humans. The greatest confusion surrounds those gracile fossils dated to about 2 mya. Particularly intriguing was the 1999 discovery in Ethiopia of a 2.5-million-year-old fossil of a gracile australopith called *Australopithecus garhi* (Asfaw et al. 1999). Not only did *A. garhi* appear

TABLE 5.2 Increase in Cranial Capacity in Hominins		
HOMININ	DATE RANGE (YEARS)	CRANIAL CAPACITY (cm³)
Sahelanthropus tchadensis	6–7 million	350
Ardipithecus ramidus	4.4–5.8 million	a
Australopithecus anamensis	4.2–3.9 million	a
Australopithecus afarensis	3.9–3.0 million	375–550
Australopithecus africanus	3–2 million	420–500
Australopithecus garhi	2.5 million	a
Australopithecus aethiopicus	2.6–2.3 million	410
Australopithecus (or *Paranthropus*) *robustus*	2.0–1.5 million	530
Australopithecus boisei	2.1–1.1 million	530
Homo habilis	2.4–1.5 million	500–800
Homo georgicus	1.8 million	600–680
Homo erectus	1.8 million–300,000	750–1,225
Homo ergaster	1.6 million	910
Homo antecessor	780,000	a
Homo heidelbergensis	500,000	1,200
Homo neanderthalensis	230,000–30,000	1,450
Homo sapiens	195,000–present	1,350

ᵃUnknown at present.

morphologically distinct from other gracile australopiths of roughly the same age, but it was also found in association with primitive stone tools 2.5 to 2.6 million years old (De Heinzelin et al. 1999). Maybe *A. garhi*, or something like it, gave rise to the genus *Homo*.

How Can Anthropologists Explain the Human Transition?

By 2 mya, bipedal hominins with specialized teeth and expanded brains were walking the open environment of the east African savannah. At least some of them made artifacts out of wood, stone, and bone and used fire. Some observers have concluded that meat eating led to a need for stone tools to kill and butcher animals and that stone-tool manufacture led natural selection to favor hominins with expanded brains. This is the "man the hunter" story about human origins and purports to explain nearly every physical and behavioral trait that makes humans human as the outcome of our ancestors' devotion to hunting. In 1968, for example, anthropologists Sherwood Washburn and C. S. Lancaster concluded that "the biological bases for killing have been incorporated into human psychology" (1968, 299–300). This story seemed to be supported by early primatological work reporting that savannah baboons lived by a rigid hierarchy in a closed society: large males with huge canines dominated much smaller females and juveniles. As primatologist Linda Fedigan remarks, this model of human origins "can be said to have been traditional and consistent with contemporary role expectations for Western men and women" (1986, 39). For those who saw such role expectations as natural rather than culturally imposed, the baboon model was highly persuasive.

Such a story is exciting, and it fits in well with many traditional Western views of human nature. But it quickly ran into trouble, both because anthropologists could not agree about how to define "hunting" and because ethnographic fieldwork showed that plant food gathered by women was more important to the survival of foraging peoples than was meat hunted by men (Fedigan 1986, 33–34). For many anthropologists, the Ju/'hoansi people of southern Africa provide helpful insights concerning the social and economic life of the first hominins (see EthnoProfile 12.7: Ju/'hoansi). Richard Lee, an ethnographer who has worked among the Ju/'hoansi since the 1960s, suggested that several "core features" of Ju/'hoansi society may have characterized the first hominin societies: a flexible form of kinship organization that recognized both the male and the female lines, group mobility and a lack of permanent attachment to territory, small group size (25–50 members) with fluctuating group membership, equitable food distribution that leads to highly egalitarian social relations, and a division of labor that leads to sharing (Lee 1974, Lee and DeVore 1968). In addition, women in foraging societies appear to arrange their reproductive lives around their productive activities, giving birth on average to one child every 3–4 years (Fedigan 1986, 49).

In sum, ethnographic evidence suggested that females played active roles in the adaptations of our early hominin ancestors. Some feminist anthropologists used this evidence to construct stories of human evolution that stressed the importance of "woman the gatherer," in which the key tools for human adaptation were digging sticks, slings to carry infants, and containers for gathered foods, all of which, they suggest, were probably invented by women. Rather than use an Old World monkey as a primate model, they used the chimpanzee. Jane Goodall's early reports from Gombe, in Tanzania, suggested that chimpanzee females were not constrained within a rigid hierarchy or dominated by aggressive males; they were active and mobile, feeding themselves and their young, and spending most of their lives apart from their mates. Their closest bonds were with their offspring, and the mother–infant group was the most stable feature of chimpanzee society. Perhaps the first human food sharing was between women and their children; perhaps even hunters would have most likely shared food with their mothers and siblings rather than with their mates. This "woman the gatherer" account—no less extremist than the "man the hunter" scenario—tested earlier assumptions about the foundations of human society and found them wanting.

All reconstructions of the lives of ancestral hominins, however, are tempered with the realization that the key features of contemporary human behavior did not all appear at the same time. As in the case of our skeletal morphology, human behavior also appears to be the product of mosaic evolution.

What Do We Know About Early *Homo* (2.4–1.5 mya)?

About 2.5–2 mya, the drying trend that had begun in Africa in the Late Miocene became more pronounced, possibly causing a wave of extinction as well as the appearance of new species. During this period, the gracile australopiths disappeared either by evolving into or being replaced by a new kind of hominin.

Expansion of the Australopith Brain

Whereas the brains of all australopith species varied within the range of 400–550 cm³, the new hominins had brains over 600 cm³. Were these merely advanced gracile australopiths, or did they belong to a new species or even a new genus? For Louis Leakey, who discovered at Olduvai in 1963 a skull with a cranial capacity of 680 cm³, the answer was clear. He asserted that the skull belonged to the genus *Homo* and named it ***Homo habilis***—"handy man." Eventually, Leakey and his allies discovered more fossils that were assigned to *H. habilis*. But some paleoanthropologists believed that these fossils showed too much internal variation for a single species, and they proceeded to sort the fossils into new categories.

How Many Species of Early *Homo* Were There?

How do paleoanthropologists decide if a gracile fossil younger than 2 million years should be placed in the genus *Homo*? The key criterion is still cranial capacity. In general, the cranial capacities of these early *Homo* fossils range from 510 to 750 cm³. Larger brains resided in larger, differently shaped skulls. Compared to the more elongated australopith cranium, the cranium of early *Homo* has thinner bone and is more rounded; the face is flatter and smaller in relation to the size of the cranium; and the teeth and jaws are less rugged, with a more parabolic arch. Most significantly, early *Homo*'s expansion in brain size was not accompanied by a marked increase in body size, meaning that the enlarged brain was a product of natural selection (Figure 5.11). We know little about the postcranial morphology of any early *Homo* species.

Today, it is widely believed that several species belonging to the genus *Homo* coexisted in eastern Africa in the early Pleistocene (Tattersall 2009, 280). The species of early *Homo* listed in Figure 5.30 are gaining increasing acceptance. And since these coexisting species of *Homo* flourished at the same time as the robust australopiths of eastern Africa (which, you recall, became extinct only 1 mya), it appears that more than one hominin genus also coexisted. This situation challenges the suppositions of phyletic gradualism but is understandable from the point of view of punctuated equilibria (see Chapter 3). Which of these early species of *Homo* might be ancestral to later humans, however, is still being debated.

Homo habilis The species of large-brained, gracile hominins 2 million years old and younger.

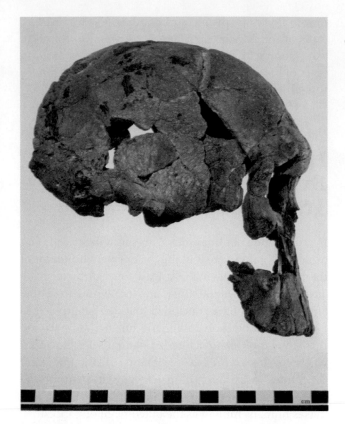

Figure 5.11 Perhaps the best-known fossil of early *Homo* is KNM-ER 1470, found by Richard Leakey and his team near Lake Turkana in northern Kenya.

Earliest Evidence of Culture: Stone Tools of the Oldowan Tradition

Stone tools are the most enduring evidence we have of culturally created human artifacts. Ian Tattersall emphasizes that the earliest hominins who made identifiable stone tools "*invented* efficient toolmaking from materials they consciously chose," something different from what any living apes have ever been observed to do (1998, 57). The oldest undisputed stone tools, found at Hadar in Ethiopia, are at least 2.5 million years old (Semaw et al. 1997; Detleinzelin et al. 1999). The oldest stone tools found in association with a fossil human ancestor also come from Ethiopia and date to 2.33 mya (Kimbel et al. 1994). Other similar tools, dating from 2.5–2 mya, have been found elsewhere in eastern and southern Africa. For the most part, these tools consist of *cores* (tennis ball–sized rocks with a few flakes knocked off to produce cutting edges) and *flakes* (chipped-off pieces of rocks that may or may not have been used as small cutting tools). This style of stone-toolmaking is called the

Figure 5.12 An Oldowan chopper with flakes removed from one side (or face).

Oldowan tradition after the Olduvai Gorge, where the first specimens were found (Figure 5.12).

Oldowan tools are extremely simple and seem indistinguishable from stones that have lost a few flakes through perfectly natural means. Given this simplicity, how can paleoanthropologists conclude that they are dealing with deliberately fashioned artifacts rather than objects modified by natural processes? Answers to such questions come from paleoanthropologists who specialize in **taphonomy**, the study of the various processes that bones and stones undergo in the course of becoming part of the fossil and archaeological records (C. K. Brain 1985). Taphonomists using a scanning electron microscope (SEM) can examine stones and bones for evidence of human activity. Stones used as tools, for example, have characteristic wear patterns along their flaked edges. Flaked rocks that lack wear patterns are not usually considered to be tools unless they are unmistakably associated with other evidence of human activity.

Paleoanthropologists Pat Shipman, Rick Potts, and Henry Bunn examined bones for marks of butchery by early hominids. Shipman learned how modern hunters butcher animals and discovered that carnivore tooth marks and stone cut marks on fresh bone look very different under the SEM (Figure 5.13). Shipman and an assistant used the SEM to examine over 2,500 2 million-year-old fossil bones from Bed I at Olduvai. They found (1) that fewer than half the cut marks seemed to be associated with meat removal; (2) that the stone-tool cut marks and carnivore tooth marks showed basically the same pattern of distribution; (3) that nearly three-quarters of the cut marks occurred on bones with little meat, suggesting they resulted from skinning; and (4) that in 8 out of 13 cases where cut marks and tooth marks overlapped, the cut marks were on top of the tooth marks. Taken together, these patterns suggested to her and her colleagues that, rather than hunting for meat, the Olduvai hominins regularly scavenged carcasses killed by carnivores, taking what they could get (Shipman 1984). It is now widely accepted that scavenging for meat was more likely than hunting among early hominins.

Taphonomists have also reexamined data from eastern African sites once thought to have been home bases, where tools were kept and to which early hominins returned to share meat. They found no convincing evidence of hearths or shelters or other structures that are found at the campsites of later human groups. In some cases, they concluded that the site in question was a carnivore lair or simply a location beside a body of water that attracted many different kinds of animals, some of whose remains ended up buried there. Modern human foragers who hunt for meat never use the same kill site for a long time, leading taphonomists to conclude that their hominin ancestors probably did not do so either. In some cases, both hominins and carnivores may have used a site, and the problem lies in determining which group of animals was responsible for which bones.

The home base hypothesis for ancient collections of tools and bones has thus been called into question. Rick Potts, however, has offered his "stone cache hypothesis" to explain how stones and bones might have accumulated at Olduvai 2 mya. Using a computer simulation, he found that the most efficient way for early hominins to get stones and animal carcasses together would be to cache (or hide) stones at various spots in areas where they hunted and bring carcasses to the nearest cache for processing. Early hominins might have created the first stone caches accidentally but would have returned to them regularly whenever stone tools were needed, thus reconstructing their niche by creating a collection of stones and animal parts. In Potts's view, stone cache sites could turn into home bases once hominins could defend these sites against carnivores. He hypothesizes that this

---

Oldowan tradition A stone-tool tradition named after the Olduvai Gorge (Tanzania), where the first specimens of the oldest human tools (2–2.5 mya) were found.

taphonomy The study of the various processes that objects undergo in the course of becoming part of the fossil and archaeological records.

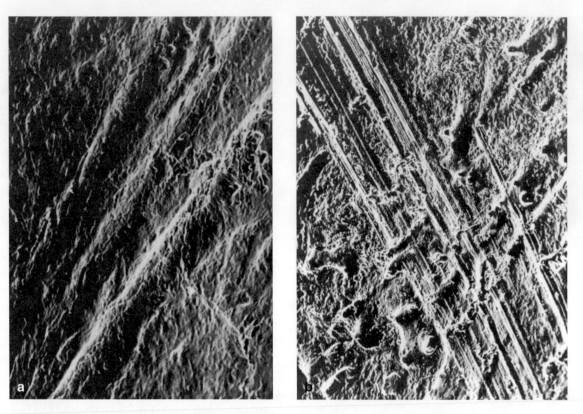

Figure 5.13 The scanning electron microscope allows taphonomists to distinguish between different kinds of marks on bones. (*a*) Hyena tooth-marks on modern bones. (*b*) V-shaped stone-tool cut marks on modern bones.

new way of using the landscape could have created the conditions favoring selection for "a large bodied, diurnal, sweaty, long-distance walking hominid" like *Homo erectus* (Potts 1993, 65).

Who Was *Homo Erectus* (1.8–1.7 mya to 0.5–0.4 mya)?

Fossils of early *Homo* disappear around the beginning of the Pleistocene, about 1.8 mya, either by evolving into or being replaced by large-brained, robust hominins called **Homo erectus** (Figure 5.14). *H. erectus* seems to have coexisted in eastern Africa with the robust australopithecines until between 1.2 and 0.7 mya, when the australopiths became extinct, and was the first hominin species to migrate out of Africa, apparently shortly after it first appeared. A *H. erectus* mandible found in the

Republic of Georgia (part of the former Soviet Union) appears to be between 1.6 million and 900,000 years old; rocks yielding *H. erectus* fossils from Java have been dated to 1.8 and 1.7 mya; and Chinese fossils, including the famous specimens from Zhoukoudian near Beijing, are from 700,000–900,000 to 250,000 years old. No agreed-upon *H. erectus* fossils have been found in western Europe, though artifacts have been found at European sites that date from the time when *H. erectus* was living in Africa and Asia (Klein 2009, 367; Boaz 1995, 33; Browne 1994).

The oldest known African *H. erectus* fossil is of a boy found at the Nariokotome III site, on the west side of Lake Turkana in 1984 (Figure 5.15). Dated to 1.7 mya, the Turkana boy is the most complete early hominin skeleton ever found and different from other *H. erectus* specimens in several ways. First, the boy was taller: it was estimated that he would have been over six feet tall had he reached adulthood. Such a tall, slim body build, found in some indigenous eastern African peoples today, is interpreted as an adaptation to tropical heat. From this, it has been argued that the Turkana boy's body was cooled by sweating and "may thus have been the first hominin species to possess a largely hairless, naked skin" (Klein 2009, 326). Second, the size and

---

Homo erectus The species of large-brained, robust hominins that lived between 1.8 and 0.4 mya.

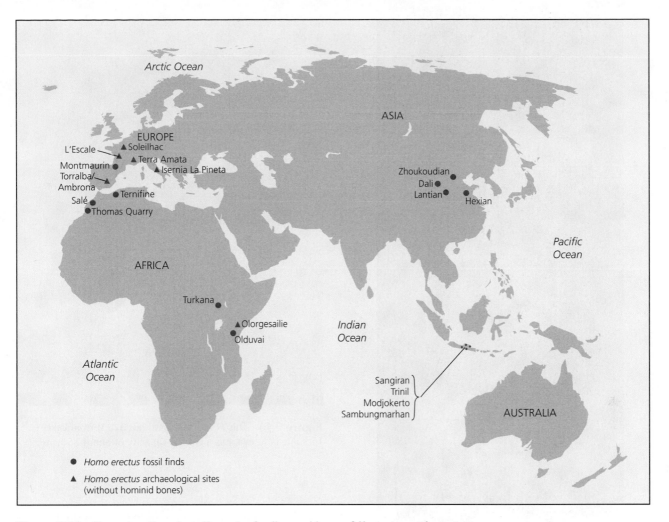

Figure 5.14   The major sites where *H. erectus* fossils or evidence of *H. erectus* settlement (without human fossils) have been found.

shape of the Turkana boy's thoracic canal is less developed than our own. Nerves passing through this bony canal control muscles used for breathing, and modern human speech makes special demands on these muscles. It appears that neural control over breathing was less developed in *H. erectus*, casting doubt on their ability to speak (Walker 1993). Third, the Turkana boy looks very different from Javanese *H. erectus* specimens. Some argue that if *H. erectus* was living in Java at the same time that the Turkana boy was living in eastern Africa, they probably belonged to separate species. Thus, paleoanthropologists have reconsidered the possible taxonomic relationships among the various fossils traditionally assigned to *H. erectus*, and they have devised new evolutionary trees (e.g., Klein 2009, 280; see Figure 5.30). This tree is controversial because it classifies early African *H. erectus* as a separate species (*H. ergaster*) and places all *H. erectus* populations outside Africa on evolutionary side branches that ended in extinction.

Morphological Traits of *H. erectus*

Morphological traits traditionally used to assign fossils to *H. erectus* involve its cranium, its dentition, and its postcranial skeleton. The cranial capacity of *H. erectus* averages around 1,000 cm^3 (Figure 5.16), a significant advance over early *Homo*, for whom cranial capacity ranged 610–750 cm^3. In addition, the skull of *H. erectus* possesses a number of distinctive morphological features, including heavy brow ridges, a five-sided cranial profile (when viewed from the rear), and a bony protuberance at the rear of the skull called a "nuchal crest." The molars of *H. erectus* are reduced in size and the jawbones less robust than those of early *Homo*. In addition, the wear patterns on teeth are different from those found on the molars of early *Homo*. The enamel of *H. erectus* is heavily pitted and scratched, suggesting that its diet was significantly different from that of previous hominins, whose tooth enamel was much smoother.

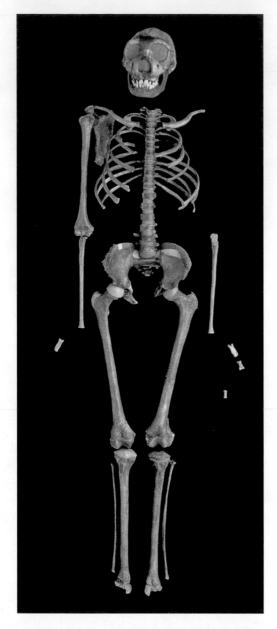

Figure 5.15 The most complete *H. erectus* skeleton ever discovered is KNM–WT 15000 from Kenya. Believed to have been a 12-year-old boy, this fossil includes a nearly complete postcranial skeleton.

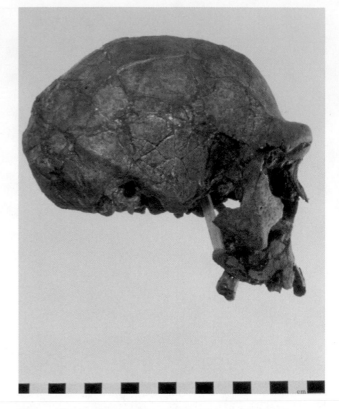

Figure 5.16 This *H. erectus* fossil (ER 3733) from Lake Turkana, in Kenya, has a cranial capacity of about 850 cm³.

The postcranial skeleton of *H. erectus* is somewhat more robust than modern human skeletons but is otherwise like our own (see Figure 5.15). In addition, sexual dimorphism is much reduced in *H. erectus*; males are only 20–30 percent larger than females. Reduced sexual dimorphism in primates is often thought to indicate reduced competition for mates among males and to be associated with monogamy and male contributions to the care of offspring. What reduced sexual dimorphism may have meant for *H. erectus*, however, is still an open question.

An assemblage of bones discovered on the Indonesian island of Flores in 2003, called *Homo floresiensis*, may have belonged to a so-called dwarf form of *Homo erectus* (Brown et al. 2004, Morwood et al. 2004, Lahr and Foley 2004). When biologists speak of "dwarf" forms of large mammals, they are describing normally proportioned but considerably smaller varieties of mammalian species that have frequently evolved on islands. Most of the bones ranged from between 38,000 and 13,000 years of age. It appears that, apart from its small stature, *H. floresiensis* used stone tools and fire like other populations of *H. erectus* and hunted dwarf elephants on the island. Since its discovery, some scholars have argued that small stature and other unusual features of the skeleton of *H. floresiensis* suggest that the bones belonged to modern *H. sapiens* individuals suffering from a pathology such as microcephaly, or, more recently, endemic cretinism (e.g., Oxnard et al. 2010). These views have been systematically challenged by others (e.g., Falk et al. 2009). Unless and until more and better preserved bones are found, it does not appear that these disagreements will be resolved; in any case, the status of *H. floresiensis* does not affect our overall understanding of human evolutionary patterns (Klein 2009, 724).

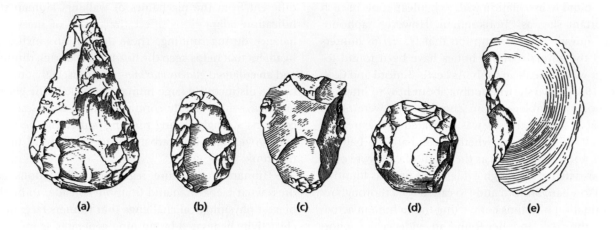

Figure 5.17 Although the biface, or "hand ax" (*a*), is the best-known tool from the Acheulean tradition, other core tools, such as scrapers (*b*), choppers (*c* and *d*), and cleavers (*e*), have also been found. For reasons that are not well understood, large bifaces are rarely found in otherwise similar Asian assemblages.

The Culture of *H. erectus*

Traditionally, the appearance of *H. erectus* in the fossil record has been linked to the appearance of a new stone-tool tradition in the archaeological record: the **Acheulean tradition**. Acheulean stone tools come in a variety of forms, but the Acheulean biface, or "hand ax," is the most characteristic (Figure 5.17). Acheulean bifaces are shaped from stone cores perhaps twice the size of Oldowan cores. Acheulean tools replaced Oldowan tools in the archaeological record shortly after the appearance of *H. erectus*. Archaeologists traditionally assign the Acheulean tradition and the Oldowan tradition to a single period known as the Lower Paleolithic in Europe and the **Early Stone Age (ESA)** in Africa.

In recent years the clear-cut association of Acheulean tools with *H. erectus* has been questioned. First, researchers have found African stone-tool assemblages between 1.5 and 1.4 million years old that contain both Oldowan and larger biface tools, but it is not known which hominins made and used these tools. Second, typical Acheulean tools continue to appear in African sites containing fossils of early *H. sapiens* over a million years later. The conclusion seems to be that there is no one-to-one correspondence between a particular stone-tool tradition and a particular hominin species. Put another way, more than one hominin species may have made and used tools that we assign to a single archaeological culture.

The Acheulean tradition in Africa and Europe changed very little over a period of slightly more than a million years, disappearing about 200,000 years ago. As long as 1 million years ago, however, stone-tool assemblages found in eastern Asia were quite different, reflecting adaptations to the very different environments invaded by

H. erectus and its descendants (Klein 1999, 256). The best-known stone-tool assemblages associated with *H. erectus* in China lack large bifaces and consist mostly of flakes. Although bifaces have been found in other east Asian early Paleolithic sites, they are few in number, more crudely made than Acheulean bifaces, and more recent in date (around 200,000 years old) (Klein 1999, 331–32). Brian Fagan (1990, 119) pointed out that areas in which large bifaces are rare coincide roughly with the distribution of bamboo and other forest materials in Asia. He argued that bamboo would have made excellent tools capable of doing the work performed elsewhere by stone bifaces.

H. erectus also used fire, the best evidence for which comes from the site of Gesher Benot Ya'akov in Israel (780,000 years ago) and Zhoukoudian, China, and Europe (between 670,000 and 400,000 years ago (Klein 2009, 412–413). Burned cobbles and bones from a southern African site suggest that African *H. erectus* (*H. ergaster*) may have had intermittent control of fire a million years earlier than this (Tattersall 2009, 192–93).

H. erectus the Hunter?

Some paleoanthropologists claimed that *H. erectus* was primarily a hunter of big game, based on the fact that the bones of animals such as elephants and giant baboons

---

Acheulean tradition A Lower Paleolithic stone-tool tradition associated with *Homo erectus* and characterized by stone bifaces, or "hand axes."

Early Stone Age (ESA) The name given to the period of Oldowan and Acheulean stone-tool traditions in Africa.

were found in association with Acheulean tools in such important sites as Zhoukoudian. However, taphonomists question the assumption that *H. erectus* hunters killed the animals whose bones have been found together with Acheulean tools. As Lewis Binford and C. K. Ho (1985) have shown, doubts about how to interpret the bone assemblages from Zhoukoudian were raised almost as soon as the site was excavated. It is extremely difficult to determine whether elephant or baboon bones got into the caves as the result of carnivore or of human activity. Although evidence of fire was found at Zhoukoudian, Binford and Ho called for a thorough re-examination of claims connecting fire to human activities in the caves; and they found no evidence to support the idea that *H. erectus* used fire to cook meat.

Many of the *H. erectus* skulls found in Zhoukoudian lacked faces and parts of the cranial base. Some scholars interpret the skull damage as evidence that *H. erectus* practiced cannibalism. However, other scholars propose that hyena activity and the compacting of natural cave deposits are more reasonable, if less lurid, explanations for the condition of those skulls.

Earlier in the chapter, we discussed the hypothesis that bipedal locomotion enabled endurance walking and daylight hunting among the australopiths. Recent research has suggested that *endurance running* may also have played a crucial role in the evolution of later hominins, linking the emergence of new forms of hunting with the appearance of *Homo erectus*. Biological anthropologist Daniel Lieberman and human biologist Dennis Bramble point out that endurance running is not found among primates other than humans and that the distinctive characteristics of human endurance running are unusual among mammals in general. For example, many people are aware that most mammals can outsprint human beings, but they may not realize that humans can outrun almost all other mammals (sometimes even horses) for marathon-length distances (Lieberman and Bramble 2007, 289). Lieberman and Bramble argue that endurance running could have been a very powerful adaptation to the environments in which later hominins such as *Homo erectus* were living (see later discussion in this chapter).

Three sets of adaptations make human endurance running possible: *energetics* (the flow and transformation of energy), *stabilization* (how the body keeps from falling), and *temperature regulation* (maintaining body temperature within limits). Human energetic adaptations include tendons and ligaments in the legs and feet that are absent or very much smaller in other primates. These anatomical structures store energy and then push the body forward in a gait that is fundamentally different from the mechanics of walking. Human stabilization adaptations affect the center of mass and balance during running. These adaptations include a ligament that helps keep the head stable during running and an enlarged *gluteus maximus* (the muscle that makes up the distinctively large human buttocks). The *gluteus maximus*, which hardly contracts during level walking, contracts strongly during running, stiffening the torso and providing a counterbalance to the forward tilt of the trunk.

Human temperature regulation adaptations address what Lieberman and Bramble consider to be the biggest physiological challenge that runners face: muscle activity generated by running generates as much as ten times more heat than does walking (2007, 289). Most mammals stop galloping after short distances because they cannot cool their body temperature fast enough to prevent *hyperthermia*, or overheating. "Humans, uniquely, can run long distances in hot, arid conditions that cause hyperthermia in other mammals, largely because we have become specialized sweaters" (2007, 289). Humans have less body hair and many more sweat glands than do other mammals, which allows for effective body cooling through evapotranspiration. By contrast, other mammals cool down by panting, which requires them to slow down from a gallop, if not stop running altogether.

When and why did humans become good at running long distances? Lieberman and Bramble (2007) argue that running emerged long after bipedal walking evolved—about 2 million years ago, at the time of the transition to *Homo erectus*. They argue that endurance running made scavenging meat and especially hunting of medium- to large-sized mammals increasingly successful. They also argue that it made persistence hunting possible: long-distance hominin runners forced prey animals to run at speeds that they could not endure for long, driving the animals to hyperthermia. The animals could then be killed by the only weapons available to hominins such as *H. erectus*—simple stone tools and sharpened, untipped, thrusting spears.

Biological anthropologist Richard Wrangham suggests that the transition to *Homo erectus* was pushed by the control of fire, which led to an increasing reliance on cooked food. In his view, cooking was of major importance in human evolution. "The newly delicious cooked diet led to their evolving smaller guts, bigger brains, bigger bodies, and reduced body hair" (2009, 194), as well as smaller teeth, since cooked foods are softer than raw foods. For Wrangham, the things that separate humanity from the other primates are the consequences of cooking.

The Evolutionary Fate of *H. Erectus*

H. erectus has long been seen as a logical link between more primitive hominins and our own species, *H. sapiens*. When paleoanthropologists assumed that evolution proceeded in a gradualistic manner, getting from *H. erectus* to *H. sapiens* seemed unproblematic. But thinking of speciation in terms of punctuated equilibria changes things. On the one hand, Richard Klein concludes that "*H. ergaster* and *H. erectus* resembled each other closely, and reasonable specialists can disagree on whether they can be separated" (2009, 329). On the other hand, Ian Tattersall contrasts the fossil record in Asia with the fossil record in Africa during the crucial period between 2 and 1.5 million years ago. During this period, he says, Africa "seems to have been a hotbed of evolutionary experimentation," producing a variety of species of early *Homo*, one of which was *H. ergaster*, whereas Asian fossils assigned to *Homo erectus* show much greater morphological similarity, suggesting little or no evolutionary experimentation (2009, 240). Phyletic gradualists could argue that very little change in *H. erectus* morphology is still more than no change at all; some trends, such as a slight increase in cranial capacity from earlier to later *H. erectus* skulls, support their argument. If, however, regional populations of *H. erectus* are better understood as separate species, this argument requires revision.

Still, the scope of evolutionary adaptation attained by *H. erectus* surpassed that of earlier *Homo* species such as *H. habilis*. The postcranial skeleton of *H. erectus* was essentially modern in form, and its brain was considerably larger than that of its precursors. These features apparently allowed populations of *H. erectus* to make more elaborate tools and to move successfully into arid, seasonal environments in Africa and cooler climates in Eurasia. As best we can tell now, it was from among these populations that the first members of our own species, *H. sapiens*, issued forth.

How Did *Homo Sapiens* Evolve?

Fossil Evidence for the Transition to Modern *H. sapiens*

The relatively rich and reasonably uniform fossil record associated with *H. erectus* disappears after about 500,000 years ago, to be replaced by a far patchier and more varied fossil record. Some 30 sites in Africa, Europe, and Asia have yielded a collection of fossils sometimes called early or **archaic *Homo sapiens*** (Figures 5.18 and 5.19). Most of these fossils consist of fragmented crania, jaws, and teeth. Postcranial bones thought to belong to archaic *H. sapiens* are robust, like those of *H. erectus*, but they are difficult to interpret because they are few in number and poorly dated and show considerable variation. Interpreting variation is particularly problematic when only a few specimens are available for analysis (Hager 1997). Arguments about interpretations of these fossils have grown heated at times, precisely because their resolution has implications for the way we understand not just the fate of *H. erectus* but also the birth of our own species.

Paleoanthropologist Günter Bräuer used cladistic methods to compare all the skulls from Africa that had been assigned to archaic *H. sapiens*. Bräuer argued that his morphological analysis showed that modern *H. sapiens* evolved from *H. erectus* only once, in Africa, and that the period of transition from archaic *H. sapiens* to modern *H. sapiens* was slow, taking some tens of thousands of years (1989, 132). Such a conclusion might be interpreted as an argument for the evolution of modern *H. sapiens* as a result of phyletic gradualism. But is a period of tens of thousands of years relatively long or relatively short, geologically speaking? G. Philip Rightmire favors a punctuationist analysis of the evolution of modern *H. sapiens*. That is, he regards *H. erectus* "as a real species, stable during a long time period" (1995, 487; see also Rightmire 1990). The appearance of modern *H. sapiens* would have followed the punctuation of this equilibrium some 200,000 years ago. If Rightmire's analysis is correct, then the period of evolutionary stability he claims for *H. erectus* would continue up to the appearance of the first anatomically modern populations of *H. sapiens*.

Paleoanthropologist Ian Tattersall also favors a punctuationist explanation for the origins of *H. sapiens*, but he does not agree that all regional populations assigned to *H. erectus* belonged to a single species. Tattersall assigns all archaic *H. sapiens* fossils from Europe to the species *Homo heidelbergensis*, which he (like Bräuer) ultimately traces to African *H. erectus* (i.e., *H. ergaster*) (Tattersall 2009, 209). In the mid-1990s, moreover, paleoanthropologists working in limestone caves in the Sierra de Atapuerca, Spain, discovered fragments of hominin bones

---

archaic *Homo sapiens* Hominins dating from 500,000 to 200,000 years ago that possessed morphological features found in both *Homo erectus* and *Homo sapiens*.

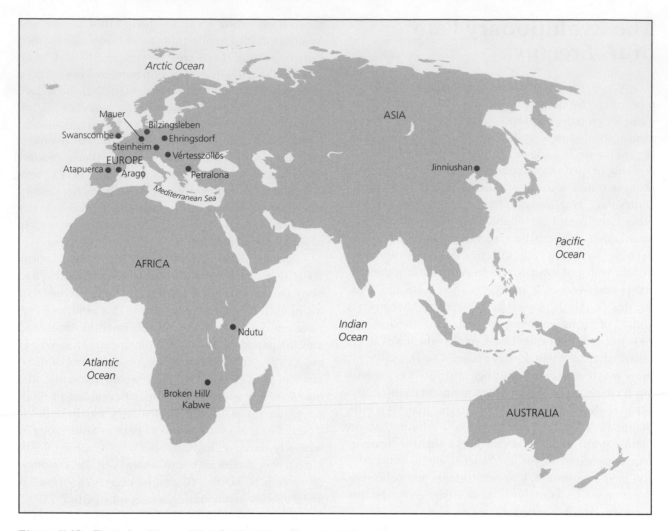

Figure 5.18   The major sites providing fossils assigned to archaic *H. sapiens*

Figure 5.19   Fossils assigned to archaic *H. sapiens* include the Broken Hill skull, from Kabwe, Zambia.

and teeth that are nearly 800,000 years old (Bermúdez de Castro et al. 1997). They argue that it is an offshoot of *Homo ergaster* (African *H. erectus*) and may be ancestral to both *H. heidelbergensis* and *H. sapiens*. Not only are these the earliest well-dated hominin fossils ever found in Europe, but they also display a mix of modern and *erectus*-like features that do not match those of *H. heidelbergensis*. As a result, the Spanish scholars assigned these fossils to a new species, *H. antecessor* (*antecessor* is Latin for "explorer, pioneer, early settler," an appropriate name for the earliest known hominin population in Europe). Other paleoanthropologists seem willing to accept *H. antecessor* as a valid species but believe that not enough evidence yet exists to link it firmly to other species that came before or after it.

The same team of Spanish paleontologists also discovered hominin fossils at Atapuerca that appear to represent a very early stage in Neandertal evolution (Arsuaga et al. 1993). In 2007, improved uranium-series dating methods showed that these fossils were at least 50,000 years old (Tattersall 2009, 230).

Today, most experts place the African and European fossils once classified as "archaic *Homo sapiens*" into the species *Homo heidelbergensis*. Tattersall describes *H. heidelbergensis* as a "truly cosmopolitan" hominin species: originating in Africa some 600,000 years ago, it "may lie close to the origin of the European and African lineages that led to the Neanderthals and modern humans, respectively" (Tattersall 2009, 281). This conclusion is based on the judgment that these fossils all show derived morphological features not present in *Homo erectus*, but none show any of the derived features that are distinctive of either Neandertals or modern humans (Stringer and Andrews 2005, 150–151). *H. heidelbergensis* "could have emerged in the same kind of rapid burst that may have produced *H. ergaster* a million years earlier" (Klein 2009, 433).

Where Did Modern *H. sapiens* Come From?

As noted above, the fossils of archaic *H. sapiens* play a crucial role in a test case for the proponents of speciation by punctuated equilibrium. Punctuationists, as we saw, view *H. erectus* as a single, long-lived, geographically dispersed species. They hypothesize that only one subpopulation of this species, probably located in Africa, underwent a rapid spurt of evolution to produce *H. sapiens* 200,000–100,000 years ago. After that, *H. sapiens* itself multiplied and moved out of Africa, gradually populating the globe and eventually replacing any remaining populations of *H. erectus* or their descendants. The factor triggering this evolutionary spurt is usually thought to be the pattern of fluctuating climate and environmental change caused by the repeated advance and retreat of ice sheets during the Late Pleistocene. The last such warm period began about 128,000 years ago; a cooling trend began about 118,000 years ago and peaked about 20,000 years ago; and then the earth's climate warmed up again and the glaciers retreated. By about 12,000 years ago, the climatic pattern we know today had been established (Fagan 1990, 12ff.). This scenario is usually called the **replacement model**.

However, some gradualists reject this scenario (Frayer et al. 1993; Thorne and Wolpoff 1992; Wolpoff 1985, 1989). Milford Wolpoff believes that evolution from *H. erectus* to *H. sapiens* occurred gradually throughout the traditional range of *H. erectus*. According to Wolpoff, as each regional population evolved from *H. erectus* to *H. sapiens*, it retained its distinct physical appearance, which was the result of adaptation to regional selection pressures. Wolpoff finds morphological similarities between European *H. erectus* and later European Neandertals, between *H. erectus* from Java and later Australian *H. sapiens*, and between Chinese *H. erectus* and later Chinese *H. sapiens*. A complex pattern of gene flow would have spread any new adaptations arising in one regional population to all the others, while at the same time preventing those populations from evolving into separate species. Wolpoff's view is usually called the **regional continuity model**.

A debate has persisted between proponents of these two models, but as paleoanthropologist Leslie Aiello points out, "neither of these hypotheses, in their extreme forms, are fully consistent with the known fossil record for human evolution in the Middle and Late Pleistocene" (1993, 73). Marta Lahr and Robert Foley (1994) proposed that regional patterns of morphological variation in anatomically modern *H. sapiens* may be the consequence of several different migrations out of Africa by phenotypically different African populations at different times and using different routes.

Taking into account these complications, biological anthropologist John Relethford (2001) proposed what has been called the "mostly out of Africa" model. Relethford agreed with advocates of the replacement model that the fossil evidence suggested an African origin for modern human *anatomy*. However, Relethford argued that this did not necessarily mean that the entire contents of the modern human *gene pool* was exclusively from Africa as well. Genetic evidence to resolve the matter was lacking at the time he wrote, but Relethford did not rule out the possibility that anatomically modern populations might have exchanged genes, to a greater or lesser degree, with archaic populations they encountered after they had left Africa for the rest of the Old World. Recent successes by scientists in recovering DNA from ancient hominin fossils is providing genetic evidence that can test some of these possibilities, as we will see later in our discussion of connections between Neandertals and anatomically modern humans.

Who Were the Neandertals (130,000–35,000 Years Ago)?

Neandertals get their name from the Neander Tal ("Neander Valley"), in Germany, where a fossil skullcap and some postcranial bones were discovered in 1856. Thereafter, paleoanthropologists used the name Neandertal

---

replacement model The hypothesis that only one subpopulation of *Homo erectus*, probably located in Africa, underwent a rapid spurt of evolution to produce *Homo sapiens* 200,000–100,000 years ago. After that time, *H. sapiens* would itself have multiplied and moved out of Africa, gradually populating the globe and eventually replacing any remaining populations of *H. erectus* or their descendants.

regional continuity model The hypothesis that evolution from *Homo erectus* to *Homo sapiens* occurred gradually throughout the traditional range of *H. erectus*.

Neandertals An archaic species of *Homo* that lived in Europe and western Asia 130,000–35,000 years ago.

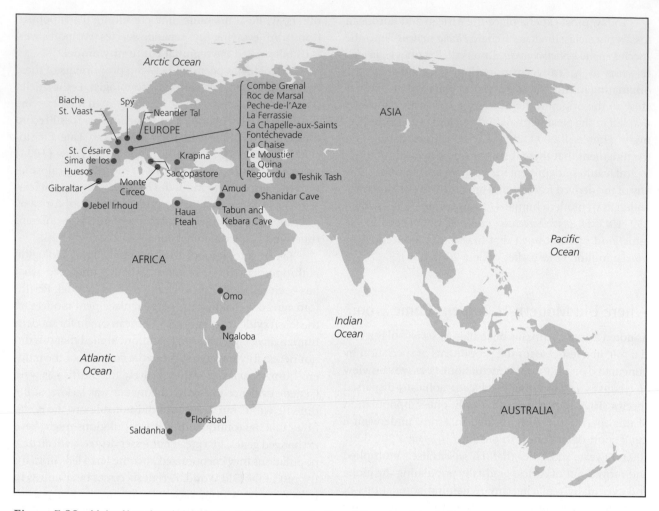

Figure 5.20   Major Neandertal sites, indicating the concentration of these hominins in Europe and southwestern Asia.

to refer to other fossils from Europe and western Asia that appeared to belong to populations of the same kind (Figure 5.20). The first Neandertals appeared about 130,000 years ago. The youngest known Neandertal fossil, from France, is about 35,000 years old; and another, from Spain, may be even younger, at 27,000 years of age (Hublin et al. 1996). After this date, Neandertals disappear from the fossil record.

Because numerous cranial and postcranial bones have been recovered, paleoanthropologists have been able to reconstruct Neandertal morphology with some confidence (Figure 5.21). Neandertals were shorter and more robust than modern *H. sapiens*, with massive skulls, continuous brow ridges, and protruding, chinless faces. Neandertal teeth are larger than those of modern human populations and have enlarged pulp cavities and fused roots, a condition known as *taurodontism*. Unlike modern human beings, Neandertal lower jaws possess a gap behind the third molar called a *retromolar space*, which results from the extreme forward placement of teeth in

the jaw. This forward placement and the characteristic wear patterns on Neandertal incisors suggest that Neandertals regularly used their front teeth as a clamp (Klein 2009, 461; Stringer and Andrews 2005, 155).

The average Neandertal cranial capacity (1,520 cm³) is actually larger than that of modern human populations (1,400 cm³); however, the braincase is elongated, with a receding forehead, unlike the rounded crania and domed foreheads of modern humans. Fossilized impressions of Neandertal brains appear to show the same pattern of difference between the left and right halves (*brain asymmetry*) that is found in modern human brains. Among other things, this suggests that Neandertals were usually right-handed. Brain asymmetries are not unique to modern human beings—or even to primates. H. L. Dibble (1989) argues that we cannot conclude that Neandertal brains functioned like ours simply because we share the same pattern of brain asymmetries. If Neandertal and anatomically modern human populations descended from the same ancestral group (i. e., some form

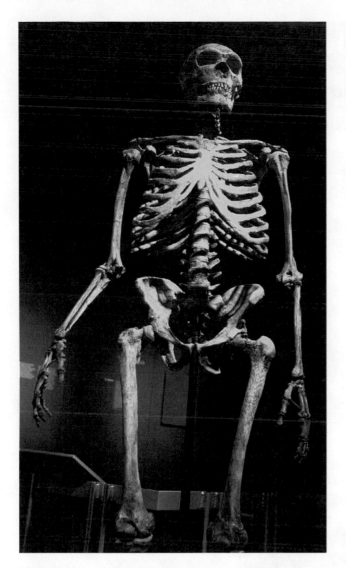

Figure 5.21 A recent reconstruction of a Neandertal skeleton.

of archaic *H. sapiens*), then it is likely that both groups inherited similarly functioning brains.

Neandertal postcranial skeletons are not significantly different from those of modern human beings, but the pelvis and femur are quite distinct (Aiello 1993, 82). Neandertal robusticity and the markings for muscle attachment on their limbs suggest that they were heavily muscled. Differences in the Neandertal hand suggest to paleoanthropologists that it had an unusually powerful grip. Some paleoanthropologists explain Neandertal robusticity as an adaptation to the stress of glacial conditions in Europe. Neandertals who lived in the far milder climate of western Asia were equally robust, however, making this explanation not entirely convincing. The Neandertal pubic bone is longer and thinner than that of modern human beings. Erik Trinkaus (1984) concluded that the Neandertal birth canal was larger as well,

but B. O. Arensburg (1989), another Neandertal expert, found no evidence for a larger birth canal. He related the length of the Neandertal pubic bone to posture and locomotion.

The morphological differences that distinguish modern human beings from the Neandertals are not considered to be greater than the differences that distinguish two subspecies within some species of mammals. This is why taxonomists continue to argue about whether Neandertals ought to be classified as a separate species (*H. neandertalensis*) or as a subspecies of *H. sapiens* (*H. sapiens neandertalensis*).

Middle Paleolithic/Middle Stone Age Culture

Late archaic human populations in Europe, Africa, and southwestern Asia are associated with a new stone-tool tradition, the **Mousterian tradition**, named after the cave in Le Moustier, France, where the first samples of these tools were discovered. Mousterian tools are assigned to the Middle Paleolithic, whereas similar tools from Africa are assigned to the **Middle Stone Age (MSA)**. They differ from the Lower Paleolithic/ESA tools in that they consist primarily of flakes, not cores. Many Mousterian flakes, moreover, were produced by the Levallois technique of core preparation. The earliest MSA tool industries in Africa are probably about 200,000 years old. The earliest Mousterian industries of Europe may be equally old, but dating is far less certain because radiometric techniques cannot provide reliable dates for this period. Although Neandertals were responsible for Mousterian tools in western Europe, similar tools were made by non-Neandertal populations elsewhere (Mellars 1996, 5).

Despite differing names and a distribution that covers more than one continent, most Mousterian/MSA stone-tool assemblages are surprisingly similar, consisting of flake tools that were retouched to make scrapers and points (Figure 5.22). Flint was the stone of choice in Europe and southwestern Asia, but quartzite and some volcanic rock types were widely used in Africa, where flint is absent. Most Mousterian/MSA sites are rock shelters located near what were once sources of fresh water.

Mousterian tradition A Middle Paleolithic stone-tool tradition associated with Neanderthals in Europe and southwestern Asia and with anatomically modern human beings in Africa.

Middle Stone Age (MSA) The name given to the period of Mousterian stone-tool tradition in Africa, 200,000–40,000 years ago.

In Their Own Words

Bad Hair Days in the Paleolithic

Modern (Re)Constructions of the Cave Man

Judith Berman has written about how Paleolithic human beings have been visually sterotyped in Western culture since the end of the nineteenth century.

The Cave Man looks as he does because he is a representation of our ideas about human nature and human origins. His image is not necessarily based on scientific data, but is rather anchored in and entwined with other tremendously puissant representations deriving from pagan and Judaeo-Christian traditions. We are readily convinced of the "truth" of Cave Man images because they seem "natural" or familiar to us; in fact, they draw on a set of conventionalized observations about the origins and natural history of humans.

Hairstyles are a clue to where on the evolutionary tree an artist or illustrator places his or her subject. Certainly a thick coat of body hair and ungroomed head hair puts an ancestor a great distance from modern humans (although we have no data on when a hairy coat was lost), while most Neanderthals have longer and untidier hair than Upper Paleolithic humans. Now these may be perfectly accurate representations of our ancestors, but we have no data on this subject until the Upper Paleolithic. Hair is our marker of evolutionary position; the further away from our animal origins, the more it is under control. (In many of the pictorial histories of humankind, later humans leave the Paleolithic behind, put on good Neolithic cloth coats, invent headbands and pageboys, and settle down on their farms.)

So far, we have delineated some of the natural history of the convention of the Cave Man and have examined the significance of his hair. But why should this Cave Man matter so to us? The Cave Man is a representation of our ancestors; the fact of evolution forces us to acknowledge that the Cave Man resides within each of us. He is our animal, primitive self, before the limits of society.

Source: Berman 1999, 297.

Charles R. Knight's 1921 painting of Neandertals for the American Museum of Natural History in New York City follows the convention Judith Berman describes, giving them ungroomed head hair to mark their great distance from modern humans.

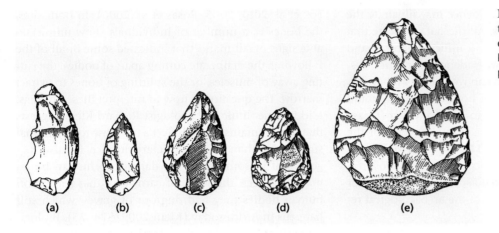

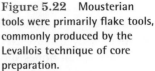

Figure 5.22 Mousterian tools were primarily flake tools, commonly produced by the Levallois technique of core preparation.

(a)   (b)   (c)   (d)   (e)

The rock shelters were probably living sites because many contained hearths as well as stone tools. Interestingly, Mousterian sites found in the European part of the former Soviet Union appear to be the earliest hominin sites that exist in these areas. This might mean that Neandertals were the first hominins capable of settling areas with such a cold, harsh climate.

Mousterian/MSA tools are more varied than the Lower Paleolithic/ESA tools that preceded them. Archaeologists have offered three different explanations for the variation found in western Europe. François Bordes identified five major Mousterian variants and thought they represented five different cultural traditions. Lewis and Sally Binford countered that what Bordes had identified were actually varied tool kits that a single group of people might have used to perform different functions or to carry out different tasks at different times of the year. Both these interpretations were rejected by H. L. Dibble and Nicolas Rolland, who saw the "variety" of Mousterian assemblages as a by-product of other factors, such as periodic resharpening (which changed the shapes of tools and reduced their size until they were discarded) or the different kinds of stone the toolmakers had used (see Mellars 1996). Archaeologist Paul Mellars reviewed the evidence for each of these arguments, and he concluded that Bordes's original interpretation is the most plausible. Each Mousterian variant has a distinct pattern of spatial and chronological distribution, and some industries are characterized by specific tools that do not occur in the other variants. For Mellars, this shows "a real element of cultural patterning" (1996, 355).

What other cultural remains are there from the Middle Paleolithic? In western Europe, Neandertals left traces of hearths, although their sites were not centered around hearths, as is typical of the Upper Paleolithic. The evidence for stone walls is ambiguous, but there is good evidence for pits and even a post hole, especially at Combe-Grenal in France, where Bordes excavated (Mellars 1996, 295).

Moreover, we know that Neandertals deliberately buried their dead, often with arms and legs folded against their upper bodies. A number of the most famous Neandertal finds, such as La Ferrassie in France and Shanidar Cave in Iraq, are grave sites. Many paleoanthropologists interpret deliberate burials as evidence for the beginnings of human religion. Accumulations of bear skulls found at some European sites have been interpreted as collections Neandertals made for use in a "cave bear cult." Flower pollen scattered over the Shanidar burial was interpreted as the remains of flowers mourners had placed on the grave. Fragments of natural red or black pigments were interpreted as possible ritual cosmetics. However, taphonomic analyses question these interpretations. For example, the cave bear skulls may simply have accumulated where cave bears died; flower pollen was found throughout the Shanidar site and may have been introduced by burrowing rodents; red and black pigments may have been used to tan hides or change the color of objects. Klein points out that Neandertals made no formal bone artifacts, and he believes some so-called Neandertal art objects may be **intrusions** from later deposits; that is, they may be artifacts made by more recent populations that accidentally found their way into Neandertal strata as the result of natural forces (2009, 528). The anatomically modern peoples who came after the Neandertals, by contrast, left a profusion of decorative objects made of bone, ivory, antler, and shell (Klein 2009, 660ff.; Stringer and Andrews 2005, 212ff.; Mellars 1996). Discoveries in Australia of engravings on stone and use of ochre pigment dating between 116,000 and 75,000 years ago, however, have reopened the debate about the creativity of early populations of *H. sapiens* (Wilford 1996).

---

intrusions Artifacts made by more recent populations that find their way into more ancient strata as the result of natural forces.

A very different kind of evidence may illustrate the humanity of the Neandertals. All the data indicate that Neandertals lived hard lives in a difficult habitat, and many Neandertal bones show evidence of injuries, disease, and premature aging. To survive as long as they did, the individuals to whom these bones belonged would have needed to rely on others to care for them (Chase 1989, 330). As Klein observes, "group concern for the old and sick may have permitted Neandertals to live longer than any of their predecessors, and it is the most recognizably human, nonmaterial aspect of their behavior that can be directly inferred from the archaeological record" (2009, 585).

Did Neandertals Hunt?

Archaeologists in Germany and Britain have discovered wooden spears that date to the period when Neandertals were the only hominins in Europe (Klein 2009, 404–05). In addition, several Mousterian stone points show what appears to be impact damage, suggesting use as a weapon. Animal remains at some sites in France and on the island of Jersey suggest that Neandertals collectively drove the animals over cliffs or engaged in other kinds of mass-killing strategies (Mellars 1996, 227–29). Archaeologists have also found the bones of hoofed mammals such as deer, bison, and wild species of oxen, sheep, goats, and horses at Eurasian Mousterian sites. As in other cases, however, it is often difficult—particularly at open-air sites—to tell how many of these bones are the remains of Neandertal meals and how many got to the site some other way. Furthermore, at some Eurasian and African sites, the bones of elephants and rhinoceros were used as building materials and their flesh may not have been eaten.

What about the flesh of other Neandertals? As we saw in our discussion of *Homo erectus*, claims that one or another hominin species practiced cannibalism are made from time to time, often on the basis of equivocal evidence. Sometimes the evidence is more straightforward—for example, at Gran Dolina in Spain, where butchered human bones were found together in 800,000-year-old deposits associated with *Homo antecessor* (Fernandez-Jalvo et al. 1999). Persuasive evidence of cannibalism in association with Neandertals has been reported from the 100,000-year-old site of Moula Guercy, in France (Defleur et al. 1993, 1999) and from the 49,000-year-old site of El Sidron, in Spain (Lalueza-

Fox et al. 2010, 2005; Rosas et al. 2006). In both sites, the bones of a number of individuals show unmistakable signs of cut marks that indicated some or all of the following: the deliberate cutting apart of bodies, the cutting away of muscles, or the splitting of bones to extract marrow. The question is how to interpret these findings. Middle Paleolithic archaeologist Richard Klein suggests that these remains might reflect a response to nutritional stress rather than a regular dietary practice. He also suggests that in some cases the damage to human bones may have been the work of carnivores that feasted on human bodies they had dug out of graves, which still happens in Africa today (Klein 2009, 574–75). Biological anthropologist Jonathan Marks reminds us that numerous contemporary human groups remove flesh from the bones of the dead, not to consume it but as part of a mortuary ritual. Making sense of these remains is complex because what it means to be human seems to ride in the balance: if Neandertals ate one another, they would appear "behaviorally nonhuman (since the consumption of human flesh lies on the symbolic boundary of human behavior)," whereas mortuary defleshing of the dead "symbolically renders them as more human, since it invokes thought and ritual" (Marks 2009, 225).

P. G. Chase argued that Neandertals were skilled hunters of large game and that their diet does not seem to have differed much from that of the modern people who eventually replaced them. He described the changes that set anatomically modern people apart from Neandertals in terms that highlighted the particular way in which they constructed their niches; that is, he emphasized the way moderns used symbolic thought and language to transform "the intellectual and social contexts in which food was obtained" (1989, 334).

What Do We Know about Anatomically Modern Humans (200,000 Years Ago to Present)?

During the period when classic Neandertal populations appeared in Europe and western Asia, a different kind of hominin appeared to the south that possessed an anatomy like that of modern human beings. They had an average cranial capacity of more than 1,350 cm³, domed foreheads, and round braincases. These early modern people also had flatter faces than Neandertals, usually with distinct chins. Their teeth were not crowded into the front of their jaws, and they lacked retromolar spaces. The postcranial skeleton of these **anatomically modern human beings** was much more lightly built than that

---

anatomically modern human beings Hominin fossils assigned to the species *H. sapiens* with anatomical features similar to those of living human populations: short and round skulls, small brow ridges and faces, prominent chins, and light skeletal build.

of the Neandertals. In Europe, where the fossil record is fullest, their skeletons gradually became smaller and less robust for about 20,000 years after they first appeared. Many paleoanthropologists believe that these changes were a by-product of niche construction as anatomically modern human beings increasingly dependent on culture buffered themselves from selection pressures that favored physical strength.

Experts long thought that anatomically modern human beings first appeared about 40,000 years ago in Europe. In the 1970s and 1980s, however, fossils of anatomically modern human beings considerably older than this were recovered from two sites in South Africa and one in southwestern Asia. The South African finds come from Border Cave and Klasies River Mouth Cave (Figure 5.23). Modern human fossils from Border Cave were found in deposits containing so little carbon 14 that radiocarbon dating was impossible. This meant that the deposits had to be more than 40,000 years old, which is the oldest date the traditional radiocarbon method can reliably yield. Because of difficulties surrounding the excavation at Border Cave, some experts suspect that the modern human fossils found there may be intrusions from more recent layers.

At Klasies River Mouth Cave, however, the situation was rather different. The anatomically modern human fossils found there also came from deposits beyond the range of radiocarbon dating, but these deposits were cross-dated using paleoclimatic and biostratigraphic methods, as well as uranium-series dating and electron spin resonance. Many paleoanthropologists

confidently assign these fossils an age of between 74,000 and 60,000 years, although others are not convinced by the cross-dating. Subsequently, modern skeletal remains about 160,000 years old were recovered from Orno and Herto in Ethiopia (Stringer and Andrews 2005, 160).

Bone harpoons found at a site in Katanda, Congo, were dated to more than 70,000 years of age using thermoluminescence and electron spin resonance. If this date stands, it would reinforce the hypothesis that anatomically modern *H. sapiens* first made Upper Paleolithic-style tools in Africa thousands of years before moving into Europe (Brooks and Yellen 1992). It is possible, however, that these bone tools are intrusions (Klein 2009, 527–28).

Until recently, archaeologists could only assign relative dates to southwestern Asian Middle Paleolithic archaeological sites based on changes in the stone-tool assemblages they contained. More recently, however, new dating techniques have been used to assign absolute dates to Mousterian sites in southwestern Asia. Deposits containing Mousterian tools associated with a Neandertal burial at Kebara, Israel, were dated by thermoluminescence to about 60,000 years ago. Deposits containing Mousterian tools associated with burials of anatomically modern people at Qafzeh Cave in Israel (Figure 5.24) were dated by thermoluminescence and cross-dated by rodent biostratigraphy and sedimentary data. All three methods suggest that the Qafzeh moderns lived about 92,000 years ago. Additional measurements using uranium-series dating and electron spin resonance

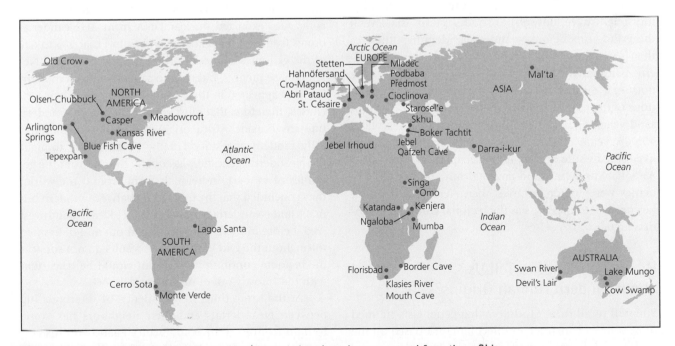

Figure 5.23 Fossils of anatomically modern human beings have been recovered from these Old World and New World sites.

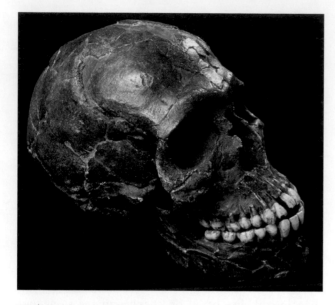

Figure 5.24 The earliest anatomically modern fossils in southwestern Asia, such as this skull, come from Qafzeh Cave, Israel. Three different dating methods confirm that the Qafzeh moderns lived about 92,000 years ago.

date Neandertal remains from Tabun and anatomically modern human remains from Qafzeh to 105,000 years ago and the modern remains from Skhul to more recent dates (McDermott et al. 1993). Tools and other cultural remains, such as hearth structures and burial patterns, likewise indicate that both southwestern Asian Neandertals and their anatomically modern neighbors used Mousterian material culture (Bar-Yosef 1989, 604; Mellars and Stringer 1989, 7).

The Qafzeh dates suggest that modern human beings might have moved into southwestern Asia several thousand years before Neandertals. Klein hypothesizes that "the Skhul/Qafzeh people were simply near modern Africans who extended their range slightly to the northeast during the relatively mild and moist conditions of the Last Interglacial, between 127 and 71 [thousand years] ago" (2009, 606). In any case, for at least 45,000 years, Neandertals and moderns apparently lived side by side or took turns occupying southwestern Asia. If Neandertals and anatomically modern human beings were contemporaries, then Neandertals cannot be ancestral to moderns as the regional continuity theorists argue.

What Can Genetics Tell Us about Modern Human Origins?

You will recall from Module 2 that geneticists claimed to be able to construct a molecular clock based on the mutation rate in human DNA. (In fact, they chose

to focus on mitochondrial DNA, known as mtDNA, which is found in the mitochondria of cells, outside the nucleus, and is only transmitted along the female line—unlike eggs, sperm are cell nuclei and only carry nuclear DNA). The results of their initial analysis suggested that the ancestors of modern humans originated in Africa some 100,000–200,000 years ago (Cann et. al. 1987, A. C. Wilson and Cann 1992). An early study of the pattern of DNA variation in the Y (i.e., the male) chromosome of different regional human populations also suggested an African origin for modern *H. sapiens* (Rouhani 1989, 53). In 1997, molecular geneticists from Germany and the United States extracted a sequence of mtDNA with 378 base pairs from the original 1856 Neandertal-type specimen and compared the Neandertal sequence with 994 human mtDNA lineages taken from a worldwide sample of living human populations. They concluded that Neandertals contributed no mtDNA to modern human populations and reasserted that the ancestor of the mtDNA pool of contemporary humans lived in Africa (Krings et al. 1997). Shortly thereafter, they concluded that the last common mtDNA ancestor of Neandertals and modern humans lived approximately half a million years ago (Krings et al. 1999).

However, Krings and his colleagues have pointed out that their results tell us nothing about whether Neandertals contributed *chromosomal* genes to modern populations.

Recent advances in the sequencing of ancient DNA are beginning to provide some answers. A major breakthrough was the publication of a draft Neandertal nuclear genome (Green et al. 2010). Green and his colleagues extracted nuclear DNA from 21 Neandertal bones from Vindija, Croatia, and found that 1% to 4% of the genomes of modern non-Africans contained Neandertal sequences, but that no sequences from modern humans appeared in the Neandertal genome. They concluded, therefore, that most genetic variation in modern humans outside Africa originated with our anatomically modern ancestors. Finally, because they thought the Neandertal genome was equally distant from the genomes of modern individuals from around the world, they concluded that the inbreeding between modern humans and Neandertals probably took place in southwest Asia, before modern humans spread out and diversified throughout the Old World. These results do not support the regional continuity model but would be consistent with the "mostly out of Africa" model.

At the same time, new evidence of interbreeding between Neandertals and their neighbors has come to light from Asia. In 2010, Svante Pääbo and his colleagues extracted both mtDNA and nuclear DNA from two tiny fossils found at Denisova Cave in Siberia. When the Denisova sequences were compared with those of Neandertal and modern sequences, three key findings emerged: (1) although they lived between 400,000 and 30,000 years ago, the Denisovans were genetically distinct from Neandertals; (2) the Denisovans and Neandertals shared a common ancestor who had left Africa nearly half a million years ago; and (3) the Denisovan genome was very similar to the genome of modern humans from New Guinea. Pääbo and his colleagues concluded that the Denisovan and Neandertal populations must have split apart after leaving Africa, but that about 50,000 years ago, the Denisovans interbred with anatomically modern humans, who took some Denisovan DNA with them when they moved into South Asia.

The collection and analysis of ancient DNA has become increasingly detailed and sophisticated. When such data are compared with genome data collected from living human populations all over the world, it is sometimes possible to tell whether genetic variants found in living human populations were part of the gene pool of these ancient populations. For example, the *FOXP2* gene found in living human populations has been implicated in our ability to speak and use language. A variant of this gene has been recovered from Neandertal bones in Spain, suggesting that limits on Neandertal language ability may have been less severe than once thought (Krause et al. 2007). In addition, a variant of the *MC1R* gene, which affects skin pigmentation in modern human populations, has been recovered from Neandertal bones in Spain and Italy; tests on its functioning suggest that Neandertals had light skin and red hair (Lalueza-Fox et al. 2007).

Although there is lingering concern that modern DNA might have contaminated some ancient fossil samples, this new genetic evidence is exciting and accumulating at an impressive rate. Still, some perspective is called for. Jonathan Marks reminds us that "while our DNA matches that of a chimpanzee at over the 98% level, it matches the DNA of the banana the chimpanzee is eating at over the 25% level. Yet there is hardly any way we can imagine ourselves to be over one-quarter banana—except in our DNA" (2011, 139). So what does it mean to share 1% to 4% of our genome with Neandertals? Many paleontologists and archaeologists are likely to be cautious about endorsing the DNA evidence until it is backed up by additional fossil evidence; as Klein observes, studies of genetic diversity are "a useful and independent means of assessment" of proposed models of human evolution, but "[t]he fossil record must be the final arbiter" when it comes to evaluating such models (2009, 631).

The Upper Paleolithic/Late Stone Age (40,000?–12,000 Years Ago)

Middle Paleolithic/MSA tools disappear in Africa and southwestern Asia by 40,000 years ago at the latest and in Europe after about 35,000 years ago. What replaces them are far more elaborate artifacts that signal the beginning of the **Upper Paleolithic** in Europe and southwestern Asia and the **Late Stone Age (LSA)** in Africa.

The stone-tool industries of the Upper Paleolithic/LSA are traditionally identified by the high proportion of blades they contain when compared with the Middle Paleolithic/MSA assemblages that preceded them. A **blade** is defined as any flake that is at least twice as long as it is wide. Blades have traditionally been associated with anatomically modern humans, who have been given credit for the development of the various cultures of the Upper Paleolithic. Indeed, the discovery of an MSA stone-tool industry in southern Africa that may be as much as 90,000 years old—the Howieson's Poort Industry (Figure 5.25)—has been viewed by some anthropologists as indirect evidence for the presence of anatomically modern humans in southern Africa at the same time (see Stringer 1989). However, Ofer Bar-Yosef and Steven L. Kuhn (1999) challenged this understanding of blades. Bar-Yosef and Kuhn identify over a dozen sites in western Eurasia and Africa that contain Middle Paleolithic or MSA stone-tool assemblages rich in blades. Drawing on their expertise in stone-tool manufacture, they point out that blades are not necessarily more difficult to make than Acheulean bifaces, nor are they necessarily superior to flakes for all purposes: after all, the very effective modern hunting and gathering peoples known in recent historical times did not use blades. Probably, blade technologies were invented again and again. There is no need to suppose that Neandertals or *H. heidelbergensis* were incapable of making blades and, therefore, no grounds for assuming that the presence of blades indicates the presence of anatomically modern humans.

At the same time, they note the rapid spread of blade-based technologies in the Upper Paleolithic/LSA, and this is a new development. During the Upper Paleolithic, blades were also regularly attached to wood, bone,

---

Upper Paleolithic/Late Stone Age (LSA) The name given to the period of highly elaborate stone-tool traditions in Europe in which blades were important, 40,000–10,300 years ago.

blades Stone tools that are at least twice as long as they are wide.

Figure 5.25 Klasies River Mouth Cave in South Africa yielded both fossils of anatomically modern human beings and blade tools, which are the characteristic tools of the European Upper Paleolithic and the African Late Stone Age

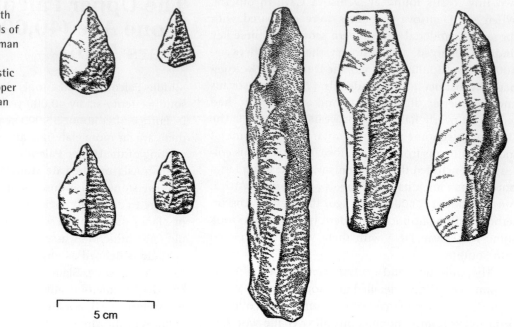

5 cm

antler, or ivory in order to form **composite tools** such as bows and arrows. Bar-Yosef and Kuhn note that composite tools require interchangeable parts, so the efficient production of standardized blades would have been advantageous and would have encouraged the spread of blade-production techniques that allowed toolmakers better control over the sizes and shapes of the blades they produced. Bar-Yosef and Kuhn conclude that Upper Paleolithic reliance on blades might ultimately have been a historical accident, but "if proliferation of blade and bladelet technologies during the Upper Paleolithic is in fact linked to composite tool manufacture, it may also reflect the emergence of novel and highly significant patterns of social and economic cooperation within human groups" (1999, 323).

Indeed, Upper Paleolithic/LSA people clearly had a new capacity for cultural innovation. Although Mousterian/MSA tool types persist with little change for over 100,000 years, several different Upper Paleolithic/LSA tool traditions replace one another over the 20,000 years or so of the Upper Paleolithic/LSA. Each industry was stylistically distinct and possessed artifact types not found in the others (Figure 5.26). For the earliest anatomically modern people to abandon the Mousterian/MSA culture that had served them well for so long, something

important must have happened. Many experts believe this something was a reorganization of the brain, producing the modern capacity for culture. This anatomical change, if it occurred, has left no fossil evidence. However, as knowledge about the genomes of living humans, other primates, and fossil hominins accumulates, it may become increasingly possible to find and date key mutations associated with brain expansion or language ability (Klein 2009, 638ff.; Tattersall 2009, 243–44). For the present, such a change must be inferred from the cultural evidence produced by anatomically modern humans after about 40,000 years ago.

What Happened to the Neandertals?

The first appearance of Upper Paleolithic culture in Europe is important because of what it can tell us about the fate of the Neandertals. If Neandertals gradually evolved into modern human beings, it is argued, then this gradual evolution should be documented in archaeological assemblages. In this search, the Châtelperronian and Aurignacian industries have attracted the most attention.

Châtelperronian assemblages from France, 35,000–30,000 years old, contain a mixture of typical Mousterian backed knives and more advanced pointed cutting tools called "burins." They also contain bone tools and pierced animal teeth. Other mixed assemblages similar to the Châtelperronian have been found in Italy, central

composite tools Tools such as bows and arrows in which several different materials are combined (e.g., stone, wood, bone, ivory, antler) to produce the final working implement.

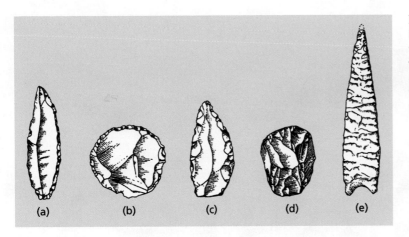

Figure 5.26 Upper Paleolithic stone-tool industries in Europe were fully developed blade technologies that show considerable stylistic variation over time. Tools *a*, *b*, and *c* are from the Perigordian culture, a variety of the Gravettian; tool *d* is from the Aurignacian; and tool *e* is from the Solutrean.

and northern Europe, and southern Russia (Mellars 1996, 417–18). Aurignacian assemblages, 34,000–30,000 years old, are Upper Paleolithic blade assemblages. We know that Neandertals were capable of making Châtelperronian tools because two Neandertal skeletons were found in 32,000-year-old Châtelperronian deposits at St. Césaire, France (Mellars 1996, 412ff.). If Neandertals invented Aurignacian technology as they evolved into anatomically modern human beings, then the Châtelperronian and other mixed assemblages might be transitional between the Mousterian and the Aurignacian.

Some archaeologists argue, however, that Neandertals may have borrowed elements of Upper Paleolithic technology from a culturally more advanced population of outsiders. For example, deposits found in some cave sites in southwestern France and northern Spain show Châtelperronian layers on top of some Aurignacian layers, suggesting that two different cultural groups coexisted and occupied the same caves at different times (Mellars 1996, 414). These archaeologists believe that anatomically modern people invented the Aurignacian industry in southwestern Asia and brought it with them when they migrated into central and western Europe 40,000–35,000 years ago. The skeletons of anatomically modern human beings begin to appear at European sites about this time, when the ice sheets had begun to melt and the climate was improving. For many archaeologists, the arrival in Europe of both modern human beings and Aurignacian culture during the same time period seems too well correlated to be an accident. No Aurignacian assemblages have been found in eastern Europe, which suggests that the Upper Paleolithic developed differently there (Klein 2009, 586–88; 605).

Even if European Neandertals borrowed Upper Paleolithic technology from southwestern Asian immigrants, they were gone a few thousand years later. What happened to them? There is no evidence that the replacement of Neandertals by modern people involved conquest and extermination, although this has been proposed from time to time. European Neandertals may have disappeared because they evolved into anatomically modern people, developing Aurignacian culture as they did so, in line with the regional continuity model. This hypothesis, however, runs afoul of the fact that Neandertals and moderns apparently originated on different continents and coexisted in southwestern Asia for 45,000 years, both of them making and using Mousterian tools. European Neandertals may have disappeared as they interbred with the in-migrating modern people and as their descendants adopted Aurignacian culture. If this happened, then contemporary European populations should share morphological traits with their alleged Neandertal ancestors. As we saw earlier, evidence for this scenario is stronger for eastern Europe and western Asia than for the classic Neandertals of western Europe. Klein concludes that "virtually every detectable aspect" of the archaeological record suggests that Neandertals "lagged their modern successors, and their more primitive behavior limited their ability to compete for game and other shared resources" (2009, 586). Neandertals may have retreated as modern people spread throughout Europe, decreasing in number until, around 30,000 years ago, they simply died out. In sum, at this time, the archaeological evidence is no more able than the fossil or genetic evidence to resolve disputes about the fate of the Neandertals.

Upper Paleolithic/Late Stone Age Cultures

Although blades are the classic tools of Upper Paleolithic/LSA culture, other tool types appear that are not found in Mousterian/MSA assemblages, such as endscrapers, burins, and numerous artifacts of bone, ivory,

Figure 5.27 Upper Paleolithic stoneworkers developed bone-, antler-, and ivory-working techniques to a high degree, as is shown by these objects from Europe.

and antler (Figure 5.27). Brian Fagan calls this technological explosion the "Swiss army knife effect": "like its modern multipurpose counterpart, the core and blade technique was a flexible artifact system, allowing Upper Paleolithic stoneworkers to develop a variety of subsidiary crafts, notably bone and antler working, which likewise gave rise to new weapons systems and tailored clothing" (1990, 157).

As we saw earlier, the most distinctive Upper Paleolithic artifacts are composite tools, such as spears and arrows, made of several different materials. The oldest undisputed evidence of wooden bows and arrows in Europe dates from 12,000–11,000 years ago; however, bows and arrows may have been used as long as 20,000 years ago in Africa and Eurasia, where researchers have found indirect evidence in the form of stone points, backed bladelets, and bone rods resembling arrow shafts (Klein 2009, 679–80). Archaeologists have also found

the skeletons of fur-bearing animals whose remains suggest they were captured for their skins, not for food; pointed bone tools that were probably used to sew skins together (the oldest eyed needles appeared between 35 and 28 Ka years old); and the remains of tailored clothing in Upper Paleolithic burials dating from between 26 and 19 Ka (Klein 2009, 673).

Evidence for regular hunting of large game is better at Upper Paleolithic sites than at sites from earlier periods, especially in Europe and Asia. In addition to hunting tools, researchers have found the bones of mammoth, reindeer, bison, horse, and antelope, animals that provided not only meat but also ivory, antler, and bone. Some animals were hunted but not for food. The mammoth, for instance, supplied bones used for building shelters. Fresh bone and animal droppings were also probably burned as fuel. The Upper Paleolithic way of life probably resembled that of contemporary foragers.

In Their Own Words

Women's Art in the Upper Paleolithic?

In a 1996 article in American Anthropologist *Catherine Hodge McCoid and LeRoy D. McDermott propose that the so-called Venus figures of the early Upper Paleolithic might be more successfully understood as women's art rather than as sex objects made from a male point of view.*

Since Édouard Piette (1895) and Salomon Reinach (1898) first described the distinctive small-scale sculptures and engravings of human figures found in the rock shelters and caves of southern France, several hundred more European Upper Paleolithic figures have been identified. The earliest of these, the so-called Stone Age Venuses or Venus figurines, constitute a distinctive class and are among the most widely known of all Paleolithic art objects. As a group they have frequently been described in the professional and popular literature. Most of the figures are about 150 millimeters in height and depict nude women usually described as obese.

In spite of many difficulties in dating, there is a growing belief that most of these early sculptures were created during the opening millennia of the Upper Paleolithic (circa 27,000–21,000 b.c.) and are stylistically distinct from those of the later Magdalenian. These first representations of the human figure are centered in the Gravettian or Upper Perigordian assemblages in France and in related Eastern Gravettian variants, especially the Pavlovian in the former Czechoslovakia, and the Kostenkian in the former Soviet Union.

Most Pavlovian-Kostenkian-Gravettian (PKG) statuettes are carved in stone, bone, and ivory, with a few early examples modeled in a form of fired loess (Vandiver et al. 1989). Carved reliefs are also known from four French Gravettian sites: Laussel, La Mouthe, Abri Pataud, and Terme Pialet. These images show a formal concern with three-dimensional sculpted masses and have the most widespread geographical distribution of any form of prehistoric art.... While considerable variation occurs among PKG figurines, claims of true diversity ignore a central tendency that defines the group as a whole. The overwhelming majority of these images reflect a most unusual anatomical structure, which André Leroi-Gourhan (1968) has labeled the "lozenge composition." What makes this structural formula so striking is that it consists of a recurring set of apparent departures from anatomical accuracy [see figure]. The characteristic features include a faceless, usually downturned head; thin arms that either disappear under the breasts or cross over them; an abnormally thin upper torso; voluminous, pendulous breasts; large fatty buttocks and/or thighs; a prominent, presumably pregnant abdomen, sometimes with a large elliptical navel coinciding with the greatest physical width of the

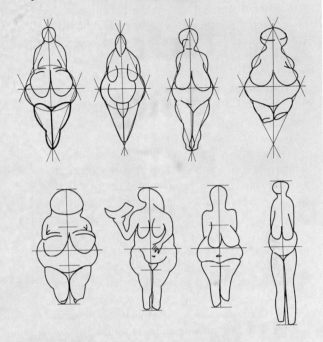

The PKG "lozenge composition." PKG images routinely elevate both the vertical midpoint and greatest width of the female body, and most make what should be one-half of the body closer to one-third. (Figures redrawn and simplified based on information in Leroi-Gourhan 1968.)

figure; and often oddly bent, unnaturally short legs that taper to a rounded point or disproportionately small feet. These deviations produce what M. D. Gvozdover (1989, 79) has called "the stylistic deformation of the natural body." Yet these apparent distortions of the anatomy become apt renderings if we consider the body as seen by a woman looking down on herself. Comparison of the figurines with photographs simulating what a modern woman sees of herself from this perspective reveals striking correspondences. It is possible that since these images were discovered, we have simply been looking at them from the wrong angle of view.

Although it is the center of visual self-awareness, a woman's face and head are not visible to her without a reflecting surface. This may explain why—although there are variations in shape, size, and position in the heads of these pieces—virtually all are rendered without facial features

(continued on next page)

In Their Own Words (continued)

Women's Art in the Upper Paleolithic?

and most seem to be turned down, as is necessary to bring the body into view. A woman looking down at herself sees a strongly foreshortened view of the upper frontal surface of the thorax and abdomen, with her breasts looming large. Such a perspective helps to explain the apparently voluminous size and distinctive pendulous elongation routinely observed in the breasts of the figurines. Viewed in this way, the breasts of the figurines possess the natural proportions of the average modern woman of childbearing age [see photographs]. Even pieces such as the one from Lespugue, in which the breasts seem unnaturally large, appear naturalistic when viewed from above.

Other apparent distortions of the upper body undergo similar optical transformations from this perspective. For example, the inability to experience the true thickness of the upper body may account for the apparently abnormal thinness seen in the torsos of many figurines. Several figurines also have what seem to be unnaturally large, elliptical navels located too close to the pubic triangle. In a foreshortened view, however, the circular navel forms just such an ellipse, and when pregnant, a woman cannot easily see the space below the navel. Thus, when viewed as women survey themselves, the apparent anatomical distortions of the upper body in these figurines vanish [see photographs].

Similarly, as a woman looks down at the lower portion of her body, those parts farthest away from the eyes look smallest. A correct representation of the foreshortened lower body would narrow toward the feet, thus explaining the small size of the feet in these figurines. It is also true that, for a pregnant woman, inspection of the upper body terminates at the navel with the curving silhouette of the distended abdomen [see photo on left]. Without bending forward, she cannot see her lower body. Thus for a gravid female, the visual experience of her body involves two separate views whose shared boundary is the abdomen at the level of the navel, which is also the widest part of the body in the visual field. The apparent misrepresentation of height and width in the figurines results from the visual experience of this anatomical necessity. The location of the eyes means that for an expectant mother the upper half of the body visually expands toward the abdomen, whereas the lower half presents a narrow, tapering form. Efforts to represent the information contained in these two views naturally resulted in the lozenge compositional formulation, which others have seen as anatomically "incorrect" proportions [see figures].

The idea that women sought to gain and preserve knowledge about their own bodies provides a direct and parsimonious interpretation for general as well as idiosyncratic features found among female representations from the middle European Upper Paleolithic. The needs of health and hygiene, not to mention coitus and childbirth, ensure that feminine self-inspection actually occurred during the early Upper Paleolithic. Puberty, menses, copulation, conception, pregnancy, childbirth, and lactation are regular events in the female cycle and involve perceptible alterations in bodily function and configuration (Marshack 1972). Mastery and control of these processes continues

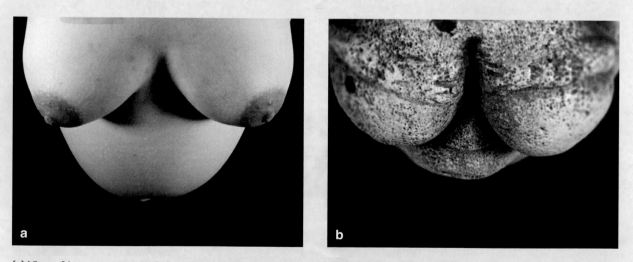

(a) View of her own upper body by a 26-year-old female who is five months pregnant and of average weight. (b) View of the upper body of the Willendorf figurine from same perspective used at left.

In Their Own Words

Women's Art in the Upper Paleolithic?

to be of fundamental importance to women today. It is possible that the emergence and subsequent propagation of these images across Europe occurred precisely because they played a didactic function with actual adaptive consequences for women. . . .

. . . These Upper Paleolithic figurines were probably made at a time when there was similarly significant population increase along with cultural and economic restructuring. The early to middle Upper Paleolithic was characterized by productive changes that harnessed energy and by reproductive changes that helped make possible the population expansion and technological changes that followed in the later European Upper Paleolithic. Could women have made a recognizable contribution to the fluorescence of art and technology seen in the opening millennia of this era? Anything they did to improve

their understanding of reproduction and thereby reduce infant and maternal mortality would clearly have contributed to this productive and reproductive change. Perhaps the figurines served as obstetrical aids, the relative sizes of the abdomens helping women to calculate the progress of their pregnancies. . . .

Theoretically, if these figurines were used to improve reproductive success, keep more women alive and healthy, and produce healthier children, then natural selection would have been acting directly on the women who made and/or used them. If these Upper Paleolithic figures are naturalistic, accurate self-representations made by women, then it is reasonable to speculate that they might have had such direct, pragmatic purposes.

Source: McCoid and McDermott 1996.

Consequently, plant foods probably formed a larger part of the diet than meat. Reliance on plant foods was probably greater among those living in warmer areas of Africa and southwestern Asia, whereas those living in the cooler climates of eastern Europe and northern Asia may have relied more on animals for food.

The richness and sophistication of Upper Paleolithic culture is documented in many other ways. Upper Paleolithic burials are more elaborate than Mousterian/MSA burials, and some of them contain several bodies (Klein 2009, 690–91). Some Upper Paleolithic sites have yielded human bones that have been shaped, perforated, or burned or that show cut marks suggesting defleshing. Again, some paleoanthropologists conclude that Upper Paleolithic peoples may have been cannibals. However, the shaped or perforated bones may have been trophies or mementos of individuals who had died for other reasons; the burned bones may be the remains of deliberate cremation or accidental charring under a hearth; and the flesh may have been removed from human bones after death for ritual purposes, a practice documented in modern ethnographic literature.

The most striking evidence for a modern human capacity for culture comes from Upper Paleolithic/LSA art. In Africa, ostrich-eggshell beads date to 38,000 years ago, while animal paintings on rocks date to at least 19,000 and possibly 27,500 years ago. Fire-hardened clay objects shaped like animals or human beings, dating to about 28,000–27,000 years ago, were recovered

at a Gravettian site in the former Czechoslovakia. This and other Gravettian sites in western and central Europe have yielded human figurines, some of which depict females with exaggerated breasts and bellies, thought to have been made between 27,000 and 20,000 years ago (see Figure 5.27). Over 200 caves in southern France and northern Spain, including Lascaux and Altamira, contain spectacular wall paintings or engravings (Figure 5.28); other painted caves exist in Italy, Portugal, and the former Yugoslavia; spectacular wall art from rock shelters in northern Australia may be especially old (Renfrew

Figure 5.28 Upper Paleolithic cave paintings, like this one from Lascaux, France, have been dated to between 15,000 and 11,000 years ago.

and Bahn 2004, 523). The European paintings portray a number of animal species now extinct and were probably painted between 15,000 and 11,000 years ago, during Magdalenian times. Recently, new techniques have permitted archaeologists to analyze the recipes of pigments used to make these wall images, while accelerator mass spectrometry can be used to date the charcoal used to make other drawings (Conkey 1993). As a result, archaeologists are increasingly able to determine when images were painted and whether all the images in a particular cave were painted at the same time.

Spread of Modern *H. Sapiens* in Late Pleistocene Times

Upper Paleolithic peoples were more numerous and more widespread than previous hominins. In Europe, according to Richard Klein, Upper Paleolithic sites are more numerous and have richer material remains than do Mousterian sites. Skeletons dating from this period show few injuries and little evidence of disease or violence, and they possess relatively healthy teeth. The presence of skeletons belonging to older or incapacitated individuals at Upper Paleolithic sites suggests that these people, like the Neandertals, cared for the old and sick. Analysis indicates that the life expectancy of Upper Paleolithic people was greater than that of the Neandertals and little different from that of contemporary foragers (Klein 2009, 695ff.).

Archaeologists have found amber, seashells, and even flint in Upper Paleolithic/LSA sites located tens to hundreds of kilometers away from the regions where these items occur naturally. They must have been deliberately transported to these sites, suggesting that Upper Paleolithic peoples, like contemporary foragers, participated in trading networks. However, no evidence of such social contacts exists for earlier times. Perhaps the linguistic and cultural capacities of fully modern humans were necessary before they could develop.

Eastern Asia and Siberia

Physically and culturally modern human beings were the first hominins to occupy the coldest, harshest climates in Asia. Upper Paleolithic blade industries developed in central Asia about 40,000–30,000 years ago (B. Fagan 1990, 195). The oldest reliable dates for human occupation in Siberia are between 35,000 and 20,000 years ago (Klein 2009, 673). Alaskan and Canadian sites with

Upper Paleolithic artifacts similar to those of northeast Siberia date to between 15,000 and 12,000 years ago. Artifacts from one of these sites, Bluefish Caves, may even be 20,000 years old. Between 25,000 and 14,000 years ago, land passage south would have been blocked by continuous ice. By 14,000 years ago, conditions for southward migration would have improved considerably.

The Americas

Genetic studies strongly support an Asian origin for Native American populations (Klein 2009, 707; Stringer and Andrews 2005, 198). The earliest known skeletal remains found in the Americas are between 11,000 and 8,000 years old, and their morphological variation suggests that the Americas may have been colonized more than once (Klein 2009, 707; Stringer and Andrews 2005, 198–99). The strongest archaeological evidence of human presence in the Americas comes after 14,000 years ago. The first anatomically modern human beings in North America, called "Paleoindians," apparently were successful hunting peoples. The oldest reliable evidence of their presence comes from sites dated between 11,500 and 11,000 years ago, which contain stone tools called Clovis points (Figure 5.29). Meadowcroft Rockshelter in Pennsylvania may represent an early Clovis site (Stringer and Andrews 2005, 197; Adovasio et al. 1978). Clovis points were finely made and probably attached to shafts to make spears. Rapidly following the Clovis culture were a series of different stone-tool cultures, all of which were confined to North America. Some experts believe that Paleoindian hunting coupled with postglacial climatic changes may have brought about the extinction of mammoth, camel, horse, and other big game species in North America; but evidence is inconclusive.

In 1997, the "Clovis barrier" of 11,200 years was finally broken when a group of archaeologists and other scientists formally announced that the South American site of Monte Verde, in Chile, was 12,500 years old (Dillehay 2000, Suplee 1997). Because it was covered by a peat bog shortly after it was inhabited, Monte Verde contained many well-preserved organic remains, including stakes lashed with knotted twine, dwellings with wooden frames, and hundreds of tools made of wood and bone. Thomas Dillehay (2000) argues that evidence from Monte Verde shows that the people who lived there were not big game hunters but, rather, generalized gatherers and hunters. A lower level at the same site, dated to 33,000 years ago, is said to contain crude stone tools. If the 33,000-year-old Monte Verde artifacts are genuine, they remain puzzling. First, these artifacts are few and extremely crude. Second, the dearth of sites in the

Figure 5.29 Stone tools made by Paleoindian peoples have been found at sites that provide the oldest reliable dates for human occupation in North America. The Clovis points pictured here were probably hafted to shafts to make spears.

Australasia

Anatomically modern human beings first arrived in Australia between 60,000 and 40,000 years ago, at a time when lower sea levels had transformed the Malayan Archipelago into a land mass called Sunda and when Australia was linked to New Guinea in a second land mass called Sahul. Nevertheless, the migrants would still have had to cross 30–90 kilometers of open water. Presumably, they used water craft, but finding the remains of boats or the sites where they landed along the now sunken continental shelf is unlikely. Modern people spread throughout the Australian interior by 25,000–20,000 years ago. They may have been connected to widespread extinctions of grass-eating marsupials in Australia between 40,000 and 15,000 years ago (Klein 2009, 714ff.).

Two Million Years of Human Evolution

By 12,000 years ago, modern human beings had spread to every continent except Antarctica, a fact that we take for granted today but which could not have been predicted 2 mya in Africa, when the first members of the genus *Homo* walked the earth. In fact, the more we learn about hominins and their primate ancestors, the more zigs and zags we perceive in our own past. Our species' origin must be regarded as "an unrepeatable particular, not an expected consequence" (Gould 1996, 4). Some paleoecologists have concluded that "human features may not be adaptations to some past environment, but exaptations . . . accidental byproducts of history, functionally disconnected from their origins" (R. Foley 1995, 47). For example, Rick Potts argues that, rather than "survival of the fittest" (i.e., of a species narrowly adapted to a specific environment), modern *H. sapiens* better illustrates "survival of the generalist" (i.e., of a species that had the plasticity, the "weedlike resilience," to survive the extremes of the rapidly fluctuating climate of the Ice Ages). In other words, our ancestors' biological capacity to cope with small environmental fluctuations was exapted to cope with larger and larger fluctuations. In Potts's view, selection for genes favoring open programs of behavior "improve an organism's versatility and response to novel conditions" (1996, 239).

Archaeologist Clive Gamble believes that the human social and cognitive skills that allowed our ancestors to survive in novel habitats were exapted by *H. sapiens* to colonize the world: "We were not adapted for filling up the world. It was instead a consequence of changes in behavior, and exaptive radiation produced by the cooption

Americas of such great age suggests that, if human beings were in the Americas 30,000 years ago, they were very thinly scattered compared to populations in Eurasia and Africa at the same period. Finally, blood group and tooth shape evidence supports the idea that the ancestors of indigenous peoples of the Americas migrated into North America from Asia. If the makers of 33,000-year-old Monte Verde artifacts also came from Asia, archaeologists must explain how these people could have reached South America from Siberia by that date. Possibly, they traveled over water and ice, but how they got to South America remains a mystery.

In 2011, evidence for pre-Clovis occupations in North America was found at the Debra L. Friedkin site near Austin, Texas: over 15,000 artifacts assigned to the Buttermilk Creek Complex, dating between 13,200 and 15,000 years ago, were discovered in soil beneath a Clovis assemblage (Waters et al. 2011). The archaeologists who discovered the tools view them as potentially representing the technology from which Clovis was developed; other archaeologists remain unconvinced. As was the case with the Monte Verde finds, it is likely that additional work, including additional finds, will be required in order to persuade the skeptics.

of existing elements in a new framework of action" (1994, 182). Gamble is sensitive to the way humanly constructed niches modified the selection pressures our ancestors faced: he argues that all the environments of Australia could never have been colonized so rapidly without far-flung social networks that enabled colonizers to depend on one another in time of need. He sees the colonization of the Pacific as a deliberate undertaking, showing planning and care (1994, 241; see also Dillehay 2000).

The role of niche construction is also implicated in the approach of Richard Klein, who lists a series of "related outcomes of the innovative burst behind the out of Africa expansion" that are detectable in the archaeological record after 50,000 years ago, ranging from standardization and elaboration of artifacts to evidence for increasing elaboration of a built environment (with campsites, hearths, dwellings, and graves) to evidence of elaborate trading networks, ritual activity, and successful colonization of challenging cold climates (Klein 2009, 742).

Paleoanthropologists and archaeologists have assembled many of the pieces of the human evolutionary puzzle, but many questions remain. Experts differ, for example, on how to reconstruct the human family tree. Figure 5.30 shows one recent attempt to summarize what is known (and what remains to be established) about the evolution of human beings. Because new data and interpretations appear in the news almost daily, you may want to find out how much this summary has been modified by the time you read this book! Another knotty problem concerns how we interpret mounting evidence that human biology and human culture evolved at different rates. Finally, within a few thousand years after the glaciers retreated, human groups in Asia and the Americas were settling in villages and domesticating plants and animals. Why they should have done so at this particular time is addressed in the next chapter.

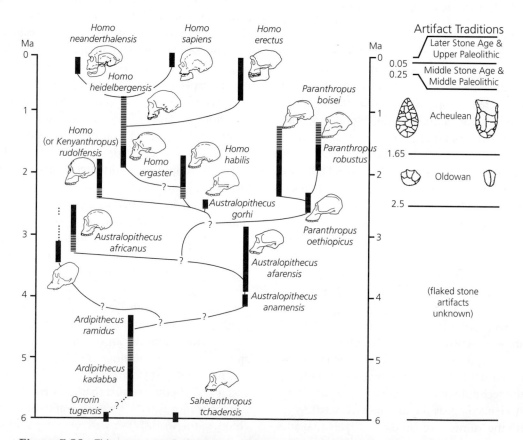

Figure 5.30 This summary of what is currently known about hominin evolution is open to modification by new data and new interpretation. (From Klein 2009, 244)

Chapter Summary

1. Bipedal hominoids that appeared in Africa at the end of the Miocene are known as hominins and are placed in the same lineage as living human beings. Bipedalism may have been favored by natural selection in hominoids exploiting food resources on the ground, outside the protection of forests. Their diet was probably omnivorous, and they could carry infants, food, and tools in their newly freed hands. The earliest hominin skeletal fossils are 6–7 million years old. The best-known early hominin fossils are 2–3 million years younger and have been placed in the genus *Australopithecus*. The earliest direct evidence of hominin bipedalism is a 3.6 million-year-old trail of fossilized footprints found in Laetoli, Tanzania.

2. Hominin adaptations apparently led to changes in dentition. The teeth of australopiths show an evolutionary trend toward smaller front teeth and enormous cheek teeth. This dental pattern is interpreted as an adaptation to diets of coarse vegetable foods that required grinding. Fossils of hominins between 3 and 2 million years old with this dental pattern have been found at southern and eastern African sites and have been classified in two groups: the gracile australopiths and the robust australopiths. Robust australopiths had more rugged jaws, flatter faces, and larger molars than the gracile forms. Apart from differences in dentition, the gracile and robust australopiths had similar postcranial skeletons and chimpanzee-sized cranial capacities.

3. The first members of the genus *Homo* appeared about 2.5 mya. Many paleontologists believe that more than one species belonging to *Homo* may have coexisted in eastern Africa in the early Pleistocene alongside the eastern African robust australopiths.

4. Fossils of early *Homo* disappear about 1.8 mya, either by evolving into or being replaced by *Homo ergaster*, the first member of the genus *Homo* to spread out of Africa, giving rise to *Homo erectus* populations in Asia. The cranium of *H. erectus* averages around 1,000 cm³, within the lower range of modern human beings. *H. erectus* may have been, to some extent, capable of speech. Wear patterns on teeth suggest that *H. erectus* had a diet different from that of previous hominins. The postcranial skeleton of *H. erectus* is more robust than that of modern humans and shows a marked reduction in sexual dimorphism. *H. erectus* was probably not primarily a hunter of big game, nor is there any evidence that *H. erectus* might have practiced cannibalism.

5. The oldest undisputed stone tools, classified in the Oldowan tradition, were found in Ethiopia, date to at least 2.5 mya, and may have been made by early *Homo*. Acheulean bifaces are associated with *H. erectus*. In recent years, however, archaeologists have concluded that it is misleading to associate individual stone-tool traditions with only one hominin species. Some archaeologists have suggested that bamboo was available for toolmaking in those areas in Asia where Acheulean bifaces are lacking. Oldowan and Acheulean traditions are usually grouped together in a single period known as the Lower Paleolithic in Europe and the Early Stone Age in Africa.

6. Between 500,000 and 200,000 years ago, *H. erectus* fossils disappear from the fossil record to be replaced by fossils that show a mosaic of features found in *H. erectus* and *H. sapiens*. Many paleoanthropologists classify these fossils as *Homo heidelbergensis*. A lively debate continues between punctuationists and gradualists about the fate of *H. erectus* and the origin of *H. sapiens*. Punctuationists and cladists favor the replacement model; gradualists favor the regional continuity model.

7. Neanderthals in Europe flourished between 130,000 and 35,000 years ago. They were shorter and more robust than anatomically modern *H. sapiens*. Their molars showed taurodontism, their jaws possessed retromolar spaces, and they may have habitually used their incisors as a clamp. Their average cranial capacity was larger than that of modern human populations, although their skull was shaped differently. Neanderthal fossils are typically associated in Europe with the Mousterian stone-tool tradition. Similar tools, found in southwestern Asia and Africa, have all been assigned to the Middle Paleolithic/Middle Stone Age, which probably began at least 200,000 years ago.

8. During the 1980s, new evidence revealed that anatomically modern *H. sapiens* appeared in Africa at the same time that Neanderthal populations were living in Europe and western Asia. Neandertals and

(continued on next page)

Chapter Summary (continued)

moderns apparently lived side by side in southwestern Asia for at least 45,000 years, and both populations used the same kinds of Mousterian tools. Whether or not Neandertals and moderns interbred continues to be disputed, although ancient DNA studies are providing some clues.

9. By 40,000 years ago in southwestern Asia and 35,000 years ago in Europe, Mousterian/Middle Stone Age tools are replaced by far more elaborate artifacts that signal the beginning of the Upper Paleolithic/Late Stone Age. Upper Paleolithic people made many different stone tools as well as tools and ornaments out of bone, ivory, and antler; composite tools, such as spears and arrows; and clothing from animal fur. They regularly hunted large game and used bones from animals such as mammoths to construct dwellings and to burn as fuel. Upper Paleolithic burials were far more elaborate than Middle Paleolithic burials. Cave paintings and personal ornaments offer the most striking evidence in the Upper Paleolithic for the modern human capacity for culture.

10. Some Upper Paleolithic assemblages, like the Châtelperronian industry from France, contain a mixture of typical Mousterian tools and more elaborate cutting tools, bone tools, and pierced animal teeth. Paleoanthropologists disagree about what these mixed assemblages represent. Some interpret the Châtelperronian industry as evidence that Neandertals gradually invented Upper Paleolithic tools on their own, which would support the regional continuity model. Others argue that Châtelperronian Neandertals borrowed Upper Paleolithic techniques from in-migrating modern people who already possessed an Upper Paleolithic technology called the Aurignacian. This view is compatible with the replacement model. If Aurignacian moderns did replace Neandertals in Europe, there is no evidence that this was the result of conquest or extermination.

11. Upper Paleolithic peoples show few signs of injury or disease, and their life expectancy was longer than that of Neandertals. Upper Paleolithic peoples apparently constructed niches that allowed them to participate in widespread trading networks. Anatomically modern people with Upper Paleolithic cultures were the first humans to migrate into the northernmost regions of Asia and into the New World, arriving at least 12,000 years ago, possibly earlier. It seems likely that the New World was populated by more than one wave of immigrants from Siberia. Anatomically modern people first arrived in Australia between 60,000 and 40,000 years ago, probably by boat.

For Review

1. Define bipedalism and explain its importance in human evolution.

2. What is distinctive about the evolution of dentition in hominins?

3. Explain the differences between robust and gracile australopiths.

4. Summarize the different arguments for explaining the evolutionary transition from early hominins to the genus *Homo*.

5. List what paleoanthropologists and archaeologists know about early *Homo* species.

6. Define taphonomy and explain why it is important for paleoanthropologists who study bones and stone tools.

7. Summarize what is known about *Homo erectus*, morphologically and culturally.

8. Describe the argument that emphasizes the importance of endurance running in human evolution.

9. What is the fossil evidence for the evolutionary transition to modern *Homo sapiens*?

10. Explain how the origins of *Homo sapiens* would be accounted for by proponents of evolution by punctuated equilibria.

11. Make a chart of the different *Homo* species currently identified, including the periods in which they lived, where they were found, and other distinctive anatomical features they display, such as brain size.

12. What is the "mostly out of Africa" model of the origin of modern *Homo sapiens*? What evidence do biological anthropologists use to defend this model? How does this model contrast with the earlier "replacement" model and the "regional continuity" model?

13. Summarize what biological anthropologists know about the Neandertals.

14. Summarize the features biological anthropologists emphasis in distinguishing anatomically modern humans from other archaic populations of *Homo*.

15. What happened to the Neandertals?

16. How do archaeology and biological anthropology contribute to our understanding of the evolution of a modern human capacity for culture?

17. Summarize anthropological evidence used to support current arguments concerning the peopling of the Americas.

Key Terms

Acheulean tradition   127
anatomically modern human beings   136
archaic *Homo sapiens*   129
bipedalism   112
blades   139
composite tools   140
cranial capacity   119

Early Stone Age (ESA)   127
Homo erectus   124
Homo habilis   122
intrusions   135
Middle Stone Age (MSA)   133

mosaic evolution   112
Mousterian tradition   133
Neandertals   131
Oldowan tradition   123
omnivorous   113
regional continuity model   131

replacement model   131
taphonomy   123
Upper Paleolithic/Late Stone Age (LSA)   139

Suggested Readings

Dahlberg, Frances, ed. 1981. *Woman the gatherer*. New Haven: Yale University Press. *A classic collection of essays challenging the "man the hunter" scenario using bioanthropological data and ethnographic evidence from four different foraging societies.*

Gamble, Clive. 1994. *Timewalkers*. Cambridge, MA: Harvard University Press. *Gamble argues that our species' ability to colonize the world was the result of exaptation of attributes we evolved for other purposes. Usefully read in conjunction with the Potts volume below.*

Lee, Richard, and Irven DeVore, eds. 1968. *Man the hunter*. New York: Aldine. *The classic collection of articles that undergirded the "man the hunter" scenario of human origins— and paradoxically offered evidence for its critique.*

Lewin, Roger. 1999. *Human evolution: An illustrated introduction*, 5th ed. Boston: Blackwell. *A highly readable introduction to human evolution. Lewin, a science journalist, has worked closely with Richard Leakey and cowritten three books about human origins with him.*

Morell, Virginia. 1996. *Ancestral passions: The Leakey family and the quest for humankind's beginnings*. New York: Simon & Schuster. *A biography of the Leakey family over several generations that brilliantly contextualizes their contributions to paleoanthropology.*

Potts, Rick. 1996. *Humanity's descent*. New York: William Morrow. *A survey of human evolution, in which evidence is presented that the great flexibility of modern* Homo sapiens *resulted from selection for the ability to survive wide fluctuations in environments, rather than adaptation to any single environment. Usefully read in conjunction with the Gamble volume above.*

Shreeve, James. 1995. *The Neandertal enigma*. New York: Avon Books. *A science journalist's account of the controversy between replacement and regional continuity theorists, all of whom we meet in this engaging volume.*

Tattersall, Ian. 2009. *The fossil trail*. New York and Oxford: Oxford University Press. *An up-to-date history of the discovery of human fossils, together with changing interpretations of their significance.*

Wolpoff, Milford, and Rachel Caspari. 1996. *Race and human evolution: A fatal attraction*. New York: Simon & Schuster. *A detailed defense of the regional continuity model by two of its most committed exponents.*

Wrangham, Richard. 2009. *Catching fire: How cooking made us human*. New York: Basic Books. *Wrangham, a biological anthropologist, makes a provocative case for the key role played by cooked food in the evolutionary success of humans.*

How Do We Know about the Human Past?

6

In this chapter, you will learn about how archaeologists reveal the remains of past human societies and interpret what they find. We will look at the increasingly important question of who owns the past. We will consider the terrible destruction that is being visited on the past through looting and the destruction of sites. We will conclude by examining some newer approaches to archaeological research.

Chapter Outline

◄ Hands painted on the wall of Hands Cave, Argentina. The painting was done more than 10,000 years ago.

Anthropologists who study the human past are of two different kinds. As we have seen, paleoanthropologists study the hominin fossil record, from its earliest beginnings through the appearance of our own species. Although archaeologists also sometimes study human skeletal remains, **archaeology** focuses primarily on the **archaeological record**—material evidence of human modification of the physical environment. Beginning with humble stone tools, the archaeological record encompasses many classes of artifacts (pottery, metalwork, textiles, and other technological developments) and nonportable material culture (architecture, irrigation canals, and ancient farm fields). This is why archaeology is sometimes called "the past tense of cultural anthropology" (Renfrew and Bahn 2008, 12). Archaeology makes many contributions to anthropology. Although it may not supply the kind of ethnographic details that are revealed by research among living groups, it does provide great time depth and reveals evidence of past forms of human culture that can no longer be seen today.

Archaeology

Archaeologists study the material remains left by our ancestors in order to interpret cultural variation and cultural change in the human past. What kinds of analytical tools do archaeologists use? Renfrew and Bahn (2008, 17) suggest that four kinds of objectives have guided archaeology at different times over its history. First came traditional approaches that focused on *reconstructing the material remains* of the past by putting together pots, reassembling statues, restoring houses. Later came the goal of *reconstructing the lifeways*—the culture—of the people who left those material remains. Since the 1960s, however, a third objective has been *explaining the cultural processes* that led to ways of life and material cultures of particular kinds. This has been the focus of what came to be known as *processual archaeology*.

Processual archaeologists "sought to make archaeology an objective, empirical science in which hypotheses about all forms of cultural variation could be tested" (Wenke 1999, 33). They integrated mathematics into their work, using statistics to analyze the distribution of artifacts at a site, the transformations of artifact usage over time, or the dimensions of trade networks. Their interest in human adaptations to various environments in the course of cultural evolution led to an interest in the field of cultural ecology, in which cultural processes must be understood in the context of climate change, the variability of economic productivity in different environments, demographic factors, and technological change. As a general rule, processual archaeologists downplayed explanations in which people play an active role as agents who are conscious to a greater or lesser degree of what is happening around them and whose activities contribute to cultural maintenance or change.

In recent years, however, archaeologists have begun to ask different questions—leading to a fourth kind of objective. Many have concluded that processual archaeology neglected human agency and the power of ideas and values in the construction of ancient cultures. A variety of new approaches, which are sometimes called *postprocessual* or *interpretive archaeology*, stress the symbolic and cognitive aspects of social structures and social relations. Some postprocessual archaeologists focus on power and domination in their explanations of certain aspects of the archaeological record; they draw attention to the ways that archaeological evidence may reflect individual human agency and internal contradictions within a society. Other postprocessual archaeologists point out that similar-looking features can mean different things to different people at different sites, which is why it can be seriously misleading to assume that all cultural variation can be explained in terms of universal processes like population growth or ecological adaptation. (We will look at varieties of postprocessual archaeology at the end of this chapter.) At the same time, increasingly precise archaeological methods and subtle archeological theorizing are worthless if there is nothing left to study. By the twenty-first century, the looting and destruction of archaeological sites had reached crisis proportions. Archaeologists have come to recognize that stewardship of the remains of the human past may be their most pressing responsibility (Fagan and DeCorse 2005, 25).

Archaeologists identify the precise geographical locations of the remains of past human activity from local **sites** of human habitation to the wider regions in which these sites were once embedded. Archaeologists pay attention not only to portable **artifacts** of human manufacture but also to nonportable remnants of material culture, such as house walls or ditches, which are called **features**. They note the presence of other remains,

---

archaeology A cultural anthropology of the human past focusing on material evidence of human modification of the physical environment.

archaeological record All material objects constructed by humans or near-humans revealed by archaeology.

site A precise geographical location of the remains of past human activity.

artifacts Objects that have been deliberately and intelligently shaped by human or near-human activity.

features Nonportable remnants from the past, such as house walls or ditches.

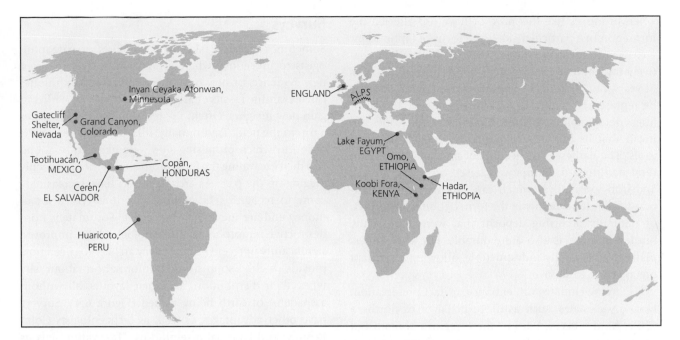

Figure 6.1   Major locations discussed in Chapter 6.

such as plant residues or animal bones connected with food provisioning, which are not themselves artifacts but appear to be the by-products of human activity (these are sometimes called *ecofacts*). When archaeologists study sites through survey or excavation, they carefully record the immediate *matrix* (e.g., gravel, sand, or clay) in which the object is found and its *provenance* (sometimes spelled *provenience*), which is the precise three-dimensional position of the find within the matrix. They also record exactly where each kind of remain is found along with any other remains found near it and any evidence that the site may have been disturbed by natural or human intervention. Sometimes they do small-scale excavation, using a shovel to dig small pits over a large area. This strong emphasis on the *context* in which artifacts are found makes scientific archaeology a holistic undertaking. Archaeological sites are important scientifically if they contain evidence that answers key questions about human migration or settlement in certain places at particular times, even when the sites themselves yield none of the elaborate artifacts valued by museums and private collectors.

Archeologists must know what to look for to identify sites and the remains that can serve as evidence. They have to think about the kinds of human behavior past populations are likely to have engaged in and what telltale evidence for that behavior might have been left behind. Sometimes the artifacts themselves tell the story: a collection of blank flint pieces, partly worked flint tools, and a heap of flakes suggest that a site was used for flint-tool manufacture. Other times,

when archaeologists are unclear about the significance of remains, they use a method called **ethnoarchaeology**, which is the study of the way present-day societies use artifacts and structures and how these objects become part of the archaeological record. Archaeologists studying how contemporary foraging people build traditional shelters—what kinds of materials are employed and how they are used in construction—can predict which materials would be most likely to survive in a buried site and the patterns they would reveal if they were excavated. If such patterns turn up in sites used by prehistoric foragers, archaeologists will already have important clues to their interpretation.

However, archaeologists must not overlook the possibility that a variety of natural and human forces may have interfered with remains once they are left behind at a site. An important source of information about past human diets may be obtained from animal bones found in association with other human artifacts; but just because hyena bones, stone tools, and human bones are found together does not in itself mean that the humans ate hyenas. Careful study of the site may show that all these remains came together accidentally after having been washed out of their original resting places by flash flooding. As we saw in the last chapter, being able to tell

---

ethnoarchaeology The study of the way present-day societies use artifacts and structures and how these objects become part of the archaeological record.

when processes like this have or have not affected the formation of a particular site is the focus of taphonomy.

Even in ideal situations, where a site has lain relatively undisturbed for hundreds, thousands, or millions of years, not all kinds of important human activity may be represented by preserved remains. Wood and plant fibers decay rapidly, and their absence at a site does not mean that its human occupants did not use wooden tools. The earliest classification of ancient human cultural traditions in Europe was based on stone, bronze, and iron tools, all of which can survive for long periods. Baked clay, whether in the form of pottery, figurines, or naturally occurring deposits that were accidentally burned in a fire, is also quite durable. Fire also renders plant seeds virtually indestructible, allowing important dietary clues to survive.

Extreme climates can enhance artifact preservation. Hot, dry climates, such as those in Egypt or northern Chile, hinder decay. Sites in these regions contain not only preserved human bodies but also other organic remains such as plant seeds, baskets, cordage, textiles, and artifacts made of wood, leather, and feathers. Cold climates provide natural refrigeration, which also hinders decay. Burial sites in northern or high-mountain regions with extremely low winter temperatures may never thaw out once they have been sealed, preserving even better than dry climates the flesh of humans and animals, plant remains, and artifacts made of leather and wood. This is well illustrated by the spectacular 1991 discovery of the so-called Ice Man, who had frozen to death in an Alpine glacier 5,300–5,200 years ago (Figure 6.2). Eyes, brain, and intestines were preserved in his dried-up body, together with his clothing, the wooden handles of his flint knife and copper ax head, an unstrung bow, two arrows, and a dozen extra shafts (Sjovold 1993).

Occasionally, archaeological sites are well preserved as a result of natural disasters, such as volcanic eruptions (Figure 6.3). Similarly, mudslides may cover sites and protect their contents from erosion, whereas waterlogged sites free of oxygen can preserve a range of organic materials that would otherwise decay. Peat bogs are exemplary airless, waterlogged sites that have yielded many plant and animal remains, including artifacts made of wood, leather, and basketry as well as the occasional human body. Log pilings recovered from Swiss lakes have been useful both for reconstructing ancient sunken dwellings and for establishing tree-ring sequences in European dendrochronology.

survey The physical examination of a geographical region in which promising sites are most likely to be found.

Surveys

Sometimes research takes archaeologists or paleontologists to museums, where scholars with new theories, new evidence, or new or more sophisticated techniques can reexamine fossils or artifacts collected years earlier to gain new insights. Often, the research problem requires a trip to the field. Traditionally, this meant surveying the region in which promising sites were likely to be found and then excavating the most promising of them—literally digging up the past. As archaeologists have increasingly come to recognize, however, excavations cost a lot of money and are inevitably destructive. Fortunately, nondestructive remote-sensing technologies have improved significantly in recent years. **Survey** archaeology can now provide highly sophisticated information about site types, their distribution, and their layouts, all without a spadeful of earth being turned (Figure 6.4). Surveys have other advantages as well, as archaeologists Colin Renfrew and Paul Bahn remind us: "Excavation tells us a lot about a little of a site, and can only be done once, whereas survey tells us a little about a lot of sites, and can be repeated" (2008, 79). As the kinds of questions archaeologists ask have changed, larger regions—entire landscapes, contrasting ecological zones, trading zones, and the like—are increasingly of interest. And for this kind of research, surveys are crucial.

Surveys can be as simple as walking slowly over a field with eyes trained on the ground. They are as important to paleontologists as to archaeologists. For example, paleontologist Donald Johanson and his colleagues discovered the bones of "Lucy" when they resurveyed a locality in the Hadar region of Ethiopia that had yielded nothing on previous visits (see Chapter 5). Between the previous visit and that one, the rainy season had come and gone, washing away soil and exposing Lucy's bones. Had Johanson or his colleagues not noticed those bones at that time, another rainy season probably would have washed away Lucy's remains (Johanson and Edey 1981). Of course, Johanson and his team were not in Hadar accidentally; they had decided to look for sites in areas that seemed promising for good scientific reasons. Archaeologists ordinarily decide where to do their field surveys based on previous work, which can give them clues about where they will most likely find suitable sites. Local citizens in the region who may know of possible sites are also important sources of information.

Aerial surveys can be used for mapping purposes or to photograph large areas whose attributes may suggest the presence of otherwise invisible sites. For example, when contemporary crops are planted in fields that were once used for other purposes, seeds sown over features such as buried walls or embankments will show growth

Figure 6.2 One of the most spectacular archaeological discoveries in recent years was the so–called Ice Man. He froze to death in an Alpine glacier more than 5,000 years ago. His remains were exposed only in 1991 as the glacier melted.

Figure 6.3 Some archaeological sites are well preserved as a result of natural disasters. This adobe house in Cerén, El Salvador (*a*), was buried under several layers of lava following a series of volcanic eruptions. Sometimes organic remains leave impressions in the soil where they decayed. These remains of a corn crib and ears of corn from Cerén (*b*) are actually casts made by pouring dental plaster into a soil cavity.

patterns different from the plants around them, casting a shadow that is easily seen in aerial photographs (Figure 6.5). Black-and-white aerial photography is the oldest and cheapest form of aerial reconnaissance and provides the highest image resolution. Infrared photography and remote-sensing techniques using false-color, heat-sensitive, or radar imaging can sometimes produce better results. In 1983, for example, archaeologists used false-color Landsat imagery to discover a vast, previously unknown network of ancient Mayan fields and several other important sites in Yucatán, Mexico. Archaeologists continue to experiment with satellite imaging technology, which is developing at an extraordinary rate. However, the resolution of images from satellites is not yet as good as that of conventional aerial photography, and satellite images can be extremely expensive.

Thanks to modern technology, archaeologists can also learn a lot about what is beneath a site's surface without actually digging. Some machines can detect buried features and gravitational anomalies using echo sounding or by measuring the electrical resistivity of the soil. Magnetic methods can detect objects made of iron or baked clay, and metal detectors can locate buried metal artifacts. In recent years, ground-penetrating radar (GPR) has become more readily available for archaeological use. GPR reflects pulsed radar waves off features below the surface. Because the radar waves pass through different kinds of materials at different rates, the echoes

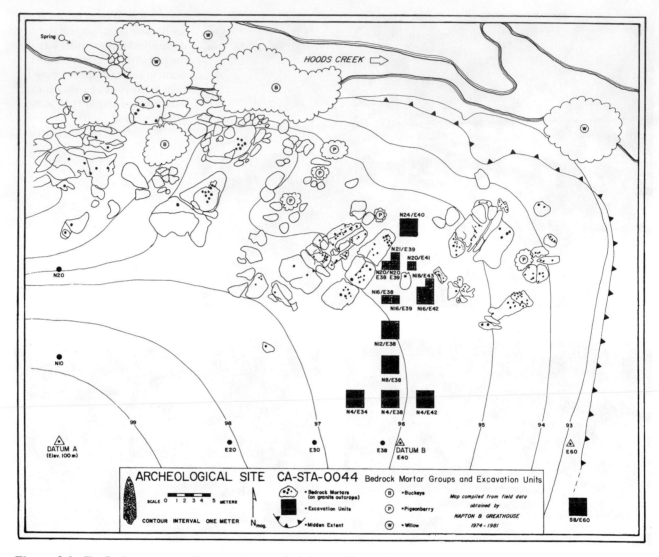

Figure 6.4 The final map representing an archaeological site usually combines several kinds of information. This map of a site in California includes cartographic data, data from aerial photography, and data photographed on the site itself.

that are picked up reflect back changes in the soil and sediment encountered as well as the depth at which those changes are found. Advances in data processing and computer power make it possible to produce large three-dimensional sets of GPR data that can be used effectively to produce three-dimensional maps of buried archaeological remains. GPR is very useful when the site to be studied is associated with people who forbid the excavation of human remains.

Geographic Information Systems (GIS) is also becoming increasingly important in archaeological research. A GIS is a "computer-aided system for the collection, storage, retrieval, analysis, and presentation of spatial data of all kinds" (Fagan and DeCorse 2005, 188). In essence, a GIS is a database with a map-based interface. Anything that can be given a location in

space—information about topography, soil, elevation, geology, climate, vegetation, water resources, site location, field boundaries, as well as aerial photos and satellite images—is entered into the database, and maps can be generated with the information the researcher wants. At the same time, statistical analysis can be done on the database, allowing archaeologists to generate new information and to study complex problems of site distribution and settlement patterns over a landscape. GIS is being used to construct predictive models, as well. That is, if certain kinds of settlement sites are found in similar places (close to water, sheltered, near specific food sources), then a GIS for an area can make it possible to predict the likelihood of finding a site at a particular location whose environmental characteristics are in the database. For archaeologists, the drawback to this kind of

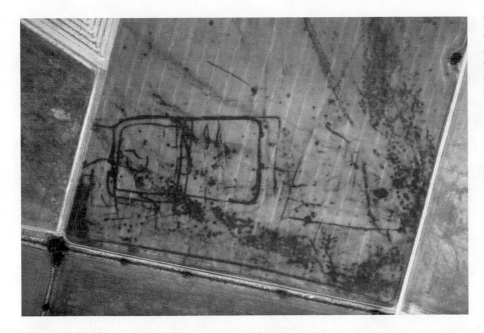

Figure 6.5 From the air, buried walls, ditches, and other features of a site may be more easily revealed than from the ground. Here, buried features became visible as the barley in this field grew.

predictive modeling is a tendency to place a very heavy weight on the environmental features as determining human settlement patterns. It is easy to measure, map, and digitize features of the natural environment. Social and cultural modifications or interpretations of the environment, however, are equally important but more difficult to handle using GIS methods.

Archaeological Excavation

When archaeologists or paleoanthropologists need to know "a lot about a little of a site," as Renfrew and Bahn put it, excavation is necessary. **Excavation** is the systematic uncovering of archaeological remains through removal of the deposits of soil and other material covering and accompanying them (Renfrew and Bahn 2008, 580). It is important to remember that excavation is a form of destruction and a site, once excavated, is gone forever. Archaeologists today will excavate only a small part of a site on the assumption that future archaeologists will have better techniques and different questions if they return to the same site. Some sites are shallow, with only one or a few levels. Other sites, especially deposits in caves that were used for centuries by successive human groups or urban sites going back thousands of years, are far more complex. In either case, however, excavators keep track of what they find by imposing on the site a three-dimensional grid system that allows them to record stratigraphic associations.

As Renfrew and Bahn point out, a multilayered site contains two kinds of information about human activities: contemporary activities that take place horizontally in space and changes in those activities that take place vertically over time (2008, 107). Artifacts and features associated with one another in an undisturbed context provide evidence for contemporary activities. As excavators uncover one stratum after another in sequence, they gradually reveal evidence for changes in human activities over time (Figure 6.6). The more levels of occupation at a site, the more likely it is that some of the levels will have been disturbed by subsequent humans, other animals, or natural forces. It then becomes the excavator's job to determine the degree of disturbance that has occurred and its effect on the site.

Only on shallow sites are archaeologists likely to expose an entire occupation level; this procedure is prohibitively expensive and destructive on large, multileveled sites. Archaeologists often use statistical sampling techniques to choose which portions of large, complex sites to excavate, aiming for a balance between major features and outlying areas (see Figure 6.4).

As the excavation proceeds, researchers record photographically and in writing all artifacts and features discovered and the stratigraphic layers exposed. Such record keeping is especially important for structures that will be destroyed as digging continues. Loose soil is sifted to recover tiny artifacts such as stone flakes or remains of plants or animals. Flotation methods allow archaeologists to separate light plant matter that will float, such as bits of wood, leaves, fibers, some seeds, stems, and charcoal,

excavation The systematic uncovering of archaeological remains through removal of the deposits of soil and other material covering them and accompanying them.

Figure 6.6 Graduate and undergraduate students work to excavate a series of stair-step units at the Paleoindian Hudson-Meng site (25SX115), Sioux County, Nebraska. All artifacts and features are recorded photographically and in writing, as are the stratigraphic layers that are exposed.

from heavier items that sink, such as rocks, sand, bones, pottery, and chipped stone. Everything is labeled and bagged for more detailed analysis in the laboratory.

Work on an archaeological dig ranges from the back-breaking shifting of dirt to the delicate brushing away of soil from a key fossil or artifact. Each dig brings special challenges. Archaeologist Robert Wenke describes his team's daily routine during the first 3 months of a 6-month field season as they searched for evidence for the emergence of agriculture after 7000 B.C.E.. at a site on the southern shore of the Fayum lake in Egypt:

> We began by making a topological map of the area we intended to work in. We then devised a sampling program and collected every artifact in the sampling units defined, that is, in the hundreds of 5 × 5 meter squares in our study area. The average temperature during much of this work was over 40°C (104°F), and by midday the stone tools were often so hot we would have to juggle them as we bagged them. Afternoons were spent sorting, drawing, and photographing artifacts, drinking warm water, and drawing each other's attention to the heat. (1999, 84)

Most of the labor of cleaning, classifying, and analyzing usually takes place in laboratories after the dig is over and frequently requires several years to complete. Researchers clean the artifacts well enough for close examination—but not so well that possible organic residues (grain kernels inside pots, traces of blood on cutting edges) are lost. They then classify the artifacts according to the materials out of which they are made, their shapes, and their surface decoration, if any, and arrange them in typologies, using ordering principles similar to those employed for fossil taxonomies. Once the artifacts are classified, researchers analyze records from the dig for patterns of distribution in space or time. It is important to underline that individual records of the excavation—notebooks, drawings, plots of artifact distributions, photographs, and computer data—are as much part of the results of the excavation as the materials excavated.

As you will recall, the artifacts and structures from a particular time and place in a site are called an *assemblage*. Cultural change at a particular site may be traced by comparing assemblages from lower levels with those found in more recent levels. When surveys or excavations at several sites turn up the same assemblages, archaeologists refer to them as an "archaeological culture." Such groupings can be very helpful in mapping cultural similarities and differences over wide areas during past ages.

The pitfall, however, which earlier generations of archaeologists did not always avoid, is to assume that archaeological cultures necessarily represent real social groups that once existed. Archaeologist Ian Hodder (1982) reminded us that archaeological cultures are the product of scientific analysis. Hodder's ethnoarchaeological research among several contemporary ethnic groups in eastern Africa showed that artifact distributions do sometimes coincide with ethnic boundaries when the items in question are used as symbols of group identity. He found, for example, that the ear ornaments worn by women of the Tugen, Njemps, and Pokot groups were distinct from one another and that women from one group would never wear ear ornaments typical of another. However, other items of material culture, such as pots or tools, which were not used as symbols of group identity, were distributed in patterns very different from those typical of ear ornaments. Such artifact distribution patterns could be misinterpreted by future researchers and result in a misleading archaeological culture.

Questions about the correspondences between archaeological cultures and present-day cultures are important to archaeologists because they would like to use archaeological evidence to explain cultural variation and cultural evolution. Burning questions for many prehistoric archaeologists concern when and why small bands of foragers decided to settle down and farm for a living and why some of these settlements grew large and complex and came to dominate their neighbors while others did not. Patterned distributions of artifacts offer clues about groups of people who might have been responsible for these developments (as we will see in Chapter 7); however, we need to remember the risks of associating these distributions too literally with real past societies.

Interpreting the Past

Subsistence Strategies

Human beings construct their ecological niches by inventing ways of using their relationships with one another and with the physical environment to make a living. *Subsistence* is the term often used to refer to the satisfaction of the most basic material survival needs: food, clothing, and shelter. The different ways that people in different societies go about meeting subsistence needs are called **subsistence strategies**.

Anthropologists have devised a typology of subsistence strategies that has gained wide acceptance (Figure 6.7). The basic division is between food collectors, or *foragers* (those who gather, fish, or hunt), and food producers (those who depend on domesticated plants or animals or both). The strategies followed by food collectors depend on the richness of the environments in which they live. Small-scale food collectors live in harsher environments and are likely to change residence often in search of resources, as the Ju/'hoansi traditionally did (see EthnoProfile 11.5). By contrast, complex food collectors live in environments richly endowed with dependable food sources and may even, like the indigenous peoples of the northwest coast of North America, build settlements with permanent architecture. As we shall see, archaeological evidence shows that some of the first food producers in the world continued food collection for many generations, raising a few crops on the side and occasionally abandoning food production to return to full-time foraging.

Food producers may farm exclusively or herd exclusively or do a little of both. Those who depend on herds are called *pastoralists*. Among those who farm, there are further distinctions. Some farmers depend primarily on human muscle power plus a few simple tools such as digging sticks or hoes or machetes. They clear plots of uncultivated land, burn the brush, and plant their crops in the ash-enriched soil that remains. Because this technique exhausts the soil after two or three seasons, the plot must then lie fallow for several years as a new plot is cleared and the process repeated. This form of cultivation is called *extensive agriculture*, emphasizing the extensive use of land as farm plots are moved every few years. Other farmers use plows, draft animals, irrigation, fertilizer, and the like. Their method of farming—known as *intensive agriculture*—brings much more land under cultivation at any one time and produces significant crop surpluses. Finally, *mechanized industrial agriculture* is found in societies in which farming or animal husbandry has become organized along industrial lines. Agribusiness "factories in the field" or animal feedlots transform food production into a large-scale, technology-dependent industry of its own.

Bands, Tribes, Chiefdoms, and States

A key task facing early anthropologists was to measure and classify the range of variation in forms of human society over time and across space, as well as to explain cultural and social change over time. In particular, accounting for the origin of the state was a key preoccupation of nineteenth-century anthropology, as seen, for example, in the work of the American Lewis Henry Morgan. Morgan was struck by certain patterns he found, in which particular forms of social and political organization seemed regularly to correlate with particular forms of economic and technological organization, which he called "the arts of subsistence." Morgan's book *Ancient Society*, published in 1877, summarized the basic orientation of what became known as *unilineal cultural evolutionism*: "The latest investigations respecting the early condition of the human race are tending to the conclusion that man-kind commenced their career at the bottom of the scale and worked their way up from savagery to civilization through the slow accumulations of experimental knowledge" ([1877] 1963, 3).

By the early twentieth century, the extravagant claims of some unilineal schemes of cultural evolutionism led most anthropologists to abandon such theorizing. Key critics in Britain were social anthropologists A. R. Radcliffe-Brown and Bronislaw Malinowski. Radcliffe-Brown argued that the evidence about social forms in past periods of human history was so incomplete that all such schemes amounted to little more than guesswork. Malinowski and his students used detailed ethnographic information to explode popular stereotypes about so-called savage peoples. In the United States, Franz Boas was highly critical of the racist assumptions in unilineal evolutionary schemes. He and his students worked to reconstruct the histories of indigenous North American

---

subsistence strategy Different ways that people in different societies go about meeting their basic material survival needs.

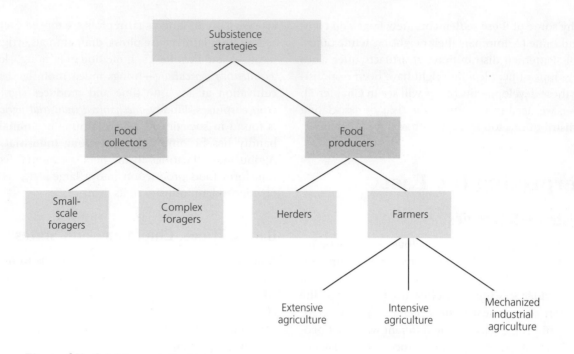

Figure 6.7 Subsistence strategies.

Figure 6.8 Extensive agriculture, sometimes known as *swidden* or *slash-and-burn horticulture*, requires a substantial amount of land, since soils are exhausted within a couple of years and may require as many as 20 years to lie fallow before they can be used again.

societies. They were struck by the links among neighboring societies, especially by the ways in which people, ideas, rituals, and material artifacts regularly flowed across porous social boundaries. Boas was quick to note that if borrowing, rather than independent invention, played an important role in cultural change, then any unilineal evolutionary scheme was doomed.

After World War II, archaeologists and cultural anthropologists in North America worked to combine archaeological and ethnographic information about a range of human societies in order to construct models of

cultural evolution that would capture key turning points in social change while avoiding the assumptions about race and progress that had marred earlier attempts. By the 1960s they had produced economic and political classifications of human social forms that mapped onto each other in interesting ways. As archaeologist Matthew Johnson summarizes,

cultural anthropologists Elman Service and Morton Fried . . . have been particularly influential on archaeologists. Service gives us a fourfold typology ranging

TABLE 6.1 Formal Categories Used by Anthropologists to Classify the Forms of Human Society	
CATEGORY	**DESCRIPTION**
Band	A small, predominantly foraging society of 50 or fewer members that divides labor by age and sex only and provides relatively equal access for all adults to wealth, power, and prestige.
Tribe	A farming or herding society, usually larger than a band, that relies on kinship as the framework for social and political life; provides relatively egalitarian social relations but may have a chief who has more prestige (but not more power or wealth) than others. Sometimes called a *rank society*.
Chiefdom	A socially stratified society, generally larger than a tribe, in which a chief and close relatives enjoy privileged access to wealth, power, and prestige and which has greater craft production but few full-time specialists.
State	An economic, political, and ideological entity invented by stratified societies; possesses specialized government institutions to administer services and collect taxes and tributes; monopolizes use of force with armies and police; possesses high level and quality of craft production. Often developed writing (particularly in early states).
Empire	Forms when one state conquers another.

along the scale of simple to complex of band, tribe, chiefdom, and state. Fried offers an alternative [political] scheme of egalitarian, ranked, stratified and state [societies]. . . . Both start and stop at the same point (they start with "simple" gatherer–hunter societies, though their definitions of such societies differ, and end with the modern state). They both also share a similar methodology. (1999, 141; see also Wenke 1999, 340–44; Table 6.1)

The **band** is the characteristic form of social organization found among foragers. Foraging groups are small, usually numbering no more than 50 people, and labor is divided ordinarily on the basis of age and sex. All adults in band societies have roughly equal access to whatever material or social valuables are locally available, which is why anthropologists call them "egalitarian" forms of society. A society identified as a **tribe** is generally larger than a band, and its members usually farm or herd for a living. Social relations in a tribe are still relatively egalitarian, although there may be a chief who speaks for the group or organizes certain group activities. The chief often enjoys greater prestige than other individuals, but this prestige does not ordinarily translate into greater power or wealth. Social organization and subsistence activities are usually carried out according to rules of kinship (see Chapter 12). However, many societies of foragers, farmers, and herders have developed what Elman Service called "pantribal sodalities" (1962, 113). **Sodalities** are "special-purpose groupings" that may be organized on the basis of age, sex, economic role, and personal interest. "[Sodalities] serve very different functions—among them police, military, medical, initiation, religious, and recreation. Some sodalities conduct their business in secret, others in public. Membership may be ascribed or it may be obtained via inheritance, purchase,

attainment, performance, or contract. Men's sodalities are more numerous and highly organized than women's and, generally, are also more secretive and seclusive in their activities" (Hunter and Whitten 1976, 362). Sodalities create enduring diffuse solidarity among members of a large society, in part because they draw their personnel from a number of "primary" forms of social organization, such as lineages (Figure 6.9).

The **chiefdom** is the first human social form to show evidence of permanent inequalities of wealth and power, in addition to inequality of **status**, or position in society. Ordinarily, only the chief and close relatives are set apart from the rest of society; other members continue to share roughly similar social status. Chiefdoms are generally larger than tribes and show a greater degree of craft production, although such production is not yet in the hands of full-time specialists. Chiefdoms also exhibit a greater degree of hierarchical political control, centered on the chief and relatives of the chief, based on their great deeds. Archaeologically, chiefdoms are

band The characteristic form of social organization found among foragers. Bands are small, usually no more than 50 people, and labor is divided ordinarily on the basis of age and sex. All adults in band societies have roughly equal access to whatever material or social valuables are locally available.

tribe A society that is generally larger than a band, whose members usually farm or herd for a living. Social relations in a tribe are still relatively egalitarian, although there may be a chief who speaks for the group or organizes certain group activities.

sodalities Special-purpose groupings that may be organized on the basis of age, sex, economic role, and personal interest.

chiefdom A form of social organization in which a leader (the chief) and close relatives are set apart from the rest of the society and allowed privileged access to wealth, power, and prestige.

status A particular social position in a group.

Figure 6.9 Members of the Oruro, Bolivia, devil sodality dance.

interesting because some, such as the southern Natufians, apparently remained as they were and then disappeared, whereas others went on to develop into states. The **state** is a stratified society that possesses a territory that is defended from outside enemies with an army and from internal disorder with police. States, which have separate governmental institutions to enforce laws and to collect taxes and tribute, are run by an elite who possesses a monopoly on the use of force.

As we shall see in Chapter 7, most archaeologists who use this general evolutionary scheme to help them interpret their findings reject the lockstep determinism which gave nineteenth-century cultural evolutionism such a bad name. Indeed, to the extent that the term *evolution* has come to refer to goal-directed, deterministic cultural processes, many archaeologists might prefer to describe what they do as cultural *history* or *prehistory* since these terms leave room for openness and contingency in human affairs, explicitly acknowledging that human cultural development does not move on rails toward a predestined outcome.

Given these qualifications, can knowledge about bands, tribes, and chiefdoms continue to be of value to anthropologists? For one thing, most archaeologists who use these categories do not think of them as sharply

divided or mutually exclusive categories but, rather, as points on a continuum. Indeed, a single social group may move back and forth between more than one of these forms over time, as was the case with the Natufians. Most anthropologists would probably agree that knowledge about human cultural prehistory is important in helping us understand what it means to be human, even if our more immediate research interests do not focus on prehistory itself. For example, knowledge that gender relations in band societies tend to be egalitarian and that human beings and their ancestors lived in bands for most of evolutionary history has been important to feminist anthropologists; knowledge that nation-states and empires are recent developments in human history that came about as a result of political, technological, and other sociocultural processes undermines the assumptions of scientific racism.

At the same time, anthropologists may continue to be interested in why certain kinds of developments came about in one place and time rather than another. Prehistorians notice that there were numerous settled villages in southwest Asia 10,000 years ago but only a few of them became cities or city-states. Some band-living hunter–gatherers settled down to become farmers or animal herders in some times in places; some of their neighbors, however, managed to find a way to continue to survive by gathering and hunting in bands right up until the end of the twentieth century. Indeed, in parts of the world, like Afghanistan, tribal organizations continue to thrive and attempts to establish centralized states regularly fail. Archaeology, history, and ethnography can help explain why these developments have (or have not)

---

state A stratified society that possesses a territory that is defended from outside enemies with an army and from internal disorder with police. A state, which has a separate set of governmental institutions designed to enforce laws and to collect taxes and tribute, is run by an elite that possesses a monopoly on the use of force.

occurred by seeking to identify social structural elements and cultural practices that may enhance, or impede, the transformation of one kind of social form into another. Nor is classification an end in itself. Today's archaeologists do not see the categories of band, tribe, chiefdom, and state as eternal forms through which all societies are fated to pass. Instead, these are understood as theoretical constructs based on available evidence and subject to critique. Their main value comes from the way in which they give structure to our ignorance.

As we will see, especially in Chapter 15, intensified processes of globalization in the late twentieth and early twenty-first centuries have revitalized the interest of many anthropologists in cultural borrowing, vindicating the Boasians' claims about the porous nature of social boundaries and the cultural adaptability of which all human societies are capable. At the same time it has become clear that not all kinds of movements across social and cultural boundaries are equally easy or equally welcome everywhere. Anthropologists continue to pay attention to those structural features of contemporary societies—such as political boundaries between nation–states and international economic structures—that continue to modulate the tempo and mode of cultural, political, and economic change.

Whose Past Is It?

As a social science discipline, archaeology has its own theoretical questions, methodological approaches, and history. In recent years, archaeologists have explicitly had to come to terms with the fact that they are not the only people interested in what is buried in the ground, how it got there, how it should be interpreted, and to whom it belongs. In some cases, archaeological sites have come to play an important role in identity formation for people who see themselves as the descendants of the builders of the site. Machu Picchu in Andean Peru, the Pyramids in Egypt, the Acropolis in Athens, Great Zimbabwe in Zimbabwe, and Masada in Israel are just a few examples of ancient monuments that have great significance for people living in modern states today. The meanings people take from them do not always coincide with the findings of current archaeological research. At the same time, these sites, and a great many others, have become major tourist destinations. Geographically remote Machu Picchu, for example, now receives about 300,000 tourists per year, a number which is both impressive and worrisome, since the constant movement of tourists may be doing permanent damage to the site (Figure 6.10). Nations, regions, and local communities have discovered that the past attracts tourists and their

money, which can provide significant income in some parts of the world. The past may even be mobilized by the entertainment industry: for example, increasingly popular "time capsule" sites invite tourists to visit places where local people wear costumes and carry out the occupations associated with a "re-created" past way of life.

Nevertheless, not all peoples welcome either archaeologists or tourists. For example, as former colonies became independent states, their citizens became interested in uncovering their own past and gaining control over their heritage. This has often meant that the artifacts discovered during archaeological research must stay in the country in which they were found. In addition, citizens of these states are now asking museums in Western countries to return cultural property—substantial quantities of material artifacts—removed long ago by colonizers. There seems to be little question that objects of special religious or cultural significance should be returned to the places from which they were

Figure 6.10 While Machu Picchu is a spectacular example of human ingenuity and achievement, it has had to endure increasing pressure from visitors who come to admire it. The Peruvian government has proposed closing the Inca trail during the rainy season to protect the sites.

taken. Some objects, for example, were considered sacred by their makers and were not intended for public view but have been openly displayed in public museums for many years. Is displaying such objects in public, even among people who do not believe in their sacredness, disrespectful to their makers? Is it just another way of representing the political power of the current owners? Renfrew and Bahn (2004, 552) suggest that the matter may be more complex:

> [One can] ask whether the interest of the great products of human endeavor does not in fact transcend the geographical boundaries of modern-day nationalism. Does it make sense that all the Paleolithic handaxes and other artifacts from Olduvai Gorge or Olorgesaillie in East Africa should remain confined within the bounds of the modern nations where they have been found? Should we not all be able to benefit from the insights they offer? And is it not a profound and important experience to be able, in the course of one day in one of the world's great museums, to be able to walk from room to room, from civilization to civilization, and see unfolded a sample of the whole variety of human experience?

But artifacts are not all that have come out of the ground over the course of a century and a half of archaeological research. Human skeletal material has also been found, usually recovered from intentional burials. For archaeologists and biological anthropologists, this skeletal material offers important data on past patterns of migration, disease, violence, family connections, social organization and complexity, technology, cultural beliefs, and many other phenomena. Constantly improving analytical techniques are increasing the quality of data that can be extracted from skeletal remains, making

this material even more valuable. Yet, these may be the remains of ancestors of peoples now living in the area from which the bones were removed, peoples who do not believe that the dead should be disturbed and have their bones analyzed.

This has been a particularly important issue for archaeology in the United States because most of the collections of skeletal materials (and sacred objects) came from Native American populations. Many, although not all, Native Americans are deeply angered by the excavation of indigenous burials. That the bones of their ancestors end up in museums, laboratories, and universities embodies for them the disrespect and domination that has been the lot of indigenous Americans since Europeans first arrived. Thus, their objections have both religious and political dimensions. These objections were recognized in the Native American Graves Protection and Repatriation Act (NAGPRA), passed by the U.S. Congress in 1990.

First, NAGPRA requires all federal agencies and institutions that receive federal funds to inventory all American Indian and Native Hawaiian human remains in their possession, as well as funerary objects, sacred objects, and "objects of cultural patrimony." These institutions must establish whether these remains or objects have a connection with any living indigenous groups. Should a connection be found, the institutions are required to notify the appropriate American Indian or Native Hawaiian group and offer to return, or "repatriate," the materials in question. In addition, if indigenous groups believe that they have a connection to remains held by an institution, they may request repatriation of those remains, even if the institution is not convinced by their claims (Figure 6.11).

Figure 6.11 Ceremony for reburial of remains of Eyak Indians in Cordova, Alaska. The bones were released by the Smithsonian Institution under NAGPRA.

Second, NAGPRA protects American Indian graves and cultural objects on all federal and tribal lands (it does not extend protection to sites on private lands). The act also requires that anyone carrying out archaeological research on federal or tribal lands must consult with the Native American people who are affiliated or may be affiliated with those lands regarding the treatment and disposition of any finds.

NAGPRA has made it necessary for archaeologists to take seriously the rights and attitudes of native peoples toward the past. While this has led to disagreements, it has also led to compromise, collaboration, and recognition of shared concerns. As Fagan and DeCorse put it, "no archaeologist in North America, and probably elsewhere, will be able to excavate a prehistoric or historic burial without the most careful and sensitive preparation. This involves working closely with native peoples in ways that archaeologists have not imagined until recently. Nothing but good can come of this" (2005, 504).

Among the positive consequences of NAGPRA have been cooperative agreements with Native American groups that are interested in developing their own museums and archaeological and historical research programs. In other cases, tribal councils or other representatives have been willing to allow archaeologists and biological anthropologists to study excavated bones or to make extremely accurate copies of them before returning them for reburial. Attempts are being made to establish working relationships based on mutual respect for the positions of all sides—respectful treatment of the ancestors and sacred objects as well as the concerns of science and education. The situation remains uncertain however. Changes in tribal council membership can lead to changes of policy positions regarding archaeology.

One case which has involved extensive legal action is that of the so-called Kennewick Man, a skeleton found in the state of Washington in 1996 (Figure 6.12). Since initial examination seemed to indicate that the remains belonged to a nineteenth-century white settler, scholars were surprised when the skeleton received a radiocarbon date of 9300 B.P. More study seemed essential to resolve the matter, but the U.S. Army Corps of Engineers intended to return the remains to the Umatilla tribe for reburial. Eight anthropologists sued the Corps of Engineers for permission to study the bones, contending that the bones could not be linked to any living tribe. The Umatilla insisted, however, that their traditions held that they had occupied the land from the beginning of time, which meant that the bones belonged to one of their ancestors and should be returned to them. In 2002, a magistrate found in favor of the scientists, but four tribes and the U.S. Department of the Interior appealed the decision. In February 2004, a U.S. court of appeals upheld the magistrate's decision, and a 10-day study of the skeletal remains was carried out in July 2005. As of this writing, promised scientific studies of Kennewick Man have yet to be published in any scientific journal (*Seattle Post Intelligencer* 2009).

Indigenous people in the United States are not the only ones concerned with the disposition of human remains unearthed by archaeologists and others. In Australia, Aboriginal people have successfully pressed for the return of the remains of their ancestors, remains that were often collected unethically, sometimes through grave robbing and even murder. In recent years, the Australian government has established programs for the repatriation of cultural material and human remains that are held in Australian museums or other institutions and has worked to secure the repatriation of Aboriginal remains from outside Australia. The Australian Archaeological Association has supported these initiatives.

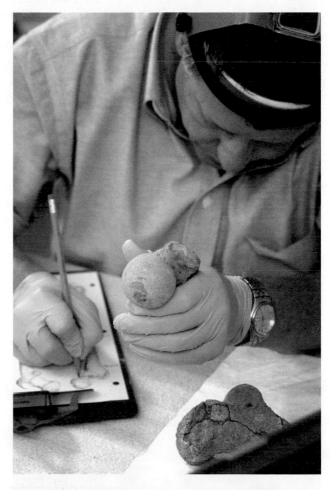

Figure 6.12 Biological anthropologist Douglas Owsley of the Smithsonian Institution, examining various features of the right femur of the Kennewick Man skeleton in order to try to determine the original position of the body in the ground.

According to the Australian government:

The aim of the program is to repatriate all ancestral remains and secret sacred objects from the eligible museums to their communities of origin. The four specific objectives are to: identify the origins of all ancestral remains and secret sacred objects held in the museums where possible; notify all communities who have ancestral remains and secret sacred objects held in the museums; arrange for repatriation where and when it is requested; appropriately store ancestral remains and secret sacred objects held in the museums at the request of the relevant community. (Department of Communications, Information Technology, and the Arts 2005)

Plundering the Past

Many people in the world were shocked and appalled in March 2001, when the extremist Taliban government of Afghanistan decided to destroy the Bamiyan Buddhas, two giant sculptures carved into the face of a cliff about 1,500 years ago (Figure 6.13). Even though almost no Buddhists live in Afghanistan today, these sculptures had long been part of the cultural heritage of the Afghan people. Despite world condemnation of this decision that included a delegation from the Islamic Conference representing 55 Muslim nations, the Taliban insisted that these human images were impious and destroyed them along with even older objects in the national museum. This act shocked many people, perhaps not only because it seemed so narrow-minded and thoughtless but also because the statues were irreplaceable examples of human creative power.

Nevertheless, destruction of the human past on a much greater scale goes on every day as a consequence of land development, agriculture, and looting for sale to collectors. The construction of roads, dams, office buildings, housing developments, libraries, subways, and so on has enormous potential to damage or destroy evidence of the past. As mechanized agriculture has spread across the world, the tractors and deep plows tear across settlement sites and field monuments. While

Figure 6.13 (a, b) Many people in the world were shocked when the Taliban leaders of Afghanistan blew up the 1,500-year-old statues of the Buddha despite worldwide requests to save these examples of the heritage of the Afghan people.

construction, development, and agriculture cannot be stopped, they can be made more sensitive to the potential damage they can do.

Unfortunately, such cannot be said for looting and the market in stolen antiquities. There is nothing really new about looting—the tombs of the pharaohs of Egypt were looted in their own day—but the scale today surpasses anything that has come before. It is safe to say that any region of the world with archaeological sites also has organized looting, and the devastation looters leave behind makes any scientific analysis of a site impossible. We have seen how important it is for archaeologists to record the precise placement of every object they excavate. When that context is destroyed, so is the archaeological value of a site. "In the American Southwest, 90 percent of the Classic Mimbres sites (c. 1000 C.E.) have now been looted or destroyed. In southwestern Colorado, 60 percent of prehistoric Anasazi sites have been vandalized. Pothunters work at night, equipped with two-way radios, scanners, and lookouts. They can be prosecuted under the present legislation only if caught red-handed, which is almost impossible" (Renfrew and Bahn 2008, 563). Looters steal to make money. Buyers, including museums and private collectors, have been willing to overlook the details of the process by which ancient objects come into their hands. While museum owners have taken some steps to make sure that they purchase (or accept as gifts) only objects that have been exported legally from their countries of origin, private collectors remain free to feed on the illegal destruction of the heritage of the world's people (Figure 6.14).

In the United States, one sign of progress has been a series of legislative actions at the federal, state, and local levels that require the consideration of environmental and cultural factors in the use of federal, state, or local funds for development. At the most basic level, projects involving federal land or federal funds (highway funds, e.g.) must file an Environmental Impact Assessment, which includes attention to cultural resources—the material record of the human past—located in affected sites. To meet this federal requirement, the archaeological specialty of cultural resource management (CRM) was developed. CRM is an attempt to insure that cultural resources threatened by projects are properly managed—"recorded, evaluated, protected, or, if necessary, salvaged" (Fagan and DeCorse 2005, 483). CRM is a multimillion-dollar undertaking, the major source of employment for archaeologists, and is practiced by private companies, federal agencies, universities, and individuals. The legal grounds for CRM developed out of a concern with conservation, rather than research. Over time, however, it has become clear that CRM archaeology contributes in a very significant way not just to the

Figure 6.14 The looting of archaeological sites continues to be a serious problem, as the heritage of the world's people is destroyed.

preservation of the past but also to basic archaeological research and theory. In this way, we see again how archaeologists have become the stewards of the past, a task that will require great energy and all their skill.

Contemporary Trends in Archaeology

As we have seen, contemporary social issues lead archaeologists to rethink how they study the human past. We now consider three examples of contemporary archaeology that illustrate these developments.

Archaeology and Gender

By the 1980s, awareness of the unequal treatment of women in modern European and American societies had led archaeologists (both women and men) to examine why women's contributions had been systematically written out of the archaeological record. Building on anthropological studies of living people, **feminist archaeology** rejected biological determinism of sex roles, arguing that cultural and historical factors were responsible for how a society allocated tasks and that this allocation could change over time. The goal was to develop a view of the past that "replaces focus on remains with a focus on people as active social agents" (Conkey and Gero 1991, 15).

Feminist archaeology did not depend on new technological breakthroughs in excavation methods to pursue this goal. Rather, by using what they already knew about living human societies, together with available historical documents, feminist archaeologists asked new kinds of questions. For example, Joan Gero (1991) drew attention to male bias in discussions of the oldest, best-known collections of human artifacts: stone tools. Gero showed how traditional archaeological discussion of stone-tool technologies focused on highly formalized, elaborately retouched, standardized core tools. This focus, together with the assumption that such tools were made by men to hunt with, turns men and their activities into the driving force of cultural evolution. It simultaneously downplays or ignores the far more numerous flake tools that were probably made and used by women in such tasks as processing food or working wood and leather. Gero cited ethnographic and historical reports that describe women as active makers of stone tools, including more elaborate core tools, exposing as false the supposition that women are not strong or smart enough to produce them.

Gero then applied her findings to her analysis of a multilayered site at Huaricoto in highland Peru. The lowest occupation level at Huaricoto dates from a period in which the site was a ceremonial center visited by foragers who apparently made elaborate biface (two-sided) core tools out of imported stone in a workshop on the site. The most recent occupation level dated from a later period, when the site was no longer a ritual center but had become a residential settlement whose inhabitants used many flake tools made of local stone for a variety of subsistence tasks. Gero pointed out that "the flake tool performs many of the same actions unceremoniously that bifaces perform in a ritualistic setting" (1991, 184). She suggests that the change from ceremonial center to

village settlement probably involved a shift not in the use of stone tools but rather in their social significance: male status may have been connected with stone-tool production during the early period but had probably become connected with some other kind of prestige goods instead (perhaps ceramics or textiles) by the later period. Stone tools continued to be made and used, but they were utilitarian flake tools, and their makers and users were most likely women.

Insights from feminist archaeology inform more recent work in **gender archaeology**, which "addresses the needs of contemporary gender studies for an understanding of how people come to understand themselves as different from others; how people represent these differences; and how others react to such claims" (Joyce 2008:17). Contemporary gender studies asks, for example, why archaeologists often assume that the meanings of artifacts from all societies across space and over time should be interpreted in terms of a universal male-female division. As Rosemary Joyce observes, "The experiences of people in the contemporary world are actually a good deal more varied than those expected under the normative two-sex/two-gender model" (2008, 18). Gender archaeologists have found that new questions can be asked about variation in sex, gender, and other kinds of human difference in past societies if attention shifts away from the universals and focuses instead on detailed contextual features of specific archaeological sites.

Focusing on site-specific details affects the kinds of interpretations that archaeologists make. First, the meaning of a common artifact, whether found in a household rubbish dump or in a burial site, cannot be assumed to remain unchanging over time. This insight was central to Gero's reinterpretation of stone tools and their use at Huaricoto. Gero's approach also illustrates a second point: archaeological analyses that focus on the highly elaborated artifact can downplay or ignore patterns that would be visible if all relevant artifacts, ordinary and extraordinary, are considered. Joyce argues that Paleolithic figurines depicting females with exaggerated breasts and bellies have been misunderstood. Because of a widely shared assumption that *all* figurines depicting human females had to be "fertility symbols," archaeologists have tended to ignore other contemporary figurines that did not easily fit such an interpretation. For examples, the 30,000-year-old central European Paleolithic site of Dolní Vestonice yielded figurines representing animals and human males as well as human females; moreover, the only figurines depicted wearing woven clothing were some of the female figurines (Figure 6.15). Since most female and all male figurines lacked any representation of clothing, archaeologists now suggest that the female figurines with clothing represent a few women at this

---

feminist archaeology A research approach that explores why women's contributions have been systematically written out of the archaeological record and suggests new approaches to the human past that include such contributions.

gender archaeology Archaeological research that draws on insights from contemporary gender studies to investigate how people come to recognize themselves as different from others, how people represent these differences, and how others react to such claims.

Figure 6.15 Sculpture head of woman, Dolní Vestonice. The Dolní Vestonice site in the Czech Republic has yielded extensive numbers of figures, some of which seem to represent women of status.

time and place who "gained individual status from their skill at producing textiles" (2008, 15). This interpretation is strengthened by evidence from contemporary burials that clothing of men and women was not differentiated by gender and did not resemble the images of clothing portrayed on figurines (2008, 15).

Third, Joyce stresses the need for archaeologists to think of material artifacts "as having had lives of their own . . . made, used, and discarded, and during which people's experiences and associations with them would have varied" (2008, 28). Focusing on the social lives of individual artifacts shifts attention away from artifacts to the individuals who made those artifacts and highlights the variety of motivations they may have had for making them the way they did. It also draws attention to the likelihood that all images were not accepted at face value but instead offered "a means for the circulation of propositions that might be contested" (2008, 16). As a result, the same images might well have meant different things to different members of the social group that produced or used them. This approach provides "a critical basis for challenges to orthodox interpretations that might otherwise ignore complexities in human societies now as much as in the past" (2008, 16,17).

The value of such an approach is displayed in the work of bioarchaeologist Sandra Hollimon, who was faced with interpreting remains of Chumash burials in California. As Joyce explains, contemporary Chumash culture traditionally recognized a third gender—"two-spirited" men whose status is neither male nor female. Moreover, as is the case in a number of Native American societies, such two-spirited individuals were often skilled craftspeople, who were given baskets in exchange for their work. Hollimon first expected that the graves of two-spirited individuals would stand out from the graves of women or other men because they would contain male skeletons accompanied by baskets. It turned out, however, that baskets were found together with the skeletal remains of both women and men. This prompted Hollimon to wonder if gender distinctions were not important in Chumash mortuary practices. She looked for other patterns of difference in the remains and discovered a typically female form of spinal arthritis in the skeletons of two young males. This form of arthritis was associated with regular use of digging sticks, typically women's work, but also the work of two-spirited men.

These two particular male skeletons had been buried both with digging stick weights and with baskets, which strengthened the conclusion that they belonged to two-spirited males. However, digging sticks and baskets were tools traditionally associated with Chumash *undertakers*, who could be either two-spirited men or postmenopausal women. Hollimon concluded that the *status* of undertaker apparently was more significant in Chumash burial practices than the *gender* of the individual being buried. "In Chumash society, these people helped the spirits of the dead make the transition to their next stage of life. To be able to do this, they needed a special spiritual status. This special status was limited to those whose sexual activity could not lead to childbirth" (Joyce 2008, 60). The lesson is clear: "not finding three burial patterns led to a realization that sex may not have been the most significant basis for the identity of these people. . . . Genders were not permanent categorical identities, but rather distinctive performances related to sexuality that could change over a person's life" (2008, 61).

Collaborative Approaches to Studying the Past

Janet Spector was one of the first archaeologists in the United States to initiate a collaborative research project with the descendants of the people who once occupied the sites she excavated. Her work in Minnesota is an example of **historical archaeology** (Figure 6.16)—the study (in this case) of post-European contact sites

Archaeology as a Tool of Civic Engagement

Barbara J. Little and Paul A. Shackel (2007) use the term *civic engagement* to refer to an important direction in contemporary archaeology. Civic engagement in archaeology refers to involvement and participation in public life, especially in directing people's attention to "the historical roots and present-day manifestations of contemporary social justice issues." Civic engagement also refers to connecting archaeologists and the work they do to the communities that are connected in one way or another to archaeological sites and the history they embody.

One example of civic engagement comes from Virginia and the site of one of the most famous episodes in U.S. popular history—the arrival in 1607 of English colonists who founded Jamestown and the supposed interactions of Chief Powhatan, John Smith, and Pocahontas. Martin Gallivan and Danielle Moretti-Langholtz (2007) have been involved with the first archaeological excavation at Werowocomoco, the site of the Powhatan chiefdom. This research has shed light on the history of Native life at the site from its founding in about 1200 C.E. to its abandonment by Powhatan in 1609 because the English colonists were too close. The research has been strongly engaged with the wider communities of Virginia, especially Native communities. The history of Native peoples in Virginia is a troubled one, in which the more prominent biracial divide between Whites and African Americans seemed to overwhelm the Native presence. Indeed, in 1924, people of Native descent were defined by the Racial Integrity Act legally as "colored persons," the same category used for people of African descent. Interracial marriage was prohibited, and Native children were forced to attend schools for "colored persons."

> The sting of the Racial Integrity Act, which remained in force until 1968, is still felt in Virginia's indigenous community. Native people were denied the right to self-identify as Native people, making it impossible for them to enter the civic arena as representatives of their respective communities. Despite the fact that the Pamunkeys and Mattaponis had long-held reservation lands within the commonwealth, official state policy maintained that there were no longer indigenous Indians in Virginia. (Gallivan and Moretti-Langholtz 2007, 54)

Finally, during the 1980s, eight Indian tribes were recognized by the Virginia Commonwealth, and when NAGPRA became law in 1990, representatives of the tribes worked closely with archaeologists in the reburial of remains that had been held in collections.

Engagements of this kind with descendant communities, served as the foundations of the Werowocomoco research project: "from its inception, the WRG [Werowocomoco Research Group] has worked toward a model of archaeological research on Native sites in the Chesapeake that includes close Native collaboration at every stage" (2007, 58). Indeed, when the WRG found the site they believed to be Werowocomoco, they requested a meeting with the Virginia Council on Indians to ensure that tribal leaders would have the information about the site and the excavation before it was announced to the public. Members of the WRG met privately with the tribal chiefs to introduce them to the research team and the owner of the property on which the site had been found. They also outlined a long-term plan to study the site with the close involvement of the Native communities. A visit to the site was scheduled, and a Native advisory board was established. Tribal representatives presented their perspectives on the site and its history. "Though these perspectives varied, several tribal leaders expressed a powerful connection to Werowocomoco as the historic center of the Powhatan chiefdom and as a modern place for renewing Virginia Indians' influence on representations of the Native past. Others encouraged us to pursue research that focuses on the power and social complexity of the Powhatan chiefdom during the years prior to 1607" (2007, 59–60).

The research team shares all information with the advisory board, including minutes from meetings and financial reports. In recent years, some Virginia Indians have gotten involved in the excavations themselves. Among other things, this has had the effect of enabling one member of the Pamunkey Tribal Council to have a better understanding of the archaeological research process when evaluating Cultural Resources Management proposals made to the tribe. On days set aside for public visitation, partners from the Pamunkey tribe speak with visitors about the excavations and about their feelings regarding archaeological research involving their ancestors (2007, 61).

But many archaeologists involved with community engagement want to go beyond public outreach. As archaeologists engage with a wide range of publics and present their research, new topics and ways of discussing old topics may emerge, and some of those discussions may contradict existing historical narratives. "Taking archaeological practice from civic engagement and toward social justice, conceived of as equity, honesty, and tolerance across segments of a society, represents a difficult challenge that we have not begun to master" (61). Gallivan and Moretti-Langholtz think that the research at Werowocomoco has the potential to expand the restrictive narratives about Native peoples in Virginia that have dominated public and academic discourse and to challenge the received stories of the past. Their research alone was not sufficient to push this transformation, but by giving descendant populations a central role in the recovery of the history of their ancestors, it opened a place for new discussions regarding the Native past. Such discussions may help create an indigenous archaeology, one in which Native peoples "become full partners in representations concerning their past" (2007, 62). This is a route for archaeology to follow in contributing to social justice in the wider societies in which archaeologists work.

Figure 6.16 Historical archaeologists, shown here excavating in the Roman Forum, supplement written documents with records of settlement patterns, structures, and artifacts, which reveal valuable information about the past that was never written down.

in North America. Like other feminist archaeologists, Spector wanted to shift attention from the artifacts to the people who made them, from a preoccupation with active men and passive women to a more realistic assessment of active women and men, and from a focus on the remains as evidence of European contact to what these remains suggested about "Indian responses or resistance to European expansion and domination" (1993, 6).

In 1980, Spector and her team began to dig at a site near Jordan, Minnesota, known by the Dakota as *Inyan Ceyak Atonwan,* or "Village at the Rapids." She examined historical documents that referred to the site for clues about what tasks were carried on by men and women at the site, as a guide to what kinds of material remains to look for. After several seasons, concerned that her work might be meaningless or offensive to the Dakota, Spector met a Dakota man who was a descendant of a man named Mazomani, one of the original inhabitants of the Village at the Rapids. Eventually, other descendants of Mazomani visited the site. By the 1985–1986 season, Dakota and non-Dakota were collaborating in teaching Dakota language, oral history, ethnobotany, ecology, and history at the site while digging continued. A Dakota

elder conducted a pipe ceremony at the site shortly before the field season began, which symbolized for Spector the Dakota people's permission to work there.

Since the early 1980s, collaborative archaeological research of this kind has become increasingly common. Renfrew and Bahn (2008), for example, report on a multidisciplinary research project inside Kakadu National Park in the Northern Territory of Australia that began in 1981. Archaeologists wanted to learn more about the earliest occupation of tropical Australia, which began more than 23,000 years ago, and Kakadu National Park was an ideal place to look: the park contains a number of rockshelters filled with rich material traces of ancient human occupation, including rock paintings as old as those found in European caves such as Lascaux. Archaeologists wanted to build on previous work and to test the proposal made by an earlier researcher, George

historical archaeology The study of archaeological sites associated with written records, frequently the study of post-European contact sites in the world

Chaloupka, who argued that the rock art in the region reflected changes in the environment triggered by rising sea levels (Renfrew and Bahn 2008, 521).

But Rhys Jones, the team leader from the Australian National University, knew that the site was legally owned by the local Aborigine community, whose permission would be needed before any excavation could begin. The Aborigine community was willing to give permission for the project, but they wanted to ensure that the dig was carried out in a way that was responsible and respectful. They insisted that one member of the community supervise the project, primarily "to protect the diggers from doing something that could bring practical or ritual danger: the totemic geography of a region contains some 'dangerous places,' into which archaeologists might stray through ignorance" (2008, 521). The archaeologists also had to agree to complete work at one site before moving on to another and to return all disturbed areas to the condition in which they had been prior to the excavation. But Aboriginal involvement in the project did not stop there. "Senior Aborigine men representing the relevant groups accompanied the team on field trips and carefully monitored the excavations, while trainee Aboriginal rangers helped in the laboratory, and were instructed in archaeological procedures" (2008, 522). When the project was completed, the researchers did indeed find evidence that verified Chaloupka's hypothesis, but two other findings were perhaps even more exciting. The first was the discovery of plant remains as much as 6,000 years old, preserved thanks to the unusual microclimate present in one rockshelter. The second came from a second rockshelter and consisted of pieces of red ochre, a pigment used by ancient human populations in many parts of the world. These pieces were 53,000 years old, had been worked by hand, and might have been the sources of pigment for some of the rock art. Renfrew and Bahn judge this project "very successful" (2008, 528), and one measure of its success was the way it provided a model—as did Spector's work—of finding a way to do archaeology while working together with an indigenous community that had its own stake in the way the project was carried out, as well as in the outcome.

Cosmopolitan Archaeologies

A variety of far-reaching changes have swept the world since the end of the Cold War in 1989. As we will see in later chapters (especially Chapter 14), these changes

have affected the way all anthropologists do research, and archaeologists are no exception. Collaborative projects between local communities and archaeologists have become increasingly common in recent years, but these collaborations themselves have been affected by a number of broader changes. For example, global tourism has mushroomed, and huge numbers of tourists from all over the world now want to visit archaeological sites such as Machu Picchu or Kakaku National Park, both of which have been named UNESCO World Heritage Sites.

As we saw in the case of Machu Picchu, a lot of money can be made managing flows of wealthy tourists to well-known cultural heritage sites (see Fig. 6.10). When tourist traffic threatens to destroy such sites, therefore, it is not merely the ruins themselves that are at stake; so are the livelihoods of local people and governments. Moreover, powerless minorities with traditional connections to these sites frequently find themselves shoved aside as national and international institutions step in and take over. In the past, most archaeologists tried to do their research while avoiding local legal and political involvements, hoping to achieve "a 'do no harm' model of coexistence" (Meskell 2009, 5). Today, many archaeologists have adopted the view that their first obligation should be to those local (and often marginalized) people with traditional connections to the archaeological sites where they work. But more and more archaeologists are finding that this kind of single-minded commitment is increasingly problematic, as they and their local allies must find a way to deal with a range of other local and global stakeholders who have their own, often conflicting, ideas about how cultural heritage should be managed.

Like many contemporary cultural anthropologists (see Chapter 8), some archaeologists have been moved by these struggles to question a view of the world that divides it up into a patchwork quilt of distinct, neatly bounded "cultures," each of which embodies a unique heritage that must be protected from change at all costs. Again, like many of their cultural anthropologist colleagues, these archaeologists have concluded that the only way forward is to cultivate a "cosmopolitan" point of view (see Chapter 15). For many cultural anthropologists, **cosmopolitanism** means being able to move with ease from one cultural setting to another. Cultural anthropologists regularly develop cosmopolitan skills and awareness as they move in and out of fieldwork situations. Moreover, people everywhere—tourists, immigrants, or refugees, for example—have crafted a variety of different kinds of cosmopolitan skills in order to cope successfully with movement from one cultural setting to another. As you will see later, these movements have become the focus of new "multisited" forms of ethnographic research.

---

cosmopolitanism   Being able to move with ease from one cultural setting to another.

For archaeologists, adopting a cosmopolitan orientation means giving up universalistic assumptions about the meaning of the past. It means acknowledging, for example, that preservation of material artifacts may in fact sometimes go against the wishes of local groups with close connections to those artifacts. Dealing with such challenges means that cosmopolitan archaeologists will no longer be able to avoid involvement in legal and political debates about the future of cultural heritage, even as they come to recognize that their views may carry less weight than the views of other stakeholders. "Cosmopolitans suppose . . . that all cultures have enough overlap in their vocabulary of values to begin a conversation. Yet counter to some universalists, they do not presume they can craft a consensus" (Meskell 2009, 7).

Archaeologist Chip Colwell-Chanthaphonh, for example, asks "Can the destruction of heritage ever be ethically justified? If so, by what principle, why, and under what conditions?" He speaks of "the preservation paradox"—that is, "the concept of preservation is itself culturally conceived," with the result that "one group's notion of cultural preservation can be another group's notion of cultural destruction" (2009, 143). Colwell-Chanthaphonh describes disagreements about the ethics of preservation of artifacts valued in different ways by different groups in the American southwest. Commitment to a "salvage ethic" led nineteenth-century collectors to "rescue" sculptures that the Zuni purposefully left to deteriorate in sacred shrines. "This is the core of the salvage ethic, the urge to 'preserve' objects by physically protecting them. But for the Zunis, such acts that aspired to cultural preservation were in fact acts of cultural destruction"(Colwell-Chanthaphonh 2009, 146).

Conflict over whether to preserve or to destroy ancient rock carvings is an issue that divides the Navajo people and the Hopi people, both of whom have lived in the American southwest for a very long time. Hopi people wish to preserve these rock carvings, which they regard as "monuments to Hopi history, proof of ancestral homelands and clan migrations" (Colwell-Chanthaphonh 2009, 149). Navajo people, however, regard all ruins from the past, including these rock carvings, as products of human evil or the activity of witches. Contact with the rock carvings is believed to cause sickness or other misfortunes, and curing ceremonies involve the destruction of the carvings. These days, moreover, the Hopi and Navajo peoples are far from being the only groups who assign meaning to carvings and ancient ruins in the American southwest (Figure 6.17). As Colwell-Chanthaphonh points out,

the ancient ruins of Chaco Canyon in New Mexico are at once a Hopi ancestral site, a locus of Navajo spiritual power, a ritual space for New Agers, an archaeological

Figure 6.17 Preservation and use of material artifacts or ruins, such as the ruins at Chaco Canyon in Arizona, can be complicated by the range of different and sometimes opposed interests that different groups bring to them.

and scientific resource, a National Historical Park of the United States, and a UNESCO World Heritage Site. . . . Clearly, in anthropological as much as ethical terms, such a complex convergence of people, communities, and institutions cannot be reduced to just intra-nationalist, nationalist, or internationalist claims. The key ethical problem . . . is not so much categorizing rights but trying to illuminate the relationships (2009, 151).

This is the reason a cosmopolitan approach appeals to him: "we must develop a sophisticated understanding of how heritage works from the individual level, to the community, to the nation and beyond it. . . . A just solution cannot simply pick out the rights of one group but must instead interweave these multiple values" (2009, 152). Colwell-Chanthaphonh recommends what he calls "the principle of complex stewardship": that is, "we should maximize the integrity of heritage objects for the good of the greatest number of people, but not absolutely" (2009, 160). To maximize the integrity of heritage objects would support those who want objects preserved. Concern for the good of the greatest number, however, would mean that the positions of other stakeholders with different views would also be included and might carry great weight, especially if they outnumbered the preservationists. Even then, however, the majority position might not necessarily carry the day because special consideration would need to be given to those whose ancestors made the objects or who are closely connected to them in other ways. The principle of complex stewardship is not a ready-made solution to disputes about the management of cultural heritage; rather, it is "a frame archaeologists can use to begin deliberations on ethical predicaments" (2009, 161). Finding solutions, for cosmopolitans, involves negotiations whose outcome cannot be predicted in advance.

Chapter Summary

1. By the end of the last Ice Age, cultural variation, not biological species differences, distinguished human populations from one another. Archaeologists interpret cultural variation and cultural change in the human past. Archaeology has changed focus over time, from reconstructing material remains or lifeways of past human groups to explaining the cultural processes that led to particular kinds of material culture to emphasizing the role of human agency and the power of ideas and values in the construction of past cultures.

2. Archaeologists trace patterns in past human cultures by identifying sites and regions of human occupation and by recovering artifacts, features, and other remains of human activity from these sites. In all cases, they are concerned with recording information about the context in which these remains are found.

3. The survival of archaeological remains depends on what they were made of and the conditions they experienced over time. Very dry and very cold climates and oxygen-free, waterlogged settings preserve many organic remains that would decay under other circumstances. Natural catastrophes, such as mudslides and lava flows, sometimes bury sites and preserve their contents remarkably well. Ethnoarchaeology and taphonomy are two methods archaeologists use to help them interpret the meaning of the remains they find.

4. Before archaeologists begin their work, they survey the region they are interested in. Surveys, whether on the ground or from the air, can yield important information that cannot be gained from excavations. Excavations are done when archaeologists want to know a lot about a little of a site. The style of excavation depends on the kind of site being excavated. As the excavation proceeds, archaeologists keep careful records to preserve contextual information. Much of the final analysis of the remains is carried out in laboratories.

5. Artifacts and structures from a particular time and place in a site are grouped together in assemblages; similar assemblages from many sites are grouped together in archaeological cultures. Archaeological cultures are constructed by archaeologists to reflect patterns in their data, so they cannot be assumed to represent specific ethnic groups that existed in the past. Archaeologically reconstructed societies are classified using a taxonomy of forms of human society that was developed in conjunction with cultural anthropologists in the middle of the twentieth century. Its major categories are bands, tribes, chiefdoms, and states.

6. In recent years, many archaeologists have rethought their traditional methods. Feminist archaeologists explored why women's contributions have been systematically written out of the archaeological record. Gender archaeologists have questioned the assumption that a male-female gender division is universal and have asked instead how variation in sex, gender, and other kinds of difference can be inferred from archaeological remains of past societies. Collaborative forms of archaeological research have increasingly involved cooperation between scientists and members of groups with past or current connections to the sites under investigation. In recent years, however, archaeological sites and artifacts have become the target of claims by a number of additional groups, including local and national governments, international institutions such as UNESCO, and tourists. These groups do not always agree about the value of cultural heritage preservation or about who has the right to decide the fate of remains from the past. Many archaeologists have concluded that it is vital to develop a cosmopolitan understanding of the claims of these varied stakeholders and to promote conversations among them, even if achieving consensus may not be possible.

For Review

1. What do archaeologists do?
2. Compare and contrast survey archaeology and excavation.
3. What kinds of questions do archaeologists ask about the human past, and what kinds of evidence do they look for in order to answer these questions?
4. List the different human subsistence strategies presented in the text. How have cultural anthropologists and archaeologists contributed to the identification of these strategies?
5. Make a table of the characteristics of bands, tribes, chiefdoms, and states. How have cultural anthropologists and archaeologists together made use of these categories in their work? How do they help? What are their drawbacks?
6. Who owns the past? In your answer, draw on the discussion of various answers to this question presented in the chapter.
7. What is NAGPRA, and why are its requirements so important to archaeologists?
8. Explain why the looting of archaeological sites is so problematic for archaeological attempts to reconstruct the human past.
9. Using case studies in which gender considerations inform archaeological work, describe feminist archaeology.
10. What are collaborative approaches to studying the past? Illustrate your answers with examples from the text.
11. What does it mean to speak of a "cosmopolitan" orientation in archaeology? Refer in your answer to the example given in the text.

Key Terms

archaeological record   154
archaeology   154
artifacts   154
band   163
chiefdom   163

cosmopolitanism   174
ethnoarchaeology   155
excavation   159
features   154
feminist archaeology   170

gender archaeology   170
historical archaeology   173
site   154
sodalities   163

state   164
status   163
subsistence strategy   161
survey   156
tribe   163

Suggested Readings

Fagan, Brian. 2002. *Archaeology: A brief introduction*, 8th ed. Englewood Cliffs, NJ: Prentice Hall. *The latest edition of a brief, classic introductory archaeology text.*

Feder, Kenneth L. 2005. *Frauds, myths, and mysteries: Science and pseudoscience in archaeology*, 5th ed. New York: McGraw-Hill. *Feder shows how scientific archaeological methods can be used to expose dubious claims about the past.*

Joyce, Rosemary A. 2008. *Ancient bodies, ancient lives: Sex, gender, and archaeology.* New York: Thames and Hudson. *A sophisticated yet accessible introduction to gender archaeology. Highly recommended.*

Price, T. Douglas, and Anne Birgitte Gebauer. 2002. *Adventures in Fugawiland: Computer simulation in archaeology*, 3rd ed. New York: McGraw-Hill. *This simulation, for Windows PC only, gives users "hands-on" experience in basic archaeological field techniques.*

Renfrew, Colin, and Paul Bahn. 2008. *Archaeology: Theories, methods, and practice*, 5th ed. New York: Thames and Hudson. *A voluminous, profusely illustrated, up-to-date introduction to all facets of modern archaeology.*

Why Did Humans Settle Down, Build Cities, and Establish States?

odern human beings took what appear in
retrospect to have been three majors steps
that profoundly transformed the lives of
their descendents: some of them settled in one place for
extended periods of time; some of them later began to
intervene in the reproductive cycle of plants and animals,
while the habitat in which they lived produced domestication and agriculture; and perhaps about 7,500 years
ago, a few peoples in the world independently developed social systems characterized by structural complexity and status inequality. In this chapter we survey what
anthropological research can tell us about the causes
and consequences of these developments.

Chapter Outline

◀ *Maya ruins at Palenque, Mexico.*

Today, many of us take settled life and dependence on agriculture for granted, but anthropologists argue that this was neither an easy nor an inevitable outcome of human history. In this chapter, we provide an overview of what anthropologists are able to say about the changes in human subsistence patterns, especially the factors responsible for the domestication of plants and animals. We then consider the impact of human dependence on culturally constructed agricultural niches for subsequent developments in human prehistory.

Human Imagination and the Material World

Human dependence on culture is as much a requirement for survival as it is a source of freedom. Human imagination and cultural experimentation can suggest which aspects of the material world to pay attention to, and these suggestions can become part of a cultural tradition. At the same time, once a group commits itself to paying attention to some parts of the material world rather than others, it locks itself into a set of relationships that it may not be able to abandon freely. These relationships become entrenched: they exert a determinant pressure on future choices. As we shall see, when people began to rely on cultivated plants and domesticated animals, not only did their use of the same landscape change, but they also found that they could not easily go back to their previous ways of using the environment to gather wild plants and hunt animals.

A good place to begin to study the relationship between human imagination and the material world is to consider how the need to make a living has led human beings to develop different forms of social organization in different natural environments. It turns out, however, that people can make a living in much the same way in different environments or in different ways in the same environment. People work in factories in the tropical coastlands of Nigeria and in the bitter cold of Siberia in Russia; in Papua New Guinea, similar environments are used for gardening by some people, whereas others have established huge plantations. Our study therefore

requires us to pay attention to factors that do not depend on the natural environment alone: features of a group's cultural tradition, for example, or external influences due to unpredictable historical encounters with other human groups. In sum, documenting and accounting for major transformations in human material adaptations require attention to ecological, economic, and sociocultural factors.

As we have seen, paleoanthropologists and archaeologists combine their knowledge with that of other scientific specialists in order to reconstruct earlier modes of human life. Based on these reconstructions, we know that our ancestors lived by gathering and hunting, at a band level of social organization, for most of human prehistory. But about 10,000 years ago, at the end of the Pleistocene, the last ice sheets retreated, sea levels rose, winds shifted, and environments changed. Human beings responded to these changes by systematically interfering with the reproduction of other species, in order to suit them better to human purposes. This process is called **domestication**, and it occurred independently in seven different areas of the world between 10,000 and 4,000 years ago (B. Smith 1995, 12–13).

To appreciate the ways human beings responded to these environmental and ecological changes, anthropologists have needed to draw upon concepts taken from the discipline of ecology. To begin with, ecologists are not content to speak vaguely of "the environment" when they discuss the relations that species develop with each other and with the material world in which they live. Rather, they look for patterns in these relations in specific geographic settings. Traditionally, a population of a species is said to have adapted to a particular local physical environment, or *habitat*, when it has found a place, or *niche*, for itself in the local community of organisms within that habitat. An **ecological niche** includes the space the population occupies and what it eats. Broader definitions also include how different populations relate to one another and the impact of their activities on the community (Figure 7.2). Many contemporary ecologists would argue that niches are best defined in terms of the activities of a particular species, including the space, time, and resources that a population utilizes on a daily or seasonal basis (Odling-Smee et al. 2003, 39).

Traditional ecological studies of animal populations in particular habitats have explained the social organization of that population's members—a troop of baboons, for example—by conceiving of space, time, and resources as limiting factors to which that population must adapt if it is to survive and reproduce successfully. Biologists studying changing adaptations over time

---

domestication Human interference with the reproduction of another species, with the result that specific plants and animals become more useful to people and dependent on them.

ecological niche Any species' way of life: what it eats and how it finds mates, raises its young, relates to companions, and protects itself from predators.

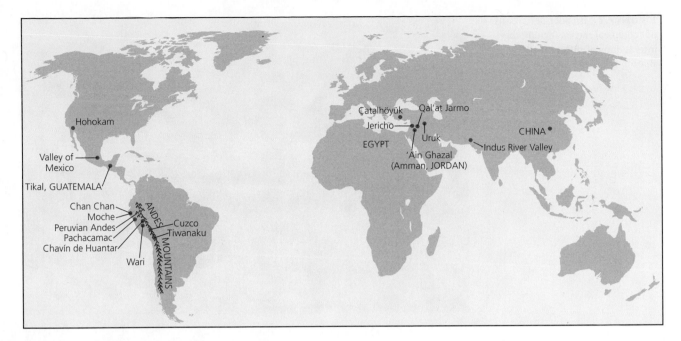

Figure 7.1   Major locations discussed in Chapter 7.

convert this ecological niche concept into an **evolution-ary niche** concept by treating "the niche of any population as the sum of all the natural selection pressures to which the population is exposed . . . that part of its niche from which it is actually earning its living, from which it is not excluded by other organisms, and in which it is either able to exclude other organisms or to compete with coexisting organisms" (Odling-Smee et al. 2003, 40). Two further ecological concepts are needed to describe the dynamics relating organisms to their niches: morphological *features*, a term ecologists apply to the phenotypic traits or characteristics of organisms, and environmental *factors*, a term which refers to subsystems of the organism's environment. "Thus, natural selection can be described as promoting a matching of features and factors" (Odling-Smee et al. 2003, 41).

Ordinarily, ecologists and evolutionary biologists assume that environmental factors are more powerful than morphological features of organisms: that is, natural selection involves an organism's adaptation *to* the environment. Ever since Darwin, it has been clear that this process of adaptation has played a powerful role in the evolution of life on earth. However, as we noted in earlier chapters and as the notion of ecological niche implies, organisms are not passive occupants of rigid environmental slots. Their activities regularly modify the factors in their habitats, as when birds build nests, gophers dig burrows, or beavers build dams. Moreover, these environmental modifications can be passed on to their descendants (or to other organisms living in their local communities). As

we saw in Chapter 2, this process is called **niche construction**. To qualify as niche construction, the modifications made by organisms to their environments must persist and/or accumulate over time, in order to affect selection pressures. The legacy of altered environments with modified selection pressures is what Odling-Smee et al. call an "ecological inheritance" (2003, 42).

How widely the process of niche construction can be successfully applied throughout the living world is controversial. But it makes excellent sense of the history of human adaptations. For example, Odling-Smee et al. argue that the effects of niche construction (or its absence) should be visible when we consider the morphologies of organisms living in particular habitats. If niche construction is absent, we should expect to find that successful organisms have adapted to their environments through modifications of their phenotypes. However, if niche construction has been present in evolution, organisms should show less phenotypic change in response to environmental changes. That is, the organisms modify their selective environments in ways that buffer them against selection for morphological changes. And they argue that this is exactly what we seem to find in

evolutionary niche Sum of all the natural selection pressures to which a population is exposed.

niche construction When an organism actively perturbs the environment or when it actively moves into a different environment, thereby modifying the selection pressures it is subject to.

Figure 7.2 Broader definitions of ecological niches include the interactions of different species sharing the same habitat.

hominin evolutionary history (2003, 348–50). People who live in extremely cold climates do not adapt by growing fur—they modify their environment by making clothing, building shelters, and heating them.

As we saw in the previous chapter, the archaeological record documents a changing legacy of human modifications to environments that, at certain points, also allowed our ancestors to make a successful living in geographical regions of the world that previously had been impenetrable to them. Particularly in the last 200,000 years, we see minor morphological change in the hominin line accompanied by dramatic elaboration of human means of environmental modification. It is within this context that questions about transitions in human adaptive patterns are most fruitfully addressed.

Is Plant Cultivation a Form of Niche Construction?

For many years, scholars have argued about the extent to which plant domestication was accidental or intentional. Biologist David Rindos, for example, suggests that domestication could have occurred without people's full awareness of what they were doing. Reminding us that human beings are just another animal species that eats plants, Rindos argues that the relationship between humans and plants is no different in principle from the relationship between a species of ant and a species of acacia. The ants live inside enlarged thorns on acacia trees. They consume a sugary substance produced at the base of the acacia leaves, and they feed modified leaf tips

to their larvae. But the ants also eat other insects that would otherwise attack acacia leaves. Ant activity is so beneficial to the acacia trees that "when ants were experimentally removed from acacias, the plants were severely attacked and all died within a year" (1984, 102).

The unintended, mutually beneficial effects of acacia trees and ants on each other modify the natural selection pressures each species experiences; this is what biologists call *mutualism*. Examples of multispecies mutualism illustrate the important fact that species need not be related to one another only as predators and prey. Indeed, mutualistic species together achieve higher biological fitnesses than either could have achieved on its own. At the same time, to focus narrowly on the mutualistic *species* themselves neglects the wider environmental context within which both species must make a living. Rindos's example needs to invoke that context in order to explain why acacia trees did so poorly when the ants were removed. It is not simply that these two species lived together in a nonpredatory manner; rather, each species served to modify significantly the ecological niche of the other species, buffering it from selective pressures that it would otherwise have been exposed to.

Clearly, ants and acacia trees were able to develop this relationship without conscious planning. But does this mean, as Robert Wenke quipped (1999, 271), that "people have proved to be excellent devices for cereals to conquer the world"? Some feminist archaeologists are wary of this way of approaching plant domestication by humans. First, to argue that domestication was an unconscious process overlooks the fact that human beings of the late Pleistocene were fully modern and bright enough to understand cause and effect concerning their

Figure 7.3 Industrial agriculture converts acres of habitat into a uniform agroecology for growing commercial crops like sunflowers.

livelihood. Thus, they surely selected deliberately those plants that were easier to harvest, more nourishing, and tastier. In this view, humans actively intervened in the gene pool of the wild plants; domestication was conscious, not unconscious. Second, women in contemporary foraging societies are primarily responsible for gathering wild plants, which makes women likely candidates for the first human ancestors to have experimented with plant domestication. To assume, therefore, that plant domestication was a passive, unconscious process looks like the imposition of a crude sexist stereotype on the subsistence behaviors of our ancestors. Third, paying attention only to the plants and the people ignores the kinds of *environmental modifications* needed to make plant domestication successful, which clearly depended on conscious, active human intervention.

Some archaeologists try to fill in this gap. T. Douglas Price and Anne Birgitte Gebauer, for example, distinguish between domestication and cultivation. *Domestication* is human interference with the reproduction of another species, with the result that specific plants and animals become both more useful to people and dependent on them. It modifies the genotypes and phenotypes of plants and animals as they become dependent upon humans. *Cultivation*, by contrast, is a deliberate cultural process involving the activities of preparing fields, sowing, weeding, harvesting, and storing and which requires a new way of thinking about subsistence and new technology to bring it about (1995, 6). That is, habitats suitable for domesticated species must be carefully constructed and maintained in order for the domesticated species to mature and be harvested successfully. Indeed, the same process is required for successful animal domestication.

From this perspective, **agriculture** is best understood as the systematic modification of "the environments of plants and animals to increase their productivity and usefulness" (Wenke 1999, 270). Price and Gebauer call this systematically modified environment (or constructed niche) the **agroecology**, which becomes the only environment within which the plants (or animals) can flourish (Figure 7.3). Bruce Smith emphasizes that activities that led to domestication were conscious, deliberate, active attempts by foraging peoples to "increase both the economic contribution and the reliability of one or more of the wild species they depended on for survival, and thus reduce risk and uncertainty" (1995, 16). Such activities include burning off vegetation to encourage preferred plants that thrive in burned-over landscapes or to attract wild animals that feed on such plants (Figure 7.4). These are clear examples of niche construction. The ancestors of domesticated seed plants like wheat were weedy generalists that, in addition to their dietary appeal, thrived in disturbed environments. Such attributes made them prime candidates for domestication.

To better understand how domestication and agriculture developed, both need to be distinguished from **sedentism** which is the process of increasingly

agriculture The systematic modification of the environments of plants and animals to increase their productivity and usefulness.

agroecology The systematically modified environment (or constructed niche) which becomes the only environment within which domesticated plants can flourish.

sedentism The process of increasingly permanent human habitation in one place.

Figure 7.4 In Australia, hunter–gatherers burn vegetation to encourage the growth of plants.

permanent human habitation in one place and contrasts with the less permanent, more nomadic patterns of habitation experienced by earlier hominins. But people do not have to become farmers in order to become sedentary. The sedentary adaptations of the indigenous people of the northwest coast of North America depended not on agriculture but on seasonally abundant salmon runs, which could be "harvested" as regularly as crops but involved minimal ecological interference and no processes of domestication.

Sedentism is probably more usefully understood as a consequence of humans choosing to depend on resources in particular kinds of constructed niches. Sedentism is a key element that modifies the selection pressures of those who come to depend on subsistence resources in a fixed location, be it a riverbank or a cultivated field or a pasture. Human beings who farm for a living may buffer themselves against periodic famine and be able to support larger populations. At the same time, they make themselves vulnerable to a variety of new selection pressures brought about by sedentary life: exposure to threats from agricultural pests and thieves, as well as disease organisms that breed and spread more successfully among settled people than they do among nomads. As we saw, the clearing of forest by the first farmers in West Africa apparently created ecological conditions favoring larger pools of standing water, which were the ideal breeding grounds for malaria-carrying mosquitoes. This, in turn, created a new selection pressure in favor of the sickle cell allele, which offers heterozygous carriers some protection against malaria (Odling-Smee et al. 2003, 251).

What obstacles faced those who first interfered in the life cycle of wild plants? If the plant was a grass, like wheat, they had to cope with that plant's reproductive pattern. The wheat kernel, both domesticated and wild, is attached to the cereal shaft by a spikelet called the "rachis" (Figure 7.5). In wild wheat, the rachis becomes extremely brittle as the kernel ripens, and the kernels on any stem ripen from bottom to top over a week or two. As each kernel ripens, the rachis can be broken by an animal walking through the stand of wheat or even by a gust of wind, dispersing the kernel into the air and eventually onto the ground. Wild wheat has two rows of kernels on each stalk. Because the kernels ripen at different times, the seeds have a greater chance of scattering in different directions and not all landing at the foot of the parent plant in a clump. The kernel of wild wheat is enclosed in a tough outer husk called a "glume," which protects the kernel from frost and dehydration and allows it to remain viable for as long as 20 years in the ground.

To be used successfully by human beings, wheat would require a much less brittle rachis, seed heads that mature at the same time, and a softer glume. It would also require a larger, more easily visible seed head (in terms of both kernel size and number of kernel rows on a stalk). Plants with these variations would have had a selective advantage once human beings began to eat them. As the genes responsible for these traits increased in the wheat plant population—changes which, given plant genetics, might have taken very few generations—the plants would have contributed more and more to the human diet. The earliest domesticated wheat shows precisely these evolutionary trends, including six rows of kernels on a stalk rather than two.

The constructed niches favorable for agriculture have also varied over time and space in several important ways, and they did not appear overnight. David Harris (1989,

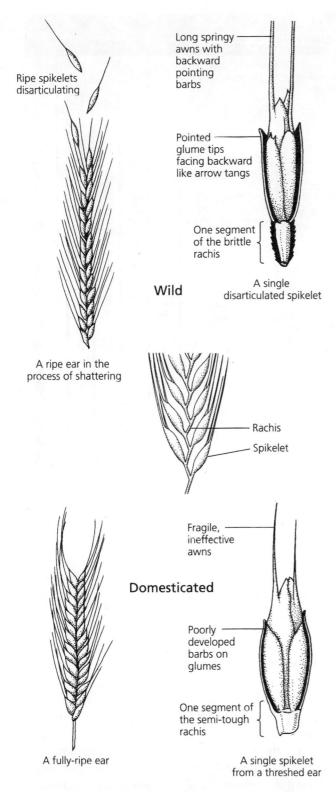

Figure 7.5 Wheat kernels form within spikelets that attach to the plant by a structure called the "rachis." The rachis of wild wheat is brittle, which aids the dispersal of seeds in the wild. The rachis of domesticated wheat is not brittle, and spikelets remain attached to the ear during harvest. (B. Smith 1995, 73)

17) provides a useful overview of these patterns and classifies the relationships between plants and people into four major food-yielding systems: (1) wild plant-food procurement, (2) wild plant-food production, (3) cultivation, and (4) agriculture (Figure 7.6). Harris notes that there are three points at which the amount of energy people put into plant-food activities increases sharply: (1) where wild plant-food production begins, (2) where cultivation begins, and (3) where agriculture begins.

Animal Domestication

Animal domestication can be defined as "the capture and taming by human beings of animals of a species with particular behavioral characteristics, their removal from their natural living area and breeding community, and their maintenance under controlled breeding conditions for mutual benefits" (Bökönyi 1989, 22). This definition views animal domestication as a consequence of people's attempts to control the animals they were hunting, which assumes active human intervention in selecting which animals to domesticate and how to domesticate them. Animals are more mobile than plants, and although culling wild herds can induce some changes in the gene pool, it is only by confining animals or maintaining them in captivity that human beings can intervene in their breeding patterns.

Of course, the innocent phrase "maintaining them in captivity" covers a range of different modifications to the environments of domesticated animals. Captive animals, especially those successfully domesticated, become dependent on the modified niche supplied to them by human beings. As we will see, these modifications may range from protecting selected animals from other predators to supplying them with food and water to close monitoring of their life cycles, from birth to slaughter, under highly artificial conditions. And again, human commitment to the construction of niches favorable to domesticated animals simultaneously modifies the selection pressures which humans experience: dependence on a reliable supply of meat and skins may mean that a human group is obliged to follow a herd wherever it chooses to go or obliged to modify their own adaptations seasonally in order to move herds to reliable supplies of water and forage. Such movements will make humans vulnerable to negative as well as positive encounters with other habitats and other species, including other human beings, with whom they will have to come to terms if their pastoral adaptation is to succeed. Not all people are pleased when herders pasture their animals in areas where cultivated plants are growing.

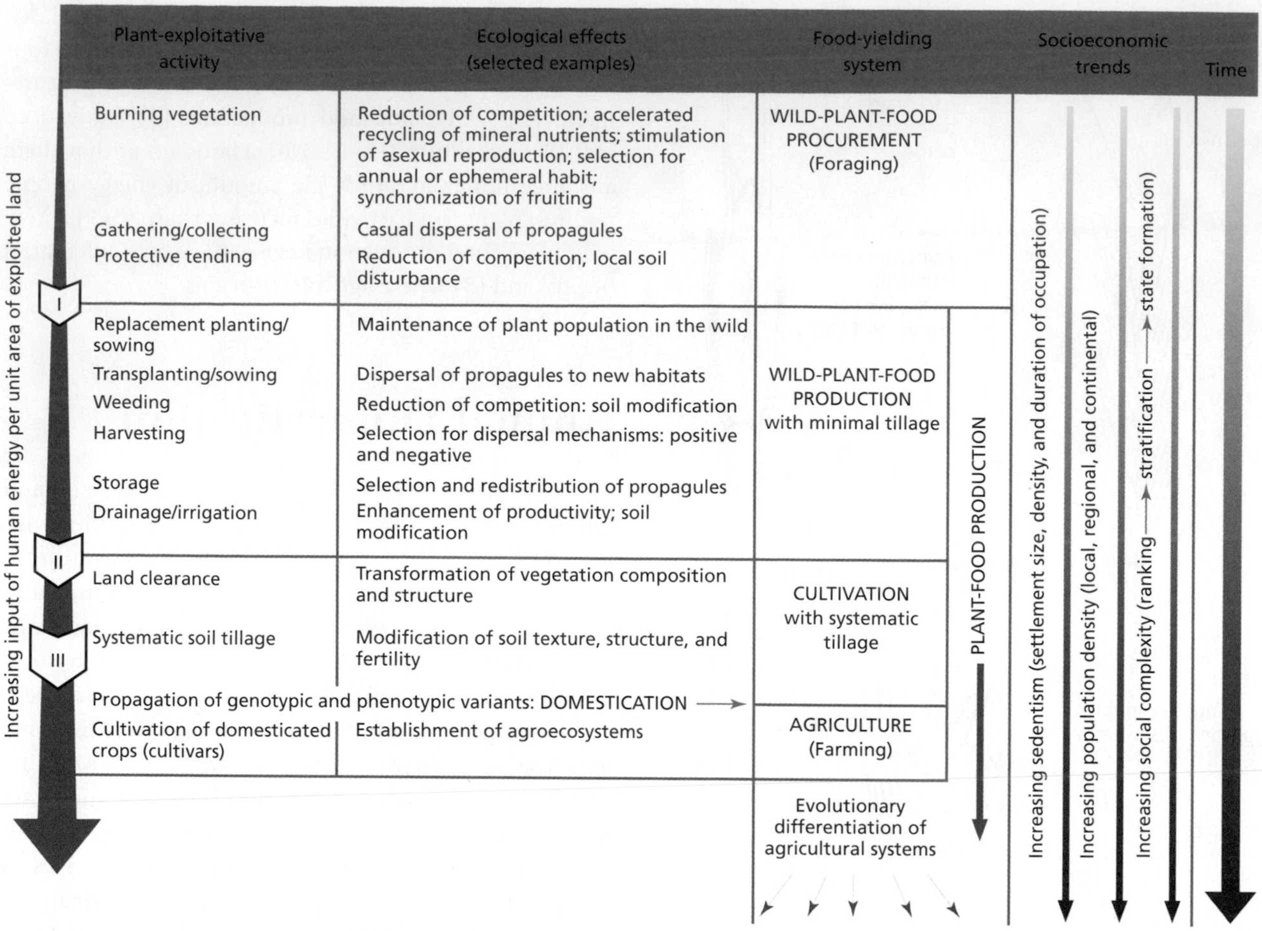

Plant-exploitative activity	Ecological effects (selected examples)	Food-yielding system	Socioeconomic trends	Time
Burning vegetation	Reduction of competition; accelerated recycling of mineral nutrients; stimulation of asexual reproduction; selection for annual or ephemeral habit; synchronization of fruiting	WILD-PLANT-FOOD PROCUREMENT (Foraging)		
Gathering/collecting	Casual dispersal of propagules			
Protective tending	Reduction of competition; local soil disturbance			
Replacement planting/ sowing	Maintenance of plant population in the wild	WILD-PLANT-FOOD PRODUCTION with minimal tillage		
Transplanting/sowing	Dispersal of propagules to new habitats			
Weeding	Reduction of competition: soil modification			
Harvesting	Selection for dispersal mechanisms: positive and negative			
Storage	Selection and redistribution of propagules			
Drainage/irrigation	Enhancement of productivity; soil modification			
Land clearance	Transformation of vegetation composition and structure	CULTIVATION with systematic tillage		
Systematic soil tillage	Modification of soil texture, structure, and fertility			
Propagation of genotypic and phenotypic variants: DOMESTICATION →				
Cultivation of domesticated crops (cultivars)	Establishment of agroecosystems	AGRICULTURE (Farming)		
		Evolutionary differentiation of agricultural systems		

Increasing input of human energy per unit area of exploited land

Stages: I, II, III

PLANT-FOOD PRODUCTION

Increasing sedentism (settlement size, density, and duration of occupation)

Increasing population density (local, regional, and continental)

Increasing social complexity (ranking → stratification → state formation)

Figure 7.6 The four major food-yielding systems according to David Harris. Energy-input/ energy-output ratios jump sharply where wild plant-food production begins, where cultivation begins, and where agriculture begins. (The *propagules* referred to in the second column are the forms by which plants are reproduced—seeds, shoots, and so on.) (Harris 1989, 17)

Animal domestication is difficult to measure with precision in the archaeological record. Wenke (1999) identifies four main classes of evidence used by archaeologists to assess animal domestication. First, the presence of an animal species outside its natural range may indicate herding. For example, because the southern Levant (the coastal area at the eastern end of the Mediterranean Sea; see Figure 7.7) is outside the area in which wild sheep evolved, scholars say that sheep remains found there constituted evidence of herding: the sheep must have been brought into the area by people. For such an argument to be effective, we must be sure we know precisely what the natural range of the wild species was.

Second, morphological changes occur in most animal populations as domestication progresses. Wenke and Olszewski (2007, 253) point out that the shape and size of sheep horns reflect the process of domestication. Wild sheep have larger, stronger horns than do domesticated sheep. In wild sheep, large horns are connected with the breeding hierarchies that males establish

through fighting. The selective pressure for these horns relaxed as sheep were domesticated, so horn size and shape changed.

Third, the abrupt population increase of some species relative to others at a site is often taken as evidence of domestication. About 9,000 years ago in southwestern Asia, the makeup of animal-bone assemblages changes. The nearly total domination of gazelle bones gives way, and the percentage of sheep and goat bones increases dramatically.

Fourth, the age and gender of the animals whose bones are fossilized are used to infer the existence of animal domestication. Researchers assume that numerous remains of immature or juvenile herd animals, especially males, represents human involvement with the herd. Why? In the wild, animals killed for meat come from a much wider age range; there is no emphasis on younger, especially younger male, animals. Also, human beings who manage herds kill immature males more readily than females because only a small number of

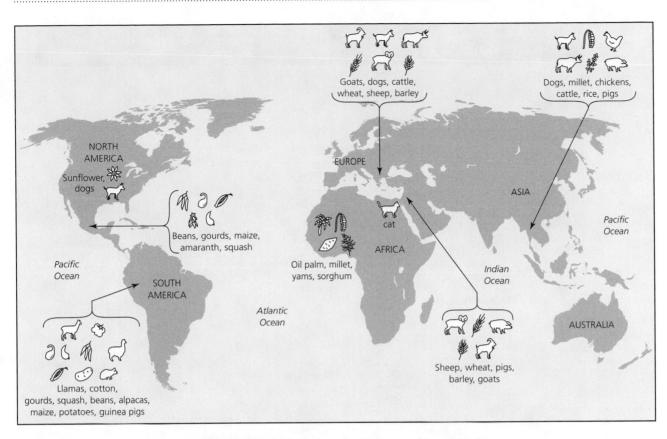

Figure 7.7 A map of probable locations where various plants and animals were domesticated.

males are required for reproduction, while larger numbers of females provide more offspring, more milk, and other products such as dung, wool, and hair. Analyses of the age and sex structure of animal remains help to establish the function of a domesticated herd: a meat herd contains a lot of adolescent and young adult animals, while a dairy herd consists mostly of adult females.

How did animal domestication begin? The earliest known domesticated animal was the dog, for which there is Old World evidence from a Magdalenian cave site in northern Spain as old as 16,000 years. Clearly, there were significant mutual advantages for both dogs and human beings to team up in the hunt. The first barely domesticated wolves must have been fearsome companions for Paleolithic hunters, but eventually the human–dog relationship became a very close one. A human grave at Mallaha, in modern Israel, dating to about 12,000 years ago, contains the remains of a puppy buried under the arm of a human corpse. Other sites in the area also have remains of dogs, rather than wolves (Figure 7.8).

It seems that other animals were domesticated to provide food rather than to help get food. Frank Hole argues that people in different areas experimented with animals found around them to determine which ones were both desirable as food and amenable to human control. Both sheep and goats were relatively harmless, gregarious

herd animals that had multiple uses for human beings and were found seasonally in the same locales as the ripening plants that people wanted to harvest.

However, the evidence, as summarized by Hole, puts sheep and goats in different ecological zones of northern Mesopotamia, and it is likely that their distribution did not overlap much, if at all (Figures 7.7 and 7.8). In other words, sheep and goats were domesticated separately and at different times. The earliest evidence for goat herding is about 11,000–10,000 years before the present, in a narrow zone along the front of the Zagros Mountains. The earliest sites for domesticated sheep were perhaps in central Anatolia (the Asian part of modern Turkey). The evidence for two other major Old World animal domesticates, cattle and pigs, is much more difficult to come by but seems to point to multiple domestication sites for cattle from China to western Europe beginning sometime after 11,000 years ago. Domesticated pig bones have been found throughout southwestern Asia as far back as 8,000 years.

As mentioned above, wild-hunted and domesticated-herded are but extreme ends of a continuum of animal–human–environment relationships. Jarman and his associates outline six stages in these relationships (1982, 51–54). The first is *random hunting*, in which hunters make no attempt to control herds but hunt

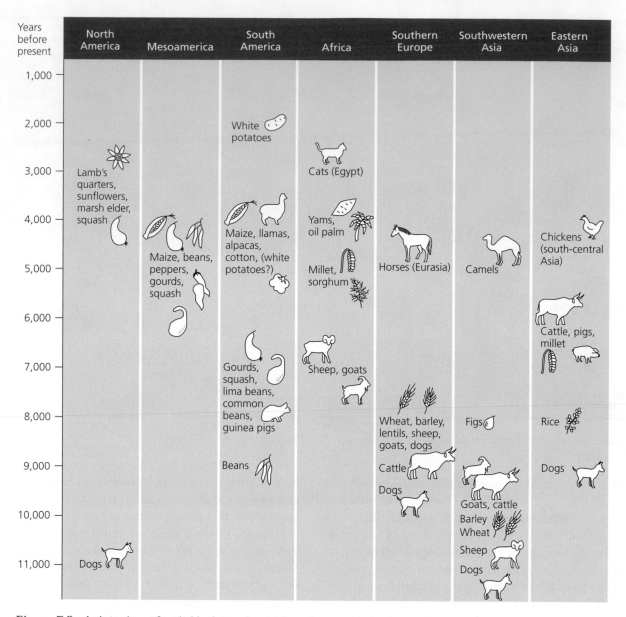

Figure 7.8   A chronology of probable dates when various plants and animals were domesticated in different regions.

animals as they find them. The second stage, *controlled hunting*, involves the selective hunting of herds—killing young males, for example. This is the beginning of regular human intervention in the herd species' gene pool. In the third stage, *herd following*, specific herds and specific groups of people begin to interact regularly; as the herd moves from place to place, the people also move. The fourth stage, *loose herding*, is when people begin to control the movements of the herd. They move the herd at various times of the year, ensuring that all of the animals move safely at the same time. They also actively intervene in the herd's gene pool through selective breeding and culling. The fifth stage, *close herding*, is the most familiar practice in much of the United States and western

Europe. The animals' mobility is limited, and their gene pool is actively managed. In the sixth stage, *factory farming*, there is very active human intervention in all aspects of the animals' lives. In some cases, animals never leave the building or feedlot in which they are raised.

Not all animals that were hunted, even in a controlled way, were domesticated. The gazelle is a good example: there is evidence that controlled hunting about 9,500 years ago in southwestern Asia led to significant changes in the gazelle gene pool, but there is no evidence of domestication. Clearly, culling herds of certain kinds of animals—male rather than female, less woolly rather than more woolly, thinner rather than fatter—affects the gene pool in ways that demonstrate that people have an influence on animals even if the animals are not fully domesticated. Thus, herd following shades almost imperceptibly into loose herding.

Richard Meadow, by contrast, argues that herding represents a complete change in human attitudes toward and relationships with animals (1989, 81). At the very least, the human focus shifts from the hunted animal to the principal product of the living animal—its offspring. This shift, he suggests, is connected to a major shift in worldview that was involved in the other cultural processes—sedentism and plant cultivation—of post-Pleistocene southwestern Asia: the development of a concern for property and its maintenance over time. Meadow argues that this change in focus was essential for the development of herding as a social and cultural phenomenon and for the development of social complexity.

Was There Only One Motor of Domestication?

About 10,000 years ago, after nearly 4 million years of hominin evolution and over 100,000 years of successful foraging by *Homo sapiens*, human beings living in distant and unconnected parts of the world nearly simultaneously developed subsistence strategies that involved domesticated plants and animals. Why? Some scholars have sought a single, universal explanation that would explain all original cases of domestication. Thus, it has been argued that domestication is the outcome of population pressure as the increasing hunting-and-gathering human population overwhelmed the existing food resources. Others point to climate change or famine as the postglacial climate got drier. Increasing archaeological research has made it clear, however, that the evidence in favor of any single-cause, universally applicable explanation is weak.

Some scholars have proposed universally applicable explanations that take several different phenomena into account. One such explanation, called **broad-spectrum foraging**, is based on a reconstruction of the environmental situation that followed the retreat of the most recent glaciers. The very large animals of the Ice Age began to die out and were replaced by increased numbers of smaller animals. As sea levels rose to cover the continental shelves, fish and shellfish became more plentiful in the warmer, shallower waters.

The effects on plants were equally dramatic as forests and woodlands expanded into new areas. Consequently, these scholars argue, people had to change their diets from big game hunting to broad-spectrum foraging for plants and animals by hunting, fishing, and gathering.

This broadening of the economy is said to have led to a more secure subsistence base, the emergence of sedentary communities, and a growth in population. In turn, population growth pressured the resource base of the area, and people were forced to eat "third-choice" foods, particularly wild grain, which was difficult to harvest and process but which responded to human efforts to increase yields. Although the broad-spectrum foraging argument seems to account for plant domestication in the New World, the most recent evidence from ancient southwestern Asia does not support it. There is also evidence for the development of broad-spectrum gathering in Europe, but domestication did not follow. Rather, domesticated crops were brought into Europe by people from southwestern Asia, where a broad-spectrum revolution had not occurred.

A very different kind of argument came from Barbara Bender (1977), who suggested that before farming began there was competition between local groups to achieve dominance over each other through feasting and the expenditure of resources on ritual and exchange, engaging in a kind of prehistoric "arms race." To meet increasing demands for food and other resources, land use was intensified, and the development of food production followed. This argument emphasizes social factors, rather than environmental or technical factors, and takes a localized, regional approach. It is supported by ethnographic accounts concerning competitive exchange activities, such as the *potlatch* of the indigenous inhabitants of the northwest coast of North America. These people were foragers in a rich environment that enabled them to settle in relatively permanent villages without farming or herding. Competition among neighboring groups led to ever more elaborate forms of competitive exchange, with increasingly large amounts of food and other goods being given away at each subsequent potlatch. As suggestive as Bender's argument is, however, it is difficult to find evidence for competitive feasting in archaeological remains.

Recently, archaeologists have avoided grand theories claiming that a single, universal process was responsible for domestication wherever it occurred. Many prefer to take a regional approach, searching for causes particular to one area that may or may not apply to other areas. Currently, the most powerful explanations seem to be *multiple strand theories* that consider the combined local effect of climate, environment, population, technology, social organization, and diet on the

---

broad-spectrum foraging A subsistence strategy based on collecting a wide range of plants and animals by hunting, fishing, and gathering.

emergence of domestication. The multiple strand approach is well illustrated in an article by McCorriston and Hole (1991), and their work forms the basis for the following case study of domestication in ancient southwestern Asia.

How Did Domestication, Cultivation, and Sedentism Begin in Southwest Asia?

Southwestern Asian domestication is thought to have begun about 12,500 years ago with the Natufian foragers, who relied on the intensive exploitation of wild cereals (notably wild wheat and barley), nuts (especially acorns, pistachios, and almonds), and wild game (especially gazelle and red deer) (Belfer-Cohen 1991, 167; Figures 7.7 and 7.8). Because of the climatic and ecological changes in the world that followed the retreat of the glaciers, the Natufians were able to exploit what were, at first, increasingly rich supplies of wild cereals and large herds of gazelle, which made sedentism possible. Although many Natufian sites are small hunting camps, researchers have discovered at least two dozen Natufian villages, or base camps, that reached a size of 1,000 m² (about a quarter of an acre) and beyond (Belfer-Cohen 1991, 176–77). Henry estimates that the Natufian hamlets ranged from 40 to 150 people (1989, 218); they were five to ten times larger than the mobile foraging camps of the peoples who preceded them.

That these early Natufian villages were more than just campsites is revealed in their architecture (Figure 7.9). Natufian houses were dug partially into the ground and had walls of stone and mud with some timber posts and probably roof beams. At the Mallaha site, archaeologists found plaster-lined storage pits in the houses. Archaeologists infer that such buildings, which required a considerable amount of labor and material to build, were not constructed for brief residence only. Archaeologists also found massive stone mortars used to grind seeds. The implication is that people could not have transported such heavy utensils, nor would they have invested the time and effort to make them if they were going to abandon them after one season's use. In addition, the remains of migratory birds and a great number of young gazelle bones indicate year-round hunting from the hamlets because migratory birds fly over the area

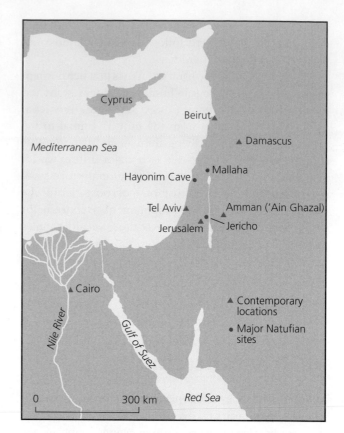

Figure 7.9   Major Natufian sites in the southern Levant in relation to other contemporary features.

during different seasons and young gazelles are born at one time only during the year.

Finally, artistic production among the Natufians was high. Anna Belfer-Cohen and others suggest that artistic activity may be viewed as indirect evidence for a sedentary way of life that forces people to interact regularly with others who are not closely related to them. In these situations, the production of such objects as personal ornaments helps to create a sense of identity among smaller groups while allowing them to participate in a larger society (Belfer-Cohen 1988, 1991; Lewis-Williams 1984). Elaborate ritual and ceremonial activities would also have soothed interactions and reduced tensions in increasingly large communities where cooperation was essential (Henry 1989, 206).

Natufian Social Organization

Information about social organization from the archaeological record is indirect, but Donald Henry (1989) believes that over time Natufian society developed social divisions with unequal access to wealth, power, and prestige. That is, Natufian society showed **social stratification**, an important sign of social complexity. His evidence comes from Natufian burials.

social stratification A form of social organization in which people have unequal access to wealth, power, and prestige.

In early Natufian times, the dead were buried together in small groups, which Henry believes corresponded to subgroups of a larger community. There is evidence that relatives lived in the same area for several generations. For example, nearly half the skeletons recovered from the Hayonim Cave site showed evidence of the genetically recessive trait, *third-molar agenesis* (failure of the third molars, or wisdom teeth, to develop). This trait occurs at much lower frequencies—on the order of 0–20 percent—in other human populations. Evidence from six other Natufian sites revealed the normal frequency of third-molar agenesis, suggesting that the group that lived at Hayonim Cave mated with other members of their own group rather than with outsiders. It seems this mating pattern continued at Hayonim Cave for about 1,000 years (Henry 1989, 208). These group burials sometimes included dentalium shell headdresses, which were decorative and valuable objects with no identifiable practical use (Figure 7.10). In other cases, elaborate grave goods were buried with children. Both these burial practices indicate the differentiation of subgroups and inherited status differences. These group burials suggest that in early Natufian times social position depended on which group a person belonged to, rather than on a communitywide set of social standards.

In late Natufian times, there were still differences in grave goods from one burial to the next but the dead were buried individually in cemeteries. The new pattern suggests that the old boundaries around descent groups had been destroyed and replaced by a new pattern in which resources were controlled by an entire community and stratification was communitywide. Some people now coordinated activities for the group as a whole and had come to occupy high-status positions that cross-cut subgroup boundaries. For these reasons, Henry suggests that Natufian social organization had come to resemble what is called a "chiefdom" in anthropological literature. *Chiefdoms*, you will recall, are societies in which a leader (the chief) and close relatives are set apart from the rest of the society and allowed privileged access to wealth, power, and prestige.

Natufian Subsistence

The Natufians obtained 98 percent of their meat protein from red deer, wild sheep, and wild goats, but especially from gazelles, whose bones make up 40–80 percent of all the animal bones recovered from Natufian sites. Henry believes entire herds of gazelle were hunted communally in game drives. Woodlands were burned to promote the growth of young plants, attractive to gazelle and deer. Henry points out that the increased attention to gazelles, wild grains, and nuts also represented specialization of subsistence activities by Natufian foragers (1989, 91). They were *complex foragers*, who live in areas of abundant resources that may have appeared inexhaustible (Price and Gebauer 1995, 7), making them different from *generalized foragers*, who live in less generous environments and cope with shortages by diversifying their subsistence activities.

Unfortunately for the Natufians, the choices they made were destabilizing in the long run. They fed an increasingly large population by intensively exploiting small areas. By settling down, they gave up mobility, the key to the long-term success of a foraging life. The short-term stability and security of sedentism and intensive collection increased the rigidity of their society, making it vulnerable to disruptive environmental changes. And changes came about 10,500 years ago: the shallow interior lakes of the southern Levant were drying up, and the Mediterranean woodlands on which they depended had shrunk to one-half the area they had covered 2,000 years earlier. Natufians in the southern part of the region abandoned their settlements and returned to simple foraging, developing what archaeologists refer to as the "Harifian culture." In the central core of the Natufian area, however, the people tried to keep the cereal plants growing in areas that were no longer ideal for them.

The first evidence for domesticated cereals in this core Natufian area dates to about 10,300 years ago. Both

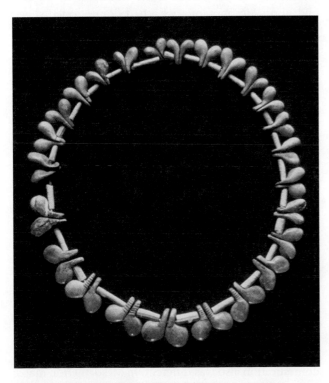

Figure 7.10 A Natufian collar from El Wad with 25 fragments of dentalia separating a type of bone bead. This collar was found in a male burial site.

wheat and barley were found at Jericho and barley alone at other sites. For archaeologists, domesticated plants signal the end of the Paleolithic and the beginning of the **Neolithic**. This transition from the Natufian culture is marked in the southern Levant by the appearance of a culture called the "Pre-Pottery Neolithic A" (PPNA), in which cultivation was practiced but pottery had not yet been invented. PPNA Jericho was much larger than the preceding Natufian settlement, with a surface area of about 2.5 hectares (about 6 acres) and perhaps 300 or more inhabitants (B. Smith 1995, 3). Henry suggests that this was due to the concentration of populations from smaller, more numerous hamlets in a setting where "large tracts of arable land, suitable for hoe cultivation, adjoined year-round water sources" (1989, 53–54).

Jericho was located on the edge of an *alluvial fan* (a fan-shaped accumulation of sediment from flowing water at the mouth of a ravine) on a permanent stream, near hills rich in gazelle, wild grains, and nuts. The stream provided clear drinking water, while the alluvial fan provided mud for bricks and its regular floods provided rich soil for plants. By about 9,300 years ago, the inhabitants of Jericho had built a stone wall, 3 meters thick, 4 meters high, and perhaps 700 meters in circumference (Figure 7.11). The wall, it is now thought, was erected as protection from the floods; similar protections from flooding are found at other PPNA sites, although none is as elaborate as the wall of Jericho (Bar-Yosef and Kislev 1989, 635).

Trade was also significant in PPNA Jericho. Obsidian is an extremely sharp and highly prized volcanic glass that is found in relatively few places worldwide (Figure 7.12). Anatolia, modern Turkey, contained the major sites for obsidian in Neolithic southwestern Asia. Archaeologists have found Anatolian obsidian in Jericho, some 700 kilometers (430 miles) from Anatolia; it is unlikely that residents traveled that distance to get it themselves. Jericho also contained marine shells from the Mediterranean Sea and the Black Sea as well as *amulets* (charms against evil or injury) and greenstone beads. These objects suggest not just trade from village to village but also trade between the settled farmers and the foraging peoples living in the semiarid regions or higher areas.

Beginning about 9,500 years ago, the PPNA culture was replaced by the Pre-Pottery Neolithic B (PPNB) culture, which represents the rapid expansion of agriculture. Although there are but a handful of PPNA sites, all in a small area around Jericho, there are more than

Figure 7.11 By about 9,300 years ago, the inhabitants of Jericho had built a stone wall, probably to protect the settlement from yearly flooding.

140 PPNB sites, many of which are very large and some of which are found in Anatolia and the Zagros Mountains. As the new farming technology moved north and east, it was adapted to fit local circumstances. At some point, farmers met herders from the Zagros Mountains and north Mesopotamia who had domesticated sheep and goats, animals that were well known in their wild state throughout the area. The agriculturalists adopted these herding techniques, which spread quickly and were incorporated into the agricultural life of the entire region. By 8,000 years ago, the farmers in southwestern Asia practiced a mixed agricultural strategy, incorporating grains and livestock.

Domestication Elsewhere in the World

The conditions under which domestication began varied around the world. In highland Mexico, for example, the predomestication population was relatively stable and sedentism had not yet occurred. There are no indications of the kinds of long-term shifts in resource density in Mexico that were characteristic of the eastern Mediterranean. As noted earlier, many scholars agree that broad-spectrum foraging was practiced prior to the transition to domestication in highland Mexico and elsewhere in the New World. The mix of crops characteristic of New World domestication also was different. In Mesoamerica, maize and squash appear between 5,000 and 4,000 years ago, with beans appearing about 2,000 years ago (B. Smith 1994). In South America, maize appears between 4,000

Neolithic The "New Stone Age," which began with the domestication of plants 10,300 years ago.

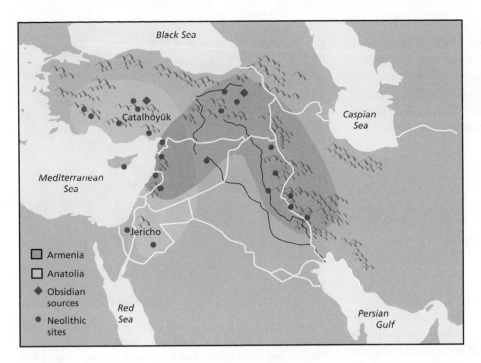

Figure 7.12 The distribution of obsidian in Neolithic southwestern Asia from sources in Anatolia (west) and Armenia (east). Obsidian is an extremely sharp and highly prized volcanic glass. Obsidian was traded widely and has been found as far as 500 miles away from its source.

and 3,000 years ago but was only one of several domesticates. In other areas of South America, soil conditions, altitude, and climate favored root crops—manioc or potatoes—as well as beans, and quinoa (a high-altitude grain), which were of greater importance. Animal domestication was far less important in the Americas than it was in the Old World, largely due to the absence of large, domesticable animals. The Andean llama is the largest animal domesticated in the New World.

Some plants and animals were also domesticated on other continents. Goosefoot, marsh elder, sunflowers, and squash were all domesticated in eastern North America (B. Smith 1995, 189–90). A variety of crops, including coffee, millet, okra, and sorghum, were domesticated in different parts of Africa. A large number of important plant domesticates came from eastern Asia, including rice, yam, tea, sugarcane, garlic, onion, apple, and carrot. Archaeologists are coming to agree that complex foragers living in areas of relatively abundant resources were probably responsible for domestication wherever it developed (Price and Gebauer 1995, 7; B. Smith 1995, 213). Rich and complex archaeological and genetic evidence from specific areas of the world downplay single-cause explanations of domestication and stress the need to consider each domestication event in its own terms. Melinda A. Zeder and Bruce D. Smith (2009) are impressed by abundant and varied data from southwestern Asia showing that during several thousand years prior to the appearance of agriculture, "people appear to have been auditioning a wide variety of region-specific plants and animals for leading roles as domesticated resources in the absence of population increase or resource

imbalance" (2009, 683). In eastern North America, the evidence is similar: climate change at the end of the Pleistocene occurred 5,000 years before initial plant domestication, 6,200 years before the development of a complex of domesticated crops, and 8,500 years before the key shift to maize agriculture. Thus climate change is "a necessary precondition rather than a central causal variable," and there is no evidence for population pressure during the 2000 years or so when plants were first being domesticated and the crop complex first being organized (Zeder and Smith 2009, 686).

In the face of such evidence, Zeder and Smith conclude that "the concept of niche construction provides a useful alternative perspective," emphasizing as it does "the engineering of local ecosystems and the manipulation of targeted resources within local biotic communities" (2009, 687). Zeder and Smith insist that humans "were actively, and with deliberate intent, shaping adaptive niches with the conscious goal of enhancing the density and productivity of desired resources" (2009, 688). Related concerns appear in the work of archaeologists who have adopted from cultural anthropology *theories of practice* that, like niche construction, "examine how humans create macroscale features such as traditions or sociopolitical institutions (structures) through their own daily actions" (Bruno 2009, 703). Bruno also emphasizes the importance for archaeologists of *historical ecology*, which also "focuses on how long-term, accumulative human activities cause observable changes in the natural environment thus creating a 'landscape'" (Bruno 2009, 704). To the extent that the process of niche construction is understood as a form of practical activity and that engineered environments/humanly shaped landscapes are understood as the outcomes of such practical activity, both approaches point in the same direction (Schultz 2009). Their incorporation into anthropological theories of cultural transitions such as the origins of agriculture or social complexity promises to shed important new light on these developments.

What Were the Consequences of Domestication and Sedentism?

Constructed agricultural niches, within which domesticated plants and animals could thrive, promoted sedentism and transformed human life in ways that still have repercussions today. First, land was no longer a free good, available to anyone; it was transformed into particular territories, collectively or individually owned, on which people raised crops and flocks. Thus, sedentism and a high level of resource extraction (whether by complex foraging or farming) led to concepts of property that were rare in previous foraging societies. Graves, grave goods, permanent housing, grain-processing equipment, as well as the fields and herds connected people to places. The human mark on the environment was larger and more obvious following sedentization and the rise of farming: people built terraces or walls to hold back floods, transforming the landscape in more dramatic ways. Second, settling down affected female fertility and contributed to a rise in population. In foraging societies, a woman's pregnancies tend to be spaced 3–4 years apart because of an extended period of breast-feeding. That is, children in foraging societies are weaned at 3 or 4 years of age but still nurse whenever they feel like it, as frequently as several times an hour (Shostak 1981, 67; Figure 7.13). This nursing stimulus triggers the secretion of a hormone that suppresses ovulation (Henry 1989, 41). Henry summarizes the effects of foraging on female fertility:

> It would appear then that a number of interrelated factors associated with a mobile foraging strategy are likely to have provided natural controls on fertility and perhaps explain the low population densities of the Paleolithic. In mobile foraging societies, women are likely to have experienced both long intervals of breastfeeding by carried children as well as the high energy drain associated with subsistence activities and periodic camp moves. Additionally, their diets, being relatively rich in proteins, would have contributed to maintaining low fat levels, thus further dampening fecundity. (1989, 43)

Figure 7.13   Ju/'hoansi mothers and children. Until recently, Ju/'hoansi women used to walk over 1,500 miles per year with children and other burdens on their backs. Children nursed for several years.

With complex foraging and increasing sedentism, these brakes on female fecundity would have been eased. This is not to say that a sedentary life is physically undemanding. Farming requires its own heavy labor, from both men and women. The difference seems to be in the kind of physical activity involved. Walking long distances while carrying heavy loads and children was replaced by sowing, hoeing, harvesting, storing, and processing grain. A diet increasingly rich in cereals would have significantly changed the ratio of protein to carbohydrate in the diet. This would have changed the levels of prolactin, increased the positive energy balance, and led to more rapid growth in the young and an earlier age for first menstruation. The ready availability of ground cereals would have enabled mothers to feed their infants soft, high-carbohydrate porridges and gruels. The analysis of infant fecal material recovered from the Wadi Kubbaniya site in Egypt seems to demonstrate that a similar practice was in use with root crops along the Nile at what may have been a year-round site by 19,000 years before the present (Hillman 1989, 230).

The influence of cereals on fertility has been observed by Richard Lee (1992b) among settled Ju/'hoansi, who recently began to eat cereals and experienced a marked rise in fertility (see EthnoProfile 11.5). Renee Pennington (1992) notes that the increase in Ju/'hoansi reproductive success also seems to be related to a reduction in infant and child mortality rates. But diets based on high-carbohydrate grains are, perhaps surprisingly, less nutritious than the diets of hunters and gatherers. Skeletons from Greece and Turkey in late Paleolithic times indicate an average height of 5 feet 9 inches for men and 5 feet 5 inches for women. With the adoption of agriculture, the average height declined sharply; by about 5,000 years ago, the average man was about 5 feet 3 inches tall and the average woman, about 5 feet. Even modern Greeks and Turks are still not, on average, as tall as the late Paleolithic people of the same region.

In the short term, agriculture was probably developed in ancient southwestern Asia, and perhaps elsewhere, to increase food supplies to support an increasing population at a time of serious resource stress. Because the agroecology created an environment favorable to the plants, farmers were able to cultivate previously unusable land. When such vital necessities as water could be brought to the land between the Tigris and Euphrates Rivers in Mesopotamia, for example, land on which wheat and barley was not native could support dense stands of the domesticated grains. The greater yield of domesticated plants per unit of ground also led to a greater proportion of cultivated plants in the diet, even when wild plants were still being eaten and were as plentiful as before. But as cultivated plants took on an increasingly large role in prehistoric diets, people became dependent on plants and the plants in turn became completely dependent on the agroecology created by the people (Figure 7.14). According to Richard Lee (1992b, 48), the Ju/'hoansi, who live in the Kalahari Desert, use over 100 plants (14 fruits and nuts, 15 berries, 18 species of edible gum, 41 edible roots and bulbs, and 17 leafy greens, beans, melons, and other foods). By contrast, modern farmers rely on no more than 20 plants, and of those, three—wheat, maize, and rice—feed most of the world's people. Historically, only one or two grain crops were staples for a specific

group of people. If hail, floods, droughts, infestations, frost, heat, weeds, erosion, or other factors destroyed the crop or reduced the harvest, the risk of starvation increased. Deforestation, soil loss, silted streams, and the loss of many native species followed domestication. In the lower Tigris–Euphrates Valley, irrigation water used by early farmers carried high levels of soluble salts, poisoning the soil and making it unusable to this day (Figure 7.15).

New features of the agroecology also created new opportunities for the spread of disease. As we saw earlier, in sub-Saharan Africa, the clearing of land for farming created standing water, which provided an excellent environment for malaria-carrying mosquitoes. As increasing numbers of people began to live near each other in relatively permanent settlements, the disposal of human (and eventually animal) waste also became increasingly problematic. Food storage was a key element in agroecological niches, but stored grains attracted pests, like rats and mice, which coevolved with the domesticated crops that attracted them. Some of these pests also spread disease-causing microorganisms that thrived in human, animal, and plant wastes. The larger the number of people

Figure 7.14 (*Left*) Corn as far as the eye can see: monocropping can provide enormous yields but exposes the field to risk. (*Right*) Tarahumara Indian father and son hoeing a multi-cropped field, where the plants provide nutrients for one another and lower the risk of catastrophic losses.

In Their Own Words

The Food Revolution

Although dietary quality declined for the earliest full-time farmers, later contact and trade among different farming societies enriched diets everywhere. Over the last 500 years, as Jack Weatherford emphasizes, foods domesticated in the New World have played a particularly important role in the "food revolution."

On Thanksgiving Day North Americans sometimes remember the Indians who gave them their cuisine by dining upon turkey with cornbread stuffing, cranberry sauce, succotash, corn on the cob, sweet potato casserole, stewed squash and tomatoes, baked beans with maple syrup, and pecan pie. Few cooks or gourmets, however, recognize the much broader extent to which American Indian cuisine radically changed cooking and dining in every part of the globe from Timbuktu to Tibet. Sichuan beef with chilies, German chocolate cake, curried potatoes, vanilla ice cream, Hungarian goulash, peanut brittle, and pizza all owe their primary flavorings to the American Indians.

The discovery of America sparked a revolution in food and cuisine that has not yet shown any signs of abating. Tomatoes, chilies, and green peppers formed the first wave of American flavorings to circle the globe, but the American Indian garden still grows a host of plants that the world may yet learn to use and enjoy. These plants may have practical uses, such as providing food in otherwise unusable land or producing more food in underused land. They also vary the daily diets of people throughout the world and thereby increase nutrition. Even in this high-tech age, the low-tech plant continues to be the key to nutrition and health. Despite all the plant improvements brought about by modern science, the American Indians remain the developers of the world's largest array of nutritious foods and the primary contributors to the world's varied cuisines.

Source: Weatherford 1988, 115.

---

living very near each other, the greater the likelihood of communicable disease transmission: by the time one person recovers from the disease, someone else reaches the infectious stage and can reinfect the first; as a result, the disease never leaves the population. Finally, the nutritional deficiencies of an agricultural diet may have reduced people's resistance to disease. Foragers could just walk away from disease, reducing the likelihood that it would spread; but this option is closed for settled people. Thus, increased exposure to epidemic disease was a major consequence of the modified selection pressures to which human populations became vulnerable as a consequence of their ancestors' construction of agroecological niches.

Maintaining an agroecology that will support domesticated plants and animals requires much more labor than does foraging. People must clear the land, plant the seeds, tend the young plants, protect them from predators, harvest them, process the seeds, store them, and select the seeds for planting the next year; similarly, people must tend and protect domesticated animals, cull the herds, shear the sheep, milk the goats, and so on. This heavy workload is not divided up randomly among members of the population. Increasing dependence on agriculture by increasing numbers of people produced an increasingly complex division of labor, which set the stage for the emergence of complex hierarchical societies with different forms of social inequality.

Insight into the processes producing these changes is offered by economic anthropologist Rhoda Halperin (1994). Borrowing concepts from economic historian Karl Polanyi, Halperin argues that every economic system can be analyzed in terms of two kinds of movements: *locational movements*, or "changes of place," and *appropriational movements*, or "changes of hands." In her view, ecological relationships that affect the economy are properly understood as changes of place, as when people must move into the grasslands, gather mongongo nuts, and transport them back to camp. Economic relationships, by contrast, are more properly understood as changes of hands, as when mongongo nuts are distributed to all members of the camp, whether or not they helped to gather them. Thus, ecological (locational) movements involve transfers of energy; economic (appropriational) movements, by contrast, involve transfers of rights (1994, 59). Analyzed in this way, people's rights to consume mongongo nuts cannot be derived from the labor they expended to gather them.

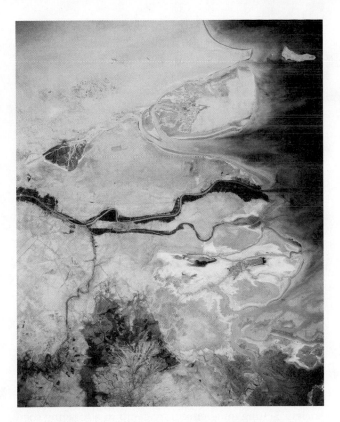

Figure 7.15 The lower Tigris–Euphrates Valley; irrigation water used by early farmers carried high levels of soluble salts, poisoning the soil and making it unusable to this day.

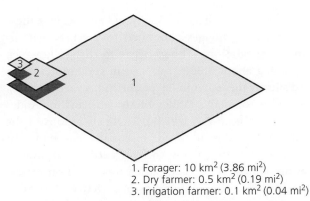

1. Forager: 10 km² (3.86 mi²)
2. Dry farmer: 0.5 km² (0.19 mi²)
3. Irrigation farmer: 0.1 km² (0.04 mi²)

Figure 7.16 Each square shows the proportionate amount of land needed to feed a single individual using three different food-getting strategies.

Another way of seeing the difference is to pay attention to the connection between food storage and food sharing. An ecologist might argue that those who gather mongongo nuts have no choice but to share them out and consume them immediately because they have no way to store this food if it is not eaten. Anthropologist Tim Ingold (1983) agreed that the obligation to share would make storage unnecessary, but he also pointed out that sharing with others today ordinarily obligates them to share with you tomorrow. Put another way, sharing food can be seen not only as a way of avoiding spoilage but also as a way of storing up IOUs for the future.

Once societies develop ways to preserve and store food and other material goods, however, new possibilities open up. Archaeological evidence indicates that the more food there is to store, the more people invest in storage facilities (e.g., pits, pottery vessels) and the more quickly they become sedentary. Large-scale food-storage techniques involve a series of "changes of place" that buffer a population from ecological fluctuations for long periods of time. But techniques of food storage alone predict nothing about the "changes of hands" that food will undergo once it has been stored. Food-storage techniques have been associated with all subsistence

strategies, including that of complex food collectors. This suggests that economic relations of consumption, involving the transfer of rights in stored food, have long been open to considerable cultural elaboration and manipulation (Halperin 1994, 178).

When people started planting grain, they could not have anticipated all of the problems to come. Initially, agriculture had several apparent advantages, the foremost of which was that farmers could extract far more food from the same amount of territory than could foragers. Put another way, to feed the same number of people, a dry farmer needs 20 times less land than a forager and an irrigation farmer needs 100 times less land (Figure 7.16). Foragers know that they will find enough food to eat, but they never know how much of any given food resource they will find or exactly when or where they will find it. By contrast, farmers can predict, with a given amount of seed—and favorable conditions—the approximate size of a harvest. Herders can predict how many lambs they will have in the spring based on the number of rams and ewes in their herds. Sedentism and a fairly reliable and predictable domesticated food supply provided new opportunities for social complexity.

What Is Social Complexity?

Early Neolithic farming and herding societies differed little from the foraging societies they replaced. For the Natufians, foraging continued to be important alongside cultivation for many generations. In the same way, the social organization of these societies differed little from that of foraging societies; although people began to settle in permanent villages, archaeological evidence suggests that no great differences in wealth, power, or prestige divided villagers initially. Put another way, these early farming villages continued to practice **egalitarian social relations**. Things began to change, however, beginning about 5,000 years ago in southwestern Asia and shortly thereafter in Egypt, the Indus Valley (India), China, Mesoamerica (Valley of Mexico), and the Andes (Peru, see Figure 7.1, p. 181). These six regions of the globe were the first to invent, essentially independently, a new way of organizing society called **social stratification**, which, as we saw earlier, was based on the assumption that different groups in society were entitled to different amounts of wealth, power, and prestige.

To move from egalitarian forms of social organization to social stratification involves the development of social complexity. Social stratification was made possible when societies produced amounts of food that exceeded the basic subsistence needs of the population. Storage of **surplus production** and control over its distribution made it possible for some members of a society to stop producing food altogether and to specialize in various occupations (e.g., weaving, pot making) or in new social roles (e.g., king, priest). In some cases, **occupational specialization** also created a wide gulf between most of society's members and a new social **class** of rulers who successfully claimed the bulk of this new wealth as their due. Societies set up in this way could support many more people than could the village societies that preceded them, not only because they successfully produced, stored, and distributed more food but also because they invented new ways of organizing people to carry out many new tasks. As a result, anthropologists refer to these as the first **complex societies** to appear in the archaeological record.

How Can Anthropologists Explain the Rise of Complex Societies?

Although the concept of a complex society seems straightforward enough, anthropologists must define this expression carefully to avoid misunderstanding. It is common to assume that the opposite of complex is simple, yet foraging and farming societies are not "simple" societies. As we saw, not even all foragers were alike; and in any case, foragers had to file away in their minds an enormously complex amount of information about different varieties of plants, seasonal habits of animals, details of kinship, and nuances of their religion and art. It was the comparatively simple technology of foragers—based on wood, stone, and bone tools that could be easily made by everyone—that was very different from the more complex technology that had to be developed and mastered in order to build massive pyramids, weave cloth, or smelt and mold metals such as copper, tin, and iron. These activities not only required highly specialized knowledge of architecture, textiles, and metallurgy but also presupposed a form of social organization that permitted some members of society to become highly specialized in certain activities while other members carried out different tasks.

Differences in technology and social organization say nothing about the complexity of the minds of the people involved. However, such differences strongly shaped the scale and texture of life in the two kinds of society. Setting up a temporary camp in a foraging society involved fewer options and fewer decisions, in terms of technology and social organization, than did the construction of a pyramid. Pyramid building required more than architectural skill; suitable materials had to be found, quarried, or produced and transported to the site. Additionally, suitable workers had to be found, trained, supervised, fed, and lodged for the duration of construction, which may have taken decades. Finally, all these specialized activities had to occur in the right order for the project to be successfully completed. Not only would a foraging band—some 50 individuals of all ages—have been too small to carry out such a project, but their traditional egalitarian social relations also would have made the giving and taking of orders impossible. Indeed, the whole idea of building massive pyramids would have probably seemed pointless to them.

A society that not only wants to build pyramids but also has the material, political, and social means to do so is clearly different from a foraging band or a Neolithic farming village. For archaeologist T. Douglas Price, a complex society has "more parts and more connections between parts" (1995, 140). Anthropologist Leslie White (1949) spoke in terms of a major change in the amount of energy a society can capture from nature and use to remodel the natural world to suit its own purposes. The members of foraging bands also depended on energy captured from the natural world but on a scale vastly smaller than that required to build pyramids. Archaeologist Robert Wenke emphasizes that, in complex societies, "the important thing is that the ability and

---

egalitarian social relations Social relations in which no great differences in wealth, power, or prestige divide members from one another.

social stratification A form of social organization in which people have unequal access to wealth, power, and prestige.

surplus production The production of amounts of food that exceed the basic subsistence needs of the population.

occupational specialization Specialization in various occupations (e.g., weaving or pot making) or in new social roles (e.g., king or priest) that is found in socially complex societies.

class A ranked group within a hierarchically stratified society whose membership is defined primarily in terms of wealth, occupation, or other economic criteria.

complex societies Societies with large populations, an extensive division of labor, and occupational specialization.

incentive to make these investments are radically different from the capacities of Pleistocene bands, in that they imply the ability of some members of society to control and organize others" (1999, 348).

What Is the Archaeological Evidence for Social Complexity?

How do archaeologists recognize social and cultural complexity when they see it? Important clues are certain kinds of remains that begin to appear in the archaeological record after about 5,000 years ago. Among the most widespread indicators of social complexity are the remains of **monumental architecture**. Contemporary monumental architecture includes such structures as the Eiffel Tower in Paris, France; the Mall of America in Bloomington, Minnesota; and the Petronas Towers in Kuala Lumpur, Malaysia (Figure 7.17). Ancient monumental architecture included public buildings, private residences, tombs, settlement walls, irrigation canals, and so on. Together with monumental architecture, however, archaeologists usually find evidence of technologically

Figure 7.18 Among the most widespread indicators of early social complexity are the remains of monumental architecture, such as the Temple of the Great Jaguar at the Mayan site of Tikal, Guatemala.

simpler constructions. Assemblages that demonstrate such architectural variability contrast with those from earlier periods, when dwellings were simpler and more uniform and monumental structures were absent.

Everywhere it is found, the earliest monumental architecture consists of raised platforms, temples, pyramids, or pyramidlike structures (Figure 7.18). Different building techniques were used to construct these monuments in different areas, and the structures did not all serve the same purpose. Therefore, archaeologists have long rejected the notion that all pyramid-building societies derived from ancient Egypt. Rather, the cross-cultural similarities of these structures appear to have a more practical explanation. None of the architects in the earliest complex societies knew how to build arches and barrel vaults. Moreover, in places like the Maya lowlands in modern Central America, builders had to work without metal, winches, hoists, or wheeled carts. Under these circumstances, the only tall structures they could have built were such basic geometric forms as squares, rectangles, and pyramids (Wenke 1999, 577).

Among the monumental structures built in the earliest complex societies were tombs. Differences in the size and construction of burials parallel differences in the size and construction of residences, and both suggest the emergence of a stratified society. Graves that are larger and built of more costly materials often contain a variety of objects, called **grave goods**, that were buried with the corpse. Smaller, modest graves occurring in the same assemblage and containing few or no grave goods

Figure 7.17 Monumental modern architecture: the Petronas Towers dwarf the surrounding city of Kuala Lumpur, Malaysia.

monumental architecture Architectural constructions of a greater-than-human scale, such as pyramids, temples, and tombs.
grave goods Objects buried with a corpse

provide evidence for social stratification. The number and quality of grave goods found with a corpse give clues as to just how highly stratified a society was. Many of the grave goods recovered from rich tombs are masterpieces of ceramics, metallurgy, weaving, and other crafts, indicating that the society had achieved a high degree of technological skill and, thus, a complex division of labor.

Archaeologists often recover evidence of complex occupational specialization directly from a site. They search for **concentrations of particular artifacts** that may indicate what sort of activity was carried out in each area. Archaeologists can distinguish garbage dumps from, say, areas where people lived, which would have been kept free of refuse. Similarly, broken pots or kilns found evenly distributed throughout a settlement might suggest that pottery was made by individual families. However, considerable evidence of pottery manufacture concentrated within a particular area strongly suggests the existence of a potter's workshop and, thus, occupational specialization. Remains of the tools used to make artifacts—potter's wheels, spindle whorls, or slag, for example—often provide important information about the degree to which craft technology developed at a particular time and place.

The emergence of complex societies seems connected almost everywhere with a phenomenal explosion of architectural and artistic creativity. Although anthropologists admire the material achievements of these ancient societies, many are struck by the "wasteful" expenditure of resources by a tiny ruling elite. Why, for example, did virtually every original complex society build monumental architecture? Why did they not invest their increasing technological and organizational power in less elaborate projects that might have benefited the ordinary members of society? Why were masterpieces of pottery, metallurgy, and weaving often hoarded and buried in the tombs of dead rulers instead of being more widely available? These excesses apparently did not develop in the early Harappan civilization of the Indus Valley, but they are so widespread elsewhere that the questions remain important.

Archaeologist Michael Hoffman, an expert on prehistoric Egypt, proposed that the key to understanding the first complex societies lies in their social organization. For the first time in human history, societies had been formed in which tremendous power was concentrated in

the hands of a tiny elite—who undoubtedly found their privileges challenged by their new subjects. Under such circumstances, the production of monumental architecture and quantities of luxury goods served as evidence of the elite's fitness to rule. Hoffman prefers to call these objects "powerfacts" rather than "artifacts" because their role was to demonstrate the superior power of the rulers (1991, 294; Hayden 1995, 67; Figure 7.19).

So far, we have described the kinds of archaeological remains that suggest that a site was once part of a complex society. But complex societies ordinarily consisted of a number of settlements organized in a hierarchy. Consequently, archaeologists survey the region to determine how any given site compares to other simultaneously occupied settlements in the same area. (See Chapter 6 for a discussion of survey techniques.) The most common and helpful surface artifacts recovered during such surveys are often pieces of broken pots called **sherds**. Different kinds of sherds found on a site's surface provide a rough inventory of the different cultural traditions followed by inhabitants over time. When the survey is completed, archaeologists tabulate and map the percentages of different kinds of sherds. A series of maps showing the distribution of each particular kind of pottery illustrates the degree to which settlement size and population changed over time. When researchers are able to accurately associate the different kinds of pottery with the stratigraphy of well-excavated sites in the region, they can devise a portrait of settlement patterns over time. Systematic survey and mapping work in southern Iraq permitted Robert Adams and Hans Nissen to show

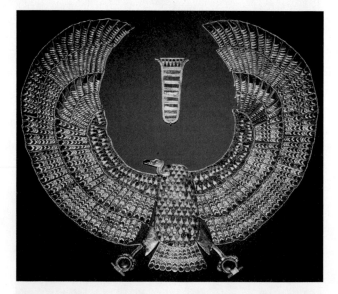

Figure 7.19 A "powerfact" from the tomb of Tutankhamen. A collar found around the neck is composed of gold, colored glass, and obsidian. There are 250 inlaid segments, and each claw is grasping a *shen*, a symbol of totality.

---

concentrations of particular artifacts Sets of artifacts indicating that particular social activities took place at a particular area in an archaeological site when that site was inhabited in the past.

sherds Pieces of broken pots.

how the small, scattered settlements that prevailed in the countryside of ancient Mesopotamia around 8,000 years ago were gradually abandoned over the centuries, such that by about 5,200 years ago virtually everyone was living in a handful of large settlements, which Adams and Nissen call "cities" (1972).

Why Did Stratification Begin?

As we saw in Chapter 6, archaeologists typically organize their findings using a set of four categories that serve as benchmarks in the history of human social organization. These categories—bands, tribes, chiefdoms, states—were developed together with cultural anthropologists and rest on insights derived from the study of living and historically documented societies of different kinds together with the material remains they all tend to leave behind (Wenke 1999, 340–44).

As we have seen, our ancestors apparently lived in foraging *bands* until some 10,000 years ago, when the last ice sheets melted, after which they began to experiment with new subsistence strategies and forms of social organization. Those who came to farm or herd for a living were able to support larger populations and are classified as *tribes*. Societies classified as tribes are enormously varied. Morton Fried (1967) preferred to call a society of this kind a "rank" society. Elman Service (1962), who was attempting to identify key turning points in the course of human prehistory, viewed tribes as a transitional form rather than a well-defined societal type. The ambiguity of terms like *rank society* or *tribe* has led some archaeologists to substitute the term *transegalitarian society* to describe all societies that are neither egalitarian nor socially stratified (Hayden 1995, 18). Seemingly poised between equality and hierarchy, transegalitarian societies have flourished at various times and places up to the present day, and they do not appear necessarily to be on the way to becoming anything else in particular.

Unlike a transegalitarian society, the *chiefdom* is an example—indeed, the earliest clear example—of a socially stratified society, as we saw among the southern Natufians. Ordinarily, only the chief and close relatives are set apart and allowed privileged access to wealth, power, and prestige; other members of the society continue to share roughly similar social status. Chiefdoms are generally larger than tribes and show a greater degree of craft production, although such production is not yet in the hands of full-time specialists. Chiefdoms also exhibit a greater degree of hierarchical political control, centered on the chief, relatives of the chief, and their great deeds. Archaeologically, chiefdoms are interesting because some, such as the southern Natufians,

apparently remained as they were and then disappeared, whereas others went on to develop into states.

The *state* is a stratified society that possesses a territory that is defended from outside enemies with an army and from internal disorder with police. States, which have separate governmental institutions to enforce laws and to collect taxes and tribute, are run by an elite that possesses a monopoly on the use of force. In early states, government and religion were mutually reinforcing: rulers were often priests or were thought to be gods themselves. State societies are supported by sophisticated food-production and -storage techniques. Craft production is normally specialized and yields a dazzling variety of goods, many of which are refined specialty items destined for the ruling elite. Art and architecture also flourish, and writing frequently has developed in state societies. Shortly after the appearance of the first state in an area, other states usually develop nearby. From time to time, one might conquer its neighbors, organizing them into a vaster political network called an *empire*.

Monumental public buildings of a religious or governmental nature, highly developed crafts (e.g., pottery, weaving, and metallurgy), and regional settlement patterns that show at least three levels in a hierarchy of social complexity are all archaeological evidence of a state. Interstate conflict is suspected when towns and cities are surrounded by high walls and confirmed by artifacts that served as weapons, by art depicting battle, and by written documents that record military triumphs. Because writing developed in most of the early states, various inscriptions often provide valuable information on social organization that supplements the archaeologist's reconstructions.

Archaeologists assume regional integration when they find unique styles in architecture, pottery, textiles, and other artifacts distributed uniformly over a wide area; such evidence is called a *cultural horizon*. For archaeologists, the term *civilization* usually refers to the flowering of cultural creativity that accompanies the rise of state societies and persists for a long time. Widespread uniformity in material culture, however, need not imply a single set of political institutions. Archaeologists who wish to speak of a state or empire, therefore, require additional evidence, such as a hierarchy of settlement patterns or written records that spell out centralized governmental policies. Cultural change in all early complex societies tended to alternate between periods of relative cultural uniformity and political unity and periods of regional differentiation and lack of political integration.

We should note that the preceding categories and the framework for cross-cultural comparison that they provide have been critiqued in recent years. Postprocessual archaeologists like Shanks and Tilley (1987), for example, argue that traditional comparisons of ancient "state" societies pay too much attention to environmental and technological similarities while ignoring or dismissing the significance of the distinct cultural patterns of meanings and values that made each of these ancient civilizations unique. Other archaeologists, however, maintain that the similarities among ancient civilizations are just as striking as their cultural differences and require explanation (Trigger 1993). While this debate continues, many archaeologists have tried to strike a balance, acknowledging the overall descriptive value of a formal category like "state" but carrying out research projects that highlight the cultural variation to be found among societies grouped together as "states" (Wenke 1999, 346).

How Can Anthropologists Explain the Rise of Complex Societies?

Given that humans lived in foraging bands for most of their history and that, in some parts of the world, village farming remained a stable, viable way of life for hundreds or thousands of years, it is not obvious why complex societies should ever have developed at all. Over the years, anthropologists have proposed a number of explanations. Some of their hypotheses (like some designed to explain our ancestors' turn to domestication or sedentism) argue for a single, uniform cause, or prime

mover, that triggered the evolution of complex society worldwide. Indeed, as we will see, many of these prime movers are the same factors suggested to explain the development of domestication and sedentism.

For a long time, scholars thought that the domestication of plants and sedentary life in farming villages offered people the leisure time to invent social and technological complexity. This explanation is questionable, however, because many farming societies never developed beyond the village level of organization. In addition, social complexity apparently can develop without the support of a fully agricultural economy, as among the Natufians. Finally, ethnographic research has shown that foraging people actually have more leisure time than most village farmers.

Other scholars suggest that social complexity depended on arid or semiarid environments (Figure 7.20). The first complex societies in Egypt, Mesopotamia, and the Indus Valley were located in dry regions crossed by a major river, which provided water for intensified agricultural production following the construction of irrigation canals. The apparent connection between farming in an arid environment, the need for irrigation water, and the rise of complex societies led Karl Wittfogel (1957) to hypothesize that complex societies first developed in order to construct and maintain large irrigation systems. Wittfogel argued that these irrigation systems could not have functioned without a ruling elite to direct operations. Thus, he sees the development of what he calls *hydraulic agriculture* as the key to the evolution of complex society. This hypothesis, although suggestive, has also been called into question. First, societies such as the

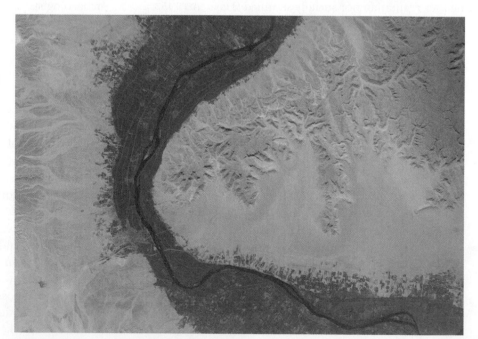

Figure 7.20 The civilization of ancient Egypt was supported by agricultural practices that relied on the regular flooding pattern of the Nile River. In this photograph taken from the Space Shuttle, the wide, dark band crossing the light desert region is the cultivated floodplain of the Nile. The river itself is the very dark, narrow line snaking its way through this cultivated area.

Hohokam of the American Southwest apparently operated an extensive irrigation system without developing social stratification or cultural complexity (Wenke 1999, 356). Second, the sorts of complex irrigation systems Wittfogel had in mind—those requiring a bureaucracy—appear late in the archaeological record of several early civilizations, long after the first appearance of monumental architecture, cities, and other signs of social complexity (see, e.g., Adams 1981, 53). Irrigation may have played a role in the development of complex societies, but it was apparently not the single prime mover that brought them into existence.

Because many early groups of village farmers never developed a high degree of social complexity, archaeologists see its appearance more as the exception, not the rule. Some suggest that population pressure was the decisive force: if the food supply could not keep up with a growing population, social chaos would have resulted unless someone were able to exercise power to allocate resources and keep the peace. This scenario is rejected, however, by those who argue that social inequality developed in societies where resources were abundant and opportunistic individuals could gain power by using surpluses to indebt others to them through competitive feasting or control of labor (Arnold 1995, Hayden 1995). Also, archaeological evidence from more than one part of the world shows that population pressure was not a problem when social complexity first appeared. Some archaeologists now suggest that human societies were able to limit population growth if they chose to do so, whether by migration, infanticide, abortion, contraception, or late marriage. Finally, the greatest decline in fertility in the modern Western world did not occur among the hungry, nor was it triggered by the invention of new birth-control technology: it was the well-fed, middle-class families in capitalist societies who began to have fewer children, not the poverty-stricken workers. The forces that change reproductive rates are far more complex than a simple population-pressure model would allow.

If population pressure did not undermine the egalitarian social relations of village farmers, perhaps conflict with other villagers was to blame. If all available farmland were settled, for example, making it impossible for people to move away at times of conflict, the only solution, apart from chaos, would have been to establish rules to resolve conflicts, thus leading to the development of more complex political structures (Nissen 1988, 60–61). Sooner or later, however, if chaos could not be contained, warfare might have broken out between neighboring villages. Indeed, Brian Hayden suggests that power-seeking individuals might well have manipulated such tensions, using economic surpluses to settle conflicts and amassing personal wealth and power

in the process. This could not occur, in his view, until people became willing to accept bloodwealth, a crucial innovation not found in egalitarian societies (1995, 32). **Bloodwealth** is economic surplus, paid by perpetrators to compensate their victims for their loss. If bloodwealth payments disproportionately favored some individuals or groups over others, their social relations would no longer be egalitarian.

Warfare, population pressure, and arid environments all play roles in Robert Carneiro's (1970) theory of the rise of the first states in Peru, Mesopotamia, and Egypt and of later, secondary states elsewhere. In Carneiro's scheme, population pressure would have led to increasing conflict between neighboring villages once it was no longer possible for villagers to cultivate new lands. This situation, which he calls *environmental circumscription*, might have been especially likely in early farming societies that grew up along river valleys running through deserts, such as those in Mesopotamia, Egypt, and coastal Peru. When the desert barrier halted village expansion, new farmlands could be obtained only by taking them away from other villages by force. Carneiro's theory has stimulated much discussion. However, the role he assigns to population pressure is open to the criticism raised earlier, and many archaeologists still have not found evidence that would confirm or refute Carneiro's hypotheses.

Clearly, any force that could destroy the egalitarian relations that prevailed in farming societies for hundreds or thousands of years would have had to be very powerful. In this connection, David Webster (1975) suggested that the turning point came in farming societies that were chiefdoms. You will recall that chiefdoms possess a limited form of social stratification that sets the chiefly line above other members of society, who continue to enjoy social equality reinforced by kinship. If warfare in such a society undermined the old relations of kinship, people might eventually be desperate for social order and accept social stratification if that restored stability.

All the prime movers discussed so far involve technological, economic, environmental, or biological factors that would have forced societies into complexity no matter what their previous cultural traditions might have been. Realizing that these external factors were less powerful than once believed, many anthropologists turned their attention to internal, sociocultural factors that might have led to the rise of social complexity: recall Barbara Bender's theory about the origin of domestication,

---

bloodwealth Material goods paid by perpetrators to compensate their victims for their loss.

In Their Own Words

The Ecological Consequences of Social Complexity

*Many people have tried to ascribe both the rise and decline of early complex societies
to factors rooted in the natural environment. Dan and Prudence Rice argue that
a closer look at Mesoamerica suggests that things were never that simple.*

It is apparent that the Maya initiated practices to reduce the regionwide processes of nutrient loss, deterioration of soil structure, destabilization of water flows, soil erosion, and loss of productive components of their environment. The results of the Maya "experiment" demonstrate that tropical forests are neither zones of unbounded fertility nor homogeneous zones in which cultivation redundancy is in order. Theirs was a multihabitat and multitechnology system that was labor intensive, a system that relied on a primary motivation for increased production—a growing population—as the source of energy to run the system. Relatively speaking, it was an ecologically efficient regime that met increased demands for production through increased labor intensity and an increased agricultural land base.

The Maya adapted to the tropical forest environment over a long period, and a key to their success was undoubtedly the opportunity for sustained experimentation and evaluation. In the Yaxha-Sacnab basins, the environmental strains caused by soil depletion and alteration of the lacustrine ecosystem developed slowly, in tandem with low rates of population growth, too slowly to act as a mechanism to reduce overall population increase until at least Late Classic times. This statement is not meant to suggest that the Maya did not suffer constraints. Their growth, expansion, and intensification forced the Maya to consider more closely the processes of degradation. No data exist at present, however, indicating that the Maya agricultural system had reached its productive limits or that reduced productivity caused the civilization's "collapse." Certainly, some habitats or technologies were more vulnerable to strain than others, and the circumstantial juxtaposition of degradation and cultural decline in the Yaxha-Sacnab basins is theoretically enticing. But Maya responses to production problems were not only technological but social, religious, and political, and effective maintenance of an agro-economic infrastructure depended on cultural forces in addition to environmental ones. Both require further investigation.

The unresolved issue of the Maya "collapse" and the long-term success of the Maya civilization may foster spurious—and dangerous—complacency toward future economic development of the tropics if the relative rates of change are not kept in perspective. Current population trends in tropical areas engender a real sense of urgency about the work ahead. Tropical environments such as the Petén must be evaluated before modern populations obscure the details of ecosystem history so that pertinent information on successful, long-term adaptive strategies can be made available while it still might have some impact on future land use.

Source: Rice and Rice 1993.

---

which has inspired Brian Hayden, among others. During the 1960s and 1970s, some anthropologists were influenced by the work of Karl Marx and his followers, who argued that attempts to resolve contradictions that develop within a particular form of social organization can lead to profound social change. Marxian analysis might suggest, for example, that external trade in luxury items by the leaders of early chiefdoms may have generated conflict between the chief's family (whose interests were served by trade) and the common people (whose interests were undermined by it) (Kipp and Schortman 1989). Such a conflict of interests might eventually have thrown a chiefdom completely out of equilibrium, leading to the kind of social transformation suggested by Webster (1975).

Written documents, when available, can sometimes provide enough detailed insight into social organization to identify social hierarchies and trace their development over time. But for ancient complex societies that lacked writing—and this includes all six of the first such societies—the marxian approach is exceedingly difficult to apply to archaeological materials. Many of the remains of the earliest complex societies are incomplete and could be compatible with more than one form of social organization. Indeed, any theory, marxian or not, that seeks to explain the rise of a complex society in terms of social relations, political culture, or religious beliefs faces the same problem. However important they may have been, such phenomena do not fossilize and cannot be reliably inferred on the basis of archaeological data alone, an uncomfortable fact that continues to frustrate archaeologists trying to reconstruct prehistory.

Anthropologists cannot offer a single, sweeping explanation of cultural evolution, although this was their hope at the end of the nineteenth century. But their attempts to test various hypotheses that promise such explanations have led to a far richer appreciation of the complexities of social and cultural change. Archaeologist Robert Wenke observes that "cultural evolution is not a continuous, cumulative, gradual change in most places. 'Fits and starts' better describes it" (1999, 336). He further emphasizes the remarkable adaptability of cultural systems, noting in a discussion of Mesoamerica that environmental and ecological analyses can only explain so much: "once we get beyond this simple ecological level of analysis, we encounter a welter of variability in sociopolitical forms, economic histories, settlement patterns, and the other elaborations of these complex societies" (609). The rest of this chapter offers a sample of some of this variability, examining evidence bearing on the rise of the first complex societies in South America.

Andean Civilization

The Andean region of South America gave birth to a rich, complex, and varied civilization that culminated in the Inka Empire, the largest political system to develop in the New World before the arrival of Europeans. The very richness and complexity of this civilization, however, coupled with insufficient funding for archaeological research, has meant that only the barest outlines of its development can be traced (Table 7.1).

The geography of the Andes is distinctive and had an important influence on the development of local complex societies. This is a region of young, steep-sided mountains and volcanoes. Along the Pacific can be found deserts on which rain has not fallen for centuries as well as a narrow, lowland coastal strip covered with lush greenery that is supported not by rain but by fog rising from the ocean. This is the zone of the *lomas*, or fog meadows, which is crossed by over two dozen short rivers flowing from the highlands. The western edge of the loma lowlands rises abruptly through several climatic zones to the highlands, or *sierra*, of the Andes Mountains. Rolling grassland areas between 3,900 and 5,000 meters form a zone called the *puna*, the highest level suitable for human habitation. Finally, the eastern slopes of the Andes descend into the humid tropical forests of the Amazon headwaters, a zone called the *selva*. In recent years, mounting evidence suggests that farming cultures in the tropical forest contributed many of the domesticated plants that later became indispensable to Andean agriculture (Chauchat 1988, Raymond 1988, Rick 1988).

The presence of humans in South America before 15,000 years ago is still being debated, but bands of foragers were definitely living along the Peruvian coast between 14,000 and 8,000 years ago and in the sierra between 11,000 and 10,000 years ago. Lowland groups took advantage of the unique upswelling of the cold coastal

TABLE 7.1 Cultural Periods of Andean Civilization			
TIME SCALE	**SELECTED CULTURE**		**PERIOD/HORIZON**
1500	Inka		Late Horizon
1250	Chimú		Late Intermediate period
1000			
	Wari	Tiwanaku	Middle Horizon
750			
500	Moche		Early Intermediate period
C.E.			
B.C.E.			
500	Chavín		Early Horizon
1000			Initial period
2000			Preceramic period
4000			
6000	Paijan		
8000	Luz		Lithic Period
10,000			

current—which kept nutrients for ocean-dwelling organisms close to the surface—to exploit a bounty of marine food resources. Between about 5,000 and 4,000 years ago, quinoa, guinea pigs, potatoes, and camelids (llamas and alpacas) were domesticated in the highlands. Neither the coastal foragers nor the earliest highland farmers made pottery however. By 3,200 years ago, the first maize appears on the Ecuadorian coast (B. Smith 1995, 157, 181).

On the Peruvian coast, between 5,000 and 4,500 years ago, villagers began to construct multiroomed buildings, which were later filled in to form pyramid-shaped mounds. Complexes of platforms, pyramids, and raised enclosures first appeared after 4,000 years ago at sites like El Paraiso on the coast and Kotosh in the highlands. There is evidence that the early coastal mound builders were not farmers but villagers who relied on food from the sea. Possibly the first mound builders in the highlands were not farmers either, but highland settlements soon became dependent on the cultivation of maize and other crops. Between 3,800 and 2,900 years ago, the number of sites with monumental architecture increased in the coastal valleys, as did the proportion of cultivated plants in the coastal diet, which suggests that irrigation agriculture had become important in coastal economies. There is also evidence during this period of increasing contact between coastal and highland settlements: the "U"-shaped plan of coastal ceremonial sites began to appear in the highlands, while llamas became important, economically and ritually, on the coast (Pineda 1988).

These early developments toward social complexity appeared among peoples with distinct cultural traditions. However, between 2,900 and 2,200 years ago, a single cultural tradition with its own styles of art, architecture, and pottery spread rapidly throughout central and northern Peru. This phenomenon is called the Chavín Horizon, and the period in which it occurred is usually called the Early Horizon because this was the first time in Andean history that so many local communities had adopted a single cultural tradition (Figure 7.21). Much is obscure about the Chavín period. It does not seem that Chavín culture spread by conquest, nor did it totally replace the local traditions of those who adopted it; but its appearance was accompanied by a new level of social and economic interaction between previously isolated local societies.

Most experts agree that the spread of Chavín culture was connected with the spread of a religious ideology, sometimes called the Chavín cult. Richard Berger (1988) suggests that this may have been a regional cult that was voluntarily adopted by a number of different ethnic groups, perhaps a forerunner of the cult of Pachacamac that flourished in sixteenth-century Peru. The Chavín cult got its name from the highland ceremonial center

Figure 7.21　Chavín culture spread widely during the Early Horizon in Peru (900–200 B.C.E.). The monumental sculpture illustrated here is the Lanzón in the Old Temple at the ceremonial complex of Chavín de Huantar.

Chavín de Huantar, which was important toward the end of the Early Horizon. The flowering of pottery, metallurgy, and textile production that marks the Chavín Horizon may have been encouraged by a religious elite eager to enhance its status among its new followers.

The Chavín cult and the regional integration that went with it fell apart after 2,200 years ago. Although this development led to the reemergence of village life in some regions, complex society did not collapse everywhere. During the Early Intermediate period (200 B.C.E.–600 C.E.), separate cultural groups followed their own paths. On the coast, over a dozen new regional states appeared, but only a few are well known archaeologically. The Moche state, for example, encompassed several river valleys on the north coast and continued the earlier pattern connecting religion, monumental architecture, and rich grave goods. The largest structures in ancient Peru that were built of sun-dried bricks (or adobe) were constructed in the Moche Valley during the Early Intermediate period, as was an elaborate system for the distribution of water. The Moche also developed a distinctive art style that appeared in ceramics, textiles, and wall paintings (Figure 7.22).

On the south coast, a complex society centered in the Nazca Valley produced monumental pyramids, terraced hills, burial areas, and walled enclosures, as well as elaborate pottery and textiles. It also produced the famous Nazca lines, monumental markings that were made by brushing away the dark, upper layer of the desert surface to expose the lighter soil beneath (Figure 7.23). The earliest markings are drawings of animals and supernatural figures, also found on textiles, whereas later markings are mostly straight lines. The exact significance of the Nazca lines is unclear. Similar structures are known elsewhere in Peru, and many experts suspect that the lines may have been memorial markers or part of a calendrical system. There is no evidence whatsoever that they were built as landing strips for aliens from outer space.

In the Andean highlands, many small, independent societies developed during the Early Intermediate period. Of these, perhaps the most significant was the tradition that grew up in the basin of Lake Titicaca in the southern highlands. Titicaca basin culture possessed distinctive traditions in architecture, textiles, and religious art that heavily influenced later complex societies in the region (Conklin and Moseley 1988).

After 600 C.E., the cultural fragmentation of the Early Intermediate period was reversed in two regions of Peru. A complex society called Tiwanaku (sometimes spelled *Tiahuanaco*) began to spread the Titicaca basin culture throughout the southern highlands of the Andes. In the central highlands and central coast, a second complex society known as Wari (sometimes spelled *Huari*) extended its influence. Both these regional powers were named after large prehistoric cities that presumably served as their capitals. The period during which these two states spread their cultural and political influence (600–1000 C.E.) is called the Middle Horizon of Andean cultural evolution.

Wari and Tiwanaku share some common cultural attributes, but archaeologists have difficulty deciphering the nature of their relationship with each other. Tiwanaku had a religiously oriented ruling hierarchy; Wari did not. The architecture of Wari administrative centers lacks residences, storehouses, and community kitchens, which were built in Tiwanaku provincial settlements for members of the religious bureaucracy. William Isbell (1988) connects the administrative structure of Wari to an earlier, nonhierarchical form of social organization that had flourished in the Ayacucho Valley during the Early Intermediate period. In that system, highland communities founded colonies in the different ecological zones that ranged between the highlands and the coast, thus providing the highland communities and their various colonies with a full range of products from each zone.

Figure 7.22 Ceramics were developed to a high level of sophistication in early states, as shown by this stirrup-spout portrait jar produced by the Moche civilization, which flourished in northern Peru between 250 and 500 C.E. It is important to note that pottery was also made and used by people who were not settled, full-time farmers.

This distinctive Andean pattern of niche construction, which integrates economic resources from a variety of environments, is called the *vertical archipelago system*.

Isbell thinks that the rulers of Wari adopted the form of centralized, hierarchical government from Tiwanaku but not the religious ideas that went with it. Wari then used these centralized political structures to transform the egalitarian vertical archipelago system of the Early Intermediate period into a socially stratified system of wealth collection for the state (1988, 182). Archaeological evidence for state-sponsored feasting in return for collective labor on state land may have been found at the Middle Horizon site of Jargampata, located 20 kilometers from Wari. Both the vertical archipelago system and facilities for state-sponsored feasts for laborers on state land were later incorporated into the society of the Inkas. Isbell (1988) also thinks that the Inka

Figure 7.23 Aerial photograph of a monkey in the Nazca Valley of Peru.

administrative system, involving regional capitals linked by highways with way stations for runners, may have first developed in Wari.

After about 1000 C.E., Wari and Tiwanaku declined, ushering in the Late Intermediate period, which lasted until the rise of the Inkas in 1476 C.E. It was during the Late Intermediate period that the pilgrimage center of Pachacamac on the central coast became fully established (Keatinge 1988). Independent regional states with distinct cultures emerged in half a dozen areas of Peru, the best known of which is the Chimú state, Chimor, on the north coast. The capital of the Chimú state, Chan Chan, is located in the Moche Valley. Chimú administered a complex irrigation system in a number of adjacent river valleys. Most of the farmers of the Chimú state appear to have lived in cities. Although the connection between hydraulic agriculture and state power seems clear in the case of Chimú, other large valleys on the central and south coast were equally well suited to hydraulic agriculture but never produced equally centralized states (Parsons and Hastings 1988).

Both Chan Chan, the Chimú capital, and Cuzco, the Inka capital, were located in areas that lay on the border between spheres of cultural and political influence during the Middle Horizon. The rise of Cuzco began in Late Intermediate times, when kingdoms that descended from Tiwanaku and Wari began to fight with one another. Warfare continued until the 1460s, when the Inkas, whose empire had begun only 20 years earlier, subdued neighboring states and brought them into their expanding empire (Parsons and Hastings 1988). By 1476, the Inkas put down the last of a series of internal rebellions, firmly establishing their empire of Tawantinsuyu, which means "world of four quarters." When the

Spanish arrived in 1525, the Inka Empire stretched from present-day Colombia to central Chile, from the Pacific coast to the rain forests of the eastern Andean slopes (Wenke 1999, 640).

During the period of Inka dominance from 1476 to 1525, known as the Late Horizon, the Inkas built on the achievements of hundreds of years of Andean civilization. They further developed the vertical archipelago system, expanded the road system, and built new monumental palaces, temples, storage facilities, barracks, and way stations on highways. They maintained control of their vast empire through military force, by moving large sections of the population from one region to another for political reasons, and by continuing to recruit labor for state projects in return for state-sponsored feasting. Unlike Chimú, which was largely urban, the Inka Empire was based in rural villages. Society was organized in large kin groups called *ayllu*, which were then grouped together into higher-level units. But the administrative system was not identical in all regions of the empire: in places like Chan Chan, the Inkas made use of preexisting administrative structures, but in areas where centralized administration did not exist, such as Huánuco Pampa in the central highlands, they built new administrative centers from the ground up (Morris 1988).

The Andes are so ecologically diverse and so much data remain unrecovered that it may seem hazardous to speculate about the rise of complex society here. If the first complex societies on the Peruvian coast were based on a steady supply of food from the sea, rather than agriculture, the notion that village agriculture must precede the rise of social complexity is dealt a blow. Moreover, the fact that these first complex coastal societies were without pottery was no more a barrier to development

Figure 7.24 The indigenous civilizations of the Andes never developed systems of writing but were able to record important information using the *quipu*, a system of knotted strings. Based on a decimal system, quipu knots were coded by size, location, relative sequence, and color.

than was the fact that the early Andean states, up to and including the Inkas, were without a written language (Figure 7.24). Carneiro's environmental circumscription hypothesis seems suggestive when we consider the rise of the first multivalley states on the coast during the Early Intermediate period, but the constant warfare required for his scheme does not become significant until much later, long after complex states had already emerged. Hydraulic agriculture was clearly important to the rise of the Chimú state, yet it emerged hundreds of years after the first complex societies on the coast. Even if hydraulic agriculture had been important during the Late Intermediate period, as we saw in comparing the Chimú with their neighbors, it cannot explain why people living in similar ecological settings in nearby valleys did not produce similar states. Much work remains to be done, but none of the current gaps in our knowledge detracts from the dazzling achievements of this unique civilization.

Chapter Summary

1. About 10,000 years ago, the retreat of the last glaciers marked the end of the Pleistocene. The earth's climate changed significantly, affecting the distribution of plants and animals and transforming the ecological settings in which human beings made their livings. Soon thereafter, human beings began to develop new ways of adapting by intervening in these changed environmental settings in order to create new niches for themselves.

2. Plant and animal domestication are usefully understood as forms of niche construction. Not only did human beings interfere with the reproduction of local species, to make them more useful for human purposes, but they also remodeled the environmental settings in which plants were grown or animals were fed and watered. When the invention of agriculture is viewed as niche construction, there is no question that it involved conscious human choice. Intelligent human beings consciously chose to domesticate wild plants that were easy to harvest, nourishing, and tasty; but they also had to consciously create the tools and plan the activities that would make cultivation of a domestic crop possible and successful.

3. The niches human beings construct to exploit plants are not all the same. Anthropologists have identified four major ways in which humans relate to plant species: wild plant-food procurement, wild plant-food production, cultivation, and

agriculture. In each successive form, the amount of energy people apply to get food from plants increases, but the energy they get back from plants increases even more.

4. Animal domestication apparently developed as people consciously attempted to control the animals that they were hunting in order to intervene in their breeding patterns. Archaeological evidence for animal domestication may be indicated in one of four ways: when an animal species is found outside its natural range, when animal remains show morphological changes that distinguish them from wild populations, when the numbers of some species at a site increase abruptly relative to other species, and when remains show certain age and gender characteristics. The earliest animal domesticated, some 16,000 years ago, was the dog. Although archaeologists can pinpoint the regions where goats were domesticated, the earliest sites for domesticated sheep are not clear. It seems that cattle and pigs were domesticated at different sites in the Old World. Domestication seems to have been slower and less important in the New World than it was in the Old World.

5. The niches humans have constructed to make use of animals vary. They include random hunting, controlled hunting, herd following, loose herding, close herding, and factory farming. Not all animals people hunted were domesticated. Once humans

(continued on next page)

Chapter Summary *(continued)*

domesticated animals, their focus shifted from dead animals to their living offspring, which may have triggered concern for private property.

6. Scholars have suggested different factors responsible for plant and animal domestication; none alone is entirely satisfactory. Today, most archaeologists prefer multiple strand theories that focus on the particular (and often different) sets of factors that were responsible for domestication in different places. One good example of a multiple strand approach to domestication is shown by recent studies of the Natufian cultural tradition in southwestern Asia, which developed about 12,500 years ago. Post-Pleistocene human niches involving sedentism and domestication had both positive and negative consequences for human beings who came to depend on them. By the time farmers became fully aware of agriculture's drawbacks, their societies had probably become so dependent on it that abandoning it for some other subsistence strategy would have been impossible.

7. Neolithic farming villages were basically egalitarian societies, like the foraging societies that had preceded them. However, beginning about 5,000 years ago in southwestern Asia and shortly thereafter in Egypt, the Indus Valley (India), China, Mesoamerica (Valley of Mexico), and the Andes (Peru), humans independently developed social stratification. Social stratification occurred when surplus food production made it possible for some members of society to stop producing food altogether and to specialize in various occupations. A wide gulf developed between most of society's members and a new social class of rulers who controlled most of the wealth. It appears that social complexity first appeared among complex foragers who lived in environments with abundant resources.

8. Archaeological evidence of social complexity includes the remains of monumental architecture, elaborate burials alongside much simpler burials, and concentrations of particular artifacts in specific areas of an archaeological site that might indicate occupational specialization. Complex societies are also normally made up of a number of settlements organized in a hierarchy: state organization is

suspected when regional settlement patterns show at least three levels in the settlement hierarchy. Art and written inscriptions may provide further information about ancient social organization. Cultural change in all early complex societies tended to alternate between periods of relative cultural uniformity and political unity and periods of regional differentiation and lack of political integration.

9. Anthropologists have devised a number of different hypotheses to explain why complex societies developed. Frequently, the hypothesis places emphasis on a single cause, or "prime mover." Although some of these causes were important in some places, they were not all important everywhere. Nevertheless, attempts to test these hypotheses about prime movers have led to a far richer appreciation of the complexities of social and cultural change in prehistory.

10. Andean civilization developed in a distinctive geographical setting. Foragers were living on the coast and in the sierra of the Andes Mountains between 14,000 and 8,000 years ago. The first monumental architecture appeared after 4,000 years ago. Irrigation agriculture became important along the coast between 3,800 and 2,900 years ago. Numerous independent states rose and fell on the coast and in the highlands until the rise of the Inka Empire in the late 1400s. During Inka times, the achievements of earlier states were consolidated and expanded. When the Spanish arrived in 1525, the Inka Empire stretched from present-day Colombia to central Chile, from the Pacific coast to the rain forests of the eastern Andean slopes.

11. The Andes are so diverse ecologically and so much information remains uncovered that it seems hazardous to speculate about the causes for the rise of complex societies there. Village agriculture was not responsible for the rise of complexity on the Peruvian coast. Environmental circumscription may explain the rise of the first states on the coast in the Early Intermediate period, but warfare and hydraulic agriculture did not become important until long after complex states had emerged. The most puzzling question is why people living in similar ecological settings in nearby valleys did not produce similar states.

For Review

1. What are ecological and evolutionary niches?

2. Why is domestication not the same as agriculture? Illustrate your answer with examples from the text.

3. Explain the basic points of animal domestication.

4. What are the different explanations offered by archaeologists for the domestication of plants and animals by humans?

5. Summarize the discussion of the beginning of domestication in Southwest Asia.

6. Who were the Natufians? What does archaeological research tell us about the processes of plant and animal domestication in Natufian society?

7. Summarize the key consequences of domestication and sedentism for human ways of life.

8. What is social complexity? What is the archaeological evidence for social complexity?

9. What were the world's first complex societies and where were they located?

10. What connections do archaeologists see between sedentism and the beginning of social stratification? Illustrate with examples.

11. What are the different explanations archaeologists offer for the beginning of complex societies?

12. Summarize the discussion in the text concerning the rise of social complexity in the Andes.

Key Terms

agriculture 183	concentrations of	grave goods 199	sedentism 183
agroecology 183	particular artifacts 200	monumental	sherds 200
bloodwealth 203	domestication 180	architecture 199	social stratification 190,
broad-spectrum	ecological niche 180	Neolithic 192	198
foraging 189	egalitarian social	niche construction 181	surplus production 198
class 198	relations 198	occupational	
complex societies 198	evolutionary niche 181	specialization 198	

Suggested Readings

Chang, K. C. 1986. *The archaeology of ancient China*, 4th ed. New Haven: Yale University Press. *A fascinating account of the rise of social complexity in China by one of the most distinguished interpreters of Chinese civilization in the United States.*

Henry, Donald. 1989. *From foraging to agriculture: The Levant at the end of the Ice Age.* Philadelphia: University of Pennsylvania Press. *A detailed, well-illustrated discussion of the archaeology of ancient southwestern Asia at the time of the emergence of agriculture. Particularly good on cultural variation.*

Hoffman, Michael. 1991. *Egypt before the pharaohs: The prehistoric foundations of Egyptian civilization.* Austin: University of Texas Press. *A highly readable account of the important developments in prehistoric Egypt that made the civilization of the pharaohs possible.*

Price, T. Douglas, and Gary M. Feinman, eds. 1995. *Foundations of social inequality.* New York: Plenum. *A fascinating collection of scholarly articles exploring the various factors responsible for institutionalizing social inequality in the first complex societies.*

Price, T. Douglas, and Anne Birgitte Gebauer, eds. 1995. *Last hunters, first farmers.* Santa Fe, NM: SAR Press. *A collection of scholarly articles exploring, among other topics, the importance of complex foraging societies in the process of domestication.*

Smith, Bruce D. 1995. *The emergence of agriculture.* New York: Scientific American Library. *An accessible, beautifully illustrated discussion of domestication throughout the world.*

Soustelle, Jacques. 1961. *Daily life of the Aztecs on the eve of the Spanish conquest.* Stanford: Stanford University Press. *A classic text that attempts to reconstruct for modern readers exactly what the title claims.*

Wenke, Robert, and Deborah Olszewski. 2006. *Patterns in prehistory: Humankind's first three million years*, 5th ed. New York: Oxford University Press. *An excellent, up-to-date, and highly readable account of the rise of social complexity in Mesopotamia, Egypt, the Indus Valley, China, Mesoamerica, and the Andes as well as a chapter on early cultural complexity in pre-European North America.*

Why Is the Concept of Culture Important?

8

In this chapter, you will examine in greater detail the concept of culture, one of the most influential ideas that anthropologists have developed. We will survey different ways that anthropologists have used the culture concept to expose the fallacies of biological determinism. We will also discuss the reasons why some anthropologists believe that continuing to use the culture concept today may be a problem.

Chapter Outline

◄ *Kindergarten children in Ofunato, Japan, observe a moment of silence for the victims of the Japanese earthquake and tsunami at 2:46 p.m. on April 11, 2011, a month after the tragedy.*

Anthropologists have long argued that the human condition is distinguished from the condition of other living species by *culture*. Other living species learn, but the extent to which human beings depend on learning is unique in the animal kingdom. Because our brains are capable of open symbolic thought and our hands are capable of manipulating matter powerfully or delicately, we interact with the wider world in a way that is distinct from that of any other species.

How Do Anthropologists Define Culture?

In Chapter 1, we defined **culture** as patterns of learned behavior and ideas acquired by people as members of society. Culture is not reinvented by each generation; rather, we learn it from other members of the social groups we belong to, although we may later modify this heritage in some way. Therefore, culture is *shared* as well as *learned*. Many things we learn, such as table manners and what is good to eat and where people are supposed to sleep, are never explicitly taught but rather are absorbed in the course of daily practical living. This kind of cultural learning is sometimes called *habitus*. The cultural practices shared within social groups always encompass the varied knowledge and skills of many different individuals. For example, space flight has been part of North American culture, and yet no individual North American could build a space shuttle from scratch.

Human cultures also appear *patterned*; that is, related cultural beliefs and practices show up repeatedly in different areas of social life. For example, in North America individualism is highly valued, and its influence can be seen in child-rearing practices (babies are expected to sleep alone, and children are reared with the expectation that they will be independent at the age of 18), economic practices (individuals are urged to get a job, to save their money, and not to count on other people or institutions to take care of them; many people would prefer to be in business for themselves; far more people commute to work by themselves in their own cars than carpool), and religious practices (the Christian emphasis on personal salvation and individual accountability before God). Cultural patterns can be traced through time: That English

and Spanish are widely spoken in North America, whereas Fulfulde (a language spoken in West Africa) is not, is connected to the colonial conquest and domination of North America by speakers of English and Spanish in past centuries. Cultural patterns also vary across space: In the United States, for example, the English of New York City differs from the English of Mississippi in style, rhythm, and vocabulary ("What? You expect me to schlep this around all day? Forget about it!" is more likely to be heard in the former than the latter!).

It is this patterned cultural variation that allows anthropologists (and others) to distinguish different "cultural traditions" from one another. But separate cultural traditions are often hard to delineate. That is because, in addition to any unique elements of their own, all contain contradictory elements, and they also share elements with other traditions. First, customs in one domain of culture may contradict customs in another domain, as when religion tells us to share with others and economics tells us to look out for ourselves alone. Second, people have always borrowed cultural elements from their neighbors, and many increasingly refuse to be limited in the present by cultural practices of the past. Why, for example, should literacy not be seen as part of Ju/'hoansi culture once the children of illiterate Ju/'hoansi foragers learn to read and write (see Ethno-Profile 11.4: Ju/'hoansi)? Thus, cultural patterns can be useful as a kind of shorthand, but it is important to remember that the boundaries between cultural traditions are always fuzzy. Ultimately, they rest on someone's judgment about how different one set of customs is from another set of customs. As we will see shortly, these kinds of contradictions and challenges are not uncommon, leading some anthropologists to think of culture not in terms of specific customs but in terms of rules that become "established ways of bringing ideas from different domains together" (Strathern 1992, 3).

So far we have seen that culture is learned, shared, and patterned. Cultural traditions are also reconstructed and enriched, generation after generation, primarily because human biological survival depends on culture. Thus, culture is also *adaptive*. Human newborns are not born with "instincts" that would enable them to survive on their own. On the contrary, they depend utterly on support and nurturance from adults and other members of the group in which they live. It is by learning the cultural practices of those around them that human beings come to master appropriate ways of thinking and acting that promote their own survival as biological organisms (Figure 8.1). Culture allows us both to adapt to and to transform the environments in which we live.

Finally, culture is *symbolic*. A **symbol** is something that stands for something else. The letters of an alphabet,

culture Sets of learned behaviors and ideas that humans acquire as members of society. Humans use culture to adapt to and transform the world in which they live.

symbol Something that stands for something else.

In Their Own Words

The Paradox of Ethnocentrism

*Ethnocentrism is usually described in thoroughly negative terms. As Ivan Karp points out,
however, ethnocentrism is a more complex phenomenon than we might expect.*

Anthropologists usually argue that ethnocentrism is both wrong and harmful, especially when it is tied to racial, cultural, and social prejudices. Ideas and feelings about the inferiority of blacks, the cupidity of Jews, or the lack of cultural sophistication of farmers are surely to be condemned. But can we do without ethnocentrism? If we stopped to examine every custom and practice in our cultural repertoire, how would we get on? For example, if we always regarded marriage as something that can vary from society to society, would we be concerned about filling out the proper marriage documents, or would we even get married at all? Most of the time we suspend a quizzical stance toward our own customs and simply live life.

Yet many of our own practices are peculiar when viewed through the lenses of other cultures. Periodically, for over fifteen years, I have worked with and lived among an African people. They are as amazed at our marriage customs as my students are at theirs. Both American students and the Iteso of Kenya find it difficult to imagine how the other culture survives with the bizarre, exotic practices that are part of their respective marriage customs. Ethnocentrism works both ways. It can be practiced as much by other cultures as by our own.

Paradoxically, ethnographic literature combats ethnocentrism by showing that the practices of cultures (including our own) are "natural" in their own setting. What appears natural in one setting appears so because it was constructed in that setting—made and produced by human beings who could have done it some other way. Ethnography is a means of recording the range of human creativity and of demonstrating how universally shared capacities can produce cultural and social differences.

This anthropological way of looking at other cultures—and, by implication, at ourselves—constitutes a major reason for reading ethnography. The anthropological lens teaches us to question what we assume to be unquestionable. Ethnography teaches us that human potentiality provides alternative means of organizing our lives and alternative modes of experiencing the world. Reading ethnographies trains us to question the received wisdom of our society and makes us receptive to change. In this sense, anthropology might be called the subversive science. We read ethnographies in order to learn about how other peoples produce their world and about how we might change our own patterns of production.

Source: Karp 1990, 74–75.

---

for example, symbolize the sounds of a spoken language. There is no necessary connection between the shape of a particular letter and the speech sound it represents. Indeed, the same or similar sounds are represented symbolically by very different letters in the Latin, Cyrillic, Hebrew, Arabic, and Greek alphabets, to name but five. Even the sounds of spoken language are symbols for meanings a speaker tries to express. The fact that we can translate from one language to another suggests that the same or similar meanings can be expressed by different symbols in different languages. But language is not the only domain of culture that depends on symbols. Everything we do in society has a symbolic dimension, from how we conduct ourselves at the dinner table to how we bury the dead. It is our heavy dependence on symbolic learning that sets human culture apart from the apparently nonsymbolic learning on which other species rely.

Human culture, then, is *learned, shared, patterned, adaptive,* and *symbolic*. And the contemporary human capacity for culture has also evolved, over millions of years. Culture's beginnings can perhaps be glimpsed among Japanese macaque monkeys who invented the custom of washing sweet potatoes and among wild chimpanzees who invented different grooming postures or techniques to crack open nuts or to gain access to termites or water (Boesch-Ackerman and Boesch 1994; Wolfe 1995, 162–63). Our apelike ancestors surely shared similar aptitudes when they started walking on two legs some 6 million years ago. By 2.5 million years ago, their descendants were making stone tools. Thereafter, our hominin lineage gave birth to a number of additional species, all of whom depended on culture more than their ancestors had. Thus, culture is not something that appeared suddenly, with the arrival of *Homo sapiens*. By the time *Homo sapiens* appeared some 200,000

Figure 8.1 Of all living organisms, humans are the most dependent on learning for their survival. From a young age, girls in northern Cameroon learn to carry heavy loads on their heads and also learn to get water for their families.

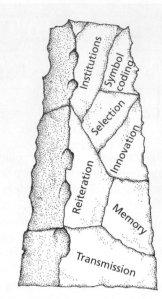

Figure 8.2 The modern human capacity for culture did not appear all at once; rather, the various pieces that make it up were added at different times in our evolutionary past.

years ago, a heavy dependence on culture had long been a part of our evolutionary heritage.

Thus, as Rick Potts puts it, "an evolutionary bridge exists between the human and animal realms of behavior. . . . Culture represents continuity" (1996, 197). Potts proposes that modern human symbolic culture and the social institutions that depend on it rest on other, more basic abilities that emerged at different times in our evolutionary past (Figure 8.2). Monkeys and apes possess many of these abilities to varying degrees, which is the reason they may be said to possess simple cultural traditions. Certainly our earliest hominin ancestors were no different.

According to Potts, the emergence of human symbolic culture and institutions could not have appeared unless our ancestors had the mental and physical capacity to copy behavior by observation or instruction (*transmission*), to remember new behaviors (*memory*), to reproduce or imitate behavior or information that has been learned (*reiteration*), to invent new behaviors (*innovation*), and to select which innovations to keep and which to discard (*selection*).

Apes apparently also possess a rudimentary capacity for *symbolic coding*, or symbolic representation, something our ancestors undoubtedly possessed as well. But new species can evolve new capacities not found in their ancestors. This occurred in the human past when our ancestors first developed a capacity for *complex symbolic representation*, including the ability to communicate freely about the past, the future, and the invisible. This ability

distinguishes human symbolic language, for example, from the vocal communication systems of apes (see Chapter 9). Biological anthropologist Terrence Deacon argues that evolution produced in *Homo sapiens* a brain "that has been significantly overbuilt for learning symbolic associations" such that "we cannot help but see the world in symbolic categories" (1997, 413, 416). Complex symbolic representation apparently was of great adaptive value for our ancestors. It created selective pressures that increased human symbolic capacities over time. Put another way, culture and the human brain *coevolved*, each furnishing key features of the environment to which the other needed to adapt (Deacon 1997, 44; Odling-Smee 1994). We have used our complex symbolic abilities, moreover, to create *institutions*—complex, variable and enduring forms of cultural practice that organize social life, also unique to our species. As a result, for *Homo sapiens*, culture has become "the predominant manner in which human groups vary from one another . . . it *swamps* the biological differences among populations" (Marks 1995, 200). We are truly biocultural organisms.

Culture, History, and Human Agency

The human condition is rooted in time and shaped by history. As part of the human condition, culture is also historical, being worked out and reconstructed in every

In Their Own Words

Culture and Freedom

Finding a way to fit human agency into a scientific account of culture has never been easy. Hoyt Alverson describes some of the issues involved.

One's assumptions concerning the existence of structure in culture, or the existence of freedom in human action, determine whether one believes that there can be a science of culture or not. Note that the possibility of developing a science of culture has nothing to do with the use of mathematics, the precision of one's assertions, or the elegance of one's models. If a phenomenon actually has structure, then a science of that phenomenon is at least conceivable. If a phenomenon exhibits freedom and is not ordered, then a science of that phenomenon is inconceivable. The human sciences, including anthropology, have been debating the issue of structure versus freedom in human cultural behavior for the past two hundred years, and no resolution or even consensus has emerged.

Some persuasive models of culture, and of particular cultures, have been proposed, both by those working with scientific, universalist assumptions, and by those working with phenomenological, relativistic assumptions.

To decide which of these approaches is to be preferred, we must have a specific set of criteria for evaluation. Faced with good evidence for the existence of both structure and freedom in human culture, no coherent set of criteria for comparing the success of these alternative models is conceivable. The prediction of future action, for example, is a good criterion for measuring the success of a model that purports to represent structure: it must be irrelevant to measuring the success or failure of a model that purports to describe freedom. For the foreseeable future, and maybe for the rest of time, we may have to be content with models that simply permit us to muddle through.

Source: Alverson 1990, 42–43.

generation. Culture is also part of our biological heritage. Our biocultural heritage has produced a living species that uses culture to surmount biological and individual limitations and is even capable of studying itself and its own biocultural evolution.

This realization, however, raises another question: Just how free from limitations are humans? Opinion in Western societies often polarizes around one of two extremes: Either we have *free will* and may do just as we please, or our behavior is completely determined by forces beyond our control. Many social scientists, however, are convinced that a more realistic description of human freedom was offered by Karl Marx, who wrote, "Men make their own history, but they do not make it just as they please; they do not make it under circumstances chosen by themselves, but under circumstances directly encountered, given and transmitted by the past" (1963, 15). That is, people regularly struggle, often against great odds, to exercise some control over their lives. Human beings active in this way are called *agents* (Figure 8.3). Human agents cannot escape from the cultural and historical context within which they act. However, they must frequently select a course of action when the "correct" choice is unclear and the outcome uncertain. Some anthropologists even liken human existence to a mine field

Figure 8.3 People regularly struggle, often against great odds, to exercise some control over their lives. During the "Dirty War" in Argentina in the 1970s and early 1980s, women whose children had been disappeared by secret right-wing death squads began, at great personal risk, to stand every Thursday in the Plaza de Mayo, the central square of Buenos Aires, with photographs of their missing children. Called the Mothers of Plaza de Mayo, they continue their weekly vigil today. They were a powerful rebuke to the dictatorship and to subsequent governments that were not forthcoming about providing information about the disappeared.

In Their Own Words

Human-Rights Law and the Demonization of Culture

Sally Engle Merry is professor of anthropology at New York University.

Why is the idea of cultural relativism anathema to many human-rights activists? Is it related to the way international human-rights lawyers and journalists think about culture? Does this affect how they think about anthropology? I think one explanation for the tension between anthropology and human-rights activists is the very different conceptions of culture that these two groups hold. An incident demonstrated this for me vividly a few months ago. I received a phone call from a prominent radio show asking if I would be willing to talk about the recent incident in Pakistan that resulted in the gang rape of a young woman, an assault apparently authorized by a local tribal council. Since I am working on human rights and violence against women, I was happy to explain my position that this was an inexcusable act, that many Pakistani feminists condemned the rape, but that it was probably connected to local political struggles and class differences. It should not be seen as an expression of Pakistani "culture." In fact, it was the local Islamic religious leader who first made the incident known to the world, according to news stories I had read.

The interviewer was distressed. She wanted me to defend the value of respecting Pakistani culture at all costs, despite the tribal council's imposition of a sentence of rape. When I told her that I could not do that, she wanted to know if I knew of any other anthropologists who would. I could think of none, but I began to wonder what she thought about anthropologists.

Anthropologists, apparently, made no moral judgments about "cultures" and failed to recognize the contestation and changes taking place within contemporary local communities around the world. This also led me to wonder how she imagined anthropologists thought about culture. She seemed to assume that anthropologists viewed culture as a coherent, static, and unchanging set of values. Apparently cultures have no contact with the expansion of capitalism, the arming of various groups by transnational superpowers using them for proxy wars, or the cultural possibilities of human rights as an emancipatory discourse. I found this interviewer's view of culture wrongheaded and her opinion of anthropology discouraging. But perhaps it was just one journalist, I thought.

However, the recent article "From Skepticism to Embrace: Human Rights and the American Anthropological Association" by Karen Engle in *Human Rights Quarterly* (23: 536–60) paints another odd portrait of anthropology

and its understanding of culture. In this piece, a law professor talks about the continuing "embarrassment" of anthropologists about the 1947 statement of the AAA Executive Board, which raised concerns about the Universal Declaration of Human Rights. Engle claims that the statement has caused the AAA "great shame" over the last fifty years (p. 542). Anthropologists are embarrassed, she argues, because the statement asserted tolerance without limits. While many anthropologists now embrace human rights, they do so primarily in terms of the protection of culture (citing 1999 AAA Statement on Human Rights at www.aaanet.org). Tensions over how to be a cultural relativist and still make overt political judgments that the 1947 Board confronted remain. She does acknowledge that not all anthropologists think about culture this way. But relativism, as she describes it, is primarily about tolerance for difference and is incompatible with making moral judgments about other societies.

But this incompatibility depends on how one theorizes culture. If culture is homogenous, integrated and consensual, it must be accepted as a whole. But anthropology has developed a far more complex way of understanding culture over the last two decades, focusing on its historical production, its porosity to outside influences and pressures, and its incorporation of competing repertoires of meaning and action. Were this conception more widely recognized within popular culture as well as among journalists and human-rights activists, it could shift the terms of the intractable debate between universalism and relativism. Instead, culture is increasingly understood as a barrier to the realization of human rights by activists and a tool for legitimating noncompliance with human rights by conservatives.

One manifestation of the understanding of culture prevalent in human-rights law is the concept of harmful traditional practices. Originally developed to describe female genital mutilation or cutting, this term describes practices that have some cultural legitimacy yet are designated harmful to women, particularly to their health. In 1990, the committee monitoring the Convention on the Elimination of All Forms of Discrimination Against Women (CEDAW), an international convention ratified by most of the nations of the world, said that they were gravely concerned "that there are continuing cultural, traditional and economic pressures which help to perpetuate harmful practices, such as female circumcision," and adopted

In Their Own Words

Human-Rights Law and the Demonization of Culture

General Recommendation 14, which suggested that state parties should take measures to eradicate the practice of female circumcision. Culture equals tradition and is juxtaposed to women's human rights to equality. It is not surprising, given this evolving understanding of culture within human-rights discourse, that cultural relativism is seen in such a negative light. The tendency for national elites to defend practices oppressive to women in the name of culture exacerbates this negative view of culture.

Human-rights activists and journalists have misinterpreted anthropology's position about relativism and difference because they misunderstand anthropology's position about culture. Claims to cultural relativism appear to be defenses of holistic and static entities. This conception of culture comes from older anthropological usages, such as the separation of values and social action advocated in the 1950s by Talcott Parsons. Since "culture" was defined only as values, it was considered inappropriate to judge one ethical system by another one. For Melville Herskovits, the leader of the AAA's relativist criticism of the Universal Declaration of Human Rights in 1947, cultural relativism meant protecting the holistic cultures of small communities from colonial intrusion (AAA 1947 Statement, AA 49: 539–43).

If culture is understood this way, it is not surprising that cultural relativism appears to be a retrograde position to human-rights lawyers. Nor is it puzzling that they find anthropology irrelevant. As human-rights law demonizes culture, it misunderstands anthropology as well. The holistic conception of culture provides no space for change, contestation or the analysis of the links between power, practices and values. Instead, it becomes a barrier to the reformist project of universal human rights. From the legal perspective on human rights, it is the texts, the documents and compliance that matter. Universalism is essential while relativism is bad. There is a sense of moral certainty which taking account of culture disrupts. This means, however, that the moral principle of tolerance for difference is lost.

When corporate executives in the U.S. steal millions of dollars through accounting fraud, we do not criticize American culture as a whole. We recognize that these actions come from the greed of a few along with sloppy institutional arrangements that allow them to get away with it. Similarly, the actions of a single tribal council in Pakistan should not indict the entire culture, as if it were a homogeneous entity. Although Pakistan and many of its communities have practices and laws that subordinate women, these are neither homogeneous nor ancient. Pakistan as a "culture" can be indicted by this particular council's encouragement to rape only if culture is understood as a homogeneous entity whose rules evoke universal compliance. Adopting a more sophisticated and dynamic understanding of culture not only promotes human-rights activism, but also relocates anthropological theorizing to the center of these issues rather than to the margins, where it has been banished.

Source: Merry 2003.

---

that we must painstakingly try to cross without blowing ourselves up. It is in such contexts, with their ragged edges, that human beings exercise their **human agency** by making interpretations, formulating goals, and setting out in pursuit of them.

Many anthropologists insist that it is possible to develop a view of human beings that finds room for culture, history, and human agency. The anthropological point of view called *holism* assumes that no sharp boundaries separate mind from body, body from environment, individual from society, my ideas from our ideas, or their traditions from our traditions. Rather, holism assumes that mind and body, body and environment, and so on, interpenetrate each other and even define each other. From a holistic perspective, attempts to divide reality into mind and matter are unsuccessful because of the complex nature of reality, which resists isolation and dissection. Anthropologists who have struggled to develop this holistic perspective on the human condition have made a contribution of unique and lasting value. Holism holds great appeal for those who seek a theory of human nature that is rich enough to do justice to its complex subject matter.

In anthropology, **holism** is traditionally understood as a perspective on the human condition in which the

---

human agency The exercise of at least some control over their lives by human beings.

holism Perspective on the human condition that assumes that mind and body, individuals and society, and individuals and the environment interpenetrate and even define one another.

whole (for example, a human being, a society, a cultural tradition) is understood to be greater than the sum of its parts. For example, from a holistic perspective, human beings are complex, dynamic living entities shaped by genes and culture and experience into entities whose properties cannot be reduced to the materials out of which they were constructed. To be sure, human organisms are closed off from the wider world in some ways by how our cells, tissues, and organs are bound into a single body. At the same time, like all living organisms, human beings are open to the world in other ways: we breathe, eat, harbor colonies of intestinal bacteria to aid our digestion, excrete waste products, and learn from experience (see Deacon 2003, 296–97). Similarly, a society is not just the sum of its individual members; people in groups develop dynamic relationships that facilitate collective actions impossible for individuals to bring about on their own. And cultural traditions are not just a list of beliefs, values, and practices; rather, different dimensions of cultural activity, such as economics and politics and religion, are knotted together in complex ways. To understand any human community requires untangling those cultural threads in order to reveal the full range of factors that shape particular cultural practices in that community.

Human beings who develop and live together in groups shaped by cultural patterns are deeply affected by shared cultural experiences. They become different from what they would have been had they matured in isolation; they also become different from other people who have been shaped by different social and cultural patterns. Social scientists have long known that human beings who grow up isolated from meaningful social interactions with others do not behave in ways that appear recognizably human. As anthropologist Clifford Geertz observed long ago, such human beings would be neither failed apes nor "natural" people stripped of their veneer of culture; they would be "mental basket cases" (1973, 40). Social living and cultural sharing are necessary for individual human beings to develop what we recognize as a *human* nature.

One useful way of thinking about the relationships among the parts that make up a whole is in terms of **coevolution**. A coevolutionary approach to the human condition emphasizes that human organisms, their physical environments, and their symbolic practices *codetermine* one another; with the passage of time, they can also

coevolve with one another. A coevolutionary view of the human condition also sees human beings as organisms whose bodies, brains, actions, and thoughts are equally involved in shaping what they become. Coevolution produces a human nature connected to a wider world and profoundly shaped by culture. These connections make us vulnerable over the courses of our lives to influences that our ancestors never experienced. The open, symbolic, meaning-making properties of human culture make it possible for us to respond to those influences in ways that our ancestors could not have anticipated.

Why Do Cultural Differences Matter?

The same objects, actions, or events frequently mean different things to people with different cultures. In fact, what counts as an object or event in one tradition may not be recognized as such in another. This powerful lesson of anthropology was illustrated by the experience of some Peace Corps volunteers working in southern Africa.

In the early 1970s, the Peace Corps office in Botswana was concerned by the number of volunteers who seemed to be "burned out," failing in their assignments, leaving the assigned villages, and increasingly hostile to their Tswana hosts. (See Figure 8.4 and EthnoProfile 8.1: Tswana.) The Peace Corps asked American anthropologist Hoyt Alverson, who was familiar with Tswana culture and society, for advice. Alverson (1977) discovered that one major problem the Peace Corps volunteers were having involved exactly this issue of similar actions having very different meanings. The volunteers complained that the Tswana would never leave them alone. Whenever they tried to get away and sit by themselves for a few minutes to have some private time, one or more Tswana would quickly join them. This made the Americans angry. From their perspective, everyone is entitled to a certain amount of privacy and time alone. To the Tswana, however, human life is social life; the only people who want to be alone are witches and the insane. Because these young Americans did not seem to be either, the Tswana who saw them sitting alone naturally assumed that there had been a breakdown in hospitality and that the volunteers would welcome some company. Here, one behavior—a person walking out into a field and sitting by himself or herself—had two very different meanings (Figure 8.5).

From this example we can see that human experience is inherently ambiguous. Even within a single cultural tradition, the meaning of an object or an action may differ, depending on the context. Quoting philosopher

---

coevolution The dialectical relationship between biological processes and symbolic cultural processes, in which each makes up an important part of the environment to which the other must adapt.

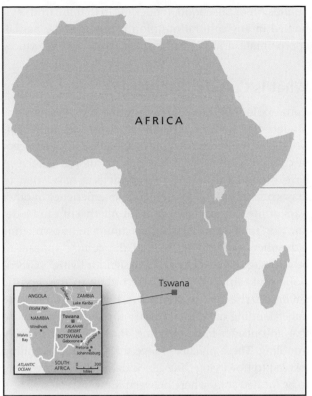

Figure 8.4 Location of Tswana. For more information, see EthnoProfile 8.1.

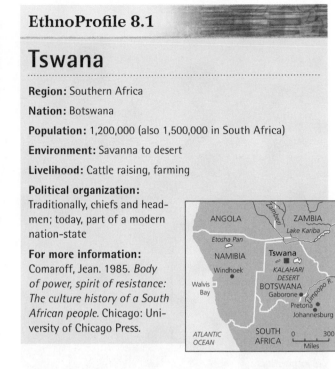

EthnoProfile 8.1

Tswana

Region: Southern Africa

Nation: Botswana

Population: 1,200,000 (also 1,500,000 in South Africa)

Environment: Savanna to desert

Livelihood: Cattle raising, farming

Political organization:
Traditionally, chiefs and headmen; today, part of a modern nation-state

For more information:
Comaroff, Jean. 1985. *Body of power, spirit of resistance: The culture history of a South African people.* Chicago: University of Chicago Press.

Gilbert Ryle, anthropologist Clifford Geertz (1973, 6) noted that there is a world of difference between a wink and a blink, as anyone who has ever mistaken one for the other has undoubtedly learned. To resolve the ambiguity, experience must be interpreted, and human beings regularly turn to their own cultural traditions in search of an interpretation that makes sense. They do this daily as they go about life among others with whom they share traditions. Serious misunderstandings may arise, however, when individuals confront the same ambiguous situation without realizing that their cultural ground rules differ.

What Is Ethnocentrism?

Ethnocentrism is the term anthropologists use to describe the opinion that one's own way of life is natural or correct, indeed the only way of being fully human. Ethnocentrism is one solution to the inevitable tension when people with different cultural backgrounds come into contact. It reduces the other way of life to a version of one's own. Sometimes we correctly identify meaningful areas of cultural overlap. But other times, we are shocked by the differences we encounter. We may conclude that if our way is right, then their way can only be

wrong. (Of course, from their perspective, our way of life may seem to be a distortion of theirs.)

The members of one society may go beyond merely interpreting another way of life in ethnocentric terms. They may decide to do something about the discrepancies they observe. They may conclude that the other way of life is wrong but not fundamentally evil and that the members of the other group need to be converted to their own way of doing things. If the others are unwilling to change their ways, however, the failed attempt at conversion may enlarge into an active dualism: us versus them, civilization versus savagery, good versus evil. The ultimate result may be war and *genocide*—the deliberate attempt to exterminate an entire group based on race, religion, national origin, or other cultural features.

Is It Possible to Avoid Ethnocentric Bias?

One way to address this question is to view relationships between individuals with different cultural backgrounds as not being fundamentally different from relationships between individuals with very similar cultural backgrounds (we pursue this further in Chapter 13). Even people with little in common can learn to get along, even if it is not always easy. Like all human relationships,

ethnocentrism The opinion that one's own way of life is natural or correct and, indeed, the only true way of being fully human.

Figure 8.5   For Tswana, human life is social life. It was difficult for Peace Corps volunteers from the United States accustomed to having "private time" to adjust to Tswana practices.

on illusion or falsehood, it does mean that the truth embodied in any cultural tradition is bound to be partial, approximate, and open to further insight and growth.

What Is Cultural Relativism?

Anthropologists must come to terms with the tensions produced by cultural differences as they do their fieldwork. One result has been the formulation of the concept of cultural relativism. Definitions of cultural relativism have varied as different anthropologists have tried to draw conclusions based on their own experience of other ways of life. For example, **cultural relativism** can be defined as "understanding another culture in its own terms sympathetically enough so that the culture appears to be a coherent and meaningful design for living" (Greenwood and Stini 1977, 182). According to this holistic definition, the goal of cultural relativism is to promote understanding of cultural practices, particularly of those that an outsider finds puzzling, incoherent, or morally troubling. These practices range from trivial (like eating insects) to horrifying (like genocide), but most are likely to be located somewhere between these extremes.

they affect all parties involved in the encounter, changing them as they learn about each other. People with a cultural background very different from your own may help you see possibilities for belief and action that are drastically at odds with everything your tradition considers possible. By becoming aware of these unsuspected possibilities, you become a different person. People from cultural backgrounds different from yours are likely to be affected in the same way.

Learning about other cultures is at once enormously hopeful and immensely threatening; once it occurs, we can no longer claim that any single culture has a monopoly on truth. Although this does not mean that the traditions in question must therefore be based entirely

---

cultural relativism   Understanding another culture in its own terms sympathetically enough so that the culture appears to be a coherent and meaningful design for living.

How Can Cultural Relativity Improve Our Understanding of Controversial Cultural Practices?

Rituals initiating girls and boys into adulthood are widely practiced throughout the world. In some parts of Africa, this ritual includes genital cutting (Figure 8.6). For example, ritual experts may cut off the foreskins of the penises of adolescent boys, who are expected to endure this operation without showing fear or pain. In the case of girls, ritual cutting may involve little more than nicking the clitoris with a knife blade to draw blood. In other cases, however, the surgery is more extreme. The clitoris itself may be cut off (or *excised*), a procedure called *clitoridectomy*. In some parts of eastern Africa, however, the surgery is even more extreme: The labia are excised along with the clitoris, and remaining skin is fastened together, forming scar tissue that partially closes the vaginal opening. This version is often called *pharaonic circumcision* or *infibulation*. When young women who have undergone this operation marry, they may require further surgery to widen the vaginal opening. Surgery may be necessary again to widen the vaginal opening when a woman gives

Figure 8.6 Among many East African people, including the Maasai, female genital cutting is an important part of the transformation of girls into women. These young women are recovering from the operation. Maasai women are proud of their new status as adults.

birth; and after she has delivered her child, she may expect to be closed up again. Many women who have undergone these procedures repeatedly can develop serious medical complications involving the bladder and colon later in life.

The removal of the male foreskin—or *circumcision*—has long been a familiar practice in Western societies, not only among observant Jews, who perform it for religious reasons, but also among physicians, who have encouraged circumcision of male newborns as a hygienic measure. The ritual practice of female genital cutting, by contrast, has been unfamiliar to most people in Western societies until recently.

Genital Cutting, Gender, and Human Rights

In 1978, radical feminist Mary Daly grouped "African female genital mutilation" together with practices such as foot binding in China and witch burning in medieval Europe and labeled all these practices patriarchal "Sado-Rituals" that destroy "the Self-affirming being of women" (1978, 111). Feminists and other cultural critics in Western societies spoke out against such practices in the 1980s. In 1992, African American novelist Alice Walker published a best-selling novel *Possessing the Secret of Joy*, in which the heroine is an African woman who undergoes the operation, suffers psychologically and

physically, and eventually pursues the female elder who performed the ritual on her. Walker also made a film, called *Warrior Marks*, that condemned female genital cutting. While many Western readers continue to regard the positions taken by Daly and Walker as formidable and necessary feminist assertions of women's resistance against patriarchal oppression, other readers—particularly women from societies in which female genital cutting is an ongoing practice—have responded with far less enthusiasm.

Does this mean that these women are in favor of female genital cutting? Not necessarily; in fact, many of them are actively working to discourage the practice in their own societies. But they find that when outsiders publicly condemn traditional African rituals like clitoridectomy and infibulation, their efforts may do more harm than good. Women anthropologists who come from African societies where female genital cutting is traditional point out that Western women who want to help are likely to be more effective if they pay closer attention to what the African women themselves have to say about the meaning of these customs: "Careful listening to women helps us to recognize them as political actors forging their own communities of resistance. It also helps us to learn how and when to provide strategic support that would be welcomed by women who are struggling to challenge such traditions within their own cultures" (Abusharaf 2000).

A better understanding of female genital cutting is badly needed in places like the United States and the European Union, where some immigrants and refugees from Africa have brought traditions of female genital cutting with them. Since the mid-1990s, growing awareness and public condemnation of the practice has led to the passage of laws that criminalize female genital cutting in 15 African states and 10 industrialized nations, including the United States and Canada (http://www.crlp.org/pub_fac_fgmicpd.html). Nonprofit legal advocacy organizations such as the Center for Reproductive and Legal Rights consider female genital cutting (which they call *female genital mutilation*, or FGM) to be a human rights violation. They acknowledge: "Although FGM is not undertaken with the intention of inflicting harm, its damaging physical, sexual, and psychological effects make it an act of violence against women and children" (http://www.crlp.org/pub_fac_fgmicpd.html). Some women have been able successfully to claim asylum or have avoided deportation by claiming that they have fled their home countries to avoid the operation. However, efforts to protect women and girls may backfire badly when immigrant or refugee mothers in the United States who seek to have their daughters ritually cut are stigmatized in the media as "mutilators" or "child abusers" and find that this practice is considered a felony punishable by up to five years in prison (Abusharaf 2000). Indeed, as we will see in Chapter 13, such efforts can backfire even when members of the receiving society attempt to be culturally sensitive.

Genital Cutting as a Valued Ritual

Female genital cutting is clearly a controversial practice about which many people have already made up their minds. In such circumstances, is there any role to be played by anthropologists? Abusharaf thinks there is. She writes: "Debates swirling around circumcision must be restructured in ways that are neither condemnatory nor demeaning, but that foster perceptions illuminated by careful study of the nuanced complexities of culture" (Abusharaf 2000, 17).

One ethnographic study that aims to achieve these goals has been written by Janice Boddy, a cultural anthropologist who has carried out field research since 1976 in the Muslim village of Hofriyat in rural northern Sudan, where female genital surgery is traditionally performed in childhood. She writes that "nothing . . . had adequately prepared me for what I was to witness" when she first observed the operation; nevertheless, "as time passed in the village and understanding deepened I came to regard this form of female circumcision in a very different light" (1997, 309). Circumcisions in Hofriyat were traditionally performed on both boys and girls, but the ritual had a different meaning for boys than it did for girls. Once circumcised, a boy takes a step toward manhood, but a girl will not become a woman until she marries. Female circumcision is required, however, to make a girl marriageable, making it possible for her "to use her one great gift, fertility" (1997, 310).

Boddy encountered a number of different explanations by scholars and other observers about the purpose of female genital cutting. In Hofriyat, female circumcision traditionally involved infibulation, the most extreme version of genital cutting. Among the justifications offered for infibulation, Boddy found that preserving chastity and curbing female sexual desire made the most sense in rural northern Sudan, where women's sexual conduct is the symbol of family honor. In practical terms, infibulation ensures "that a girl is a virgin when she marries for the first time" (313). Women who undergo the procedure do indeed suffer a lot, not only at the time of circumcision, but whenever they engage in sexual intercourse, whenever they give birth, and, over time, as they become subject to recurring urinary infections and difficulties with menstruation. What cultural explanation could make all this suffering meaningful to women?

The answer lies in the connection rural northern Sudanese villagers make between the infibulated female body and female fertility. Boddy believes that the women she knew equated the category of "virgin" more with fertility than with lack of sexual experience and believed that a woman's virginity and her fertility could be renewed and protected by the act of reinfibulation after giving birth. Women she knew described infibulated female bodies as clean and smooth and pure (313). Boddy concluded that the ritual was best understood as a way of socializing female fertility "by dramatically de-emphasizing their inherent sexuality" and turning infibulated women into potential "mothers of men." This means they are eligible, with their husbands, to found a new lineage section by giving birth to sons. Women who become "mothers of men" are more than mere sexual partners or servants of their husbands and may attain high status, their name remembered in village genealogies (314).

Boddy discovered that the purity, cleanliness, and smoothness associated with the infibulated female body is also associated with other activities, concepts, and objects in everyday village customs. For example, Boddy discovered that "clean" water birds, "clean food" such as eggs, ostrich eggshells, and gourds shaped like ostrich eggshells all were associated with female fertility. Indeed, "the shape of an ostrich egg, with its tiny orifice, corresponds to the idealized shape of the circumcised woman's womb" (317). Fetching water is traditionally considered women's work, and the ability of an object to retain moisture is likened to its ability to retain fertility. A dried egg-shaped gourd with seeds that rattle inside it is like the womb of an infibulated woman that contains and mixes her husband's semen with her own blood. The traditional house in Hofriyat itself seems to be a symbol for the womb, which is called the "house of childbirth" (321). In the same way that the household enclosure "protects a man's descendants, so the enclosed womb protects a woman's fertility . . . the womb of an infibulated woman is an oasis, the locus of appropriate human fertility" (321).

Evidence like this leads Boddy to insist that, for the women of Hofriyat, pharaonic circumcision is "an assertive symbolic act." The experience of infibulation, as well as other traditional curing practices teach girls to associate pure female bodies with heat and pain, making them meaningful. Such experiences become associated with the chief purpose women strive for—to become mothers of men—and the lesson is taught them repeatedly in a variety of ways when they look at waterbirds or eggs or make food or move around the village. Boddy's relativistic account demonstrates how the meanings associated with female infibulation are reinforced by so many different aspects of everyday life that girls who grow up, marry, and bear children in Hofriyat come to consider the operation a dangerous but profoundly necessary and justifiable procedure that enables them to help sustain all that is most valued in their own world.

Culture and Moral Reasoning

A relativistic understanding of female genital cutting, therefore, accomplishes several things. It makes the practice comprehensible and even coherent. It reveals how a physically dangerous procedure can appear perfectly acceptable—even indispensable—when placed in a particular context of meaning. It can help us see how some of the cultural practices that we take for granted, such as the promotion of weight loss and cosmetic surgery among women in our own society, are equally dangerous—from "Victorian clitoridectomy" (Sheehan 1997) to twenty-first century cosmetic surgery. In the March 1, 2007, issue of the *New York Times*, for example, reporter Natasha Singer observes, "Before braces, crooked teeth were the norm. Is wrinkle removal the new orthodontics?" (Singer 2007, 3). Media and marketing pressure for cosmetic treatments that stop the visible signs of aging bombard middle-aged women. People are living longer, and treatments like Botox injections are becoming more easily available, with the result that "the way pop culture perceives the aging face" is changing, leaving women "grappling with the idea of what 60 looks like" (2007, E3). Moreover, pressure to undergo antiaging treatments, including plastic surgery, is not simply a matter of vanity. "At the very least, wrinkles are being repositioned as the new gray hair—another means to judge attractiveness, romantic viability, professional competitiveness and social status" (2007, E3). Singer quotes a 33-year-old real estate broker who has had Botox injections, chemical peels and laser treatments who said, "If you want to sell a million-dollar house, you have to look good . . . and you have to have confidence that you look good" (2007, E3). In Sudan, people say that virgins are "made, not born" (Boddy 1997, 313); perhaps in the United States, youth is also "made, not born." In the United States today, the media message to women is that success in life requires not an infibulated body, but a face that never ages. In both cases, cultural practices recommend surgical intervention in the female life cycle to render permanent certain aspects of youthful female bodies that are otherwise transient (fertility and unlined faces, respectively).

Did Their Culture Make Them Do It?

Do these examples imply that women support "irrational" and harmful practices simply because "their culture makes them do it?" For some people, this kind of

explanation is plausible, even preferable, to alternative explanations, because it absolves individual people of blame. How can one justify accusing immigrant African women of being mutilators or abusers of children and throw them into prison if they had no choice in the matter, if their cultures conditioned them into believing that female circumcision was necessary and proper and they are powerless to resist?

Nevertheless, such an explanation is too simplistic to account for the continued practice of infibulation in Hofriyat. First, the villages of northern Sudan are not sealed off from a wider, more diverse world. Northern Sudan has experienced a lively and often violent history as different groups of outsiders, including the British, have struggled to control the land. Boddy describes the way rural men regularly leave the village as migrant workers and mix with people whose customs—including sexual customs—are very different from the ones they left behind; and outsiders, like anthropologists, also may come to the village and establish long-lasting relationships with those whom they meet. Second, Boddy's account makes clear that the culture of Hofriyat allows people more than one way to interpret their experiences. For example, she notes that although men in Sudan and Egypt are supposed to enjoy sexual intercourse with infibulated women more than with noninfibulated women, in fact these men regularly visit brothels where they encounter prostitutes who have not undergone the surgery.

Third, and perhaps most significantly, Boddy observes that a less radical form of the operation began to gain acceptance after 1969, and "men are now marrying—and what is more, saying that they prefer to marry—women who have been less severely mutilated," at least in part because they find sexual relations to be more satisfying (312). Finally, as these observations also show, Boddy's account emphatically rejects the view that women or men in Hofriyat are passive beings, helpless to resist cultural indoctrination. As Abusharaf would wish, Boddy listened to women in Hofriyat and recognized them "as political actors forging their own communities of resistance." Specifically, Boddy showed how increasing numbers of women (and men) continued to connect female genital cutting with properly socialized female fertility—but they no longer believed that infibulation was the only procedure capable of achieving that goal.

Understanding something is not the same as approving of it or excusing it. People everywhere may be repelled by unfamiliar cultural practices when they first encounter them. Sometimes when they understand these practices better, they change their minds. They may conclude that the practices in question are more suitable for the people who employ them than their own practices would be. They might even recommend incorporating practices from other cultures into their own society. But the opposite may also be the case. It is possible to understand perfectly the cultural rationale behind such practices as slavery, infanticide, headhunting, and genocide—and still refuse to approve of these practices. Insiders and outsiders alike may not be persuaded by the reasons offered to justify these practices, or they may be aware of alternative arrangements that could achieve the desired outcome via less drastic methods. In fact, changing practices of female circumcision in Hofriyat seem to be based precisely on the realization that less extreme forms of surgery can achieve the same valued cultural goals. This should not surprise us: It is likely that any cultural practice with far-reaching consequences for human life will have critics as well as supporters within the society where it is practiced. This is certainly the case in the United States, where abortion and capital punishment remain controversial issues.

A sensitive ethnographic account of a controversial cultural practice, like Boddy's account of infibulation in Hofriyat, will address both the meaningful dimensions of the practice and the contradictions it involves. As Boddy concludes,

> Those who work to eradicate female circumcision must, I assert, cultivate an awareness of the custom's local significances and of how much they are asking people to relinquish as well as gain. The stakes are high and it is hardly surprising that efforts to date have met with little success. It is, however, ironic that a practice that—at least in Hofriyat—emphasizes female fertility at a cultural level can be so destructive of it physiologically and so damaging to women's health overall. That paradox has analogies elsewhere, in a world considered "civilized," seemingly far removed from the "barbarous East." Here too, in the west from where I speak, feminine selfhood is often attained at the expense of female well-being. In parallels like these there lies the germ of an enlightened approach to the problem (322).

Cultural relativism makes moral reasoning more complex. It does not, however, require us to abandon every value our own society has taught us. Every cultural tradition offers more than one way of evaluating experience. Exposure to the interpretations of an unfamiliar culture forces us to reconsider the possibilities our own tradition recognizes in a new light and to search for areas of intersection as well as areas of disagreement. What cultural relativism does discourage is the easy solution of refusing to consider alternatives from the outset. It also does not free us from sometimes facing difficult choices between alternatives whose rightness or wrongness is less than clear-cut. In this sense, "cultural relativism is a 'toughminded' philosophy" (Herskovits 1973, 37).

Does Culture Explain Everything?

We believe that our view of the concept of culture as presented in this chapter is widely shared among contemporary cultural anthropologists. Nevertheless, in recent years the concept of culture has been critically reexamined as patterns of human life have undergone major dislocations and reconfigurations. The issues are complex and are more fully explored in later chapters, but we offer here a brief account to provide some historical context.

For at least the past 50 years, many anthropologists have distinguished between Culture (with a capital C) and cultures (plural with a lowercase c). *Culture* has been used to describe an attribute of the human species as a whole—its members' ability, in the absence of highly specific genetic programming, to create and to imitate patterned, symbolically mediated ideas and activities that promote the survival of our species. By contrast, the term *cultures* has been used to refer to particular, learned *ways of life* belonging to specific groups of human beings. Given this distinction, the human species as a whole can be said to have Culture as a defining attribute, but actual human beings would only have access to particular human cultures—either their own or other people's.

It is the plural use of cultures with a lowercase c that has been challenged. The challenge may seem puzzling, however, because many anthropologists have viewed the plural use of the culture concept not only as analytically helpful but as politically progressive. Their view reflects a struggle that developed in nineteenth-century Europe: Supporters of the supposedly progressive, universal civilization of the Enlightenment, inaugurated by the French Revolution and spread by Napoleonic conquest, were challenged by inhabitants of other European nations, who resisted both Napoleon and the Enlightenment in what has been called the Romantic Counter-Enlightenment. Romantic intellectuals in nations like Germany rejected what they considered to be the imposition of "artificial" Enlightenment *civilization* on the "natural" spiritual traditions of their own distinct national *cultures* (Kuper 1999; Crehan 2002).

This political dynamic, which pits a steamroller civilization against vulnerable local cultures, carried over into the usage that later developed in anthropology, particularly in North America. The decades surrounding the turn of the twentieth century marked the period of expanding European colonial empires as well as westward expansion and consolidation of control in North

America by European settlers. At that time, the social sciences were becoming established in universities, and different fields were assigned different tasks. Anthropology was allocated what Michel-Rolph Trouillot (1991) has called "the savage slot"—that is, the so-called "primitive" world that was the target of colonization. Anthropologists thus became the official academic experts on societies whose members suffered racist denigration as "primitives" and whose ways of life were being undermined by contact with Western colonial "civilization."

Anthropologists were determined to denounce these practices and to demonstrate that the "primitive" stereotype was false. Some found inspiration in the work of English anthropologist E. B. Tylor, who, in 1871, had defined "culture or civilization" as "that complex whole which includes knowledge, belief, art, morals, law, custom, and any other capabilities and habits acquired by man as a member of society" (1958 [1871]:1). This definition had the virtue of blurring the difference between "civilization" and "culture," and it encouraged the view that even "primitives" possessed "capabilities and habits" that merited respect. Thus, in response to stereotypes of "primitives" as irrational, disorganized, insensitive, or promiscuous, anthropologists like Franz Boas and Bronislaw Malinowski were able to show that, on the contrary, so-called "primitives" possessed "cultures" that were reasonable, orderly, artistically developed, and morally disciplined. The plural use of culture allowed them to argue that, in their own ways, "primitives" were as fully human as "civilized" people.

By the end of the twentieth century, however, some anthropologists became concerned about the way the plural concept of culture was being used. That is, the boundary that was once thought to protect vulnerability was starting to look more like a prison wall, condemning those within it to live according to "their" culture, just as their ancestors had done, like exhibits in a living museum, whether they wanted to or not. But if some group members criticize a practice, such as female genital cutting, that is part of their cultural tradition, does this mean that the critics are no longer "authentic" members of their own culture? To come to such a conclusion overlooks the possibility that alternatives to a controversial practice might already exist *within* the cultural tradition and that followers of that tradition may *themselves* decide that some alternatives make more sense than others in today's world. The issue then becomes not just which traditions have been inherited from the past—as if "authentic" cultures were monolithic and unchanging—but, rather, which traditional practices *ought* to continue in a contemporary world—and who is entitled to make that decision.

Culture Change and Cultural Authenticity

It is no secret that colonizing states have regularly attempted to determine the cultural priorities of those whom they conquered. Sending missionaries to convert colonized peoples to Christianity is one of the best-known practices of Western cultural imperialism. In North America in the 1860s, for example, escalating struggles between settlers and Native American groups led federal policymakers to place federal Indian policy in the hands of Christian reformers "who would embrace the hard work of transforming Indians and resist the lure of getting rich off the system's spoils" (Lassiter et al. 2002, 22). And although missionaries were initially resisted, eventually they made many converts, and Christianity remains strong among indigenous groups like the Comanches and Kiowas today. But how should this religious conversion be understood?

Doesn't the fact that Kiowas are Christians today show that federal officials and missionaries succeeded in their policies of Western Christian cultural imperialism? Maybe not: "Taking the 'Jesus Way' is not necessarily the story of how one set of beliefs replace another one wholesale, or of the incompatibility of Kiowa practices with Christian ones. Rather, it is a more complex encounter in which both sides make concessions" (Lassiter et al. 2002,19). True, missionaries arrived as the buffalo were disappearing and Kiowa people were being confined to reservations, and in 1890 the U.S. government used military force to put an end to the Kiowa Sun Dance, the centerpiece of Kiowa ceremonies. And yet, Lassiter tells us, "For many Kiowas—as for Indian people generally—Christianity has been, and remains, a crucially important element in their lives as Native people. Its concern for community needs, its emphasis on shared beliefs, and its promise of salvation have helped to mediate life in a region long buffeted by limited economic development, geographic isolation, and cultural stress" (Lassiter et al. 2002, 18).

One reason it succeeded was that missionaries did not insist that the Kiowa give up all traditional ways (2002, 53). Prominent individuals adopted Christianity, and Kiowa converts were trained to become missionaries and ministers, which proved attractive (2002, 57; Figure 8.7). Especially persuasive were women missionaries who "lived in the Kiowa camps, ate their food, and endured the privations of life on the plains with impressive strength" (2002, 59). Missionaries, in turn, actively sought to adapt Christian practices to traditional Kiowa ways. For example, "Missions were historically located in and around established camps and communities," with

Figure 8.7 Among the Kiowa, prominent individuals, like Chief Lone Wolf, adopted Christianity and invited missionaries to train Kiowa ministers.

the result that "churches were the natural extension of traditional Kiowa camps" and eventually took their place at the center of Kiowa life (2002, 61). "People would often camp on the grounds or stay with relatives for weeks at a time. . . . Services with Kiowa hymns and special prayers often extended into the evening" (2002, 62).

It might be as accurate to say that the Kiowa "kiowanized" Christianity, therefore, as it would be to say that missionaries "Christianized" the Kiowa. One of Lassiter's Kiowa collaborators, Vincent Bointy, insists that Christianity is not the same as "the white man's way" and explains that "the elders didn't say 'Christian.' . . . They said 'this is the way of God'" (Lassiter et al. 2002, 63). Kiowa identity and Christian values are so closely intertwined for Bointy that "he believes that he can express the power of Christianity better in Kiowa than in English." And this is why Kiowa hymns are so important. Unlike other Kiowa songs, Kiowa hymns are sung in the Kiowa language, which is spoken less and less in other settings. Kiowa hymns "give life to a unique Kiowa experience, preserve the language, and affirm an ongoing (and continually unfolding) Kiowa spirituality. Indeed, Kiowa Indian hymns are as much Kiowa (if not more) as they are "Christian" (Lassiter 2004, 205).

The way in which Kiowa Christians have been able to transform what began as an exercise in cultural imperialism into a reaffirmation of traditional Kiowa values challenges the presumption that "authentic cultures" never change. Such an inflexible concept of culture can accommodate neither the agency of Kiowa Christians nor the validity of the "ongoing" and "continually unfolding" cultural traditions they produce.

Today a variety of groups, from indigenous activists in Amazonia to immigrant activists in Europe, have incorporated the plural use of culture into their own self-definitions, and in some cases anthropologists defend this move as valuable and progressive. In addition, scholarly disciplines outside anthropology, from cultural studies to cognitive science, have incorporated "culture" into their own technical vocabularies. On the one hand, this can be seen (perhaps ironically) as a measure of the success of earlier generations of anthropologists in demonstrating the value of the culture concept. On the other hand, it means that today, "culture" is sometimes used in ways that anthropologists find objectionable but that they cannot control.

Attempts by anthropologists to deal with these complications are a focus in future chapters, especially in our discussions of anthropological approaches to ethnicity and nationalism (Chapter 14), globalization and multiculturalism (Chapter 15), and democracy and identity politics (Chapter 12).

The Promise of the Anthropological Perspective

The anthropological perspective on the human condition is not easy to maintain. It forces us to question the commonsense assumptions with which we are most comfortable. It only increases the difficulty we encounter when faced with moral and political decisions. It does not allow us an easy retreat, for once we are exposed to the kinds of experience that the anthropological undertaking makes possible, we are changed. We cannot easily pretend that these new experiences never happened to us. There is no going back to ethnocentrism when the going gets rough, except in bad faith. So anthropology is guaranteed to complicate your life. Nevertheless, the anthropological perspective can give you a broader understanding of human nature and the wider world, of society, culture, and history, and thus help you construct more realistic and authentic ways of coping with those complications.

Chapter Summary

1. Anthropologists have argued that culture distinguishes the human condition from the condition of other living species. Human culture is learned, shared, patterned, adaptive, and symbolic. It did not emerge all at once but evolved over time.

2. Many anthropologists have long thought holistically about human culture. Anthropological holism argues that objects and environments interpenetrate and even define each other. Thus, the whole is more than the sum of its parts. Human beings and human societies are open systems that cannot be reduced to the parts that make them up. The parts and the whole mutually define, or codetermine, each other and coevolve. This book adopts a coevolutionary approach to human nature, human society, and the human past. Human beings depend on symbolic cultural understandings to help them resolve the ambiguities inherent in everyday human experience.

3. Anthropologists believe that ethnocentrism can be countered by a commitment to cultural relativism, an attempt to understand the cultural underpinnings of behavior. Cultural relativism does not require us to abandon every value our society has taught us; however, it does discourage the easy solution of refusing to consider alternatives from the outset. Cultural relativism makes moral decisions more difficult because it requires us to take many things into account before we make up our minds.

4. Human history is an essential aspect of the human story. Culture is worked out over time and passed on from one generation to the next. The cultural beliefs and practices we inherit from the past or borrow from other people in the present make some things easier for us and other things more difficult. At the same time, culture provides resources human beings can make use of in the pursuit of their own goals. Thus, the anthropological understanding of human life recognizes the importance of human agency.

5. Many anthropologists have criticized using the term *cultures* to refer to particular, learned ways of life belonging to specific groups of human beings. Critics argue that this way of talking about culture seems to endorse a kind of oppressive cultural determinism. Supporters, however, argue that in some cases this version of the culture concept can be used to defend vulnerable social groups against exploitation and oppression by outsiders.

For Review

1. What are the five key attributes of human culture that are highlighted in this chapter?
2. What are complex symbolic representation and institutions, and why are they especially important to human culture?
3. What is human agency? How does attention to human agency affect the way anthropologists interpret cultural phenomena?
4. What do anthropologists mean by holism?
5. Describe the problems U.S. Peace Corps volunteers were having in Botswana and the explanation that was provided by anthropologist Hoyt Alverson.

6. Explain ethnocentrism and cultural relativism.
7. Summarize in your own words how cultural relativity can improve outsiders' understanding of a cultural practice that is unfamiliar and disturbing to them, such as female genital cutting.
8. Distinguish between Culture (with a capital C) and culture(s) (with a lowercase c). What does this difference reflect for anthropologists?
9. Summarize the case study on Kiowa Christianity. What does this case study reveal about human cultural processes?

Key Terms

coevolution 220	culture 214	holism 219	symbol 214
cultural relativism 222	ethnocentrism 221	human agency 219	

Suggested Readings

Gamst, Frederick, and Edward Norbeck. 1976. *Ideas of culture: Sources and uses.* New York: Holt, Rinehart & Winston. *A useful collection of important articles about culture. The articles are arranged according to different basic approaches to culture.*

Geertz, Clifford. 1973. Thick description: Towards an interpretive theory of culture *and* The impact of the concept of culture on the concept of man. In *The interpretation of cultures.* New York: Basic Books. *Two classic discussions of culture from a major figure in American anthropology. These works have done much to shape the discourse about culture in anthropology.*

Kuper, Adam. 1999. *Culture: The anthropologists' account.* Cambridge, MA: Harvard University Press. *A critical history of the use of the culture concept in anthropology, which traces its links to earlier Western ideas about culture and analyzes the work of several late twentieth-century anthropologists who made the concept central to their scholarship. Based on his experience with the abuse of the culture concept in apartheid South Africa, Kuper recommends that anthropologists drop the term entirely from their professional vocabulary.*

Voget, Fred. 1975. *A history of ethnology.* New York: Holt, Rinehart & Winston. *A massive, thorough, and detailed work. For the student seeking a challenging read.*

Module 3: On Ethnographic Methods

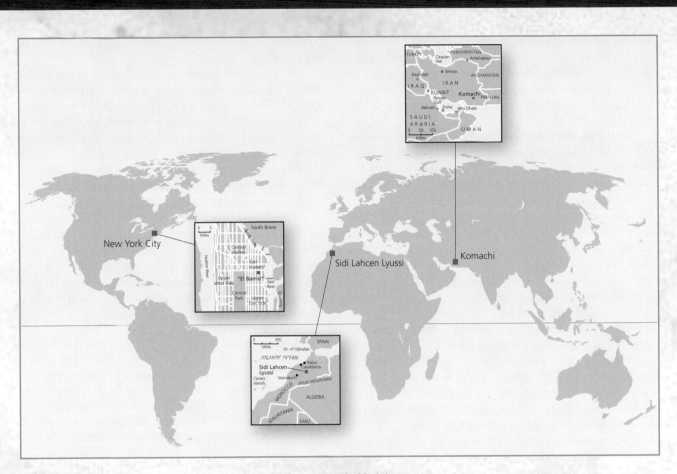

Figure M3.1 Locations of societies whose EthnoProfiles appear in Module 3.

A Meeting of Cultural Traditions

Ethnographic **fieldwork** is an extended period of close involvement with the people whose way of life interests an anthropologist. This is the period in which anthropologists collect most of their data. Fieldwork deliberately brings together people from different cultural backgrounds, an encounter that makes misunderstandings, understandings, and surprises likely. It is nevertheless through such encounters that fieldwork generates much of what anthropologists come to know about people in other societies.

Gathering data while living for an extended period in close contact with members of another social group is called **participant-observation**. Cultural anthropologists also gather data by conducting interviews and administering surveys, as well as by consulting archives and previously published literature relevant to their research. But participant-observation, which relies on face-to-face contact with people as they go about their daily lives, was pioneered by cultural anthropologists and remains characteristic of anthropology as a discipline. Participant-observation allows anthropologists to interpret what people say and do in the wider context

of social interaction and cultural beliefs and values. Sometimes they administer questionnaires and psychological tests as part of their fieldwork, but they would never rely solely on such methods because, by itself, the information they produce cannot be contextualized and may be misleading. Participant-observation is perhaps the best method available to scholars who seek a holistic understanding of culture and the human condition.

Single-Sited Fieldwork

For most cultural anthropologists, ethnographic fieldwork is the key experience that characterizes the discipline. Anthropologists sometimes gain field experience as undergraduates

---

fieldwork An extended period of close involvement with the people in whose language or way of life an anthropologist is interested, during which anthropologists ordinarily collect most of their data.

participant-observation The method anthropologists use to gather information by living as closely as possible to the people whose culture they are studying while participating in their lives as much as possible.

231

Module 3: On Ethnographic Methods (continued)

or early in their graduate studies by working on research projects or in field schools run by established anthropologists. An extended period of fieldwork is the final phase of formal anthropological training, but most anthropologists hope to incorporate additional periods of field research into their subsequent careers.

Beginning anthropologists usually decide during graduate school where and on what topic they wish to do their research. These decisions are based on their interests, their readings, the courses they have taken, the interests of their professors, and current debates in cultural anthropology. Success depends on being able to obtain both permission to work in a particular place in the form of approvals from academic and governmental offices in the host country and the funds to support one's research. Getting grants from private or government agencies involves, among other things, persuading them that your work will focus on a topic of current interest within anthropology and is connected to their funding priorities. As a result, "field sites end up being defined by the crosshatched intersection of visa and clearance procedures, the interests of funding agencies, and intellectual debates within the discipline and its subfields" (Gupta and Ferguson 1997, 11). Because there is a great demand for grants, not all topics of current interest can be funded, so some anthropologists pay for their research themselves by getting a job in the area where they want to do fieldwork or by supplementing small grants out of their own pockets.

Classic cultural anthropological fieldwork emphasized working "abroad"—that is, doing fieldwork in societies that were culturally and geographically distant from that of the ethnographer. This orientation bears undeniable traces of its origins under European colonialism, but it continues to be a valuable means of drawing attention to ways of life and parts of the world that elite groups in powerful Western nations have traditionally dismissed and marginalized. It also forces the fieldworker to recognize differences that might not be so obvious at home. More recent discussions of anthropological fieldwork have drawn attention to the significance of working "at home"—including paying attention to the forms of social differentiation and marginalization present in the society to which the ethnographer belongs. This orientation has the virtue of emphasizing ethnographers' ethical and political accountability to those among whom they work, especially when the anthropologists are themselves members of the groups they study. Such an orientation incorporates traditions of anthropological research that have developed in countries like Mexico, Brazil, India, and Russia, where fieldwork at home has long been the norm. At the beginning of the twenty-first century, these developments are helping to create "decolonized anthropology in a deterritorialized world" that will be enriched by varied contributions of anthropologists trained in different traditions, working at home and abroad.

Participant-observation requires living as closely as possible to the people whose culture you are studying. Anthropologists who work among remote peoples in rain forests, deserts, or tundra may need to bring along their own living quarters. In other cases, an appropriate house or apartment in the village, neighborhood, or city where the research is to be done becomes the anthropologist's home. In any case, living conditions in the field can themselves provide major insights into the culture under study. This is powerfully illustrated by the experiences of Charles and Bettylou Valentine, whose field site was a poor neighborhood they called "Blackston," located in a large city in the northern United States (see EthnoProfile M3.1: Blackston). The Valentines lived for the last field year on one-quarter of their regular income; during the final 6 months, they matched their income to that of welfare families:

> For five years we inhabited the same decrepit rat- and roach-infested buildings as everyone else, lived on the same poor quality food at inflated prices, trusted our health and our son's schooling to the same inferior institutions, suffered the same brutality and intimidation from the police, and like others made the best of it by some combination of endurance, escapism, and fighting back. Like the dwellings of our neighbors, our home went up in flames several times, including one disaster caused by the carelessness or ill will of the city's "firefighters." For several cold months we lived and worked in one room without heat other than what a cooking stove could provide, without hot water or windows, and with only one light bulb. (C. Valentine 1978, 5)

Not all field sites offer such a stark contrast to the middle-class backgrounds of many fieldworkers, and indeed some can be almost luxurious. But physical and mental dislocation and stress can be expected anywhere. People from temperate climates who find themselves in the tropics have to adjust to the heat; fieldworkers in the Arctic have to adjust to the cold. In hot climates especially, many anthropologists encounter plants, animals, insects, and diseases with which they have had no previous experience. In any climate, fieldworkers need to adjust to local water and food.

In addition, there are the cultural differences—which is why the fieldworkers came. Yet the immensity of what they will encounter is difficult for them to anticipate. Initially, just getting through the day—finding a place to stay and food to eat—may seem an enormous accomplishment; but there are also data to gather, research to do! Sometimes, however, the research questions never become separate from the living

Blackston

Region: North America

Nation: United States

Population: 100,000

Environment: Urban ghetto

Livelihood: Low-paying full-time and temporary jobs, welfare

Political organization: Lowest level in a modern nation-state

For more information: Valentine, Bettylou. 1978. *Hustling and other hard work.* New York: Free Press.

El Barrio

Region: North America

Nation: United States (New York City)

Population: 110,000

Environment: Urban ghetto

Livelihood: Low-paying full-time and temporary jobs, selling drugs, welfare

Political organization: Lowest level in a modern nation-state

For more information: Bourgois, Philippe. 1995. *In search of respect: Selling crack in El Barrio.* Cambridge: Cambridge University Press.

---

arrangements. Philippe Bourgois, who studied drug dealers in East Harlem in New York City, had to learn to deal not only with the violence of the drug dealers but also with the hostility and brutality that white police officers directed toward him, a white man living in *El Barrio* (see EthnoProfile M3.2: *El Barrio*). His experiences on the street pressed him to consider how the situation he was studying was a form of what he calls "inner-city apartheid" in the United States (Bourgois 1995, 32).

Multisited Fieldwork

In many ways, Bourgois's fieldwork in Spanish Harlem was very much in keeping with the fieldwork tradition inherited from Malinowski and Boas. That is, he engaged in what remains the most common mode of fieldwork in anthropology: "the intensively-focused-upon single site of ethnographic observation and participation" (Marcus 1995, 96). Much valuable work continues to be done in this mode. But changes in the world in the past 30 years have led many anthropologists to undertake fieldwork projects that include more than a single site.

Multisited fieldwork focuses on cultural processes that are not contained by social, ethnic, religious, or national boundaries, and the ethnographer follows the process from site to site, often doing fieldwork at sites and with persons who traditionally were never subjected to ethnographic analysis. As Marcus describes it, "Multi-sited research is designed around chains, paths, threads, conjunctions, or juxtapositions of locations" as ethnographers trace "a complex cultural phenomenon . . . that turns out to be contingent and malleable as one traces it" (1995, 105–6). Multisited ethnographers follow people, things, metaphors, plots, and lives (Marcus 1995, 107). Examples of this kind of ethnography will appear throughout the book, but here are a few:

Ethnographers who follow people include those who study tourists or migrants. Indeed, Philippe Bourgois's ethnography of Spanish Harlem (1995) also involved multisited research: although his day-to-day fieldwork was mostly focused on the neighborhood where the crack dealers lived, he followed them outside *El Barrio* when they sought employment in other parts of New York City. He also visited the sites in Puerto Rico from which their parents and grandparents had emigrated to the United States, in order to gain a first-hand understanding of that setting. And he supplemented present-day participant-observation with research on the history of Spanish Harlem from its first settlement up to the present day, thus locating it within the changing context of New York City and shaped by wider processes of immigration and employment and job loss.

Michelle Bigenho (2002) was interested in "authenticity" in Bolivian musical performances and in how Bolivian identities and music were connected. Studying this topic took her to Bolivia for 2 years plus several subsequent summers, where she performed with one musical ensemble in

---

multisited fieldwork Ethnographic research on cultural processes that are not contained by social, ethnic, religious, or national boundaries, in which the ethnographer follows the process from site to site, often doing fieldwork at sites and with persons who traditionally were never subjected to ethnographic analysis.

Figure M3.2 *El Barrio*, the part of New York City in which Philippe Bourgois did his research, is a socially complex, dynamic urban neighborhood.

La Paz, studied a nongovernmental organization in La Paz dedicated to cultural projects related to music, and worked in two highland indigenous communities in the south. She also traveled to France to perform at an international folk festival with the Bolivian ensemble in which she played. This kind of topic could not have been pursued except as a multisited ethnography. As she herself puts it, "I moved through multiple places to conduct research on the narratives of Bolivian nations as experienced through several music performance contexts" (2002, 7).

Collecting and Interpreting Data

Fieldwork is not just participating and observing—it also involves writing. It seems as though fieldworkers always have a notebook somewhere handy and, whenever possible, jot down notes on what they are seeing, hearing, doing, or wondering. These days, laptops, digital cameras, video cameras, and digital recorders are usually considered essential to accurate recording of what the ethnographer is learning. We cannot really trust our memories to keep track of the extraordinary range of information that comes at us in the field, so effective note taking is required. But note taking is not sufficient. The quickly jotted scrawls in notebooks must be turned into field notes, and as a result, anthropologists spend a lot of their time in front of their computers, writing as complete and coherent a set of notes as possible. Most ethnographers try to write up field notes on a daily basis, and also try to code the information as well, so that they can find it later. There are very useful field manuals for neophyte ethnographers to consult to assist them in developing workable and straightforward coding systems (e.g., Bernard 2011, DeWalt and DeWalt 2002).

As fieldworkers type up their notes, places for further inquiry become plain and a back-and-forth process begins. The ethnographer collects information, writes it down, thinks about it, analyzes it, and then takes new questions and interpretations back to the people with whom he or she is working to see if these questions and interpretations are more accurate than the previous ones.

Figure M3.3 Multisited field research is increasingly important in contemporary anthropology. As part of her research in Bolivia, Michelle Bigenho played violin with an ensemble in La Paz (*left*) and spent time in participant-observation—here helping with planting—while studying music in the small town of Yura (*right*).

The Dialectic of Fieldwork: Interpretation and Translation

Fieldwork in cultural anthropology is a risky business. Fieldworkers not only risk offending their informants by misunderstanding their way of life but also face the shock of the unfamiliar and their own vulnerability. Indeed, they must embrace this shock and cultivate this vulnerability if they are to achieve any kind of meaningful understanding of their informants' culture.

In the beginning, fieldworkers can be reassured by some of the insights that anthropological training provides. Since all human beings are members of the same biological species, ethnographers can expect to find in all human groups the same range of variation with regard to such human potentialities as intelligence. This can fortify them against ethnocentric impulses by recalling "that if what we observe appears to be odd or irrational, it is probably because we do not understand it and not because it is a product of a 'savage' culture in which such nonsense is to be expected" (Greenwood and Stini 1977, 185).

Anthropologist Michael Agar uses the expression "rich points" for those unexpected moments when problems in cross-cultural understanding emerge. Rich points may be words or actions that signal the gaps between the local people's out-of-awareness assumptions about how the world works and those of the anthropologist. For Agar, rich points

are the raw material of ethnography, challenging researchers but also offering opportunities for insight. As he says, "it is this distance between two worlds of experience that is exactly the problem that ethnographic research is designed to locate and resolve" (1996, 31). Ethnographers work hard to situate rich points within the local cultural world, continually testing their interpretations in a variety of settings, with different people, in order to see if those interpretations are or are not confirmed.

Interpreting Actions and Ideas

How does one go about interpreting the actions and ideas of other human beings? Paul Rabinow addressed this problem in a book based on reconsideration of his own fieldwork experiences. In *Reflections on Fieldwork in Morocco* (1977), Rabinow suggested that what goes on in ethnographic research is interpretation. As we come to grasp the meaning of the other's cultural self, we simultaneously learn something of the meaning of our own cultural identity.

The gulf between self and other may seem unbridgeable in the context of cross-cultural ethnography. Yet, anthropologists and informants engaged in participant-observation share at least one thing: the fieldwork situation itself. They are in physical proximity, observing and discussing the same material objects and activities. At first, they may talk past one another as each describes these activities from a different perspective using a different language. However, all

Figure M3.4 Anthropologists use different technologies for different research purposes. Anthropologist Ryan Cook videotapes the spectators and ritual performers at the Popocatepetl volcano in Mexico.

cultures and languages are open enough to entertain a variety of viewpoints and a variety of ways to talk about them. Continued discussion allows anthropologists and informants to search for ways to communicate about what is going on around them. Any overlap or intersection that promotes mutual understanding, however small, can form the foundation on which anthropologist and informant may build a new intersubjective symbolic language of their own. This process of building a bridge of understanding between self and other is what Rabinow refers to as the **dialectic of fieldwork** (1977, 39). Both fieldworker and informant may begin with little or nothing in the way of shared experience that could allow them to figure one another out with any accuracy. But if they are motivated to make sense of one another and willing to work together, steps toward valid interpretation and mutual understanding can be made.

For example, traditional fieldwork often begins with collecting data on how people in the local community believe themselves to be related to each other. A trained anthropologist comes to the field with knowledge of a variety of possible forms of social organization in mind. These ideas derive

dialectic of fieldwork The process of building a bridge of understanding between anthropologists and informants so that each can begin to understand the other.

reflexivity Critically thinking about the way one thinks, reflecting on one's own experience.

in part from the anthropologist's own personal experiences of social relations, but they will also be based on research and theorizing about social relations by other anthropologists. As the fieldworker begins to ask questions about social relations, he or she may discover that the informants have no word in their language that accurately conveys the range of meaning carried by a term like *kinship* or *ethnic group*. This does not mean that the anthropologist must give up. Rather, the anthropologist must enter into the dialectic process of interpretation and translation.

In the dialectic of fieldwork, both anthropologist and informant are active agents. Each party tries to figure out what the other is saying. For example, the anthropologist asks about "ethnic groups" using a term in the informants' language that seems close to "ethnic group" in meaning. Informants then try to interpret the anthropologist's question in a way that makes sense. That is, each informant has to be reflexive, thinking about how people in his or her society think about the topic which they believe is addressed by the anthropologist's question. This thinking about thinking is called **reflexivity**. Having formulated an answer, informants respond in terms they think the anthropologist will understand. Now it is the anthropologist's turn to interpret this response, to decide if it makes sense and carries the kind of information he or she was looking for.

If there is goodwill on the part of both, each party also tries to provide responses that make sense to the other. That is, anthropological fieldwork is also translation, and translation is a complicated and tricky process, full of false starts and misunderstandings. As time passes, each participant learns more about the other: the anthropologist gains skill at asking questions that make sense to the informant, and the informant becomes more skilled at answering those questions in terms relevant to the anthropologist. The validity of this ongoing translation is anchored in the setting of ongoing cultural activities in which both anthropologist and informant are participant-observers. Out of this mutual effort comes knowledge about the informant's culture that is meaningful to both anthropologist and informant. This is new cultural knowledge, a hybrid product of common understandings that emerges from the collaboration of anthropologist and informant.

Informants are equally involved in this dialogue and may end up learning as much or more about anthropologists as anthropologists learn about them. But it is important to emphasize that in field situations the dialogue is initiated by anthropologists. Anthropologists come to the field with their own sets of questions, which are determined not by the field situation but by the discipline of anthropology itself (see Karp and Kendall 1982, 254). Furthermore, when anthropologists are finished with a particular research project, they are often free to break off the dialogue with informants and resume discussions with fellow professionals. The only links between these two sets of dialogues—between particular anthropologists and the people with whom they work and among anthropologists in general—are the particular anthropologists themselves.

In recent years, members of indigenous societies have begun to speak powerfully on their own behalf as political advocates for their people, as lawyers, as organizers, as professionals. Language and other barriers often prevent many such individuals from speaking to an audience of professional scholars on complex topics, nor are their interests necessarily the same as those of professional scholars. Fieldwork thus involves differences of power and thereby places a heavy burden of responsibility on ethnographers. They are accountable not only to their informants but also to the discipline of anthropology, which has its own theoretical and practical concerns and ways of reasoning about ethnographic data. For these reasons, Arjun Appadurai calls for a "deparochialization of the research ethic" that would involve collaboration with colleagues outside the United States such as grassroots activists, who often lack the kinds of institutional resources and professional experience that scholars in the United States take for granted. With the right support, such colleagues could become equal partners in "a conversation about research" in which they "bring their own ideas of what counts as new knowledge" as well as their own ideas of how to measure the researcher's accountability to those among whom they work (2002, 281). Luke Eric Lassiter's work with Kiowa elders, discussed in Chapter 8, is a successful example of such collaboration.

Anthropologists feel strongly that their informants' identities should be protected. The need for protection is all the greater when informants belong to marginal and powerless groups that might suffer retaliation from more powerful members of their society. However, because some informants wish to express their identity and their ideas openly, anthropologists have experimented with forms of ethnographic writing in which they serve primarily as translators and editors of the voices and opinions of individual informants (e.g., Keesing 1983, Shostak 1981). Increasingly, anthropologists working in their own societies write about their fieldwork both as observers of others and as members of the society they are observing (e.g., D. Foley 1989, Kumar 1992).

The Dialectic of Fieldwork: An Example

Daniel Bradburd writes about the give and take of cross-cultural learning in his discussion of fieldwork among the Komachi, a nomadic people in Iran with whom he and his wife,

EthnoProfile M3.3

Komachi (mid-1970s)

Region: Southwest Asia

Nation: Iran

Population: 550

Environment: Varied—mountain valleys, lowland wooded areas

Livelihood: Nomadic herders

Political organization:
Part of modern nation-state

For more information:
Bradburd, Daniel. 1998. *Being there: The necessity of fieldwork*. Washington DC: Smithsonian Institution Press.

Anne Sheedy, lived in the mid-1970s (see Figure M3.5 and EthnoProfile M3.3: Komachi). Bradburd had gone to Iran to study the process of active decision making among nomadic herding people, and he was therefore quite interested in when people would move their camps and why they would do it. His first experience with moving was not what he had expected. After a month in one place, he started to hear talk about moving. Why? he asked. To be closer to the village and because the campsite was dirty. When? Soon. When is soon? When Tavakoli comes. This answer made no sense until further questioning revealed that Tavakoli was the son of the leader of the camp.

Eventually, their hosts told them that the move would be the next day; but when the next day came, there were no signs of activity in the camp. Finally, when it became clear that they would not be moving that day, Bradburd began asking why they had not moved. The answer was *ruz aqrab*. When they looked up *aqrab* in the dictionary, the answer made even less sense than the previous one: they were not moving because it was the day of the scorpion.

As was often the case, we felt as though we had moved one step forward and two steps back. We had an answer, but we hadn't the faintest idea what it meant. We were pretty certain it didn't have anything to do with real scorpions, because we hadn't seen any. We were also pretty certain that we hadn't heard any mention of them. So back we trudged to Qoli's tent, and we

Figure M3.5 Daniel Bradburd and Komachi camels packed for moving.

started asking more questions. Slowly it became clear. The scorpion was not a real, living one; it was the constellation Scorpio, which Qoli later pointed out to us on the horizon. (Bradburd 1998, 41)

After more questioning and more thinking, Bradburd and Sheedy finally concluded that the Komachi believed it was bad luck to undertake a new activity on days when it appeared that Scorpio would catch the rising moon. On checking back with their informants, they found that their conclusion was correct, but they were still puzzled. On the day that they had been told the move would be the next day, the Komachi in their camp had been fully aware that Scorpio and the rising moon would be in conjunction the next day. Eventually, Bradburd and Sheedy decided that "ruz aqrab" was a reasonable excuse for not moving, but they never did figure out the real reason for not moving that day. In fact, over the course of many such experiences, Bradburd and Sheedy came to realize that the Komachi did not have specific reasons for not moving. Rather, they still had one or another thing to do where they were, the weather was uncertain, the route to take was not clear yet, and so on. As a result of Bradburd's questions and the Komachi's responses, his interpretations and their responses to those, he gradually concluded that the Komachi decision-making process was an attempt to minimize the risks they had to take. Rather than being heroic nomads, masters of their fate, the Komachi made decisions only when they had to.

The Effects of Fieldwork

Fieldwork changes both anthropologists and informants. What kinds of effects can the fieldwork experience have on informants? Anthropologists have not always been able to

report on this. In some cases, the effects of fieldwork on informants cannot be assessed for many years. In other cases, it becomes clear in the course of fieldwork that the anthropologist's presence and questions have made the informants aware of their own cultural selves in new ways that are both surprising and uncomfortable.

As he reflected on his own fieldwork in Morocco, Rabinow recalled some cases in which his informants' new reflexivity led to unanticipated consequences (Figure M3.6). One key informant, Malik, agreed to help Rabinow compile a list of landholdings and other possessions of the villagers of Sidi Lahcen Lyussi (see EthnoProfile M3.4: Sidi Lahcen Lyussi). As a first step in tracing the economic status of the middle stratum in society, Rabinow suggested that Malik list his own possessions. Malik appeared to be neither rich nor poor; in fact, he considered himself "not well off." "As we began to make a detailed list of his possessions, he became touchy and defensive. . . . It was clear that he was not as impoverished as he had portrayed himself. . . . This was confusing and troubling for him. . . . Malik began to see that there was a disparity between his self-image and my classification system. The emergence of this 'hard' data before his eyes and through his own efforts was highly disconcerting for him" (1977, 117–18).

Malik's easy understanding of himself and his world had been disrupted, and he could not ignore the disruption. He would either have to change his self-image or find some way to assimilate this new information about himself into the old self-image. In the end, Malik managed to reaffirm his conclusion that he was not well off by arguing that wealth lay not in material possessions alone. Although he might be rich in material goods, his son's health was bad, his own father was dead, he was responsible for his mother and unmarried

Figure M3.6 Paul Rabinow's reflections on his fieldwork experiences in a Moroccan village much like this one led him to reconceptualize the nature of anthropological fieldwork.

brothers, and he had to be constantly vigilant in order to prevent his uncle from stealing his land (117–19).

What are the consequences of fieldwork for the fieldworker? Graduate students in anthropology who have not yet been in the field sometimes develop an idealized narrative about fieldwork: at first, the fieldworker is a bit disoriented and potential informants are suspicious, but uncertainty soon gives way to understanding and trust as the anthropologist's good intentions are made known and accepted. The fieldworker succeeds in establishing rapport. In fact, the fieldworker becomes so well loved and trusted, so thoroughly accepted, that he or she is incorporated as an equal and allowed access to cultural secrets. Presumably, all this happens as a result of the personal attributes of the fieldworker. If you have what it takes, you will be taken in and treated like one of the family. If this does not happen, you are obviously cut out for some other kind of work.

But much more than the anthropologist's personality is responsible for successful fieldwork. Establishing rapport with the people being studied is an achievement of anthropologist and informants together. Acceptance is problematic, rather than ensured, even for the most gifted fieldworkers. After all, fieldworkers are usually outsiders with no personal ties to the community in which they will do their research. According to Karp and Kendall (1982), it is therefore not just

EthnoProfile M3.4

Sidi Lahcen Lyussi

Region: Northern Africa

Nation: Morocco

Population: 900

Environment: Mountainous terrain

Livelihood: Farming, some livestock raising

Political organization: Village in a modern nation-state

For more information: Rabinow, Paul. 1977. *Reflections on fieldwork in Morocco*. Berkeley: University of California Press.

naive to think that the locals will accept you as one of them without any difficulty; it is also bad science.

Rabinow recalled the relationship he formed with his first Moroccan informant, a man called Ibrahim, whom he hired to teach him Arabic. Rabinow and Ibrahim seemed to get along well together, and, because of the language lessons, they saw each other a great deal, leading Rabinow to think of Ibrahim as a friend. When Rabinow planned a trip to another city, Ibrahim offered to go along as a guide and stay with relatives. This only confirmed Ibrahim's friendliness in Rabinow's eyes. But things changed once they arrived at their destination. Ibrahim told Rabinow that the relatives with whom he was to stay did not exist, that he had no money, and that he expected Rabinow to pay for his hotel room. When Rabinow was unable to do so, however, Ibrahim paid for it himself. Rabinow was shocked and hurt by this experience, and his relationship with Ibrahim was forever altered. Rabinow remarks: "Basically I had been conceiving of him as a friend because of the seeming personal relationship we had established. But Ibrahim, a lot less confusedly, had basically conceptualized me as a resource. He was not unjustly situating me with the other Europeans with whom he had dealings" (1977, 29).

Rabinow's experience illustrates what he calls the "shock of otherness." Fieldwork institutionalizes this shock. Having to anticipate **culture shock** at any and every turn, anthropologists sometimes find that fieldwork takes on a tone that is anything but pleasant and sunny. For many anthropologists, what characterizes fieldwork, at least in its early stages, is anxiety—the anxiety of an isolated individual with nothing familiar to turn to, no common sense on which to rely, and no relationships that can be taken for granted. There is a reason anthropologists have reported holing up for weeks at a time reading paperback novels and eating peanut butter sandwiches. One of us (E. A. S.) recalls how difficult it was every morning to leave the compound in Guider, Cameroon. Despite the accomplishments of the previous day, she was always convinced that no one would want to talk to her *today* (see EthnoProfile 14.3: Guider).

Good ethnography should allow readers to *experience* the informants' full humanity. This privileged position, the extraordinary opportunity to experience "the other" as human beings while learning about their lives, is an experience that comes neither easily nor automatically. It must be cultivated, and it requires cooperation between and effort from one's informants and oneself. We have made an important first step if we can come to recognize, as Paul Rabinow did, that "there is no primitive. There are other [people] living other lives" (1977, 151).

Multisited ethnography can complicate the picture by simultaneously offering rich, fieldwork-based portraits of other people living other lives as variously situated as AIDS patients and corporate managers and by demonstrating, moreover, that members of these groups share important cultural commitments. In the best ethnographic writing, we can grasp the humanity—the greed, compassion, suffering, pleasure, confusions, and ambivalences—of the people who have granted the anthropologist the privilege of living with them for an extended period of time. Because of such experiences, it may become more natural for us to talk about cultural differences by saying "not 'they,' not 'we,' not 'you,' but some of us are thus and so" (W. Smith 1982, 70).

The Production of Anthropological Knowledge

Anthropologist David Hess defines **fact** as a widely accepted observation, a taken-for-granted item of common knowledge (1997, 101–2). Ethnographers' field notebooks will be full of facts collected from different informants, as well as facts based on their own cultural experiences and professional training. But what happens when facts from these various sources contradict one another?

Facts turn out to be complex phenomena. On the one hand, they assert that a particular state of affairs about the world is true. On the other hand, reflexive analysis has taught us that *who* tells us that *x* is a fact is an extremely important thing to know. This is because, as we saw in Module 1, facts do not speak for themselves. They speak only when they are interpreted and placed in a context of meaning that makes them intelligible. What constitutes a cultural fact is ambiguous. Anthropologists and informants can disagree; anthropologists can disagree among themselves; informants can disagree among themselves. The facts of anthropology exist neither in the culture of the anthropologist nor in the culture of the informant. "Anthropological facts are cross-cultural, because they are made across cultural boundaries" (Rabinow 1977, 152). In short, facts are not just out there, waiting for someone to come along and pick them up. They are made and remade (1) in the field, (2) when fieldworkers reexamine field notes and reflect

---

culture shock The feeling, akin to panic, that develops in people living in an unfamiliar society when they cannot understand what is happening around them.

fact A widely accepted observation, a taken-for-granted item of common knowledge. Facts do not speak for themselves but only when they are interpreted and placed in a context of meaning that makes them intelligible.

on the field experience at a later time, and (3) when the fieldworkers write about their experiences or discuss them with other anthropologists.

For Daniel Bradburd, fieldwork begins with "being there." But simply being there is not enough. As Bradburd puts it, "my experiences among the Komachi shaped my understanding of them, and that part of field experience consists of a constant process of being brought up short, of having expectations confounded, of being forced to think very hard about what is happening, right now, with me and them, let alone the thinking and rethinking about those experiences when they have—sometimes mercifully—passed" (1998, 161–62). After all, fieldwork is fieldwork—there are notes to be taken, interviews to be carried out, observations to make, interpretations to be made. There is also the transformation of the experiences of being there into what Bradburd calls "elements of an understanding that is at once incomplete and impossible to complete, but also wonderfully capable of being improved" (164). According to Harry Wolcott (1999, 262), it is what ethnographers do with data— "making considered generalizations about how members of a group tend to speak and act, warranted generalizations appropriate for collectivities of people rather than the usual shoot-from-the-hip stereotyping adequate for allowing us to achieve our individual purposes"—that makes fieldwork experience different from just experience and turns it into doing ethnography.

Multisited fieldwork elaborates on and further complicates this experience because it involves being "here and there." In the course of the movement from site to site, new facts come into view that would otherwise never be known, adding a further layer to the thinking and rethinking that all fieldwork sets in motion. What happens if you find that your activism in support of the urban poor at one site works against the interests of the indigenous people you have supported at a different site? "In conducting multisited research," Marcus says, "one finds oneself with all sorts of cross-cutting commitments" that are not easily resolved (Marcus 1995, 113).

Anthropological Knowledge as Open-Ended

Cultivating reflexivity allows us to produce less distorted views of human nature and the human condition, yet we remain human beings interpreting the lives of other human beings. We can never escape from our humanity to some point of view that would allow us to see human existence and human experience from the outside. Instead, we must rely on our common humanity and our interpretive powers to show us the parts of our nature that can be made visible.

If there truly is "no primitive," no subsection of humanity that is radically different in nature or in capacity from the anthropologists who study it, then the ethnographic record of anthropological knowledge is perhaps best understood as a vast commentary on human possibility. As with all commentaries, it depends on an original text—in this case, human experience. But that experience is ambiguous, speaking with many voices, capable of supporting more than one interpretation. Growth of anthropological knowledge is no different, then, from the growth of human self-understanding in general. It ought to contribute to the domain of human wisdom that concerns who we are as a species, where we have come from, and where we may be going.

Like all commentaries, the ethnographic record is and must be unfinished: human beings are open systems, human history continues, and problems and their possible solutions change. There is no one true version of human life. For anthropologists, the true version of human life consists of all versions of human life. This is a sobering possibility. It makes it appear that "the anthropologist is condemned to a greater or lesser degree of failure" in even trying to understand another culture (Basham 1978, 299). Informants would equally be condemned to never know fully even their own way of life. But total pessimism does not seem warranted. We may never know everything, but it does not follow that our efforts can teach us nothing. "Two of the fundamental qualities of humanity are the capacity to understand one another and the capacity to be understood. Not fully certainly. Yet not negligibly, certainly. . . . There is no person on earth that I can fully understand. There is and has been no person on earth that I cannot understand at all" (W. Smith 1982, 68–69).

Moreover, as our contact with the other is prolonged and as our efforts to communicate are rewarded by the construction of intersubjective understanding, we can always learn more. Human beings are open organisms, with a vast ability to learn new things. This is significant, for even if we can never know everything, it does not seem that our capacity for understanding ourselves and others is likely to be exhausted soon. This is not only because we are open to change but also because our culture and our wider environment can change, and all will continue to do so as long as human history continues. The ethnographic enterprise will never be finished, even if all nonindustrial ways of life disappear forever, all people move into cities, and everyone ends up speaking English. Such a superficial homogeneity would mask a vast heterogeneity beneath its bland surface. In any case, given the dynamics of human existence, nothing in human affairs can remain homogeneous for long.

Module 3: On Ethnographic Methods (continued)

Module Summary

1. Anthropological fieldwork has traditionally involved participant-observation, extended periods of close contact at a single site with members of another society. Anthropologists were expected to carry out research in societies different from their own, but in recent years increasing numbers have worked in their own societies. Each setting has its own advantages and drawbacks for ethnographers.

2. Many contemporary anthropologists have begun to carry out fieldwork in a number of different sites. Such multisited fieldwork is usually the outcome of following cultural phenomena wherever they lead, often crossing local, regional, and national boundaries in the process. Such fieldwork allows anthropologists to understand better many cultural processes that link people, things, metaphors, plots, and lives that are not confined to a single site.

3. Contemporary ethnographers still take field notes by hand, but most also rely on electronic forms of data collection, including laptop computers, digital cameras, video cameras, and digital recorders. Because all this information needs to be organized and interpreted, ethnographers tack back and forth between their various sources of data, seeking feedback whenever possible from the people among whom they work before finally writing up and publishing their findings in ethnographies.

4. When human beings study other human beings, scientific accuracy requires that they relate to one another as human beings. Successful fieldwork involves anthropologists who think about the way they think about other cultures. Informants also must reflect on the way they and others in their society think and try to convey their insights to the anthropologist. This is basic to the reflexive approach to ethnographic research, which sees participant-observation as a dialogue about the meaning of experience in the informant's culture. Fieldworkers and informants work together to construct an intersubjective world of meaning.

5. Taking part in ethnographic fieldwork has the potential to change informants and researchers in sometimes unpredictable ways. In some cases, anthropologists have worked with their informants to bring about social changes, although not all anthropologists agree that this is appropriate. In other cases, anthropologists argue that their main task is to figure out and explain to others how people in particular places at particular moments engage with the world.

6. Because cultural meanings are intersubjectively constructed during fieldwork, cultural facts do not speak for themselves. They speak only when they are interpreted and placed in a context of meaning that makes them intelligible. Multisited fieldwork complicates this because it involves the anthropologist in crosscutting commitments in different contexts, where the same cultural facts may be differently understood or valued.

7. The ethnographic record of anthropological knowledge is perhaps best understood as a vast unfinished commentary on human possibility. We will surely never learn all there is to know, but we can always learn more.

For Review

1. Explain the basic elements of ethnographic fieldwork.
2. Describe multisited fieldwork and explain why many anthropologists undertake it.
3. What is the dialectic of fieldwork, and why is it important for ethnographic research?
4. Using the examples in the text, explain how ruptures of communication in fieldwork may turn out to have positive consequences for the ethnographer.
5. What are some of the ways that fieldwork may affect informants?
6. What are some of the ways that fieldwork affects the researcher?
7. What is the importance of "being there" for ethnographic fieldwork?
8. In your view, what are the strengths and weaknesses of ethnographic fieldwork?

Key Terms

culture shock 240	multisited fieldwork 233
dialectic of	participant-
fieldwork 236	observation 231
fact 240	reflexivity 236
fieldwork 231	

Suggested Readings

Bernard, H. Russell. 2011. *Research Methods in Anthropology*, 5th ed. Lanham, MD: AltaMira Press. *An enduring classic of methods books, detailed and thorough.*

Bigenho, Michelle. 2002. *Sounding indigenous: Authenticity in Bolivian musical performance.* New York: Palgrave Macmillan. *A recent multisited ethnography that follows Bolivian and non-Bolivian members of a Bolivian musical ensemble through different settings on more than one continent, chronicling varied understandings of what counts as "indigenous" Bolivian music.*

Bradburd, Daniel. 1998. *Being there: The necessity of fieldwork.* Washington DC: Smithsonian Institution Press. *An engaging personal study of how the many seemingly small details of experience during field research add up to anthropological understanding.*

Lévi-Strauss, Claude. 1974. *Tristes tropiques.* New York: Pocket Books. *Originally published in French in 1955, this book (with an untranslatable title) is considered by some to be the greatest book ever written by an anthropologist (although not necessarily a great anthropology book). This is a multifaceted work about voyaging, fieldwork, self-knowledge, philosophy, and much more. It is a challenging read in some places but highly rewarding overall.*

Rabinow, Paul. 1977. *Reflections on fieldwork in Morocco.* Berkeley: University of California Press. *An important, brief, powerfully written reflection on the nature of fieldwork. Very accessible and highly recommended.*

Valentine, Bettylou. 1978. *Hustling and other hard work.* New York: Free Press. *An innovative, provocative, and now classic study of African American inner-city life. Reads like a good novel.*

Why Is Understanding Human Language Important?

Only human beings have symbolic language, and it is so deeply part of our lives that we rarely even think about how unusual it is. In this chapter, you will learn about what makes human symbolic language different from other forms of animal communication. You will also explore its deep connections to other symbolic dimensions of social and cultural life, including the ways your patterns of thought, your sense of self, and even your personality are shaped by experiences in different kinds of symbolically shaped settings.

Chapter Outline

◀ *Communication takes many forms.*

As we saw in Chapter 4, primates depend on learned behavior to survive, and some primate species appear to have developed their own cultural traditions. Primates also communicate with one another in a variety of ways, most obviously by relying on vocal calls to alert one another about significant aspects of their environment, from presence of food to the threat of a predator. In the past, some anthropologists hypothesized that human language was simply an elaboration of the call system of our ancestors, but this hypothesis proved to be incorrect. In fact, the more anthropologists and other scientists learned about human language, the more obvious it has become that human languages are very different from primate call systems. Indeed, they have shown that human language is a *second* system of communication that evolved in our lineage *alongside* the call system we inherited from our primate ancestors. Humans still possess a simple, species-specific system of calls, as we will see. But because of their complex dependence on *symbols*, the languages we speak are distinct from our own—and all other—primate call systems.

In Chapter 8, we defined a **symbol** as something that stands for something else. Human symbolic language is perhaps the clearest illustration of the central role played by symbols in all of human culture. Indeed, it is the dependence of human language on symbols that makes it such a flexible and creative system of communication—and far more powerful than any primate call system could ever be. So when anthropologists talk about human language, they always mean human *symbolic* language. This is why we define **language** as the system of arbitrary symbols human beings use to encode and communicate about their experience of the world and of one another. The role played by symbols in human language sets it apart from the apparently nonsymbolic communication systems of other living species. Symbolic language has also made many singular human achievements possible. And yet, language is double-edged: it allows people to communicate with one another, but it also creates barriers to communication. There are some 3,000 mutually unintelligible languages spoken in the world today (Figure 9.1). This chapter explores the ambiguity, limitations, and power of human language and its connections to other forms of human symbolic activity.

symbol Something that stands for something else. A symbol signals the presence of an important domain of experience.

language The system of arbitrary symbols people use to encode their experience of the world and of others.

linguistics The scientific study of language.

How Are Language and Culture Related?

Human language is a biocultural phenomenon. The human brain and the anatomy of the mouth and throat make language a biological possibility. At the same time, no human language can be restricted only to the sounds that come out of people's mouths. Languages are clearly cultural products embedded in meanings and behavioral patterns that stretch beyond individual bodies, across space, and over time. Anthropologists have long been particularly attentive to the multiple powerful dimensions of language, especially when ethnographic fieldwork in societies presented them with the challenge of learning unwritten languages without formal instruction. At the same time, anthropologists who transcribed or tape-recorded speech could lift it out of its cultural context to be analyzed on its own. Their analyses revealed grammatical intricacies and complexities suggesting that language might be a good model for the rest of culture. It also became obvious that the way people use language provides important clues to their understanding of the world and of themselves. Indeed, some theories of culture are explicitly based on ideas taken from **linguistics**, the scientific study of language.

As with the culture concept, the concept of "language" has regularly involved a distinction between *Language* and *languages*. *Language* with a capital *L* (like *Culture* with a capital *C*) has often been viewed as an abstract property belonging to the human species as a whole, not to be confused with the specific *languages* of concrete groups of people. This distinction initially enabled the recognition that all human groups possessed fully developed *languages* rather than "primitive," "broken," or otherwise defective forms of vocal communication. Today, however, linguistic anthropologists realize that totalizing views of "languages" can be as problematic as totalizing views of "cultures." The difficulties associated with demarcating the boundaries between one language and another or with distinguishing between dialects and languages become particularly obvious in studies of pidgins and creoles, as we will see.

If we take a broad view of *human communication* as the transfer of information from one person to another, it immediately becomes clear that humans can communicate without the use of spoken words. People communicate with one another nonverbally all the time, sending messages with the clothes they wear, the way they walk, or how long they keep other people waiting for them. Even when people do make use of verbal communication, it is important to distinguish *language* from

Figure 9.1   In 1918, Krazy Kat asks the question, "Why is 'lenguage'?"

speech. Many people often equate language with *spoken* language (speech), but English can be communicated in writing, Morse code, or American Sign Language, to name just three nonspoken media.

Nevertheless, all human linguistic communication, regardless of the medium, depends on more than words alone. Native speakers of a language share not just vocabulary and grammar but also a number of assumptions about how to speak that may not be shared by speakers of a different language. Students learning a new language discover early on that word-for-word translation from one language to another does not work. Sometimes there are no equivalent words in the second language; but even when there appear to be such words, a word-for-word translation may not mean in language B what it meant in language A. For example, when English speakers have eaten enough, they say "I'm full." This may be translated directly into French as "Je suis plein." To a native speaker of French, this sentence (especially when uttered at the end of a meal) has the nonsensical meaning "I am a pregnant [male] animal." Alternatively, if uttered by a man who has just consumed a lot of wine, it means "I'm drunk."

Learning a second language is often frustrating and even unsettling; someone who once found the world simple to talk about suddenly turns into a babbling fool. Studying a second language, then, is less a matter of learning new labels for old objects than it is of learning how to identify new objects that go with new labels. The student must also learn the appropriate contexts in which different linguistic forms may be used: a person can be "full" after eating in English but not in French. Knowledge about context is cultural knowledge.

How Do People Talk about Experience?

Each natural human language is adequate for its speakers' needs, given their particular way of life. Speakers of a particular language tend to develop larger vocabularies to discuss those aspects of life that are of importance to them. The Aymara, who live in the Andes of South America, have invented hundreds of different words for the many varieties of potato they grow (see Figure 9.2 and EthnoProfile 9.1: Aymara). By contrast, speakers of English have created an elaborate vocabulary for discussing computers. However, despite differences in vocabulary and grammar, all natural human languages ever studied by linguists prove to be equally complex. Just as there is no such thing as a "primitive" human culture, there is no such thing as a "primitive" human language.

Traditionally, languages are associated with concrete groups of people called *speech communities.* Nevertheless, because all languages possess alternative ways of speaking, members of particular speech communities do not all possess identical knowledge about the language (or languages) they share, nor do they all speak the same way. Individuals and subgroups within a speech community make use of linguistic resources in different ways. Consequently, there is a tension in language between diversity and commonality. Individuals and subgroups attempt to use the varied resources of a language to create unique, personal voices or ways of speaking. These efforts are countered by pressures to negotiate shared codes for communication within larger social groups. In this way, language patterns are produced, imitated, or modified through the activity of speakers. A particular language that we isolate at any given moment is but a snapshot of a continuing process.

Figure 9.2 Locations of societies whose EthnoProfiles appear in Chapter 9.

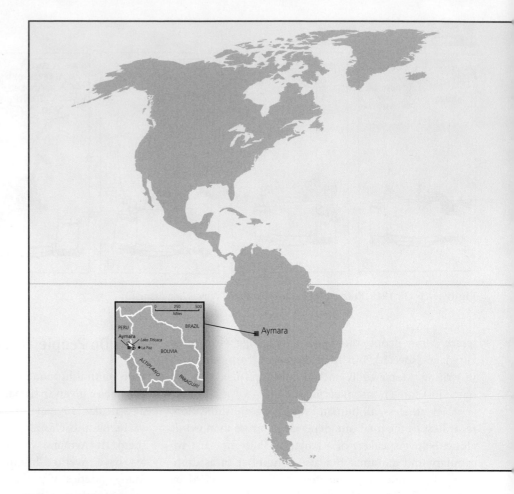

EthnoProfile 9.1

Aymara

Region: South America

Nation: Bolivia, Peru, Chile

Population: 2,000,000

Environment: High mountain lake basin

Livelihood: Peasant farmers

Political organization: Preconquest state societies conquered first by Inkas and later by Spanish; today, part of a modern nation-state

For more information: Miracle, Andrew. 1991. Aymara joking behavior. *Play and Culture* 4:144–52.

There are many ways to communicate our experiences, and there is no absolute standard favoring one way over another. Some things that are easy to say in language A may be difficult to say in language B, yet other aspects of language B may appear much simpler than equivalent aspects of language A. For example, English ordinarily requires the use of determiners (*a, an, the*) before nouns, but this rule is not found in all languages. Likewise, the verb *to be*, called the "copula" by linguists, is not found in all languages, although the relationships we convey when we use *to be* in English may still be communicated. In English, we might say "There *are* many people in the market." Translating this sentence into Fulfulde, the language of the Fulbe of northern Cameroon, we get "Him'be boi 'don nder luumo," which, word-for-word, reads "people-many-there-in-market" (Figure 9.3). No single Fulfulde word corresponds to the English *are* or *the*.

Differences across languages are not absolute. In Chinese, for example, verbs never change to indicate tense; instead, separate expressions referring to time are used. English speakers may conclude that Chinese speakers cannot distinguish between past, present, and future. This structure seems completely different from English structure. But consider such English sentences as

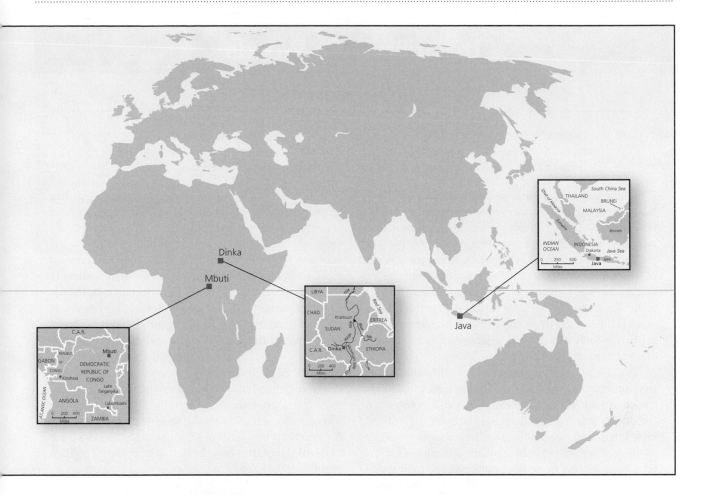

Figure 9.3 Him'be boi 'don nder luumo.

"Have a hard day at the office today?" and "Your interview go well?" These abbreviated questions, used in informal English, are very similar to the formal patterns of Chinese and other languages of southeastern Asia (Akmajian et.al. 1979, 194–95).

This kind of overlap between two very different languages demonstrates at least four things. First, it shows the kind of cross-linguistic commonality that forms the foundation both for learning new languages and for translation. Second, it highlights the variety of expressive

In Their Own Words

Cultural Translation

Linguistic translation is complicated and beset with pitfalls, as we have seen. Cultural translation, as David Parkin describes, requires knowledge not just of different grammars but also of the various different cultural contexts in which grammatical forms are put to use.

Cultural translation, like translation from one language to another, never produces a rendering that is semantically and stylistically an exact replica of the original. That much we accept. What is not often recognized, perhaps not even by the translators themselves, is that the very act of having to decide how to phrase an event, sentiment, or human character engages the translator in an act of creation. The translator does not simply represent a picture made by an author. He or she creates a new version, and perhaps in some respects a new picture—a matter that is often of some great value.

So it is with anthropologists. But while this act of creation in reporting on "the other" may reasonably be regarded as a self-sustaining pleasure, it is also an entry into the pitfalls and traps of language use itself. One of the most interesting new fields in anthropology is the study of the relationship between language and human knowledge, both among ourselves as professional anthropologists and laypeople, and among peoples of other cultures. The study is at once both reflexive and critical.

The hidden influences at work in language use attract the most interest. For example, systems of greetings have many built-in elaborations that differentiate subtly between those who are old and young, male and female, rich and poor, and powerful and powerless. When physicians discuss a patient in his or her presence and refer to the patient in the third-person singular, they are in effect defining the patient as a passive object unable to enter into the discussion. When anthropologists present elegant accounts of "their" people that fit the demands of a convincing theory admirably, do they not also leave out [of] the description any consideration of the informants' own fears and feelings? Or do we go too far in making such claims, and is it often the anthropologist who is indulged by the people, who give him or her the data they think is sought, either in exchange for something they want or simply because it pleases them to do so? If the latter, how did the anthropologist's account miss this critical part of the dialogue?

Source: Parkin 1990, 290–91.

resources to be found in any single language. We learn that English allows us to use either tense markers on verbs (*-s, -ed*) or unmarked verbs with adverbs of time (*have + today*). Third, we learn that the former grammatical pattern is associated with formal usage, whereas the latter is associated with informal usage. Fourth, it shows that the same structures can have different functions in different languages. As anthropological linguist Elinor Ochs observes, most cross-cultural differences in language use "turn out to be differences in *context* and/or *frequency of occurrence*" (1986, 10).

What Makes Human Language Distinctive?

In 1966, anthropological linguist Charles Hockett listed 16 different *design features* of human language that, in his estimation, set it apart from other forms of animal communication. Six of these design features seem especially

helpful in defining what makes human language distinctive: openness, displacement, arbitrariness, duality of patterning, semanticity, and prevarication.

Openness indicates that human language is productive. Speakers of any given language not only can create new messages but also can understand new messages created by other speakers. Someone may have never said to you "Put this Babel fish in your ear," but knowing English, you can understand the message. Openness might also be defined as "the ability to understand the same thing from different points of view" (Ortony 1979, 14). In language, this means being able to talk about the same experiences from different perspectives, to paraphrase using different words and various grammatical constructions. Indeed, it means that the experiences themselves can be differently conceived, labeled, and discussed. In this view, no single perspective would necessarily emerge as more correct in every respect than all others.

The importance of openness for human verbal communication is striking when we compare, for example, spoken human language to the vocal communication systems (or *call systems*) of monkeys and apes. Biological anthropologist Terrence Deacon (1977) points out that, in addition to spoken symbolic language, modern human beings possess a set of six calls: laughing, sobbing, screaming with fright, crying with pain, groaning, and sighing. Linguistic anthropologist Robbins Burling also emphasizes the difference between call systems and symbolic language: "Language . . . is organized in such utterly different ways from primate or mammalian calls and it conveys such utterly different kinds of meanings, that I find it impossible to imagine a realistic sequence by which natural selection could have converted a call system into a language . . . We will understand more about the origins of language by considering the ways in which language differs form the cries and gestures of human and nonhuman primates than by looking for ways in which they are alike" (2005, 16). In Deacon's view, human calls appear to have *coevolved alongside* symbolic language, together with gestures and the changes in speech rhythm, volume, and tonality that linguists call *speech prosody*. This would explain why calls and speech integrate with one another so smoothly when we communicate vocally with one another.

Nonhuman primates can communicate in rather subtle ways using channels of transmission other than voice. However, these channels are far less sophisticated than, say, American Sign Language. The number of calls in a call system ranges from 15 to 40, depending on the species; and the calls are produced only when the animal finds itself in a situation including such features as the presence of food or danger, friendly interest and the desire for company, or the desire to mark a location or to signal pain, sexual interest, or the need for maternal care. If the animal is not in the appropriate situation, it does not produce the call. At most, it may refrain from uttering a call in a situation that would normally trigger it. In addition, nonhuman primates cannot emit a signal that has some features of one call and some of another. For example, if the animal encounters food and danger at the same time, one of the calls takes precedence. For these reasons, the call systems of nonhuman primates are said to be *closed* when compared to open human languages.

Closed call systems also lack *displacement*, our human ability to talk about absent or nonexistent objects and past or future events as easily as we discuss our immediate situations. Although nonhuman primates clearly have good memories, and some species, such as chimpanzees, seem to be able to plan social action in advance (such as when hunting for meat), they cannot use their call systems to discuss such events.

Closed call systems also lack *arbitrariness*, the fact that there is no universal, necessary link between particular linguistic sounds and particular linguistic meanings. For example, the sound sequence /boi/ refers to a "young male human being" in English but means "more" or "many" in Fulfulde, a major language in Northern Cameroon. One aspect of linguistic creativity is the free, creative production of new links between sounds and meanings. Thus, arbitrariness and openness imply each other: if all links between sound and meaning are open, then any particular links between particular sounds and particular meanings in a particular language must be arbitrary. In nonhuman primate call systems, by contrast, links between the sounds of calls and their meanings appear fixed, and there is no easy slippage between sounds and what they stand for from one population to the next.

Arbitrariness is evident in the design feature of language *duality of patterning*. Human language, Hockett claimed, is patterned on two different levels: sound and meaning. On the first level, the arrangement of the small set of meaningless sounds (or *phonemes*) that characterize any particular language is not random but systematically patterned to create meaning-bearing units (or *morphemes*): in English, the final /ng/ sound in *song*, for example, is never found at the beginning of a sound sequence, although other languages in the world do allow that combination. The result is that from any language's set of phonemes (in English, there are some 36 phonemes) a very large number of correctly formed morphemes can be created. On the second level of patterning, however, the rules of **grammar** allow for the arrangement and rearrangement of these single morphemes into larger units—utterances or sentences—that can express an infinite number of meanings ("*The boy bit the dog*" uses the same morphemes as "*The dog bit the boy*," but the meaning is completely different). Since Hockett first wrote, many linguists have suggested that there are more than just two levels of patterning in language— that there are levels of morphemes, of sentence structure (*syntax*), meaning (*semantics*), and use (*pragmatics*). In each case, patterns that characterize one level cannot be reduced to the patterns of any other level but can serve as resources for the construction of more comprehensive levels. For example, units at the level of sound, patterned in one way, can be used to create units of meaning (or morphemes) at a different level, patterned in a different way. Morphemes, in turn, can be used to create units at a different level (sentences) by means of syntactic rules that are different from the rules that create morphemes,

---

grammar A set of rules that aim to describe fully the patterns of linguistic usage observed by speakers of a particular language.

and syntactic rules are again different from the rules that combine sentences into discourse. Ape call systems, by contrast, appear to lack multilevel patterning of this kind (Wallmann 1992).

Arbitrariness shows up again in the design feature of *semanticity*—the association of linguistic signals with aspects of the social, cultural, and physical world of a speech community. People use language to refer to and make sense of objects and processes in their world (remember Aymara and potatoes, as well as computer users in the United States). Nevertheless, any linguistic description of reality is always somewhat arbitrary because all linguistic descriptions are selective, highlighting some features of the world and downplaying others. (Semanticity is not the same thing as *semantics*, which refers to the formal study of linguistic meaning.)

Perhaps the most striking consequence of linguistic openness is the design feature *prevarication*. Hockett's remarks about this design feature deserve particular attention: "Linguistic messages can be false, and they can be meaningless in the logician's sense" (1966). In other words, not only can people use language to lie but, in addition, utterances that seem perfectly well formed grammatically may yield nonsense. An example is this sentence invented by linguist Noam Chomsky: "Colorless green ideas sleep furiously" (1957, 15). This is a grammatical sentence on one level—the right kinds of words are used in the right places—but on another level it contains multiple contradictions. The ability of language users to prevaricate—to make statements or ask questions that violate convention—is a major consequence of open symbolic systems. Apes using their closed call systems can neither lie nor formulate theories.

What Does It Mean to "Learn" a Language?

Years ago studies of child language amounted to a list of errors that children make when attempting to gain what Chomsky calls **linguistic competence**, or mastery of adult grammar. For some time, however, linguists who study children's verbal interactions in social and cultural contexts have drawn attention to what children can do very well. "From an early age they appear to

---

linguistic competence A term coined by linguist Noam Chomsky to refer to the mastery of adult grammar.

communicative competence A term coined by anthropological linguist Dell Hymes to refer to the mastery of adult rules for socially and culturally appropriate speech.

---

communicate very fluently, producing utterances which are not just remarkably well-formed according to the linguist's standards but also appropriate to the social context in which the speakers find themselves. Children are thus learning far more about language than rules of grammar. [They are] acquiring communicative competence" (Elliot 1981, 13).

Communicative competence, or mastery of adult rules for socially and culturally appropriate speech, is a term introduced by American anthropological linguist Dell Hymes (1972). As an anthropologist, Hymes objected to Chomsky's notion that linguistic competence consisted only of being able to make correct judgments of sentence grammaticality (Chomsky 1965, 4). Hymes observed that competent adult speakers do more than follow grammatical rules when they speak. They are also able to choose words and topics of conversation appropriate to their social position, the social position of the person they are addressing, and the social context of interaction.

How Does Context Affect Language?

Anthropologists are very much aware of the influence of context on what people choose to say. For example, consider the issue of using personal pronouns appropriately when talking to others. In English, the problem almost never arises because native speakers address all people as "you." But any English speaker who has ever tried to learn French has worried about when to address an individual using the second-person plural (*vous*) and when to use the second-person singular (*tu*). To be safe, most students use *vous* for all individuals because it is the more formal term and they want to avoid appearing too familiar with native speakers whom they do not know well. But if you are dating a French person, at which point in the relationship does the change from *vous* to *tu* occur, and who decides? Moreover, sometimes—for example, among university students—the normal term of address is *tu* (even among strangers); it is used to indicate social solidarity. Native speakers of English who are learning French wrestle with these and other linguistic dilemmas. Rules for the appropriate use of *tu* and *vous* seem to have nothing to do with grammar, yet the choice between one form and the other indicates whether the speaker is someone who does or does not know how to speak French.

But French seems quite straightforward when compared with Javanese, in which all the words in a sentence must be carefully selected to reflect the social relationship between the speaker and the person addressed (see EthnoProfile 9.2: Java). In the 1950s, when Clifford Geertz first did fieldwork in Java, he discovered that it was impossible to say anything in Javanese without also communicating your social position relative to the person to whom you are speaking. Even a simple request—like "Are you going to eat rice and cassava now?"—required that speakers know at least five different varieties of the language in order to communicate socially as well as to make the request (Figure 9.4). This example illustrates the range of diversity present in a single language and how different varieties of a language are related to different subgroups within the speech community.

How Does Language Affect How We See the World?

During the first half of the twentieth century, two American anthropological linguists, Edward Sapir and Benjamin Whorf, observed that the grammars of different languages often described the same situation in different ways. They concluded that language has the power to shape the way people see the world. This claim has been called the **linguistic relativity principle**, or the "Sapir-Whorf hypothesis." This principle has been highly controversial because it is a radical proposition that is difficult to test and, when it has been tested, the results have been ambiguous.

The so-called strong version of the linguistic relativity principle is also known as *linguistic determinism*. It is a totalizing view of language that reduces patterns of thought and culture to the grammatical patterns of the language spoken. If a grammar classifies nouns in male and female gender categories, for example, linguistic determinists claim that speakers of that language are forced to think of males and females as radically different kinds of beings. By contrast, a language that makes no grammatical distinctions on the basis of gender supposedly trains its speakers to think of males and females as exactly the same. If linguistic determinism is correct, then a change in grammar should change thought patterns: if English speakers replaced *he* and *she* with a new, gender-neutral third-person singular pronoun, such as *te*, then, linguistic determinists predict, English speakers would begin to treat men and women as equals.

There are a number of problems with linguistic determinism. In the first place, there are languages such as Fulfulde in which only one third-person pronoun is used for males and females (*o*); however, male-dominant social patterns are quite evident among Fulfulde speakers. In the second place, if language determined thought in this way, it would be impossible to translate from one language to another or even to learn another language with a different grammatical structure. Because human beings do learn foreign languages and translate from one language to another, the strong version of the linguistic

EthnoProfile 9.2

Java

Region: Southeastern Asia

Nation: Indonesia

Population: 120,000,000

Environment: Tropical island

Livelihood: Intensive rice cultivation

Political organization: Highly stratified state

For more information: Geertz, Clifford. 1960. *The religion of Java.* New York: Free Press.

relativity principle cannot be correct. Third, even if it were possible to draw firm boundaries around speech communities (which it is not), every language provides its native speakers with alternative ways of describing the world. Finally, in most of the world's societies, people learn to speak more than one language fluently. Yet people who grow up bilingual do not also grow up unable to reconcile two contradictory views of reality. Indeed, bilingual children ordinarily benefit from knowing two languages, do not confuse them, can switch readily from one to another, and even appear to demonstrate greater cognitive flexibility on psychological tests than do monolinguals (Elliot 1981, 56) (Figure 9.5).

In the face of these objections, other researchers offer a "weak" version of the linguistic relativity principle that rejects linguistic determinism but continues to claim that language shapes thought and culture. Thus, grammatical gender might not determine a male-dominant social order, but it might facilitate the acceptance of such a social order because the grammatical distinction between *he* and *she* might make separate and unequal gender roles seem "natural." Because many native speakers of English also are strong promoters of gender equality, however, the shaping power of grammar would seem far too weak to merit any scientific attention.

Neither Sapir nor Whorf favored linguistic determinism. Sapir argued that language's importance lies in

---

linguistic relativity principle A position, associated with Edward Sapir and Benjamin Whorf, that asserts that language has the power to shape the way people see the world.

Speaking to persons of:	Level	"Are	you	going	to eat	rice	and	cassava	now?"	Complete sentence
Very high position	3a		pandjenengan		ḍahar					Menapa pandjenengan baḍé ḍahar sekul kalijan kaspé samenika?
		menapa		baḍé			kalijan		samenika	
High position	3					sekul				Menapa sampéjan baḍé neḍa sekul kalijan kaspé samenika?
Same position, not close	2	napa	sampéjan	adjéng	neḍa			kaspé	saniki	Napa sampéjan adjéng neḍa sekul lan kaspé saniki?
Same position, casual acquaintance	1a						lan			Apa sampéjan arep neḍa sega lan kaspé saiki?
		apa		arep	sega				saiki	
Close friends of any rank; also to lower status (basic language)	1		kowé		mangan					Apa kowé arep mangan sega lan kaspé saiki?

Figure 9.4 The dialect of nonnoble, urbanized, somewhat educated people in central Java in the 1950s. (Geertz 1960)

the way it directs attention to some aspects of experience rather than to others. He was impressed by the fact that "it is generally difficult to make a complete divorce between objective reality and our linguistic symbols of reference to it" (Sapir [1933] 1966, 9, 15). Whorf's views have been more sharply criticized by later scholars. His discussions of the linguistic relativity principle are complex and ambiguous. At least part of the problem arises from Whorf's attempt to view grammar as the linguistic pattern that shapes culture and thought. Whorf's contemporaries understood grammar to refer to rules for combining sounds into words and words into sentences. Whorf believed that grammar needed to be thought of in broader terms (Schultz 1990), but he died before working out the theoretical language to describe such a level.

In recent years, interest in the "Whorfian question" has revived, and scholars have recognized that there are several different ways to ask about the relationship of language to thought. Especially exciting is the new perspective that comes from focusing on the influence of language in pragmatic contexts of use. Dan Slobin's "thinking for speaking" hypothesis, for example, suggests that the influence of linguistic forms on thought may be greatest when people prepare to speak to others

on a specific topic in a specific setting. "One fits one's thoughts into available linguistic forms . . . 'Thinking for speaking' involves picking those characteristics that (a) fit some conceptualization of the event, and (b) are readily encodable in the language" (Slobin 1987, 435). Slobin points out that related challenges are faced by speakers involved in "thinking for writing" or "thinking for translating." Thinking for translating is especially intriguing, particularly when translators must render features that are grammatically encoded in one language into a second language in which they are not encoded, or vice versa (Slobin 2003).

For example, an English speaker who is trying to say "I like fast food" in Spanish will have to use a passive encoding—*me gusta la comida rápida* ("fast food pleases me."). This encoding is not easy for many English speakers to learn, precisely because it is not the standard English way to encode the thought.

Dedre Gentner and Susan Goldin-Meadow (2003) point out that some researchers still take a traditional Whorfian approach, viewing language as a lens through which people view the world. Others think of language as a tool kit, a set of resources that speakers make use of to build more elaborate conceptual structures. Still others

Figure 9.5 Canada is officially a bilingual country, and signs are in both French and English.

think of language as a category maker, influencing the way people classify experiences and objects in the world. They note that the research that produces the most consistent evidence of the influence of language on thought comes from those who view language as a tool kit—that is, as a set of resources that speakers make use of for conceptual or communicative purposes (2003, 10). Nevertheless, they emphasize that defining the research question in such variable ways means that "we are unlikely to get a yes-or-no answer to the whole of Whorf's thesis. But if we have delineated a set of more specific questions for which the answer is no to some and yes to others, we will have achieved our goal" (2003, 12).

Pragmatics: How Do We Study Language in Contexts of Use?

Pragmatics can be defined as the study of language in the context of its use. Each context offers limitations and opportunities concerning what we may say and how we may say it. Everyday language use is thus often characterized by a struggle between speakers and listeners over definitions of context and appropriate word use. Linguistic anthropologist Michael Silverstein (1976, 1985) was one of the first to argue that the referential meaning of certain expressions in language cannot be determined unless we go beyond the boundaries of a sentence and place the expressions in a wider context of use. Two kinds of context must be considered. *Linguistic context* refers to the other words, expressions, and sentences that surround the expression whose meaning we are trying to determine. The meaning of *it* in the sentence "I really enjoyed it" cannot be determined if the sentence is considered on its own. However, if we know that the previous sentence was "My aunt gave me this book," we have a linguistic context that allows us to deduce that *it* refers

to *this book. Nonlinguistic context* consists of objects and activities that are present in the situation of speech at the same time we are speaking. Consider the sentence "Who is that standing by the door?" We need to inspect the actual physical context at the moment this sentence is uttered to find the door and the person standing by the door and thus give a referential meaning to the words *who* and *that*. Furthermore, even if we know what a door is in a formal sense, we need the nonlinguistic context to clarify what counts as a door in this instance (e.g., it could be a rough opening in the wall) (Figure 9.6).

By going beyond formal grammatical analysis, pragmatics directs our attention to **discourse**, understood as a stretch of speech longer than a sentence united by a common theme. Discourse may be a series of sentences uttered by a single individual or a series of rejoinders in a conversation among two or more speakers. Many linguistic anthropologists accept the arguments of M. M. Bakhtin (1981) and V. N. Voloshinov (see, e.g., Voloshinov [1926] 1987) that the series of verbal exchanges in conversation is the primary form of discourse. In this view, the speech of any single individual, whether a simple *yes* or a book-length dissertation, is only one rejoinder in an ongoing dialogue.

Ethnopragmatics

Linguistic anthropologists pay attention not only to the immediate context of speech, linguistic and nonlinguistic, but also to broader contexts that are shaped by unequal social relationships and rooted in history (Brenneis and Macauley 1996, Hill and Irvine 1992). Alessandro Duranti calls this **ethnopragmatics**, "a study of language use which relies on ethnography to illuminate the ways in which speech is both constituted by and constitutive of social interaction" (1994, 11). Such a study focuses on *practice*, human activity in which the rules of grammar, cultural values, and physical action are all conjoined (Hanks 1996, 11). Such a perspective locates the source of meaning in everyday routine social activity, or *habitus*, rather than in grammar. As a result, phonemes, morphemes, syntax, and semantics are viewed as *linguistic resources* people can make use of, rather than rigid forms that determine what people can and cannot think or say (see Module 4).

pragmatics The study of language in the context of its use.

discourse A stretch of speech longer than a sentence united by a common theme.

ethnopragmatics The study of language use that relies on ethnography to illuminate the ways in which speech is both constituted by and constitutive of social interaction.

Figure 9.6   To answer the question "What is that on the door?" requires that we examine the actual physical context at the moment we are asked the question in order to try to determine what "that" refers to. Is it the locks? the door handles? the studs on the door? Also, what part of the structure is the "door"?

If mutual understanding is shaped by shared routine activity and not by grammar, then communication is possible even if the people interacting with one another speak mutually unintelligible languages. All they need is a shared sense of "what is going on here" and the ability to negotiate successfully who will do what (Hanks 1996, 234). Such mutually coengaged people shape *communicative practices* that involve spoken language but also include values and shared habitual knowledge that may never be put into words. Because most people in most societies regularly engage in a wide range of practical activities with different subgroups, each one will also end up knowledgeable about a variety of different communicative practices and the linguistic habits that go with them. For example, a college student might know the linguistic habits appropriate to dinner with her parents, to the classroom, to worship services, to conversations in the dorm with friends, and to her part-time job in a restaurant. Each set of linguistic habits she knows is called a *discourse genre*. Because our student simultaneously knows a multiplicity of different discourse genres she can choose among when she speaks, her linguistic knowledge is characterized by what Bakhtin called *heteroglossia* (Bakhtin 1981).

For Bakhtin, heteroglossia is the normal condition of linguistic knowledge in any society with internal divisions. Heteroglossia describes a coexisting multiplicity of linguistic norms and forms, many of which are anchored in more than one social subgroup. Because we all participate in more than one of these subgroups, we inevitably become fluent in many varieties of language, even if we speak only English! Our capacity for heteroglossia is an example of linguistic openness: it means that our thought and speech are not imprisoned in a single set of grammatical forms, as linguistic determinists argued. Indeed, if our college student reflects on the overlap as well as the contrasts between the language habits used in the dorm with those used in the restaurant, she might well find herself raising questions about what words really mean. To the extent, however, that her habitual ways of speaking are deeply rooted in everyday routine activity, they may guide the way she typically thinks, perceives, and acts. And to that extent, the linguistic relativity hypothesis may be correct—not on the level of grammatical categories but on the level of discourse (Hanks 1996, 176, 246; Schultz 1990).

What Happens When Languages Come into Contact?

In local communities where they know each other well, speakers and listeners are able, for the most part, to draw upon knowledge of overlapping language habits in order to converse or argue about moral and political issues. Sometimes, however, potential parties to a verbal exchange find themselves sharing little more than physical proximity to one another. Such situations arise when members of communities with radically different language traditions and no history of previous contact with one another come face to face and are forced to communicate. There is no way to predict the outcome of such enforced contact on either speech community, yet from these new shared experiences, new forms of practice, including a new form of language—pidgin—may develop.

"When the chips are down, meaning is negotiated" (Lakoff and Johnson 1980, 231). The study of pidgin languages is the study of the radical negotiation of new meaning, the production of a new whole (the pidgin language) that is different from and reducible to none of the languages that gave birth to it. The shape of a pidgin reflects the context in which it arises—generally one of colonial conquest or commercial domination. Vocabulary is usually taken from the language of the dominant group, making it easy for that group to learn. The system of pronunciation and sentence structure may be similar to the subordinate language (or languages), however, making it easier for subordinated speakers to learn. Complex grammatical features marking the gender or number of nouns or the tenses of verbs tend to disappear (Holm 1988).

What Is the Difference Between a Pidgin and a Creole?

Pidgins are traditionally defined as reduced languages that have no native speakers. They develop, in a single generation, between groups of speakers that possess distinct native languages. When speakers of a pidgin language pass that language on to a new generation, linguists have traditionally referred to the language as a *creole*. As linguists studied pidgins and creoles more closely, they discovered that the old distinction between pidgins and creoles did not seem to hold up. In the Pacific, for example, linguists have discovered pidgin dialects, pidgin languages used as main languages of permanently settled groups, and pidgins that have become native languages. Moreover, creolization can take place at any time after a pidgin forms, creoles can exist without having been preceded by pidgins, pidgins can remain pidgins for long periods and undergo linguistic change without acquiring native speakers, and pidgin and creole varieties of the same language can coexist in the same society (Jourdan 1991, 192ff.). In fact, it looks as if heteroglossia is as widespread among speakers of pidgins and creoles as among speakers of other languages.

How Is Meaning Negotiated?

More information has been gathered about the historical and sociocultural contexts within which pidgins first formed. Here, as elsewhere in linguistic anthropology, the focus has turned to communicative practice. From this perspective, creolization is likely when pidgin speakers find themselves in new social contexts requiring a new language for *all* the practical activities of everyday life; without such a context, it is unlikely that creoles will

Figure 9.7 Tok Pisin, a pidgin language that developed in New Guinea following colonization by English speakers, has become a major medium of communication in New Guinea. The news in Tok Pisin is available on the Internet at http://www.abc.net.au/ra/tokpisin/.

emerge. Accordingly, a pidgin is now defined as a secondary language in a speech community that uses some other main language, and a creole is understood as a main language in a speech community, whether or not it has native speakers (Jourdan 1991, 196).

Viewing pidgin creation as a form of communicative practice means that attention must be paid to the role of pidgin creators as agents in the process (Figure 9.7). As we negotiate meaning across language barriers, it appears that all humans have intuitions about which parts of our speech carry the most meaning and which parts can be safely dropped. Neither party to the negotiation, moreover, may be trying to learn the other's language; rather, "speakers in the course of negotiating communication use whatever linguistic and sociolinguistic resources they have at their disposal, until the shared meaning is established and conventionalized" (Jourdan 1991, 200).

What Is Linguistic Inequality?

Pidgins and creoles turn out to be far more complex and the result of far more active human input than we used to think, which is why they are so attractive to linguists and linguistic anthropologists as objects of study.

---

pidgin A language with no native speakers that develops in a single generation between members of communities that possess distinct native languages.

Where they coexist, however, alongside the language of the dominant group (e.g., Hawaiian Pidgin English and English), they are ordinarily viewed as defective and inferior languages. Such views can be seen as an outgrowth of the situation that led to the formation of most of the pidgins we know about: European colonial domination. In a colonial or postcolonial setting, the language of the colonizer is often viewed as better than pidgin or creole languages, which are frequently thought to be broken, imperfect versions of the colonizer's language. The situation only worsens when formal education, the key to participation in the European-dominated society, is carried out in the colonial language. Speakers of pidgin who remain illiterate may never be able to master the colonial tongue and may find themselves effectively barred from equal participation in the civic life of their societies.

To take one language variety as the standard against which all other varieties are measured might be described as "linguistic ethnocentrism," and such a standard may be applied to any language, not just pidgins and creoles. This is one kind of linguistic inequality: making value judgments about other people's speech in a context of dominance and subordination. A powerful example of the effects of linguistic inequality is found in the history and controversies surrounding African American English in the United States.

What Are Language Habits of African Americans?

In the 1960s, some psychologists claimed that African American children living in urban areas of the northern United States suffered from linguistic deprivation. They argued that these children started school with a limited vocabulary and no grammar and thus could not perform as well as European American children in the classroom—that their language was unequal to the challenges of communication. Sociolinguist William Labov (1972) and his colleagues found such claims incredible and undertook research of their own, which demonstrated two things. First, they proved that the form of English spoken in the inner city was not defective pseudolanguage. Second, they showed how a change in research setting permitted inner-city African American children to display a level of linguistic sophistication that the psychologists had never dreamed they possessed.

When African American children were in the classroom (a European American–dominated context) being interrogated by European American adults about topics of no interest to them, they said little. This did not necessarily mean, Labov argued, that they had no language. Rather, their minimal responses were better

understood as defensive attempts to keep threatening European American questioners from learning anything about them. For the African American children, the classroom was only one part of a broader racist culture. The psychologists, due to their ethnocentrism, had been oblivious to the effect this context might have on their research.

Reasoning that reliable samples of African American speech had to be collected in settings where the racist pressure was lessened, Labov and his colleagues conducted fieldwork in the homes and on the streets of the inner city. They recorded enormous amounts of speech in African American English (AAE) produced by the same children who had had nothing to say when questioned in the classroom. Labov argued that AAE was a variety of English that had certain rules not found in Standard English. This is a strictly linguistic difference: most middle-class speakers of Standard English would not use these rules, but most African American speakers of AAE would. However, neither variety of English should be seen as "defective" as a result of this difference. This kind of linguistic difference, apparent when speakers of two varieties converse, marks the speaker's membership in a particular speech community. Such differences distinguish the language habits of most social subgroups in a society, like that of the United States, that is characterized by heteroglossia.

From the perspective of communicative practice, however, African American English is distinctive because of the historical and sociocultural circumstances that led to its creation. For some time, linguists have viewed AAE as one of many creole languages that developed in the New World after Africans were brought there to work as slaves on plantations owned by Europeans. Dominant English-speaking elites have regarded AAE with the same disdain that European colonial elites have accorded creole languages elsewhere. Because African Americans have always lived in socially and politically charged contexts that questioned their full citizenship, statements about their language habits are inevitably thought to imply something about their intelligence and culture. Those psychologists who claimed that inner-city African American children suffered from linguistic deprivation, for example, seemed to be suggesting either that these children were too stupid to speak or that their cultural surroundings were too meager to allow normal language development. The work of Labov and his colleagues showed that the children were not linguistically deprived, were not stupid, and participated in a rich linguistic culture. But this work itself became controversial in later decades when it became clear that the rich African American language and culture described was primarily that of adolescent males. These young men saw themselves

In Their Own Words

Varieties of African American English

The school board of Oakland, California, gained national attention in December 1996 when its members voted to recognize Ebonics as an official second language. What they called Ebonics is also known as Black English Vernacular (BEV), Black English (BE), African American English Vernacular (AAEV), and African American English (AAE). The school board decision generated controversy both within and outside the African American community because it seemed to be equating Ebonics with other "official second languages," such as Spanish and Chinese. This implied that Standard English was as much a "foreign language" to native speakers of Ebonics as it was to native speakers of Spanish and Chinese and that Oakland school students who were native speakers of Ebonics should be entitled not only to the respect accorded native Spanish- or Chinese-speaking students but also, perhaps, to the same kind of funding for bilingual education. The uproar produced by this dispute caused the school board to amend the resolution a month later. African American linguistic anthropologist Marcyliena Morgan's commentary highlights one issue that many disputants ignored: namely, that the African American community is not monoglot in Ebonics but is in fact characterized by heteroglossia.

After sitting through a string of tasteless jokes about the Oakland school district's approval of a language education policy for African American students, I realize that linguists and educators have failed to inform Americans about varieties of English used throughout the country and the link between these dialects and culture, social class, geographic region and identity. After all, linguists have been a part of language and education debates around AAE and the furor that surrounds them since the late 1970s. Then the Ann Arbor school district received a court order to train teachers on aspects of AAE to properly assess and teach children in their care.

Like any language and dialect, African American varieties of English—ranging from that spoken by children and some adults with limited education to those spoken by adults with advanced degrees—are based on the cultural, social, historical and political experiences shared by many US people of African descent. This experience is one of family, community and love as well as racism, poverty and discrimination. Every African American does not speak AAE. Moreover, some argue that children who speak the vernacular, typically grow up to speak both AAE as well as mainstream varieties of English. It is therefore not

surprising that the community separates its views of AAE, ranging from loyalty to abhorrence, from issues surrounding the literacy education of their children. Unfortunately, society's ambivalent attitudes toward African American students' cognitive abilities, like Jensen's 1970s deficit models and the 1990s' *The Bell Curve*, suggest that when it comes to African American kids, intelligence and competence in school can be considered genetic.

African American children who speak the vernacular form of AAE may be the only English-speaking children in this country who attend community schools in which teachers not only are ignorant of their dialect but refuse to accept its existence. This attitude leads to children being marginalized and designated as learning disabled. The educational failure of African American children can, at best, be only partially addressed through teacher training on AAE. When children go to school, they bring not only their homework and textbooks but also their language, culture and identity. Sooner rather than later, the educational system must address its exclusion of cultural and dialect difference in teacher training and school curriculum.

Source: M. Morgan 1997, 8.

as bearers of authentic African American language habits and dismissed African Americans who did not speak the way they did as "lames." This implied that everyone else in the African American community was somehow not genuinely African American, a challenge that those excluded could not ignore. Linguists like Labov's team, who thought their work undermined racism, were thus bewildered when middle-class African Americans, who

spoke Standard English, refused to accept AAE as representative of "true" African American culture (M. Morgan 1995, 337).

From the perspective of linguistic anthropology, this debate shows that the African American community is not homogeneous, linguistically or culturally, but is instead characterized by heteroglossia (Figure 9.8). At a minimum, language habits are shaped by social class,

Figure 9.8 The language habits of African Americans are not homogeneous but vary according to gender, social class, region, and situation.

age cohort, and gender. Moreover, members of all of these subgroups use both Standard English and AAE in their speech. Morgan reports, for example, that upper middle-class African American students at elite colleges who did not grow up speaking AAE regularly adopt many of its features and that hip-hop artists combine the grammar of Standard English with the phonology and morphology of AAE (1995, 338). This situation is not so paradoxical if we recall, once again, the politically charged context of African American life in the United States. African Americans both affirm and deny the significance of AAE for their identity, perhaps because AAE symbolizes both the oppression of slavery and resistance to that oppression (M. Morgan 1995, 339). Forty years ago, Claudia Mitchell-Kernan described African Americans as "bicultural" and struggling to develop language habits that could reconcile "good" English and AAE (1972, 209). That struggle continues at the beginning of the twenty-first century.

What Is Language Ideology?

Building on earlier work on linguistic inequality, linguistic anthropologists in recent years have developed a focus on the study of **language ideology**—ways of representing the intersection "between social forms and forms of talk" (Woolard 1998, 3). While the study of language ideology discloses speakers' sense of beauty or morality or basic understandings of the world, it also provides evidence of the ways in which our speech is always embedded in a social world of power differences. Language

---

language ideology A marker of struggles between social groups with different interests, revealed in what people say and how they say it.

---

ideologies are markers of struggles between social groups with different interests, revealed in what people say and how they say it. The way people monitor their speech to bring it into line with a particular language ideology illustrates that language ideologies are "active and effective . . . they transform the material reality they comment on" (Woolard 1998, 11). In settings with a history of colonization, where groups with different power and different languages coexist in tension, the study of language ideologies has long been significant (Woolard 1998, 16). The skills of linguistic anthropologists especially suit them to study language ideologies because their linguistic training allows them to describe precisely the linguistic features (e.g., phonological, morphological, or syntactic) that become the focus of ideological attention and their training in cultural analysis allows them to explain how those linguistic features come to stand symbolically for a particular social group.

Linguistic anthropologist Marcyliena Morgan has studied the language ideology held by African Americans about AAE. Her research reveals that perhaps the key element of African American language ideology is the importance of *indirectness* (2002, 25). Indirectness of communication was vital for African Americans living under conditions of slavery and legal segregation. In conditions of extreme political inequality, African Americans had to contend with a set of unwritten rules that governed how they were supposed to communicate with whites, such as speaking only when permission was granted, without questioning or contradicting what whites said to them, and bowing their heads and saying "yes, sir" or "yes, ma'am." Following these rules publicly confirmed the subordinate status of African Americans in the racial hierarchy, while breaking the rules was severely punished.

African Americans spoke differently when not in the company of whites. But they also developed ways of speaking when whites were present that allowed them to demonstrate their agency in a way that was "very much above ground . . . cloaked and unseen by those in power" (2002, 23). That is, African Americans developed a *counterlanguage* based on indirectness that could only be fully enacted before an audience that included both people who had been socialized within the African American setting and outsiders who had not. The most highly valued instances of this counterlanguage were ambiguous speech performances that were usually puzzling or unintelligible to outsiders but easily understood by the African Americans who were present. Successful performances depend on participation by the audience as well as the speaker and on everyone's mastery of local heteroglossia: "the knowledge that language varieties exist and represent different positions of power, politics, and history" (2002, 38).

Language Revitalization

Many linguists and linguistic anthropologists who specialize in the study of the indigenous languages of North America are increasingly involved in collaborating with the speakers of those languages to preserve and revive them in the face of threatened decline or extinction with the spread of English. Leanne Hinton is a linguist at the University of California, Berkeley, who has worked for many years to help revitalize the languages of the indigenous peoples of California (Table 9.1, Figure 9.9). In 1998, she wrote:

> Of at least 98 languages originally spoken in what are now the political confines of the state, 45 (or more) have no fluent speakers left, 17 have only one to five speakers left, and the remaining 36 have only elderly speakers. Not a single California Indian language is being used

(continued on page 263)

Figure 9.9 A map of indigenous languages of California prior to Western European settlement. From California Indian Library Collections, Ethnic Studies Library, University of California, Berkeley.

TABLE 9.1 California Languages and Their Classification (adapted from Hinton 1994: 83–85)		
STOCK	**FAMILY/BRANCH**	**LANGUAGES IN CALIFORNIA**
Hokan		Chimariko*
		Esselen*
		Karuk
		Salinan*
		Washo
	Shastan	Shasta,* New River Shasta,* Okwanuchu,* Konomihu*
	Palaihnihan	Achumawi (Pit River), Atsugewi (Hat Creek) (<5)
	Yanan	Northern Yana,* Central Yana,* Southern Yana,* Yahi*
	Pamoan	Northern (<5), Northeastern,* Eastern (<5), Central, Southeastern (<5), Southern (<5), Kashaya Pomo
	Yuman	Quechan, Mojave, Cocopa, Kumeyaay, Ipai, Tipai
	Chamashan	Obispeño,* Barbareño,* Ventureño,* Purisimeño,* Ynezeño,* Island*
Penutian	Costanoan (Ohlone)	Karkin,* Chochenyo,* Tamyen,* Ramaytush,* Awaswas,* Chalon,* Rumsen,* Mutsun*
	Wintun	Wintu, Nomlaki,* Patwin (<5)
	Maiduan	Maidu (<5), Konkow (<5), Nisenan (<5)
	Miwokan*	Lake Miwok (<5), Coast Miwok (<5), Bay Miwok,* Saclan,* Plains Miwok (<5), Northern Sierra Miwok, East Central Sierra Miwok, West Central Sierra Miwok, Southern Sierra Miwok
	Yokutsan	Choynumni, Chukchansi, Dumna (<5), Tachi (<5), Wukchumi, Yowlumni, Gashowu (<5) (at least 6 other extinct Yokutsan major dialects or languages)*
	Klamath-Modoc	Klamath, Modoc (<5)
Algic		Yurok
		Wiyot*
Na-Dené	Athabascan	Tolowa (<5), Hupa, Mattole,* Wailaki-Nongatl-Lassik-Sinkyone-Cahtco* (a group of related dialects, all without known speakers)
Uto-Aztecan	Numic	Mono, Owens Valley Paiute, Northern Paiute, Southern Paiute, Shoshoni, Kawaiisu, Chemehuevi
	Takic	Serrano, Cahuilla, Cupeño (<5), Luiseño, Ajachemem* (Juaneño), Tongva* (Gabrielino), Tataviam,* San Nicolas,* Kitanemuk,* Vanyume*
		Tubatulabal
Yukian		Yuki,* Wappo

*Starred languages have no known fluent native speakers (although some of them have semispeakers). Languages with five or fewer speakers are marked "(<5)" (Hinton 1998, 217).

Source: Hinton, Leanne. 1998. Language loss and devitalization in California: overview. In Blum, Susan (ed), *Making Sense of Language.* New York: Oxford University Press, 216–222.

now as the language of daily communication. The elders do not in actuality speak their language—rather, they remember how to speak their language (1998, 216).

Language loss began with the arrival of European American settlers in the nineteenth century, especially in connection with the California Gold Rush. In later years, indigenous Californians were subjected to a range of disruptive and oppressive practices that undermined their cultures and reduced their numbers severely. By the 1870s, populations began to increase again, but the possibilities of preserving indigenous language and culture were bleak: most tribes had no land base, their children had been sent to boarding schools to forget indigenous traditions, and most California Indians were forced to find work in the wider, English-speaking society. "Thus, California Indians are now immersed in English. There is little or no space in the present-day way of life for the use of indigenous languages" (Hinton 1998, 218).

Recent decades have brought change, however. In the 1970s, government funds became available to support bilingual education programs for some indigenous groups. By the 1990s, laws such as the Native American Languages Act were providing additional funds for such projects. But private individuals were also attempting language revival outside these settings. In 1997 a new journal called *News from Native California* helped connect members of California tribes with one another, and a main focus of their interest became language revitalization. A few years later, the Native California Network was formed to fund projects related to traditional culture, and language became its focus as well. This network gave birth to the Advocates for Indigenous California Language Survival (AICLS), an organization that has brought many California language activists together over the years. AICLS sponsors a range of workshops and other programs that are concerned in one way or another with language revitalization.

One of the major successes of this organization has been the Master-Apprentice Language Learning Program with which Hinton has been involved. As the AICLS website explains,

> An elder and a younger tribal member who are committed to learning the language are trained in one-on-one immersion techniques. The trained team members are then paid stipends so that they can devote the 10 to 20 hours per week necessary to do the work.
>
> Key to the program is the concept that the team live their daily lives together in the language. The teams keep journals and AICLS monitors them by phone and site visits. (http://www.aicls.org/)

In addition to these formal programs, many informal efforts have been made to devise new writing systems for indigenous languages, to write books and educational materials in indigenous languages, and to offer language classes, immersion camps, or other gatherings in which students can practice their new language skills.

Those who participate in these language revitalization programs do not end up speaking their heritage languages exactly the way they used to be spoken by their ancestors. As Hinton notes, "Learners have an accent and exhibit many grammatical simplifications and influences from English, their dominant language" (Hinton 1998, 220). Although this is disappointing to some, others are determined to do the best they can under the circumstances. "A number of learners have expressed the notion that even if the future of their language takes on a pidginized form, the social value of using their language far exceeds the detriments of the change" (Hinton 1998, 220).

Morgan collected samples of African American discourse and drew upon African American language ideology to explain the significance of what is said and what is not said. For example, she examined a narrative provided by Rose and Nora, two elderly African American women, whom she interviewed about the 1919 race riot in Chicago. Morgan reproduced the transcript of their conversation and then pointed to significant passages that reveal the disciplined indirectness of these women's speech. For example, when Morgan asked them *how* the riot started, Nora replied by saying *where* it started, "on the beach." While to an outsider this answer may seem unrelated to the question, in fact it is an indirect response that signals the correct answer to listeners in the know: "The location is in fact the reason for the riot. The 31st Street beach included an imaginary line in the water separating black and white swimmers. A young white man accused a young black man of swimming across the border" (2002, 109). Rose and Nora referred only to "the whites" as being the attackers, although historical sources suggest that the main group involved were Irish. At the same time, the women explicitly stated that "the Italians" living on certain named streets helped to calm things down. Again, to those in the know, the named streets indirectly signal that Italians were living on some of the same streets as African Americans, which also indirectly suggests why they might have been motivated to calm things down. Finally, when Morgan asked the two women why the riot happened, Rose answered that she still had not figured it out, that the type of mattress they were sleeping on must have caused it (2002, 109). This answer seems completely inappropriate, but Morgan is able to show that such explanations for the harshness of life under white supremacy conform to another pattern of indirectness: statements like this at the end of a narrative of this kind signify "that there is no explanation for racist acts . . . The riot happened because white supremacy exists. If one does not want the truth, the mattress is as good an explanation as any" (2002, 110).

How Are Language, Culture, and Thought Connected?

Since the time of Sapir and Whorf, linguists, anthropologists, and psychologists have pondered the relationship between language, culture, and human thought. Today, there is abundant evidence that human psychology, like human language, is an open system. Human beings not only talk about the world in a variety of ways but also think and feel about it (and take action within it) in a variety of ways. The "same" object can mean different things in different contexts (consider what a butcher knife means lying on a cutting board in your kitchen next to a pile of mushrooms or wielded by an intruder who has cornered you in your kitchen in the middle of the night). And if no one way of thinking, feeling, or acting is obligatory, then any particular way of thinking, feeling, or acting depends on (or is *contingent* on) unforeseen events or opportunities that arise in the present and attention patterns, values, and skills we have acquired in the past. As a result, different groups in a society—with different histories and experiences—are likely to develop unique points of view, pay attention to different things, and feel and behave differently toward them, all of which recalls the linguistic design feature of semanticity. When we learn from this culturally shaped experience, we can use previous categories and habits to help us interpret new experiences. This is a version of the linguistic design feature called displacement. All our senses can play tricks on us, moreover, and if they are clever enough, people can trick other people into perceiving something that "does not exist." Prevarication is thus a built-in feature of general human psychological processes, just as it is of language.

Human psychological openness is perhaps best illustrated by research that requires human subjects to

deal with ambiguity. We will briefly review work on human perception, cognition, and practical action that highlights the kinds of ambiguity people regularly encounter in their lives and how culture becomes an indispensable tool for resolving ambiguity. We will then describe how groups of people are able to organize their interpretations and cultural practices into encompassing pictures of the way the world works.

Perception

Perception has long been understood as a psychological process that links people to the world around them or within them by means of the five senses: we perceive size, color, texture, loudness, odor, pain, and so on. Studies of perception flourished in the 1950s and 1960s, but their results remain significant for correcting persistent misunderstandings about the way human perception works. Anthropologists have always insisted that, as Bock puts it, "culture enters into every step of the perceptual process, initially by providing patterned material for perception . . . and later, through verbal and nonverbal means, by suggesting (or insisting on) the proper labeling of and responses to perceived patterns" (1994, xi). Although it is often difficult to pinpoint the general effects of a particular cultural background on perception, researchers have been able to identify some of the ways in which meaning is mapped onto our experiences (Bock 1994, xii).

Chunks of experience that appear to hang together as wholes, exhibiting the same properties in the same configuration whenever they recur, are called **schemas**. As human beings grow up, they gradually become aware of the schemas that their culture (or subculture) recognizes. Such schemas are often embedded in practical activities and labeled linguistically, and they may serve as a focus for discourse. People living in the United States, for example, cannot avoid a schema called "Christmas," a chunk of experience that recurs once every year. The Christmas schema can include features like cold and snowy weather and activities like baking cookies, singing carols, going to church, putting up a Christmas tree, and buying and wrapping gifts. In the experience of a child, all these elements may appear to be equally relevant parts of a seamless whole. It may take time and conditioning for Christian parents to persuade children what the "true meaning of Christmas" really is. Some adults who celebrate Christmas disagree about its true meaning. Non-Christians living in the United States must also come to terms with this schema and may struggle to explain to their children why the activities associated with it are not appropriate for them.

People take for granted most of the schemas that their culture recognizes, using them as simplified

---

perception The processes by which people organize and experience information that is primarily of sensory origin.

schemas Patterned, repetitive experiences.

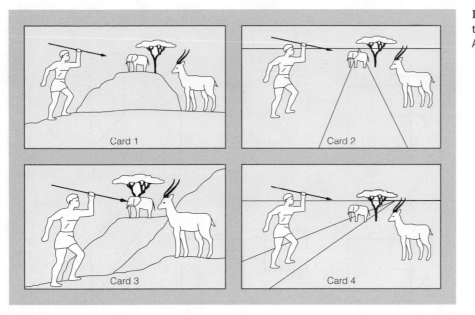

Figure 9.10   Pictures used for the study of depth perception in Africa.

interpretive frameworks for judging new experiences as typical or not, human or not (D'Andrade 1992, 48). That is, they learn to use schemas as **prototypes**. Prototypes of various sorts appear to be central to the way meaning is organized in human language. The words we use refer to typical instances, typical elements or relations, and are embedded in (or scaffolded by) language patterns associated with routine cultural practices. When we organize experience and assign meaning on the basis of prototypes, however, the categories we use have fuzzy boundaries. And because our experiences do not always neatly fit our prototypes, we are often not sure which prototype applies. Is a tossed salad a prototypical tossed salad if, in addition to lettuce and tomatoes and onions, it contains raisins and apple slices? Is a library a prototypical library when it contains fewer books than DVDs, videotapes, and electronic databases? In cases like this, suggests linguist R. A. Hudson (1980), a speaker must simply recognize the openness of language and apply linguistic labels creatively. Similarly, when confronted with novel perceptions, experiences for which no ready-made cultural interpretation is to hand, thinking and feeling human beings must extrapolate creatively to make sense of what is going on around them. As we will see in later chapters, such psychological creativity and resiliency is called upon with particular urgency in situations of extreme social suffering or violent trauma.

Classic research on variations in perception has attempted to relate people's descriptions of their experiences, or their performances on psychological tests, to their understandings of context. For example, nonliterate South African mine workers were tested using two-dimensional line drawings of three-dimensional objects

(Figure 9.10). The test results indicated that the mine workers consistently interpreted the drawings in two dimensions. When asked at which animal the man was pointing his spear on card 1, subjects would usually respond "the elephant." The elephant is, in fact, directly in line with and closest to the spear point in the drawing. However, the elephant ought to be seen as standing on top of the distant hill if the subjects interpret the drawings three-dimensionally. Did their responses mean that these Africans could not perceive in three dimensions?

J. B. Deregowski devised the following test. He presented different African subjects with the same drawings, asked them to describe what they saw, and received two-dimensional verbal reports. Next, he presented the same subjects with the line drawings in Figure 9.11. This time, he gave his subjects craft materials and asked them to construct models based on the drawings. His subjects had no difficulty producing three-dimensional models.

In these tests, the "correct" solution depended on the subject's mastery of a Western convention for interpreting two-dimensional drawings and photographs. For the drawings in Figure 9.10, the Western convention includes assumptions about perspective that relate the size of objects to their distance from the observer. Without such a convention in mind, it is not obvious that the size of a drawn object has any connection with distance. Far from providing us with new insights about African perceptual abilities, perhaps the most interesting result

---

prototypes Examples of a typical instance, element, relation, or experience within a culturally relevant semantic domain.

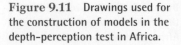

Figure 9.11 Drawings used for the construction of models in the depth–perception test in Africa.

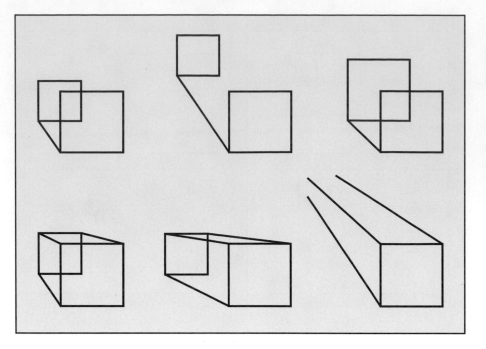

of such tests is what they teach us about Western perceptual conventions. That is, drawings do not necessarily speak for themselves. They can make sense to us only once we accept certain rules for interpreting them (Cole and Scribner 1974).

Illusion

If you examine Figure 9.12, you will see that marks on a piece of paper can be ambiguous. The signals we receive from the outside world tend to be open to more than one interpretation, whether they are patterns of light and dark striking the retinas of our eyes, smells, tastes, shapes, or words. Just as studies of metaphor provide insight into the nature of literal language, so studies of visual illusions provide insight into the nature of visual perception. Indeed, the contrast between literal and metaphorical language is not unlike the contrast between reality and illusion as it relates to perception. In both cases, knowledge of context permits us to distinguish between the literal and the metaphorical, the real and the illusory.

Richard Gregory is a cognitive psychologist who has spent most of his career studying visual illusions. In his view, illusions are produced by *misplaced procedures*: perfectly normal, ordinary cognitive processes that have somehow been inappropriately selected and applied to a particular set of extraordinary visual signals. For him, perceptions are symbolic representations of reality, not direct samples of reality. Perceivers must often work very hard to make sense of the visual signals they receive. When they are wrong, they are subject to illusion.

Consider the visual illusion Gregory (1981) calls "distortion": what you see appears larger or smaller, longer or shorter, and so on, than it really is. Look at the Ponzo illusion in Figure 9.13. Typically, the upper parallel line appears to be longer than the lower one when, in fact, they are equal. The standard explanation of this illusion is that we are looking at a two-dimensional drawing but interpreting it as if it were in three dimensions. In other words, the Ponzo illusion plays on our ability to see three-dimensional space in a two-dimensional drawing.

This explanation helps us understand the responses of the African mine workers to the drawings reproduced in Figure 9.10. Western observers interpret that drawing as a two-dimensional representation of three-dimensional

Figure 9.12 Ambiguous marks.

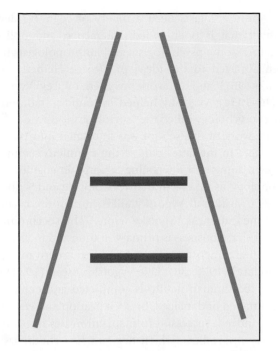

Figure 9.13 An example of distortion: the Ponzo illusion.

EthnoProfile 9.3

Mbuti

Region: Central Africa

Nation: Democratic Republic of the Congo (Zaire)

Population: 40,000

Environment: Dense tropical forest

Livelihood: Nomadic hunting and gathering

Political organization: Traditionally, communal bands of 7 to 30 families (average 17 families); today, part of a modern nation-state

For more information: Turnbull, Colin. 1961. *The forest people.* New York: Simon & Schuster.

reality. In the Ponzo illusion, the shapes trick us because they are very similar to what we perceive when we stand on a railroad track and look toward its vanishing point on the horizon. Africans are also familiar with railroad tracks, but they did not attempt to interpret the Ponzo-like lines on card 2 of Figure 9.10 as representations of three-dimensional reality. On the contrary, they seemed to work very hard to keep the relationships between objects in two dimensions, even if this meant that the sizes of the objects themselves appeared distorted. When we compare the Western interpretation of the Ponzo illusion with the African interpretation of the pictures in Figure 9.10, we discover something important: both sets of drawings are ambiguous, and both are potentially open to distortion. How people interpret them depends on preexisting experiences and cultural conventions.

Colin Turnbull was an anthropologist who worked for many years among the Mbuti of northeastern Democratic Republic of the Congo (Zaire) (see EthnoProfile 9.3: Mbuti). He discovered that people who live all their lives in a dense forest have no experience of distance greater than a few feet and are therefore not accustomed to taking distance into consideration when estimating the size of an object in the visual field. Turnbull took one of his informants, Kenge, on a trip that brought them out of the forest and into a game park. For the first time in his life, Kenge faced vast, rolling grasslands nearly empty of trees. Kenge's response to this experience was dramatic: "When Kenge topped the rise, he stopped dead. Every smallest sign of mirth suddenly left his face.

He opened his mouth but could say nothing. He moved his head and eyes slowly and unbelievingly" (1961, 251). When Kenge finally saw the far-off animals grazing on the plain, he asked Turnbull what insects they were. When told that they were buffalo, Kenge laughed and accused Turnbull of lying. Then he strained to see better and inquired what kind of buffalo could be so small. Later, when Turnbull pointed out a fishing boat on the lake, Kenge scoffed at him and insisted it was a floating piece of wood (252). Significantly, Kenge was soon able to adjust to these unprecedented (for him) physical surroundings, which itself illustrates the openness, flexibility, and adaptability of human perceptual processes.

When people in another culture fail to see similarities between people or objects that we think ought to be obvious to any observer, we are apt to become impatient. Yet, in the United States, where racist stereotypes influence perceptions of mixed peoples, many people are subject to similar blindness. Puerto Ricans, for example, experience racial distinctions in Puerto Rico in terms of a continuum of phenotypes and skin shades. When they move to the United States, however, they often find that their cultural identity as Puerto Ricans is ignored and they are classified as either "white" or "black" (Rodriguez 1994).

Cognition

The study of illusion demonstrates that there can be a gulf between what we see and what we know, what we perceive and what we conceive. Nevertheless, in the ordinary contexts of everyday life, these discrepancies seem to be manageable: there is coherence between perceptions and conceptions. Moreover, because our link with the world comes not just through our minds but also through the rest of our bodies, there is often no sharp boundary (or conflict) separating what we perceive, what we conceive, and the material features of the world with which we interact. Not only can new perceptions or interactions lead us to modify our conceptions and skills (i.e., we learn), but new conceptions and skills can also lead us to perceive aspects of the world around us that we did not pay attention to before (Ingold 2000). We are active meaning-makers, mentally and physically striving to make sense of our experiences. As a result, **cognition** is perhaps best understood as a tangle of connections "between the mind at work and the world in which it works" (Lave 1988, 1).

What Are Symbolic Practices?

Children use their own bodies and brains to explore the world. But from their earliest days, as we have seen, other people are actively working to steer their activity and attention in particular directions. Two terms in the social sciences refer to this process of culturally and socially shaped cognitive development. The first, *socialization*, is the learning process by which individuals develop the skills they need to interact successfully with other members of the social groups to which they belong. The second term, *enculturation*, refers to the learning process by which individuals come to terms with the ways of thinking and feeling that are considered appropriate in their respective cultures. These processes are intertwined because human children develop interaction skills and habits of thought, feeling, and speech while participating with others in joint, culturally shaped activities. We will use the term **socialization/enculturation** to represent these processes. Socialization/enculturation produces a skilled, socially and culturally constructed *self* capable of functioning successfully in society.

---

cognition (1) The mental process by which human beings gain knowledge. (2) A tangle of connections between the mind at work and the world in which it works.

socialization/enculturation The learning process by which individuals develop the skills they need to interact successfully with other members of the social groups to which they belong and come to terms with the ways of thinking and feeling that are considered appropriate in their respective cultures.

Anthropologists need a theory of cognitive development that is open-ended, interactive, and holistic; therefore, some psychologists and anthropologists have been attracted to the ideas of George Herbert Mead (1863–1931) and to work inspired by Lev Vygotsky (1896–1934). Vygotsky helped to found a tradition of Soviet psychology called the "sociohistorical school." After the work of this school was translated into Western languages in the latter part of the twentieth century, it inspired some very interesting research in cognitive anthropology, as we saw in the work of Cole and Scribner.

For Mead and Vygotsky alike, human life is social from the outset. As Vygotsky wrote, "The social dimension of consciousness is primary in time and in fact. The individual dimension of consciousness is derivative and secondary" (1978, 30). Like Vygotsky, Mead (1934) believed that human nature is completed and enhanced, not curtailed or damaged, by socialization and enculturation. Indeed, successful humanization lies in people's mastery of symbols, which begins when children start to learn language. As children come to control the symbolic systems of their cultures, they gain the ability to distinguish objects and relationships in the world. Most important, they come to see themselves as objects as well as subjects.

For Vygotsky, acquisition takes place in a context of face-to-face interactions between, typically, a child and an adult. When children learn about the world in such a context, they are not working on their own; on the contrary, they are learning about the world as they learn the symbolic forms (usually language) that others use to represent the world.

This learning process creates in the child a new plane of consciousness resting on the dialogue-based, question-and-answer format of social interaction. From this, Vygotsky inferred that our internal thought processes would also take the format of a dialogue. Mead suggested something similar when he spoke of every person as being able to carry on internal conversations between the *I* (the unsocialized self) and the *me* (the socially conditioned self). Only on this basis can an individual's sense of identity develop as the self is distinguished from the conversational other.

One interesting Vygotskian concept is the *zone of proximal development*, which is the distance between a child's "actual development level as determined by independent problem solving" and the level of "potential development as determined through problem solving under adult guidance or in collaboration with more capable peers" (Vygotsky 1978, 86) (Figure 9.14). Psychologists everywhere have long been aware that children can often achieve more when they are coached than when they work alone. Western psychologists, with

Figure 9.14 The zone of proximal development is the distance between what a child can do on her own and what she can do under adult guidance. Here, a woman helps a girl with Chinese calligraphy.

their individualist bias, have viewed this difference in achievement as contamination of the testing situation or as the result of cheating. Vygotsky and his followers see it as an indispensable measure of potential growth that simultaneously demonstrates how growth is rooted in social interaction, especially in educational settings (Moll 1990). The concept of the zone of proximal development enables anthropologists and comparative psychologists to link cognitive development to society, culture, and history because practices of coaching or formal instruction are shaped by social, cultural, and historical factors. To the extent that these factors vary from society to society, we can expect cognitive development to vary as well.

How Are Symbolic Practices and Worldviews Connected?

Anthropological approaches to language and cognition offer insight into the resources human beings use to make sense of the wider world on a comprehensive scale. Cultural resources may come from different times and places, and no set of cultural practices in any society is perfectly integrated and without contradiction. Still, anthropologists have good evidence that culture is not just a hodgepodge of unrelated elements. Cultural creativity can develop in widely different directions from one group to the next, but in any particular society, culture tends to be coherent and patterned. Thus, an individual's everyday attempts to account for experience do not occur in a vacuum. Members of the same society

make use of shared assumptions, habits, and material culture in their efforts to understand the way the world works. The encompassing pictures of reality that result are called **worldviews**. Multiple worldviews may coexist in a single society.

What Are Symbols?

As they develop complex understandings of themselves and the wider world, people regularly devise symbols to organize this knowledge. As we saw earlier a *symbol*—such as a word, an image, or an action—is something that stands for something else. Symbols signal the presence and importance of given domains of experience.

Some symbols, which anthropologist Sherry Ortner calls *summarizing symbols*, sum up, express, represent for people "in an emotionally powerful . . . way what the system means to them" (1973, 1339). To many people, for example, the American flag stands for the American way (Figure 9.15). But the American way is a complex collection of ideas and feelings that includes such things as patriotism, democracy, hard work, free enterprise, progress, national superiority, apple pie, and motherhood. As Ortner points out, the flag focuses our attention on all these things at once. It does not encourage us, say, to reflect on how the American way affects non-Americans. But the symbolic power of the flag is double-edged. For some people, Americans included, this same flag stands for imperialism, racism, opposition to the legitimate struggle of exploited peoples, and support for right-wing dictatorships. Perhaps stranger still, for many Americans, the flag sums up all these things at once, contradictory though they are!

What Ortner calls *elaborating symbols* are essentially analytic. They allow people to sort out and label complex and undifferentiated feelings and ideas into comprehensible and communicable language and action. Elaborating symbols provide people with categories for thinking about how their world is ordered. For the Dinka, a cattle-herding people of eastern Africa, cattle are a key elaborating symbol (see Figure 9.16 and Ethno-Profile 9.4: Dinka). According to Godfrey Lienhardt, cattle provide the Dinka with most of the metaphors they use for thinking about and responding to experience. For instance, Dinka perceptions of color, light, and shade are connected to the colors they see in cattle. They even liken how their society is put together to how a bull is put together (Lienhardt 1961, Ortner 1973).

worldviews Encompassing pictures of reality created by the members of societies.

In Their Own Words

The Madness of Hunger

Medical anthropologist Nancy Scheper-Hughes describes how symptoms of a rural Brazilian folk ailment can be understood as a form of protest against physical exploitation and abuse.

Among the agricultural wage laborers living in the hillside shantytown of Alto do Cruzeiro, on the margins of a large, interior market town in the plantation zone of Pernambuco, Brazil, and who sell their labor for as little as a dollar a day, socioeconomic and political contradictions often take shape in the "natural" contradictions of angry, sick, and afflicted bodies. In addition to the wholly expectable epidemics of parasitic infections and communicable fevers, there are the more unexpected outbreaks and explosions of unruly and subversive symptoms that will not readily materialize under the health station's microscope. Among these are the fluid symptoms of nervos (angry, frenzied nervousness): trembling, fainting, seizures, hysterical weeping, angry recriminations, blackouts, and paralysis of face and limbs.

These nervous attacks are in part coded metaphors through which the workers express their dangerous and unacceptable condition of chronic hunger and need . . . and in part acts of defiance and dissent that graphically register the refusal to endure what is, in fact, unendurable and their protest against their availability for physical exploitation and abuse. And so, rural workers who have cut sugarcane since the age of seven or eight years will sometimes collapse, their legs giving way under an ataque de nervos, a nervous attack. They cannot walk, they cannot stand upright; they are left . . . without a leg to stand on.

In "lying down" on the job, in refusing to return to the work that has overly determined their entire lives, the cane cutters' body language signifies both surrender and defeat. But one also notes a drama of mockery and refusal. For if the folk ailment nervos attacks the legs and the face, it leaves the arms and hands intact and free for less physically ruinous work. Consequently, otherwise healthy young men suffering from nervous attacks press their claims as sick men on their various political bosses and patrons to find them alternative work, explicitly "sitting down" work, arm work (but not clerical work for these men are illiterate).

The analysis of nervos does not end here, for nervous attack is an expansive and polysemic (having multiple meanings) form of disease. Shantytown women, too, suffer from nervos—both the nervos de trabalhar muito, "overwork" nerves from which male cane cutters suffer, and also the more gender-specific nervos de sofrir muito, the nerves of those who have endured and suffered much. "Sufferers' nerves" attacks those who have endured a recent, especially a violent, tragedy. Widows of husbands and mothers of sons who have been abducted and violently "disappeared" are prone to the mute, enraged, white-knuckled shaking of "sufferers' nerves."

Source: Scheper-Hughes 1994, 236–37.

Figure 9.15 For U.S. citizens, the flag of the United States is a summarizing symbol that brings together and evokes for them a range of images and emotions, positive and negative, about their country.

Figure 9.16 For pastoral people such as the Dinka and their neighbors the Nuer, cattle are elaborating symbols of paramount power.

EthnoProfile 9.4

Dinka

Region: Eastern Africa

Nation: Sudan

Population: 2,000,000

Environment: Savanna

Livelihood: Principally cattle herding, also agriculture

Political organization:
Traditionally, egalitarian with noble clans and chiefs; today, part of a modern nation-state

For more information:
Deng, Francis Madeng. 1972. *The Dinka of the Sudan.* New York: Holt, Rinehart and Winston.

How Are Selves Shaped by Symbolic Practices?

The experiences of socialization and enculturation produce a **self**, capable of functioning successfully in society. But what sort of entity is a self? Many Western psychologists have assumed that the mature self was a bounded, independent, self-contained entity with a clear and non-contradictory sense of identity that persisted through time. Anthropologists working in other societies, however, often found that the development of such an independent self was not recognized as the goal of socialization and enculturation. On the contrary, socialization and enculturation were often designed to shape selves that did *not* think of themselves as independent and self-sufficient; the mature individual was one motivated to look out for others and to work for the well-being of the family or the lineage rather than in pursuit of his or her own self-interest.

---

self The result of the process of socialization/enculturation for an individual.

Anthropology in Everyday Life

Lead Poisoning among Mexican American Children

In the summer of 1981, a Mexican American child was treated for lead poisoning in a Los Angeles emergency room. When the child's stomach was pumped, a bright orange powder was found. It was lead tetroxide, more than 90 percent elemental lead. Lead in that form is not usually found in lead poisoning cases in the United States. When questioned by health professionals, the mother revealed that her child had been given a folk remedy in powdered form— azarcón. Azarcón was used to treat an illness called *empacho*, part of the Mexican American set of culturally recognized diseases. Empacho is believed to be a combination of indigestion and constipation.

This case prompted a public health alert that was sent out nationally to clinics and physicians. The alert turned up another case of lead poisoning from azarcón in Greeley, Colorado. A nurse had read about the Los Angeles case and asked if the mother was treating the child for empacho. She was. Additional investigation revealed widespread knowledge of azarcón in both Mexican American communities. The U.S. Public Health Service decided that an anthropological study of azarcón would be useful.

The Public Health Service in Dallas called Dr. Robert Trotter, who had done research on Mexican American folk medicine. Trotter had never heard of azarcón and could not find it in south Texas. But a short time later, he received information from the Los Angeles County Health Department, which had discovered that azarcón was not the only name for the preparation. When he asked for *greta*, he was sold a heavy yellow powder that turned out to be lead oxide with an elemental lead content of approximately 90 percent. The shop owners said it was used to treat empacho. Here was confirmation that two related lead-based remedies were being used to treat empacho. Trotter discovered that a wholesale distributor in Texas was selling greta to over 120 herb shops.

Trotter was asked to work in a health education project designed to reduce the use of these lead-based remedies. Because of the complex nature of the problem, he had six different clients with somewhat different needs and responsibilities. The first client was the Public Health Service office in Dallas, which sponsored the first study he did.

The second client was the task force that had been formed to create and implement a health education project in Colorado and California. Task force members wanted to reduce the use of azarcón—but they did not want to attack or denigrate the folk medical system that promoted its use. The goal of the task force became product substitution—to convince people to switch from greta or azarcón to another, harmless remedy for empacho that was already part of the folk medical system.

The Food and Drug Administration (FDA), Trotter's third client, decided it needed basic ethnographic information on the use of greta. The FDA had never considered that lead oxide could be a food additive or a drug, and it needed verifiable data that the compound was being used in this way. As a result of Trotter's research, the FDA concluded that greta was a food additive. It issued a Class I recall to ban the sale of greta as a remedy.

Client number four was the Texas regional office of the Department of Health and Human Services. It needed assistance in creating and carrying out a survey along the United States-Mexico border. Trotter's survey indicated that as many as 10 percent of the Mexican American households along the border had at one time used greta or azarcón. The survey also turned up several other potentially toxic compounds that were in use.

Trotter's fifth client was the Hidalgo County Health Care Corporation, a local migrant clinic. It needed a survey that would compare the level of greta and azarcón usage in the local population in general with the level of usage among the people who came to the clinic. Trotter found that the two groups did not differ significantly in their knowledge about and use of the two preparations; however, the clinic population was more likely to treat folk illnesses with folk medicines than was the population at large.

The sixth client was the Migrant Health Service. It needed to know whether it was necessary to design a nationwide lead project. Based on the research that Trotter and others did, it became clear that such a major project was not necessary; rather, health projects were targeted and health professionals notified in the areas of high greta and azarcón use only.

Two years after the project began, both greta and azarcón were hard to find in the United States. In addition, the various surveys Trotter carried out led to better screening procedures for lead poisoning. Information on traditional medications is now routinely gathered when lead poisoning is suspected, and several other potentially toxic compounds have been discovered. Health professionals were able to learn about the current use of traditional medications in their areas and about the specific health education needs of their clients.

Trotter brought to the project the skills of the anthropologist; his principal focus was on culture. He took a holistic, comparative approach, and he was willing to innovate, to look for explanations in areas in which investigators from other disciplines had not thought to look. This is typical for medical anthropologists, who struggle with the friction generated when biomedical approaches encounter cultural practices that begin with different assumptions about the way the world works.

Early psychological anthropologists often spoke of individual **personality** rather than the self. Philip Bock points out that for these anthropologists "personality involves the relative *integration* of an individual's perceptions, motives, cognitions, and behavior within a sociocultural matrix. (The subjective view of this unity is more often referred to as the *self*) . . . Personality is thus revealed as part of a dynamic interactive system between a human organism and its physical–social environment" (1994, xiv). Many psychological anthropologists, including Bock himself, have argued that an individual's personality, understood in this way, is not merely a reflection of a culturally ideal type but is regularly shaped by such factors as "the individual's position in the social structure, including his or her social class, gender, occupational role, and even birth order. . . . These quasi-universal structural constraints cut across conventional divisions into 'cultures' and even nations" (Bock 1994, xiv).

The notion of an integrated personality, or self, harks back to Enlightenment ideas; as a result, it is hardly surprising that the postmodern critique of Enlightenment ideas questioned the existence of integrated, harmonious personalities or selves. The idea of a centered, integrated self was viewed as an illusion or an effect of powerful political ideologies that worked to mask the heterogeneity and contradictory features of individual experience. Rather than possessing a single unified self that did not change from one social setting to the next, people were said to have "decentered" selves, with different dimensions of the self emerging (or disappearing) in different social settings.

Contemporary scholars in many fields continue to disagree about the extent to which anyone's self is integrated or coherent, and few anthropologists would defend an unreflective Enlightenment view of the self. In psychological anthropology, these developments have led to a focus on the role of external, social discourse about people's behavior in the shaping of selves, and a rejection of approaches that attempt to understand an individual's behavior as the outward manifestation of an internally coherent self. This leaves the nature of one's internal self unspecified, while suggesting that "culture is (largely) created by people in the discourse justifying their behavior as rational and moral" (Bock 1994, xv). Still, anthropologists who recognize the uneven and contradictory features of individual self-experience also often draw attention to the attempts individuals make, even in the most difficult or bewildering situations, to impose meaning on their experiences. We struggle to find meaning, strive to achieve ordered, coherent understandings of the world and of ourselves, even if the world is disorderly and even if our understandings are inevitably imperfect and partial.

In recent years, many psychological anthropologists and others have come to speak not of individual personality or individual self but of individual **subjectivity**. Medical anthropologists Veena Das and Arthur Kleinman, for example, define *subjectivity* as "the felt interior experience of the person that includes his or her positions in a field of relational power" (2000, 1). To think of individuals as subjects has much to recommend it. First, it points to individual agency: each of us is, to some degree, the initiating subject of our actions. Second, however, individual agency is not understood as absolute: we are not free to chart our own destinies unimpeded; quite the contrary, our agency is circumscribed by various limitations that result from the deployment of social, economic, and political power in the societies in which we live. These limitations may be greater or lesser, depending on who we are (remember Bock's urging that we pay attention to the effects of such social variables as class, gender, occupation, and birth order and their impact on our developing sense of self). That is, we are *subject to* the workings of institutionalized power in the various *subject positions* we occupy. The fact that all people in all societies occupy a variety of different subject positions reflects our decentered selves: a particular individual may, in different contexts, be positioned in terms of gender, ethnicity, occupation, class, or some combination of these positions. At the same time, however, all of us can potentially play the insights gained from each subject position off against the others and thus gain a measure of reflexive awareness and understanding of our own situations.

Individual subjectivity is heavily influenced by socialization and enculturation. But social and cultural expectations are sometimes overturned by experiences that intrude on predictable daily routines, and these, too, will have a powerful role in shaping the subjectivities of the individuals who are affected. Among the most powerful such experiences are those occasioned by violence and trauma that originates in social struggles within and between societies. Social and political conflicts that push people out of their original societies, or that allow their own governments to oppress or persecute them, have been all too frequent in the late twentieth and early twenty-first centuries. For those who live under such disordered circumstances, orderly, harmonious daily life is not taken for granted. Human meaning-making processes, however, rooted in our linguistic and symbolic practices, are central to their attempts to create purpose and order, to survive and adapt, as we shall see.

---

personality The relative integration of an individual's perceptions, motives, cognitions, and behavior within a sociocultural matrix.

subjectivity "The felt interior experience of the person that includes his or her positions in a field of relational power." (Das and Kleinman 2000)

In Their Own Words

American Premenstrual Syndrome

*Anthropologist Alma Gottlieb explores some of the contradictions surrounding
the North American biocultural construction known as PMS.*

To what extent might PMS be seen as an "escape valve," a means whereby American women "let off steam" from the enervating machine of the daily domestic grind? To some extent this explanation is valid, but it tells only part of the story. It ignores the specific contours of PMS and its predictable trajectory; moreover it puts PMS in a place that is peripheral to the American vision of womanhood, whereas my contention is that the current understanding of PMS (and, before its creation, of the menstrual period itself) is integral to how we view femininity. Even if it occupies a small portion of women's lives (although some women may see the paramenstruum as occupying half the month), and even if not all women suffer from it, I contend that the contemporary vision of PMS is so much a part of general cultural consciousness that it constitutes, qualitatively, half the female story. It combines with the other part of the month to produce a bifurcated vision of femininity whose two halves are asymmetrically valued.

Married women who suffer from PMS report that during the "normal" phase of the month they allow their husbands' myriad irritating acts to go uncriticized. But while premenstrual they are hyper-critical of such acts, sometimes "ranting and raving" for hours over trivial annoyances. Unable to act "nice" continually, women break down and are regularly "irritable" and even "hostile." Their protest is recurrent but futile, for they are made to feel guilty about it, or, worse, they are treated condescendingly. "We both know you're going to have your period tomorrow so why don't we just go to bed?" one husband regularly tells his wife at the first sign of an argument, thereby dismissing any claim to legitimate disagreement. Without legitimacy, as Weber taught us long ago, protests are doomed to failure; and so it is with PMS.

I suggest that these women in effect choose, however unconsciously, to voice their complaints at a time that they know those complaints will be rejected as illegitimate. If complaints were made during the non-premenstrual portion of the month, they would have to be taken seriously. But many American women have not found a voice with which to speak such complaints and at the same time retain their feminine allure. They save their complaints for that "time of the month" when they are in effect permitted to voice them yet by means of hormones do not have to claim responsibility for such negative feelings. In knowing when their complaints will not be taken seriously yet voicing them precisely during such a time, perhaps women are punishing themselves for their critical thoughts. In this way, and despite the surface-level aggression they display premenstrually, women continue to enact a model of behavior doomed to failure, as is consistent with what some feminists have argued is a pervasive tendency among American women in other arenas. . . .

So long as American society recreates its unrealistic expectations of the female personality, it is inevitable that there will be a PMS, or something playing its role: a regular rejection of the stringent expectations of female behavior. But PMS masks the protest even as it embodies it: for, cast in a biological idiom, PMS is made to seem an autonomous force that is often uncontrollable . . . ; or if it can be controlled, it is only by drugs not acts of personal volition. Thus women's authorship of their own states of mind is denied them. As women in contemporary America struggle to find their voices, it is to be hoped that they will be able to reclaim their bodies as vehicles for the creation of their own metaphors, rather than autonomous forces causing them to suffer and needing to be drugged.

Source: Gottlieb 1988.

Chapter Summary

1. Symbolic language is a uniquely human faculty that both permits us to communicate with one another and sets up barriers to communication. The anthropological study of languages reveals the cultural factors that shape language use. In every language, there are many ways to communicate our experiences, and there is no absolute standard favoring one way over another. Individual efforts to create a unique voice are countered by pressures to negotiate a common code within a larger speech community.

2. Of Charles Hockett's 16 design features of language, six are particularly important: openness, arbitrariness, duality of patterning, displacement, semanticity, and prevarication.

3. Early linguistic anthropologists like Edward Sapir and Benjamin Whorf suggested that language has the power to shape the way people see the world. This is called the "linguistic relativity principle." How this shaping process works is still investigated by some linguistic anthropologists, who argue that linguistic relativity should not be confused with linguistic determinism, which they reject.

4. Ethnopragmatics locates linguistic meaning in routine practical activities, which turn grammatical features of language into resources people can use in their interactions with others. It pays attention both to the immediate context of speech and to broader contexts that are shaped by unequal social relationships and rooted in history.

5. Because linguistic meaning is rooted in practical activity, which carries the burden of meaning, different social groups engaged in different activities generate different communicative practices. The linguistic habits that are part of each set of communicative practices constitute discourse genres. People normally command a range of discourse genres, which means that each person's linguistic knowledge is characterized by heteroglossia.

6. The study of pidgin languages is the study of the radical negotiation of new meaning. Pidgin languages exhibit many of the same linguistic features as nonpidgin languages. Studies of African American English illustrate the historical circumstances that can give rise to creoles and provide evidence of the ways in which human speech is always embedded in a social world of power differences.

7. Language ideologies are unwritten rules shared by members of a speech community concerning what kinds of language are valued. Language ideologies develop out of the cultural, social, and political histories of the groups to which they belong. Knowing the language ideology of a particular community can help listeners make sense of speech that otherwise would seem inappropriate or incomprehensible to them.

8. The design features of human language, particularly openness, seem to characterize human thought processes in general. The work of psychological anthropologists on human perception, cognition, and practical action overwhelmingly sustains the view that human psychological processes are open to a wide variety of influences.

9. Human psychological perception always takes place in a cultural context. Researchers use concepts like "schemas" and "prototypes" to describe some of the ways in which meaning is mapped onto our experience. Classic research on cross-cultural variations in perception showed that variation in responses to psychological tests depended on the meanings subjects brought to the testing situation, especially whether they understood the tests the same way Western subjects typically understood them. Alternative understandings are possible because of the ambiguity of many perceptual signals.

10. Human beings are active meaning-makers, striving to make sense of experiences, which is a focus of anthropological studies of cognition. At the same time, humans must learn to pattern and adapt behavior and ways of thinking and feeling to the standards considered appropriate in their respective cultures. Vygotsky's concept of the zone of proximal development stresses that cognitive development results from a dialogue. Children progress through that process at different rates and in different directions, depending on the amount and kind of coaching they receive by others. This concept makes it possible to explain why people in different cultural subgroups are socialized and enculturated in different ways. Patterns of socialization and enculturation are sometimes overturned by experiences that intrude on predictable daily routines, such as war or political persecution. Some contemporary psychological anthropologists study

(continued on next page)

Chapter Summary *(continued)*

the effects of social trauma on psychological and social functioning.

11. People attempting to account for their experiences make use of shared cultural assumptions about how the world works. The encompassing pictures of reality that result are called "worldviews." Symbols that stand for an entire semantic domain are called "summarizing symbols." Elaborating symbols, by contrast, are analytic and allow people to sort out complex and undifferentiated feelings and ideas associated with a particular semantic domain.

12. A single society may have members who subscribe to different worldviews. Knowledge, like power, is not evenly distributed throughout a society. More powerful individuals and groups often impose

their preferred key metaphors on the rest of society. Those without power can resist this imposition by creating their own contrasting metaphors and alternative worldviews.

13. Because anthropologists understand individuals' senses of themselves to be mediated by symbolic meanings and worldviews embedded in power relations, they have long been critical of ideas of the individual self that assume it to be a bounded independent entity with a clear and noncontradictory sense of identity that persists through time. Some anthropologists prefer to speak not of personality or self but of individual subjectivity, which focuses on the internal experiences of individuals as they are shaped by their positions in a field of power.

For Review

1. What are the three reasons given in the text to explain why language is of interest to anthropologists?

2. Distinguish among language, speech, and communication.

3. Summarize the key points for each of the six design features of language discussed in the text (openness, displacement, arbitrariness, duality of patterning, semanticity, and prevarication).

4. What is the difference between closed call systems and open symbolic languages?

5. Describe the differences between linguistic competence and communicative competence.

6. Why do linguistic anthropologists emphasize the importance of context in language use?

7. What is the linguistic relativity principle? Summarize the problems with linguistic determinism and describe the steps that contemporary linguists and linguistic anthropologists have taken to address these problems.

8. Explain the differences between pidgins and creoles.

9. Summarize the research done by William Labov and subsequent scholars on African American speech patterns.

10. What is language ideology? Summarize the case studies in this section of the text that anlayze the language ideology of specific speech communities.

11. What is language revitalization? What are some of the difficulties in implementing language revitalization?

12. Distinguish between schemas and prototypes.

13. What kinds of studies have been carried out in order to test the nature of human perception in Western and non-Western societies? Based on the results of these studies, what conclusions can anthropologists draw about human perception?

14. Describe the differences between European American and African American responses to test-taking situations, and discuss how these responses can be explained from an anthropological perspective.

15. What are the differences between socialization and enculturation, and why are they combined in the text?

16. Explain the zone of proximal development.

17. Summarize the major points of the discussion of symbolism in the text.

18. Explain the differences among self, personality, and subjectivity.

Key Terms

Suggested Readings

Akmajian, A., R. Demers, A. Farmer, and R. Harnish. 2010. *Linguistics*, 6th ed. Cambridge, MA: MIT Press. *A fine introduction to the study of language as a formal system.*

Blum, Susan, ed. 2008. *Making Sense of Language: Readings in Culture and Communication.* New York: Oxford University Press. *An engaging and accessible collection of original essays by a wide range of scholars, inside and outside anthropology, past and present, who explore the many dimensions of human language.*

Bock, Philip K. 1999. *Rethinking psychological anthropology: Continuity and change in the study of human action*, 2nd ed. Prospect Heights, IL: Waveland Press. *A thorough introduction to psychological anthropology, tracing developments from the early twentieth century to current directions in the field.*

Brenneis, Donald, and Ronald K. S. Macauley, eds. 1996. *The matrix of language.* Boulder, CO: Westview Press. *A wide-ranging collection of essays by anthropologists studying linguistic habits in their sociocultural contexts.*

Burling, Robbins. 2005. *The talking ape.* Oxford: Oxford University Press. *A lively, up-to-date introduction for nonspecialists to the nature and evolution of human language, written by a distinguished linguistic anthropologist.*

Casy, Conerly, and Robert B. Edgertien. 2005. *A companion to psychological anthropology.* Walden, MA: Blackwell. *A recent collection of articles by anthropologists who consider the impact of globalization on the traditional concerns of psychological anthropology.*

Cole, Michael, and Sylvia Scribner. 1974. *Culture and thought: A psychological introduction.* New York: Wiley. *A classic survey of the literature and case studies on the cultural shaping of cognition.*

Smitherman, Geneva. 1977. *Talkin and testifyin: The language of black America.* Detroit: Wayne State University Press. *An engaging introduction to Black English Vernacular, for native and nonnative speakers alike, with exercises to test your mastery of African American English.*

Module 4: Components of Language

Linguistic anthropologists are trained in cultural anthropology but must also master the finer points of language structure, which is the focus of formal linguistics. This module offers brief introductions to four key areas of specialization in formal linguistics: phonology, morphology, syntax, and semantics.

Linguistic study involves a search for patterns in the way speakers use language; linguists aim to describe these patterns by reducing them to a set of rules called a **grammar**. As Edward Sapir once commented, however, "all grammars leak" (1921, 38). Over time linguists came to recognize a growing number of language components; each new component was an attempt to plug the "leaks" in an earlier grammar, to explain what had previously resisted explanation. The following discussion pinpoints the various leaks linguists have recognized (as well as their attempts to plug the leaks) and demonstrates how culture and language influence each other.

Phonology: Sounds

The study of the sounds of language is called **phonology**. The sounds of human language are special because they are produced by a set of organs, the speech organs, that belong only to the human species (Figure M4.1). The sounds that come out of our mouths are called *phones*, and they vary continuously in acoustic properties. However, speakers of a particular language hear that language's variant phones within a particular range as functionally equivalent sounds (e.g., we hear different pronunciations of the word *pecan* as meaning the same thing).

Part of the phonologist's job is to map out possible ways that human beings use speech organs to create the sounds of language. Another part is to examine individual languages to discover the particular sound combinations they contain and the patterns into which those sound combinations are organized. No language makes use of all the many sounds the human speech organs can produce, and no two languages use exactly the same set. American English uses only 38 sounds. Most work in phonology has been done from the perspective of the speaker, who produces, or articulates, the sounds of language using the speech organs. Although all languages rely on only a handful of what are called *phonemes*—classes

of functionally equivalent sounds—no two languages use exactly the same set. Furthermore, different speakers of the same language often differ from one another in the way their phonemes are patterned, producing "accents," which constitute one kind of variety within a language. This variety is not random; the speech sounds characteristic of any particular accent follow a pattern. Speakers with different accents are usually able to understand one another in most circumstances, but their distinctive articulation is a clue to their ethnic, regional, or social class origins.

Morphology: Word Structure

Morphology, the study of how words are put together, developed as a subfield of linguistics as soon as linguists realized that the rules they had devised to explain sound patterns in language could not explain the structure of words. What is a word? English speakers tend to think of words as the building blocks of sentences and of sentences as strings of words. But words are not all alike: some words (e.g., *book*), cannot be broken down into smaller elements; others (e.g., *bookworm*) can. The puzzle becomes more complex when we try to translate words from one language into another. Sometimes expressions that require only one word in one language require more than one word in another (e.g., *préciser* in French is *to make precise* in English). Other times, we must deal with languages whose utterances cannot easily be broken down into words at all. Consider the utterance *nikookitepeena* from Shawnee (an indigenous North American language), which translates into English as "I dipped his head in the water" (Whorf 1956, 172). Although the Shawnee utterance is composed of parts, the parts do not possess the characteristics we attribute to words in, say, English or French (Table M4.1). To make sense of the structure of languages such as Shawnee, anthropological linguists needed a concept that could refer to both words (like those in the English sentence given) and the parts of an utterance that could not be broken down into words. This need led to the development of the concept of *morphemes*, traditionally defined as "the minimal units of meaning in a language." The various parts of a Shawnee utterance or an English word can be identified as morphemes. Describing minimal units of meaning as morphemes, and not as words, allows us to compare the morphology of different languages. Morphemic patterning in languages such as Shawnee may seem hopelessly complicated to native English speakers, yet the patterning of morphemes in English is equally complex. Why is it that some morphemes can stand alone as words (e.g., *sing*, *red*) and others cannot (*-ing*, *-ed*)? What determines a word boundary in the first place? Words, or the morphemes

---

grammar A set of rules that aim to describe fully the pattern of linguistic usage observed by speakers of a particular language.

phonology The study of the sounds of language.

morphology In linguistics, the study of the minimal units of meaning in a language.

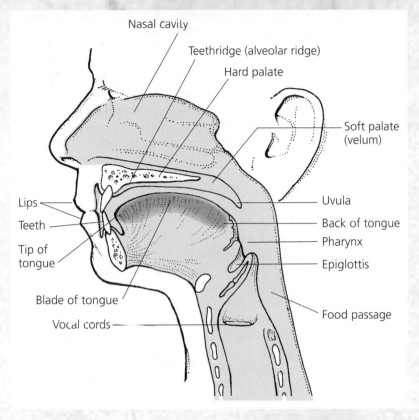

Nasal cavity

Teethridge (alveolar ridge)

Hard palate

Soft palate (velum)

Lips

Teeth

Tip of tongue

Blade of tongue

Vocal cords

Uvula

Back of tongue

Pharynx

Epiglottis

Food passage

TABLE M4.1 Morphemes of Shawnee Utterance and Their Glosses				
ni	kooki	tepe	en	a
I	immersed in water	point of action at head	by hand action	cause to him

they contain, represent the fundamental point at which the arbitrary pairing of sound and meaning occurs.

Syntax: Sentence Structure

A third component of language is **syntax**, or sentence structure. Linguists such as Noam Chomsky began to study syntax when they discovered that morphological rules alone could not account for certain patterns of morpheme use. In languages such as English, for example, rules governing word order cannot explain what is puzzling about the following English sentence: "Smoking grass means trouble." For many native speakers of American English, this sentence exhibits what linguists call *structural ambiguity*. That is, we must ask

ourselves what *trouble* means here: is it the act of smoking grass (marijuana) or observing grass (the grass that grows on the prairie) that is giving off smoke? In the first reading, *smoking* is a verb functioning as a noun; in the second, it is a verb functioning as an adjective. We can explain the ambiguity by assuming that a word's role in a sentence depends on sentence structure and not on the structure of the word itself. Thus, sentences can be defined as ordered strings of words, and those words can be classified as parts

syntax The study of sentence structure.

of speech in terms of the function they fulfill in a sentence. But these two assumptions cannot account for the ambiguity in a sentence such as "The father of the girl and the boy fell into the lake." How many people fell into the lake? Just the father, or the father and the boy? Each reading of the sentence depends on how the words of the sentence are grouped together. Linguists discovered numerous other features of sentence structure that could not be explained in terms of morphology alone, leading to a growth of interest in the study of syntactic patterns in different languages. Although theories of syntax have changed considerably since Chomsky's early work, the recognition that syntax is a key component of human language structure remains central to contemporary linguistics.

Semantics: Meaning

For many years linguists avoided **semantics**, the study of meaning, because *meaning* is a highly ambiguous term. What do we mean when we say that a sentence means something? We may be talking about what each individual word in the sentence means, or what the sentence as a whole means, or what I mean when I utter the sentence, which may differ from what someone else would mean even if uttering the same sentence.

In the 1960s, however, formal semantics took off when Chomsky argued that grammars needed to represent all of the linguistic knowledge in a speaker's head and that word meanings were part of that knowledge. Formal semanticists focused attention on how words are linked to one another within a language, exploring relations such as *synonymy*, or "same meaning" (e.g., *old* and *aged*); *homophony*, or "same sound, different meaning" (e.g., *would* and *wood*); and *antonymy*, or "opposite meaning" (e.g., *tall* and *short*). They also defined words in terms of *denotation*, or what they referred to in the "real world."

The denotations of such words as *table* or *monkey* seem fairly straightforward, but this is not the case with such words as *truth* or *and*. Moreover, even if we believe a word can be linked to a concrete object in the world, it may still be difficult to decide exactly what the term refers to. (Anthropological linguist Charles Hockett elaborated on this issue

semantics The study of meaning.

metaphor A form of figurative or nonliteral language that violates the formal rules of denotation by linking expressions from unrelated semantic domains.

in describing the *semanticity* feature of human language.) Suppose we decide to find out what *monkey* refers to by visiting the zoo. In one cage we see small animals with grasping hands feeding on fruit. In a second cage are much larger animals that resemble the ones in the first cage in many ways, except that they have no tails. And in a third cage are yet other animals who resemble those in the first two cages except that they are far smaller and use their long tails to swing from the branches of a tree. Which of these animals are monkeys? To answer this question, the observer must decide which features of similarity or difference are important and which are not. Having made this decision, it is easier to decide whether the animals in the first cage are monkeys and whether the animals in the other cages are monkeys as well.

But such decisions are not easy to come by. Biologists have spent the last 300 years or so attempting to classify all living things on the planet into mutually exclusive categories. To do so they have had to decide which traits matter out of all the traits that living things exhibit. They have therefore constructed meaning in the face of ambiguity.

Formal linguistics, on the other hand, tries to deal with ambiguity by eliminating it, by "disambiguating" ambiguous utterances. To find a word's "unambiguous" denotation, we might consult a dictionary. According to the *American Heritage Dictionary*, for example, a pig is "any of several mammals of the family *Suidae*, having short legs, cloven hoofs, bristly hair, and a cartilaginous snout used for digging." A formal definition of this sort indirectly relates the word *pig* to other words in English, such as *cow* and *chicken*.

To complicate the matter, however, words also have *connotations*, additional meanings that derive from the typical contexts in which they are used in everyday speech. In the context of antiwar demonstrations in the 1960s, for example, a *pig* was a police officer. From a denotative point of view, to call police officers *pigs* is to create ambiguity deliberately, to muddle rather than to clarify. It is an example of **metaphor**, a form of figurative or nonliteral language that violates the formal rules of denotation by linking expressions from unrelated semantic domains. Metaphors are used all the time in everyday speech. Does this mean, therefore, that people who use metaphors are talking nonsense? What can it possibly mean to call police officers *pigs*?

We cannot know until we place the statement into some kind of context. If we know, for example, that protesters in the 1960s viewed the police as the paid enforcers of racist elites responsible for violence against the poor and that pigs are domesticated animals, not humans, who are often viewed as fat, greedy, and dirty, then the metaphor "police are pigs" begins to make sense. This interpretation, however, does not reveal the meaning of the metaphor for all time. In a different context, the same phrase might be used, for example, to distinguish the costumes worn by police officers to a charity function from the costumes of other groups of government functionaries. Our ability to use the same words in different ways (and different words in the same way) is the hallmark of the *openness* feature of language (Hockett, 1966), and formal semantics is powerless to contain it. Much of the referential meaning of language escapes us if we neglect the context of language use.

For Review

Prepare a chart listing the components of language identified by linguists, and explain the significance of each component.

Key Terms

grammar   278

metaphor   280

morphology   278

phonology   278

semantics   280

syntax   279

How Do We Make Meaning?

10

Human beings are creative, not just in their use of language, but in a variety of symbolic forms. We look at several different kinds of creative symbolic forms in this chapter, including play, art, myth, ritual, and religion. But human cultural creativity is never entirely unconstrained. You will also learn about how symbolic forms are shaped by power relations in different social settings.

Chapter Outline

◀ *A group of Costa Rican dancers in a festive end-of-the-year parade, December 2005.*

Building on the discussion of language and symbolism from the previous chapter, this chapter looks at human play, art, myth, ritual, and religion—dimensions of human experience in which the interplay of openness and creativity encounters rules and constraints, enabling people to produce powerful and moving symbolic practices that transform the character of human life.

What Is Play?

In Chapter 9, we explored the concept of "openness" in relation to language and cognition. *Openness* was defined as the ability to talk or think about the same thing in different ways and different things in the same way. If we expand openness to include all behavior—that is, the ability not just to talk or think about but also to *do* the same thing in different ways or different things in the same way—we begin to define **play**. All mammals play, and humans play the most and throughout their lives.

Robert Fagen (1981, 1992, 2005) looks at play as a product of natural selection that may have significant fitness value for individuals in different species. Play gives young animals (including young human beings) the exercise they need to build up the skills necessary for physical survival as adults: fighting, hunting, or running away when pursued. Play may be important for the development of cognitive and motor skills and may be connected with the repair of developmental damage caused by either injury or trauma. It may also communicate the message "all's well," signaling "information about short-term and long-term health, general well-being, and biological fitness to parents, littermates, or other social companions" (R. Fagen 1992, 51). In species with more complex brains, playful exploration of the environment aids learning and allows for the development of behavioral versatility. Fagen (2005) suggests that play reflects natural selection for unpredictability. That is, to be able to produce unpredictable behaviors can be advantageous for an intelligent species faced with unanticipated adaptive challenges.

---

play A framing (or orienting context) that is (1) consciously adopted by the players, (2) somehow pleasurable, and (3) systemically related to what is nonplay by alluding to the nonplay world and by transforming the objects, roles, actions, and relations of ends and means characteristic of the nonplay world.

metacommunication Communication about the process of communication itself.

framing A cognitive boundary that marks certain behaviors as "play" or as "ordinary life."

reflexivity Critical thinking about the way one thinks; reflection on one's own experience.

What Do We Think about Play?

Moving from everyday reality to the reality of play requires a radical transformation of perspective. To an outside observer, the switch from everyday reality to play reality may go undetected. However, sometimes the switch can have serious consequences for other people and their activities. In this case, play and nonplay must be signaled clearly so that one is not mistaken for the other.

According to Gregory Bateson (1972), shifting into or out of play requires **metacommunication**, or communication about communication. Metacommunication provides information about the relationship between communicative partners. In play there are two kinds of metacommunication. The first, called **framing**, sends a message that marks certain behaviors either as play or as ordinary life. Dogs, for example, have a *play face*, a signal understood by other dogs (and recognizable by some human beings) indicating a willingness to play. If dogs agree to play, they bare their fangs and one animal attacks the other, but bites become nips. Both dogs have agreed to enter the *play frame*, an imaginative world in which bites do not mean bites. Within the play frame, a basic element of Western logic—that $A = A$—does not apply; the same thing is being treated in different ways. Human beings have many ways of marking the play frame: a smile, a particular tone of voice, a referee's whistle, or the words "Let's pretend." The marker says that "everything from now until we end this activity is set apart from everyday life." The second kind of metacommunication involves **reflexivity**. Play offers us the opportunity to think about the social and cultural dimensions of the world in which we live. By suggesting that ordinary life can be understood in more than one way, play can be a way of speculating about what can be rather than about what should be or what is (Handelman 1977, 186). When we say that jokes keep us from taking ourselves too seriously, for example, we are engaging in reflexive metacommunication. Joking allows us to consider alternative, even ridiculous, explanations for our experience.

What Are Some Effects of Play?

Helen Schwartzman has demonstrated how play, through satire and clowning, may allow children to comment on and criticize the world of adults (1978, 232–45). A powerful example of this kind of commentary is described by anthropologist Elizabeth Chin, who studied African American girls and their dolls in Newhallville, a working-class and poor neighborhood in New Haven, Connecticut. Although "ethnically correct" dolls are on the market, very few of the girls had them because they cost too much. The poor children Chin knew in Newhallville had white dolls. But in their play these girls transformed their dolls in a powerful way by giving them hairstyles like their own. The designers gave the dolls smooth, flowing hair to be brushed over and over again and put into a ponytail. But the girls' dolls had beads in their hair, braids held at the end with twists of aluminum foil or barrettes, and braids that were themselves braided together (Chin 1999, 315). As Chin observes, "In some sense, by doing this, the girls bring their dolls into their own worlds, and whiteness here is not absolutely defined by skin and hair, but by style and way of life. The complexities of racial references and racial politics have been much discussed in the case of black hair simulating the look of whiteness; what these girls are creating is quite the opposite: white hair that looks black" (315). It is not that the girls did not realize that their dolls were white; it is that through their imaginative and material work they were able to integrate the dolls into their own world. The overt physical characteristics of the dolls—skin color, facial features, hair—did not force the girls into treating the dolls in ways that obeyed the boundaries of racial difference. Their transformative play does not make the realities of poverty, discrimination, and racism disappear from the worlds in which they live; but Chin points out that "in making their white dolls live in black worlds, they . . . reconfigure the boundaries of race" and in so doing "challenge the social construction not only of their own blackness, but of race itself as well" (318) (Figure 10.1).

Figure 10.1 Play enables this girl in Guider, Cameroon, to incorporate her European doll into the world she knows.

What Is Art?

In Western societies, art includes sculpture, drawing, painting, dance, theater, music, and literature, as well as such similar processes and products as film, photography, mime, mass media production, oral narrative, festivals, and national celebrations. These are the kinds of objects and activities that first caught the attention of anthropologists who wanted to study art in non-Western societies. Whether non-Western peoples referred to such activities or products as "art," however, is a separate question. People everywhere engage in these kinds of playful creativity, yet activities defined as "art" differ from free play because they are circumscribed by rules. Artistic rules direct particular attention to, and provide standards for evaluating, the *form* of the activities or objects that artists produce.

Is There a Definition of Art?

Anthropologist Alexander Alland defines **art** as "play with form producing some aesthetically successful transformation-representation" (1977, 39). For Alland, *form* refers to the rules of the art game: the culturally appropriate restrictions on the way this kind of play may be organized in time and space. We can also think about form in terms of style and media. A *style* is a schema (a distinctive patterning of elements) that is recognized within a culture as appropriate to a given medium. The media themselves in which art is created and executed are culturally recognized and characterized (R. L. Anderson 1990, 272–75). A painting is a form: it is two-dimensional; it is done with paint; it is intentionally made; it represents or symbolizes something in the world outside the canvas, paper, or wood on which it is created. There are different kinds of paintings as well. There is the painting form called "portrait"—a portrait depicts a person, it resembles the person in some appropriate way, it is done with paint, it can be displayed, and more.

By "aesthetic," Alland means appreciative of, or responsive to, form in art or nature (1977, xii). "Aesthetically successful" means that the creator of the piece of art (and possibly its audience) responds positively or negatively to it ("I like this," "I hate this"). Indifference is the sign of something that is aesthetically unsuccessful. It is probably the case that the aesthetic response is a universal feature in all human societies.

art Play with form producing some aesthetically successful transformation-representation.

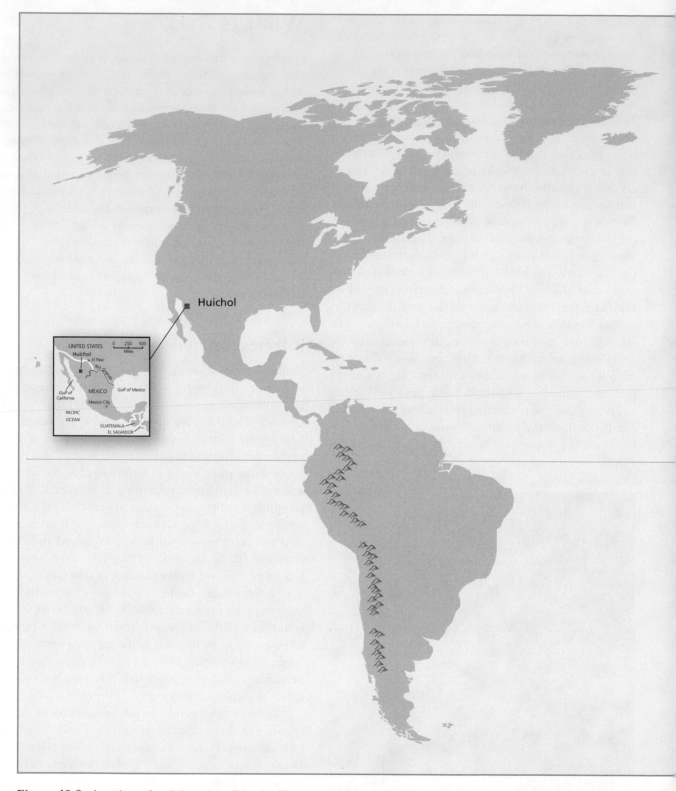

Figure 10.2 Locations of societies whose EthnoProfiles appear in Chapter 10.

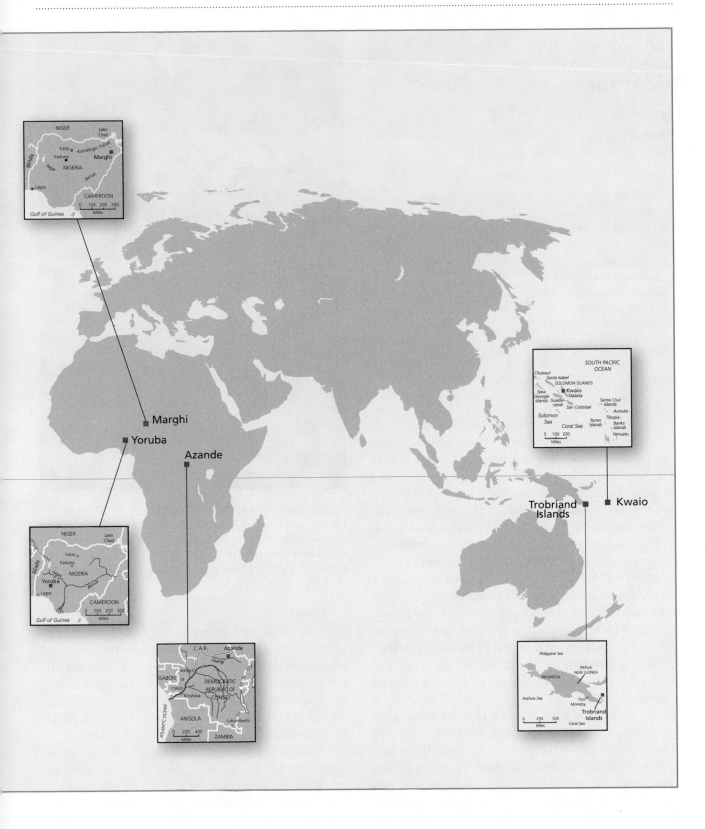

Figure 10.3 One of the great mythic heros of Javanese *wajang* is represented here in a beautifully painted flat leather shadow puppet. The color of the image, the angle of the head, the shape of the eye, the position of the fingers, and the style, color, and quantity of clothing all represent the inner state of the hero.

EthnoProfile 10.1

Marghi

Region: Western Africa

Nation: Nigeria

Population: 100,000 to 200,000 (1960s)

Environment: Mountains and plains

Livelihood: Farming, selling surplus in local markets

Political organization:
Traditionally, kingdoms; today, part of a modern nation-state

For more information:
Vaughan, James. 1970. Caste systems in the western Sudan. In *Social stratification in Africa*, edited by Arthur Tuden and Leonard Plotnikov, 59–92. New York: Free Press.

Aesthetic value judgments guide the artist's choice of form and material; they also guide the observers' evaluations. This implies that art involves more than just objects. V. N. Voloshinov argues that art is a creative "event of living communication" involving the work, the artist, and the artist's audience ([1926] 1987, 107). Artists create their works with an audience in mind, and audiences respond to these works as if the works were addressed to them. Sometimes their response is enthusiastic; sometimes it is highly critical. In addition, if aesthetic creation involves more than just the end product, such as a painting or a poem, attention needs to be paid to the process through which some product is made. James Vaughan (1973, 186) pointed out, for example, that the Marghi of northeastern Nigeria do not appreciate a folktale as a story per se but rather enjoy the *performance* of it (see EthnoProfile 10.1: Marghi).

To understand what Alland means by "transformation-representation," we can recall that the link between a symbol and what it represents is arbitrary. This means that symbols can be separated from the object or idea represented and appreciated for their own sake. They may also be used to represent a totally different meaning. Because transformation and representation depend on each other, Alland (1977, 35) suggests that they be referred to together (i.e., as transformation-representation). When a Javanese leather-puppet maker makes a puppet of the great mythic hero Arjuna, for example, he is representing the traditional form of the hero in his work, but he is also transforming a three-dimensional human form into

a two-dimensional flat puppet made of buffalo hide, in which the colors, style, inclination of the head, and adornment stand for the internal state of the hero at a specific moment (Figure 10.3). At the same time, he is carrying out this work more or less skillfully and is representing in his work the meanings that Arjuna carries for his Javanese audience (see EthnoProfile 9.2: Java).

Alland's definition of art attempts to capture something universal about human beings and cultural creativity. Similarly, anthropologist Shelly Errington observes that all human cultures have "'symbolic forms': artifacts, activities, or even aspects of the landscape that humans view as densely meaningful" (1998, 84). One dramatic example in the United States that demonstrates the power of art as a densely meaningful landscape is the Vietnam Veterans Memorial in Washington, D.C. (Figure 10.4). This work by architect Maya Lin not only has impressed art critics but also continues to have a profound

Figure 10.4 The Vietnam Veterans Memorial is a powerfully affecting work of art that speaks directly to central issues in the culture of the United States.

aesthetic and emotional impact on hundreds of thousands of people who visit it each year. The memorial continues to draw offerings by visitors, not just wreaths or flowers but also messages of all kinds remembering those memorialized and even communicating with them. Letters from friends and families, a hand-lettered sign from a fortieth high school reunion in a small Indiana town, tracings of names, intensely private grief, and respectful silence in its presence are all testimony to the success of this piece of art.

"But Is It *Art*?"

Many people—anthropologists included—have resisted the notion that art is only what a group of Western experts define as art. To highlight the ethnocentrism of Western art experts, they stressed that the division into categories of art and nonart is not universal. In many societies, there is no word that corresponds to "art," nor is there a category of art distinct from other human activities. On the other hand, convinced that all people were endowed with the same aesthetic capacities, anthropologists felt justified in speaking of art and of artists in non-Western societies. Their goal was to recognize a fully human capacity for art in all societies but to redefine art until it became broad enough to include on an equal basis aesthetic products and activities that Western art experts would qualify, at best, as "primitive," "ethnic," or "folk" art.

For example, some anthropologists focused on the evaluative standards that artists use for their own work and other work in the same form and how these may differ from the standards used by people who do not themselves perform such work. Anthony Forge (1967), for example, noted that Abelam carvers in New Guinea discuss carvings in a language that is more incisive than that of noncarvers. Forge and other anthropologists pointed out that artists in traditional non-Western societies created objects or engaged in activities that reinforced the central values of their culture. Thus, their work helped to maintain the social order, and the artists did not see themselves (nor were they understood to be) avant garde critics of society as they often are in modern Western societies. Forge (1967) tells us that Abelam artworks are statements about male violence and warfare, male nurturance, and the combination of the two. These statements about the nature of men and their culture are not made by other means of communication, such as speech. Moreover, these statements are essential to Abelam social structure.

Recent work in the anthropology of art, however, has prompted many anthropologists to rethink this position. They have turned their attention to the way certain kinds of material objects made by tribal peoples flow into a global art market, where they are transformed into "primitive" or "ethnic" art. Some anthropologists, like Shelly Errington, point out that even in the West most of the objects in fine arts museums today, no matter where they came from, were not intended by their makers to be "art." They were intended to be, for example, masks for ritual use, paintings for religious contemplation, reliquaries for holding the relics of saints, ancestor figures, furniture, jewelry boxes, architectural details, and so on. They are in fine arts museums today because at some point they were claimed to be art by someone with the authority to put them in the museum (Figure 10.5).

For these reasons, Errington distinguishes "art by intention" from "art by appropriation." Art by intention includes objects that were made to be art, such as Impressionist paintings. Art by appropriation, however, consists of all the other objects that "became art" because at a certain moment certain people decided that they belonged to the category of art. Because museums, art dealers, and art collectors are found everywhere in the world today, it is now the case that potentially any material object crafted by human hands can be appropriated by these institutions as "art."

To transform an object into art, Errington argues, it must have *exhibition value*—someone must be willing to display it. Objects that somehow fit into the Western definition of art will be selected for the art market as "art." Looking at the collection of objects that over the years have been defined as "art," Errington sees that the vast majority show certain elements to be embedded rather deeply in the Western definition of art: the objects are "portable (paintings, preferred to murals), durable (bronze preferred to basketry), useless for practical purposes in the secular West (ancestral effigies and Byzantine icons preferred to hoes and grain grinders), representational (human and animal figures preferred to, say, heavily decorated ritual bowls)" (1998, 116–17). In other words, for Errington, art requires that someone *intend* that the objects be art, but that someone does not have to be the object's creator.

It can be fruitful to talk about art as a kind of play. Like play, art presents its creators and participants with alternative realities, a separation of means from ends, and the possibility of commenting on and transforming the everyday world. In today's global art market, however, restrictions of an entirely different order also apply. Errington observes that the people who make "primitive art" are no longer "tribal" but have become

> modern-day peasants or a new type of proletariat. . . . They live in rain forests and deserts and other such formerly out-of-the-way places on the peripheries . . . within national and increasingly global systems of buying and selling, of using natural and human resources, and of marketing images and notions about products. Some lucky few of them make high ethnic art, and sell

Figure 10.5 Non-Western sculpture is transformed into art when it is displayed like Western art in a museum and viewed by a public that has the opportunity to look at it intensively (in this case, by French president Jacques Chirac).

In Their Own Words

Tango

Anthropologist Julie Taylor describes the traditional cultural understandings that inform the contexts in which the Argentine tanguero, or tango-man, dances the tango.

Traditionally, Argentines will not dance to a tango that is sung. If they danced they could not attend properly to the music and lyrics, or hear their own experience and identity revealed in the singer's and musicians' rendering of quintessential Argentine emotions. The singer of the tango shares his personal encounter with experiences common to them all. He does not need bold pronouncement or flamboyant gesture. His audience knows what he means and his feelings are familiar ones. They listen for the nuances—emotional and philosophical subtleties that will tell them something new about their guarded interior worlds.

When they dance to tangos, Argentines contemplate themes akin to those of tango lyrics, stimulating emotions that, despite an apparently contradictory choreography, are the same as those behind the songs. The choreography also reflects the world of the lyrics, but indirectly. The dance portrays an encounter between the powerful and completely dominant male and the passive, docile, completely submissive female. The passive woman and the rigidly controlled but physically aggressive man contrast poignantly with the roles of the sexes depicted in the tango lyrics. This contrast between two statements of relations between the sexes aptly mirrors the insecurities of life and identity.

An Argentine philosophy of bitterness, resentment, and pessimism has the same goal as a danced statement of machismo, confidence, and sexual optimism. The philosopher elaborates his schemes to demonstrate that he is a man of the world—that he is neither stupid nor naive. In the dance, the dancer acts as though he has none of the fears he cannot show—again proving that he is not gil. When an Argentine talks of the way he feels when dancing a tango, he describes an experience of total aggressive dominance over the girl, the situation, the world—an experience in which he vents his resentment and expresses his bitterness against a destiny that denied him this dominance. Beyond this, it gives him a moment behind the protection of this facade to ponder the history and the land that have formed him, the hopes he has treasured and lost. Sábato echoes widespread feeling in Argentina when he says "Only a gringo would make a clown of himself by taking advantage of a tango for a chat or amusement."

While thus dancing a statement of invulnerability, the somber tanguero sees himself, because of his sensitivity, his great capacity to love, and his fidelity to the true ideals of his childhood years, as basically vulnerable. As he protects himself with a facade of steps that demonstrate perfect control, he contemplates his absolute lack of control in the face of history and destiny. The nature of the world has doomed him to disillusionment, to a solitary existence in the face of the impossibility of perfect love and the intimacy this implies. If by chance the girl with whom he dances feels the same sadness, remembering similar disillusion, the partners do not dance sharing the sentiment. They dance together to relive their disillusion alone. In a Buenos Aires dance hall, a young man turned to me from the fiancee he had just relinquished to her chaperoning mother and explained, "In the tango, together with the girl—and it does not matter who she is—a man remembers the bitter moments of his life, and he, she, and all who are dancing contemplate a universal emotion. I do not like the woman to talk to me while I dance tango. And if she speaks I do not answer. Only when she says to me, 'Omar, I am speaking,' I answer, 'And I, I am dancing.'"

Source: Taylor 1987, 484–85.

it for good prices, and obtain a good portion of the proceeds. Others make objects classed as tourist or folk art, usually for much less money, and often through a middleperson. (1998, 268)

Others fulfill orders from elsewhere, "producing either masses of 'folk art' or expensive handmade items designed by people in touch with world taste and world markets" (269). Errington points out the bitter irony that international demand for "exotic" objects is growing at the very moment when the makers of these objects are severely threatened by international economic policies and resource-extraction projects that impoverish them and undermine the ways of life that give the objects they make their "exotic" allure. It should also be noted that what counts as fashionable decoration this year—"world taste"—may be out of fashion next year, leaving the producers with very little to fall back on.

"She's Fake": Art and Authenticity

Michelle Bigenho is an anthropologist and violinist whose multisited ethnography, mentioned in Module 3, examines music performance in Bolivia, in part through her experiences performing with Música de Maestros (Figure 10.6). This ensemble performs the works of master Bolivian composers of the past and attempts to re-create accurate performances of contemporary original music that they have studied in the countryside (Bigenho 2002, 4). The ensemble included both classically trained and traditionally trained musicians, and three were foreigners: a Japanese who played the Andean flute, a Cuban who played violin, and Bigenho, from the United States, who also played violin. Along with a local dance ensemble, the musicians were invited to represent Bolivia in a folklore festival in France. As the bands were lining up, a member of the Belgian delegation walked over to Bigenho and announced, in French, "She's fake." The Belgian woman then "pointed to one of the Bolivian dancers dressed in her dancing costume with her long fake braids worked into her short brown hair. As she pointed, she said, 'She's real'" (88).

In this way, Bigenho raises the issue of the connection between "authenticity" and so-called folk art. How do the images that people in dominant nations have of "folk" or indigenous peoples affect the production and circulation of indigenous art? Can a Bolivian band include musicians from Japan, Cuba, and the United States and still be Bolivian? And who gets to decide what is authentic? Bigenho discusses a kind of authenticity that she calls "unique authenticity," which refers to the individual artist's new, innovative, and personal production,

such as the original compositions of creative musicians. Unique authenticity is "the founding myth of modern concepts of authorship and copyright" (Bigenho 2002, 20). It concerns who owns cultural products and raises the issue of whether it is possible to talk about collective creation and ownership of the music of a community, a people, an ethnic group.

Bigenho came face to face with this issue when she compiled a cassette of music from one of the villages in which she worked. While the villagers recognized that the music they played was composed by individuals, they felt strongly that ownership of the music was collective. In doing so, they moved from uniquely authentic individual compositions—intellectual property—to collective ownership of a "culturally authentic representation"—cultural property (Bigenho 2002, 217). She discussed with the villagers how to register the copyright on the cassette. When Bigenho went to La Paz to register the copyright, however, she found that it was impossible to register the cassette under collective authorship or ownership. Ironically, *she* as the compiler could register the work but the people who created the work could not, unless they were willing to be recognized as individuals. According to Bolivian law, the music on the cassette was legally folklore, "the set of literary and artistic works created in national territory by unknown authors or by authors who do not identify themselves and are presumed to be nationals of the country, or of its ethnic communities, and that are transmitted from generation to generation, constituting one of the fundamental elements of traditional cultural patrimony of the nation" (221). As a result, the music was part of the "national patrimony" and belonged to the nation-

Figure 10.6 Música de Maestros in costume performing in a folklore festival in France.

state. Given the context of Bolivian cultural and ethnic politics, Bigenho reports that the villagers decided to try to gain visibility and connections as a collective indigenous entity, which they believed would provide them with possible economic advantages; whether this belief was accurate remains to be seen. But similar struggles over the relationship between art and authenticity can be found all over the world.

What Is Myth?

We have suggested that play lies at the heart of human creativity. However, because the openness of play seems random, and thus just as likely to undermine the social order as to enhance it, societies tend to surround play with cultural rules, channeling it in directions that appear less destructive. Rules designed to discipline artistic expression are one result of this channeling process. As we have seen, artists in various media are permitted a wide range of expression as long as they adhere to rules governing the form that expression takes. Societies differ in how loose or strict the rules of artistic form may be. Artists who challenge the rules, however, are often viewed negatively by those in power, who believe they have the right to restrict artistic expressions that question social, religious, or sexual precepts that ought not to be questioned.

In fact, all societies depend on the willingness of their members to not question certain assumptions about the way the world works. Because the regularity and predictability of social life might collapse altogether if people were free to imagine and act upon their own understandings of the world, most societies find ways to restrict the available options through the use of myth. As we saw in Module 1, many people take the word *myth* to mean something that is false. But for anthropologists, **myths** are stories that recount how various aspects of the world came to be the way they are. The power of myths comes from their ability to make life meaningful for those who accept them. The truth of myths seems self-evident because they do such a good job of integrating personal experiences with a wider set of assumptions about how the world works. As stories that involve a teller and an audience, myths are products of high verbal art (and increasingly of cinematic art). Frequently, the official myth-tellers are the ruling groups in society: the elders, the political leaders, the religious specialists. They may also be considered master storytellers. The content of myths usually concerns past events (usually at the beginning of time) or future events (usually at the end of time). Myths are socially important because, if

they are taken literally, they tell people where they have come from and where they are going and, thus, how they should live right now (Figure 10.7).

Societies differ in the degree to which they permit speculation about key myths. In complex Western societies such as that of the United States, many different groups, each with its own mythic tradition, often live side by side. Ironically, Americans' rights to do so without state interference are guaranteed in mythic statements from documents crafted at the time of this country's founding. Consider the "self-evident" truths proclaimed in the U.S. Declaration of Independence: "that all men are created equal, that they are endowed by their Creator with certain inalienable rights, that among these rights are life, liberty, and the pursuit of happiness." Despite the imperfect realization of these rights over the centuries, Americans still appeal to the "self-evident truths" enshrined in the Declaration of Independence in ongoing struggles to establish the equality of all citizens under the law. That is, U.S. citizens are striving to bring their lived reality in line with the Declaration's mythic proclamation, the truth of which remains unquestioned.

Myths and related beliefs that are taken to be self-evident truths are sometimes codified in an explicit manner. When this codification is extreme and deviation from the code is treated harshly, we sometimes speak of **orthodoxy** (or "correct doctrine"). Societies differ in the degree to which they require members to adhere to orthodox interpretations of key myths. But even societies that place little emphasis on orthodoxy are likely to exert some control over the interpretation of key myths because myths have implications for action. They may justify past action, explain present action, or generate future action. To be persuasive, myths must offer plausible explanations for our experience of human nature, human society, and human history.

The success of Western science has led many members of Western societies to dismiss nonscientific myths as flawed attempts at science or history. Only recently have some scientists come to recognize the similarities between scientific and nonscientific storytelling about such events as the origin of life on earth. Scientific stories about origins, *origin myths*, must be taken to the natural world to be matched against material evidence;

---

myths Stories that recount how various aspects of the world came to be the way they are. The power of myths comes from their ability to make life meaningful for those who accept them. The truth of myths seems self-evident because they effectively integrate personal experiences with a wider set of assumptions about how the world works.

orthodoxy "Correct doctrine"; the prohibition of deviation from approved mythic texts.

Figure 10.7   A vase painting illustrating part of the Popul Vuh, the Mayan creation story.

the success of this match determines whether they are accepted or rejected. By contrast, nonscientific origin myths get their vitality from how well they match up with the social world.

How Does Myth Reflect— and Shape—Society?

Early in the twentieth century, anthropologist Bronislaw Malinowski introduced a new approach to myth. He believed that to understand myths we must understand the social context in which they are embedded. Malinowski argued that myths serve as "charters" or "justifications" for present-day social arrangements. In other words, a myth operates much like the Declaration of Independence. That is, the myth contains some "self-evident" truth that explains why society is as it is and why it cannot be changed. If the social arrangements justified by the myth are challenged, the myth can be used as a weapon against the challengers.

Malinowski's famous example is of the origin myths of the Trobriand Islanders ([1926] 1948; see Ethno-Profile 10.2: Trobriand Islanders). Members of every significant kinship grouping knew, marked, and retold the history of the place from which their group's ancestress and her brother had emerged from the depths of the earth. These origin myths were set in the time before history began. Each ancestress-and-brother pair brought a distinct set of characteristics that included special objects and knowledge, as well as various skills, crafts, spells, and the like. On reaching the surface, the pair took possession of the land. That is why, Malinowski was told, the people on a given piece of land had rights to it. It is also why they possessed a particular set of spells, skills, and crafts. Because the original sacred beings were a woman and her brother, the origin myth could also be used to endorse present-day membership in a Trobriand clan, which depends on a person's ability to trace kinship links through women to that clan's original ancestress. A brother and a sister represent the prototypical members of a clan because they are both descended from the ancestress through female links. Should anyone question the wisdom of organizing society in this way, the myth could be cited as proof that this is indeed the correct way to live.

In Trobriand society, Malinowski found, clans were ranked relative to one another in terms of prestige. To account for this ranking, Trobrianders referred to another myth. In the Trobriand myth that explains rank, one clan's ancestor, the dog, emerged from the earth before another clan's ancestor, the pig, thus justifying ranking the dog clan highest in prestige. To believe in this myth, Malinowski asserted, is to accept a transcendent justification for the ranking of clans. Malinowski made it clear, however, that if social arrangements change, the myth changes too—in order to justify the new arrangements. At some point, the dog clan was replaced in prominence by the pig clan. This social change resulted in a change in the mythic narrative. The dog was said to have eaten food that was taboo. In so doing, the dog gave up its claim to higher rank. Thus, to understand a myth and its transformations, one must understand the social organization of the society that makes use of it.

Do Myths Help Us Think?

Beginning in the mid-1950s, a series of books and articles by the French anthropologist Claude Lévi-Strauss (1967) transformed the study of myth. Lévi-Strauss argues that myths have meaningful structures that are worth studying in their own right, quite apart from the uses to which the myths may be put. He suggested that myths should

EthnoProfile 10.2

Trobriand Islanders

Region: Oceania

Nation: Papua New Guinea

Population: 8,500 (1970s)

Environment: Tropical island

Livelihood: Yam growing

Political organization:
Traditionally, chiefs and others of rank; today, part of a modern nation-state

For more information:
Weiner, Annette. 1988. *The Trobrianders of Papua New Guinea.* New York: Holt, Rinehart and Winston.

be interpreted the way we interpret musical scores. In a piece of music, the meaning emerges not just from the melody but also from the harmony. In other words, the structure of the piece of music, the way in which each line of the music contributes to the overall sound and is related to other lines, carries the meaning.

For Lévi-Strauss, myths are tools for overcoming logical contradictions that cannot otherwise be overcome. They are put together in an attempt to deal with the oppositions of particular concern to a particular society at a particular moment in time. Using a linguistic metaphor, Lévi-Strauss argues that myths are composed of smaller units—phrases, sentences, words, relationships—that are arranged in ways that give both a linear, narrative (or "melodic") coherence and a multilevel, structural (or "harmonic") coherence. These arrangements represent and comment on aspects of social life that are thought to oppose each other. Examples include the opposition of men to women; opposing rules of residence after marriage (living with the groom's father or the bride's mother); the opposition of the natural world to the cultural world, of life to death, of spirit to body, of high to low, and so on.

The complex syntax of myth works to relate those opposed pairs to one another in an attempt to overcome their contradictions. However, these contradictions can never be overcome; for example, the opposition of death to life is incapable of any earthly resolution. But myth can transform an insoluble problem into a more accessible, concrete form. Mythic narrative can then provide the concrete problem with a solution. For example, a

culture hero may bridge the opposition between death and life by traveling from the land of the living to the land of the dead and back. Alternatively, a myth might propose that the beings who transcend death are so horrific that death is clearly preferable to eternal life. Perhaps a myth describes the journey of a bird that travels from the earth, the home of the living, to the sky, the home of the dead. This is similar to Christian thought, where the death and resurrection of Jesus may be understood to resolve the opposition between death and life by transcending death.

From this point of view, myths do not just talk about the world as it is but also describe the world as it might be. To paraphrase Lévi-Strauss, myths are good to think with; mythic thinking can propose other ways to live our lives. Lévi-Strauss insists, however, that the alternatives that myths propose are ordinarily rejected as impossible. Thus, even though myths allow for play with self-evident truths, this play remains under strict control.

Is Lévi-Strauss correct? There has been a great deal of debate on this issue since the publication in 1955 of his article "The Structural Study of Myth" (see Lévi-Strauss 1967). But even those who are most critical of his analyses of particular myths agree that mythic structures are meaningful because they display the ability of human beings to play with possibilities as they attempt to deal with basic contradictions at the heart of human experience.

For Malinowski, Lévi-Strauss, and their followers, those who believe in myths are not conscious of how their myths are structured or of the functions their myths perform for them. More recent anthropological thinking takes a more reflexive approach. This research recognizes that ordinary members of a society often *are* aware of how their myths structure meaning, allowing them to manipulate the way myths are told or interpreted in order to make an effect, to prove a point, or to buttress a particular perspective on human nature, society, or history.

What Is Ritual?

Play allows unlimited consideration of alternative perspectives on reality. Art permits consideration of alternative perspectives, but certain limitations restricting the form and content are imposed. Myth aims to narrow radically the possible perspectives and often promotes a single, orthodox perspective presumed to be valid for everyone. It thus offers a kind of intellectual indoctrination. But because societies aim to shape action as well as thought to orient all human faculties in the approved direction, art, myth, and ritual are often closely associated with one another. In this section, we will look at ritual as a form of action in a variety of societies.

How Can Ritual Be Defined?

For many people in Western societies, rituals are presumed to be religious—for example, weddings, Jewish bar mitzvahs, Hmong sacrifices to the ancestors, or the Catholic Mass. For anthropologists, however, rituals also include practices such as scientific experiments, college graduation ceremonies, procedures in a court of law, and children's birthday parties.

In order to capture this range of activities, our definition of **ritual** has four parts. First, ritual is a repetitive social practice composed of a sequence of symbolic activities in the form of dance, song, speech, gestures, the manipulation of certain objects, and so forth. Second, it is set off from the social routines of everyday life. Third, rituals in any culture adhere to a characteristic, culturally defined schema. This means that members of a culture can tell that a certain sequence of activities is a ritual even if they have never seen that particular ritual before. Fourth, ritual action is closely connected to a specific set of ideas that are often encoded in myth. These ideas might concern, for example, the relationship of human beings to the spirit world, how human beings ought to interact with one another, or the nature of evil. The purpose for which a ritual is performed guides how these ideas are selected and symbolically enacted. What gives rituals their power is that the people who perform them assert that the authorization for the ritual comes from outside themselves—from the state, society, a divine being, god, the ancestors, or "tradition." They have not made up the ritual themselves; rather, it connects them to a source of power that they do not control but that controls them.

How Is Ritual Expressed in Action?

A ritual has a particular sequential ordering of acts, utterance, and events: that is, ritual has a *text*. Because ritual is action, however, we must pay attention to the way the ritual text is performed. The performance of a ritual

---

ritual A repetitive social practice composed of a sequence of symbolic activities in the form of dance, song, speech, gestures, or the manipulation of objects; adhering to a culturally defined ritual schema; and closely connected to a specific set of ideas that are often encoded in myth.

rite of passage A ritual that serves to mark the movement and transformation of an individual from one social position to another.

---

cannot be separated from its text; text and performance shape each other. Through ritual performance, the ideas of a culture become concrete, take on a form, and, as Bruce Kapferer (1983) puts it, give direction to the gaze of participants. At the same time, ritual performers are not robots but active individuals whose choices are guided by, but not rigidly dictated by, previous ritual texts; ritual performance can serve as a commentary on the text and even transform it. For example, Jewish synagogue ritual following the reading from the Torah (the five books of Moses, the Hebrew Bible) includes lifting the Torah scroll, showing it to the congregation, and then closing it and covering it. In some synagogues, a man and a woman, often a couple, are called from the congregation to lift and cover the Torah: the man lifts it and, after he seats himself, the woman rolls the scroll closed, places the tie around it, and covers it with the mantle that protects it. One of the authors once observed a performance of this ritual in which the woman lifted the Torah and the man wrapped it; officially, the ritual text was carried out, but the performance became a commentary on the text—on the role of women in Judaism, on the Torah as an appropriate subject of attention for women as well as for men, on the roles of men and women overall, and so on. The performance was noteworthy—indeed, many of the regular members of the congregation seemed quite surprised—precisely because it violated people's expectations and in so doing directed people's attention toward the role of men and women in religious ritual at the end of the twentieth century as well as toward the Torah as the central symbol of the Jewish people.

What Are Rites of Passage?

Graduating from college, getting married, joining the military, and other "life cycle" rituals share certain important features, most notably that people begin the ritual as one kind of person (e.g., student, single, recruit), and by the time the ritual is over, they have been transformed into a different kind of person (e.g., graduate, spouse, soldier). These rituals are called **rites of passage**. At the beginning of the twentieth century, the Belgian anthropologist Arnold Van Gennep noted that certain kinds of rituals around the world had similar structures. These were rituals associated with the movement (or passage) of people from one position in the social structure to another. They took place at births, initiations, confirmations, weddings, funerals, and the like (Figure 10.8).

Van Gennep (1960) found that all these rituals began with a period of *separation* from the old position and

In Their Own Words

Video in the Villages

Patricia Aufderheide describes how indigenous peoples of the Amazonian rain forest in Brazil have been able to master the video camera and use it for their own purposes.

The social role and impact of video is particularly intriguing among people who are new to mass-communications technologies, such as lowlands Amazonian Indians. One anthropologist has argued persuasively that a naive disdain for commercial media infuses much well-meaning concern over the potential dangers of introducing mass media and that "indigenous media offers a possible means—social, cultural, and political—for reproducing and transforming cultural identity among people who have experienced massive political, geographic, and economic disruption." . . . In two groups of Brazilian Indians, the Nambikwara and the Kayapo, this premise has been tested.

The Nambikwara became involved with video through Video in the Villages, run by Vincent Carelli at the Centro de Trabalho Indigenista in São Paulo. This project is one example of a trend to put media in the hands of people who have long been the subjects of ethnographic film and video. . . . While some anthropologists see this resort as a "solution" to the issue of ethnographic authority, others have focused on it as part of a struggle for indigenous rights and political autonomy. . . . Many of the groups Carelli has worked with have seized on video for its ability to extensively document lengthy rituals that mark the group's cultural uniqueness rather than produce a finished product. . . .

Carelli coproduced a project with a Nambikwara leader, documenting a cultural ritual. After taping, the Nambikwara viewed the ritual and offered criticisms, finding it tainted with modernisms. They then repeated the ritual in traditional regalia and conducted, for the first time in a generation, a male initiation ceremony—taping it all. (This experience is recounted in a short tape, Girls' Puberty Ritual, produced by Carelli with a Nambikwara leader for outsiders.) Using video reinforced an emerging concept of "traditional" in contrast to Brazilian culture—a concept that had not, apparently, been part of the Nambikwara's repertoire before contact but that had practical political utility.

The Kayapo are among the best-known Brazilian Indians internationally, partly because of their video work, promoted as a tool of cultural identification by the anthropologist who works most closely with them. Like other tribes such as the Xavante who had extensive contact with Brazilian authorities and media, the Kayapo early seized on modern media technologies. . . . Besides intimidating authorities with the evidence of recording equipment . . . , the Kayapo quickly grasped the symbolic expectations of Brazilian mass media for Indians. They cannily played on the contrast between their feathers and body paint and their recording devices to get coverage. Even staging public events for the purpose of attracting television crews, they were able to insert, although not ultimately control, their message on Brazilian news by exploiting that contrast. . . . Using these techniques, Kayapo leaders became international symbols of the ironies of the postmodern age and not incidentally also the subjects of international agitation and fundraising that benefited Kayapo over other indigenous groups and some Kayapo over others.

Kayapo have also used video to document internal cultural ceremonies in meticulous detail; to communicate internally between villages; to develop an archive; and to produce clips and short documentaries intended for wide audiences. Their video work, asserts anthropologist Terence Turner, has not merely preserved traditional customs but in fact transformed their understanding of those customs as customs and their culture as a culture. Turner also found that video equipment, expertise, and products often fed into existing factional divisions. Particular Kayapo leaders used the equipment in their own interests, sometimes as a tool to subdue their enemies, sometimes as evidence of personal power. . . .

Source: Aufderheide 1993, 587–89.

from normal time. During this period, the ritual passenger leaves behind the symbols and practices of his or her previous position. For example, military recruits leave their families behind and are moved to a new place. They are forced to leave behind the clothing, activities, and even the hairstyle that marked who they were in civilian life.

The second stage in rites of passage involves a period of *transition*, in which the ritual passenger is neither in the old life nor yet in the new one. This period is marked by rolelessness, ambiguity, and perceived danger. Often, the person involved is subjected to ordeal by those who have already passed through. In the military service, this

Figure 10.8 Rites of passage are rituals that enable people to move from one position in the social structure to another. Here, in June 2004, an Apache girl, accompanied by her godmother and a helper, moves into adulthood through the Sunrise Dance.

is the period of basic training, in which recruits (not yet soldiers but no longer civilians) are forced to dress and act alike. They are subjected to a grinding-down process, after which they are rebuilt into something new.

During the final stage—*reaggregation*—the ritual passenger is reintroduced into society in his or her new position. In the military, this involves graduation from basic training and a visit home but this time as a member of the armed forces, in uniform and on leave—in other words, as a new person. Other familiar rites of passage in youth culture in the United States include high school graduation and the informal yet significant ceremonies associated with the twenty-first birthday, both of which are understood as movements from one kind of person to another.

The work of Victor Turner greatly increased our understanding of rites of passage. Turner concentrated on the period of transition, which he saw as important both for the rite of passage and for social life in general. Van Gennep (1960) referred to this part of a rite of passage as the "liminal period," from the Latin *limen* ("threshold"). During this period, the individual is on the threshold, betwixt and between, neither here nor there, neither in nor out. Turner notes that the

symbolism accompanying the rite of passage often expresses this ambiguous state. **Liminality**, he tells us, "is frequently likened to death, to being in the womb, to invisibility, to darkness, to bisexuality, to the wilderness, and to an eclipse of the sun or moon" (1969, 95). People in the liminal state tend to develop an intense comradeship with each other in which their nonliminal distinctions disappear or become irrelevant. Turner calls this kind of social relationship communitas, which is best understood as an unstructured or minimally structured community of equal individuals.

Turner contends that all societies need some kind of **communitas** as much as they need structure. Communitas gives "recognition to an essential and generic human bond, without which there could be no society" (1969, 97). That bond is the common humanity that underlies all culture and society. However, periods of communitas (often in ritual context) are brief. Communitas is dangerous, not just because it threatens structure but because it threatens survival itself. During the time of communitas, the things that structure ensures—production of food and physical and social reproduction of the society—cannot be provided. But someone always has to take out the garbage and clean up after the party. Thus, communitas gives way again to structure, which in turn generates a need for a new release of communitas. The feeling of communitas can also be attained by means of play and art. Indeed, it may well be that for people in contemporary nation-states the experience of communitas comes through the climactic winning moments of a sports team, attendance at large-scale rock concerts, or participation in

liminality The ambiguous transitional state in a rite of passage in which the person or persons undergoing the ritual are outside their ordinary social positions.

communitas An unstructured or minimally structured community of equal individuals found frequently in rites of passage.

mass public events like Carnival in Rio de Janeiro, the Greenwich Village Halloween parade, or Mardi Gras in New Orleans.

How Are Play and Ritual Complementary?

How does the logic of ritual differ from the logic of play? Play and ritual are complementary forms of metacommunication (Handelman 1977). The movement from nonplay to play is based on the premise of metaphor ("Let's make believe"); the movement to ritual is based on the premise of literalness ("Let's believe"). From the perspective of the everyday social order, the result of these contrasting premises is the "inauthenticity" of play and the "truth" of ritual.

Because of the connection of ritual with self-evident truth, the metacommunication of the ritual frame ("This is ritual") is associated with an additional metacommunication: "All messages within this frame are true." It is ritual that asserts *what should be* to play's *what can be*. The ritual frame is more rigid than the play frame. Consequently, ritual is the most stable liminal domain, whereas play is the most flexible. Players can move with relative ease into and out of play, but such is not the case with ritual.

Finally, play usually has little effect on the social order of ordinary life. This permits play a wide range of commentary on the social order. Ritual is different: its role is explicitly to maintain the status quo, including the prescribed ritual transformations. Societies differ in the extent to which ritual behavior alternates with everyday, nonritual behavior. When nearly every act of everyday life is ritualized and other forms of behavior are strongly discouraged, we sometimes speak of **orthopraxy** ("correct practice"). Traditionally observant Jews and Muslims, for example, lead a highly ritualized daily life, attempting from the moment they awaken until the moment they fall asleep to carry out even the humblest of activities in a manner that is ritually correct. In their view, ritual correctness is the result of God's law, and it is their duty and joy to conform their every action to God's will.

Margaret Drewal argues that, at least among the Yoruba, play and ritual overlap (see EthnoProfile 10.3: Yoruba). Yoruba rituals combine spectacle, festival, play, sacrifice, and so on and integrate diverse media—music, dance, poetry, theater, sculpture (1992, 198). They are events that require improvisatory, spontaneous individual moves; as a result, the mundane order is not only inverted and reversed but may also be subverted through power play and gender play. For example, gender roles are rigidly structured in Yoruba

EthnoProfile 10.3

Yoruba

Region: Western Africa

Nation: Nigeria

Population: 40,000,000

Environment: Coastal and forest

Livelihood: Farming, commerce, modern professions

Political organization: Traditionally, kingdoms; today, part of a modern nation-state

For more information: Bascom, William. 1969. *The Yoruba of southwestern Nigeria.* New York: Holt, Rinehart and Winston.

society. Yoruba rituals, however, allow some cross-dressing by both men and women, providing institutionalized opportunities for men and women to cross gender boundaries and to express the traits that the Yoruba consider to be characteristic of the opposite sex, sometimes as parody but sometimes seriously and respectfully (190).

How Are Worldview and Symbolic Practice Related?

Our previous discussions of language, play, art, myth, and ritual provided an overview of some of the ways human beings use culture to construct rich understandings of everyday experiences. In this section, we build on those insights and describe how human beings use cultural creativity to make sense of the wider world on a more comprehensive scale as they construct encompassing pictures of reality called **worldviews**.

---

orthopraxy "Correct practice"; the prohibition of deviation from approved forms of ritual behavior.

worldviews Encompassing pictures of reality created by the members of societies.

What Is Religion?

For many readers of this text, the most familiar form of worldview is probably religion. The anthropological concept of religion, like many analytic terms, began as a description of a certain domain of Western culture. As a result, it has been very difficult for anthropologists to settle on a definition of religion that is applicable in all human societies. Scholars have often argued that a religion differs from other kinds of worldviews because it assumes the existence of a supernatural domain: an invisible world populated by one or more beings who are more powerful than human beings and able to influence events in the "natural" human world. The problem with this definition is that the distinction between "natural" and "supernatural" was originally made by nonreligious Western observers in order to distinguish the real "natural" world from what they took to be the imaginary "supernatural" world. Many anthropologists who study different religious traditions believe that it is less distorting to begin with their informants' statements about what exists and what does not. In this way, they are in a better position to understand the range of forces, visible and invisible, that religious devotees perceive as being active in their world.

For these reasons, John Bowen proposes that anthropologists approach religion in a way that begins broadly but that allows for increasing specificity as we learn more about the details of particular religious traditions. Bowen defines **religion** as "ideas and practices that postulate reality beyond that which is immediately available to the senses" (2008, 4). In individual societies, this may take the shape of beliefs in spirits and gods, in impersonal forces that affect the world, in the correct practice of ritual, or in the awareness that their ancestors continue to be active in the world of the living. It is important to note that this definition encompasses both practices and ideas; religions involve actions as well as beliefs (Figure 10.9). Indeed, anthropologist A. F. C. Wallace (1966) proposed a set of "minimal categories of religious behavior" that describe many of the practices usually associated with religions. Several of the most important are as follows:

1. *Prayer.* Where there are personified cosmic forces, there is a customary way of addressing them, usually by speaking or chanting out loud. Often, people pray in public, at a sacred location, and with special apparatus: incense, smoke, objects (e.g., rosary beads or a prayer wheel), and so on (Figure 10.9a).

2. *Physiological exercise.* Many religious systems have methods for physically manipulating psychological states to induce an ecstatic spiritual state. Wallace suggests four major kinds of manipulation: (1) drugs; (2) sensory deprivation; (3) mortification of the flesh by pain, sleeplessness, and fatigue; and (4) deprivation of food, water, or air. In many societies, the experience of ecstasy, euphoria, dissociation, or hallucination seems to be a goal of religious effort (Figure 10.9b).

3. *Exhortation.* In all religious systems, certain people are believed to have closer relationships with the invisible powers than others, and they are expected to use those relationships in the spiritual interests of others. They give orders, they heal, they threaten, they comfort, and they interpret.

4. *Mana.* Mana refers to an impersonal superhuman power that is sometimes believed to be transferable from an object that contains it to one that does not. The laying on of hands, in which the power of a healer enters the body of a sick person to remove or destroy an illness, is an example of the transmission of power. In Guider, Cameroon, some people believe that the ink used to copy passages from the Qur'an has power (See Ethno-Profile 14.3: Guider). Washing the ink off the board on which the words are written and drinking the ink transfers the power of the words into the body of the drinker. All these examples illustrate the principle that sacred things are sometimes to be touched so that their power may be transferred to human beings.

5. *Taboo.* Objects or people that may not be touched are taboo. Some people believe that the cosmic power in such objects or people may "drain away" if touched or may injure the toucher. Many religious systems have taboo objects. Traditionally, Catholics were not to touch the Host during communion. Jews may not touch the handwritten text of the biblical scrolls. In ancient Polynesia, commoners could not touch the chief's body; even an accidental touch resulted in the death of the commoner. Food may also be taboo; many societies have elaborate rules concerning the foods that may or may not be eaten at different times or by different kinds of people.

6. *Feasts.* Eating and drinking in a religious context is very common. The Holy Communion of

---

religion "Ideas and practices that postulate reality beyond that which is immediately available to the senses" (Bowen 2008).

Figure 10.9 (*a*) The joint pilgrimage by Hindu worshipers to the Ganges River illustrates the social nature of religion. (*b*) This participant in the Hindu Thaipusam ritual pilgrimage in Singapore in 2004 has agreed to carry a kavadi for religious benefit. Kavadi can weigh 60 pounds (27 kg).

Catholics and Protestants is a meal set apart by its religious context. The Passover Seder for Jews is another religious feast. For the Huichol of Mexico, the consumption of peyote is set apart from other meals by its religious context (see Ethno-Profile 10.4: Huichol). Even everyday meals may be seen to have a religious quality if they begin or end with prayer.

7. *Sacrifice.* Giving something of value to the invisible forces or their agents is a feature of many religious systems. This may be an offering of money, goods, or services. It may also be the immolation of animals or, very rarely, human beings. Sacrifices may be made in thanks to the cosmic forces, in hopes of influencing them to act in a certain way, or simply to gain general religious merit.

How Do People Communicate in Religion?

Those who are committed to religious worldviews are convinced of the existence and active involvement in their lives of beings or forces that are ordinarily invisible. Some of the most highly valued religious practices, such as religious ecstasy or trance, produce outer symptoms that may be perceived by others; but their most powerful effects can be experienced only by the individual who undergoes them personally. What if you wanted to know what it felt like to experience religious ecstasy? What if you were someone who had had such

---

EthnoProfile 10.4

Huichol

Region: Latin America

Nation: Mexico

Population: 20,000

Environment: Mountainous terrain

Livelihood: Corn farming, deer hunting in recent past

Political organization:
Traditionally, no formal organization, some men with influence; today, part of a modern nation-state

For more information:
Myerhoff, Barbara. 1974. *Peyote hunt.* Ithaca, NY: Cornell University Press.

---

an experience and wanted to tell others about it? What if you were convinced that the supreme power in the universe had revealed itself to you and you wanted to share this revelation with others? How would you proceed?

You might well begin by searching for metaphors based on experiences already well known to your audience. Thus, one Hindu Tamil worshiper in Kuala Lumpur who successfully went into trance during the festival of Thaipusam described his experience as "floating in the air, followed by the wind" (*Floating in the Air* 1973). And the Hebrew poet who wrote the twenty-third psalm tried to express his experience of the power and love of his god by comparing God to his shepherd and himself to a sheep. Many contemporary theologians argue that the language human beings use to talk about God is inevitably full of everyday metaphors (e.g., see Gillman 1992). Even those who claim to have had personal experience of the reality of God, of ancestral spirits, or of witchcraft will probably still find themselves forced to resort to poetic, metaphorical language if they want to explain that experience to other people—and perhaps even to themselves.

How Are Religion and Social Organization Related?

Anthropological research suggests that members of many religious traditions base their understanding of the structure of the universe on the structure of the society in which they live. One consequence of this mode of understanding is that forces in the universe are personalized. Thus, people seeking to influence those forces must handle them as they would handle powerful human beings. Communication is perhaps the central feature of how we deal with human beings: when we address each other, we expect a response. The same is true when we address personalized cosmic forces.

Maintaining contact with invisible cosmic powers is a tremendously complex undertaking. It is not surprising, therefore, that some societies have developed complex social practices to ensure that it is done properly. In other words, religion becomes institutionalized. Social positions are created for specialists who supervise or embody correct religious practice.

Anthropologists have identified two broad categories of religious specialists: shamans and priests. A **shaman** is a part-time religious practitioner who is believed to have the power to contact invisible powers directly on behalf of individuals or groups. Shamans are often thought to be able to travel to the cosmic realm to communicate with the beings or forces that dwell there. They often plead with those beings or forces to act in favor of their people and may return with messages for them. The Ju/'hoansi, for example, recognize that some people are able to develop an internal power that enables them to travel to the world of the spirits—to enter "half death"—in order to cure those who are sick (see EthnoProfile 11.5: Ju/'hoansi).

In many societies, the training that a shaman receives is long and demanding and may involve the use of powerful psychotropic substances. Repeatedly entering altered states of consciousness can produce long-lasting effects on shamans themselves, and shamans may be viewed with suspicion or fear by others in the society. This is because contacting cosmic beings to persuade them to heal embodies dangerous ambiguities: someone who can contact such beings for positive benefits may also be able to contact them to produce negative outcomes like disease or death.

The term *shaman* comes from the Tungus of eastern Siberia, where, at a minimum, it referred to a religious specialist who has the ability to enter a trance through which he or she is believed to enter into direct contact with spiritual beings and guardian spirits for the purposes of healing, fertility, protection, and aggression in a ritual setting (Bowie 2006, 175; Hultkrantz 1992,

---

shaman A part-time religious practitioner who is believed to have the power to contact supernatural forces directly on behalf of individuals or groups.

Figure 10.10 Using smoke from a juniper twig, Siberian shaman Vera heals a patient possessed by evil spirits.

Figure 10.11 The complex organization of the Roman Catholic Church was illustrated at the funeral for Pope John Paul II in 2005.

10). The healing associated with Siberian shamanism was concerned with the idea that illness was caused by soul loss and healing through recovery of the soul (Figure 10.10). Thus, the shaman was responsible for dealing with spirits that were, at best, neutral and at worst actively hostile to human beings. The shaman could travel to the spirit world to heal someone by finding the missing soul that had been stolen by spirits. But a shaman who was jealous of a hunter, for example, was believed to be able to steal the souls of animals so that the hunter would fail. In these societies, shamans are dangerous.

Shamanic activity takes place in the trance séance, which can be little more than a consultation between shaman and patient, or it can be a major public ritual, rich in drama. Becoming a shaman is not undertaken for personal development. In the societies in which shamanism is important, it is said that the shaman has no choice but to take on the role; the spirits demand it. It can take a decade or more to become fully recognized as a shaman, and it is assumed that the shaman will be in service to the society (for good or ill) for the rest of his or her life.

A **priest**, by contrast, is skilled in the practice of religious rituals, which are carried out for the benefit of the group or individual members of the group. Priests do not necessarily have direct contact with cosmic forces. Often their major role is to mediate such contact by ensuring that the required ritual activity has been properly performed. Priests are found in hierarchical societies, and they owe their ability to act as priests to the

hierarchy of the religious institution (Figure 10.11). Status differences separating rulers and subjects in such societies are reflected in the unequal relationship between priest and laity.

Worldviews in Operation: Two Case Studies

We have been discussing how worldviews are constructed, but most of us encounter them fully formed, both in our own society and in other societies. We face a rich tapestry of symbols, rituals, and everyday practices linked to one another in what often appears to be a seamless web. Where do we begin to sort things out?

Coping with Misfortune: Witchcraft, Oracles, and Magic among the Azande

Anthropologist E. E. Evans-Pritchard, in his classic work *Witchcraft, Oracles, and Magic among the Azande* ([1937] 1976), showed how Azande beliefs and practices concerning witchcraft, oracles, and magic were related to one another (see EthnoProfile 10.5: Azande). He describes how Azande in the 1920s used witchcraft beliefs to explain

priest A religious practitioner skilled in the practice of religious rituals, which he or she carries out for the benefit of the group.

EthnoProfile 10.5

Azande

Region: Central Africa

Nation: Sudan, Democratic Republic of the Congo (Zaire), Central African Republic

Population: 1,100,000

Environment: Sparsely wooded savanna

Livelihood: Farming, hunting, fishing, chicken raising

Political organization: Traditionally, highly organized, tribal kingdoms; today, part of modern nation-states

For more information: Evans-Pritchard, E. E. [1937] 1976. *Witchcraft, oracles, and magic among the Azande*, abridged ed. Oxford: Oxford University Press.

unfortunate things that happened to them and how they employed oracles and magic to exert a measure of control over the actions of other people. Evans-Pritchard was impressed by the intelligence, sophistication, and skepticism of his Azande informants. For this reason, he was all the more struck by their ability to hold a set of beliefs that many Europeans would regard as superstitious.

Azande Witchcraft Beliefs The Azande Evans-Pritchard knew believed that *mangu* (translated by Evans-Pritchard as **witchcraft**) was a substance in the body of witches, generally located under the sternum.[1] Being a part of the body, the witchcraft substance grew as the body grew; therefore, the older the witch, the more potent his or her witchcraft. The Azande believed that children inherited witchcraft from their parents. Men or women might be witches. Men practiced witchcraft against other men, women against other women. Witchcraft worked when

---

witchcraft The performance of evil by human beings believed to possess an innate, nonhuman power to do evil, whether or not it is intentional or self-aware.

magic A set of beliefs and practices designed to control the visible or invisible world for specific purposes.

oracles Invisible forces to which people address questions and whose responses they believe to be truthful.

its "soul" removed the soul of a certain organ in the victim's body, usually at night, causing a slow, wasting disease. Suffering such a disease was therefore an indication that an individual had been bewitched.

Witchcraft was a basic concept for the Azande, one that shaped their experience of adversity. All deaths were due to witchcraft and had to be avenged by **magic**. Other misfortunes were also commonly attributed to witchcraft unless the victim had broken a taboo, had failed to observe a moral rule, or was believed to be responsible for his own problems. Suppose I am an incompetent potter and my pots break while I am firing them. I may claim that witchcraft caused them to break, but everyone will laugh at me because they know I lack skill. Witchcraft was believed to be so common that the Azande were neither surprised nor awestruck when they encountered it. Rather, their usual response was anger.

To the Azande, witchcraft was a completely natural explanation for events. Consider the classic case of the collapsing granary. Azandeland is hot, and people seeking shade often sit under traditional raised granaries, which rest on logs. Termites are common in Azandeland, and sometimes they destroy the supporting logs, making a granary collapse. Occasionally, when a granary collapses, people sitting under it are killed. Why does this happen? The Azande are well aware that the termites chew up the wood until the supports give way, but to them that is not answer enough. Why, after all, should that particular granary have collapsed at that particular moment? To skeptical observers, the only connection is coincidence in time and space. Western science does not provide any explanation for why these two chains of causation intersect. But the Azande did: witchcraft caused the termites to finish chewing up the wood at just that moment, and that witchcraft had to be avenged by magic.

Dealing with Witches To expose the witch, the Azande consulted **oracles** (invisible forces to which people address questions and whose responses they believe to be truthful). Preeminent among these was the poison oracle. The poison was a strychninelike substance imported into Azandeland. The oracle "spoke" through the effect the poison had on chickens. When witchcraft was suspected, a relative of the afflicted person took some

---

[1]Beliefs and practices similar to those associated with Azande mangu have been found in many other societies, and it has become traditional in anthropology to refer to them as "witchcraft." This technical usage must not be confused with everyday uses of the word in contemporary Western societies, still less with the practices of followers of movements like Wicca, which are very different.

young chickens into the bush along with a specialist in administering the poison oracle. This person fed poison to one chicken, named a suspect, and asked the oracle to kill the chicken if that person were the witch. If the chicken died, a second chicken was fed poison, and the oracle was asked to spare the chicken if the suspect just named was indeed the witch. Thus, the Azande double-checked the oracle carefully; a witchcraft accusation was not made lightly.

People did not consult the oracle with a long list of names. They needed only to consider those who might wish them or their families ill: people who had quarreled with them, who were unpleasant, who were antisocial, or whose behavior was somehow out of line. Indeed, witches were always neighbors because neighbors were the only people who know you well enough to wish you and your family ill.

Once the oracle identified the witch, the Azande removed the wing of the chicken and had it taken by messenger to the compound of the accused person. The messenger presented the accused witch with the chicken wing and said that he had been sent concerning the illness of so-and-so's relative. "Almost invariably the witch replies courteously that he is unconscious of injuring anyone, that if it is true that he has injured the man in question he is very sorry, and that if it is he alone who is troubling him then he will surely recover, because from the bottom of his heart he wishes him health and happiness" (Evans-Pritchard [1937] 1976, 42). The accused then called for a gourd of water, took some in his mouth, and sprayed it out over the wing. He said aloud, so the messenger could hear and repeat what he said, that if he was a witch he was not aware of it and that he was not intentionally causing the sick man to be ill. He addressed the witchcraft in him, asking it to become cool, and concluded by saying that he made this appeal from his heart, not just from his lips (42).

People accused of witchcraft were usually astounded; no Azande thought of himself or herself as a witch. However, the Azande strongly believed in witchcraft and in the oracles; and if the oracle said someone was a witch, then it must be so. The accused witch was grateful to the family of the sick person for being informed. Otherwise, if the accused had been allowed to murder the victim, all the while unaware of it, the witch would surely be killed later by vengeance magic. The witchcraft accusation carried a further message: the behavior of the accused was sufficiently outside the bounds of acceptable Azande behavior to have marked him or her as a potential witch. Only the names of people who you suspected of wishing you ill were submitted to the oracle. The accused witch, then, was being told to change his or her behavior.

Are There Patterns of Witchcraft Accusation?

Compared with the stereotypes of European American witchcraft—old hags dressed in black, riding on broomsticks, casting spells, causing milk to sour or people to sicken—Azande witchcraft seems quite tame. People whose impression of witchcraft comes from Western European images may believe that witchcraft and witch-hunting tear at the very fabric of society. Yet, anthropological accounts like Evans-Pritchard's suggest that practices such as witchcraft accusation can sometimes keep societies together. Anthropologist Mary Douglas looked at the range of witchcraft accusations worldwide and discovered that they fall into two basic types (1970, xxvi–xxvii): in some cases, the witch is an evil outsider; in others, the witch is an internal enemy, either the member of a rival faction or a dangerous deviant. These different patterns of accusation perform different functions in a society. If the witch is an outsider, witchcraft accusations can strengthen in-group ties. If the witch is an internal enemy, accusations of witchcraft can weaken in-group ties; factions may have to regroup, communities may split, and the entire social hierarchy may be reordered. If the witch is a dangerous deviant, the accusation of witchcraft can be seen as an attempt to control the deviant in defense of the wider values of the community. Douglas concluded that how people understand witchcraft is based on the social relations of their society.

Coping with Misfortune: Seeking Higher Consciousness among the Channelers

Anthropologist Michael F. Brown spent several years studying the beliefs and practices of "alternative," or "New Age," spirituality, focusing particularly on channeling, the use of altered states of consciousness to contact spirits, "or, as many of its practitioners say, to experience spiritual energy captured from other times and dimensions" (1997, viii). The practitioners of channeling, called "channels," believe that they can "use altered states of consciousness to connect to wisdom emanating from the collective unconscious or even from other planets, dimensions, or historical eras" (6). Brown was fascinated to see how channeling brings together several important strands of North American culture: individualism, the personal recovery movement, and women-centered spirituality meld with features of nineteenth-century spiritualism to provide practitioners and followers with meaning, coherence, and a sense of control over events in what Brown refers to as "an anxious age" (Figure 10.12).

In Their Own Words

For All Those Who Were Indian in a Former Life

Andrea Smith challenges members of the New Age movement who, in her view, trivialize the situation of women like herself "who are Indian in this life."

The New Age movement completely trivializes the oppression we as Indian women face: Indian women are suddenly no longer the women who are forcibly sterilized and tested with unsafe drugs such as Depo Provera; we are no longer the women who have a life expectancy of 47 years; and we are no longer the women who generally live below the poverty level and face a 75 percent unemployment rate. No, we're too busy being cool and spiritual.

This trivialization of our oppression is compounded by the fact that nowadays anyone can be Indian if s/he wants to. All that is required is that one be Indian in a former life, or take part in a sweat lodge, or be mentored by a "medicine woman," or read a how-to book.

Since, according to this theory, anyone can now be "Indian," then the term Indians no longer regresses specifically to those people who have survived five hundred years of colonization and genocide. This furthers the goals of white supremacists to abrogate treaty rights and to take away what little we have left. When everyone becomes "Indian," then it is easy to lose sight of the specificity of oppression faced by those who are Indian in this life. It is no wonder we have such a difficult time finding non-Indians to support our struggles when the New Age movement has completely disguised our oppression.

The most disturbing aspect about these racist practices is that they are promoted in the name of feminism. Sometimes it seems that I can't open a feminist periodical without seeing ads promoting white "feminist" practices with little medicine wheel designs. I can't seem to go to a feminist conference without the woman who begins the conference with a ceremony being the only Indian presenter. Participants then feel so "spiritual" after this opening that they fail to notice the absence of Indian women in the rest of the conference or Native American issues in the discussions. And I certainly can't go to a feminist bookstore without seeing books by Lynn Andrews and other people who exploit Indian spirituality all over the place. It seems that, while feminism is supposed to signify the empowerment of all women, it obviously does not include Indian women.

If white feminists are going to act in solidarity with their Indian sisters, they must take a stand against Indian spiritual abuse. Feminist book and record stores should stop selling these products, and feminist periodicals should stop advertising these products. Women who call themselves feminists should denounce exploitative practices wherever they see them.

Source: A. Smith 1994, 71.

Figure 10.12 Gerry Bowman channeling John the Baptist at the Harmonic Convergence of the Planets, celebrated in California in 1987.

If one can speak of a theology of channeling, Brown concludes that it is based on four key assumptions. First, channels and their followers believe that human beings are in essence gods. Individuals are referred to as "fragments of the God-head" or "Christed beings." These metaphors imply not only that humans share in the divinity that created the universe but also that they are immortal, inherently good, and fully able to create their own reality (1977, 47). Second, channels and their clients generally believe that human beings undergo a series of reincarnations in order to acquire important learning experiences. This evolutionary process may involve previous lives lived on earth or on different planets or in different dimensions. Third, channels and their clients believe that each of us is responsible for creating our own reality. In their view, thoughts shape reality and the impact of any thought is magnified when a critical mass of like-minded people share it (47–48). From their perspective, if enough people "visualize world peace," it will suddenly happen. Fourth, channels and their clients believe in the transcendent value of holism. "The purpose of channeling is to bring together elements of life ripped apart by Western civilization: male and female, reason and intuition, thought and matter. . . . Channels and their clients see the universe as a single interconnected field. Just as the thought patterns of individuals can reshape the cosmos, so shifts in the cosmos affect individuals" (48–49).

What follows from this theology is a moral framework in which the existence of evil is called into question. As we have seen, the Azande explain misfortune in terms of witchcraft. Channels and their clients explain misfortune—illness, poverty, or other forms of suffering—in one of two ways. On the one hand, misfortune occurs because the victims cannot or will not envision the world in ways that protect them from it. "Calamity originates in a failure of individual attitude or thought" (M. F. Brown 1997, 65). On the other, channels assert that victims have chosen their own fate, usually at a "deep soul level" that is beyond their own conscious awareness. The logic here is that the reincarnating soul chooses certain challenges as part of its growth process. Thus, a person with cancer has, at some level, chosen to have it because the experience is important or necessary to the development of a higher consciousness over the course of the many lives that soul will live.

While some observers regard this as a form of blaming the victim, channels see their position as a way of asserting control. Channels see themselves "explicitly reacting against the contemporary American cult of victimhood. . . . Channeling's theological framework rejects victimhood because of its connotation of powerlessness, arguing instead that everyone suffers indignities on their way to higher consciousness. These painful episodes are important learning experiences, but nothing is gained by dwelling on them" (M. F. Brown 1997, 67).

Thus, people drawn to channeling believe that they are the authors of their own fate. If people are divine actors, then their temporary setbacks and troubles must be part of a master plan that they themselves have designed; thus, they are inevitably responsible to some degree for their own misfortunes (M. F. Brown 1997, 68). Among other things, this way of explaining misfortune totally rejects the social nature of human experience. As opposed to Azande witchcraft beliefs, where misfortune is due to the ill will of others, channeling is a belief system of and for individuals. Although claiming to offer a corrective to the sense of isolation that many people feel, ironically, channeling isolates individuals from one another even more, by making each of us a universe unto ourselves.

Maintaining and Changing a Worldview

What makes a worldview stable? Why is a worldview rejected? Changes in worldview are regularly connected to the practical everyday experiences of people in a particular society. Stable, repetitive experiences reinforce the acceptability of any traditional worldview that has successfully accounted for such experiences in the past. When experiences become unpredictable, however, thinking people in any society may become painfully aware that past experiences can no longer be trusted as guides for the future and traditional worldviews may be undermined (see Horton 1982, 252).

How Do People Cope with Change?

Drastic changes in experience lead people to create new interpretations that will help them cope with the changes. Sometimes the change is an outcome of local or regional struggles. The Protestant Reformation, for example, adapted the Christian tradition to changing social circumstances in northern Europe during the Renaissance by breaking ties to the pope, turning church lands over to secular authorities, allowing clergy to marry, and so forth. Protestants continued to identify themselves as Christians, even though many of their religious practices had changed.

In Guider, Cameroon, lone rural migrants to town frequently abandoned their former religious practices and took on urban customs and a new identity through conversion to Islam. However, similar conflicts between new and old ways do not everywhere lead to religious conversion. Sometimes the result is a creative synthesis of old religious practices and new ones, a process called **syncretism**. Under the pressure of Christian missionizing, indigenous people of Central America identified some of their own pre-Christian, personalized superhuman beings with particular Catholic saints. Similarly, Africans brought to Brazil identified Catholic saints with African gods, to produce the syncretistic religion Candomblé.

Anthropologists have debated the nature of syncretistic practices, noting that, while some may be viewed as a way of resisting new ideas imposed from above, others may be introduced from above by powerful outsiders deliberately making room for local beliefs within their own more encompassing worldview. The Romans, for example, made room for local deities within their imperial pantheon, and post–Vatican II Catholicism explicitly urged non-European Catholics to worship using local cultural forms (Stewart and Shaw 1994).

When groups defend or refashion their own way of life in the face of outside encroachments, anthropologists sometimes describe their activities as **revitalization**—a deliberate, organized attempt by some members of a society to create a more satisfying culture (Wallace 1972, 75). Revitalization arises in times of crisis, most often among groups who are facing oppression and radical transformation, usually at the hands of outsiders (e.g., colonizing powers). Revitalization movements engage in a "politics of religious synthesis" that produces a range of outcomes (Stewart and Shaw 1994). Sometimes syncretism is embraced. Other times it is rejected in favor of **nativism**, or a return to the old ways. Some nativistic movements expect a messiah or prophet, who will bring back a lost golden age of peace, prosperity, and harmony, a process often called *revivalism, millenarianism,* or *messianism.*

A classic New World example of a millenarian movement is the Ghost Dance movement among indigenous peoples of the Great Plains of the United States in the late 1880s to 1890. When the buffalo were exterminated, indigenous Plains dwellers lost their independence and were herded onto reservations by numerically superior and better-armed European Americans. Out of this final crisis emerged Wovoka, a prophet who taught that the existing world would soon be destroyed and that a new crust would form on the earth. All settlers and indigenous people who followed the settlers' ways would become buried. Those indigenous people who abandoned the settlers' ways, led pure lives, and danced the Ghost Dance would be saved. As the new crust formed, the buffalo would return, as would all the ancestors of the believers. Together, all would lead lives of virtue and joy.

Because the world was going to change by itself, violence against the oppressors was not a necessary part of the Ghost Dance. Nevertheless, the movement frightened settlers and the U.S. Army, which suspected an armed uprising. Those fears and suspicions led to the massacre at Wounded Knee, in which the cavalry troopers killed all the members of a Lakota (Sioux) band, principally women and children, whom they encountered off the reservation.

Nativistic movements, however, may represent resistance to, rather than escape from, the outside world, actively removing or avoiding any cultural practices associated with those who seek to dominate them. One such "antisyncretistic" group is the Kwaio, living on the island of Malaita in the Solomon Islands (see EthnoProfile 10.6: Kwaio). Almost all their neighbors have

---

syncretism The synthesis of old religious practices (or an old way of life) with new religious practices (or a new way of life) introduced from outside, often by force.

revitalization A conscious, deliberate, and organized attempt by some members of a society to create a more satisfying culture in a time of crisis.

nativism A return to the old ways; a movement whose members expect a messiah or prophet who will bring back a lost golden age of peace, prosperity, and harmony.

EthnoProfile 10.6

Kwaio

Region: Oceania (Melanesia)

Nation: Solomon Islands (Malaita)

Population: 7,000 (1970s)

Environment: Tropical island

Livelihood: Horticulture and pig raising

Political organization:
Traditionally, some men with influence but no coercive power; today, part of a modern nation-state

For more information:
Keesing, Roger. 1992. *Custom and confrontation.* Chicago: University of Chicago Press.

In Their Own Words

Custom and Confrontation

In the following passage, the late Roger Keesing recorded the words of one of his Kwaio informants, Dangeabe'u, who defends Kwaio custom.

The government has brought the ways of business, the ways of money. The people at the coast believe that's what's important, and tell us we should join in. Now the government is controlling the whole world. The side of the Bible is withering away. When that's finished, the government will rule unchallenged. It will hold all the land. All the money will go to the government to feed its power. Once everything—our lands, too—are in their hands, that will be it.

I've seen the people from other islands who have all become Christians. They knew nothing about their land. The white people have gotten their hands on their lands. The whites led them to forget all the knowledge of their land, separated them from it. And when the people knew nothing about their land, the whites bought it from them and made their enterprises. . . .

That's close upon us too. If we all follow the side of the Bible, the government will become powerful here too, and will take control of our land. We won't be attached to our land, as we are now, holding our connections to our past. If the government had control of our land, then if we wanted to do anything on it, we'd have to pay them. If we wanted to start a business—a store, say—we'd have to pay the government. We reject all that. We want to keep hold of our land, in the ways passed down to us.

Source: Keesing 1992, 184.

converted to Christianity, and the nation of which they are a part is militantly Christian. Members of other groups wear clothing, work on plantations or in tourist hotels, attend schools, and live in cities. The Kwaio have refused all this: "Young men carry bows and arrows; girls and women, nude except for customary ornaments, dig taro in forest gardens; valuables made of strung shell beads are exchanged at mortuary feasts; and priests sacrifice pigs to the ancestral spirits on whom prosperity and life itself depend" (Keesing 1982, 1).

Roger Keesing (1992) admits that he does not know exactly why the Kwaio responded in this way. He suspects that precolonial social and political differences between the Kwaio and their coastal neighbors influenced later developments. The colonial encounter itself was certainly relevant. In 1927, some Kwaio attacked a British patrol, killing the district officer and 13 Solomon Island troops. The subsequent massacre of many Kwaio by a police force made up of other Malaitans, followed by marginalization and persecution by the colonial government, also clearly contributed to Kwaio resistance.

It is important to emphasize that the Kwaio maintain their old ways deliberately, in the face of alternatives; their traditional way of life is therefore lived in a modern context. "In the course of anticolonial struggle, 'kastomu' (custom) and commitment to ancestral ways have become symbols of identity and autonomy" (Keesing 1992, 240). In the eyes of the Kwaio, the many Solomon Islanders who became Christianized and acculturated lost their cultural ties and thereby their ties to the land and to their past, becoming outsiders in their own homeland. Maintaining traditional ways is thus a form of political protest. From this perspective, many contemporary antisyncretistic movements in the world, from fundamentalism of various religions to movements for national identity and cultural autonomy, can be understood as having aims very similar to those of the Kwaio, sparked by many of the same forces.

How Are Worldviews Used as Instruments of Power?

Within any particular cultural tradition, different worldviews often coexist. How then does a particular picture of reality become the "official" worldview for a given society? And once that position is achieved, how is it maintained? To be in the running for the official picture of reality, a worldview must be able, however minimally, to make sense of some people's personal and social experiences. Sometimes, however, it may seem to some members of society that barely credible views of reality have triumphed over alternatives that seem far more plausible. Thus, something more than persuasive ability alone must be involved, and that something is power. Powerless people may be unable to dislodge the official worldview of their society. They can, however, refuse to accept the imposition of someone else's worldview and develop an unofficial worldview based on metaphors that reflect their own condition of powerlessness (Scott 1990).

How can worldviews be mobilized as instruments of power and control? First, a religious symbol can be invoked as a guarantee of self-evident truths when people in power seek to eliminate or impose certain forms of conduct. Holy books, like the Qur'an, may be used in this way. For example, a legal record from Guider, Cameroon, indicates that a son once brought suit against his father for refusing to repay him a certain amount of money. The father claimed that he had paid. Both father and son got into an increasingly heated argument in which neither would give ground. Finally, the judge in the case asked the father to take a copy of the Qur'an in his hand and swear that he was telling the truth. This he did. The son, however, refused to swear on the Qur'an and finally admitted that he had been lying. In this case, the status of the Qur'an as the unquestioned word of God, which implied the power of God to punish liars, controlled the son's behavior.

Second, a symbol may be under the direct control of a person wishing to affect the behavior of others. Consider the role of official interpreters of religious or political ideology, such as priests or kings. Their pronouncements define the bounds of permissible behavior. As Roger Keesing points out:

> Senior men, in Melanesia as elsewhere in the tribal world, have depended heavily on control of *sacred knowledge* to maintain their control of earthly politics. By keeping in their hands relations with ancestors and other spirits, by commanding magical knowledge, senior men could maintain a control mediated by the supernatural. Such religious ideologies served too, by defining rules in terms of ancient spirits and by defining the nature of men and women in supernatural terms, to reinforce and maintain the roles of the sexes—and again to hide their nature. (1982, 219)

Keesing's observations remind us that knowledge, like power, is not evenly distributed throughout a society. Different kinds of people know different things.

Figure 10.13 Senior Dogon men carrying out fox trail divination. The knowledge and skills of elderly men, based on experience gained over a lifetime, provide their interpretations with an authority that those of people with less experience would not have.

In some societies, what men know about their religious system is different from what women know and what older men know may be different from what younger men know. Keesing suggested that men's control over women and older men's control over younger men are based on differential access to knowledge (1982, 14). It is not just that these different kinds of people know different things; rather, the different things they know (and do not know) enable them (or force them) to remain in the positions they hold in the society (Figure 10.13).

Worldviews represent comprehensive ideas about the structure of the world and the place of one's own group, or one's own self, within that world. The ethnographic record offers a broad array of different worldviews, each testifying to the imaginative, meaning-making cultural capacity of humans. These models of the world, moreover, do not exist apart from everyday social practices; on the contrary, they are heavily implicated in our interactions with others. And when those interactions lead to crisis, humans respond by, among other things, seeking a way of making the crisis appear meaningful and therefore manageable. We are meaning-making, meaning-using, meaning-dependent organisms; and that is nowhere more clear than when a meaningful way of life is under assault.

Chapter Summary

1. Play is a generalized form of behavioral openness: the ability to think about, speak about, and do different things in the same way or the same thing in different ways. Play can also be thought of as a way of organizing activities. We put a frame that consists of the message "This is play" around certain activities, thereby transforming them into play. Play also permits reflexive consideration of alternative realities by setting up a separate reality and suggesting that the perspective of ordinary life is only one way to make sense of experience. The functions of play include exercise, practice for the real world, increased creativity in children, and commentary on the real world.

2. Art is a kind of play that is subject to certain culturally appropriate restrictions on form and content. It aims to evoke a holistic, aesthetic response from the artist and the observer. It succeeds when the form is culturally appropriate for the content and is technically perfect in its realization. Aesthetic evaluations are culturally shaped value judgments. We recognize art in other cultures because of its family resemblance to what we call art in our own culture. Although people with other cultural understandings may not have produced art by intention, we can often successfully appreciate what they have created as art by appropriation. These issues are addressed in ethnographic studies that call into question received ideas about what counts as "authentic" art.

3. Myths are stories whose truth seems self-evident because they do such a good job of integrating personal experiences with a wider set of assumptions about the way the world works. The power of myths comes from their ability to make life meaningful for those who accept them. As stories, myths are the products of high verbal art. A full understanding of myth requires ethnographic background information.

4. Ritual is a repetitive social practice composed of sequences of symbolic activities such as speech, singing, dancing, gestures, and the manipulation of certain objects. In studying ritual, we pay attention not just to the symbols but also to how the ritual is performed. Cultural ideas are made concrete through ritual action. Rites of passage are rituals in which members of a culture move from one position in the social structure to another. These rites are marked by periods of separation, transition, and reaggregation. During the period of transition, individuals occupy a liminal position. All those in this position frequently develop an intense comradeship and a feeling of oneness, or communitas.

5. Ritual and play are complementary. Play is based on the premise "Let us make believe," while ritual is based on the premise "Let us believe." As a result, the ritual frame is far more rigid than the play frame. Although ritual may seem overwhelming and all-powerful, individuals and groups can sometimes manipulate ritual forms to achieve nontraditional ends.

6. Anthropological studies of religion tend to focus on the social institutions and meaningful processes with which it is associated. Followers of religions can address personalized forces symbolically and expect them to respond. Maintaining contact with cosmic forces is very complex, and societies have complex social practices designed to ensure that this is done properly. Two important kinds of religious specialists are shamans and priests.

(continued on next page)

Chapter Summary *(continued)*

7. Many anthropologists have attempted to display the rich, coherent tapestries of symbols, rituals, and everyday practices that make up particular worldviews and to demonstrate the high degree to which worldviews vary from one another. They have also studied the ways in which drastic changes in people's experiences lead them to create new meanings to explain the changes and to cope with them. This can be accomplished through elaboration of the old system to fit changing times, conversion to a new worldview, syncretism, revitalization, or resistance.

8. Because religious knowledge is not distributed evenly among the members of societies, those who control such knowledge may use it as an instrument of power to control other members of society.

For Review

1. Take the definition of play in the running glossary at the bottom of page 284, and explain the importance of each feature of this complex definition.
2. What are the consequences of play for animals?
3. What is metacommunication?
4. How does the case study by Elizabeth Chin about African American girls and their dolls in New Haven, Connecticut, illustrate the importance of play for understanding human symbolic practices?
5. What are the main components of the definition of art offered in the text, and why is each component important?
6. Distinguish "art by intention" from "art by appropriation."
7. What argument is made in the text concerning the role of "authenticity" in art? How does the case study illustrate these points?
8. What are myths?
9. Compare Malinowski's view of myth with the view of Claude Lévi-Strauss.
10. Explain the significance of each of the major components of the definition of ritual given in the text.
11. How may a child's birthday party be understood as a ritual?
12. Describe each stage of a rite of passage.
13. How are play and ritual complementary?
14. List A. F. C. Wallace's minimal categories of religion, and define and illustrate each of them.
15. Explain the differences anthropologists recognize between shamans and priests.
16. Compare the Azande and the channelers with regard to the way members of each group explain misfortune.
17. What is syncretism?
18. Explain how worldviews can be used as instruments of power.

Key Terms

art 285	myths 293	priest 303	ritual 296
communitas 298	nativism 308	reflexivity 284	shaman 302
framing 284	oracles 304	religion 300	syncretism 308
liminality 298	orthodoxy 293	revitalization 308	witchcraft 304
magic 304	orthopraxy 299	rite of passage 296	worldviews 299
metacommunication 284	play 284		

Suggested Readings

Alland, Alexander. 1977. *The artistic animal.* New York: Doubleday Anchor. *An introductory look at the biocultural bases for art. This work is very well written, very clear, and fascinating.*

Bowen, John. 2008. *Religions in practice: An approach to the anthropology of religion,* 4th ed. Needham Heights, MA: Allyn & Bacon. *An up-to-date introduction of the anthropology of religion focusing on religious practice and interpretation, with a very wide range of case studies.*

Errington, Shelly. 1998. *The death of authentic primitive art and other tales of progress.* Berkeley: University of California Press. *A sharp and witty book about the production, distribution, interpretation, and selling of "primitive art."*

Evans-Pritchard, E. E. [1937] 1976. *Witchcraft, oracles, and magic among the Azande,* abridged ed. Oxford: Oxford University Press. *An immensely influential and very readable anthropological classic.*

Keesing, Roger. 1992. *Custom and confrontation: The Kwaio struggle for cultural autonomy.* New York: Columbia University Press. *Based on 30 years of research, Keesing's final book provides a clear, readable, and committed discussion of Kwaio resistance.*

Lambek, Michael. 2008. *A reader in the anthropology of religion.* 2nd ed. Malden, MA: Blackwell. *An excellent collection of classic and contemporary readings in the anthropology of religion.*

Schwartzman, Helen. 1978. *Transformations: The anthropology of children's play.* New York: Plenum. *A superlative work that considers how anthropologists have studied children's play, with some insightful suggestions about how they might do this in the future.*

Turner, Victor. 1969. *The ritual process.* Chicago: Aldine. *An important work in the anthropological study of ritual, this text is an eloquent analysis of rites of passage.*

Vogel, Susan. 1997. *Baule: African art/Western eyes.* New Haven, CT: Yale University Press. *A book of extraordinary photographs and beautifully clear text, this work explores both Baule and Western views of Baule expressive culture.*

Why Do Anthropologists Study Economic Relations?

11

All human groups have to organize themselves to make available to their members the material things they need for survival, such as food, shelter, and clothing. This chapter explores the variety of economic patterns human societies have developed over the millennia. It also draws attention to the way large-scale connections forged by trade or conquest continue to shape—and be reshaped by—the local economic practices of societies throughout the world.

Chapter Outline

◀ *Aymara farmer Mario Alanoca shows a quinoa field in Cotimbora, in Oruro, Bolivia, February 2011.*

Human beings are material organisms, and the seemingly endless meaningful ways we can imagine to live must always come to terms with the material realities of day-to-day existence. Culture contributes to the way human beings organize their social lives to meet such challenges. **Social organization** can be defined as the patterning of human interdependence in a given society through the actions and decisions of its members. This chapter and the two that follow will explore the ways anthropologists have investigated differences in human social organization in three key domains: economic relations, political relations, and more intimate forms of human relatedness associated with kin and families. The variation these forms of human social organization display across space and over time is truly remarkable, but that does not mean that people are free to do or be whatever they like. Rather, the adaptive flexibility of long-lived, large-brained social animals such as ourselves develops over the life cycle in response to a range of sometimes unpredictable experiences. This kind of developmental response would be impossible if human behavior were rigidly programmed by genes, firmly circumscribed by environments, or strictly limited by technologies.

How Do Anthropologists Study Economic Relations?

Forty years ago, I. M. Lewis (1967, 166ff.) pointed out that the northern Somalis and the Boran Galla lived next to each other in semiarid scrubland and even herded the same animals (goats, sheep, cattle, camels) (see EthnoProfiles 11.1: Somalis [Northern] and 11.2: Boran). Despite these similarities, the Somali and the Boran were quite different in social structure: The Boran engaged in much less fighting and feuding than the Somali; Boran families split up to take care of the animals, whereas the Somali did not; and lineage organization was less significant among the Boran. Economic and political anthropologists have attempted to explain why this should be.

> **social organization** The patterning of human interdependence in a given society through the actions and decisions of its members.
>
> **economic anthropology** The part of the discipline of anthropology that debates issues of human nature that relate directly to the decisions of daily life and making a living.

Ethno Profile 11.1

Somalis (Northern)

Region: Eastern Africa

Nation: Somalia, Djibouti, Ethiopia, Kenya

Population: 600,000 (3,250,000 total; 2,250,000 in Somalia)

Environment: Harsh, semidesert

Livelihood: Herding of camels, sheep, goats, cattle, horses

Political organization: Traditionally, lineage-based, ad hoc egalitarian councils; today, part of modern nation-states

For more information:
Lewis, I. M. 1967. *A pastoral democracy: A study of pastoralism and politics among the northern Somali of the Horn of Africa.* Oxford: Oxford University Press.

What Are the Connections between Culture and Livelihood?

Although our physical survival depends on our making adequate use of the resources around us, our culture tells us which resources to use and how to use them. Economic anthropologists study the many variations in human livelihood which anthropologists have found in different societies. Richard Wilk has defined **economic anthropology** as "the part of the discipline that debates issues of *human nature* that relate directly to the decisions of daily life and making a living" (1996, xv).

In ordinary conversation, when we speak of making a living, we usually mean doing what is necessary to obtain the material things—food, clothing, shelter—that sustain human life. Making a living thus encompasses what is generally considered economic activity. However, anthropologists and other social scientists disagree about just what the term *economy* ought to represent. The rise of the capitalist market led to one view of what economy might mean: buying cheap and selling dear. That is, economy means maximizing utility—obtaining as much satisfaction as possible for the smallest possible cost. This view is based on the assumption of scarcity. Many economists and economic anthropologists believe that people's resources (e.g., money) are not, and never will be, great enough for them to obtain all the goods they want. This view of economy also assumes that economic analysis should focus on *individuals* who must maximize

EthnoProfile 11.2

Boran

Region: Eastern Africa

Nation: Kenya and Ethiopia

Population: 80,000 (1970s)

Environment: Adequate rangeland, scrub, and desert

Livelihood: Herding of cattle by preference, also sheep and goats

Political organization: Traditionally, a kinship-based organization with a set of six elders who have certain responsibilities for maintaining order; today, part of a modern nation-state

For more information:
Baxter, P. T. W., and Uri Almagor, eds. 1978. *Age, generation and time.* New York: St. Martin's Press.

How Do Anthropologists Study Production, Distribution, and Consumption?

Anthropologists generally agree that economic activity is usefully subdivided into three distinct phases: production, distribution, and consumption. Production involves transforming nature's raw materials into products useful to human beings. Distribution involves getting those products to people. Consumption involves using up the products—for example, by eating food or wearing clothing. When analyzing economic activity in a particular society, however, anthropologists differ in the importance they attach to each phase. For example, the distributive process known as *exchange* is central to the functioning of capitalist free enterprise. Some anthropologists have assumed that exchange is equally central to the functioning of all economies and have tried to explain the economic life of non-Western societies in terms of exchange. Anthropologists influenced by the work of Karl Marx, however, have argued that exchange cannot be understood properly without first studying the nature of *production*. They point out that production shapes the context in which exchange can occur, determining which parties have how much of what kind of goods to exchange. Other anthropologists have suggested that neither production nor exchange patterns make any sense without first specifying the *consumption* priorities of the people who are producing and exchanging. Consumption priorities, they argue, are certainly designed to satisfy material needs. But the recognition of needs and of appropriate ways to satisfy them is shaped by historically contingent cultural patterns. Finally, as noted in Chapter 7, many would agree that patterns of production, exchange, and consumption are seriously affected by the kind of *storage* in use in a particular society (Figure 11.2).

How Are Goods Distributed and Exchanged?

The discipline of economics was born in the late 1700s, during the early years of the Industrial Revolution in western Europe. At that time, such thinkers as Adam Smith and his disciples struggled to devise theories to explain the

their utility under conditions of scarcity. An economizing individual is supposed to set priorities and to allocate resources according to those priorities: this is what economists mean by economic "rationality." To accept this view implies that economic anthropologists should clarify the different priorities set by different societies and study how these priorities affect the maximizing decisions of individuals who live in those societies.

Other economic anthropologists, however, regard this way of thinking about economic life as ethnocentric. They present evidence to show that different societies use different principles to organize economic life, and they argue that the job of economic anthropologists should be to describe and explain these cultural variations. This view of economy focuses on **institutions**: complex, variable, and enduring forms of cultural practice that organize social life. From an institutional point of view, a society's economy consists of the culturally specific processes its members use to provide themselves with material resources. Therefore, economic processes cannot be considered apart from the other cultural institutions in which they are embedded and by which they are scaffolded or sustained. And because institutional scaffolding relies on human decisions—or choices—of daily life and making a living, economic anthropologists need to pay attention to the conditions that shape these choices.

---

institutions Complex, variable, and enduring forms of cultural practices that organize social life.

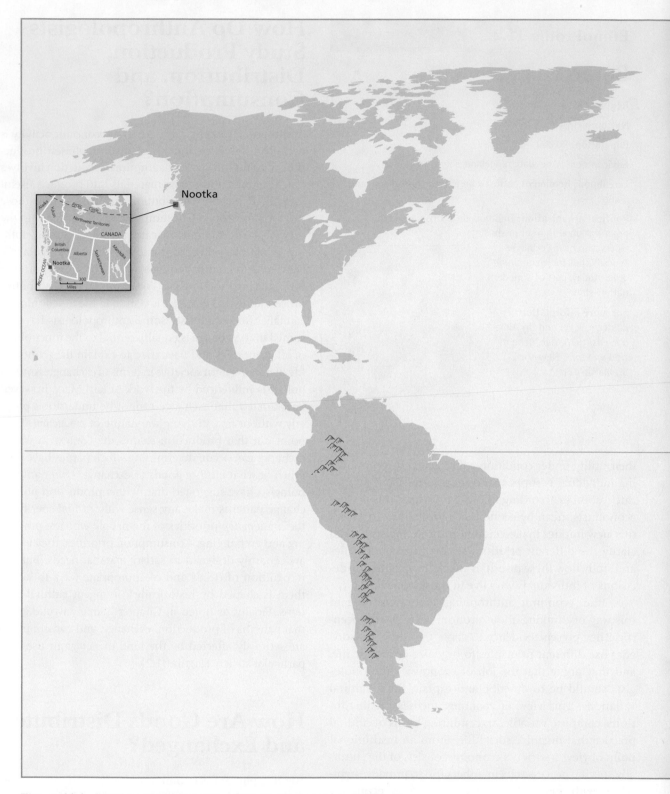

Figure 11.1   Locations of societies whose EthnoProfiles appear in Chapter 11.

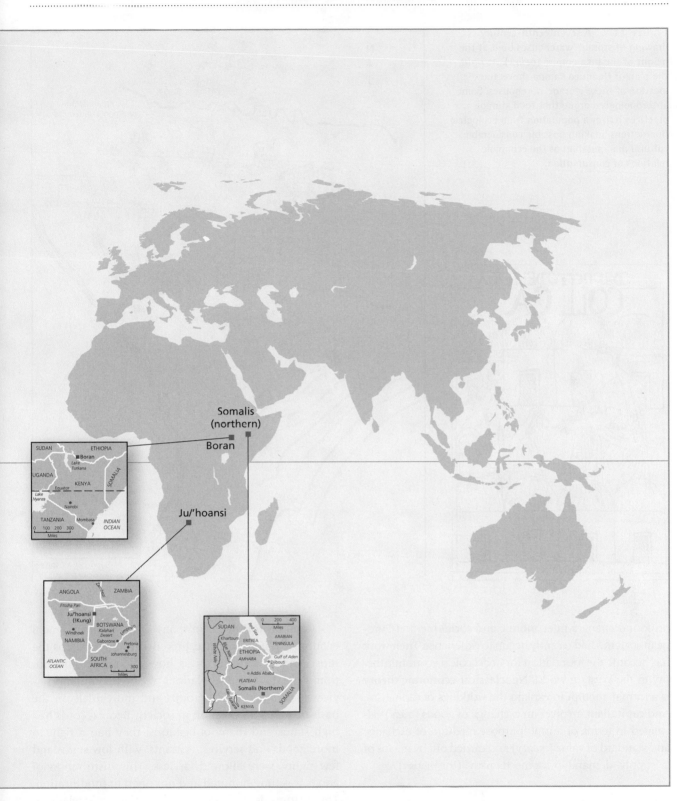

Figure 11.2 A seventeenth-century drawing of storage warehouses built at the height of the Inka empire (*below*). At *right*, the plan of Huánuco Pampa shows the location of these storage warehouses. Some anthropologists argue that food storage practices buffer a population from ecological fluctuations, making possible considerable cultural manipulation of the economic relations of consumption.

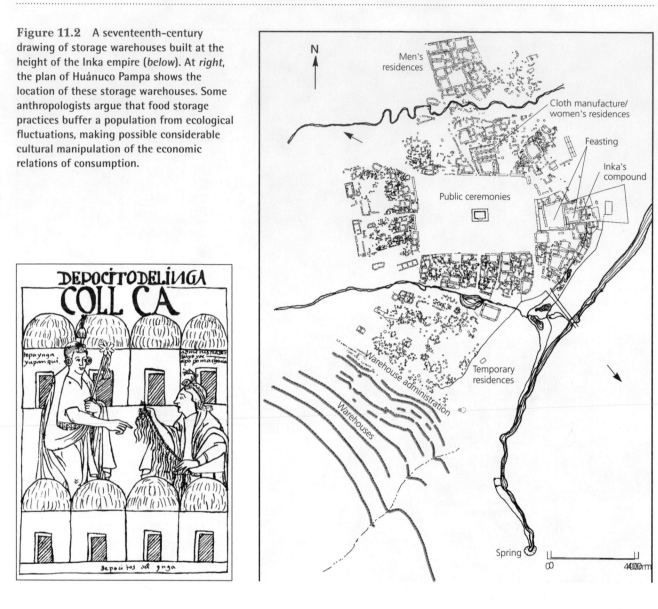

profound changes in economic and social life that European societies had recently begun to experience. Their work has become the foundation for neoclassical economic theory in the Western world. **Neoclassical economic theory** is a formal attempt to explain the workings of capitalism. And **capitalism** involves an exchange of goods (*trade*) calculated in terms of a multipurpose medium of exchange and standard of value (*money*) and carried out by means of a "supply–demand–price mechanism" (the *market*).

neoclassical economic theory A formal attempt to explain the workings of capitalist enterprise, with particular attention to distribution.

capitalism An economic system dominated by the supply–demand–price mechanism called the "market"; an entire way of life that grew in response to and in service of that market.

status A particular social position in a group.

Capitalism differed in many ways from the feudal economic system that had preceded it, but perhaps the most striking difference was how it handled distribution. Feudal economic relations allotted goods and services to different social groups and individuals on the basis of **status**, or position in society. Because lords had high status and many obligations, they had a right to more goods and services. Peasants, with low status and few rights, were allowed far less. This distribution of goods was time-honored and not open to modification. The customs derived from capitalist economic relations, by contrast, were considered "free" precisely because they swept away all such traditional restrictions. As we shall see in our discussion of "Sedaka" Village, Malaysia, capitalism also swept away traditional protections (see EthnoProfile 12.5: "Sedaka" Village). In any case, distribution under capitalism was negotiated between buyers and sellers in the market.

Capitalist market exchange of goods for other goods, for labor, or (increasingly) for cash was an important development in Western economic history. It is not surprising, therefore, that Western economic theory was preoccupied with explaining how the capitalist market worked. Markets clearly had a new, decisive importance in capitalist society, which they had not possessed in feudal times. Western neoclassical economics is based on the assumption that market forces are the central forces determining levels of both production and consumption in society. But is it legitimate to argue that market forces have played the same role in *all* human societies?

What Are Modes of Exchange?

Some anthropologists argued that taking self-interested, materialistic decision making in the capitalist market as the prototype of human rationality was ethnocentric. They pointed out that the capitalist market is a relatively recent cultural invention in human history. Western capitalist societies distribute material goods in a manner that is consistent with their basic values, institutions, and assumptions about human nature. So too non-Western, noncapitalist societies might be expected to have devised alternative modes of exchange that distribute material goods in ways that are in accord with their basic values, institutions, and assumptions about human nature. In the early twentieth century, for example, French anthropologist Marcel Mauss ([1950] 2000) contrasted noncapitalist **gift exchanges** (which are deeply embedded in social relations and always require a return gift) with impersonal **commodity exchanges** typical of the capitalist market (in which goods are exchanged for cash and exchange partners need have nothing further to do with one another). Later, Marshall Sahlins (1972) drew on the work of economic historian Karl Polanyi (e.g., 1977) to propose that three **modes of exchange** could be identified historically and cross-culturally: reciprocity, redistribution, and market exchange.

The most ancient mode of exchange was **reciprocity**. Reciprocity is characteristic of egalitarian societies, such as the Ju/'hoansi once were (see EthnoProfile 11.4: Ju/'hoansi). Sahlins identified three kinds of reciprocity. *Generalized reciprocity* is found when those who exchange do so without expecting an immediate return and without specifying the value of the return. Everyone assumes that the exchanges will eventually balance out. Generalized reciprocity usually characterizes the exchanges that occur between parents and their children. In the United States, for example, parents ordinarily do not keep a running tab on what it costs them to raise their children and then present their children with repayment schedules when they reach the age of 18. *Balanced reciprocity* is found

when those who exchange expect a return of equal value within a specified time limit (e.g., when cousins exchange gifts of equal value with one another at Christmastime). Lee notes that the Ju/'hoansi distinguish between barter, which requires an immediate return of an equivalent, and *hxaro*, which is a kind of generalized reciprocity that encourages social obligations to be extended into the future (1992b, 103). Finally, *negative reciprocity* is an exchange of goods and services in which at least one party attempts to get something for nothing without suffering any penalties. These attempts can range from haggling over prices to outright seizure, as with cattle rustling.

Redistribution, the second mode of exchange, requires some form of centralized social organization. Those who control the central position receive economic contributions from all members of the group. It is then their responsibility to redistribute the goods they receive in a way that provides for every member of the group. The Internal Revenue Service is probably the institution of redistribution that people in the United States know best. A classic anthropological example of redistribution is the *potlatch* of the indigenous peoples of the northwest coast of North America. In the highly stratified fishing and gathering society of the Nootka, for example, nobles sought to outdo one another in generosity by giving away vast quantities of objects during the potlatch ceremony (see EthnoProfile 11.3: Nootka). The noble giving the potlatch accumulated goods produced in one village and redistributed them to other nobles attending the ceremony. When the guests returned to their own villages, they in turn redistributed the goods among their followers.

Market exchange, invented in capitalist society, is the most recent mode of exchange, according to Polanyi

---

gift exchanges Noncapitalist forms of economic exchange that are deeply embedded in social relations and always require a return gift.

commodity exchanges Impersonal economic exchanges typical of the capitalist market in which goods are exchanged for cash and exchange partners need have nothing further to do with one another.

modes of exchange Patterns according to which distribution takes place: reciprocity, redistribution, and market exchange.

reciprocity The exchange of goods and services of equal value. Anthropologists distinguish three forms of reciprocity: *generalized*, in which neither the time nor the value of the return is specified; *balanced*, in which a return of equal value is expected within a specified time limit; and *negative*, in which parties to the exchange hope to get something for nothing.

redistribution A mode of exchange that requires some form of centralized social organization to receive economic contributions from all members of the group and to redistribute them in such a way as to provide for every group member.

market exchange The exchange of goods (trade) calculated in terms of a multipurpose medium of exchange and standard of value (money) and carried out by means of a supply–demand–price mechanism (the market).

Figure 11.3 Shirts for sale at the market in Guider, Cameroon. Markets can be found in many societies, but capitalism links markets to trade and money in a unique way.

EthnoProfile 11.3

Nootka

Region: North America

Nation: Canada (Vancouver Island)

Population: 6,000 (1970s)

Environment: Rainy, relatively warm coastal strip

Livelihood: Fishing, hunting, gathering

Political organization: Traditionally, ranked individuals, chiefs; today, part of a modern nation-state

For more information:
Rosman, Abraham, and Paula G. Rubel. 1971. *Feasting with mine enemy: Rank and exchange among northwest coast societies.* New York: Columbia University Press.

(1977) (Figure 11.3). Polanyi was well aware that trade, money, and market institutions had developed independently of one another historically. He also knew that they could be found in societies outside the West. The uniqueness of capitalism was how all three institutions were linked to one another in the societies of early modern Europe.

According to Polanyi (1977), different modes of exchange often coexist within a single society, although he argued that only one functions as the society's overall mode of economic integration. The United States, for example, is integrated by the market mode of exchange, yet redistribution and reciprocity have not disappeared. Within the family, parents who obtain income from the market redistribute that income, or goods obtained with that income, to their children. Generalized reciprocity also characterizes much exchange within the family: as noted earlier, parents regularly provide their children with food and clothing without expecting any immediate return.

Some economic anthropologists, however, argued that exchange could not properly be understood without a prior knowledge of production. Like earlier critics of capitalism, such as Karl Marx, they insisted that people who meet to exchange have different kinds and amounts of resources to use in bargaining with one another. Those differences in resources, Marx argued, are shaped by the process of economic production.

Does Production Drive Economic Activities?

Some economic anthropologists have argued that production is the driving force behind economic activity, creating supplies of goods which must accommodate people's demand, thereby determining levels of consumption. Anthropologists who take this view borrow their perspective, as well as many key concepts, from the works of Karl Marx. They argue that studying production explains important economic processes ignored by views that emphasize market exchange as the driving force of economic activity.

In Their Own Words

"So Much Work, So Much Tragedy . . . and for What?"

Angelita P. C. (the author's surnames were initialed to preserve her anonymity) describes traditional labor for farmers' wives in Costa Rica during the 1930s. Her account was included in a volume of peasant autobiographies published in Costa Rica in 1979.

The life of farmers' wives was more difficult than the life of day laborers' wives; what I mean is that we work more. The wife of the day laborer, she gets clean beans with no rubbish, shelled corn, pounded rice, maybe she would have to roast the coffee and grind it. On the other hand, we farm wives had to take the corn out of the husk, shuck it; and if it was rice, generally we'd have to get it out of the sack and spread it out in the sun for someone to pound it in the mortar. Although we had the advantage that we never lacked the staples: tortillas, rice, beans, and sugar-water. When you had to make tortillas, and that was every day, there were mountains of tortillas, because the people who worked in the fields had to eat a lot to regain their strength with all the effort they put out. And the tortilla is the healthiest food that was eaten—still is eaten—in the countryside. Another thing we had to do often was when you'd get the corn together to sell it, you always had to take it off the cob and dry it in the sun: the men spread it out on a tarp, maybe two or three sackfuls, and they would go and bring the corn, still in the husks, up from the cornfield or the shack where it was kept. Well, we women had to guard it from the chickens or the pigs that were always in the house, but the rush we had when it started to rain and the men hadn't gotten back! We had to fill the sacks with corn and then a little later haul it in pots to finish filling them; that's if the rain gave us time. If not, all of us women in the house would have to pick up the tarps—sometimes the neighbor-women would get involved in all the bustle—to carry the corn inside. We looked like ants carrying a big worm! The thing was to keep the corn from getting wet.

It didn't matter if you threw out your spine, or if your uterus dropped, or you started hemorrhaging, or aborted, but since none of that happened immediately, it was the last thing we thought of. So much work, so much tragedy and that was so common that it seemed like just a natural thing, and for what? To sell corn at about 20 colones or at most at 24 colones per fanega [about 3 bushels] of 24 baskets! What thankless times for farm people!

Source: Autobiografías campesinas. 1979, 36 (translation from the original Spanish by Robert H. Lavenda).

Labor

Labor is perhaps the most central marxian concept these anthropologists have emphasized. **Labor** is the activity linking human social groups to the material world around them: human beings must actively struggle together to transform natural substances into forms they can use. Human labor is therefore always *social* labor. Marx emphasized the importance of human physical labor in the material world, especially in the production of food, clothing, shelter, and tools. But Marx also recognized the importance of mental or cognitive labor: human intelligence allows us to reflect on and organize productive activities in different ways.

Modes of Production

Marx attempted to classify the ways different human groups carry out production. Each way is called a **mode of production**. Anthropologist Eric Wolf defined a mode of production as "a specific, historically occurring set of social relations through which labor is deployed to wrest energy from nature by means of tools, skills, organization, and knowledge" (1982, 75). Tools, skills, organization, and knowledge constitute what Marx called the **means of production**. The social relations linking human beings who use a given means of production within a particular mode of production are called the **relations of production**. That is, different productive tasks (clearing the bush, planting, harvesting, and so on) are

labor The activity linking human social groups to the material world around them; from the point of view of Karl Marx, labor is therefore always social labor.

mode of production A specific, historically occurring set of social relations through which labor is deployed to wrest energy from nature by means of tools, skills, organization, and knowledge.

means of production The tools, skills, organization, and knowledge used to extract energy from nature.

relations of production The social relations linking the people who use a given means of production within a particular mode of production.

Producing Sorghum and Millet in Honduras and the Sudan

Applied anthropologists carry out much work in international development, often in agricultural programs. The U.S. Agency for International Development (AID) is the principal instrument of U.S. foreign development assistance. One direction taken by AID in the mid-1970s was to create multidisciplinary research programs to improve food crops in developing countries. An early research program dealt with sorghum and millet, important grains in some of the poorest countries in the world (Figure 11.5). This was the International Sorghum/Millet Research Project (INTSORMIL). Selected American universities investigated one of six areas: plant breeding, agronomy, plant pathology, plant physiology, food chemistry, and socioeconomic studies.

Anthropologists from the University of Kentucky, selected for the socioeconomic study, used ethnographic field research techniques to gain firsthand knowledge of the socioeconomic constraints on the production, distribution, and consumption of sorghum and millet among limited-resource agricultural producers in the western Sudan and in Honduras. They intended to make their findings available to INTSORMIL as well as to scientists and government officials in the host countries. They believed sharing such knowledge could lead to more effective research and development. This task also required ethnographic research and anthropological skill.

The principal investigators from the University of Kentucky were Edward Reeves, Billie DeWalt, and Katherine DeWalt. They took a holistic and comparative approach, called *Farming Systems Research* (FSR). This approach attempts to determine the techniques used by farmers with limited resources to cope with the social, economic, and ecological conditions under which they live. FSR is holistic because it examines how the different crops and livestock are integrated and managed as a system. It also relates farm productivity to household consumption and off-farm sources of family income (Reeves, DeWalt, and DeWalt 1987, 74). This is very different from the traditional methods of agricultural research, which grow and test one crop at a time in an experiment station. The scientists at INTSORMIL are generally acknowledged among the best sorghum and millet researchers in the world, but their expertise comes from traditional agricultural research methods. They have spent little time working on the problems of limited-resource farmers in Third World countries.

The anthropologists saw their job as facilitating "a constant dialog between the farmer, who can tell what works best given the circumstances, and agricultural scientists, who produce potentially useful new solutions to old problems" (Reeves, DeWalt, and DeWalt 1987, 74–75). However, this was easier said than done in the sorghum/millet project. The perspectives of farmers and scientists were very different from one another. The anthropologists found themselves having to learn the languages and the conceptual systems of both the farmers and the scientists for the two groups to be able to communicate.

The anthropologists began research in June 1981 in western Sudan and in southern Honduras. They were in the field for 14 months of participant-observation and in-depth interviewing, as well as survey interviewing of limited-resource farmers, merchants, and middlemen. They discovered that the most significant constraints the farmers faced were uncertain rainfall, low soil fertility, and inadequate labor and financial resources (Reeves, DeWalt, and DeWalt 1987, 80). Equally important were the social and cultural systems within

assigned to different social groups, which Marx called **classes**, all of which must work together for production to be successful. Wolf notes that Marx speaks of at least eight different modes of production in his own writings, although he focused mainly on the capitalist mode.

Wolf finds the concept of mode of production useful and suggests that three modes of production have been particularly important in human history: (1) a *kin-ordered mode* (Figure 11.4), in which social labor is deployed on the basis of kinship relations (e.g., husbands/fathers clear the fields, the whole family plants, mothers/wives weed, children keep animals out of the field); (2) a *tributary mode*, "in which the primary producer, whether cultivator or herdsman, is allowed access to the means of production while tribute [a payment of goods or labor] is exacted from him by political or military means" (1982, 79); and (3) the *capitalist mode*, which has three main features: the means of production are private property owned by members of the capitalist class, workers must sell their labor power to the capitalists in order to survive, and surpluses of wealth are produced that capitalists may retain as profit or reinvest in production, to increase output and generate further surpluses and higher profits.

The kin-ordered mode of production is found among foragers and those farmers and herders whose political organization does not involve domination by one group.

---

classes Ranked groups within a hierarchically stratified society whose membership is defined primarily in terms of wealth, occupation, or other economic criteria.

Figure 11.5 INTSORMIL has been involved in the improvement of the cultivation of sorghum and millet. This is sorghum.

which the farmers were embedded. Farmers based their farming decisions on their understanding of who they were and what farming meant in their own cultures.

As a result of the FSR group's research, it became increasingly clear that "real progress in addressing the needs of small farmers in the Third World called for promising innovations to be tested at village sites and on farmers' fields under conditions that closely approximated those which the farmers experience" (Reeves, DeWalt, and DeWalt 1987, 77). Convincing the scientists and bureaucrats of this required the anthropologists to become advocates for the limited-resource farmers. Bill DeWalt and Edward Reeves ended up negotiating INTSORMIL's contracts with the Honduran and Sudanese governments and succeeded in representing the farmers. They had to learn enough about the bureaucracies and the agricultural scientists so they could put the farmers' interests in terms the others could understand.

As a result of the applied anthropologists' work, INTSORMIL scientists learned to understand how small farmers in two countries made agricultural decisions. They also learned that not all limited-resource farmers are alike.

The INTSORMIL staff was so impressed that it began funding long-term research directed at relieving the constraints that limited-resource farmers face. Rather than trying to develop and then introduce hybrids, INTSORMIL research aimed to modify existing varieties of sorghum. The goal is better-yielding local varieties that can be grown together with other crops.

In summary, Reeves, DeWalt, and DeWalt point out that without the anthropological research, fewer development funds would have been allocated to research in Sudan and Honduras. More important, the nature of the development aid would have been different.

Figure 11.4 This drawing from 1562 shows Native American men breaking the soil and Native American women planting, a gender-based division of labor.

In Their Own Words

Solidarity Forever

Anthropologist Dorinne Kondo, who worked alongside Japanese women in a Tokyo sweets factory, describes how factory managers, almost despite their best efforts, managed to engender strong bonds among women workers.

Our shared exploitation sometimes provided the basis for commonality and sympathy. The paltry pay was often a subject of discussion. . . . My co-workers and I were especially aware, however, of the toll our jobs took on our bodies. We constantly complained of our sore feet, especially sore heels from standing on the concrete floors. And a company-sponsored trip to the seashore revealed even more occupational hazards. At one point, as we all sat down with our rice balls and our box lunches, the part-timers pulled up the legs of their trousers to compare their varicose veins. In our informal contest, Hamada-san and Iida-san tied for first prize. The demanding pace and the lack of assured work breaks formed another subject of discussion. At most of the factories in the neighborhood where I conducted extensive interviews, work stopped at ten in the morning and at three in the afternoon, so workers could have a cup of tea and perhaps some crackers. Nothing of the sort occurred at the Satō factory, although the artisans were, if the pace of work slackened, able to escape the workroom, sit on their haunches, and have a smoke, or grab a snack if they were out doing deliveries or running up and down the stairs to the other divisions. Informal restrictions on the part-timers' movement and time seemed much greater. Rarely, if ever, was there an appropriate slack period where all of us could take a break. Yet our energy, predictably, slumped in the afternoon.

After my first few months in wagashi, Hamada-san began to bring in small containers of fruit juice, so we could take turns having a five-minute break to drink the juice and eat some seconds from the factory. Informal, mutual support enabled us to keep up our energies, as we each began to bring in juice or snacks for our tea breaks.

The company itself did nothing formally in this regard, but informal gestures of thoughtfulness and friendliness among co-workers surely redounded to the company's benefit, for they fostered our sense of intimacy and obligation to our fellow workers. The tea breaks are one example, but so are the many times we part-timers would stop off at Iris, our favorite coffee house, to sip banana juice or melon juice and trade gossip. We talked about other people in the company, about family, about things to do in the neighborhood. On one memorable occasion, I was sitting with the Western division part-timers in a booth near the window. A car honked as it went by, and Sakada-san grimaced and shouted loudly, "Shitsurei yarō—rude bastard!" The offender turned out to be her husband. In subsequent weeks, Sakada-san would delight in recounting this tale again and again, pronouncing shitsurei yarō with ever greater relish, and somehow, we never failed to dissolve in helpless laughter.

Source: Kondo 1990, 291–92.

The tributary mode is found among farmers or herders living in a social system that is divided into classes of rulers and subjects. Subjects produce both for themselves and for their rulers, who take a certain proportion of their subjects' produce or labor as tribute. The capitalist mode, the most recent to develop, can be found in the industrial societies of North America and western Europe beginning in the seventeenth and eighteenth centuries. The concept of mode of production thus draws attention to many of the same features of economic life highlighted in traditional anthropological discussions of subsistence strategies. Yet, the concept emphasizes forms of social and political organization as well as material productive activities and shows how they are interconnected. That is, the kin-ordered mode of production is distinctive as much for its use of the kinship system to allocate labor to production

as for the kind of production undertaken, such as farming. In a kin-ordered mode of production, the *relations of kinship* serve as the *relations of production* that enable a particular *mode of production* to be carried out. Farm labor organized according to kin-ordered relations of production, where laborers are relatives to whom no cash payment is due, is very different from farm labor organized according to capitalist relations of production, where laborers are often nonrelatives who are paid a wage.

What Is The Role of Conflict in Material Life?

Anthropologists traditionally have emphasized the important links between a society's organization (kinship groups, chiefdom, state) and the way that society meets its subsistence needs, either to demonstrate the stages of cultural evolution or to display the functional interrelationships between its parts. In both cases, however, the emphasis of the analysis has been on the harmonious fashion in which societies operate. For some observers, this carried the additional message that social stability was "natural" and should not be tampered with. Social change was possible, but it would take place in an orderly fashion, in the fullness of time, according to laws of development beyond the control of individual members of society.

Many anthropologists, however, have not been persuaded that social organization is naturally harmonious or that social change is naturally orderly. They find the marxian approach useful precisely because it treats conflict and disorder as a natural part of the human condition. The concept of mode of production makes a major contribution to economic anthropology precisely because it acknowledges that the potential for conflict is built into the mode of production itself. And the more complex and unequal is the involvement of different classes in a mode of production, the more intense is the struggle between them likely to be. The links between economic and political relations become particularly obvious and must be addressed (see Chapter 12).

Why Do People Consume What They Do?

Consumption usually refers to the using up of material goods necessary for human survival. These goods include—at a minimum—food, drink, clothing, and shelter; they can and often do include much more. Until quite recently, the study of consumption by economists and others has been much neglected, especially when compared to distribution or production. To some extent, this is because many observers assumed that there were no interesting questions to ask about consumption. That is, it seemed clear either that people consume goods for obvious reasons (i.e., because they need to eat and drink to survive) or that they consume goods as a result of idiosyncratic personal preferences (e.g., "I like the flavor of licorice and so I eat a lot of it, but my neighbor hates the flavor and would never put it into his mouth"). In either case, studying consumption seemed unlikely to reveal any interesting cultural patterns. As we will see below, however, anthropologists have always noticed striking differences in consumption patterns in different societies that seemed hard to reconcile with accepted economic explanations. Historically, anthropologists have taken three basic approaches to account for these patterns: (1) the internal explanation, (2) the external explanation, and (3) the cultural explanation.

The Internal Explanation: Malinowski and Basic Human Needs

The internal explanation for human consumption patterns comes from the work of Bronislaw Malinowski. Malinowski's version of functionalist anthropology explains social practices by relating them to the basic human needs that each practice supposedly fulfills. Basic human needs can be biological or psychological. Whatever their origin, if these needs go unmet, Malinowski argued, a society might not survive. Malinowski proposed a list of basic human needs, which includes nourishment, reproduction, bodily comforts, safety, movement, growth, and health. Every culture responds in its own way to these needs with some form of the corresponding institutions: food-getting techniques, kinship, shelter, protection, activities, training, and hygiene (Malinowski 1944, 91).

Malinowski's approach had the virtue of emphasizing the dependence of human beings on the physical world in order to survive. In addition, Malinowski was able to show that many customs that appear bizarre to uninitiated Western observers make sense once it is seen how they help people satisfy their basic human needs. However, Malinowski's approach fell short of explaining why all societies do not share the same consumption patterns. After all, some people eat wild fruit and nuts and wear clothing made of animal skins, others eat bread made from domesticated wheat and wear garments woven from the hair of domesticated sheep, and still others eat millet paste and meat from domesticated cattle and go naked. Why should these differences exist?

The External Explanation: Cultural Ecology

A later generation of anthropologists was influenced by evolutionary and ecological studies. They tried to answer this question with an external explanation for the diversity of human consumption patterns. As we saw in earlier chapters, ecology has to do with how living species relate to one another and the physical environment. To explain patterns of human consumption (as well as production and distribution), cultural ecologists have often turned to the resources available in the particular habitats exploited by particular human groups. Hence, the particular

---

consumption The using up of material goods necessary for human survival.

In Their Own Words

Questioning Collapse

In the last 15 years, geographer Jared Diamond has published two books that have enjoyed wide popular success, Guns, Germs, and Steel *(1997) and* Collapse: How Societies Choose to Fail or Succeed *(2005). At the same time, some anthropologists—including those who admire Diamond's achievements—are concerned by the selective way in which he makes use of anthropological data to support his arguments. These issues are explored in* Questioning Collapse *(2010), a recent volume of essays edited by Mesoamerican archaeologist Patricia A. McAnany and Near Eastern archaeologist Norman Yoffee.*

What's the Beef Between Scholars and Popular Writers?

Among the issues we wanted to explore in our AAA [American Anthropological Association] symposium and in our subsequent seminar were the reasons for the incredible success of Jared Diamond's books. After all, Diamond is a professor of geography at UCLA, not an anthropologist, archaeologist, or historian. He obviously reads prolifically the obscure (to most laypersons and students) publications of historians, archaeologists, and sociocultural anthropologists and can present their research with verve and clarity and as important knowledge for a larger public. In *Guns, Germs, and Steel*, Diamond confronts racist views of the past that claim that Western superiority is due to the genes and genius of Westerners. In *Collapse* he warns of real and potential environmental destruction in the present by arguing that past societies and cultures collapsed because they damaged their environments. His successful writing style of distilling simple points from complex issues is a remarkable gift; it is no wonder that his books win prizes and are used in classrooms . . . .

In this book most of the chapters are critical of Diamond's stories. This is why the AAA session was organized in the first place. Whereas we are indebted to Diamond for drawing together so much material from our own fields of research and for emphasizing how important anthropological and historical knowledge is for the modern world, as scholars we want to get things right. We also want to write in such a way that the public can grasp not only the significance of research findings but also how we do research and why we think that some stories are right, whereas others are not as right or are incomplete, and still others are dead wrong.

Thanks to Diamond's provoking inquiries and more generally those of the popular media, we focus this book on several questions: (1) Why do we portray ancient societies—especially those with indigenous descendants—as successes or failures, both in scholarship and in the popular media? We want to get the story of social change right, and descendants of the ancient societies we study demand it. (2) How do we characterize people who live today in the aftermath of empires? Today's world is the product of past worlds, and the consequences of the past cannot be ignored. (3) How are urgent climatic and environmental issues today similar to those faced by our ancestors? Can we learn from the past? . . .

The Question of Societal Collapse

Over two decades ago the sociologist Shmuel Eisenstadt wrote that societal collapse seldom occurs if collapse is taken to mean "the complete end of those political systems and their accompanying civilizational framework." Indeed, studying collapse is like viewing a low-resolution digital photograph: it's fine when small, compact, and viewed at a distance but dissolves into disconnected parts when examined up close. More recently, Joseph Tainter, after a search for archaeological evidence of societal "overshoot" and collapse, arrived at a conclusion similar to Eisenstadt's: there wasn't any. When closely examined, the overriding human story is one of survival and regeneration. Certainly crises existed, political forms changed, and landscapes were altered, but rarely did societies collapse in an absolute and apocalyptic way. Even the examples of societal collapse often touted in the media—Rapa Nui (Easter Island), Norse Greenland, Puebloan U.S. Southwest, and the Maya Lowlands—are also cases of societal resilience when examined carefully, as authors do in the chapters in this book (see Figure 11.6). Popular writers' tendency to approach the past in terms of a series of societal failures and collapses—while understandable in terms of providing drama and mystery—falls apart in light of the information and fresh perspectives presented in this book.

Abandoned ruins—the words themselves evoke a romantic sense of failure and loss to which even archaeologists—most of whom are reared in the Western tradition—are not immune. But why is it that when we visit Stonehenge we don't feel a twinge of cultural loss, but simply a sense that things were very different 5,000 years ago? Is it because Stonehenge is somehow part of *our* civilization? On the other hand, the Great Houses of Chaco Canyon, the soaring pyramids of ancestral Maya cities, the fallen colossal heads of Rapa Nui tend to invoke a sense of mysterious loss and cultural failure, and

In Their Own Words

Figure 11.6 One case study by Jared Diamond that has been criticized by anthropologists is that of Rapa Nui (Easter Island), where enormous human figures were carved between the years 1250 and 1500.

a notion that something must have gone terribly wrong environmentally. For many of us these places and people are not part of the Western experience. Moreover, descendant communities—in all three cases—live marginalized on the edge of nation-states without the resources and connections to worldwide media that are needed to tell their own story, at least to an English-speaking audience. Might these abandoned places, in many cases, be just as accurately viewed as part of a successful strategy of survival, part of human resilience? . . . Abandonment also can be read as indicative of opportunity elsewhere and of the societal flexibility to seize that opportunity. . . .

Although it would be wonderful to feel that scholarly understanding of abandonment stood outside contemporary social concerns, it is pretty clear that today's worries about the future make their way into our explanations of the past. . . . Historians and archaeologists, who are not immune to seeing the past through modern lenses, try to test the relevance of their ideas by looking for multiple lines of evidence that point to the same conclusion.

In our chapters we hold interpretations of past environmental abuse up to critical scrutiny for two reasons. First, because the fit between ideas and evidence is never straightforward. Second (and for better or worse), humans have a long history of both interacting assertively with their environments and coalescing into fragile political groups that fission easily. Archaeologists such as Sander van der Leeuw have shown that landscape alteration has occurred in human societies since the end of the Pleistocene (Ice Age), 10,000 years ago. It is not difficult to find evidence of preindustrial landscape alteration . . . but it is another matter altogether to link that evidence in a convincing and rigorous fashion to site abandonment

or changes in political forms. The notion that the present recapitulates the past is not necessarily true. We ask how long human societies have possessed the technological ability to profoundly change and destroy their environment and bring down their societies.

In concluding comments to this book and elsewhere, J. R. McNeill amasses a formidable body of evidence suggesting that the human ability to impact environment on a global scale is newfound and cannot be pushed back beyond the Industrial Revolution of the 1800s. . . .

Choice and Geographic Determinism

In his book on societal collapse, Jared Diamond proposes that societies choose to succeed or fail. On the other hand, in *Guns, Germs, and Steel*, there was no choice: today's inequalities among modern nation-states are argued to be the result of geographic determinism. In the first scenario, societies (or power brokers within societies) make the decisions that result in long-term success or failure. . . . At the root of this thesis is the modern neoliberal theory of self-interested motivation as well as the assumption of unconstrained and rational choice. . . . Many economists view the motivational assumptions of self-interest and rational choice as lacking explanatory power, even when applied to Western societies. When applied globally and into deep time, this theory has particular difficulties. . . .

If we are to understand global events today, we must perceive that the basis of intentionality and motivation can differ profoundly across the globe. . . . For those of us studying early states, archaeologists and historians alike, it isn't easy to discern intentions and their effects in the remote past. . . . Many current global inequalities indisputably are the product of historical colonialism and its enduring legacy. . . .

If one takes a long view, as archaeologists and historians are wont to do, then the situation in the year 2009 seems less the manifestation of a geographic destiny than it is a temporary state of affairs. Can anyone say that the present balance of economic and political power will be the same in 2500 as it is today? For example, in the year 1500 some of the most powerful and largest cities in the world existed in China, India, and Turkey. In the year 1000, many of the mightiest cities were located in Peru, Iraq, and Central Asia. In the year 500 they could be found in central Mexico, Italy, and China. In 2500 B.C.E., the most formidable rulers lived in Iraq, Egypt, and Pakistan. What geographic determinism can account for this? Is history a report card of success or failure?

Source: McAnany and Yoffee 2009, 4–10.

consumption patterns found in a particular society cannot depend just on the obvious, internal hunger drive, which is the same for all people everywhere; instead, people depend on the particular external resources present in the local habitat to which their members must adapt.

How Is Consumption Culturally Patterned?

Why do people X raise peanuts and sorghum? The internal, Malinowskian explanation would be to meet their basic human need for food. The external, cultural ecological explanation would be because peanuts and sorghum are the only food crops available in their habitat that, when cultivated, will meet their subsistence needs. Both these answers sound reasonable, but they are also incomplete. To be sure, people must consume something to survive, and they will usually meet this need by exploiting plant and animal species locally available. However, Malinowski and many cultural ecologists seem to assume that patterns of consumption are dictated by an iron environmental necessity that permits only narrow adaptive options. They further seem to assume that human beings are by and large powerless to modify what the environment offers (at least, it is sometimes implied, until the invention of modern technology).

But we have seen that human beings (along with many other organisms) are able to construct their own niches, buffering themselves from some kinds of selection pressures while exposing themselves to other kinds. This means that human populations, even those with foraging technologies, are not passive in the face of environmental demands. On the contrary, people have the agency to produce a range of cultural inventions—tools, social relations, domesticated crops, agroecologies. Or as Marshall Sahlins put it, human beings are *human* "precisely when they experience the world as a concept (symbolically). It is not essentially a question of priority but of the unique quality of human experience as meaningful experience. Nor is it an issue of the reality of the world; it concerns *which worldly dimension becomes pertinent*, and in what way, to a given human group" (1976, 142; emphasis added). Because human beings construct their own niches, they construct their patterns of consumption as well.

What Is the Original Affluent Society? Many Westerners long believed that foraging peoples led the most miserable of existences, spending all their waking hours in a food quest that yielded barely enough to keep them alive. To test this assumption in the field, Richard Lee went to live among the Dobe Ju/'hoansi, a foraging people of southern Africa (see EthnoProfile 11.4: Ju/'hoansi). Living in the central Kalahari Desert of southern Africa in

EthnoProfile 11.4

Ju/'hoansi (!Kung)

Region: Southern Africa

Nation: Botswana and Namibia

Population: 45,000

Environment: Desert

Livelihood: Hunting and gathering

Political organization: Traditionally, egalitarian bands; today, part of modern nation-states

For more information: Lee, Richard B. 1992b. *The Dobe Ju/'hoansi.* 2d ed. New York: Holt, Rinehart and Winston.

the early 1960s, the Ju/'hoansi of Dobe were among the few remaining groups of San still able to return to full-time foraging when economic ties to neighboring herders became too onerous. Although full-time foraging has been impossible in the Dobe area since the 1980s and the Ju/'hoansi have had to make some difficult adjustments, Lee documented a way of life that contrasts vividly with their current settled existence.

Lee accompanied the Ju/'hoansi as they gathered and hunted in 1963, and he recorded the amounts and kinds of food they consumed. The results of his research were surprising. It turned out that the Ju/'hoansi provided themselves with a varied and well-balanced diet based on a selection from among the food sources available in their environment. At the time of Lee's fieldwork, the Ju/'hoansi classified more than 100 species of plants as edible, but only 14 were primary components of their diet (1992b, 45ff.). Some 70 percent of this diet consisted of vegetable foods; 30 percent was meat. Mongongo nuts, a protein-rich food widely available throughout the Kalahari, alone made up more than one-quarter of the diet. Women provided about 55 percent of the diet, and men provided 45 percent, including the meat. The Ju/'hoansi spent an average of 2.4 working days—or about 20 hours—per person per week in food-collecting activities. Ju/'hoansi bands periodically suffered from shortages of their preferred foods and were forced to consume less desired items. Most of the time, however, their diet was balanced and adequate and consisted of foods of preference (1992b, 56ff.; Figure 11.7).

Figure 11.7 Ju/'hoansi women returning from foraging with large quantities of mongongo nuts.

Marshall Sahlins coined the expression "the original affluent society" to refer to the Ju/'hoansi and other foragers like them. In an essay published in 1972, Sahlins challenged the traditional Western assumption that the life of foragers is characterized by scarcity and near-starvation (see Sahlins 1972). **Affluence**, he argued, is having more than enough of whatever is required to satisfy consumption needs. There are two ways to create affluence. The first, to *produce much*, is the path taken by Western capitalist society; the second, to *desire little*, is the option, Sahlins argues, that foragers have taken. Put another way, the Ju/'hoansi foragers used culture to construct a niche within which their wants were few but abundantly fulfilled by their local environment. Moreover, it is not that foragers experience no greedy impulses; rather, according to Sahlins, affluent foragers live in societies whose institutions do not reward greed. Sahlins concluded that, for these reasons, foragers cannot be considered poor, even though their material standard of living is low by Western measures.

Original affluent foraging societies emphasize the long-standing anthropological observation that the concept of economic "needs" is vague (Douglas and Isherwood 1979). Hunger can be satisfied by beans and rice or steak and lobster. Thirst can be quenched by water or beer or soda pop. In effect, human beings in differently constructed niches define needs and provide for their satisfaction according to their own *cultural* logic, which is reducible to neither biology nor psychology nor ecological pressure. In every case, the human need for food is met but selectively, and the selection humans make carries a social message. But what about cases of consumption that do not involve food and drink?

Banana Leaves in the Trobriand Islands Anthropologist Annette Weiner traveled to the Trobriand Islands in the 1970s, more than half a century after Malinowski carried out his classic research there (see EthnoProfile 10.2: Trobriand Islanders). To her surprise, she discovered a venerable local tradition involving the accumulation and exchange of banana leaves, which were known locally as "women's wealth" (Figure 11.8). Malinowski had never described this tradition, even though there is evidence from photographs and writing that it was in force at the time of his fieldwork. Possibly, Malinowski overlooked these transactions because they are carried out by women, and Malinowski did not view women as important actors in the economy. However, Malinowski might also have considered banana leaves to be an unlikely item of consumption because he recognized as "economic" only those activities that satisfied biological

affluence The condition of having more than enough of whatever is required to satisfy consumption needs.

survival needs, and banana leaves are inedible. Transactions involving women's wealth, however, turn out to be crucial for the stability of Trobrianders' relationships to their relatives.

Banana leaves might be said to have a "practical" use because women make skirts out of them. These skirts are highly valued, but the transactions involving women's wealth more often involve the bundles of leaves themselves. Why bother to exchange great amounts of money or other goods to obtain bundles of banana leaves? This would seem to be a classic example of irrational consumption. Yet, "as an economic, political, and social force, women's wealth exists as the representation of the most fundamental relationships in the social system" (Weiner 1980, 289).

Trobrianders are *matrilineal* (i.e., they trace descent through women; see Chapter 13), and men traditionally prepare yam gardens for their sisters. After the harvest, yams from these gardens are distributed by a woman's brother to her husband. Weiner's research suggests that what Malinowski took to be the *redistribution* of yams, from a wife's kin to her husband, could be better understood as a *reciprocal exchange* of yams for women's wealth. The parties central to this exchange are a woman, her brother, and her husband. The woman is the person through whom yams are passed from her own kin to her husband and through whom women's wealth is passed from her husband to her own kin.

Transactions involving women's wealth occur when someone in a woman's kinship group dies. Surviving relatives must "buy back," metaphorically speaking, all the yams or other goods that the deceased person gave to others during his or her lifetime. Each payment marks a social link between the deceased and the recipient,

and the size of the payment marks the importance of their relationship. All the payments must be made in women's wealth.

The dead person's status, as well as the status of her or his family, depends on the size and number of the payments made; and the people who must be paid can number into the hundreds. Women make women's wealth themselves and exchange store goods to obtain it from other women, but when someone in their matrilineage dies, they collect it from their husbands. Indeed, a woman's value is measured by the amount of women's wealth her husband provides. Furthermore, "if a man does not work hard enough for his wife in accumulating wealth for her, then her brother will not increase his labor in the yam garden. . . . The production in yams and women's wealth is always being evaluated and calculated in terms of effort and energy expended on both sides of production. The value of a husband is read by a woman's kin as the value of his productive support in securing women's wealth for his wife" (Weiner 1980, 282).

Weiner argues that women's wealth upholds the kinship arrangements of Trobriand society. It balances out exchange relationships between lineages linked by marriage, reinforces the pivotal role of women and matriliny, and publicly proclaims, during every funeral, the social relationships that make up the fabric of Trobriand society. The system has been stable for generations, but Weiner suggests that it could collapse if cash ever became widely substitutable for yams. Under such conditions, men might buy food and other items on the market. If they no longer depended on yams from their wives' kin, they might refuse to supply their wives' kin with women's wealth. This had not yet happened at the time of Weiner's research, but she saw it as a possible future development.

Figure 11.8 In the Trobriand Islands, women's wealth, made from banana leaves, is displayed during a funeral ritual called the *sagali*, which serves to reaffirm the status of the women's kinship group.

In Their Own Words

Fake Masks and Faux Modernity

Christopher Steiner addresses the perplexing situation all of us face in the contemporary multicultural world: given mass reproduction of commodities made possible by industrial capitalism, how can anybody distinguish "authentic" material culture from "fake" copies? The encounter he describes took place in Ivory Coast, western Africa.

In the Plateau market place, I once witnessed the following exchange between an African art trader and a young European tourist. The tourist wanted to buy a Dan face mask which he had selected from the trader's wooden trunk in the back of the market place. He had little money, he said, and was trying to barter for the mask by exchanging his Seiko wrist watch. In his dialogue with the trader, he often expressed his concern about whether or not the mask was "real." Several times during the bargaining, for example, the buyer asked the seller, "Is it really old?" and "Has it been worn?" While the tourist questioned the trader about the authenticity of the mask, the trader, in turn, questioned the tourist about the authenticity of his watch. "Is this the real kind of Seiko," he asked, "or is it a copy?" As the tourist examined the mask—turning it over and over again looking for the worn and weathered effects of time—the trader scrutinized the watch, passing it to other traders to get their opinion on its authenticity.

Although, on one level, the dialogue between tourist and trader may seem a bit absurd, it points to a deeper problem in modern transnational commerce: an anxiety over authenticity and a crisis of misrepresentation. While the shelves in one section of the Plateau market place are lined with replicas of so-called "traditional" artistic forms, the shelves in another part of the market place—just on the other side of the street—are stocked with imperfect imitations of modernity: counterfeit Levi jeans, fake Christian Dior belts, and pirated recordings of Michael Jackson and Madonna. Just as the Western buyer looks to Africa for authentic symbols of a "primitive" lifestyle, the African buyer looks to the West for authentic symbols of a modern lifestyle. In both of their searches for the "genuine" in each other's culture, the African trader and the Western tourist often find only mere approximations of "the real thing"—tropes of authenticity which stand for the riches of an imagined reality.

Source: Steiner 1994, 128–29.

How Is Consumption Being Studied Today?

The foregoing examples focus attention on distinctive consumption practices in different societies and demonstrate that the Western market is not the measure of all things. These studies also encourage respect for alternative consumption practices that, in different times and places, have worked as well as or better than capitalist markets to define needs and provide goods to satisfy those needs. But many anthropologists also draw attention to the way in which the imposition of Western colonialism has regularly undermined such alternatives, attempting to replace them with new needs and goods defined by the capitalist market. This helps explain why, as Daniel Miller summarizes, "much of the early literature on consumption is replete with moral purpose," emphasizing the ways in which vulnerable groups have resisted commodities or have developed ritual means of "taming" them, based on an awareness at some level of the capacity of those commodities to destroy (1995, 144–45). At the beginning of the twenty first century, however, the consumption of market commodities occurs everywhere in the world. Moreover, not only are Western commodities sometimes

embraced by those we might have expected to reject them (e.g., video technology by indigenous peoples of the Amazon), but this embrace frequently involves making use of these commodities for local purposes, to defend or to enrich local culture, rather than to replace it (e.g., the increasing popularity of sushi in the United States).

Daniel Miller has therefore urged anthropologists to recognize that these new circumstances require that they move beyond a narrow focus on the destructive potential of mass-produced commodities to a broader recognition of the role commodities play in a globalizing world. But this shift does not mean that concern about the negative consequences of capitalist practices disappears. In a global world in which everyone everywhere increasingly relies on commodities provided by a capitalist market, Miller believes that critical attention needs to be refocused on "inequalities of access and the deleterious impact of contemporary economic institutions on much of the world's population" (143).

Coca-Cola in Trinidad The change of focus promoted in Miller's writing about anthropological studies of consumption is nowhere better in evidence than in his own research on the consumption of Coca-Cola in Trinidad (1998). He points out that for many observers of global consumption, Coca-Cola occupies the status of a *meta-symbol*: "a symbol that stands for the debate about the materiality of culture" (169). That is, Coca-Cola is often portrayed as a Western/American commodity that represents the ultimately destructive global potential of all forms of capitalist consumption. Extracting profits from dominated peoples by brainwashing them into thinking that drinking Coke will improve their lives, the powerful controllers of capitalist market forces are accused of replacing cheaper, culturally appropriate, locally produced, and probably more nutritious beverages with empty calories. Based on his own fieldwork, however, Miller is able to show that this scenario grossly misrepresents the economic and cultural role which Coca-Cola plays in Trinidad, where it has been present since the 1930s.

First, Coca-Cola is not a typical example of global commodification because it has always spread as a franchise, allowing for flexible arrangements with local bottling plants. Second, the bottling plant that originally produced Coca-Cola in Trinidad was locally owned (as is the conglomerate that eventually bought it). Third, apart from the imported concentrate, the local bottler was able to obtain all the other key supplies needed to produce the drink (e.g., sugar, carbonation, bottles) from local, Trinidadian sources. Fourth, this bottling company exports soft drinks to other islands throughout the Caribbean, making it an important local economic force that accounts for a considerable proportion of Trinidad's foreign exchange earnings. Fifth, the bottler of Coca-Cola also bottled other drinks and has long competed with several other local bottling companies. Decisions made by these companies, rather than by Coca-Cola's home office, have driven local production decisions about such matters as the introduction of new flavor lines. Sixth, and perhaps most importantly, Coca-Cola has long been incorporated into a set of local, Trinidadian understandings about beverages that divides them into two basic categories: "red sweet drinks" and "black sweet drinks"; in this framework, Coke is simply an upmarket black, sweet drink, and it has traditionally been consumed, like other black sweet drinks, as a mixer with rum, the locally produced alcoholic beverage. Finally, the Trinidadian categories of "sweet drinks" do not correspond to the Coca-Cola company's idea of "soft drinks," a distinction which has baffled company executives. For example, executives were taken by surprise when Trinidadians objected to attempts to reduce the sweetness of Coca-Cola and other beverages since this did not correspond to the trend they were familiar with from the United States, where taste has shifted away from heavily sugared soft drinks in recent years (Figure 11.9).

Beverage consumption in Trinidad is connected with ideas of cultural identity. "Red sweet drinks" have been associated with the Trinidadian descendants of indentured laborers, originally from the Indian subcontinent, and "black sweet drinks," with Trinidadian descendants of enslaved Africans. But this does not mean that the drinks are consumed exclusively by members of those communities. On the contrary, both kinds of sweet drink

Figure 11.9 The soft-drink market in Trinidad is both complex and idiosyncratic, reflecting Trinidadian understandings of beverage categories.

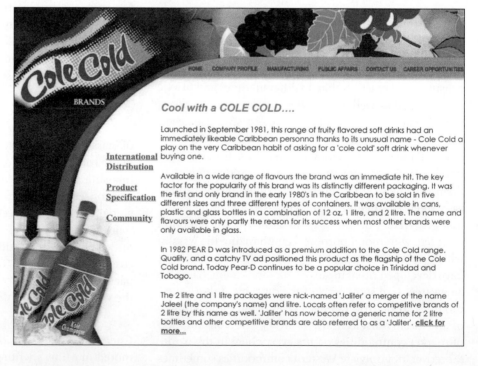

make sense as elements in a more complex image of what it means to be Trinidadian: "a higher proportion of Indians drink Colas, while Kola champagne as a red drink is more commonly drunk by Africans. Many Indians explicitly identify with Coke and its modern image," while "In many respects the 'Indian' connoted by the red drink today is in some ways the Africans' more nostalgic image of how Indians either used to be or perhaps still should be" (D. Miller 1998, 180). There is no simple connection between the political parties which different segments of the Trinidadian population support and the owners of different local bottling companies producing red or black sweet drinks. Finally, the Trinidadians Miller knew emphatically did *not* associate drinking Coke with trying to imitate Americans. "Trinidadians do not and will not choose between being American and being Trinidadian. Most reject parochial nationalism or neo-Africanized roots that threaten to diminish their sense of rights of access to global goods, such as computers or blue jeans. But they will fiercely retain those localisms they wish to retain, not because they are hypocritical but because inconsistency is an appropriate response to contradiction" (185). Miller concludes, therefore, that it is a serious mistake to use Coca-Cola as a meta-symbol of the evils of commodity consumption. As we will see in our discussion of globalization in Chapter 15, Miller's conclusion is reinforced by studies of consumption that focus on the many ways in which global commodities are incorporated into locally defined cultural practices.

The Anthropology of Food and Nutrition

One of the most recent areas of anthropological specialization centers on studies of food and nutrition. For some time biological anthropologists have carried out cross-cultural comparisons of nutrition and growth in different societies, and cultural anthropologists, such as Daniel Miller, have written detailed studies of particular local or ethnic food habits. Today, however, the anthropology of food and nutrition is increasingly concerned with the way the global capitalist food market works, favoring the food security of some consumers over others. At the same time, exploring links between food and culture in a globally complex world exposes changing understandings of fatness and thinness, and it reveals the many ways different kinds of food and cooking can be embraced by different groups in society to bolster their gender, sexual, racial, ethnic, class, or national identities.

Carole Counihan is a pioneering anthropologist of food and nutrition whose work was initially inspired by a feminist desire to give an ethnographic voice to women. She found that food was an aspect of culture that many women used to express themselves when other avenues were blocked. Beginning in 1970, she lived and worked in Italy for fourteen years. During this time she developed a "long term relationship with a Florentine I call Leonardo," and most of the data for her book *Around the Tuscan Table* (2004) comes "from fifty-six hours of food-centered life histories tape-recorded in Italian with Leonardo's twenty-three living relatives in 1982–84" (2004, 2).

Counihan began collecting food-centered life histories from women but eventually collected them from men as well. Because these life histories came from individuals from different generations, they reflected historical changes in the political economy of food that had shaped the lives of her interview subjects over time. For example, situating the food memories of the oldest members of her sample required reconstructing the traditional *mezzadria* sharecropping system in Tuscany. This system was based on large landholdings worked by peasant laborers whose households were characterized by a strict division of labor by gender: the patriarch (male head of the family) managed food production in the fields, and his wife supervised food preparation for the large extended family. The *mezzadria* system would disappear in the early twentieth century, but it constituted the foundation of Tuscan food practices that would follow.

Counihan's interviewees ate a so-called "Mediterranean" diet consisting of "pasta, fresh vegetables, legumes, olive oil, bread, and a little meat or fish" (2004, 74) (Figure 11.10). Food was scarce in the first part of the twentieth century but more abundant after World War II. "This diet, however, was already being modified by the postmodern, ever-larger agro-food industry that continued to grow in 2003, but which Florentines and other Italians shaped by alternative food practices" (2004, 4).

The postwar capitalist market also drew younger Florentines into new kinds of paid occupations, which led to modifications of the earlier gendered division of labor, without eliminating it entirely. Counihan describes the struggles of Florentines of her generation, especially women, who needed to work for wages but who were still expected to maintain a household and a paying job at the same time and often could not count on assistance from their husbands with domestic chores, including cooking. Counihan is especially critical about Italian child-rearing practices that allow boys to grow up with no responsibilities around the house, learning to expect their sisters (and later their wives) to take care of them, explaining away their incompetence at housekeeping tasks as a natural absence of talent or interest. She also describes men who cook on a regular basis but who often do not take on the tasks of shopping for ingredients or cleaning up

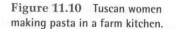

Figure 11.10 Tuscan women making pasta in a farm kitchen.

and who tend to dismiss cooking as easy, thereby diminishing the status of work that has long been central to Florentine women's sense of self-worth.

Food-centered life histories from Counihan's oldest interviewees traced nearly a century of changing Tuscan food practices and revealed, surprisingly, older people's nostalgia for the more constrained patterns of food consumption in their youth. "When my older subjects were young before and during the second world war, consumption was highly valued because it was scarce and precarious. Yet their children, born after the war in the context of the Italian economic miracle, grew up in a world where consumption was obligatory, taken for granted, and essential to full personhood—a transformation lamented by older people" (2004, 5).

Even as Counihan's research documents continuities in Tuscan diet and cuisine, it also demonstrates the way deeply rooted consumption practices were upended by the Italian state under Mussolini in the 1920s and 1930s and by the international cataclysm of World War II. Anthropologists have long argued that economic life cannot be considered apart from political relations in any society.

Chapter Summary

1. Contemporary cultural anthropologists are interested in how cultures change, but they are suspicious of evolutionary schemes that give the impression that social arrangements could not have been—or could not be—other than the way they are. They also point out that no society anywhere is static. The power that human beings have to reproduce or to change their social organization is an important focus of anthropological study. Anthropological approaches can provide insights often overlooked by other disciplines.

2. Human economic activity is usefully divided into three phases—production, distribution, and consumption—and is often shaped in important ways by storage practices. Formal neoclassical economic theory developed in Europe in order to explain how capitalism works, and it emphasizes the importance of market exchange. Economic anthropologists showed that noncapitalist societies regularly relied on nonmarket modes of exchange, such as reciprocity and redistribution, which still play restricted roles in societies dominated by the capitalist market.

3. Marxian economic anthropologists view production as more important than exchange in determining the patterns of economic life in a society. They classify societies in terms of their modes of production. Each mode of production contains within it the potential for conflict between classes of people who receive differential benefits and losses from the productive process.

4. In the past, some anthropologists tried to explain consumption patterns in different societies either by arguing that people produce material goods to satisfy basic human needs or by connecting consumption patterns to specific material resources available to people in the material settings where they lived. Ethnographic evidence demonstrates that both these explanations are inadequate because they ignore how culture defines our needs and provides for their satisfaction according to its own logic.

5. Particular consumption preferences that may seem irrational from the viewpoint of neoclassical economic theory may make sense when the wider cultural practices of consumers are taken into consideration. In the twenty-first century, those whom Western

observers might have expected to reject Western market commodities often embrace them, frequently making use of them to defend or enrich their local culture rather than to replace it. In a global world in which everyone everywhere increasingly relies on commodities—including food—provided by a capitalist market, some anthropologists focus on inequalities of access and the negative impact of contemporary economic institutions on most of the world's population.

For Review

1. Explain the connection between culture and livelihood.
2. Describe each of the three models presented by Wilk and Cliggett.
3. Define production, distribution, and consumption.
4. What is neoclassical economic theory?
5. Describe each of the three modes of exchange.
6. What is a mode of production? What are the three modes of production that Eric Wolf found useful?
7. Explain how conflict is built into the mode of production.
8. Define consumption. Summarize each of the explanations offered in the text for human consumption patterns.
9. Explain the significance of food storage and food sharing in economic activity.
10. What are the key elements in Marshall Sahlins's argument about "the original affluent society"?
11. The text offers two case studies about the cultural construction of human needs—the original affluent society and banana leaves in the Trobriand Islands. Explain how each of these illuminates the cultural construction of human needs.
12. Summarize Miller's argument about the significance of Coca-Cola in Trinidad.
13. Discuss the connections between gender and food in Italy, as presented by Carole Counihan.

Key Terms

affluence   331
capitalism   320
classes   324
commodity
   exchanges   321
consumption   327

economic
   anthropology   316
gift exchanges   321
institutions   317
labor   323
market exchange   321

means of production   323
mode of production   323
modes of exchange   321
neoclassical economic
   theory   320
reciprocity   321

redistribution   321
relations of
   production   323
social organization   316
status   320

Suggested Readings

Counihan, Carole. 2004. *Around the Tuscan table*. New York and London: Routledge. *Food-centered life histories allow Counihan to re-create a century of changing food practices—and social relations—in central Italy. Counihan analyzes the historically changing food ways of Tuscany to reveal changes in Tuscan (and Italian) understandings of gender and family relations.*

Counihan, Carole, and Penny van Esterik, eds. 2008. *Food and culture: A reader*, 2nd edition. New York and London: Routledge. *A collection of classic and recent essays on a range of topics currently investigated by anthropologists who study the anthropology of food and nutrition.*

Douglas, Mary, and Baron Isherwood. 1996. *The world of goods: Towards an anthropology of consumption*, rev. ed. New York: Routledge. *A discussion of consumption, economic theories about consumption, and what anthropologists can contribute to the study of consumption.*

Ensminger, Jean, ed. 2002. *Theory in economic anthropology.* Walnut Creek, CA: AltaMira Press. *An introductory volume that addresses the contributions that economic anthropology can make to understanding a globalized world economy.*

Lee, Richard. 2002. *The Dobe Ju/'hoansi*, 3rd ed. Belmont, CA: Wadsworth. *This highly readable ethnography contains important discussions about foraging as a way of making a living and traces political and economic changes in Ju/'hoansi life since Lee began fieldwork in Dobe in the 1960s.*

Sahlins, Marshall. 1972. *Stone Age economics.* Chicago: Aldine. *A series of classic essays on economic life, written from a substantivist position. Includes "The Original Affluent Society."*

Wilk, Richard, and Lisa Cliggett. 2007. *Economies and cultures.* Boulder, CO: Westview. *A current, accessible "theoretical guidebook" to the conflicting views of human nature that underlie disputes in economic anthropology.*

How Do Anthropologists Study Political Relations?

12

H uman societies are able to organize human interdependency successfully only if they find ways to manage relations of power among the different individuals and groups of which they are composed. In this chapter, we survey approaches anthropologist take to the study of political relations in different societies.

Chapter Outline

◄ *February 11, 2011: Demonstrators in Alexandria, Egypt, wave the flag during the Egyptian revolution.*

Anthropologists have long been interested in the role of power in human societies. Why are members of some societies able to exercise power on roughly equal terms, whereas other societies sharply divide the powerful from the powerless? In societies where access to power is unequal, how can those with little power gain more? What, in fact, is power?

Human societies are able to organize human interdependency successfully only if they find ways to manage relations of power among the different individuals and groups they comprise. **Power** may be understood broadly as "transformative capacity" (Giddens 1979, 88). When the choice affects an entire social group, scholars speak of *social power*. In this chapter, you will learn about the approaches anthropologists take to the study of political relations in different societies. Eric Wolf (1994) describes three different modes of social power: the first, *interpersonal power*, involves the ability of one individual to impose his or her will on another individual; the second, *organizational power*, highlights how individuals or social units can limit the actions of other individuals in particular social settings; the third, *structural power*, organizes social settings themselves and controls the allocation of social labor. To lay bare the patterns of structural power requires paying attention to the large-scale and increasingly global division of labor among regions and social groups, the unequal relations between these regions and groups, and the way these relations are maintained or modified over time. The way in which clothing is manufactured now—in factories in Indonesia or El Salvador, Romania or China—for markets in Europe, the United States, and Japan is an example of structural power. People are hired to work long hours for low wages in unpleasant conditions to make clothing that they cannot afford to buy, even if it were available for sale in the communities where they live (Figure 12.1).

How Are Culture and Politics Related?

The study of social power in human society is the domain of **political anthropology**. In a recent overview, Joan Vincent argues that political anthropology continues to be vital because it involves a complex interplay

between ethnographic fieldwork, political theory, and critical reflection on political theory (2002, 1). Vincent divides the history of political anthropology into three phases. The first phase, from 1851 to 1939, she considers the "formative" era, in which basic orientations and some of the earliest anthropological commentaries on political matters were produced. The second phase, from 1942 to about 1971, is the "classic" era in the field. It is most closely associated with the flourishing of British social anthropology rooted in functionalist theory and produced well-known works by such eminent figures as E. E. Evans-Pritchard, Max Gluckman, Fredrik Barth, and Edmund Leach. This phase developed in the context of the post–World War II British Empire through the period of decolonization in the 1950s and 1960s. Topics of investigation during this period were also the "classic" topics of political anthropology: the classification of preindustrial political systems and attempts to reconstruct their evolution; displaying the characteristic features of different kinds of preindustrial political systems and demonstrating how these functioned to produce political order; studying local processes of political strategizing by individuals in non-Western societies (see, e.g., Lewellyn 1983). Decolonization drew attention to emerging national-level politics in new states and the effects of "modernization" on the "traditional" political structures that had formerly been the focus of anthropological investigation. The turbulent politics of the 1960s and early 1970s, however, called this approach into question.

Beginning in the 1960s, political anthropologists developed new ways of thinking about political issues and new theoretical orientations to guide them, inaugurating in the 1970s and 1980s a third phase in which the anthropology of politics posed broader questions about power and inequality (Vincent 2002, 3). Under conditions of globalization, anthropologists interested in studying power have joined forces with scholars in other disciplines who share their concerns and have adopted ideas from influential political thinkers such as Antonio Gramsci and Michel Foucault to help them explain how power shapes the lives of those among whom they carry out ethnographic research. The cross-cultural study of political institutions reveals the paradox of the human condition. On the one hand, open cultural creativity allows humans to imagine worlds of pure possibility; on the other hand, all humans live in material circumstances that make many of those possibilities profoundly unrealistic. We can imagine many different ways to organize ourselves into groups, but, as Marx pointed out long ago, the past weighs like a nightmare on the brain of the living—and the opportunity to remake social organization is ordinarily quite limited.

---

power Transformative capacity; the ability to transform a given situation
political anthropology The study of social power in human society.

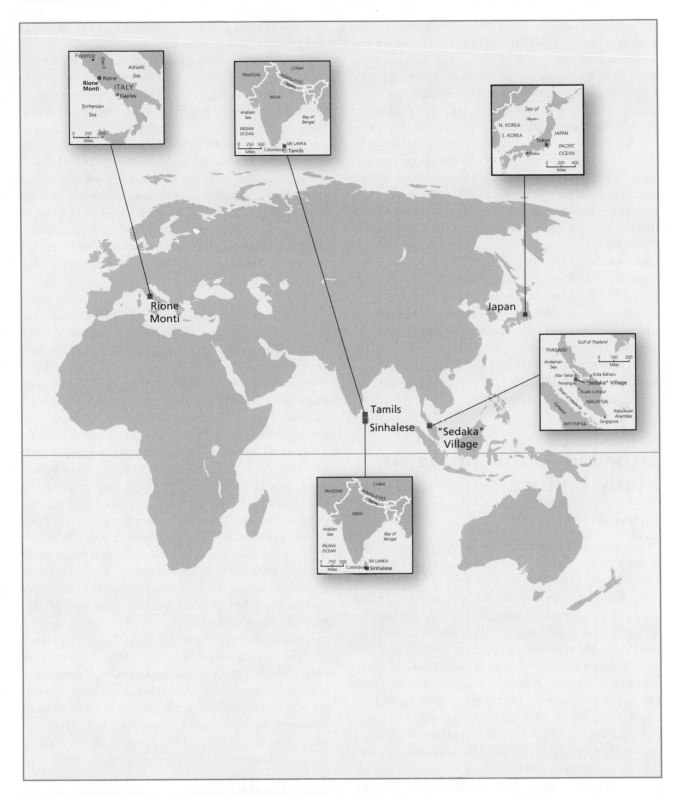

Figure 12.1   Location of societies whose EthnoProfiles appear in Chapter 12.

Human beings actively work to reshape the environments in which they live to suit themselves. Because the resources available in any environment can be used to sustain more than one way of life, however, human beings must choose which aspects of the material world to depend on. This is why, inevitably, questions about human economic activity are intimately intertwined with questions about the distribution of power in society. Some archaeologists have suggested, as we saw in Chapter 7, that population growth is a constant aspect of the human condition that determines forms of social organization. Marshall Sahlins (1976, 13) pointed out, however, that population pressure determines nothing more than the number of people that can be supported when the environment is used in a particular way. Members of a society can respond to that pressure in any of various ways: they can try to get along on less, intensify food production by inventing new technology, reduce their numbers by inventing new social practices (infanticide or other forms of birth control), or migrate elsewhere. Indeed, the manner in which a group might choose to implement any of these options is equally undetermined by population pressure. Which members of the group will have to do with less? Which members will control technological innovation? Who will be expected to migrate? And will the ultimate decision be imposed by force or voluntarily adopted?

The answers offered to these questions by members of any particular society describe the niche they have constructed for themselves. By building social and political alliances and mobilizing technology and material resources in order to make a living, ways of life are scaffolded and sustained over time.

How Do Anthropologists Study Politics?

Coercion

In the beginning, political anthropologists were strongly influenced by earlier Western thinkers who had assumed that the state was the prototype of "civilized" social power. For them, the absence of a state could mean only *anarchy*, disorderly struggles for power among individuals—what the English philosopher Thomas Hobbes (1588–1679) called the "war of all against all." This view assumes that power is best understood as physical force, or *coercion*. A fistfight might be seen as a typical, "natural" manifestation of attempts by individuals to exercise physical coercion. Although states that monopolize the use of force often perpetrated injustice or exploitation as a side effect, Hobbes and others viewed this as the necessary price for social order. Their assumption was that cooperative social living is not natural for human individuals because they are born with **free agency**—instincts that lead them to pursue their own self-interest above everything else and to challenge one another for dominance.

Discussions of power as coercion tend to see political activity as competition between individual free agents over political control. When free agents make decisions, no larger groups, no historical obligations, no collective beliefs can or ought to stand in their way. For some, cultural evolution took a giant leap forward when our ancestors first realized that sticks and stones could be used as weapons not only against nonhuman predators but especially against human enemies. In this view, human history is a chronicle of the production of better and better weapons. The civilizations we are so proud of have been born and sustained in violence. But this is not the only way to understand human agency, as we will see.

Coercion in Societies without States? Early anthropologists such as Lewis Henry Morgan showed that kinship institutions could organize orderly social life in societies without states, and his observations were confirmed by later political anthropologists, such as E. E. Evans-Pritchard, based on his work among the Azande. Evans-Pritchard's description of social life among the Azande ([1937] 1976) in no way resembled a war of all against all, even though the Azande lived in a stateless society and held a complex set of beliefs about witchcraft, oracles, and magic (see EthnoProfile 10.5: Azande). Evans-Pritchard observed that Azande people discussed witchcraft openly, and if they believed they were bewitched, they were likely to be angry rather than afraid. This kind of attitude made sense because most Azande subscribed to a worldview in which witchcraft had a meaningful place. In addition, they did not feel helpless because their society also supplied them with practical remedies, like vengeance magic, that they could use to defend themselves if they thought they had been bewitched. Here, we see an example of what Wolf called organizational power that does not depend on state coercion. Instead, it depends on *persuasion*. Scaffolded by particular social institutions and practices, the belief system continues to appear natural and rational to members of the society; this is why ordinary, rational people support it.

What Are Domination and Hegemony? Anthropologists who consider both coercive and persuasive forms of power have to come to terms with the ambiguity of power both as a concept and as a phenomenon threaded into the fabric of everyday life. Perhaps people do submit to institutionalized power because they have been coerced and fear punishment. But perhaps they submit because they believe that the power structures in

---

free agency The freedom of self-contained individuals to pursue their own interests above everything else and to challenge one another for dominance.

their society are legitimate, given their understandings about the way the world works. What could lead people to accept coercion by others as legitimate (Figure 12.2)? A worldview that justifies the social arrangements under which people live is sometimes called an **ideology**. Karl Marx argued that rulers consolidate their power by successfully persuading their subjects to accept an ideology that portrays domination by the ruling class as legitimate; dominated groups who accept the ruling class ideology were said to suffer from *false consciousness*. The concept of false consciousness is problematic, however, since it views people as passive beings incapable of withstanding ideological indoctrination. As we discussed in Chapter 8, this is not a plausible view of human nature.

More promising is the approach taken by Antonio Gramsci (1971). Writing in the 1930s, Gramsci pointed out that coercive rule—what he called **domination**—is expensive and unstable. Rulers do better if they can persuade the dominated to accept their rule as legitimate, both by providing some genuine material benefits to their subjects and by using schools and other cultural institutions to disseminate an ideology justifying their rule. If they achieve all this—while also ensuring that none of these concessions seriously undermines their privileged position—they have established what Gramsci called **hegemony**. Hegemony is never absolute but always vulnerable to challenges: struggles may develop between rulers trying to justify their domination and subordinate groups who exercise agency by challenging "official" ideologies and practices that devalue or exclude them. Hegemony may be threatened if subordinate groups maintain or develop alternative, or *counter-hegemonic*, cultural practices. Successful hegemony, by contrast, involves linking the understandings of dominant and subordinate groups into what appears to be mutual accommodation.

The concept of hegemony is attractive to many anthropologists because it draws attention to the central role of cultural beliefs and symbols in struggles to consolidate social organization and political control. Gramsci's contrast between domination (rule by coercive force) and hegemony (rule by persuasion) was central to his own analysis of the exercise of power (Crehan 2002, 153), and it has been helpful to anthropologists who study the exercise of power in societies with and without traditional state institutions. In attempting to extend Gramsci's insights to nonstate settings, anthropologists are able to avoid some of the implausible accounts of power that depend on fear of punishment or false consciousness. In place of such arguments, attention can be drawn to the verbal dexterity and personal charisma of leaders with limited coercive force at their disposal who can nonetheless persuade

Figure 12.2 Prior to colonial conquest by outsiders, Muslim emirs from northern Cameroon had coercive power.

others to follow them by skillfully aligning shared meanings, values, and goals with a particular interpretation of events or proposed course of action.

Consider, for example, the Azande belief that people use witchcraft only against those they envy. The psychological insight embodied in this belief makes it highly plausible to people who experience daily friction with their neighbors. At the same time, however, this belief makes it impossible to accuse Azande chiefs of using witchcraft against commoners—because, as the Azande themselves say, why would chiefs envy their subjects? In this way, hegemonic ideology deflects challenges that might be made against those in power.

---

ideology A worldview that justifies the social arrangements under which people live.

domination Coercive rule.

hegemony The persuasion of subordinates to accept the ideology of the dominant group by mutual accommodations that nevertheless preserve the rulers' privileged position.

Power and National Identity: A Case Study

Gramsci himself was particularly interested in how hegemony is (or is not) successfully established in state societies. In a postcolonial and globalizing world, where all people are presumed to be citizens of one or another nation-state, understanding the effects of decisions and actions of state authorities becomes crucial for making sense of many events at the local level. Anthropologists have often focused on the processes by which ruling groups in former colonies attempt to build a new national identity (we will explore this more fully in Chapter 14). For example, the British colony of Ceylon became independent in 1948, later changing its name to Sri Lanka. The residents of Ceylon belonged to two major populations: the Tamils, concentrated in the northern part of the island and the larger population of Sinhalese, who lived everywhere else (see EthnoProfiles 12.1: Sinhalese and 12.2: Tamils). After independence, however, new Sinhalese rulers worked to forge a national identity rooted in their version of local history, which excluded the Tamils. In 1956, Sinhala was made the only official language; in the 1960s and 1970s, Tamils' access to education was restricted and they were barred from the civil service and the army (Daniel 1997, 316). When some Tamils began to agitate for a separate state of their own, the Sri Lankan government responded in 1979 with severe, violent repression against Tamils, sending many into exile and stimulating the growth of the nationalist Liberation Tigers of Tamil Eelam (LTTE), which grew "into one of the most dreaded militant organizations in the world" (Daniel 1997, 323). By May of 2009, however, the Sri Lankan government army had retaken all territory once controlled by the Tamil Tigers. Since the 1980s, however, thousands have died in ethnic violence.

> The exclusion of the Tamil residents from the Sri Lankan state has thus been pursued by means of violent coercion. But violence has also been used by the government against Sinhalese citizens who objected to state policies. Between 1987 and 1990, Indian troops were brought into Sri Lanka to supervise a peace agreement between Tamils and Sinhalese. These troops found themselves fighting the LTTE in the north, but they were also resisted violently in Sinhalese areas, where the rest of the country was convulsed by a wave of terror as young members of a group called the JVP (*Janata Vimukti Peramuna*, or People's Liberation Front) attacked the government not only for betraying the nation by allowing the Indian presence, but also for its own unjust political and economic policies. . . . The government responded with a wave of terror, directed at young males in particular, which reached its climax with the capture and murder of the JVP leadership in

EthnoProfile 12.1

Sinhalese

Region: Southern Asia

Nation: Sri Lanka (city: Galle)

Population: 15,000,000 (population of Galle: 95,000)

Environment: Tropical island

Livelihood: Farming, urban life

Political organization: Highly stratified state

For more information: Kapferer, Bruce. 1983. *A celebration of demons.* Bloomington: Indiana University Press.

late 1989. As far as we can tell, the government won the day by concentrated terror—killing so many young people, whether JVP activists or not, that the opposition ran out of resources and leadership. (Spencer 2000, 124–25)

After 1990, violence directed by the state against Sinhalese lessened, and in 1994, a new government promised to settle the ethnic conflict by peaceful means. But even before then, Sri Lankan government efforts to create national unity had not rested entirely on violence. Leaders also tried to exercise persuasive power to convince Sinhalese citizens that the state had their welfare in mind and was prepared to take steps to improve their lives. For example, anthropologist Michael Woost (1993) described how the government of Sri Lanka has used a wide range of cultural media (television, radio, newspapers, the school system, public rituals, and even a lottery) to link the national identity to development. National development strategies are presented as attempts to restore Sinhalese village society to its former glory under the precolonial rule of Sinhalese kings. The ideal village, in this view, is engaged in rice paddy cultivation carried out according to the harmonious principles of Sinhala Buddhist doctrine.

The villagers Woost knew could hardly escape this nationalist development discourse, but they did not resist it as an unwelcome imposition from the outside. On the contrary, all of them had incorporated development goals into their own values and had accepted that state-sponsored development would improve their lives. This

EthnoProfile 12.2

Tamils

Region: South Asia

Nation: Sri Lanka

Population: 3,500,000 (several hundred thousand have fled the country)

Environment: Low plains; tropical monsoon climate

Livelihood: Planation agriculture, clothing manufacture

Political organization: Modern nation-state. Long-term armed dispute between government and Tamil separatists.

For more information:
Trawick, Margaret. 2002. Reasons for violence: A preliminary ethnographic account of the LTTE. In *Conflict and community in contemporary Sri Lanka*, ed. Siri Gamage and I. B. Watson. Thousand Oaks, CA: Sage.

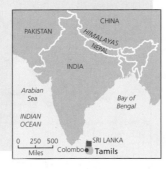

might suggest that the state's attempt to establish hegemony had succeeded. But collaboration with the state was undermined as three different village factions selectively manipulated development discourse in their struggle to gain access to government resources. For example, nationalistic rhetoric connected development with "improvement of the land." One village faction claimed it had been the first in the village to "improve the land" by building houses or planting tree crops. A second faction claimed that it had "improved the land" first by introducing paddy cultivation in the village. A third faction claimed it had "improved the land" first since its members had intermarried with other early settlers who had planted a large mango tree, a sign of permanent residence. Each faction made what the other factions interpreted as unjust claims, and each blamed the lack of village unity on the un-Buddhist greed of its opponents. These disagreements eventually led the state to withdraw its offer of resources, ultimately preventing the implementation of a village development scheme that all factions wanted!

Woost argues that the outcome of this political wrangling demonstrates the contradictory and fragile nature of the hegemonic process: paradoxically, the villagers' active appropriation of nationalist ideology undermined efforts to establish the very social order it was supposed to create. Gramsci himself was well aware that establishing successful hegemony in a nation-state was a difficult process whose outcome was not assured; it

was the very inability of Italians to achieve this goal that stimulated many of his reflections on domination and hegemony. Indeed, Gramsci's own description of a *colonial* state, emphasized by Indian historian Ranajit Guha, as dominance *without* hegemony (Crehan 2002, 125) is brought to mind by the repeated resort of the Sri Lankan state to violent coercion.

Biopower and Governmentality Is there a way to bring into existence and sustain a peaceful, prosperous nation-state in places like Sri Lanka? French historian Michel Foucault (1991) looked at the way European thinkers from the end of the Middle Ages onward had posed (and attempted to answer) similar questions. Together with colleagues, he identified the emergence of a new form of power in the nineteenth century. This form of power he called **biopower** or *biopolitics*, and it was preoccupied with bodies, both the bodies of citizens and the social body itself (Hacking 1991, 183). As Colin Gordon summarizes, biopower refers to "forms of power exercised over persons specifically insofar as they are thought of as living beings; a politics concerned with subjects as members of a *population*, in which issues of individual sexual and reproductive conduct interconnect with issues of national policy and power" (1991, 4–5).

Before the 1600s, according to Foucault (1991), European states were ruled according to different political understandings. At that time, politics was focused on making sure that an absolute ruler maintained control of the state. Machiavelli's famous guide *The Prince* is the best known of a series of handbooks explaining what such an absolute ruler needed to do to maintain himself in power. But by the seventeenth century, this approach to state rule was proving increasingly inadequate. Machiavelli's critics began to speak instead about *governing* a state, likening such government to the practices that preserved and perpetuated other social institutions.

The example of household management was a preferred model of government. But running a state as if it were a household meant that rulers would need more information about the people, goods, and wealth that needed to be managed. How many citizens were there? What kinds of goods did they produce, and in what quantities? How healthy were they? What could a state do to manage the consequences of misfortunes such as famines, epidemics, and death? In the 1700s, state bureaucrats began to count and measure people and things subject to state control, thereby inventing the discipline of *statistics*.

biopower Forms of power preoccupied with bodies, both the bodies of citizens and the social body of the state itself.

In this way, according to Foucault (1991), European states began to govern in terms of biopolitics, using statistics to manage the people, goods, and wealth within their borders. This, in turn, led to the birth of a new art of governing appropriate to biopolitics, which Foucault calls governmentality. **Governmentality** involves using the information encoded in statistics to govern in a way that promotes the welfare of populations within a state. To exercise governmentality, for example, state bureaucrats might use statistics to determine that a famine was likely and to calculate how much it might cost the state in the suffering and death of citizens and in other losses. They would then come up with a plan of intervention—perhaps a form of insurance—designed to reduce the impact of famine on citizens, protect economic activity within the state, and thereby preserve the stability of the state and its institutions.

Governmentality is a form of power at work in the contemporary world, and institutions that rely on it count and measure their members in a variety of ways (Figure 12.3). Although, as Ian Hacking insists, not all bureaucratic applications of such statistical knowledge are evil (1991, 183), the fact remains that providing the government (or any bureaucratic institution) with detailed vital statistics can be very threatening, especially in cases where people are concerned that the state does not have their best interests at heart. After all, states want to tax citizens, vaccinate and educate their children, restrict their activities to those that benefit the state, control their movements beyond (and sometimes within) state borders, and otherwise manage what their citizens do. In a globalizing world full of nation-states, anthropologists are increasingly likely to encounter in their fieldwork both the pressures of governmentality and attempts to evade or manipulate governmentality.

Can Governmentality Be Eluded?

This was the experience of Aihwa Ong (2002), who carried out research among a dispersed population of wealthy Chinese merchant families. In explaining how these Chinese became so successful, Ong focused on the different forms of governmentality characteristic of nation-states, the capitalist market, and Chinese kinship and family. These three forms of governmentality possess rules for disciplining individual conduct in ways that are connected to the exercise of power appropriate to each of them. Ong argues that in the late nineteenth

governmentality The art of governing appropriately to promote the welfare of populations within a state.

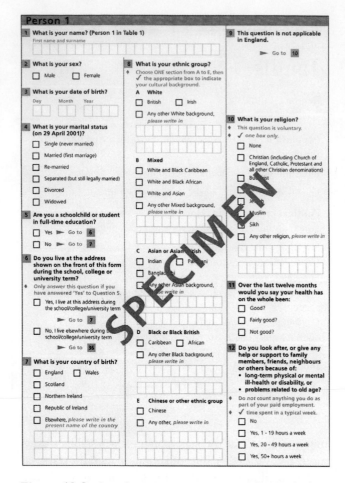

Figure 12.3 In order to govern, a state must know who it is governing. Censuses are one way in which the information a state believes it needs can be collected.

century some managed to evade the governmentality of Chinese kinship and family by moving physically out of China and into merchant cities under European imperial control elsewhere in Asia and Southeast Asia. Under these circumstances, the traditional obligations to one's lineage were effectively severed, and the individual family and its members, under the control of males, became the virtually unique focus of loyalty among kin. But such families have had to deal with two other forms of governmentality in this new setting. One of these was the governmentality of particular states. Moving from one state to the next involved making oneself or one's family subject to different forms of biopower: for example, for wealthy residents of Hong Kong, "citizenship becomes an issue of handling the diverse rules or 'governmentality' of host societies where they may be economically correct in terms of human capital, but culturally incorrect in terms of ethnicity" (2002, 340).

Finally, the prosperity of these overseas Chinese families depends on doing business according to the governmentality of the capitalist market. But the

In Their Own Words

Reforming the Crow Constitution

Anthropologist Kelly Branam has worked for many years among the Apsáalooke, or Crow, Indian nation in central Montana, and she was able to witness complex negotiations as they struggled in 2001 to reform their constitution. In this passage, Branam discusses some of the reasons why the constitutional process has been so complex and difficult for Crow people.

With the turmoil facing the Apsáalooke, or Crow, Indian nation in central Montana at the turn of the twenty-first century, including the distrust of their political leaders, a decade of increased chairman decision-making power under "Resolution 90-35," and the lack of large-scale resource development, it is not surprising that the discourse surrounding the 2000 tribal elections included constitutional reform. With the promise of "returning the voice to the tribal council," a new chairman was elected in 2000. In 2001, under this new leadership, the Crow Indian nation accepted a new constitution and a representative democracy. For over 50 years, the Crow Indian nation had been governed under the 1948 Constitution, which maintained a pure democracy system with executive offices of chairman, vice-chairman, secretary, and vice secretary. Why was this system no longer working for the Crow people? Why was a new constitution needed?

For many legal theorists, the importance of constitutions lies in the fact that constitutions outline the relationship the government has to its people. Constitutions restrict governmental power and often ensure citizens' rights. "The theoretical justification for the creation of an independent American nation included, at its center, an assumption that there existed some proper relationship between government and the subjects of government" (Kay 1998, 17). No doubt this is true in other constitutional instances as well. However, when it comes to the unique position of American Indian nations to the U.S. government, it is important to contemplate the meaning of their constitutions. American Indian tribal constitutions exist not only to outline the relationship tribal governments have to their people, but to outline the relationship the tribal government has to the federal government.

In today's global society, having a written form of a polity's rules outlining the ways in which those rules are made, enforced, and maintained is quintessential for national survival. Despite and often because of Indian nations' "domestic dependent nation" (*Cherokee Nation v Georgia* 1831) status within the U.S. federal framework, more and more Indian nations are reformulating their tribal governing structures. "If tribal communities want to assert greater control over their economic, political, and cultural lives, they will need more effective forms of government. For many communities there is a growing sense of crisis and movement to remake tribal constitutions" (Champagne 2006, 11). Many Indian nations, including the Apsáalooke, have found constitutions crucial to the maintenance and expansion of their sovereignty.

Analysis of the Crow constitution-making processes reveals the ways in which the Crow Indian nation has resisted federal Indian policies. They have fought to maintain their sovereignty and control their political identity. Through this process, "traditional" notions of governance were redefined, district identity became more important, kinship alliances remained crucial to the political process, and the Crow Indian nation took new steps in defining and asserting their sovereignty in relation to the U.S. government. The ways in which Crows have used constitutions to resist federal assimilationist polices may provide an example for other Indian nations who are also trying to exist under the federal sphere yet maintain traditional notions of governance.

Source: Branam 2012

governmentality of the market is hard to evade because it reaches beyond families or nation-states. As a result, overseas Chinese families would try whenever possible to move their members from country to country, as needed, to take advantage of fresh opportunities for business. Such mobility, in turn, depended on being able to evade or manipulate the bureaucratic rules of nation-states whenever these threatened to limit mobility. Thanks to

their wealth, overseas Chinese families found this sort of evasion or manipulation was frequently possible: "international managers and professionals have the material and symbolic resources to manipulate global schemes of cultural difference, racial hierarchy, and citizenship to their own advantage . . . in environments controlled and shaped by nation-states and capitalist markets" (Ong 2002, 339).

Doing Business in Japan

Anthropologist Richard Reeves-Ellington (1993) designed and implemented a cross-cultural training program for a North American company doing business in Japan (see EthnoProfile 12.3: Japan). He found that many of the traditional methods of anthropology—cultural understanding, ethnographic data, and participant-observation—helped managers conduct business in Japan. Reeves-Ellington began the training program by having employees first gather general cultural information artifacts ("How are things classified or what are the artifacts of an agreed classification system?"), social knowledge ("What are proper principles for behavior? What are the values that drive the categories and artifacts?"), and cultural logic. Social knowledge or values are based on an underlying, taken-for-granted cultural logic. Coming to understand Japanese cultural logic is of great importance to foreigners wishing to live and work in Japan.

The managers at the company decided to learn how to carry out introductions, meetings, leave-taking, dinner, and drinking in Japan (Figure 12.4). Each practice was analyzed according to the framework of artifacts, social knowledge, and cultural logic and was taught by a combination of methods that included the general observations that the managers collected while visiting Japanese museums, theaters, shrines, baseball games, and business meetings. The managers analyzed these observations and discussed stories that show how badly things can go when cultural knowledge is not sufficient. For example, one thing Reeves-Ellington's students needed to learn about introductions involved the presentation of the business card (*meishi*). The proper presentation and use of the meishi is the central element in the practice of making introductions at business meetings. Reeves-Ellington explained that, to a Japanese businessperson, the meishi is an extension of the self. Damage to the card is damage to the individual. Therefore, mistreatment of a meishi will ruin a relationship. Reeves-Ellington notes that his colleagues did not fully appreciate the consequences of these beliefs until he told them a story:

> A major U.S. company was having problems with one of its distributors, and the parties seemed unable to resolve their differences. The president of the U.S. company decided to visit Japan, meet with his counterpart in the wholesaler organization, and attempt to resolve their differences. The two had not met previously and, upon meeting, each followed proper *meishi* ritual. The American, however, did not put the Japanese counterpart's *meishi* on the table; instead he held on to it. As the conversation became heated, the American rolled

EthnoProfile 12.3

Japan

Region: Northeastern Asia

Nation: Japan

Population: 118,000,000

Environment: Temperate climate

Livelihood: Full range of occupations to be found in a core industrial nation-state

Political organization: Highly urbanized nation-state

For more information: Kondo, Dorinne, 1990. *Crafting selves.* Chicago: University of Chicago Press.

up the *meishi* in his hand. Horror was recorded on the face of the Japanese businessman. The American then tore the *meishi* into bits. This was more than the Japanese could stand; he excused himself from the meeting. Shortly afterward the two companies stopped doing business with each other. (209)

Table 12.1 shows the information regarding introductions and the use of the meishi that Reeves-Ellington's students derived from their work based on their analytic framework of artifacts, social knowledge, and cultural logic.

On three critical measures—effective working relationships with Japanese executives, shortened project times, and improved financial returns—the anthropologically based training program that Reeves-Ellington designed was a success. Both employees and their Japanese counterparts felt more comfortable in working with each other. Prior to the program, joint projects required an average of fifteen months to complete; projects run by executives applying the methodologies of the program cut completion time to an average of eight months. Financial returns based on contracts negotiated by personnel who had not participated in the program averaged gross income of 6 percent of sales whereas those negotiated by personnel applying the anthropological techniques averaged gross income equal to 18 percent of sales.

Figure 12.4 Japanese and North American businesspeople negotiating pickup. Japanese and U.S. businesspeople negotiate better when they understand something of each other's culture.

TABLE 12.1 Introductions at Business Meetings		
ARTIFACTS	**SOCIAL KNOWLEDGE**	**CULTURAL LOGIC**
Technology	• Once given, a card is kept—not discarded.	**Human relations**
• Business cards	• Meishi are not exchanged a second time unless there is a position change.	• Meishi provide understanding of appropriate relations between parties.
• Meishi	• Before the next meeting between parties, the meishi are reviewed for familiarization with the people attending the meeting.	• Meishi take uncertainty out of relationships.
Visual behavior	• The meishi provides status for the owner.	**Environment**
• Presentation of meishi by presenting card, facing recipient.		• Meishi help establish insider/outsider environment.
• Senior people present meishi first.		• Meishi help establish possible obligations to environment.
• Guest presents first, giving name, company affiliation, and bowing.		**Human activity**
• Host presents meishi in same sequence.		• Meishi help to establish human activities.
• Upon sitting at conference table, all meishi are placed in front of recipient to assure name use.		

Source: Reeves-Ellington 1993.

How Are Politics, Gender, and Kinship Related?

Formal electoral politics in many countries seems to be the domain of men—few women run for office, and some countries have prohibited women from voting. Anthropologist Katherine Bowie has analyzed a local election in Thailand to show "how anthropological insights into kinship systems can provide important avenues into understanding the gender dynamics of electoral politics" (2008, 136). Her point is that it is impossible to understand local electoral politics in Thailand without paying attention to local practices of matrilocality and matrilineal kinship (Figure 12.5).

In northern Thailand, people belong to social groups called matrilineages, which are created by links made through women, and both men and women belong to the same matrilineage as their mother. (Matrilineages are discussed at greater length in Chapter 13.) People there also practice matrilocal residence after marriage—that is, the new couple goes to live with or near the wife's mother, a residence practice found in many matrilineal societies. In northern Thailand, a man leaves his mother's house and goes to live in his wife's parents' home. Because members of the same matrilineage tend to live near one another, entire sections of villages—and sometimes entire villages—are made up of related women and their in-marrying husbands.

Cooperative labor exchanges are essential for transplanting and harvesting rice, maintaining irrigation systems, and helping build houses in these communities. Because of the matrilocal residence pattern, it is the wife's matrilineal kinship network that provides labor and other resources for these activities, and labor exchanges are made both within and across matrilines. Kin groups also depend on one another to share the costs of various expensive ritual events. In any neighborhood there, it is women who keep these connections harmonious and functioning well—after all, it is their matriline that is being maintained: the village or neighborhood is composed of related women and their husbands, who are "strangers."

In-marrying men feel a certain stress as strangers: even though they have formal authority as head of the household, they are dependent on their wives' families; and because everyone in the village is a stranger to them, they are isolated in the village. At the same time, stranger status frees men to engage in local politics, because men who are strangers have less at stake when engaging in political conflict at the village level. By contrast, women members of the local matrilineages appear

Figure 12.5   A woman in northern Thailand votes. In local elections, kin relations are entangled with local electoral politics.

neutral in local elections, which allows them to mediate the tensions that build as a result of the political activities of in-marrying men. They are able to transmit information and maintain networks, even while appearing to have no political interests of their own. In fact, they do have interests in mobilizing votes for specific candidates, but they are also committed to "their efforts to achieve unity within their villages and to heal divisions both within and across their villages" (148).

In July 2005, Bowie was able to observe a local election to choose two village representatives from nine candidates. Almost everyone in the village was related to all nine candidates in some way. Villagers were willing to reveal that one of their votes would go to their closest relative, but they would not commit to the second vote, instead just describing each candidate's relative strengths. "When I delicately probed into who might win, the standard response was a politic refrain, 'depends on their kinship network'" (148). Indeed, Bowie argues that as women embedded male leaders within their matrilines, the political networks provided by wives, sisters, and mothers were fundamental to a successful campaign. "At the village level, the art of neutral partisanship enables women to pursue the broader interests of their matrilines and safeguard village harmony. . . . In the politics of matrilineal kinship, conflict is the arena for ignorant, drunken husbands and sons-in-law; resolving conflict is the arena for knowledgeable, sober wives and mothers. If formal politics is necessarily divisive, women's political role is in avoiding conflict and healing division. The processes are diametrically opposed, but each is political" (148).

Thus, kinship continues to play a significant role in people's political lives, even in contemporary settings, in which it would not necessarily be expected to do so. It is the holistic approach of anthropology that makes such connections visible.

How Are Immigration and Politics Related in the New Europe?

One of the more interesting things about the early twenty-first century is that Europe—the continent that gave birth to the Enlightenment, to colonial empires, and (along with North America) to anthropology itself—has become a living laboratory for the study of some of the most complex social and cultural processes to be found anywhere in the world.

During the last half of the twentieth century, the countries of Europe, including Italy, were the target of large waves of migration from all over the world. Visitors to Rome regularly make stops at the ancient ruins in the center of the city. One venerable working-class Roman neighborhood, only a short walk from the Colosseum, is Rione Monti, which has a fascinating history of its own (EthnoProfile 12.4: Rione Monti). In 1999, anthropologist Michael Herzfeld (2003) moved into Rione Monti to explore social change in the uses of the past. Long-time residents of Monti share a common local culture, which includes use of the *romanesco* dialect rather than standard Italian and a strong sense of local identity that distinguishes them from "foreigners," including diplomats and non-Roman Italians. Their identity survived Mussolini's demolition of part of the neighborhood in the early twentieth century. They successfully dealt with a local criminal underworld by mastering a refined urbane code of politeness. The underworld had faded away by the 1970s, but beginning in the 1980s, residents began to face two new challenges to their community. First, historic Roman

neighborhoods became fashionable, and well-to-do Italians began to move into Rione Monti, pushing many workers into cheaper housing elsewhere. Second, in the 1990s, another group of newcomers arrived: immigrants from eastern Europe.

Italy is one of the more recent destinations of immigration into Europe, reversing the country's historical experience as a source, rather than a target, of immigration. However, after Germany, France, and Britain passed laws curtailing immigration in the 1970s, Italy became an increasingly popular destination for immigrants from Africa, Asia, and Latin America; after the end of the Cold War came immigrants from outside the European Union (EU), including eastern Europe. Until recently, laws regulating immigration were few and the country appeared welcoming. But this is changing. "Italy has not historically been a racist country, but intolerant attitudes towards immigrants have increased. To a large extent, this seems to be the result of a long-standing underestimation of the magnitude of the changes and thus poor policy implementation for a lengthy period, in spite of the best intentions officially proclaimed" (Melotti 1997, 91).

Umberto Melotti contrasts the distinctive ways in which immigration is understood by the governments of France, Britain, and Germany. According to Melotti, the French project is "ethnocentric assimilationism": since early in the nineteenth century, when French society experienced a falling birthrate, immigration was encouraged and immigrants were promised all the rights and

EthnoProfile 12.4

Rione Monti (Rome)

Region: Europe

Nation: Italy

Population: 15,300

Environment: Central neighborhood in Rome

Livelihood: Urban occupations, ranging from tourism and factory work to restaurants, small businesses, bureaucratic, executive

Political organization: Neighborhood in a modern nation-state

For more information: http://www.rionemonti.net/

privileges of native-born citizens as long as they adopted French culture completely, dropping other ethnic or cultural attachments and assimilating the French language and character (1997, 75). The British project, by contrast, is "uneven pluralism": that is, the pragmatic British expect immigrants to be loyal and law-abiding citizens, but they do not expect immigrants to "become British" and they tolerate private cultivation of cultural differences as long as these do not threaten the British way of life (79–80). Finally, Melotti describes the German project as "the institutionalization of precariousness," by which he means that, despite the fact that Germany has within its borders more immigrants than any other European country and began receiving immigrants at the end of the nineteenth century, its government continues to insist that Germany is not a country of immigrants. Immigrants were always considered "guest workers," children born to guest workers are considered citizens of the country from which the worker came, and it remains very difficult for guest workers or their children born in Germany to obtain German citizenship. (This contrasts with France, for example, where children of immigrants born on French soil automatically become French citizens.)

Coming to terms with increasing numbers of Muslims living in countries where Christianity has historically been dominant is a central theme in political debates within Europe. Although all European states consider themselves secular in orientation (see Asad 2003), the relation between religion and state is far from uniform. France is unusual because of its strict legal separation between religion and state. In Britain, the combination of a secular outlook with state funding of the established Anglican Church has allowed citizens to support forms of religious inclusion that first involved state funding of Catholic schools for Irish immigrants and now involve state funding of Muslim schools for Muslim immigrants (Modood 1997, P. Lewis 1997). In Germany, where a secular outlook also combines with state-subsidized religious institutions, the state has devised curricula for elementary schools designed to teach all students about different religious traditions, including Islam, in ways that emphasize the possibility of harmonizing one's religious faith with one's obligations as a citizen. Although this approach may seem presumptuous or paternalistic, its supporters counter that its advantages outweigh its costs. Perhaps as a result of their own history, many contemporary Germans have less faith than the British that a civic culture of religious tolerance will automatically lead to harmony without state intervention and less faith than the French in the existence of a separate secular sphere of society from which religion can be safely excluded (Schiffauer 1997).

These are, of course, thumbnail sketches of more complex attitudes and practices. But they illustrate the fact that there is no single "European" approach to the challenges posed by immigration. In a way, each European state, with its own history and institutions, is experimenting with different ways of coping with the challenges it presents; and their failures and successes will influence the kinds of cultural institutions that develop in the twenty-first century. This is particularly significant in light of the fact that European nation-states have joined together in the EU, a continent-wide superstate with 25 members. Reconciling the diverse interests and needs of member states poses enormous challenges for EU members, and issues surrounding immigration are among them.

Tariq Modood points out, for example, that European multiculturalism requires supporting conceptions of citizenship that allow the "right to assimilate" as well as the "right to have one's 'difference' . . . recognized and supported in the public and the private spheres"; multiculturalism must recognize that "participation in the public or national culture is necessary for the effective exercise of citizenship" while at the same time defending the "right to widen and adapt the national culture" (1997, 20).

Anthropologist John Bowen's recent fieldwork in France documents the process Modood describes. Bowen has worked among the many French Muslims who are not interested in terrorism but "who wish to live fulfilling *and* religious lives in France" (2010, 4). He has paid particular attention to the work of a number of French Muslim religious teachers and scholars, whom he calls "Islamic public actors." Other French Muslims come to them for religious instruction and for advice about how to cope with the difficulties of living in a non-Muslim country. In turn, the Islamic public actors Bowen knew are working to craft solutions that, in their view, are true both to the laws of the French republic and to the norms and traditions of Islam.

For example, many French Muslims are concerned about how to contract a valid marriage in France. Ever since the French Revolution, France has refused to accept the legality of religious marriages and recognizes only civil marriages contracted at city hall (Figure 12.7). Yet Muslims who want to marry are often confused about whether a "secular" marriage at city hall is appropriate or necessary. Indeed, some Muslims have argued that city hall marriages are un-Islamic because they did not exist at the time of the Prophet Muhammad. But other Muslims, including some of Bowen's consultants, disagree with this position. They argue that there was no need for civil marriages at the time of the Prophet because, in those days, tribal life made it impossible to avoid the

Figure 12.6 Rione Monti is a neighborhood in central Rome where longtime residents and new immigrants are negotiating new forms of relationship.

obligations of the marriage contract. But things are different today for Muslims in urban France: Bowen's consultants have seen many tragic outcomes when young women who thought they had a valid Muslim marriage were left by their husbands, only to discover that the French state did not recognize their marriage and could offer them no legal redress.

Because this was not the outcome that Islamic marriage was intended to produce, the Muslim scholars Bowen knew looked beyond traditional Islamic marriage practices in order to clarify the larger purposes that Islamic marriage was supposed to achieve. They then asked if these purposes could be achieved using the French institution of civil marriage. One scholar told Bowen: "I say that if you marry at the city hall, you have already made an Islamic marriage, because all the conditions for that marriage have been fulfilled" (2010, 167). Those conditions include the fact that both Islamic marriages and French civil marriages are contracts; that both require the consent of the spouses; and that the legal requirements imposed on the spouses by French civil marriage further the Islamic goal of keeping the spouses together. Given that this kind of reasoning is further strengthened by appealing to opinions on marriage drawn from the four traditional Sunni schools of Islamic law, many Islamic public intellectuals believe that a way can be found to craft acceptable practices for French Muslims in many areas of daily life.

Because Bowen agrees with Modood that accommodation has to go in both directions, he also shows how

some French legal scholars are working to craft solutions to the challenges Muslim marriage practices present to French law. Most French judges agree, for example, that Islamic marriages or divorces contracted outside France remain valid when the parties involved move to France. But French judges can refuse to accept international rules for resolving legal conflicts if they decide that the solution would violate French "public order." Bowen found that the concept of public order is basic to the French legal system, referring "both to the conditions of social order and to basic values, and it limits the range of laws that a legislator may pass and the decisions that a judge may make" (2010, 173).

Violations of public order may include customs from outside France that are judged to "offend the morality and values" of French law. Some French jurists argue that consequences following from Muslim practices of marriage and divorce should not be recognized in France if they violate French and European commitments to the equality of women and men. Other French jurists, however, point to the practical problems that this argument creates: not recognizing the validity of Islamic divorces in France, for example, would mean that a woman divorced according to Islamic law abroad could not remarry if she came to France. Similarly, refusing to recognize polygamous marriage in France would deprive the children of all but a man's first wife of their rights under French and European law. In recent years, Bowen reports, French judges have devised two ways of crafting a solution to these

Figure 12.7 A Turkish bride and groom in Clichy-sous-Bois, a poor suburb of Paris. Islamic and French legal scholars are both working to harmonize French and Islamic marriage practices.

unwelcome consequences. One has been to modify the concept of public order by making so-called "practical exceptions" for Muslims who emigrate to France. The other is to be more flexible with Muslim marriage and family practices as long as these arrangements involve individuals who are not French citizens. These pragmatic solutions are an improvement over what Bowen calls the "more blunt-instrument approach" associated with the older understanding of public order. Bowen concludes that in France today, Muslim and French jurists alike are both struggling to craft "the legal conditions for common life that are capacious enough to 'reasonably accommodate' people living in differing conditions and with differing beliefs, yet unitary enough to retain the hope that such a common life is conceivable" (2010, 178).

Thus, the struggles and dilemmas facing residents of Rione Monti are widespread across the new Europe. But the specifics of their situation and the cultural resources at their disposal have their own particularity. Thus, the traditionally left-wing Monti residents have resisted attempts by neofascist politicians to get them to turn against immigrant families in the neighborhood. Still, they are unhappy with the location of the Ukrainian church in a building that overlooks the neighborhood's central square because church-goers gather there twice a week, invading "their" space (Herzfeld 2003, 150; Figure 12.6). Herzfeld reports that the residents of Monti, like other Romans, claim not to be racist (which accords with Melotti's views of Italians in general) and that they seem less hostile to immigrants of color than

to Ukrainians. But Ukrainians are more numerous in Monti and more threatening because they look like local people but in fact are competing with local people for work and space in the neighborhood (151). At the same time, the Monti code of politeness "underlies the facility with which democratically inclined residents today construct a popular street democracy, a system of neighbourhood associations" (148). Currently, immigrants are not able to deploy this code, a fact that signals their outsider status and can lead to misunderstandings and bad feelings. If they could learn to use the code, however, fresh opportunities for political cooperation might be forged.

Hidden Transcripts and the Power of Reflection

The power that people have to invest their experiences with meanings of their own choosing suggests that a ruler's power of coercion is limited, which was Gramsci's key insight. Thought alone may be unable to alter the fact of material coercion, yet it has the power to transform the meaning of material coercion for those who experience it.

Any hegemonic establishment runs the risk that the dominated may create new, plausible accounts of their experiences of domination. Political scientist James Scott (1990) refers to these unofficial accounts as "hidden transcripts." Occasionally, those who are dominated may be able to organize themselves socially in order to transform their hidden transcripts into a counterhegemonic discourse aimed at discrediting the political establishment. Those who are dominated may be able to persuade some or all of those around them that their counterhegemonic interpretation of social experience is better than the hegemonic discourse of the current rulers. Such challenges to incumbent political power are frequently too strong to be ignored and too widespread to be simply obliterated by force. When coercion no longer works, what remains is a struggle between alternative accounts of experience.

Scott carried out 2 years of ethnographic research among peasant rice farmers in a Malaysian village called "Sedaka" (a pseudonym, see EthnoProfile 12.5: "Sedaka" Village). Poor Malaysian peasants are at the bottom of a social hierarchy dominated locally by rich farmers and nationally by a powerful state apparatus. According to Scott, these peasants are not kept in line by some form of state-sponsored terrorism; rather, the context of their lives is shaped by what he calls "routine repression": "occasional arrests, warnings, diligent police work, legal restrictions, and an Internal Security Act that allows for indefinite preventive detention and proscribes much political activity" (1987, 274).

Scott wanted to find out how this highly restrictive environment affected political relations between members of dominant and subordinate classes in the village. He quickly realized that the poor peasants of "Sedaka" were not about to rise up against their oppressors. But this was not because they accepted their poverty and low status as natural and proper. For one thing, organized overt defense of their interests was difficult because local economic, political, and kinship ties generated conflicting loyalties. For another, the peasants knew that overt political action in the context of routine repression would be foolhardy. Finally, they had to feed their families. Their solution was to engage in what Scott calls "everyday forms of peasant resistance": this included "foot dragging, dissimulation, desertion, false compliance, pilfering, feigned ignorance, slander, arson, sabotage, and so forth" (1987, xvi). These actions may have done little to alter the peasants' situation in the short run; however, Scott argues, in the long run they may have been more effective than overt rebellion in undercutting state repression.

What we find in everyday forms of peasant resistance are indirect attempts to challenge local hegemony. Scott says, "The struggle between rich and poor in Sedaka is not merely a struggle over work, property rights, grain, and cash. It is also a struggle over the appropriation of symbols, a struggle over how the past and present shall

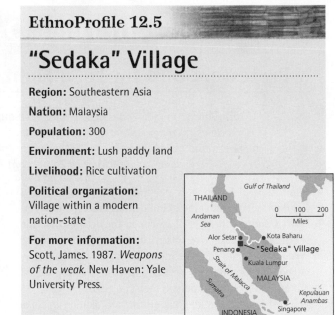

EthnoProfile 12.5

"Sedaka" Village

Region: Southeastern Asia

Nation: Malaysia

Population: 300

Environment: Lush paddy land

Livelihood: Rice cultivation

Political organization: Village within a modern nation-state

For more information: Scott, James. 1987. *Weapons of the weak.* New Haven: Yale University Press.

be understood and labeled, a struggle to identify causes and assess blame" (1987, xvii). When peasants criticize rich landowners or rich landowners find fault with peasants, the parties involved are not just venting emotion. According to Scott, each side is simultaneously constructing a worldview. Rich and poor alike are offering "a critique of things as they are as well as a vision of things as they should be. . . . [They are writing] a kind of social text on the subject of human decency" (23).

Scott describes the dynamics of this struggle during the introduction of mechanized rice harvesting in "Sedaka." Traditionally, rice harvesting was manual labor. It regularly allowed poor peasants to earn cash and receive grain from their employers as a traditional form of charitable gift (Figure 12.8). In the late 1970s, however, the introduction of combine harvesters eliminated the rich farmers' need for hired labor, a loss that dealt poor families a severe economic blow. When the rich and poor talked about the harvesters, each side offered a different account of their effect on economic life in the village.

Scott tells us that both sides agreed that using the machines hurt the poor and helped the rich. When each side was asked whether the benefits of the machines outweighed their costs, however, consensus evaporated. The poor offered practical reasons against the use of combine harvesters: they claimed that the heavy machines were inefficient and that their operation destroyed rice paddies. They also offered moral reasons: they accused the rich of being "stingy," of ignoring the traditional

In Their Own Words

Protesters Gird for Long Fight over Opening Peru's Amazon

Latin American Indigenous people have been organizing in recent years to protect their lands, sometimes from agricultural invasion, sometimes against oil exploration and drilling, sometimes to assert land claims. These are not always peaceful. Simon Romero reports for the New York Times, *June 12, 2009 (Andrea Zarate contributed reporting from Lima, Peru).*

Iquitos, Peru—Faced with a simmering crisis over dozens of deaths in the quelling of indigenous protests last week, Peru's Congress this week suspended the decrees that had set off the protests over plans to open large parts of the Peruvian Amazon to investment. Senior officials said they hoped this would calm nerves and ease the way for oil drillers and loggers to pursue their projects.

But instead, indigenous groups are digging in for a protracted fight, revealing an increasingly well-organized movement that could be a tinderbox for President Alan García. The movement appears to be fueled by a deep popular resistance to the government's policies, which focused on luring foreign investment, while parts of the Peruvian Amazon have been left behind.

The broadening influence of the indigenous movement was on display Thursday in a general strike that drew thousands of protesters here to the streets of Iquitos, the largest Peruvian city in the Amazon, and to cities and towns elsewhere in jungle areas. Protests over Mr. García's handling of the violence in the northern Bagua Province last Friday also took place in highland regions like Puno, near the Bolivian border, and in Lima and Arequipa on the Pacific coast.

"The government made the situation worse with its condescending depiction of us as gangs of savages in the forest," said Wagner Musoline Acho, 24, an Awajún Indian and an indigenous leader. "They think we can be tricked by a maneuver like suspending a couple of decrees for a few weeks and then reintroducing them, and they are wrong."

The protesters' immediate threat—to cut the supply of oil and natural gas to Lima, the capital—seems to have subsided, with protesters partly withdrawing from their occupation of oil installations in the jungle. But as anger festers, indigenous leaders here said they could easily try to shut down energy installations again to exert pressure on Mr. García.

Another wave of protests appears likely because indigenous groups are demanding that the decrees be repealed and not just suspended. The decrees would open large jungle areas to investment and allow companies to bypass indigenous groups to obtain permits for petroleum exploration, logging and building hydroelectric dams. A

Peruvian indigenous leaders Alberto Pizango (*R*) and Servando Puerta Pena (*L*) at a press conference in Lima, Peru, in June 2009, requesting an investigation of the clashes in the north of the country that left an undetermined number of people dead.

stopgap attempt to halt earlier indigenous protests in the Amazon last August failed to prevent them from being reinitiated more forcefully in April.

The authorities said that nine civilians were killed in the clashes that took place last Friday on a remote highway in Bagua. But witnesses and relatives of missing protesters contend that the authorities are covering up details of the episode, and that more Indians died. Twenty-four police officers were killed on the highway and at an oil installation.

Indigenous representatives say at least 25 civilians, and perhaps more, may have been killed, and some witnesses say that security forces dumped the bodies of protesters into a nearby river. At least three Indians who were wounded said they had been shot by police officers as they waited to talk with the authorities.

"The government is trying to clean the blood off its hands by hiding the truth," said Andrés Huaynacari Etsam, 21, an Awajún student here who said that five of his relatives had been killed on June 5 and that three were missing.

Senior government officials repudiate such claims. "There is a game of political interests taking place in which

In Their Own Words

some are trying to exaggerate the losses of life for their own gain," said Foreign Minister José García Belaunde.

He said the ultimate aim of the protesters was to prevent Peru from carrying out a trade agreement with the United States, because one of the most contentious of the decrees that were suspended on Thursday would bring Peru's rules for investment in jungle areas into line with the trade agreement.

"But," Mr. García Belaunde insisted, "the agreement is not in danger."

Still, the government's initial response to the violence seems to have heightened resentment. A television commercial by the Interior Ministry contained graphic images of the bodies of some police officers who were killed while being held hostage by protesters. The commercial said that the killings were proof of the "ferocity and savagery" of indigenous activists, but an uproar over that depiction forced the government to try to withdraw the commercial.

The authorities are struggling to understand a movement that is crystallizing in the Peruvian Amazon among more than 50 indigenous groups. They include about 300,000 people, accounting for only about 1 percent of Peru's population, but they live in strategically important and resource-rich locations, which are scattered throughout jungle areas that account for nearly two-thirds of Peru's territory.

So far, alliances have proved elusive between Indians in the Amazon and indigenous groups in highland areas, ruling out, for now, the kind of broad indigenous protest movements that helped oust governments in neighboring Ecuador and Bolivia earlier in the decade.

In contrast to some earlier efforts to organize indigenous groups, the leaders of this new movement are themselves indigenous, and not white or mestizo urban intellectuals. They are well organized and use a web of radio stations to exchange information across the jungle. After one prominent leader, Alberto Pizango, was granted asylum in Nicaragua this week, others quickly emerged to articulate demands.

"There has been nothing comparable in all my years here in terms of the growth of political consciousness among indigenous groups," said the Rev. Joaquín García, 70, a priest from Spain who arrived in Iquitos 41 years ago and directs the Center of Theological Studies of the Amazon, which focuses on indigenous issues.

"At issue now," he said, "is what they decide to do with the newfound bargaining power in their hands."

Source: Romero 2009.

---

obligation of rich people to help the poor by providing them with work and charity. The rich denied both the practical and the moral objections of the poor. They insisted that using harvesters increased their yield. They accused the poor people of bad faith. They claimed that the poor suffered because they were bad farmers or lazy, and they attributed their own success to hard work and prudent farm management.

Rich rice farmers would never have been able to begin using combine harvesters without the outside assistance of both the national government and the business groups that rented the machines to them at harvest time. Poor peasants were aware of this, yet they directed their critique at the local farmers and not at the government or outside business organizations. After all, the rich farmers "are a part of the community and therefore *ought* not to be indifferent to the consequences of their acts for their neighbors" (Scott 1987, 161). The stinginess of the rich did not just bring economic loss; it also attacked the social identity of the poor, who vigorously resisted being turned into nonpersons. The poor insisted on being accorded the "minimal cultural decencies in this small community" (xviii). The only weapon they controlled in this struggle was their ability, by word and deed, to undercut the prestige and reputation of the rich.

This strategy worked in "Sedaka" because rich local farmers were not ready to abandon the traditional morality that had regulated relations between rich and poor. They had not yet become so Westernized that they no longer cared what other villagers thought of them. A shrewd campaign of character assassination may have caused at least some of the rich to hesitate before ignoring their traditional obligations. The improvement might have been minor in strictly economic terms, but it would have been major in terms of the ability of the poor to defend their claims to citizenship in the local

Figure 12.8   Until recently, rice harvesting in rural Malaysia was manual labor that regularly allowed poor peasants to earn cash and receive grain from their employers as a traditional form of charitable gift.

community. In addition, the wider political arena could always change in the future. Scott was convinced that many of the poor peasants he knew might well engage in open, active rebellion if routine repression disappeared.

When disputes are settled in this manner, experience is transformed. As Scott observes, "The key symbols animating class relations in "Sedaka"—generosity, stinginess, arrogance, humility, help, assistance, wealth, and poverty—do not constitute a set of given rules or principles that actors simply follow. They are instead the normative raw material that is created, maintained, changed, and above all manipulated by daily human activity" (1987, 309). Worldviews articulated in language by different social subgroups aim "not just to convince but to control; better stated, they aim to control by convincing" (1987, 23).

The power to invest experience with one's own meanings is very real. Yet, many anthropologists are divided about the effectiveness of resistance as a solution to the problems of those at the very bottom of society. While there is much ethnographic evidence documenting the

ability of some individuals and groups to assert themselves and their view of the world in the face of tremendous oppression, there is also much evidence that other individuals and groups have been destroyed by such oppression. Political anthropologist John Gledhill has observed that it would be "dangerous to be over-optimistic. 'Counter-hegemonic' movements exist, but much of the world's population is not participating in them" (1994, 198). He is particularly skeptical about the power of everyday forms of peasant resistance: the ability of such practices to undermine the local elite, he warns, may "merely provide the scenario for the replacement of one elite by another, more effective, dominant group" (92). At the beginning of the twenty-first century, with no utopian solutions in sight, the most that anthropologists may be able to do is agree with historian A. R. Tawney, who wrote about the agrarian disturbances in sixteenth-century England: "Such movements are a proof of blood and sinew and of a high and gallant spirit. . . . Happy the nation whose people has not forgotten how to rebel" (quoted in Wallerstein 1974, 357).

Human Terrain Teams and Anthropological Ethics

Recently, an ethical dispute has emerged among anthropologists about the Human Terrain System, a U.S. Army program that hires small teams of civilian anthropologists and other social scientists to become embedded with U.S. combat brigades in Iraq and Afghanistan. These teams are intended to provide relevant sociocultural information about the particular neighborhoods and village communities in which the U.S. military is operating. Backed by an elaborate 24-hour research center in the United States, the Human Terrain System attempts to improve relations between U.S. military personnel and Iraqis and Afghans they might encounter, to gather information on development needs, and to generate culturally informed strategic advice (Figure 12.9). The hope is that providing U.S. military forces with a greater understanding of social and cultural contexts will help reduce misunderstandings and unintentional insults and ultimately help prevent bloodshed. This program was instantly controversial: is this an appropriate use of anthropological knowledge?

A number of anthropologists have been concerned that the service of anthropologists in military units, almost like spies, could compromise the integrity of the discipline. Anthropologist Hugh Gusterson was quoted as saying, "The prime directive is you do no harm to informants . . . [but] data collected by [Human Terrain Team] members can also be accessed by military intelligence operatives who might use the same information for targeting Taliban operatives" (Caryl 2009). Indeed, it might be used to target *supposed* Taliban sympathizers. As Gusterson puts it, "The product generated by the Human Terrain Teams is inherently double-edged" (Caryl 2009). The interests of the military units may not be the same as the interests of the embedded anthropologists. How can the anthropologists prevent their research from being used for purposes to which they object? Could working for the military betray informants' trust?

Further, some have argued that the Human Terrain System may undermine anthropological research anywhere, all of which depends on the trust anthropologists develop with the people with whom they work. If some anthropologists are working for the U.S. military, how can community members be sure that an anthropologist in their community is not also working for the U.S. military?

Should anthropologists work for military organizations? Is it better to stand on the sidelines and criticize or to take part and risk compromising the integrity of anthropological work? Who "owns" anthropological knowledge? These are not simple issues. What would you do?

Figure 12.9 U.S. civilian anthropologist talking to Afghan national army soldiers, who were providing security both for the April 2009 elections and for Human Terrain Team interviews with local people.

Chapter Summary

1. Contemporary cultural anthropologists are interested in how cultures change, but they are suspicious of evolutionary schemes that give the impression that social arrangements could not have been—or could not be—other than the way they are. They also point out that no society anywhere is static. The power that human beings have to reproduce or to change their social organization is an important focus of political anthropology.

2. The ability to act implies power. The study of power in human society is the domain of political anthropology. In most societies at most times, power can never be reduced to physical force, although this is the Western prototype of power. Power in society operates according to principles that are cultural creations. As such, those principles are affected by history and may differ from one society to another.

3. Western thinkers traditionally assumed that without a state social life would be chaotic, if not impossible. They believed that people were free agents who would not cooperate unless forced to do so. Anthropologists have demonstrated that power is exercised both by coercive and by persuasive means. They have been influenced by the works of Antonio Gramsci and Michel Foucault. Gramsci argued that coercion alone is rarely sufficient for social control, distinguishing coercive domination from hegemony. Rulers always face the risk that those they dominate may create counterhegemonic accounts of their experience of being dominated, acquire a following, and unseat their rulers. Foucault's concept of governmentality addresses practices developed in Western nation-states in the nineteenth century that aimed to create and sustain peaceful and prosperous social life by exercising biopower over persons who could be counted, whose physical attributes could be measured statistically, and whose sexual and reproductive behaviors could be shaped by the exercise of state power.

4. Anthropological research in societies without states has shown how social obligations can restrict individuals from pursuing their own self-interest to the detriment of the group. Individuals cannot be coerced but must be persuaded to cooperate. Individuals use the constraints and opportunities for action open to them, however limited they may be. They are not free agents, but they are empowered to resist conforming to another's wishes.

For Review

1. Define power and the three different kinds of power described by Eric Wolf.
2. What are the different theoretical orientations and subject matters that have interested political anthropology over its history?
3. Explain how power may be understood as physical force, or coercion.
4. Compare hegemony and domination.
5. Why is hegemony a useful term for anthropologists?
6. What does the perspective of political anthropology highlight about the history of nationalism in Sri Lanka?
7. What is biopower?
8. Following Foucault, how does governing a state differ from ruling a state?
9. Summarize how kinship affects politics in northern Thailand.
10. What are hidden transcripts? Where do they come from and how do they function?
11. Summarize the argument in the text concerning the powers of the weak, and illustrate your summary with references to the Tswana and Bolivian examples.
12. Summarize the key points concerning multicultural politics in contemporary Europe, with particular attention to the different ways in which the United Kingdom, France, and Germany deal with immigration.
13. How does ethnographic research illuminate the challenges faced by French Muslims who wish to contract a valid marriage?
14. What are everyday forms of peasant resistance? How does James Scott connect them with the political relations of dominant and subordinate categories of people in "Sedaka," Malaysia?

Key Terms

Suggested Readings

Arens, W., and Ivan Karp, eds. 1989. *Creativity of power: Cosmology and action in African societies.* Washington, DC: Smithsonian Institution Press. *Contains 13 essays exploring the relationship among power, action, and human agency in African social systems and cosmologies.*

Fogelson, Raymond, and Richard N. Adams, eds. 1977. *The anthropology of power.* New York: Academic Press. *A classic collection of 28 ethnographic essays on the varied ways power is understood all over the world. Also contains two important essays based on case studies.*

Herzfeld, Michael. 2009. *Evicted from eternity: The restructuring of modern Rome.* Chicago: University of Chicago Press. *An extended study of the politics of the new Europe as experienced in one historic neighborhood in Rome.*

Keesing, Roger. 1983. *'Elota's story.* New York: Holt, Rinehart and Winston. *The autobiography of a Kwaio Big Man, with interpretive material by Keesing. First-rate, very readable, and involving.*

Lewellen, Ted. 2003. *Political anthropology,* 3rd ed. New York: Praeger. *The latest edition of a standard introductory text in political anthropology, covering leading theories, scholars, and problems in the field.*

Vincent, Joan, ed. 2002. *The anthropology of politics.* New York: Wiley-Blackwell. *An excellent collection of texts that illustrate the development of political anthropology over time and showcase important achievements by influential political anthropologists today.*

Where Do Our Relatives Come From and Why Do They Matter?

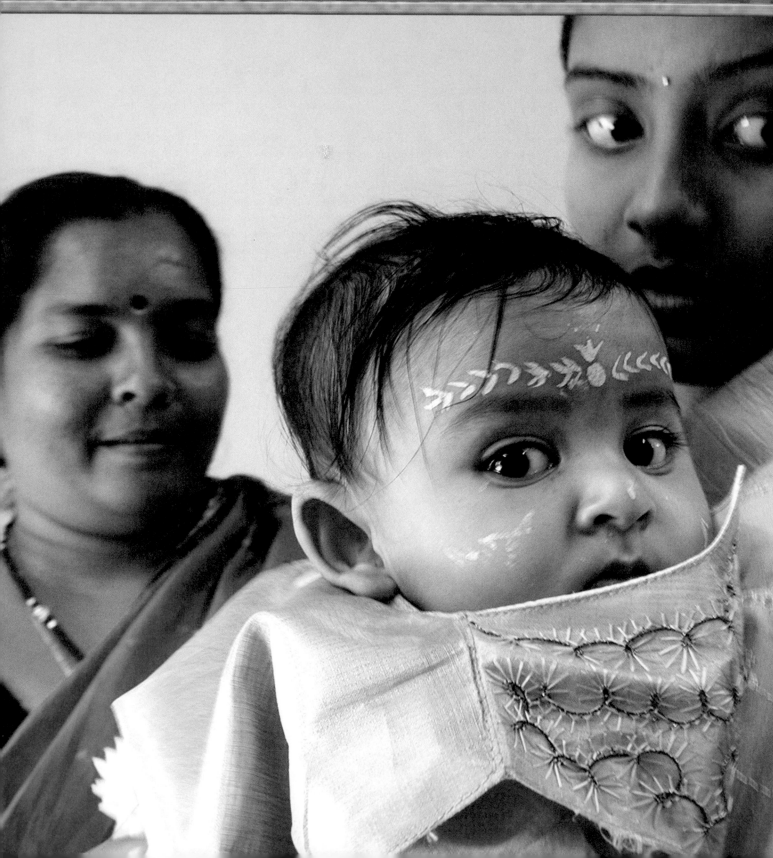

One of the major ways in which people sustain their connections to each other is by asserting that they are in some way related. In this chapter, we will look at some important social rules and patterns that result from different ways of understanding human relatedness: kinship, adoption, marriage, where to live after marriage, family, and sexuality. As examples in this chapter illustrate, all of these forms of relatedness show a great deal of worldwide variation.

Chapter Outline

◄ *Relatives carrying baby during the Annaprashana rituals in Kolkata, West Bengal, India. This is the ceremony for the first feeding of cooked rice, performed when the baby is weaned at six months of age.*

Human life is group life. How we choose to organize ourselves is open to creative variation, as we have seen. But each of us was born into a society whose political, economic, and cultural practices were already well established when we arrived. These traditional practices make some kinds of social connections more likely than other kinds. As a result, much can be predicted about a child's probable path in life just by knowing the kind of social groups into which he or she is born. This chapter focuses on how such human experiences as sexuality, conception, birth, and nurturance are selectively interpreted and shaped into shared cultural practices that anthropologists call **relatedness**. Relatedness takes many forms—friendship, marriage, parenthood, shared links to a common ancestor, workplace associations, and so on. And these intimate everyday relationships are always embedded in, and shaped by, broader structures of power, wealth, and meaning.

For more than a century, anthropologists have studied those forms of relatedness believed to come from shared substance and its transmission (Holy 1996, 171). The substance believed to be shared may be a bodily one (blood, genes, or mother's milk, for example) or a spiritual one (soul, spirit, nurturance, or love, for example); sometimes more than one substance is thought to be shared. Systems of relatedness based on ideas of shared substance are called **kinship systems**. In the West as well as in many other parts of the world, people are thought to share a common substance because it was transmitted to them via the act of sexual intercourse between their parents that led to their conception and birth. Such ideas were close enough to Western beliefs for many anthropologists to conclude that all people everywhere based their kinship systems on the biology of reproduction. It was but a short step to conclude that Western beliefs about which people counted as one's "real" relatives were universally valid. In the early days, kinship studies in anthropology were based on the assumption that all societies recognized the same basic genealogical

relationships between mothers and fathers, children and parents, sisters and brothers, and so on. But over the years, ethnographic evidence accumulated indicating that quite often people's understanding of kin ties was strikingly at odds with these genealogical relationships. In other cases, these genealogical relationships turned out to form but a small subset of the ways in which people created enduring connections with one another.

What Is Kinship?

Anthropologists call culturally recognized relationships based on mating **marriage** and those based on birth **descent**. Although nurturance is ordinarily seen to be closely connected with mating and birth, it need not be, and all societies have ways of acknowledging a relationship based on nurturance alone, which is called **adoption** in English. Although marriage is based on mating, descent on birth, and adoption on nurturance, marriage is not the same thing as mating, descent is not the same thing as birth, and adoption is not the same thing as nurturance. This is because the human experiences of mating, birth, and nurturance are ambiguous. Systems of relatedness in different societies highlight some features of these experiences while downplaying or even ignoring others. Europeans and North Americans know that in their societies mating is not the same as marriage, although a culturally valid marriage encourages mating between the married partners. Similarly, all births do not constitute valid links of descent: children whose parents have not been married according to accepted legal or religious specifications do not fit the cultural logic of descent, and many societies offer no positions that they can properly fill. Finally, not all acts of nurturance are recognized as adoption: consider, for example, foster parents in the United States, whose custody of foster children is officially temporary. Put another way, through culturally created ties of kinship, a society emphasizes certain aspects of human experience, constructs its own theory of human nature, and specifies "the processes by which an individual comes into being and develops into a complete (i.e., mature) social person" (Kelly 1993, 521).

Marriage, descent, and adoption are selective institutions. One society may emphasize women as the bearers of children and base its kinship system on this fact, paying little formal attention to the male's role in conception. Another society may trace connections through men, emphasizing the paternal role in conception and reducing the maternal role. A third society may

---

relatedness The socially recognized ties that connect people in a variety of different ways.

kinship systems Social relationships that are prototypically derived from the universal human experiences of mating, birth, and nurturance.

marriage An institution that transforms the status of the participants, carries implications about permitted sexual access, perpetuates social patterns through the birth of offspring, creates relationships between the kin of partners, and is symbolically marked.

descent The principle based on culturally recognized parent–child connections that define the social categories to which people belong.

adoption Kinship relationships based on nurturance, often in the absence of other connections based on mating or birth.

Figure 13.1 Cross-cultural research repeatedly demonstrates that physical indicators of sex difference do not allow us to predict the roles that females or males will play in any particular society. In Otavalo, Ecuador, men were traditionally weavers (*a*), while traditional Navajo weavers were women (*b*).

encourage its members to adopt not only children but also adult siblings, blurring the link between biological reproduction and family creation. Even though they contradict one another, all three understandings can be justified with reference to the panhuman experiences of mating, birth, and nurturance.

Sex, Gender, and Kinship

Kinship is based on, but is not reducible to, biology. It is a cultural interpretation of the culturally recognized "facts" of human reproduction. One of the most basic of these "facts," recognized in some form in all societies, is that two different kinds of human beings must cooperate sexually to produce offspring (although what they believe to be the contribution of each party to the outcome varies from society to society). Anthropologists use the term **sex** to refer to the observable physical characteristics that distinguish the two kinds of human beings, females and males, needed for reproduction. People everywhere pay attention to *morphological sex* (the appearance of external genitalia and observable secondary sex characteristics, such as enlarged breasts in females). Scientists further distinguish females from males on the basis of *gonadal sex* (the presence of ovaries in females, testes in males) and *chromosomal sex* (two X chromosomes in females, one X and one Y chromosome in males).

At the same time, cross-cultural research repeatedly demonstrates that physical sex differences do not allow us to predict the roles that females or males will play in any particular society (Figure 13.1). Consequently, anthropologists distinguish sex from **gender**—the cultural construction of beliefs and behaviors considered appropriate for each sex. As Barbara Miller puts it,

> In some societies, people with XX chromosomes do the cooking, in others it is the XY people who cook, in others both XX and XY people cook. The same goes for sewing, transplanting rice seedlings, worshipping deities, and speaking in public. Even the exclusion of women from hunting and warfare has been reduced by recent studies from the level of a universal to a generality. While it is generally true that men hunt and women do not, and that men fight in wars and women do not, important counter cases exist. (1993, 5)

In fact, the outward physical features used to distinguish females from males may not be obvious either. Sometimes genetic or hormonal factors produce ambiguous external genitalia, a phenomenon called

sex Observable physical characteristics that distinguish two kinds of humans, females and males, needed for biological reproduction.

gender The cultural construction of beliefs and behaviors considered appropriate for each sex.

Figure 13.2   Location of societies whose EthnoProfiles appear in Chapter 13.

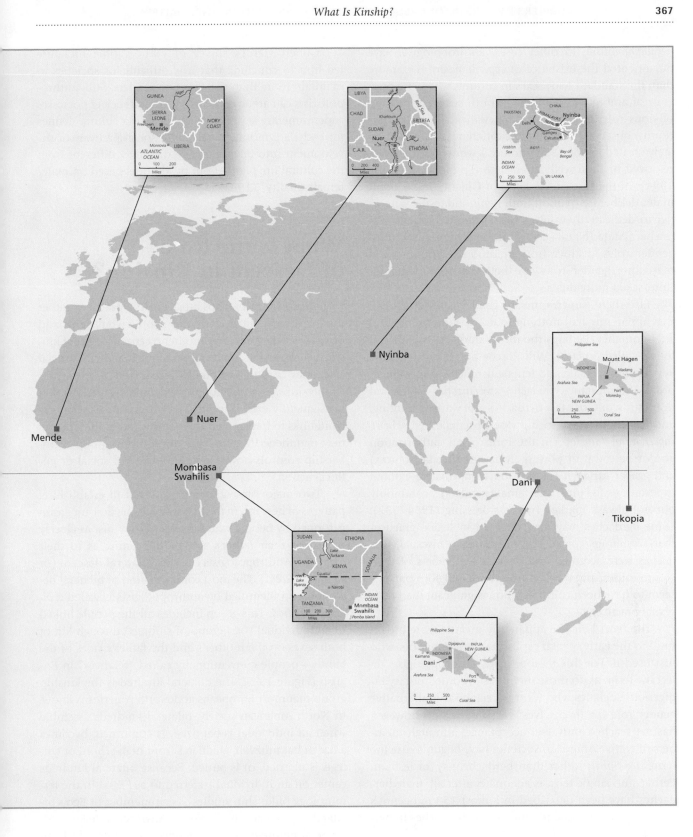

hermaphroditism. In other cases, anthropologists have documented the existence of *supernumerary* (i.e., more than the standard two) sexes in cultures where the presence of ambiguous genitalia at birth seems to play no obvious role. In the Byzantine civilization of late antiquity, observable phenotypic differences were deliberately created in the case of eunuchs, whose testicles were removed or destroyed, often before puberty (Ringrose 1994). In the case of the *hijras* of Gujarat, India, adult males deliberately cut off both penis and testicles in order to dedicate themselves to the mother goddess Bahuchara Mata (Nanda 1994). In both these cases, third gender roles distinct from traditional feminine and masculine gender roles are believed appropriate for third-sexed individuals.

Elsewhere, supernumerary gender roles developed that apparently had nothing to do with morphological sex anomalies. Perhaps the most famous case is that of the so-called *berdache*. Will Roscoe points out that "the key features of male and female berdache roles were, in order of importance, *productive specialization* (crafts and domestic work for male berdaches and warfare, hunting, and leadership roles in the case of female berdaches), *supernatural sanction* (in the form of an authorization and/or bestowal of powers from extrasocietal sources) and *gender variation* (in relation to normative cultural expectations for male and female genders)," commonly but not always marked by cross-dressing (1994, 332). Some berdaches may have engaged in sexual practices that Westerners consider homosexual or bisexual. Berdaches were accepted and respected members of their communities, and their economic and religious pursuits seem to have been culturally more significant than their sexual practices.

The term *berdache* apparently meant "male prostitute" to the early French explorers in the Americas, who first used it. For this reason, many anthropologists reject the term, as do those members of contemporary indigenous societies who want to reclaim this alternative gender role for themselves. No single term, however, has yet reached universal acceptance, although members of Native American societies have begun to use the term *Two Spirits* rather than berdache, gay, or lesbian. Perhaps no single term is adequate; after all, male berdaches have been described in almost 150 indigenous North American societies and female berdaches in perhaps half that number.

---

bilateral descent The principle that a descent group is formed by people who believe they are related to each other by connections made through their mothers and fathers equally (sometimes called *cognatic descent*).

Gilbert Herdt's survey of ethnographic literature led him to conclude that it is difficult for societies to maintain more than two sexes or genders. Still, anthropologists can argue convincingly that a society possesses supernumerary sexes or genders when a culture defines for each "a symbolic niche and a social pathway of development into later adult life distinctly different from the cultural life plan set out by a model based on male/female duality" (1994, 68).

What Is the Role of Descent in Kinship?

In many societies, perhaps most, kinship practices, rather than written statutes, clarify for people what rights and obligations they owe one another A central aspect of kinship is descent—the cultural principle that defines social categories through culturally recognized parent–child connections. Descent groups are defined by ancestry and consequently exist in time. Descent groups use parent–child links to transmit group identity and to incorporate new members. In some societies, descent group membership controls how people mobilize for social or political action.

Two major strategies are employed in establishing patterns of descent. In the first strategy, the descent group is formed by people who believe they are just as closely related to their father's side of the family as to their mother's. Anthropologists call this **bilateral descent** (or *cognatic descent*). The most common kind of bilateral descent group identified by anthropologists is called a *bilateral kindred*. This group includes all the people linked to an individual (or a group of siblings) through kin of both sexes on the mother's and the father's sides of the family—people conventionally called "relatives" in English (Figure 13.3). The bilateral kindred is the kinship group that most Europeans and North Americans know. In North American society, bilateral kindreds assemble when an individual is baptized, is confirmed, becomes a bar or bat mitzvah, graduates from high school or college, is married, or is buried. Because bilateral kindreds center on an individual (referred to as "Ego" in the terminology of kinship studies), each member of Ego's bilateral kindred also has his or her own separate kindred. Bilateral kindreds can be extended indefinitely to form broad overlapping networks of people who are somehow related to one another. Such flexible group boundaries offer advantages in an individualistic society like that of the United States. However, flexible group boundaries can become a liability when social action requires the formation of groups with clear-cut memberships that are

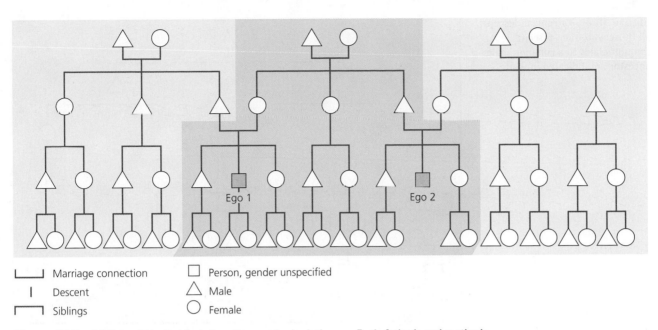

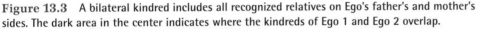

⊔ Marriage connection	□ Person, gender unspecified
| Descent	△ Male
⊓ Siblings	○ Female

Figure 13.3 A bilateral kindred includes all recognized relatives on Ego's father's and mother's sides. The dark area in the center indicates where the kindreds of Ego 1 and Ego 2 overlap.

larger than individual families. This can happen, for example, when conflicting claims to land and labor must be resolved and groups seek to perpetuate limitations on membership over time. In societies that face such challenges, unilineal descent groups are usually formed.

What Roles Do Lineages Play in Descent?

Unilineal descent is based on the assumption that a person's most significant kin relationships come either through one's mother or through one's father. **Lineages** are unilineal descent groups whose members believe they can specify all the parent–child links that unite them. Lineages that are made up of links traced through a father are called *patrilineal*; those traced through a mother are called *matrilineal*. In a patrilineal society, women and men belong to a **patrilineage** formed by father–child links (Figure 13.4); similarly, in a matrilineal society, men and women belong to a **matrilineage** formed by mother–child connections (Figure 13.5). Lineages in some societies may have from 20 or 30 members to several hundred. Before 1949, some Chinese lineages contained more than 1,000 members.

Lineage Membership

The most important feature of lineages is that they are *corporate* in organization—that is, a lineage has a single

legal personality. As the Ashanti put it, a lineage is "one person"; that is, from the point of view of outsiders, all members of a lineage are equal *in law* to all others (Fortes 1953). For example, in the case of a blood feud, the death of any opposing lineage member avenges the death of the person whose death triggered the feud. Lineages are also corporate in that they control property, specifically land, as a unit. Such groups are found only in societies where rights to use land are crucial and must be monitored over time. Lineages are also the main political associations in the societies that have them. People have relatives who are not members of their own lineage, but they recognize that their individual political or legal status comes only through the lineage to which they belong.

Lineages provide for the "perpetual exercise of defined rights, duties, office and social tasks vested in the lineage" (Fortes 1953, 165). In societies where they are found, the system of lineages can serve as a foundation of social life. Lineage membership is transmitted in a direct line from father or mother to child. This means that in societies in which no other form of organization lasts lineages can endure as long as people can remember

---

lineages The consanguineal members of descent groups who believe they can trace their descent from known ancestors.

patrilineage A social group formed by people connected by father–child links.

matrilineage A social group formed by people connected by mother–child links.

Figure 13.4 Patrilineal descent; all those who trace descent through males to a common male ancestor are indicated in white.

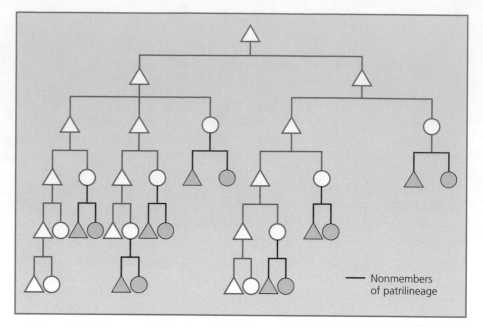

Figure 13.5 Matrilineal descent; all those who trace descent through females to a common female ancestor are indicated in white.

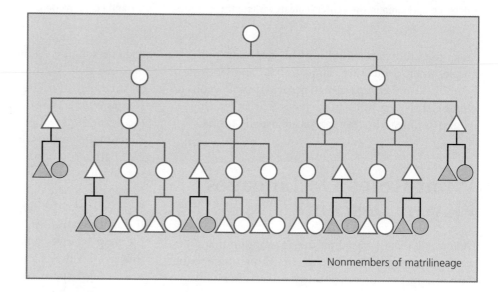

from whom they are descended. Most lineages have a time depth of about five generations: grandparents, parents, Ego, children, and grandchildren. When members of a group believe that they can no longer accurately specify the genealogical links that connect them but believe that they are "in some way" connected, we find what anthropologists call "clans." A **clan** is usually made up of lineages that the society's members believe to be related to each other through links that go back into mythic times. Sometimes the common ancestor of each clan is said to be an animal that lived at the beginning of time. The important point is that lineage members can specify all the generational links back to their common ancestor, whereas clan members ordinarily cannot. The clan is thus larger than any lineage and more diffuse in both membership and the hold it has over individuals.

Patrilineages

By far the most common form of lineage organization is the patrilineage, which consists of all the people (male and female) who believe themselves related to each other because they are related to a common male ancestor by links through men. The prototypical kernel of

---

clan A descent group formed by members who believe they have a common (sometimes mythical) ancestor, even if they cannot specify the genealogical links.

EthnoProfile 13.1

Nuer

Region: Eastern Africa

Nation: Ethiopia and Sudan

Population: 300,000

Environment: Open grassland

Livelihood: Cattle herding and farming

Political organization: Traditionally, egalitarian tribes, no political offices; today, part of modern nation-states

For more information:
Evans-Pritchard, E. E. 1940. *The Nuer.* Oxford: Oxford University Press; and Hutchinson, Sharon. 1996. *Nuer dilemmas.* Berkeley: University of California Press.

a patrilineage is the father–son pair. Although female members of patrilineages normally leave the lineages when they marry, they do not relinquish their interest in their own lineages. Indeed, in a number of societies, they play an active role in the affairs of their own patrilineages for many years.

A classic patrilineal system was found among the Nuer of the Sudan and Ethiopia (see EthnoProfile 13.1: Nuer). At the time of his fieldwork in the 1930s, English anthropologist E. E. Evans-Pritchard (1940) noted that the Nuer were divided into at least 20 clans. Evans-Pritchard defined *clan* as the largest group of people who (1) trace their descent patrilineally from a common ancestor, (2) cannot marry each other, and (3) consider sexual relations within the group to be incestuous. The clan is subdivided, or segmented, into smaller lineages that are themselves linked to each other by presumed ties of patrilineal descent. The most basic level of lineage segmentation is the minimal lineage, which has a time depth of three to five generations.

Evans-Pritchard (1940) observed that the Nuer kinship system worked as a set of nested lineages: members of lineages A and B might consider themselves related because they believed that the founder of lineage A had been the older brother of the founder of lineage B. These two *minimal lineages*, as Evans-Pritchard called them, together formed a *minor lineage*—all those descended from a common father, believed to be the father of the two founders of A and B. Minor lineages connect to other

minor lineages by yet another presumed common ancestor one more level back, forming *major lineages*. These major lineages are also believed to share a common ancestor and thus form a *maximal lineage*. The members of two maximal lineages believe their founders had been the sons of the clan ancestor; thus, all members of the clan are believed to be patrilineally related.

According to Evans-Pritchard (1940), disputes among the Nuer emerged along the lines created by lineages. Suppose a quarrel erupted between two men whose minimal lineages were in different minor lineages. Each man could recruit allies both from his own minimal lineage and from all the other minimal lineages that belonged in his major lineage. When members of the quarreling minor lineages acknowledged (or were made to acknowledge by a mediator) that they were all part of the same major lineage, the dispute would be resolved. Similarly, the minor lineages belonging to one major lineage would ally if a dispute broke out that involved members of another, opposed major lineage. This process of nested groups moving apart or coming together in order to oppose one another at different levels of a hierarchy is called **segmentary opposition**, and it is a very common social process.

Evans-Pritchard (1940) noted that lineages were important to the Nuer for political purposes. Members of the same lineage in the same village were conscious of being in a social group with common ancestors and symbols, corporate rights in territory, and common interests in cattle. When a son in the lineage married, these lineage members helped provide the **bridewealth** cattle, the symbolically valuable goods paid to the bride's lineage in compensation for the loss of her services. If the son were killed, they—indeed, all members of his patrilineage, regardless of where they lived—would avenge him and would hold the funeral ceremony for him. Nevertheless, relationships among the members of a patrilineage were not necessarily harmonious:

> A Nuer is bound to his paternal kin from whom he derives aid, security, and status, but in return for these benefits he has many obligations and commitments. Their often indefinite character may be both evidence of, and a reason for, their force, but it also gives ample scope for disagreement. Duties and rights easily

---

segmentary opposition A mode of hierarchical social organization in which groups beyond the most basic emerge only in opposition to other groups on the same hierarchical level.

bridewealth The transfer of certain symbolically important goods from the family of the groom to the family of the bride on the occasion of their marriage. It represents compensation to the wife's lineage for the loss of her labor and childbearing capacities.

conflict. Moreover, the privileges of [patrilineal] kinship cannot be divorced from authority, discipline, and a strong sense of moral obligation, all of which are irksome to Nuer. They do not deny them, but they kick against them when their personal interests run counter to them. (Evans-Pritchard 1951, 162)

Although the Nuer were patrilineal, they recognized as kin people who were not members of their lineage. In the Nuer language, the word *mar* referred to "kin": all the people to whom a person could trace a relationship of any kind, including people on the mother's side as well as on the father's side. In fact, at such important ceremonial occasions as a bridewealth distribution after a woman in the lineage had been married, special attention was paid to kin on the mother's side. Certain important relatives, such as the mother's brother and the mother's sister, were given cattle. A man's mother's brother was his great supporter when he was in trouble. The mother's brother was kind to him as a boy and even provided a second home after he reached manhood. If he liked his sister's son, a mother's brother would even be willing to help pay the bridewealth so that he could marry. "Nuer say of the maternal uncle that he is both father and mother, but most frequently that 'he is your mother'" (Evans-Pritchard 1951, 162).[1]

What Are Matrilineages?

In matrilineages, descent is traced through women rather than through men. Recall that in a patrilineage a woman's children are not in her lineage. In a matrilineage, a man's children are not in his.

Certain features of matrilineages make them more than just mirror images of patrilineages. First, the prototypical kernel of a matrilineage is the sister–brother pair; a matrilineage may be thought of as a group of brothers and sisters connected through links made by women. Brothers marry out and often live with the family of their wives, but they maintain an active interest in the affairs of their lineage. Second, the most important man in a boy's life is not his father (who is not in his lineage) but his mother's brother, from whom he will receive his lineage inheritance. Third, the amount of power women exercise in matrilineal societies is still hotly debated in anthropology. A matrilineage is not the same thing as a *matriarchy* (a society in which women rule); brothers often retain what appears to be a controlling interest in the lineage. Some anthropologists claim that the male members of a matrilineage run the lineage even though

---

EthnoProfile 13.2

Navajo

Region: North America

Nation: United States (northwestern New Mexico, northeastern Arizona, southeastern Utah)

Population: 100,000

Environment: Rugged landscape

Livelihood: Farming, sheepherding, silver work, arts

Political organization: Traditionally, clans, public consensus; today, a tribal council

For more information: Witherspoon, Gary. 1975. *Navajo kinship and marriage*. Chicago: University of Chicago Press.

there is more autonomy for women in matrilineal societies than in patrilineal ones—that the day-to-day exercise of power tends to be carried out by the brothers or sometimes the husbands. A number of studies, however, have questioned the validity of these generalizations. Saying anything about matrilineal societies in general is difficult. The ethnographic evidence suggests that matrilineages must be examined on a case-by-case basis.

The Navajo are a matrilineal people (see EthnoProfile 13.2: Navajo). The basic unit of Navajo social organization is the subsistence residential unit, composed of a head mother, her husband, and some of their children with their spouses and children (Witherspoon 1975, 82; Figure 13.6). The leader of the unit is normally a man, usually the husband of the head mother. He directs livestock and agricultural operations and is the one who deals with the outside world: "He speaks for the unit at community meetings, negotiates with the traders and car salesmen, arranges marriages and ceremonies, talks to visiting strangers, and so on." He seems to be in charge. But it is the head mother around whom the unit is organized:

> [The head mother] is identified with the land, the herd, and the agricultural fields. All residence rights can be traced back to her, and her opinions and wishes are always given the greatest consideration and usually prevail. In a sense, however, she delegates much of her role and prestige to the leader of the unit. If we think of the unit as a corporation, and the leader as its president, the head mother will be the chairman of the board.

---

[1] Readers interested in what has happened to Nuer kinship and relatedness as a consequence of the civil war in the Sudan should look at Hutchinson 1996 or 2002.

In Their Own Words

Outside Work, Women, and Bridewealth

Judith M. Abwunza took life histories from and interviewed many women among the Logoli of western Kenya about their lives, and has allowed many of those women to speak for themselves in her 1997 book, Women's Voices, Women's Power: Dialogues of Resistance from East Africa. *Here, Abwunza introduces us to Alice, a 24-year-old secondary school teacher.*

Alice's father is relatively affluent, as all his children are in school or working, his land is well-kept and fully utilized and the yard has cows, chickens, and goats. Alice's motivation to get a job was that she wanted to assist her family. She said that everyone in the family depends upon her for money, a burden that she finds to be "overwhelming." Alice has been living with her husband, who is also a teacher, since January, 1987. They have seven-month-old twins, a boy and a girl. Uvukwi [bridewealth] discussion has taken place and her in-laws and her relatives have agreed on 23,000 shillings and five cows. A 3,000 shilling "down payment" has been given, and her marriage occurred in January, 1988. Alice discusses her situation in English:

> We live in a house supplied by the school. We have electricity and water and a gas cooker. We have a small house plot in my husband's yard at Bunyore, and six acres in the scheme in Kitale. We hire people to dig there, as we are teaching. So far, we have not sold cash crops. We are only beginning. On the schemes, workers are paid between five and six hundred shillings a month to dig, so it is expensive. There is no need of paying uvukwi. Am I a farm to be bought? It is unfortunate the parents are poor. Parents ought to contribute to the newly married to start them off. But there is nothing we can do; it's a custom. Also uvukwi is not the end of assistance to parents. Some men mistreat after buying, that is paying uvukwi. Some men refuse to help parents any more after uvukwi, think that's enough. On the other hand, if you don't pay uvukwi, the husbands think you are not valued by parents. You are cheap. It's a tug of war.
>
> People who get jobs in Kenya have been to school, these are the elite. They are able to integrate various situations. They are analytical and choosing courses of action. They have developed decision-making skills; this gives access to wage labour. Most women are not this; many men are not. Things have changed for women, but still it is very difficult; they must work very hard. In the old days, customs did not allow men in the kitchen; now they do. It's absurd to see milk boiling over in the kitchen while I'm taking care of the baby and he is reading. A more even distribution of labour is needed. Women need a word of appreciation for their hard work, in the home and caring for children. Here in Maragoli we cannot develop: the population is too high. The government is suggesting that maternity leave will not be given after the fourth child. This is a good thing but it has not been passed yet. I will not be abused in my marriage. I will leave. My job is difficult. Children are beaten, sent from school for fees, for harambee this, harambee that. Seldom do I have my entire class to teach. Some are always missing. I have had to chase them for fees. This is not my role; my job is to teach them, so they may better their lives. I refuse to beat them. I try not to upset them. I want them to learn. But many do not want to. Girls only want to chase boys, and boys the girls. But a few learn. Teaching is difficult.

[Abwunza concludes:] Alice takes a different position from most Logoli women. She complains of having to follow traditional ways in these difficult economic times, even as she adheres to them. Although many people complained about the "high cost" of uvukwi, on no other occasion did women suggest that parents should assist a newly married couple and not follow the custom of uvukwi. Alice's feeling is not typical of Logoli people. It comes about at least in part because Alice's uvukwi is quite high and both she and her husband will have to contribute to its payment, as she says, "at the expense of our own development." She sees that she is caught in a bind. Not following the traditions will place her in a position of being without a good reputation and thus at risk in the community.

Source: Abwunza 1997, 77–78.

Figure 13.6 The head mother of a Navajo subsistence residential unit is identified with the land, the herd, and the agricultural fields.

She usually has more sheep than the leader does. Because the power and importance of the head mother offer a deceptive appearance to the observer, many students of the Navajo have failed to see the importance of her role. But if one has lived a long time in one of these units, one soon becomes aware of who ultimately has the cards and directs the game. When there is a divorce between the leader and the head, it is always the leader who leaves and the head mother who returns, even if the land originally belonged to the mother of the leader. (Witherspoon, 1975, 82–83)

Overall, evidence from matrilineal societies reveals some domains of experience in which men and women are equal, some in which men are in control, and some in which women are in control. Observers and participants may disagree about which of these domains of experience is more or less central to Navajo life.

What Are Kinship Terminologies?

People everywhere use special terms to refer to people they recognize as related to them. Kinship terminologies suggest both the external boundaries and internal

---

affinity Connection through marriage.

collaterality A criterion employed in the analysis of kinship terminologies in which a distinction is made between kin who are believed to be in a direct line and those who are "off to one side," linked to the speaker by a lineal relative.

bifurcation A criterion employed in the analysis of kinship terminologies in which kinship terms referring to the mother's side of the family are distinguished from those referring to the father's side.

---

divisions of kinship groups, and they outline the structure of rights and obligations assigned to different members of the society. They also provide clues about how the vast and undifferentiated world of potential relations may be divided.

What Criteria Are Used for Making Kinship Distinctions?

Anthropologists have identified several criteria that people use to indicate how people are related to one another. From the most common to the least common, these criteria include the following:

- *Generation.* Kin terms distinguish relatives according to the generation to which the relatives belong. In English, the term *cousin* conventionally refers to someone of the same generation as Ego.

- *Gender.* The gender of an individual is used to differentiate kin. In Spanish, *primo* refers to a male cousin and *prima* to a female cousin. In English, cousins are not distinguished on the basis of gender, but *uncle* and *aunt* are distinguished on the basis of both generation and gender.

- *Affinity.* A distinction is made on the basis of connection through marriage, or **affinity**. This criterion is used in Spanish when *suegra* (Ego's spouse's mother) is distinguished from *madre* (Ego's mother). In matrilineal societies, Ego's mother's sister and father's sister are distinguished from one another on the basis of affinity. The mother's sister is a direct, lineal relative; the father's sister is an affine; and they are called by different terms.

- *Collaterality.* A distinction is made between kin who are believed to be in a direct line and those who are "off to one side," linked to Ego through a lineal relative. In English, the distinction of **collaterality** is exemplified by the distinction between *mother* and *aunt* or *father* and *uncle*.

- *Bifurcation.* The distinction of **bifurcation** is employed when kinship terms referring to the mother's side of the family differ from those referring to the father's side.

- *Relative age.* Relatives of the same category may be distinguished on the basis of whether they are older or younger than Ego. Among the Ju/'hoansi, for example, speakers must separate "older brother" (*!ko*) from "younger brother" (*tsin*).

- *Gender of linking relative.* This criterion is related to collaterality. It distinguishes *cross relatives* (usually cousins) from *parallel relatives* (also usually cousins). Parallel relatives are linked through two

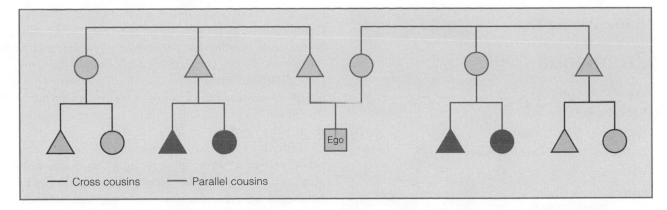

Figure 13.7 Cross cousins and parallel cousins. Ego's cross cousins are the children of Ego's father's sister and mother's brother. Ego's parallel cousins are the children of Ego's father's brother and mother's sister.

brothers or two sisters. **Parallel cousins**, for example, are Ego's father's brother's children or mother's sister's children. Cross relatives are linked through a brother-sister pair. Thus, **cross cousins** are Ego's mother's brother's children or father's sister's children. The gender of either Ego or the cousins does not matter; rather, the important factor is the gender of the linking relative (Figure 13.7).

By the early 1950s, kinship specialists in anthropology had identified six major patterns of kinship terminology, based on how cousins were classified. In recent years, however, anthropologists have become quite skeptical of the value of these idealized models, in large measure because they are highly formalized, neglect all kin categories except cousins, and fail to consider the full range of people's actual kinship practices. Perhaps the main value to come from formal kinship studies is the fact that they took seriously the ways other people classified their relatives and were able to display the logic that informed such classifications.

What Is Adoption?

Kinship systems sometimes appear to be fairly rigid sets of rules that use the accident of birth to thrust people into social positions laden with rights and obligations they cannot escape. Social positions that people are assigned at birth are sometimes called **ascribed statuses**, and positions within a kinship system have long been viewed as the prototypical ascribed statuses in any society. Ascribed statuses are often contrasted with **achieved statuses**, those social positions that people

may attain later in life, often as the result of their own (or other people's) effort, such as becoming a spouse or college graduate. All societies have ways of incorporating outsiders into their kinship groups, however, which they achieve by converting supposedly ascribed kinship statuses into achieved ones, thus undermining the distinction between them. We will use the term *adoption* to refer to these practices which allow people to transform relationships based on nurturance into relations of kinship.

Adoption in Highland Ecuador

Mary Weismantel is an anthropologist who carried out fieldwork among indigenous farmers living outside the community of Zumbagua in highland Ecuador (1995) (see EthnoProfile 13.3: Zumbagua). The farmers' households were based on lifelong heterosexual relationships, but she discovered that Zumbaguans recognized kin ties that were very different from those found in European American cultures. Most striking was her discovery that every adult seemed to have several kinds of parents and several kinds of children.

In some societies, like that of ancient Rome, people distinguish between Ego's biological father (or *genitor*) and social father (or *pater*); they may also distinguish

---

parallel cousins The children of a person's parents' same-gender siblings (a father's brother's children or a mother's sister's children).

cross cousins The children of a person's parents' opposite-gender siblings (a father's sister's children or a mother's brother's children).

ascribed statuses Social positions people are assigned at birth.

achieved statuses Social positions people may attain later in life, often as the result of their own (or other people's) effort.

EthnoProfile 13.3

Zumbagua

Region: South America

Nation: Ecuador

Population: 20,000 (parish)

Environment: Andean mountain valley

Livelihood: Farming

Political organization:
Peasant village and parish in modern nation-state

For more information:
Weismantel, Mary. 2001. *Food, gender, and poverty in the Ecuadorian Andes.* Prospect Heights, IL: Waveland Press.

between Ego's biological mother (or *genetrix*) and social mother (or *mater*). Social parents are those who nurture a child, and they are often the child's biological parents as well. Zumbaguans use the Quichua term *tayta* for both genitor and pater and *mama* for both genetrix and mater. In their society, however, genitor, pater, genetrix, and mater are often entirely different people.

Weismantel learned that this use of kin terms was related to local forms of adoption, most of which occur within the family. In 1991, for example, a young girl named Nancy moved into the household of her father Alfonso's prosperous, unmarried older sister, Heloisa, whom Nancy called *tía* ("aunt"). By 1993, however, Nancy was calling Heloisa "mama." Everyone concerned viewed this transition positively, a way of strengthening family solidarity in a difficult economic situation, and no one seemed worried about whether Heloisa was Nancy's "natural" mother or not.

People also often adopted children who were not kin. In both cases, however, the bond of adoption was created through nurturing, symbolized by the provision of food. Heloisa became Nancy's adoptive mama because she took care of her and fed her. Men in Zumbagua can also become the adoptive tayta of children by feeding them in front of witnesses, who verbally proclaim what a "good father" the man is. However, the adoptive relationship does not gain recognition unless the adoptive parent continues feeding the child regularly for a

long time. Weismantel discovered that the Zumbaguan family consists of those who eat together. The kinship bond results, they believe, because people who regularly eat the same food together eventually come to share "the same flesh," no matter who gave birth to them. Weismantel points out that feeding children is every bit as "biological" as giving birth to them: it is simply a different aspect of biology.

Indeed, in Zumbagua, a woman's biological tie to her offspring is given no greater weight than a man's biological tie to his. In other words, enduring kin ties in Zumbagua are achieved, not merely ascribed, statuses. Many Zumbaguans are closer to their adopted family than they are to their biological parents. If genitor and genetrix are young and poor, they run a very real risk that they will lose their children to adoption by older, wealthier individuals.

European American Kinship and New Reproductive Technologies

Western medicine has developed new reproductive technologies, such as in vitro fertilization, sperm banks, and surrogate motherhood, that are creating challenges not only for law and morality but also for Western concepts of kinship (Figure 13.8). Marilyn Strathern (1992) observes that in the European American world, kinship is understood as the social construction of natural facts, a logic that both combines and separates the social and natural worlds. That is, European Americans recognize kin related by blood and kin related by marriage, but they also believe that procreation—the process that brings kin into existence—is part of nature. "The rooting of social relations in natural facts traditionally served to impart a certain quality to one significant dimension of kin relations . . . these relations were at base non-negotiable" (Strathern 1992, 28). Yet, the new reproductive technologies make clear that everything is negotiable: even the world of natural facts is subject to social intervention.

As Janet Dolgin (1995) reports, contemporary ambiguities surrounding kinship in the United States have put pressure on the courts to decide what constitutes biological parenthood and how it is related to legal parenthood. She examined two sets of court cases, the first involving the paternal rights of unwed supposed fathers and the second focusing on the rights of parties involved in surrogate motherhood agreements. In two cases involving supposed unwed fathers, courts reasoned that biological maternity automatically made a woman a social mother but biological paternity did not automatically make a man a social father. Because the

Figure 13.8 In vitro fertilization, one of the new reproductive technologies, is already having an effect on what it means to be a "natural" parent. Over 1,000 IVF babies gathered in 2003 to celebrate the twenty-fifth anniversary of the birth of the first IVF baby, Louise Brown (center front).

men in these two cases had failed to participate in rearing their children, their paternity rights were not recognized. In another case, the biological father had lived with his child and her mother for extended periods during the child's early years and had actively participated in her upbringing. However, the child's mother had been married to another man during this period, and the law proclaimed her legal husband to be the child's father. Although the genitor had established a supportive relationship with his daughter, the court labeled him "the adulterous natural father," arguing, in effect, that a genitor can never be a pater unless he is involved in an ongoing relationship with the child's mother, something that was clearly impossible because she was already married to someone else.

The surrogacy cases demonstrate directly the complications that can result from new reproductive technologies. The "Baby M" situation was a traditional surrogacy arrangement in which the surrogate, Mary Beth Whitehead, was impregnated with the sperm of the husband in the couple who intended to become the legal parents

of the child she bore. Whitehead was supposed to terminate all parental rights when the child was born, but she refused to do so. The court faced a dilemma. Existing law backed Whitehead's maternal rights, but the court was also concerned that the surrogacy agreement looked too much like baby selling or womb rental, which were against the law. The court's opinion focused on Whitehead's attempt to break the surrogacy contract to justify terminating her legal rights, although she was awarded visitation rights.

More complicated than traditional surrogacy, *gestational surrogacy* deconstructs the role of genetrix into two roles that can be performed by two different women. In a key case, the Calverts, a childless married couple, provided egg and sperm that were used in the laboratory to create an embryo, which was then implanted in Anna Johnson's uterus. But when Johnson gave birth to the baby, she refused to give it up. As Dolgin points out, this case "provided a context in which to measure the generality of the assumption that the gestational role both produces and constitutes maternity" (1995, 58).

As we have seen, other court cases emphasized the role of gestation in forming an indissoluble bond between mother and child. In this case, however, the court referred to Anna Johnson "as a 'gestational carrier,' a 'genetic hereditary stranger' to the child, who acted like a 'foster parent'" (1995, 59). The court declared the Calverts and the child a family unit on genetic grounds and ruled that the Calverts were the baby's "natural" and legal parents.

Dolgin notes that in all of these cases the courts awarded legal custody to those parties whose living arrangements most closely approximated the traditional middle-class, North American two-parent family. "Biological facts were called into judicial play only . . . when they justified the preservation of traditional families" (1995, 63). Biological facts that might have undermined such families were systematically overlooked. Perhaps the clear-cut biological basis of North American kinship is not so clear-cut after all.

How Does Organ Transplantation Create New Relatives?

Equally curious and provocative are the new kinds of kin ties that have emerged in the United States, following the increasingly widespread use of biomedical and surgical techniques that allow bodily organs to be salvaged from brain-dead individuals and transplanted into the bodies of others. Lesley Sharp reports that professionals who manage the many steps involved in organ transplantation have, until very recently, attempted to keep the families of organ donors from finding out the identities of organ recipients. The rather paternalistic justification given was that keeping people ignorant would be good for their psychic health. But Sharp reports that donor kin and organ recipients have found ways to find each other and meet face-to-face, and her research contradicted the fears of the professionals: Out of 30 recorded cases of such meetings, only one failed (2006, 191).

An important outcome of the bringing together of donor kin and organ recipients has been the development of kinship relationships linking donor kin to those who received organs from their relatives. Affected individuals struggle with the question of what Sharp calls "donor ownership": "What rights do surviving kin have to trace the whereabouts of the remains of the lost loved one? Can one, for instance, assert claims of access—or postmortem visiting rights?" (2006, 190). Sharp's research showed her that

> donor kin and recipients alike share the understanding that transplanted organs, as donor fragments, carry with them some essence of their former selves, and this persists in the bodies of recipients. The donor then becomes a transmigrated soul of sorts, one that generates compelling dilemmas for involved parties. . . . At risk here is the further shattering of each person's world; yet, as successful encounters reveal, potentially each party is partially healed in the process. (2006, 190)

One example Sharp offers involves Sally and Larry. Both had been involved in activities promoting organ donation and had known each other for several years, before they learned that Sally's son had provided the heart now beating inside Larry's body. When Sharp interviewed them, Sally was in her mid-fifties and a widow; Larry was a dozen years older and married. Right after his transplant surgery, and against the advice of his doctors, Larry had begun trying to find the family of the teenager who had provided his heart, and his wife, "Bulldog," helped him find Sally. Larry and Sally exchanged letters and met three years later. As they got to know one another, Larry, Sally, and Sally's daughter began to use kin terms to refer to one another.

> For example, Larry addresses Sally's daughter as "Sis," and she calls him "Bro." After Larry's own birth mother died, he then began to address Sally as "Mom," and she now calls him "Son." As Sally explained, Larry now sends her a Mother's Day card. These terms have facilitated the establishment of an elaborate joking relationship. . . . They are mildly troubled by the adulterous overtones of their relationship, one laced, too, I would assert, with the incestuous, given that Larry now harbors part of Charlie inside his body. (188)

Sharp found that, of all kinship statuses, the role of the donor mother was particularly important among those whom she interviewed (Figure 13.9). In this case, emphasizing Sally's role as donor mother helped Sally and Larry deal with the "adulterous" or "incestuous" overtones in their relationship. "In assuming the role of donor mother to Larry, she eliminates the discomfort that arises when one considers their proximity in age. In essence, the mother–son bond trumps age" (2006, 190). Interestingly, traditionally North American understandings about "blood" relations extend to Larry but not to his wife: "Today, Sally, Larry, and Bulldog are dear to one another," but "there is no special term of address reserved for Bulldog. . . . Structurally, she is simply 'Larry's wife,' whereas Larry, in embodying Charlie's heart, is now embraced as blood kin" (2006, 190).

Figure 13.9 The families of organ donors and the recipients of those organs have begun to meet face-to-face in the United States. A heart recipient (center, facing camera) embraces the mother of the young man whose heart he received; his wife (*right*) and the young man's sister (*left*) look on.

Marriage

The forms of relatedness we have just described are intimately connected with another widespread social process—marriage. Marriage and household formation provide significant forms of social support that enable people to take part in wider patterns of social life. In many places, they also facilitate important economic and political exchanges between the kinship groups to which the marriage partners belong. Even when marriage is not connected with lineage or clan relations, marriage patterns provide frameworks for linking previously unrelated people to one another, embedding individuals within groups, and organizing individual emotional commitments and economic activities.

Toward a Definition of Marriage

Marriage and *family* are two terms anthropologists use to describe how mating and its consequences are understood and organized in different societies. Getting married involves more than living together or having sexual relations. In most societies, marriage also requires involvement and support from the wider social groups to which the spouses belong—first and foremost, from their families.

Nowhere in the world is *marriage* synonymous with *mating,* but some criteria are common in most societies; we concentrate on these in our own definition of marriage. A prototypical **marriage** (1) transforms the status of the participants; (2) stipulates the degree of sexual

access the married partners are expected to have to each other, ranging from exclusive to preferential; (3) perpetuates social patterns through the production or adoption of offspring, who also have rights and obligations; (4) creates relationships between the kin of the partners; and (5) is symbolically marked in some way, from an elaborate wedding to simply the appearance of a husband and wife seated one morning outside her hut.

Ordinarily, a prototypical marriage involves a man and a woman. But what are we to make of the following cases?

Woman Marriage and Ghost Marriage among the Nuer

Among the Nuer, as E. E. Evans-Pritchard observed during his fieldwork in the 1930s, a woman could marry another woman and become the "father" of the children the wife bore (see EthnoProfile 13.1: Nuer). This practice, which also appears in some other parts of Africa, involves the distinction between pater and genitor. The female husband (the pater) had to have some cattle of her own to use for bridewealth payments to the wife's lineage. Once the bridewealth had been paid, the marriage was established. The female husband then got a

---

marriage An institution that transforms the status of the participants, carries implications about permitted sexual access, perpetuates social patterns through the birth of offspring, creates relationships between the kin of partners, and is symbolically marked.

male kinsman, friend, or neighbor (the genitor) to impregnate the wife and to help with certain tasks around the homestead that the Nuer believed could be done only by men.

Generally, Evans-Pritchard (1951) noted, a female husband was unable to have children herself "and for this reason counts in some respects as a man." Indeed, she played the social role of a man. She could marry several wives if she was wealthy. She could demand damage payment if those wives engaged in sexual activity without her consent. She was the pater of her wives' children. On the marriage of her daughters, she received the portion of the bridewealth that traditionally went to the father, and her brothers and sisters received the portions appropriate to the father's side. Her children were named after her, as though she were a man, and they addressed her as "Father." She administered her compound and her herds as a male head of household would, and she was treated by her wives and children with the same deference shown a male husband and father.

More common in Nuer social life was what Evans-Pritchard called the "ghost marriage." The Nuer believed that a man who died without male heirs left an unhappy and angry spirit who might trouble his living kin. The spirit was angry because a basic obligation of Nuer kinship was for a man to be remembered through and by his sons: his name had to be continued in his lineage. To appease the angry spirit, a kinsman of the dead man—a brother or a brother's son—would often marry a woman "to his name." Bridewealth cattle were paid in the name of the dead man to the patrilineage of a woman. She was then married to the ghost of the dead man but lived with one of his surviving kinsmen. In the marriage ceremonies and afterward, this kinsman acted as though he were the true husband. The children of the union were referred to as though they were the kinsman's, but officially they were not. That is, the ghost husband was their pater and his kinsman, their genitor. As the children got older, the name of their ghost father became increasingly important to them. The ghost father's name, not his stand-in's name, would be remembered in the history of the lineage. The social union between the ghost and the woman took precedence over the sexual union between the ghost's surrogate and the woman.

Ghost marriage serves to perpetuate social patterns. Although it was common for a man to marry a wife "to his kinsman's name" before he himself married, it became difficult, if not impossible, for him to marry later in his own right. His relatives would tell him he was "already married" and that he should allow his younger brothers to use cattle from the family herd so they could marry. Even if he eventually accumulated enough cattle to afford to marry, he would feel that those cattle should provide the bridewealth for the sons he had raised for his dead kinsman. When he died, he died childless because the children he had raised were legally the children of the ghost. He was then an angry spirit, and someone else (in fact, one of the sons he had raised for the ghost) had to marry a wife to *his* name. Thus, the pattern continued, as, indeed, it does to the present day.

Why Is Marriage a Social Process?

Like all formal definitions, our definition of marriage is somewhat rigid. Thinking of marriage as a social process rather than a rigid form, however, is more inclusive of all forms of marriage, even those that may not perfectly fit the definition (Figure 13.10). For example, mating alone does not create in-laws, nor does it set up a way of locating the offspring in space and time as members of a particular social group. Marriage does both; it embeds human mating within an elaborately constructed social and cultural niche. A marriage sets up new relationships that bring together the kin of both spouses. These are called **affinal relationships** (based on *affinity*—relationships created via marriage) and contrast with **consanguineal relationships** (based on "blood" ties, i.e., on descent).

Marriage mediates relationships based on affinity and consanguinity and thus can play an important role in the formation of social groups. Marriage marks a major transformation of social position. It affects not only the newly married couple and their families but also the wider community, which is responsible for acknowledging the legitimacy of every new union. Every society has its own forms of matchmaking. Sometimes marriages must be contracted within a particular social group, a pattern called **endogamy**. In other cases, marriage partners must be found outside a particular group, a pattern called **exogamy**. In Nuer society, for example, a person had to marry outside his or her lineage. In the United States, where the ideology of individualism leads many people to conclude that they can marry whomever they want, statistically people tend to marry within the bounds of certain groups. For example, young people

---

affinal relationships Kinship connections through marriage, or affinity.

consanguineal relationships Kinship connections based on descent.

endogamy Marriage within a defined social group.

exogamy Marriage outside a defined social group.

Figure 13.10 Marriage is a social process that creates social ties and involves more than just the people getting married. Family and friends recognize the new couple after the formal ceremony in Venice.

are often told to marry "your own kind," which usually means someone in their own ethnic, racial, or religious group or social class. In all societies, some close kin are off limits as spouses or as sexual partners. This exogamous pattern is known as the *incest taboo*.

Patterns of Residence after Marriage

Once married, a couple must live somewhere. There are four major patterns of postmarital residence. Most familiar to North Americans is **neolocal residence**, in which the new couple sets up an independent household at a place of their own choosing. Neolocal residence tends to be found in societies that are more or less individualistic in their organization.

When the married couple lives with (or near) the husband's father's family, the pattern is called **patrilocal residence**, which is observed by more societies in the contemporary world than any other residence pattern. It produces a characteristic social grouping of related men: a man, his brothers, and their sons (along with in-marrying wives) all live and work together. This pattern is common in both herding and farming societies; some anthropologists argue that survival in such societies depends on activities that are best carried out by groups of men who have worked together all their lives.

When the married couple lives with (or near) the family in which the wife was raised, the pattern is called **matrilocal residence**, which is usually found in association with matrilineal kinship systems. Here, the core of the social group consists of a woman, her sisters, and

their daughters (along with in-marrying husbands). This pattern is most common among groups practicing extensive agriculture.

Less common, but also found in matrilineal societies, is the pattern known as **avunculocal residence**. Here, the married couple lives with (or near) the husband's mother's brother. The most significant man in a boy's matrilineage is his mother's brother, from whom he will inherit. Avunculocal residence emphasizes this relationship.

Single and Plural Spouses

The number of spouses a person may have varies cross-culturally. Anthropologists distinguish forms of marriage in terms of how many spouses a person may have. **Monogamy** is a marriage form in which a person may have only one spouse at a time, whereas **polygamy** is a

---

neolocal residence A postmarital residence pattern in which a married couple sets up an independent household at a place of their own choosing.

patrilocal residence A postmarital residence pattern in which a married couple lives with (or near) the husband's father.

matrilocal residence A postmarital residence pattern in which a married couple lives with (or near) the wife's mother.

avunculocal residence A postmarital residence pattern in which a married couple lives with (or near) the husband's mother's brother (from avuncular, "of uncles").

monogamy A marriage pattern in which a person may be married to only one spouse at a time.

polygamy A marriage pattern in which a person may be married to more than one spouse at a time.

In Their Own Words

Two Cheers for Gay Marriage

Roger Lancaster is professor of anthropology and director of cultural studies at George Mason University. In this essay from the Anthropology News *of September 2004, he discusses some of the issues involved with gay marriage.*

Announcing his support for a proposed constitutional amendment to ban same-sex marriages, President Bush pronounced marriage, or more specifically the union of one man and one woman, to be "the most fundamental institution of civilization." Actually, it can hardly be said that monogamous heterosexual marriage is the sole form of union "honored and encouraged in all cultures and by every religious faith," as Bush claims. That's Anthropology 101. Nor can it be said that the idea of gay marriage runs counter to 5000 years of moral teaching, as spokespersons for the Christian right insist.

What careful scholarship and "millennia of human experience" actually show is that marriage cannot be forever fixed into a one-size-fits-all formula. There's more than one way to live, to love, and to set up home and hearth.

Just What Is Marriage?

Marriage sometimes involves a formal union marked by a public announcement or a ritual—like a wedding. Or it might have the informal character of a union gradually acquired or consolidated over a period of time. What North Americans and Europeans call "common-law marriage" is the prevailing form of union in many parts of Latin America and elsewhere. For these (and other) reasons, anthropologists often avoid using baggage-laden terms like "marriage" when describing the broad sweep of institutions related to affinity, residency, and kinship, opting instead for more portable (if off-putting) technical terms like "union" or "alliance."

Just how many forms of same-sex union one discerns across cultures and throughout human history will depend on what one counts as "same sex" and "union." Bonds of same-sex friendship, publicly announced and ritually marked by an officiating authority, amount to something very much like "marriage" in a great number of cultures. So do other forms of same-sex group affiliation, such as orders of nuns, certain priesthoods,

the Band of Thebes, any number of warrior castes, and highly organized groups of women who lived collectively on the Chinese Kwantung delta in the nineteenth century. Ironically, the very wedding vows that the president wants to "protect" derive from early Greek Christian same-sex commitment ceremonies, as historian John Boswell has shown in his final book, *Same-Sex Unions in Premodern Europe.*

Modern Love

What most Americans think of as "marriage" actually turns out not to be a universal institution but a relatively recent invention. If you read St. Paul or St. Augustine, for instance, you'll see that the fathers of the early Christian Church were quite hostile to marriage. Far from celebrating the sexual union of one man and one woman, St. Paul recommended celibacy for everyone and only grudgingly accepts marriage as a back-up plan: "Better to marry than to burn."

Although archaic texts sometimes refer to wedding feasts, marriage rituals involving the exchange of vows appear to develop fairly late in medieval Europe. The idea that an officiating authority—a priest—ought to be present during those vows comes later still. Later yet, the Church starts to keep records. And much later, the state becomes involved.

The revolutionary notion that one might marry not in the political or economic interests of extended kin groups, but voluntarily and out of love, is an idea of distinctly modern vintage—one whose implications our culture continues to digest. And that's where we find ourselves today: in the throes of ongoing changes and contestations.

Social conservatives lament the decline of traditional families, the rise of divorce rates, the spread of cohabiting arrangements, the emergence of new family forms and, perhaps especially, the growing visibility of lesbian and gay relationships. They tap pervasive feelings of unease

In Their Own Words

about the new arrangements. But logically, you can't have love without heartache. You probably can't have the idea that love is the sole legitimate basis for marriage without also having modern divorce rates. (Levelheaded people entered into the spirit of this arrangement in the 1970s, when they began vowing "as long as we both shall love.") All said, these aspects of sexual modernity would seem to follow, more or less logically, from the idea that our relationships, like other contracts in a market economy, ought to be entered into freely. They would seem to follow from the idea that marriage ought to be based on love.

And once you have a modern culture of love, linked to that consummate American right, "the pursuit of happiness," it becomes difficult to justify arbitrarily excluding people from it.

Where Do We Go from Here?

Obviously, who's in and who's out of official kinship really matters. It counts in ways that are more than symbolic. There are real social, economic, and health-care implications. It's thus important to modernize the official definitions of marriage. But like most members of the gay left, I do worry about the fetishization of marriage and family in U.S. political culture—a phenomenon not notably vented in a single other industrial democracy. Claims about the supposed benefits of marriage, anguish over how to strengthen the family, and endless talk about "individual responsibility" have become panaceas in an era of declining wages, skyrocketing health-care costs, vindictive welfare reform, and social insecurity in general.

These collective fantasies distill a distinctly neoliberal picture of the world: the family, shored up by monogamous marriage (and sometimes enhanced by "covenant marriage"), is to act as a sort of state within the state, providing for individual members' welfare—precisely at a time when the state has renounced its historic responsibilities for social welfare (as I have shown in *The Trouble with Nature*).

In this skewed and surreal context, advocates of gay marriage sometimes sound more conservative than the conservatives. They sometimes present an astonishingly unrepresentative and unrealistic picture of gay and lesbian relationships. In a recent *Nation* article, Lisa Duggan pulls this quote from "The Roadmap to Equality," published by the Lambda Legal Defense and Education Fund and Marriage Equality in California: "Gay people are very much like everyone else. They grow up, fall in love, form families, and have children. They mow their lawns, shop for groceries, and worry about making ends meet. They want good schools for their children, and security for their families as a whole."

Frankly, I doubt that this suburban picture of children, school worries, lawnmowers, and domestic bliss really applies to more than a very small minority—perhaps as small as 3 or 4 percent—of the gay and lesbian community. I certainly want no part of America's deranged culture of lawn care. I also chafe at the idea, floated in the same guide, that denying marriage rights to lesbian and gay couples keeps them in a state of permanent adolescence. . . . I don't feel like a permanent adolescent, and palaver like this makes me deeply ashamed for Lambda Legal Defense.

I've lived with my lover for over 15 years. I'd like some legal recognition of our relationship. I'd like the right to file joint taxes, if married couples are going to have that option, and the right to inherit each other's pensions and social security benefits. But I have no interest in quasi-religious rigmarole or moralizing platitudes. I don't feel that our relationship would benefit from the exchange of vows. And like most sound people of my generation, I'm skeptical of claims about the moral and existential benefits of being "shackled by forgotten words and bonds/ And the ink stains that are dried upon some line" (as John Hartford once put it).

We need gay marriage, and we should fight for it. But we also need recognition of the true existent variety of ways people live and love. And everybody—whether they take the plunge or not—ought to have access to basic health care, affordable housing, and a decent retirement. A one-size institution won't fit all. We need more options, not less. We need to be as radical as reality about these matters.

Source: Lancaster, 2004

marriage system that allows a person to have more than one spouse. Within the category of polygamy are two subcategories: **polygyny**, or multiple wives, and **polyandry**, or multiple husbands. Most societies in the world permit polygyny.

Monogamy Monogamy is the only legal spousal pattern of the United States and most industrialized nations. (Indeed, in 1896, a condition of statehood for the territory of Utah was the abolition of polygyny, which had been practiced by Mormon settlers for nearly 50 years.) There are variations in the number of times a monogamous person can be married. Before the twentieth century, people in western European societies generally married only once unless death intervened. Today, some observers suggest that we practice *serial monogamy*—we may be married to several different people but only one at a time.

Polygyny Polygynous societies vary in the number of wives a man may have. Islam permits a man to have as many as four wives but only on the condition that he can support them equally. Some Muslim authorities today argue, however, that equal support must be emotional and affective, not just financial. Convinced that no man can feel the same toward each of his wives, they have concluded that monogamy must be the rule. Other polygynous societies have no limit on the number of wives a man may marry. Nevertheless, not every man can be polygynous. There is a clear demographic problem: for every man with two wives, there is one man without a wife. Men can wait until they are older to marry and women can marry very young, but this imbalance cannot be eliminated. Polygyny is also expensive, for a husband must support all his wives as well as their children (Figure 13.11).

Polyandry Polyandry is the rarest of the three marriage forms. In some polyandrous societies, a woman may marry several brothers. In others, she may marry men who are not related to each other and who all will live together in a single household. Sometimes a woman is allowed to marry several men who are not related, but she will live only with the one she most recently married. Studies of polyandry have shed new light on the dynamics of polygyny and monogamy, as well.

The traditional anthropological prototype of polyandry is based on marriage practices among some groups in Nepal and Tibet, where a group of brothers marry one woman. This is known as *fraternal polyandry*. During a wedding, one brother, usually the oldest, serves as the groom. All brothers (including those yet to be born to the husbands' parents) are married by this wedding, which establishes public recognition of the marriage. The wife and her husbands live together, usually patrilocally. All brothers have equal sexual access to the wife, and all act as fathers to the children. In some cases—notably among the Nyinba of Nepal (Levine 1980, 1988)—each child is recognized as having one particular genitor, who may be a different brother from the genitor of his or her siblings (see EthnoProfile 13.4: Nyinba). In other cases, all the brothers are considered jointly as the father, without distinguishing the identity of the genitor.

There appears to be little sexual jealousy among the men, and the brothers have a strong sense of solidarity with one another. Levine (1988) emphasizes this point for the Nyinba. If the wife proves sterile, the brothers may marry another woman in hopes that she may be fertile. All brothers also have equal sexual access to the new wife and are treated as fathers by her children. In societies that practice fraternal polyandry, marrying sisters (or *sororal polygyny*) may be preferred or permitted. In this system, a group of brothers could marry a group of sisters.

According to Levine, Nyinba polyandry is reinforced by a variety of cultural beliefs and practices (1988, 158ff.). First, it has a special cultural value. Nyinba myth provides a social charter for the practice because the legendary ancestors are polyandrous, and they are praised for the harmony of their family life. Second, the solidarity of brothers is a central kinship ideal. Third, the corporate, landholding household, central to Nyinba life, presupposes the presence of a single wife with multiple husbands. Fourth, the closed corporate structure of Nyinba villages is based on a limited number of households, and polyandry is highly effective at checking the proliferation of households. Fifth, a household's political position and economic viability increase when its resources are concentrated.

The Distinction between Sexuality and Reproductive Capacity Polyandry demonstrates how a woman's sexuality can be distinguished from her reproductive capacity. This distinction is absent in monogamous or purely polygynous systems, in which polyandry is not permitted; such societies resist perceiving women's sexual and reproductive capacities as separable (except, perhaps, in prostitution), yet they usually accept such separation for men without question. "It may well be a fundamental feature of the [worldview] of polyandrous peoples that they recognize such a distinction for *both*

---

polygyny A marriage pattern in which a man may be married to more than one wife at a time.

polyandry A marriage pattern in which a woman may be married to more than one husband at a time.

Figure 13.11 The wives and children of a polygynous family.

EthnoProfile 13.4

Nyinba

Region: Central Asia

Nation: Nepal

Population: 1,200

Environment: Valleys

Livelihood: Agriculture, herding

Political organization: Traditionally, headmen; today, part of a modern nation-state

For more information:
Levine, Nancy. 1988. *The dynamics of polyandry: Kinship, domesticity, and population on the Tibetan border.* Chicago: University of Chicago Press.

How Is Marriage an Economic Exchange?

In many societies, marriage is accompanied by the transfer of certain symbolically important goods. Anthropologists have identified two major categories of marriage payments, usually called *bridewealth* and *dowry*.

Bridewealth is most common in patrilineal societies that combine agriculture, pastoralism, and patrilocal marriage, although it is found in other types of societies as well (Figure 13.12). When it occurs among matrilineal peoples, a postmarital residence rule (avunculocal, for example) usually takes the woman away from her matrilineage.

As we noted earlier, the goods exchanged as bridewealth have significant symbolic value to the people concerned. They may include shell ornaments, ivory tusks, brass gongs, bird feathers, cotton cloth, and animals. Bridewealth in animals is prevalent in eastern and southern Africa, where cattle have the most profound symbolic and economic value. Cash may also be used. In these societies, a man's father, and often his entire patrilineage, give a specified number of cattle (often in installments) to the patrilineage of the man's bride. Anthropologists view bridewealth as a way of compensating the bride's relatives for the loss of her labor and childbearing capacities.

men and women" (Levine and Sangree 1980, 388). In the better-known polyandrous groups, a woman's sexuality can be shared among an unlimited number of men but her childbearing capacities cannot. Indeed, among the Nyinba (Levine 1980), a woman's childbearing capacities are carefully controlled and limited to one husband at a time. But she is free to engage in sexual activity outside her marriage to the brothers as long as she is not likely to get pregnant.

> **bridewealth** The transfer of certain symbolically important goods from the family of the groom to the family of the bride on the occasion of their marriage. It represents compensation to the wife's lineage for the loss of her labor and childbearing capacities.

Figure 13.12 This photograph illustrates a bridewealth ceremony in southern Africa. Bridewealth is usually understood as a way of compensating the bride's relatives for the loss of her labor and childbearing capacities. Cash may also be used for bridewealth, as here among the Lese of the Democratic Republic of Congo.

When the bride leaves her home, she goes to live with her husband and his lineage. She will be working and producing children for his people, not her own.

Bridewealth transactions create affinal relations between the relatives of the wife and those of the husband. The wife's relatives, in turn, may use the bridewealth they receive for her to find a bride for her brother in yet another kinship group. In many societies in eastern and southern Africa, a woman gains power and influence over her brother because her marriage brings the cattle that allow him to marry and continue their lineage. This is why Jack Goody and Stanley Tambiah describe bridewealth as "a societal fund, a circulating pool of resources, the movement of which corresponds to the movement of rights over spouses, usually women" (1973, 17). Or, as the Southern Bantu put it, "cattle beget children" (Kuper 1982, 3).

Dowry, by contrast, is typically a transfer of family wealth, usually from parents to their daughter, at the time of her marriage. It is found primarily in the agricultural societies of Europe and Asia but has been brought to some parts of Africa with the arrival of religions like Islam that support the practice. In societies where both women and men are seen as heirs to family wealth,

dowry is sometimes regarded as the way women receive their inheritance. Dowries are often considered the wife's contribution to the establishment of a new household, to which the husband may bring other forms of wealth. In stratified societies, the size of a woman's dowry often ensures that when she marries she will continue to enjoy her accustomed style of life. The goods included in dowries vary in different societies and may or may not include land (Goody and Tambiah 1973).

What Is a Family?

A minimal definition of a **family** would be that it consists of a woman and her dependent children.[2] While some anthropological definitions of family require the presence of an adult male, related by either marriage or descent (husband or brother, for example), recent feminist and primatological scholarship has called this requirement into question. As a result, some anthropologists prefer to distinguish the **conjugal family**, which is a family based on marriage—at its minimum, a husband and wife (a spousal pair) and their children—from the **nonconjugal family**, which consists of a woman and her children. In a nonconjugal family, the husband/father

---

dowry The wealth transferred, usually from parents to their daughter, at the time of her marriage.

family Minimally, a woman and her dependent children.

conjugal family A family based on marriage; at a minimum, a husband and wife (a spousal pair) and their children.

nonconjugal family A woman and her children; the husband/father may be occasionally present or completely absent.

---

[2] In the contemporary United States, where many men as well as women are single parents, the view that a man with his children constitute a family is widely shared. This illustrates the ongoing reconfiguration of North American family relations, other features of which are described below.

In Their Own Words

Dowry Too High. Lose Bride and Go to Jail

In some parts of the world, discussions of bridewealth or dowry seem so divorced from reality as to appear "academic." But elsewhere, these topics remain significant indeed. In May 2003, news media all over the world reported the story of a bride in India who called the police when a battle erupted over demands for additional dowry payments at her wedding. The New York Times *reports.*

Noida, India, May 16—The musicians were playing, the 2,000 guests were dining, the Hindu priest was preparing the ceremony and the bride was dressed in red, her hands and feet festively painted with henna.

Then, the bride's family says, the groom's family moved in for the kill. The dowry of two televisions, two home theater sets, two refrigerators, two air-conditioners and one car was too cheap. They wanted $25,000 in rupees, now, under the wedding tent.

As a free-for-all erupted between the two families, the bartered bride put her hennaed foot down. She reached for the royal blue cellphone and dialed 100. By calling the police, Nisha Sharma, a 21-year-old computer student, saw her potential groom land in jail and herself land in the national spotlight as India's new overnight sensation.

"Are they marrying with money, or marrying with me?" Ms. Sharma asked today, her dark eyes glaring under arched eyebrows. In the next room a fresh wave of reporters waited to interview her, sitting next to the unopened boxes of her wedding trousseau.

After fielding a call from a comic-book artist who wanted to bring her act of defiance last Sunday night to a mass market, she said, "I'm feeling proud of myself."

"It Takes Guts to Send Your Groom Packing," a headline in *The Times of India* read.

Rashtriya Sahara, a major Hindi daily, said in a salute, "Bravo: We're Proud of You."

"She is being hailed as a New Age woman and seen as a role model to many," the newspaper *Asian Age* wrote next to a front-page drawing of Ms. Sharma standing in front of red and green wedding pennants while flashing a V sign to cameras and wearing a sash over her blue sari with the words *Miss Anti-Dowry*.

"This was a brave thing for a girl dressed in all her wedding finery to do," said Vandana Sharma, president of the Women's Protection League, one of many women's rights leaders and politicians to make a pilgrimage this week to this eastern suburb of Delhi. "This girl has taken a very dynamic step." India's new 24-hour news stations have propelled Nisha Sharma to Hindi stardom. One television station set up a service allowing viewers to "send a message to Nisha." In the first two days, 1,500 messages came in.

Nisha Sharma, surrounded by some of the dowry with which her family had intended to endow her.

Illegal for many decades in India, dowries are now often disguised by families as gifts to give the newlyweds a start in life. More than a media creation, Ms. Sharma and her dowry defiance struck a chord in this nation, whose expanding middle class is rebelling against a dowry tradition that is being overfed by a new commercialism.

"Advertisements now show parents giving things to make their daughters happy in life," Brinda Karat, general secretary of the All India Democratic Women's Association, a private group, said, referring to television commercials for products commonly given in dowries.

"It is the most modern aspects of information technology married to the most backward concepts of subordination of women," Ms. Karat continued in a telephone interview. Last year, she said, her group surveyed 10,000 people in 18 of India's 26 states. "We found an across-the-board increase in dowry demand," she said.

Much of the dowry greed is new, Ms. Karat added. In a survey 40 years ago, she noted, almost two-thirds of Indian communities reported that the local custom was for the groom to pay the bride's family, the reverse of the present dominant custom. According to government statistics, husbands and in-laws angry over small dowry payments killed nearly 7,000 women in 2001.

(continued on next page)

In Their Own Words (continued)

Dowry Too High. Lose Bride and Go to Jail

When Ms. Sharma's parents were married in 1970, "my father-in-law did not demand anything," her mother, Hem Lata Sharma, said while serving hot milk tea and cookies to guests.

For the Sharma family, the demands went far beyond giving the young couple a helping hand.

Dev Dutt Sharma, Nisha's father, said his potential in-laws were so demanding that they had stipulated brands. "She specified a Sony home theater, not a Philips," Mr. Sharma, an owner of car battery factories,

said of Vidya Dalal, the mother of the groom, Munish Dalal, 25.

Sharma Jaikumar, a telecommunications engineer and friend of the Sharma family, said as the press mob ebbed and flowed through the house: "My daughter was married recently and there was no dowry. But anyone can turn greedy. What can be more easy money than a dowry? All you have to do is ask."

Source: Brooke 2003.

may be occasionally present or completely absent. Non-conjugal families are never the only form of family organization in a society and, in fact, cross-culturally are usually rather infrequent. In some large-scale industrial societies, including the United States, however, nonconjugal families have become increasingly common. In most societies, the conjugal family is coresident—that is, spouses live in the same dwelling, along with their children—but there are some matrilineal societies in which the husband lives with his matrilineage, the wife and children live with theirs, and the husband visits his wife and children.

What Is the Nuclear Family?

The structure and dynamics of neolocal monogamous families are familiar to North Americans. They are called *nuclear families,* and it is often assumed that most people in the United States live in them (although in 2000 only about one-quarter of the U.S. population did). For anthropologists, a **nuclear family** is made up of two generations: the parents and their unmarried children. Each member of a nuclear family has a series of evolving relationships with every other member: husband and wife, parents and children, and children with each other. These are the lines along which jealousy, competition, controversy, and affection develop in neolocal monogamous families; sibling rivalry, for example, is a form of competition characteristic of nuclear families that is shaped by the relationships between siblings and between siblings and their parents.

nuclear family A family pattern made up of two generations: the parents and their unmarried children.

What Is the Polygynous Family?

A polygynous family includes, at a minimum, the husband, all his wives, and their children. Polygynous families are significantly different from nuclear families in their internal dynamics. Each wife has a relationship with her cowives as individuals and as a group (Figure 13.13). Cowives, in turn, individually and collectively, interact with the husband. In addition, an important distinction is made between children with the same mother and children with a different mother. Where there is a significant inheritance, these relationships serve as the channels for jealousy and conflict. The children of the same mother, and especially the children of different mothers, compete with one another for their father's favor. Each mother tries to protect the interests of her own children, sometimes at the expense of her cowives' children.

Competition in the Polygynous Family Although the relationships among wives in a polygynous society may be very close, among the Mende of Sierra Leone, cowives eventually compete with each other (see Ethno-Profile 13.5: Mende). Caroline Bledsoe (1993) explains that this competition is often focused on children: how many each wife has and how likely it is that each child will obtain things of value, especially education. Husbands in polygynous Mende households are supposed to avoid overt signs of favoritism, but their wives do not all have equal status. To begin with, wives are ranked by order of marriage. The senior wife is the first wife in the household, and she has authority over junior wives. Marriage-order ranking structures the household but also lays the groundwork for rivalries. Wives are also ranked, however, in terms of the status of the families from which they came. Serious conflicts arise if the husband

Figure 13.13 Cowives in polygynous households frequently cooperate in daily tasks, such as food preparation.

EthnoProfile 13.5

Mende

Region: Western Africa

Nation: Sierra Leone

Population: 12,000,000

Environment: Forest and savanna

Livelihood: Slash-and-burn rice cultivation, cash cropping, diamond mining

Political organization: Traditionally, a hierarchy of local chiefdoms; today, part of a modern nation-state

For more information: Little, Kenneth. 1967. *The Mende of Sierra Leone.* London: Routledge and Kegan Paul.

shows favoritism by paying for the education of the children of a wife from a high-status family before educating the older children of other wives or the children of wives higher in the marriage-order ranking.

The level of her children's education matters intensely to a Mende woman because her principal claim to her husband's land or cash and her expectations of future support after he dies come through her children. She depends not only on the income that a child may earn to support her but also on the rights her children have to inherit property and positions of leadership from their father. Nevertheless, education requires a significant cash outlay in school fees, uniforms, books, and so on. A man may be able to send only one child to school, or he may be able to send one child to a prestigious private school only if he sends another to a trade apprenticeship. These economic realities make sense to husbands but can lead to bitter feuds among cowives and even divorce, when wives blame their husband for disparities in the accomplishments of their children. In extreme cases, cowives are said to use witchcraft to make their rivals'

children fail their exams. To avoid these problems, children are frequently sent to live with relatives who will send them to school. Such competition is missing in monogamous households unless they include adopted children or spouses who already have children from a previous marriage.

Extended and Joint Families

Within any society, certain patterns of family organization are considered proper. In American nuclear families, two generations live together. In some societies, three generations—parents, married children, and grandchildren—are expected to live together in a vertical **extended family**. In still other societies, the extension is horizontal: brothers and their wives (or sisters and their husbands) live together in a **joint family**. These are ideal patterns, which all families may not be able or willing to emulate. It is important to emphasize that extended families do not operate the way joint families operate, and neither can be understood as just several nuclear families that happen to overlap. Extended and joint families are fundamentally different from nuclear families with regard to the rights and obligations they engender among their members.

---

extended family A family pattern made up of three generations living together: parents, married children, and grandchildren.

joint family A family pattern made up of brothers and their wives or sisters and their husbands (along with their children) living together.

In Their Own Words

Law, Custom, and Crimes against Women

John van Willigen and V. C. Channa describe the social and cultural practices surrounding dowry payments that appear to be responsible for violence against women in some parts of India.

A 25-year-old woman was allegedly burnt to death by her husband and mother-in-law at their East Delhi home yesterday. The housewife, Mrs. Sunita, stated before her death at the Jaya Prakash Narayana Hospital that members of her husband's family had been harassing her for bringing inadequate dowry.

The woman told the Shahdara subdivisional magistrate that during a quarrel over dowry at their Pratap Park house yesterday, her husband gripped her from behind while the mother-in-law poured kerosene over her clothes.

Her clothes were then set ablaze. The police have registered a case against the victim's husband, Suraj Prakash, and his mother.

—Times of India,
February 19, 1988

This routinely reported news story describes what in India is termed a "bride-burning" or "dowry death." Such incidents are frequently reported in the newspapers of Delhi and other Indian cities. In addition, there are cases in which the evidence may be ambiguous, so that deaths of women by fire may be recorded as kitchen accidents, suicides, or murders. Dowry violence takes a characteristic form. Following marriage and the requisite giving of dowry, the family of the groom makes additional demands for the payment of more cash or the provision of more goods. These demands are expressed in unremitting harassment of the bride, who is living in the household of her husband's parents, culminating in the murder of the woman by members of her husband's family or by her suicide. The woman is typically burned to death with kerosene, a fuel used in pressurized cook stoves, hence the use of the term "bride-burning" in public discourse.

Dowry death statistics appear frequently in the press and parliamentary debates. Parliamentary sources report the following figures for married women 16 to 30 years of age in Delhi: 452 deaths by burning for 1985; 478 for 1986 and 300 for the first six months of 1987. There were 1,319 cases reported nationally in 1986 (*Times of India*, January 10, 1988). Police records do not match hospital records for third degree burn cases among younger married women; far more violence occurs than the crime reports indicate.

There is other violence against women related both directly and indirectly to the institution of dowry. For example, there are unmarried women who commit suicide so as to relieve their families of the burden of providing a dowry. A recent case that received national attention in the Indian press involved the triple suicide of three sisters in the industrial city of Kanpur. A photograph was widely published showing the three young women hanging from ceiling fans by their scarves. Their father, who earned about 4000 Rs. [rupees] per month, was not able to negotiate marriage for his oldest daughter. The grooms were requesting approximately 100,000 Rs. Also linked to the dowry problem is selective female abortion made possible by amniocentesis. This issue was brought to national attention with a startling statistic reported out of a seminar held in Delhi in 1985. Of 3000 abortions carried out after sex determination through amniocentesis, only one involved a male fetus. As a result of these developments, the government of the state of Maharashtra banned sex determination tests except those carried out in government hospitals.

Source: van Willigen and Channa 1991, 369–70.

How Are Families Transformed over Time?

Families change over time: they have a life cycle and a life span. The same family takes on different forms and provides different opportunities for the interaction of members at different points in its development. New households are formed and old households change through divorce, remarriage, the departure of children, and the breakup of extended families.

Divorce and Remarriage

Most societies make it possible for married couples to separate. In some societies, the process is long, drawn out, and difficult, especially when bridewealth must be returned; a man who divorces a wife in such societies or whose wife leaves him expects some of the bridewealth back. But for the wife's family to give the bridewealth back, a whole chain of marriages may have to be broken up. Brothers of the divorced wife may have to divorce to get back enough bridewealth from their in-laws. Sometimes a new husband will repay the bridewealth to the former husband's line, thus relieving the bride's relatives of this expense.

Grounds for Divorce Depending on the society, nagging, quarreling, cruelty, stinginess, or adultery may be cited as causes for divorce. In almost all societies, childlessness is grounds for divorce as well. For the Ju/'hoansi, most divorces are initiated by women, mainly because they do not like their husbands or do not want to be married (Lee 1992b, Shostak 1981; see EthnoProfile 11.5: Ju/'hoansi). After what is often considerable debate, a couple that decides to break up merely separates. There is no bridewealth to return, no legal contract to be renegotiated. Mutual consent is all that is necessary. The children stay with the mother. Ju/'hoansi divorces are cordial, Richard Lee (1992b) tells us, at least compared with the Western norm. Ex-spouses may continue to joke with each other and even live next to each other with their new spouses.

Separation among the Inuit Among the northwestern Inuit, the traditional view is that all kin relationships, including marital ones, are permanent (Burch 1970) (see EthnoProfile 13.6: Alaskan Inuit). Thus, although it is possible to deactivate a marriage by separating, a marriage can never be permanently dissolved. (Conversely, reestablishing the residence tie is all that is needed to reactivate the relationship.) A husband and wife who stop living together and having sexual relations with each other are considered to be separated and ready for

another marriage. If each member of a separated couple remarried, the two husbands of the wife would become cohusbands and the two wives of the husband, cowives; the children of the first and second marriages would become cosiblings. In effect, a "divorce" among the Inuit results in more, not fewer, connections.

Blended Families In recent years in the United States, anthropologists have observed the emergence of a new family type: the **blended family**. A blended family is created when previously divorced or widowed people marry, bringing with them children from their previous marriages. The internal dynamics of the new family—which can come to include his children, her children, and their children—may resemble the dynamics of polygynous families as the relations among the children and their relations to each parent may be complex and negotiated over time.

How Does International Migration Affect the Family?

Migration to find work in another country has become increasingly common worldwide and has important effects on families. Anthropologist Eugenia Georges (1990) examined its effects on people who migrated to the United States from Los Pinos, a small town in the Dominican Republic (see EthnoProfile 13.7: Los Pinos). Migration divided these families, with some members moving to New York and some remaining in Los Pinos. Some parents stayed in the Dominican Republic while their children went to the United States. A more common pattern was for the husband to migrate and the wife to stay home. Consequently, many households in Los Pinos were headed by women. In most cases, however, the spouse in the United States worked to bring the spouse and children in Los Pinos there.

This sometimes took several years because it involved completing paperwork for the visa and saving money beyond the amount regularly sent to Los Pinos. Children of the couple who were close to working age also came to the United States, frequently with their mother, and younger children were sent for as they approached working age. Finally, after several years in the United States,

EthnoProfile 13.6

Alaskan Inuit

Region: North America

Nation: United States (northwestern Alaska)

Population: 11,000 (1960s)

Environment: Arctic: mountains, foothills, coastal plain

Livelihood: Hunting, wage labor, welfare

Political organization:
Traditionally, families; today, part of a modern nation-state

For more information:
Burch, Ernest S., Jr. 1975. *Eskimo kinsmen: Changing family relationships in northwest Alaska*. American Ethnological Society Monograph, no. 59. St. Paul: West.

---

blended family A family created when previously divorced or widowed people marry, bringing with them children from their previous families.

EthnoProfile 13.7

Los Pinos

Region: Caribbean

Nation: Dominican Republic

Population: 1,000

Environment: Rugged mountain region

Livelihood: Peasant agriculture (tobacco, coffee, cacao) and labor migration

Political organization: Part of a modern nation-state

For more information: Georges, Eugenia. 1990. *The making of a transnational community: Migration, development, and cultural change in the Dominican Republic.* New York: Columbia University Press.

Figure 13.14   As migration from the Dominican Republic to the United States has increased, more Dominicans are staying and bringing their families or creating families in the United States. Such celebrations of ethnic pride as Dominican Day in New York have increased in recent years.

the couple who started the migration cycle would often take their savings and return home to the Dominican Republic. Their children stayed in the United States and continued to send money home. Return migrants tended not to give up their residence visas and, therefore, had to return to the United States annually. Often, they stayed for a month or more to work. This also provided them with the opportunity to buy household goods at a more reasonable cost, as well as other items—clothing, cosmetics, and the like—to sell to neighbors, friends, and kin in the Dominican Republic (Figure 13.14).

Georges observes that the absent family member maintained an active role in family life despite the heavy psychological burden of separation. Although he might be working in a hotel in New York, for example, the husband was still the breadwinner and the main decision maker in the household. He communicated by visits, letters, and occasional telephone calls. Despite the strains of migration, moreover, the divorce rate was actually slightly lower in migrant families than in families whose members never migrated. This was in part because the exchange of information between Los Pinos and New York was both dense and frequent but also because strong ties of affection connected many couples. Finally, "the goal of the overwhelming majority of the migrants [from Los Pinos] I spoke with was permanent return to the Dominican Republic. Achievement of this goal was hastened by sponsoring the migration of dependents, both wives and children, so that they could work and

save as part of the reconstituted household in the United States" (Georges 1990, 201). This pressure also helped keep families together.

In recent years, the Internet has come to play an increasingly important role in the lives of families that are separated by migration, education, work, and so on. Daniel Miller and Don Slater (2000) studied Internet use in Trinidad, finding that e-mail and Instant Messaging have considerably strengthened both nuclear and extended families, allowing closer relations between distant parents and children, among siblings, and among other relatives.

Families by Choice

In spite of the range of variation in family forms that we have surveyed, some readers may still be convinced that family ties depend on blood and that blood is thicker than water. It is therefore instructive to consider the results of research carried out by Kath Weston (1991) on family forms among gays and lesbians in the San Francisco Bay Area during the 1980s. A lesbian herself, Weston knew that a turning point in the lives of most gays and lesbians was the decision to announce their sexual orientation to their parents and siblings. If blood truly were thicker than water, this announcement should not destroy family bonds; and many parents have indeed been supportive of their children after the announcement. Often enough, however, shocked parents have turned away, declaring that this person is no longer their son or daughter. Living through—or even contemplating—such an experience has been enough to force gays and lesbians to think seriously about the sources of family ties.

Caring for Infibulated Women Giving Birth in Norway

Female genital cutting has generated enormous publicity—and enormous conflict. Coping with this practice across difference is complex. People in Western societies often have very little grasp of how the operation fits into the cultural practices of those who perform it. Even women from societies with the tradition find themselves on opposing sides: Some seek asylum to avoid it, while others are prosecuted because they seek to have it performed on their daughters. Many governments have declared it a human rights violation.

Norway has struggled with these issues ever since 1991, when it became the home of a large number of refugees from civil war in Somalia (Figure 13.15). Norwegian health care is free, and Norway has one of the lowest infant mortality rates in the world. Nevertheless, despite the efforts of dedicated health care workers to be culturally sensitive, outcomes for Somali women are not always optimal. Medical anthropologist R. Elise B. Johansen tried to find out why (Johansen 2006, 516).

In contemporary Norway, Johansen reports, giving birth is considered a positive, "natural" process that women are expected to be able to handle with minimal medical intervention. As a result, "midwives are preferred to obstetricians, medication and incisions are avoided whenever possible,

partners are allowed to be present in the delivery room to support the birthing mother, newborns are immediately placed on the mother's belly, and mothers are encouraged to breast feed immediately" (2006, 521). At the same time, Norwegian health workers believe that giving birth "naturally" is hard for Norwegian women, because their "natural female essence" is "buried under layers of modernity" (521). Norwegian women nevertheless support "natural" birth practices out of concern for the health of the child, and they expect to manage the pain of unmedicated labor assisted by nothing more than their own physical stamina. Midwives also usually leave women alone until the expulsion phase of labor begins, a practice connected to their idea of what constitutes a "natural" delivery: "Women are expected to take charge of their own deliveries. Health workers explained restricted interference as a gesture of respect for women's strength and ability to deliver by themselves," an attitude that is possibly also reinforced by the Norwegian values of independence and privacy (538).

What happens when midwives with these expectations encounter Somali women about to give birth? The high value they place on "natural" birthing has led some to regard African immigrant women as "more natural than most Norwegians"

(continued on next page)

Figure 13.15 These Somali women are returned refugees. Political turmoil in their country has led many Somalis to flee to other countries, including Norway.

Caring for Infibulated Women Giving Birth in Norway

and "in closer contact with their female essence" (2006, 521). As a result, health care workers sometimes assume that African women are "naturally" equipped with the skills they need to deliver and care for their babies. Only "modern" Norwegian women require such things as medication or child care instruction.

At the same time, Somali women present a paradox: They are African, but they have been infibulated, and infibulation is thought by most health workers to be "the ultimate expression of female oppression and male dominance" (522). As a result, "infibulated women in the delivery ward present a confusing mixture because 'the natural wild' has culturally constructed genitals." Johansen saw this paradox as "central to understanding the challenges facing health workers in looking after infibulated women during delivery" (522).

Midwives thought of infibulation as a social stigma: It marked infibulated women "as incomplete, disfigured, and oppressed." Johansen concludes that health care workers are at once troubled by infibulation and concerned that this discomfort not interfere with their "professionalism." Their solution is simply *not to speak about infibulation*, a decision that "seems to increase discomfort in both health workers and birthing women. It also reduces the parties' chances of exchanging vital information" (523).

Although the midwives Johansen interviewed knew about infibulation, they had not been formally trained to provide care for infibulated women giving birth, because guidelines were not yet available. This lack of training, coupled with the midwives' unwillingness to talk with Somali women about infibulation, had two unfortunate, interconnected effects. First, it made many Somali women unsure about whether they would be properly cared for during their deliveries, adding to their own anxieties about childbirth. Second, it allowed health care workers to draw their own silent, *mistaken* conclusions about the "cultural meaning" of infibulation for Somali women. Midwives assumed without asking, for example, that Somali women would not want to be defibulated—that is, to have the infibulation scar cut to widen the vaginal opening. They further assumed without asking that Somali women would also oppose the use of *episiotomies*—cuts used to widen the vaginal passage for the child during delivery. Such cuts,

which are sewn up afterwards, are a standard practice in Western obstetrics.

Since many health care workers assumed that Somali values dictated that Somali women remain infibulated through life, they were concerned that defibulation would violate those values. Why had one midwife chosen to perform three episiotomies to avoid defibulating one Somali woman, even though episiotomies involve cutting through muscular and blood-filled tissue? Had the midwife asked the woman if she preferred defibulation? The surprised midwife replied, "No! Of course she wants to remain the way she is" (526). Because the midwife assumed that Somali women want to remain infibulated and because the midwife wanted to respect this wish, to ask this Somali woman if she wanted defibulation made no sense to the midwife.

Had the midwives actually spoken with Somali women, Johansen reports, much discomfort and misunderstanding could have been avoided on both sides. Midwives would have learned that almost all Somali women *wanted* to be defibulated and *did not want* to be reinfibulated—and that nearly two-thirds of their husbands did not want their wives to be reinfibulated either (527). Midwives would also have learned that Somali infibulation practices were different from infibulation practices elsewhere in Africa. As we saw from Boddy's ethnography in Chapter 8, lifelong infibulation is a traditional practice in Sudan. Johansen discovered that "infibulation as practiced in Sudan has been taken to represent infibulation in general, so that the practice of reinfibulation in Sudan is taken as evidence that reinfibulation must also be common in all other societies practicing infibulation. However, as we have seen, this is not always the case" (529).

Johansen's research shows how even attempts to be culturally sensitive can generate a wall of misconceptions. These can circumvent actual conversation with those individuals whose culture is the focus of attention. There is no question that the midwives were trying to do right by the women they attended. Ironically, however, from a Norwegian perspective, to respect the dignity and autonomy of Somali women meant that one left Somali women alone and *did not ask them questions*. In situations like this, medical anthropologists can play an important role as cultural brokers who see situations from a fresh perspective, ease the friction, and help to build a bridge across difference.

In Their Own Words

Why Migrant Women Feed Their Husbands Tamales

Brett Williams suggests that the reasons Mexican migrant women feed their husbands tamales may not be the stereotypical reasons that outside observers often assume.

Because migrant women are so involved in family life and so seemingly submissive to their husbands, they have been described often as martyred purveyors of rural Mexican and Christian custom, tyrannized by excessively masculine, crudely domineering, rude and petty bullies in marriage, and blind to any world outside the family because they are suffocated by the concerns of kin. Most disconcerting to outside observers is that migrant women seem to embrace such stereotypes: they argue that they should monopolize their foodways and that they should not question the authority of their husbands. If men want tamales, men should have them. But easy stereotypes can mislead; in exploring the lives of the poor, researchers must revise their own notions of family life, and this paper argues that foodways can provide crucial clues about how to do so.

The paradox is this: among migrant workers both women and men are equally productive wage earners, and husbands readily acknowledge that without their wives' work their families cannot earn enough to survive. For migrants the division of labor between earning a living outside the home and managing household affairs is unknown; and the dilemma facing middle-class wives who may wish to work to supplement the family's income simply does not exist. Anthropologists exploring women's status cross-culturally argue that women are most influential when they share in the production of food and have some control over its distribution. If such perspectives bear at all on migrant women, one might be led to question their seemingly unfathomable obsequiousness in marriage.

Anthropologists further argue that women's influence is even greater when they are not isolated from their kinswomen, when women can cooperate in production and join, for example, agricultural work with domestic duties and childcare. Most migrant women spend their lives within large, closely knit circles of kin and their work days with their kinswomen. Marriage does not uproot or isolate a woman from her family, but rather doubles the relatives each partner can depend on and widens in turn the networks of everyone involved. The lasting power of marriage is reflected in statistics which show a divorce rate of 1 percent for migrant farmworkers from Texas, demonstrating the strength of a union bolstered by large numbers of relatives concerned that it go well. Crucial to this concern is that neither partner is an economic drain on the family, and the Tejano pattern of early and lifelong marriages establishes some limit on the whimsy with which men can abuse and misuse their wives.

While anthropology traditionally rests on an appreciation of other cultures in their own contexts and on their own terms, it is very difficult to avoid class bias in viewing the lives of those who share partly in one's own culture, especially when the issue is something so close to home as food and who cooks it. Part of the problem may lie in appreciating what families are and what they do. For the poor, public and private domains are blurred in confusing ways, family affairs may be closely tied to economics, and women's work at gathering and obligating or binding relatives is neither trivial nor merely a matter of sentiment. Another problem may lie in focusing on the marital relationship as indicative of a woman's authority in the family. We too often forget that women are sisters, grandmothers, and aunts to men as well as wives. Foodways can help us rethink both of these problematic areas and understand how women elaborate domestic roles to knit families together, to obligate both male and female kin, and to nurture and bind their husbands as well.

Source: Williams 1984.

By the 1980s, some North American gays and lesbians had reached two conclusions: (1) that blood ties *cannot* guarantee the "enduring diffuse solidarity" supposedly at the core of North American kinship (Schneider 1968); and (2) that new kin ties *can* be created over time as friends and lovers demonstrate their genuine commitment to one another by creating families of choice. "Like their heterosexual counterparts, most gay men and lesbians insisted that family members are people who are 'there for you,' people you can count on emotionally and materially" (Weston 1991, 113). Some gay kinship ideologies now argue that "whatever endures is real" as a way of claiming legitimacy for chosen families that were not the product of heterosexual marriages. Such a definition of family is compatible with understandings of kinship based on nurturance. Lesbian and gay activists have used this similarity as a resource in their struggles to obtain for long-standing families by choice some of the same legal rights enjoyed by traditional heterosexual families, such as hospital visiting privileges, joint adoption, and property rights (Weston 1995, 99).

Friendship

Anthropologist Robert Brain cites a dictionary definition of *friend* as "one joined to another in intimacy and mutual benevolence independent of sexual or family love" (1976, 15). He quickly points out that the Western belief that friendship and kinship are separate phenomena often breaks down in practice. Today, for example, some husbands and wives in Western societies consider each other "best friends." Similarly, we may become friends with some of our relatives while treating others the same way we treat nonrelatives. Indeed, as we have just seen, families can become constituted by friendship—"that which endures is real," as Kath Weston's informants told her (Weston 1991, 113). Presumably, we can be friends with people over and above any kinship ties we might have with them. Indeed, primatologist Joan Silk points out that close human friendships, especially the kind we find in Western societies, are unlike relationships called "friendship" in primate species like baboons and do not correspond to any of the classic patterns of reciprocity recognized in formal evolutionary models (2003, 42). "People establish close cooperative relationships with nonrelatives, care about reciprocity, but avoid keeping careful count of benefits given and received" (51). Although this would seem to make us vulnerable to exploitation, Silk is impressed by evidence that human beings are nevertheless strongly committed to friendships with exactly these attributes.

Sandra Bell and Simon Coleman suggest that typical "markers" for **friendship** are the relatively "unofficial" bonds that people construct with one another (see Figure 13.16). These tend to be bonds that are personal, affective, and, to a varying extent from society to society, a matter of choice. The line between friendship and kinship is often a very fuzzy one since there may be an affective quality to kinship relations (we can like our cousins and do the same things with them that we would do with friends), since sometimes friends are seen after a long time as being related, and since some societies have networks of relatedness that can

Figure 13.16 These two young men in Cameroon were the best of friends.

be activated or not for reasons of sentiment, not just for pragmatic reasons. Friendship has been difficult for some anthropologists to study since in the past they have concentrated on trying to find regular long-term patterns of social organization in societies with non-centralized forms of political organization (Bell and Coleman 1999, 4). Bell and Coleman also note that the importance of friendship seems to be increasing: "In many shifting social contexts, ties of kinship tend to be transformed and often weakened by complex and often contradictory processes of globalization. At the same time new forms of friendship are emerging" (5). This is illustrated in a striking way in Rio de Janeiro by Claudia Barcellos Rezende (1999), who observed the ways in which middle-class women and their maids could come to refer to each other as "friends." Within this hierarchical relationship, the distinctions that separated the women were not questioned in themselves but the "friendship" consisted of the affection, care, and consideration that both sets of women valued in their work relationship. It was a way of establishing trust: "What friendship invokes . . . is the affinity that brings these people together as parts of the same social world" (93).

How Are Sexual Practices Organized?

Some anthropologists seem to regard marriage as an abstract formal system and say little about human **sexual practices**, the emotional or affectional relationships between sexual partners and the physical activities they engage in with one another. But sexual intercourse is part of almost all marriages. And because in many societies

---

friendship The relatively "unofficial" bonds that people construct with one another that tend to be personal, affective, and often a matter of choice.

sexual practices Emotional or affectional relationships between sexual partners and the physical activities they engage in with one another.

EthnoProfile 13.8

Tikopia

Region: Oceania (Polynesia)

Nation: Solomon Islands

Population: 1,200 (1928)

Environment: Tropical island

Livelihood: Horticulture and pig raising

Political organization: Traditionally, chiefs; today, part of a modern nation-state

For more information: Firth, Raymond. [1936] 1984. *We, the Tikopia.* Reprint. Stanford, CA: Stanford University Press.

EthnoProfile 13.9

Dani

Region: Oceania (New Guinea)

Nation: Indonesia (Irian Jaya)

Population: 100,000 (1960s)

Environment: Valley in central highlands

Livelihood: Horticulture and pig raising

Political organization: Traditionally, some men with influence but no coercive power; today, part of a modern nation-state

For more information: Heider, Karl. 1979. *Grand Valley Dani.* New York: Holt, Rinehart and Winston.

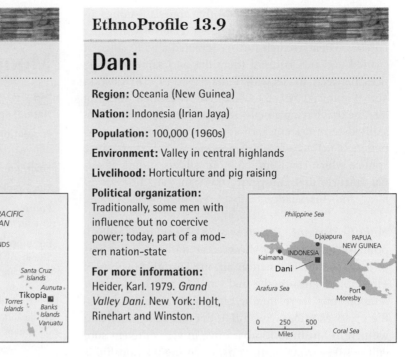

marriage is the formal prerequisite for becoming sexually active (at least for females), a desire for sex is a strong motivation for getting married (Spiro 1977, 212).

Ranges of Heterosexual Practices

The range of sexual practice in the world is vast. In many Oceanian societies—Tikopia, for example—the young could expect to have a great deal of sexual experience before marriage (see EthnoProfile 13.8: Tikopia). In the early twentieth century, anthropologist Raymond Firth observed that young men and young women began having sexual relations at an early age, and having several lovers was considered normal for the young. Getting married, however, was a key move toward adulthood and represented a great change for both partners. The woman was to give up sexual freedom, but she replaced it with what Firth called "a safe and legalized sexual cohabitation" ([1936] 1984, 434). The man was theoretically free to continue to have affairs, but in practice he also "settled down." This pattern is quite common cross-culturally, but it is not universal.

Karl Heider's research (1979) among the Dani, a people of highland New Guinea, revealed yet another pattern (see EthnoProfile 13.9: Dani). Heider discovered that the Dani had extraordinarily little interest in sex. For 5 years after the birth of a child, the parents do not have sexual intercourse with each other. This practice, called a *postpartum sex taboo*, is found in all cultures, but in most societies it lasts for a few weeks or months.

(In North America, we say that the mother needs time to heal; other societies have other justifications.) What could explain a postpartum sex taboo that lasts 5 years? Heider points out that Westerners assume that the sex drive is so powerful that if it is not satisfied directly in sexual activity, then some other outlet will be found. In fact, some suggest that the Dani's high levels of outgroup aggression may be connected with their low level of sexual intercourse. The Dani are not celibate, and they certainly have sexual intercourse often enough to reproduce biologically; yet, they do not seem very interested in sex (Heider 1979, 78–81). The Dani, who are not abnormal physically or mentally, represent an extreme in the cultural construction of sexuality.

Other Sexual Practices

The traditional anthropological focus on what European Americans call "heterosexual relationships" is understandable. People in every society are concerned about perpetuating themselves, and most have developed complex ideological and ritual structures to ensure that this occurs. The fact that elaborate cultural constructions seem necessary to encourage heterosexual practices, however, suggests that human sexual expression would resist such confinement if it were not under strict control. For example, anthropologists Evelyn Blackwood and Saskia Wieringa have studied the cultural shaping of female desires. They found that female bodies are assigned different cultural meanings in different historical and ethnographic settings and that those meanings affect the way females constitute their relations with other females. Their research further revealed a wide range of "varied and rich cultural identities and same-sex practices between those with female bodies" (Blackwood and Wieringa 1999, ix). This sort of research does not assume that having a male body or a female body necessarily determines any individual's traits, feelings, or experiences (x). As a result, it provides a vital comparative context which can illuminate our understanding of sexual practices that European Americans call "homosexuality" and "bisexuality."

Female Sexual Practices in Mombasa Anthropologist Gil Shepherd shows that traditional patterns of male–female interaction among Swahili Muslims in Mombasa, Kenya, make male and female homosexual relationships there intelligible (1987) (see EthnoProfile 13.10: Mombasa Swahilis). For one thing, men and women in Muslim Mombasa live in very different subcultures. For women, the most enduring relationship is between mothers and daughters, mirrored in the relationship between an older married sister and a younger unmarried sister. By contrast, relationships between mothers and sons and between brothers and sisters are more distant. Except in the case of young, modern, educated couples, the relationship between husband and wife is often emotionally distant as well. Because the worlds of men and women overlap so little, relationships between the sexes tend to be one-dimensional. Men and women join a variety of sex-segregated groups for leisure-time activities such as dancing or religious study. Within these same-sex groups, individuals compete for social rank.

Of the some 50,000 Swahili in Mombasa, about 5,000 could be called homosexual. The number is misleading, however, because men and women shift between what European Americans call "homosexuality" and "heterosexuality" throughout their lives. Women are allowed to choose other women as sexual partners only after they have been married. Therefore, all such women in Mombasa are married, widowed, or divorced. Both men and women are open about their same-sex relationships, and "nobody would dream of suggesting that their sexual choices had any effect on their work capabilities, reliability, or religious piety" (Shepherd 1987, 241). Moreover, many women were quite clear about the practical reasons that had led them into sexual relationships with other women. Women with little money are unlikely to marry men who can offer them jewelry, shoes, new dresses, status, or financial security, but a wealthy lesbian lover can offer them all these things. Also, a poor young woman in an unhappy marriage may have no way

to support herself if she leaves her husband unless she has a lesbian lover.

According to Islamic law, a wealthy, high-ranking Muslim woman can only marry a man who is her equal or superior. A marriage of this kind brings a great deal of seclusion, and her wealth is administered by her husband. The wealthy partner in a lesbian relationship, however, is freed from these constraints. "Thus if she wishes to use her wealth as she likes and has a taste for power, entry into a lesbian relationship, or living alone as a divorced or widowed woman, are virtually her only options" (Shepherd 1987, 257). Financial independence for a woman offers the chance to convert wealth to power. If she pays for the marriages of other people or provides financial support in exchange for loyalty, a woman can create a circle of dependents. Shepherd points out that a few women, some lesbians, have achieved real political power in Mombasa in this way (1987, 257).

Still, it is not necessary to be a lesbian to build a circle of dependents. Why do some women follow this route? The answer, Shepherd tells us, is complicated. It is not entirely respectable for a woman under 45 or 50 to be unmarried. Some women can maintain autonomy by making a marriage of convenience to a man who already lives with a wife and then living apart from him. Many women, however, find this arrangement both lonely and sexually unsatisfying. Living as a lesbian is less respectable than being a second, nonresident wife, but it is more respectable than not being married at all.

EthnoProfile 13.10

Mombasa Swahilis

Region: Eastern Africa

Nation: Kenya

Population: 50,000 Swahili among 350,000 total population of city (1970s)

Environment: Island and mainland port city

Livelihood: Various urban occupations

Political organization: Part of a modern nation-state

For more information: Shepherd, Gil. 1987. Rank, gender and homosexuality: Mombasa as a key to understanding sexual options. In *The cultural construction of sexuality*, ed. Pat Caplan, 240–70. London: Tavistock.

The lesbian sexual relationship does not reduce the autonomy of the wealthy partner "and indeed takes place in the highly positive context of the fond and supportive relationships women establish among themselves anyway" (1987, 258).

Shepherd suggests that the reason sexual relationships between men or between women are generally not heavily stigmatized in Mombasa is because social rank takes precedence over all other measures of status. Rank is a combination of wealth, the ability to claim Arab ancestry, and the degree of Muslim learning and piety. Rank determines marriage partners as well as relations of loyalty and subservience, and both men and women expect to rise in rank over a lifetime. Although lesbian couples may violate the prototype for sexual relations, they do not violate relations of rank. Shepherd suggests that a marriage between a poor husband and a rich wife might be more shocking than a lesbian relationship between a dominant rich woman and a dependent poor one. It is less important that a woman's lover be a male than it is for her to be a good Arab, a good Muslim, and a person of wealth and influence.

Anthropologists working in Africa have described a range of relations between females (woman marriage, e.g.) that have been likened to European or American models of lesbian relationships, but disputes have arisen about whether such relationships always include an erotic involvement between the female partners. In a survey of this evidence, Wieringa and Blackwood note that woman marriage can take many forms, some of which are more likely than others to include sexuality between the female partners. Among those where such sexual relations appear more likely are cases like that described by Shepherd, "in which a woman of some means, either married (to a man) or unmarried, pays bride-price for a wife and establishes her own compound" (Wieringa and Blackwood 1999, 5).

Such evidence is not merely of academic interest. In the contemporary world of intensified global communication and exchange, Western and non-Western same-sex practices are becoming increasingly entangled with one another, leading to the emergence of local movements for "lesbian" and "gay" rights in Africa and elsewhere. In this context, in the late 1990s, the presidents of Zimbabwe, Kenya, and Namibia declared that homosexuality is "un-African." Based on the ethnographic evidence, however, Wieringa and Blackwood side with those arguing that, on the contrary, it is homophobia that is "un-African": "President Mandela from South Africa is a striking exception to the homophobia of his colleagues. The South African constitution specifically condemns discrimination on the basis of sexual orientation" (1999, 27).

Male Sexual Practices in Nicaragua Anthropologist Roger Lancaster spent many months during the 1980s studying the effects of the Sandinista Revolution on the lives of working people in Managua, Nicaragua (see EthnoProfile 13.11: Managua). While he was there, he learned about *cochones. Cochón* could be translated into English as *homosexual*, but this would be highly misleading. As Lancaster discovered, working-class Nicaraguans interpret sexual relations between men differently from North Americans, and their interpretation is central to the traditional Nicaraguan ideas about masculinity that have been called *machismo.*

To begin with, a "real man" (or *macho*) is widely admired as someone who is active, violent, and dominant. In sexual terms, this means that the penis is seen as a weapon used violently to dominate one's sexual partner, who is thereby rendered passive, abused, and subordinate. North Americans typically think of machismo as involving the domination of women by men, but as Lancaster shows, the system is equally defined by the domination of men over other men. Indeed, a "manly man" in working-class Nicaragua is defined as one who is the active, dominant, penetrating sexual partner in encounters with women *and* men. A "passive" male who allows a "manly man" to have sexual intercourse with him in this way is called a cochón.

A North American gay man himself, Lancaster found that Nicaraguan views of male–male sexual encounters differ considerably from contemporary North American ideas about male homosexuality. In Nicaragua, for example, the people Lancaster knew assumed that men

EthnoProfile 13.11

Managua

Region: Central America

Nation: Nicaragua

Population: 1,000,000 (1995 est.)

Environment: Tropical city

Livelihood: Modern stratified city

Political organization: City in modern nation-state

For more information: Lancaster, Roger. 1992. *Life is hard: Machismo, danger, and the intimacy of power in Nicaragua.* Berkeley: University of California Press.

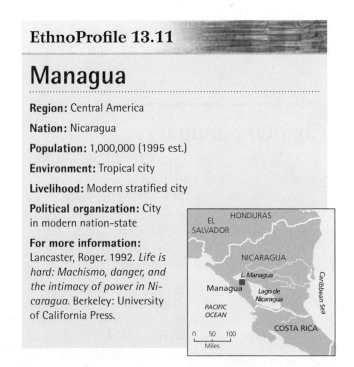

"would naturally be aroused by the idea of anally penetrating another male" (1992, 241). Only the "passive" cochón is stigmatized, whereas males who always take the "active" role in sexual intercourse with other males and with females are seen as "normal." Nicaraguans, moreover, find hate crimes such as gay-bashing inconceivable: cochones may be made fun of, but they are also much admired performers during Carnival. In the United States, by contrast, the active–passive distinction does not exist, and anal intercourse is not the only form that male homosexual expression may take. Both partners in same-sex encounters are considered homosexual and equally stigmatized, and gay-bashing is a sometimes deadly reality, probably because it is *not* assumed that "normal" males will naturally be aroused by the idea of sex with another man.

In Nicaragua, public challenges for dominance are a constant of male–male interaction even when sexual intercourse is not involved. The term *cochón* may be used as an epithet not only for a man who yields publicly to another man but also for cats that do not catch mice or, indeed, anything that somehow fails to perform its proper function. In Lancaster's view, cochones are made, not born: "Those who consistently lose out in the competition for male status . . . discover pleasure in the passive sexual role or its social status: these men are made into cochones. And those who master the rules of conventional masculinity . . . are made into machistas" (1992, 249).

These ideas about gender and sexuality created an unanticipated roadblock for Sandinistas who wanted to improve the lives of Nicaraguan women and children. The Sandinista government passed a series of New Family Laws, which were designed to encourage men to support their families economically and to discourage irresponsible sex, irresponsible parenting, and familial dislocation. When Lancaster interviewed Nicaraguan men to see what they thought of these laws, however, he repeatedly got the following response: "First the interrogative: 'What do the Sandinistas want from us? That we should all become cochones?' And then the tautological: 'A man has to be a man.' That is, a man is defined by what he is not—a cochón" (1992, 274).

Sexuality and Power

The physical activity that we call "sexual intercourse" is not just doing what comes naturally. Like so much else in human life, sex does not speak for itself, nor does it have only one meaning. Sexual practices can be used to give concrete form to more abstract notions we have about the place of men and women in the world. They may serve as a metaphor for expressing differential power within a society. This is particularly clear in the sexual practices that embody Nicaraguan machismo or North American date rape and family violence. That is, sexual practices can be used to enact, in unmistakable physical terms, the reality of differential power. This is equally clear in the arguments over "gay marriage" in the United States since marriage in a nation-state has legal consequences and protections, as well as embodying the legitimacy of the couple's commitment to each other. This reminds us that marriages, families, and sexual practices never occur in a vacuum but are embedded in other social practices such as food production, political organization, and kinship.

Chapter Summary

1. Human life is group life; we depend upon one another to survive. People organize their interdependence by means of various forms of relatedness, including friendship, marriage, parenthood, shared links to a common ancestor, workplace associations, and so on. Forms of relatedness are always embedded in, and shaped by, politics, economics, and worldviews.

2. One of the key forms of relatedness studied by anthropologists is kinship. Kinship systems focus on ideas about shared substance and its transmission, often thought to take place in the process of sexual reproduction. Cross-cultural comparison, however, shows that kinship is not a direct reflection of biology. Kinship principles are based on, but not reducible to, the universal biological experiences of mating, birth, and nurturance. Kinship systems help societies maintain social order without central government. Although female-male duality is basic to kinship, many societies have developed supernumerary sexes or genders.

3. Descent links members of different generations with one another. Patterns of descent in kinship systems are selective. Bilateral descent results in the formation of groups called "kindreds" that include all relatives from both parents' families. Unilineal descent results in the formation of groups called "lineages" that trace descent through either the mother or the father. Unlike kindreds, lineages are corporate groups. Lineages control important property, such as land, that collectively belongs to their members. In many societies, the language of lineage is the idiom of political discussion and lineage relationships are of political significance.

4. Kinship terminologies pay selective attention to certain attributes of people that are then used to define different classes of kin. The attributes most often recognized include, from most to least common, generation, gender, affinity, collaterality, bifurcation, relative age, and the gender of the linking relative. Achieved kinship statuses can be converted into ascribed ones by means of adoption. In Zumbagua, Ecuador, most adults have several kinds of parents and several kinds of children, some adopted and some not. Zumbaguan adoptions are based on nurturance—in this case, the feeding by the adoptive parent of the adopted child.

5. Marriage may be defined as a social process that transforms the status of a man and woman, stipulates the degree of sexual access the married partners may have to each other, establishes the legitimacy of children born to the wife, and creates relationships between the kin of the wife and the kin of the husband. However, woman marriage and ghost marriage demonstrate that the social roles of husband and father or wife and mother may be independent of the gender of the persons who fill them. There are four major patterns of postmarital residence: neolocal, patrilocal, matrilocal, and avunculocal.

6. A person may be married to only one person at a time (*monogamy*) or to several (*polygamy*). Polygamy can be further subdivided into *polygyny*, in which a man is married to two or more wives, and *polyandry*, in which a woman is married to two or more husbands. The study of polyandry reveals the separation of a woman's sexuality and her reproductive capacity, something not found in monogamous or polygynous societies. Most human societies permit marriages to end by divorce, although it is not always easy. In most societies, childlessness is grounds for divorce. Sometimes nagging, quarreling, adultery, cruelty, and stinginess are causes. In some societies, only men may initiate a divorce. In very few societies is divorce impossible.

7. Bridewealth is a payment of symbolically important goods by the husband's lineage to the wife's lineage. Anthropologists see this as compensation to the wife's family for the loss of her productive and reproductive capacities. A woman's bridewealth payment may enable her brother to pay bridewealth to get a wife. Dowry is typically a transfer of family wealth from parents to their daughter at the time of her marriage. Dowries are often considered the wife's contribution to the establishment of a new household.

8. Different family structures produce different internal patterns and tensions. There are three basic family types: nuclear, extended, and joint. Families may change from one type to another over time and with the birth, growth, and marriage of children. Families have developed ingenious ways of keeping together even when some members live abroad for extended periods. Gays and lesbians in North America have created families by choice, based on nurturance, which they believe are as enduring as families based on marriage and birth.

9. Friendship is a form of relatedness that is apparently unique to human beings. In some societies, the link between best friends may be ritually confirmed. Under conditions of globalization, older forms of relatedness such as kinship are transformed and new forms of friendship are developing.

10. Sexual practices vary greatly worldwide, from the puritanical and fearful to the casual and pleasurable. In some societies, young men and women begin having free sexual relations from an early age until they are married. Sexual practices that North Americans call "homosexuality" or "bisexuality" may be understood very differently in different societies. In the contemporary globalizing world, Western and non-Western same-sex practices are becoming increasingly entangled with one another, leading to the emergence of local movements for "lesbian" and "gay" rights on many continents.

For Review

1. What is relatedness?
2. Define kinship, marriage, and adoption, and explain how these are based on, but not reducible to, biology.
3. List the major attributes of human kinship systems, as presented in the section "What Is Kinship?"
4. How have anthropologists traditionally distinguished between sex and gender?
5. Describe the major strategies human beings have used to establish patterns of descent.
6. Compare bilateral kindreds and unilineal descent groups.
7. What is the technical difference anthropologists recognize between a lineage and a clan?
8. Summarize the key points in the text about patrilineages.
9. Summarize the key points in the text about matrilineages.
10. Prepare a chart of the key criteria used to distinguish different categories of kin within kinship terminologies, with a brief explanation (and example) of each criterion.
11. Explain the differences between ascribed and achieved status.
12. Explain how the flexibility of relatedness is illustrated by the case studies on adoption in Zumbagua, European American new reproductive technologies, and organ transplants.
13. Define marriage and explain each of the five points of the definition given in the text.
14. Explain woman marriage and ghost marriage among the Nuer. Why is it important to distinguish *pater* and *genitor*?
15. What are affinal relationships? What are consanguineal relationships?
16. Distinguish between endogamy and exogamy.
17. Summarize the different kinds of residence rules that newly married couples have been expected to observe in different societies.
18. Describe monogamy, polygyny, and polyandry.
19. Discuss how different marriage patterns reflect variation in social understandings of male and female sexuality.
20. What are the differences between bridewealth and dowry?
21. What is a family?
22. Summarize the major forms of the family that are discussed in the text.
23. Discuss the ways in which families change over time, as discussed in the text.
24. Describe the effects of international migration on families.
25. Compare and contrast friendship and kinship.
26. Using the case studies in the text, discuss how anthropologists understand human sexual practices.

Key Terms

achieved statuses   375
adoption   364
affinal relationships   380
affinity   374
ascribed statuses   375
avunculocal
   residence   381
bifurcation   374
bilateral descent   368
blended family   391
bridewealth   371, 385
clan   370

collaterality   374
conjugal family   386
consanguineal
   relationships   380
cross cousins   375
descent   364
dowry   386
endogamy   380
exogamy   380
extended family   389
family   386
friendship   396

gender   365
joint family   389
kinship systems   364
lineages   369
marriage   364, 379
matrilineage   369
matrilocal residence   381
monogamy   381
neolocal residence   381
nonconjugal family   386
nuclear family   388

parallel cousins   375
patrilineage   369
patrilocal residence   381
polyandry   384
polygamy   381
polygyny   384
relatedness   364
segmentary
   opposition   371
sex   365
sexual practices   396

Suggested Readings

Capsten, Jane, ed. 2000. *Cultures of relatedness: New approaches to the study of kinship.* Cambridge: Cambridge University Press. *An excellent collection of very current articles on relatedness.*

Ginsburg, Faye D. 1998. *Contested lives: The abortion debate in an American community,* updated ed. Berkeley: University of California Press. *A study of gender and procreation in the context of the abortion debate in Fargo, North Dakota, in the 1980s.*

Ginsburg, Faye D., and Rayna Rapp, eds. 1995. *Conceiving the new world order: The global politics of reproduction.* Berkeley: University of California Press. *An important collection of articles by anthropologists who address the ways human reproduction is structured across social and cultural boundaries.*

Kahn, Susan Martha. 2000. *Reproducing Jews: A cultural account of assisted conception in Israel.* Durham, NC: Duke University Press. *An exceptionally interesting ethnographic study of the effects of new reproductive technologies on kinship in Israel.*

Lancaster, Roger. 1992. *Life is hard: Machismo, danger, and the intimacy of power in Nicaragua.* Berkeley: University of California Press. *A stunning analysis of machismo in Nicaragua, in which sexual practices that North Americans consider homosexual are interpreted very differently.*

Parlain, Robert, and Linda Stone, eds. 2004. *Kinship and family: An anthropological reader.* Malden, MA: Blackwell. *A distinguished collection of classic and contemporary articles.*

Sharp, Lesley. 2006. *Strange harvest: Organ transplants, denatured bodies, and the transformed self.* Berkeley: University of California Press. *In addition to her discussion of post-transplant forms of kinship, Sharp addresses a range of related issues, raised by organ transplantation, all of which—as her subtitle indicates—call into question traditional Western notions of natural bodies and autonomous selves.*

Shostak, Marjorie. 1981. *Nisa: The life and words of a !Kung woman.* New York: Vintage. *The story of a Ju/'hoansi (!Kung) woman's life in her own words. Shostak provides background for each chapter. There is much here on marriage and everyday life.*

Stone, Linda. 2010. *Kinship and gender,* 4th ed. Boulder, CO: Westview Press. *A recent discussion of human reproduction and the social and cultural implications of male and female reproductive roles.*

Suggs, David, and Andrew Miracle, eds. 2004. *Culture, biology, and sexuality.* Athens, GA: University of Georgia Press. *A collection of important articles from a variety of theoretical perspectives on the nature and culture of human sexuality.*

What Can Anthropology Tell Us about Social Inequality?

14

Not all human groups are equal to one another in terms of wealth, power, or prestige. Indeed, in complex human societies, a variety of forms of social inequality are regularly passed on from generation to generation. This chapter looks at forms of social inequality based on gender, class, caste, ethnicity, and nationalism. We also explore some of the ways different societies regularly attempt to justify forms of inequality by attempting to make them appear unchangeable and eternal, rather than the outcome of historically contingent cultural and political practices.

Chapter Outline

◀ *Local fishermen head out to sea in Labadee, Haiti, as a luxury cruise ship leaves in the background.*

In Chapter 12, we observed that most people in the world today come under the authority of one or another nation-state and that all nation-states are socially stratified. But inequality within nation-states may be constructed out of multiple categories arranged in different, and sometimes contradictory, hierarchies of stratification. We shall focus in this chapter on six such categories: gender, class, caste, race, ethnicity, and nationality. It is important to emphasize from the outset that *every one of these categories is a cultural invention* designed to create boundaries around one or another imagined community. *None* of these categories maps onto permanent biological subdivisions within the human species, although members of societies that employ these categories often will invoke "nature" to shore up their legitimacy.

Some of these patterns of inequality (e.g., gender, class, caste) reach back thousands of years into human history. Others (e.g., race, ethnicity, and nationality) are far more recent in origin and closely associated with changes that began in Europe some 500 years ago. The spread of capitalism and colonialism reshaped forms of stratification that predated their arrival, as well as introducing new forms of stratification into formerly independent, egalitarian societies. Anthropologists and other social scientists have argued with one another about how these categories should be defined and whether or not they can be usefully applied cross-culturally, and we will look at some of their arguments. But these observations are quite abstract, so we begin with an ethnographic example to illustrate the issues involved.

Inequality and Structural Violence in Haiti

The entire world focused on Haiti in January 2010, when a devastating earthquake struck the country, killing tens of thousands of people, rendering perhaps a million people homeless, and turning much of the built environment to rubble. Paul Farmer is an anthropologist and medical doctor who has worked in Haiti since 1983. The organization he founded, Partners in Health, provided care to many who suffered in the earthquake and is active in efforts to rebuild and improve medical facilities that were lost (see the Partners in Health website for details: http://www.pih.org/pages/haiti/).

One reason the effects of the earthquake were so devastating is that most Haitians live under precarious circumstances. Farmer's activities as a physician have exposed him to extreme forms of human suffering that have long been taken-for-granted aspects of everyday life for those at the bottom of Haitian society (see Figure 14.2 and EthnoProfile 14.1: Haiti). Farmer describes this suffering as the outcome of structural violence. **Structural violence** is a product of the way that political and economic forces structure people's risks for various forms of suffering within a population. Much structural violence takes the form of infectious and parasitic disease. But it can also include other forms of extreme suffering, such as hunger, torture, and rape (Farmer 2002, 424). Structural violence circumscribes the spaces in which the poorest and least powerful members of Haitian society must live and subjects them to highly intensified risks of all kinds. The *structural* aspect of this violence must be emphasized since most Western outside observers (even those who want to alleviate suffering) often focus only on individuals and their personal experiences and are often tempted to blame the victims for their own distress.

Farmer's work as a physician allowed him to see firsthand the suffering of poor Haitians he knew, including one young woman who died of AIDS and one young man who died from injuries he received in the course of a beating by the police. As Farmer says, these two individuals "suffered and died in exemplary fashion," and he shows how state-supported political violence operating on inequalities of gender, social class, and race conspired "to constrain agency" and "crystallize into the sharp, hard surfaces of individual suffering" (2002, 425).

Acéphie Joseph was the woman who died of AIDS at 25, in 1991, one of the first in her rural village. Her parents had been prosperous peasant farmers selling produce in village markets until 1956, when the fertile valley in which they lived was flooded after a dam was built to generate electricity. They lost everything and became "water refugees," forced to try to grow crops on an infertile plot in the village where they were resettled. Farmer writes that Acéphie's "beauty and her vulnerability may have sealed her fate as early as 1984" (2002, 426). She began to help her mother carry produce to the market along a road that went past the local military barracks, where soldiers like to flirt with the passing women, and one soldier in particular approached her. "Such flirtation is seldom unwelcome, at least to all appearances. In rural Haiti, entrenched poverty made the soldiers—the region's only salaried men—ever so much more attractive" (427). Although Acéphie knew he had a wife and children, she nevertheless did not rebuff him; indeed, he visited her family, who approved of their liaison. "'I could tell that the old people were uncomfortable, but

---

structural violence Violence that results from the way that political and economic forces structure risk for various forms of suffering within a population.

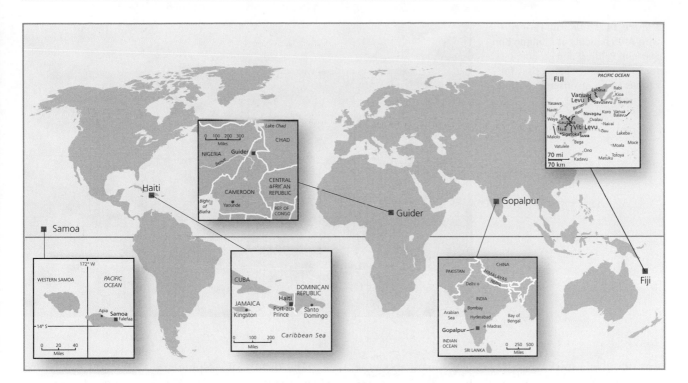

Figure 14.1   Location of societies whose EthnoProfiles appear in Chapter 14.

they didn't say no . . . I never dreamed he would give me a bad illness . . . it was a way out, that's how I saw it,'" Acéphie explained. Only a few weeks after the beginning of their sexual relationship, the soldier died. Eventually, Acéphie found work as a maid, began a relationship with a young man, and planned to marry. After 3 years, Acéphie became pregnant and went home to her village to give birth, but she had a very difficult delivery; when she finally sought medical help for a series of infections, she was diagnosed with AIDS. After her death, her father hanged himself.

Chouchou Louis grew up in a village on the Central Plateau of Haiti. He attended primary school briefly and then worked with his father and older sister to raise produce after his mother died. In the 1980s, times were especially difficult under the repressive dictatorship of Jean-Claude Duvalier. Those Haitians who tried to flee by boat to the United States were termed *economic* rather than *political* refugees and, thanks to a 1981 treaty between Duvalier and President Ronald Reagan, were promptly returned to Haiti. By 1986, a prodemocracy movement had grown powerful enough in Haiti to force Duvalier to leave the country, but he was replaced in power by the military. Although the U.S. government based its hopes for the introduction of democracy on this military government and supplied it with over $200 million in aid, poor peasants like Chouchou Louis and his family continued to be subject to military violence. An election in 1990 brought the popular leader Father

Jean-Bertrand Aristide to power with over 70 percent of the vote, but in 1991 he was ousted in a coup. Anger in the countryside at this coup "was soon followed by sadness, then fear, as the country's repressive machinery, dismantled during the seven months of Aristide's tenure, was hastily reassembled under the patronage of the army" (Farmer 2002, 429). Soon thereafter Chouchou

EthnoProfile 14.1

Haiti

Region: Caribbean

Nation: Haiti

Population: 7,500,000

Livelihood: Rough, mountainous terrain, tropical to semi-arid climate. About 80 percent of the population lives in extreme poverty

Political organization: Multiparty, nation-state

For more information: Farmer, Paul. 1992. *AIDS and accusation: Haiti and the geography of blame.* Berkeley, University of California Press.

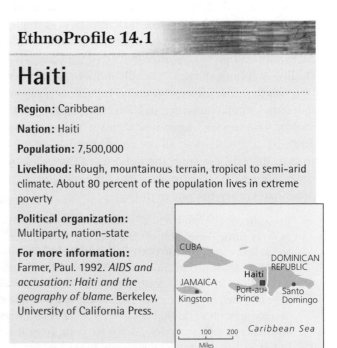

Figure 14.2 Dr. Paul Farmer with AIDS patients at Clinique Bon Sauveur. Political and economic forces structure people's risks for various forms of suffering in Haiti as elsewhere.

was riding in a truck when he made a remark about the poor state of the roads that might have been interpreted as a veiled criticism of the coup. On the same truck was an out-of-uniform soldier, who, at the next checkpoint, had Chouchou dragged from the truck and beaten. Although he was let go, he lived in fear of another arrest, which came several months later, with no explanation, when he was visiting his sister. He was taken to the nearest military checkpoint and tortured. Three days later, he was dumped in a ditch to die; the day after, Farmer was brought in to treat him, but his injuries were too severe. He died 3 days later.

Acéphie and Chouchou are individuals, so it is natural to ask how representative their experiences might be. Farmer's experience among many poor women with AIDS allowed him to recognize that all of their cases, including Acéphie's, showed "a deadly monotony." Farmer observes that "the agony of Acéphie and Chouchou was in a sense, 'modal' suffering. In Haiti, AIDS and political violence are two leading causes of death among young adults" (2002, 431). And all the key events that contributed to their deaths, from the flooding of the valley to the funding of the Haitian army, were the consequences of human agency. Because of this,

> the agency of Acéphie and Chouchou was . . . curbed at every turn. These grim biographies suggest that the social and economic forces that have helped to shape the AIDS epidemic are, in every sense, the same forces that led to Chouchou's death and to the larger repression in which it was eclipsed. What is more, both were "at risk" of such a fate long before they met the soldiers who altered their destinies. *They* were both, from the outset, victims of structural violence. (431)

The deaths of Acéphie and Chouchou can be explained if their ethnographic and historical context is articulated, as Farmer tries to do. It is also important to identify specifically the relations of power in which each of them was embedded, for these contributed to the likelihood that their suffering and death would take the forms they took. For example, "gender helps explain why Acéphie died of AIDS whereas Chouchou died from torture . . . also . . . why the suffering of Acéphie is much more commonplace than that of Chouchou" (433). Race or ethnicity helps explain why illness is more likely to be suffered by the descendants of enslaved Africans, and social class helps explain why they were more likely to be poor. To understand why the Haitian state should need or receive massive aid from the United States, as well as why it should use violence against its citizens, requires a consideration of the structure of the Haitian state and its position within a global system of nation-states. In what follows, we explore each of these dimensions of inequality—and a bit more besides.

Gender

As we saw in the previous chapter, anthropological research on issues involving sex and gender increased enormously in the last third of the twentieth century, especially in the work of feminist anthropologists. Research focused not only on reproductive roles and sexuality but also on the question of gender inequality. Beginning in the 1970s, feminist anthropologists dissatisfied with gender inequality in their own societies closely examined the ethnographic record to determine whether male dominance was a feature of all human societies. Early work seemed to suggest that male dominance was in fact universal. For example, Sherry Ortner (1974) suggested that male dominance was rooted in a form of binary cultural thinking that opposed male to female; males were ranked higher than females because females were universally seen as "closer to nature" by virtue of the fact that they gave birth and nursed their young. Yet, Jane Collier, Michelle Rosaldo, and Sylvia Yanagisako (1997) were able to show that the roles of men and women within families—even the very idea of what constituted a "family"—varied enormously, cross-culturally and historically. They concluded that the "nuclear family" of father, mother, and children was far from universal and, in fact, best understood as a relatively recent historical consequence of the rise of industrial capitalism in western European societies. Attention to history also led Marxist-feminist anthropologists like Eleanor Leacock to argue that women's subordination to men was not inevitable but could be connected explicitly to the rise of private property and the emergence of the state. She used ethnographic and historical evidence from North America and South America, Melanesia, and Africa to show how Western capitalist colonization had transformed egalitarian precolonial indigenous gender relations into unequal, male-dominated gender relations (Leacock 1983).

More recently, anthropologists like Marilyn Strathern (1988) have argued that the particular relations between males and females in society need to be recognized as just one example of gender symbolism. Strathern defines *gender* as "those categorizations of persons, artifacts, events sequences, and so on which draw upon sexual imagery—upon the ways in which the distinctiveness of male and female characteristics make concrete people's ideas about the nature of social relations" (1988, ix). Thinking of gender in this way helps make sense of the fact that in some societies gendered forms of inequality not only are applied to phenotypic males and females but also may be used to structure relations between different categories of men, as in the Nicaraguan contrast of "manly men" and *cochones* described in Chapter 13. Similarly, Roy Richard Grinker found that male village-dwelling Lese householders of the Democratic Republic of Congo distinguished themselves from their forest-dwelling Efe pygmy trading partners using the same unequal gender categories that they used to distinguish themselves from their wives. From the point of view of Lese men, Efe partners and Lese wives were subordinate to them because both had been incorporated within the households of Lese men (Grinker 1994). Anthropologist Ann Stoler studied the effects of Dutch

colonialism in Indonesia, and has compared it with colonialism elsewhere. She has shown that the relationship between white European colonizers and the nonwhite indigenous males was regularly conceived in terms both of "racial" inequality and of gender inequality. That is, colonizers constructed a "racial" divide between colonizer and colonized that ranked "white" colonial males above "nonwhite" indigenous males. At the same time, by violently punishing any hint of sexual involvement between indigenous males and "white" women, while allowing themselves unrestricted sexual access to indigenous women, white male colonizers "feminized" indigenous males—constructing them as less than fully male because they had been unable to defend either their land or "their women" from more powerful white outsiders. Stoler points out that white male colonizers struggled to shore up these racialized and gendered colonial hierarchies whenever indigenous males organized politically in ways that threatened colonial rule.

Haiti, of course, began as a colony of France and achieved its independence following a successful revolt of black slaves against their white colonial masters. As Nina Glick Schiller and Georges Fouron argue, however, "Haiti has its own particular and mixed messages about gender that give to women and men both rights and responsibilities to family and nation" (2001, 133). Women appear in official stories about the Haitian Revolution, and some of them are even portrayed as heroines; most, however, are usually portrayed as silent wives and mothers. Moreover, the founders of the Haitian state borrowed from their former French masters "a patriarchal idea of family as well as a civil code that gave men control of family life, wealth, and property" (134). Women belonged to the Haitian nation, but "state officials and the literate elite envisioned women as able to reproduce the nation only in conjunction with a Haitian man" (134). Until recently, Haitian women who married foreigners lost their Haitian citizenship. High-status Haitian women are those who are supported economically by their Haitian husbands and who stay home with their children. Schiller and Fouron argue that many Haitians "still believe that to live by these values is to uphold not only family but also national honor"(135) (Figure 14.3).

By contrast, Haitian women who cannot live by these values are accorded low status. On the one hand, this means that they are not confined to the domestic sphere. On the other hand, for this very reason, they are assumed to be always sexually available. "Men in Haiti see women alone or in the workplace as willing and able to trade their sexuality for other things they need. Men may ask rather than take, but often they are making an offer that women cannot afford to refuse" (Schiller and

Figure 14.3 The founders of the Haitian state borrowed from their former French masters an idea of gender that gave men control of family life. Women belonged to the Haitian nation, but until recently, Haitian women who married foreigners lost their Haitian citizenship and their children would not be considered Haitians.

Fouron 2001, 139–40). This describes well the structural constraints with which Acéphie Joseph had to contend; options open to women of higher social position were not available to her. To understand why, however, we need to look more closely at what anthropologists have to say about the connections between social class and social inequality.

Class

In general, **classes** are hierarchically arranged social groups defined on economic grounds. That is, higher-ranked social classes have disproportionate access to sources of wealth in the society, whereas the members of low-ranked classes have much more limited access to wealth (Figure 14.4).

The concept of class has a double heritage in modern anthropology, one stemming from Europe and the other from the United States. European social scientists lived in states with a long history of social class divisions reaching back into the Middle Ages and, in some cases, even into earlier times. In their experience, social classes are well-entrenched and relatively closed groups. In the late 1700s, both the Industrial Revolution and the

French Revolution promised to end the oppressive privileges of the ruling class and to equalize everyone's access to wealth. However, class divisions did not wither away in Europe during the nineteenth century; they just changed their contours. Followers of Marx judged that, at best, an old ruling class had been displaced by a new one: feudal aristocrats had been replaced by bourgeois capitalists. The lowest level in European societies—rural peasants—were partially displaced as well, with the appearance of the urban working class. But the barriers separating those at the top of the class hierarchy from those at the bottom seemed just as rigid as ever.

As we saw in Chapter 11, Marx defines classes in terms of their members' different relations to the means of production. This means that as long as a particular set of unequal productive relations flourishes in a society, the classes defined by these unequal roles in the division of labor will also persist. The French Revolution had triggered the displacement of aristocrats and peasants who had played the key roles in European feudalism. They were replaced by new key classes—industrial entrepreneurs and the industrial working class—who were linked together within the capitalist mode of production. In time, Marx predicted, these industrial workers would become the new "leading class," rising up to oust capitalists when the socialist revolution came.

As Marx was well aware, all those who are linked to the means of production in the same way (e.g., as workers) often do not recognize what they have in common and may therefore fail to develop the kind of solidarity among themselves—the "class consciousness"—that could, in Marx's view, lead to revolution. Indeed, the possibility of peasant- or working-class solidarity in many of the stratified societies studied by anthropologists is actively undercut by institutions of clientage. According to anthropologist M. G. Smith, **clientage** "designates a variety of relationships, which all have inequality of status of the associated persons as a common characteristic" ([1954] 1981, 31). Clientage is a relationship between *individuals* rather than groups. The party of superior status is the patron, and the party of inferior status is the client. Stratified societies united by links of clientage can be very stable. Low-status clients believe their security depends on finding a high-status individual who can protect them. For example, clientage is characteristic of *compadrazgo*, or ritual coparenthood relationships, found throughout Latin America. The Latin American societies in which compadrazgo flourishes are class societies, and parents who are peasants or workers often seek landowners or factory owners to serve as *compadres*, or godparents, at the baptism of their children. When the baptism ritual is completed, the parents and godparents of the child now have a new, more relaxed

class A ranked group within a hierarchically stratified society whose membership is defined primarily in terms of wealth, occupation, or other economic criteria.

clientage The institution linking individuals from upper and lower levels in a stratified society.

Figure 14.4 Social classes often live within easy sight of one another. Here, luxury apartments and squatter settlements rub shoulders in Caracas, Venezuela.

relationship. They call each other "compadre" and can feel freer to seek one another out for support in times of need. While the lower-status biological parents may seek out their higher-status compadres for economic relief, the higher-status individuals might seek out their lower-status compadres for political support.

Marx's view of class is clearly different from the hegemonic view of class in the United States. For generations the "American Dream" has been that in the United States individuals may pursue wealth, power, and prestige unhampered by the unyielding class barriers characteristic of "Old World" societies. As a result, many social scientists trained in the United States (including cultural anthropologists) have tended to define social classes primarily in terms of income level and to argue that such social classes are open, porous, and permeable, rather than rigid and exclusionary. Upward class mobility is supposed to be, in principle, attainable by all people, regardless of how low their social origins are. Even poor boys like Abraham Lincoln, born in a log cabin on the frontier, can grow up to be president.

But the promise of the American Dream of equal opportunity for upward class mobility has not been realized by all those living in the United States. In the early twentieth century, both black and white social scientists concluded that an unyielding "color bar" prevented upward class mobility for U.S. citizens with African ancestry. One participant in these studies, a sociologist named W. Lloyd Warner, argued in 1936 that the color bar looked more like the rigid barrier reported to exist between castes in India than the supposedly permeable boundary separating American social classes. That is to say, membership in a **caste** is ascribed

at birth and each ranked caste is closed such that individuals are not allowed to move from one caste into another. Membership in social classes is also ascribed at birth, according to Warner; but unlike castes, classes are not closed and individual social mobility from one class into another is possible (Sharma 1999, 15; Harrison 1995, 1998; Warner 1936). Warner's distinction between *caste* and *class* became standard for decades in American cultural anthropology.

Is this a plausible contrast? The aspect of caste that impressed Warner was the reported rigidity of the barrier between castes, which seemed much like the barrier separating blacks and whites in the United States. But in 1948, an African American sociologist named Oliver Cromwell Cox rejected an equation between caste and race. Cox pointed out that many authorities on caste in India claimed that Hindu castes were harmoniously integrated within a *caste system* shaped by Hindu religious beliefs about purity and pollution. Most importantly, it appeared that members of low-ranked "impure" castes did not challenge the caste system even though it oppressed them. If this were true, Cox concluded, caste relations were *unlike* race relations in the United States because whites had imposed the color bar by force and only by force had they been able to repress black resistance to the injustice of the system. Ursula Sharma (1999) points out, however, that both Warner and Cox were relying on an understanding of Hindu castes that

---

caste A ranked group within a hierarchically stratified society that is closed, prohibiting individuals to move from one caste to another.

today is considered highly misleading. In order not to be led astray ourselves, it is necessary to spend some time considering what anthropologists have learned about caste as a form of social inequality.

Caste

The word *caste* comes from the Portuguese word *casta*, meaning "chaste." Portuguese explorers applied it to the stratification systems they encountered in south Asia in the fifteenth century. They understood that these societies were divided into a hierarchy of ranked subgroups, each of which was "chaste" in the sense that sexual and marital links across group boundaries were forbidden. That is, in anthropological terms, castes were endogamous, and many anthropologists agree that caste is fundamentally a form of kinship (Guneratne 2002). Most Western scholars have taken the stratification system of India as the prototype of caste stratification, and some insist that caste cannot properly be said to exist outside India. However, anthropologists often use the term *caste* to describe societies outside India when they encounter one of two features: (1) endogamous occupational groupings whose members are looked down on by other groups in the society or (2) an endogamous ruling elite who set themselves above those they rule. Anthropologist James Vaughan (1970; see also Tamari 1991) reviewed the data on western African caste systems. The presence of endogamous, stigmatized occupational groupings was common in all societies of the Sahara and in the western Sudan (the band of territory between Senegal and Lake Chad that lies south of the Sahara and north of the coastal rain forest). Vaughan also found castes in a second cultural area located in the mountain ranges that lie along the modern border between Nigeria and Cameroon. In this region, many societies had endogamous groups of "blacksmiths" whose status was distinct from that of other members of society. These "blacksmiths" were not despised however; if anything, they were feared or regarded with awe.

The concept of "caste" was also used by anthropologist Jacques Maquet (1970) to describe the closed, endogamous ranked strata of Tutsi, Hutu, and Twa in the central African kingdom of Rwanda prior to 1959. Pierre van den Berghe (1970) documents the history of caste-like relationships dating from the beginnings of white settlement in southern Africa that culminated in the twentieth-century "color caste" system distinguishing Whites, Asians, Coloreds, and Bantu that was enforced in apartheid South Africa. De Vos and Wagatsuma (1966) used the term *caste* to describe the *burakumin* of

Japan, low-ranking endogamous groups traditionally associated with polluting occupations, who have been subjected to dehumanizing stereotypes and residential segregation from other Japanese. Ursula Sharma suggests that the concept of "caste" might be fruitfully used to characterize the relations between the Rom (or Gypsies) of Europe and their non-Rom neighbors, who for centuries have subjected the Rom to stigmatization, social segregation, and economic exclusion (1999, 85–86). To better understand why these examples of social inequality have been called "caste," we will look more closely at the best-studied example of caste in the ethnographic literature.

Caste in India

The term *caste*, as most Western observers use it, combines two distinct south Asian concepts. The first term, *varna*, refers to the widespread Hindu notion that Indian society is ideally divided into priests, warriors, farmers, and merchants—four functional subdivisions analogous to the estates of medieval and early modern Europe (Sharma 1999, Guneratne 2002). The second term, *jati*, refers to localized, named, endogamous groups. Although jati names are frequently the names of occupations (e.g., farmer, saltmaker), there is no universally agreed-upon way to group the many local jatis within one or another of the four varnas. This is why members of different jatis can disagree about where their own jatis ought to belong. In any case, varna divisions are more theoretical in nature, whereas jati is the more significant term in most of the local village settings where anthropologists have traditionally conducted fieldwork.

Villagers in the southern Indian town of Gopalpur defined a jati for anthropologist Alan Beals (see Ethno-Profile 14.2: Gopalpur). They said it was "a category of men thought to be related, to occupy a particular position within a hierarchy of jatis, to marry among themselves, and to follow particular practices and occupations" (Beals 1962, 25). Beals's informants compared the relationship between jatis of different rank to the relationship between brothers. Ideally, they said, members of low-ranking jatis respect and obey members of high-ranking jatis, just as younger brothers respect and obey older brothers.

Villagers in Gopalpur were aware of at least 50 different jatis, although not all were represented in the village. Because jatis have different occupational specialties that they alone can perform, villagers were sometimes dependent on the services of outsiders. For example, there was no member of the washerman jati in Gopalpur. As a result, a member of that jati from another village had to be employed when people in Gopalpur

In Their Own Words

Burakumin: Overcoming Hidden Discrimination in Japan

Tomoe Kawasaki is a college staff member in Japan and identifies herself as a Buraku. While the Japanese government has passed laws prohibiting discrimination against Burakumin, prejudice remains. On the website globalcompassion.com, which features photos, videos, and writings about our human condition, Tomoe tells her story.

My parents didn't tell me much about Buraku, and they raised me as far away from the Buraku as possible. They didn't want me to suffer any discrimination. Upon taking a class about Buraku issues in college, I started to face my family roots—roots that I was forgetting. I sometimes wrestled with my parents' protective love, and it made me anxious; I wondered if other people would accept me having a Buraku origin. At the same time, it was overwhelmingly joyful for me to learn so much about myself in the contexts of history, culture, and people. Now I often visit my hometown, the Buraku [town] where I lived until the age of 7. Now I am weaving a story that leads to me through the people I was reunited with there. When I took the plunge and faced my roots, and then leaped further into my past, I found a world so wonderful.

*Source:*http://www.globalcompassion.com/2008/05/19/masaru-goto/. Accessed August 8, 2011.

Tomoe Kawasaki

---

wanted their clothes cleaned ritually or required clean cloth for ceremonies.

Jatis are distinguished in terms of the foods they eat as well as their traditional occupations. These features have a ritual significance that affects interactions between members of different jatis. In Hindu belief, certain foods and occupations are classed as pure and others as polluting. In theory, all jatis are ranked on a scale from purest to most polluted (Figure 14.5). Ranked highest of all are the vegetarian Brahmins, who are pure enough to approach the gods. Carpenters and Blacksmiths, who also eat a vegetarian diet, are also assigned a high rank. Below the vegetarians are those who eat "clean," or "pure," meat. In Gopalpur, this group of jatis included Saltmakers, Farmers, and Shepherds, who eat sheep, goats, chicken, and fish but not pork or beef. The lowest-ranking jatis are "unclean" meat eaters, who include Stoneworkers and Basketweavers (who eat pork) as well as Leatherworkers (who eat pork and beef). Occupations that involve slaughtering animals or touching polluted things are themselves polluting. Jatis that traditionally carry out such activities as butchering and

EthnoProfile 14.2

Gopalpur

Region: Southern Asia

Nation: India

Population: 540 (1960)

Environment: Center of a plain, some fertile farmland and pasture

Livelihood: Intensive millet farming, some cattle and sheep herding

Political organization: Caste system in a modern nation-state

For more information: Beals, Alan. 1962. *Gopalpur, a south Indian village.* New York: Holt, Rinehart, and Winston.

In Their Own Words

As Economic Turmoil Mounts, So Do Attacks on Hungary's Gypsies

Ethnic conflict in Europe takes a variety of forms, but one that has a long history is prejudice against Roma, the Gypsies. In April 2009, reporter Nicholas Kulish filed this story with the New York Times.

Jeno Koka was a doting grandfather and dedicated worker on his way to his night-shift job at a chemical plant last week when he was shot dead at his doorstep. To his killer, he was just a Gypsy, and that seems to have been reason enough.

Prejudice against Roma—widely known as "Gypsies" and long among Europe's most oppressed minority groups—has swelled into a wave of violence. Over the past year, at least seven Roma have been killed in Hungary, and Roma leaders have counted some 30 Molotov cocktail attacks against Roma homes, often accompanied by sprays of gunfire.

But the police have focused their attention on three fatal attacks since November that they say are linked. The authorities say the attacks may have been carried out by police officers or military personnel, based on the stealth and accuracy with which the victims were killed.

In addition to Mr. Koka's death, there were the slayings of a Roma man and woman, who were shot after their house was set ablaze last November in Nagycsecs, a town about an hour's drive from Tiszalok in northeastern Hungary. And in February, a Roma man and his 4-year-old son were gunned down as they tried to escape from their home, which was set on fire in Tatarszentgyorgy, a small town south of Budapest.

Jozsef Bencze, Hungary's national police chief, said in an interview on Friday with the daily newspaper *Nepszabadsag* that the perpetrators, believed to be a group of four or more men in their 40s, were killing "with hands that are too confident." Military counterintelligence is taking part in the investigation, Hungarian radio reported, and Mr. Bencze said the pool of suspects included veterans of the Balkan Wars and Hungarian members of the French Foreign Legion.

Experts on Roma issues describe an ever more aggressive atmosphere toward Roma in Hungary and elsewhere in Central and Eastern Europe, led by extreme right-wing parties, whose leaders are playing on old stereotypes of Roma as petty criminals and drains on social welfare systems at a time of rising economic and political turmoil. As unemployment rises, officials and Roma experts fear the attacks will only intensify.

"One thing to remember, the Holocaust did not start at the gas chambers," said Lajos Korozs, senior state

Funeral for Robert Csorba, 27, and his son Robert, Jr., 4, in Tatarszentgyorgy, Hungary. The Csorbas were shot dead in February 2009 while fleeing their home, which had been set on fire.

secretary in the Ministry of Social Affairs and Labor, who works on Roma issues for the government. . . .

"In the past five years, attitudes toward Roma in many parts of Eastern Europe have hardened, and new extremists have started to use the Roma issue in a way that either they didn't dare to or didn't get an airing before," said

In Their Own Words

Michael Stewart, coordinator of the Europe-wide Roma Research Network.

The extreme-right party Jobbik has used the issue of what its leaders call "Gypsy crime" to rise in the polls to near the 5 percent threshold for seats in Hungary's Parliament in next year's election, which would be a first for the party. Opponents accuse the Hungarian Guard, the paramilitary group associated with the party, of staging marches and public meetings to stir up anti-Roma sentiment and to intimidate the local Roma population.

The group held a rally last year in Tiszalok and in 2007 in Tatarszentgyorgy, the town where the father and son were killed in February, an act that some residents deplored while in the same breath complaining about a spate of break-ins in town that they blamed on Roma.

"The situation is bad because of the many Roma," said Eva, 45, a non-Roma Hungarian in Tatarszentgyorgy who declined to give her last name, out of what she said was fear of reprisals. "When the guard was here, for a while they weren't so loud. It helped."

Since the attacks in Tatarszentgyorgy, some local residents have joined their terrified Roma neighbors in nighttime patrols, looking for strange cars armed with nothing but searchlights.

"We are living in fear, all the Roma people are," said Csaba Csorba, 48, whose son Robert, 27, and grandson, also named Robert, were killed by a blast from a shotgun shortly after midnight in the February attack. They were buried together in one coffin, the little boy laid to rest on his father's chest.

The child's death in particular shook Roma here. "It proved to us it doesn't matter whether we are good people or bad people," said Agnes Koka, 32, the niece and goddaughter of Mr. Koka, who relatives said loved to bring candy and fruit to his grandchildren. "It only matters that we are Gypsy," Ms. Koka said.

Source: Kulish, 2009.

---

washing dirty clothing are ranked below jatis whose traditional work does not involve polluting activities.

Hindu dietary rules deal not only with the kinds of food that may be eaten by different jatis but also with the circumstances in which members of one jati may accept food prepared by members of another. Members of a lower-ranking jati may accept any food prepared by members of a higher-ranking jati. Members of a higher-ranking jati may accept only certain foods prepared by a lower-ranking jati. In addition, members of different jatis should not eat together.

In practice, these rules are not as confining as they appear. In Gopalpur, "'food' referred to particular kinds of food, principally rice. 'Eating together' means eating from the same dish or sitting on the same line. . . . Members of quite different jatis may eat together if they eat out of separate bowls and if they are facing each other or turned slightly away from each other" (Beals 1962, 41). Members of jatis that are close in rank and neither at the top nor at the bottom of the scale often share food and eat together on a daily basis. Strict observance of the rules is saved for ceremonial occasions.

The way in which non-Hindus were incorporated into the jati system in Gopalpur illuminates the logic of the system. For example, Muslims have long ruled the region surrounding Gopalpur; thus, political power has been a salient attribute of Muslim identity. In addition, Muslims do not eat pork or the meat of animals that have not been ritually slaughtered. These attributes, taken together, led the villagers in Gopalpur to rank Muslims above the Stoneworkers and Basketweavers, who eat

Figure 14.5 Gautam Ganu Jadhao, a city worker, removes a cart full of sewage waste from a Bombay neighborhood in July 2005. People like him whose occupations are characterized as polluting are ranked at the bottom of the Hindu caste system.

pork. All three groups were considered to be eaters of unclean meat, however, because Muslims do eat beef.

There is no direct correlation between the status of a jati on the scale of purity and pollution and the class status of members of that jati. Beals noted, for example, that the high status of Brahmins meant that "there are a relatively large number of ways in which a poor Brahmin may become wealthy" (1962, 37). Similarly, members of low-status jatis may find their attempts to amass wealth curtailed by the opposition of their status superiors. In Gopalpur, a group of Farmers and Shepherds attacked a group of Stoneworkers who had purchased good rice land in the village. Those Stoneworkers were eventually forced to buy inferior land elsewhere in the village. In general, however, regardless of jati, a person who wishes to advance economically "must be prepared to defend his gains against jealous neighbors. Anyone who buys land is limiting his neighbor's opportunities to buy land. Most people safeguard themselves by tying themselves through indebtedness to a powerful landlord who will give them support when difficulties are encountered" (Beals 1962, 39).

Although the interdependence of jatis is explained in theory by their occupational specialties, the social reality is a bit different. For example, Saltmakers in Gopalpur are farmers and actually produce little salt, which can be bought in shops by those who need it. It is primarily in the context of ritual that jati interdependence is given full play. Recall that Gopalpur villagers required the services of a Washerman when they needed ritually clean garments or cloth; otherwise, most villagers washed their own clothing.

> To arrange a marriage, to set up the doorway of a new house, to stage a drama, or to hold an entertainment, the householder must call on a wide range of jatis. The entertainment of even a modest number of guests requires the presence of the Singer. The Potter must provide new pots in which to cook the food; the Boin from the Farmer jati must carry the pot; the Shepherd must sacrifice the goat; the Crier, a Saltmaker, must invite the guests. To survive, one requires the cooperation of only a few jatis; to enjoy life and do things in the proper manner requires the cooperation of many. (Beals 1962, 41)

Beals's study of Gopalpur documented three dimensions of caste relations in India that have become increasingly significant over time. First, Beals describes a rural village in which jati membership mattered most on ritual occasions. In the last 30 years, cultural practices associated with caste have become even more attenuated or have disappeared as increasingly large numbers of Indians have moved to large cities where they are surrounded by strangers whose caste membership they do not know (Sharma 1999, 37). Migrants still use the idiom of purity and pollution to debate the status of particular castes, but otherwise their understanding of caste usually has nothing to do with ritual status.

Second, Beals describes members of middle-ranking jatis in Gopalpur who treated one another as equals outside of ritual contexts. Subrata Mitra points out that "By the 1960s, electoral mobilization had led to a new phenomenon called horizontal mobilization whereby people situated at comparable levels within the local caste hierarchy came together in caste associations," many of which formed new political parties to support their own interests (1994, 61). Moreover, increased involvement of Indians in capitalist market practices has led to "a proliferation of modern associations that use traditional ties of jati and varna to promote collective economic well-being" (65). For example, a housing trust set up for Brahmins in the Indian state of Karnataka recruits Brahmins from throughout the Karnataka region in an effort to overcome "jati-based division into quarrelling sects of Brahmins" (66). The interests that draw jatis into coalitions of this kind "often turn out to be class interests. . . . This does not mean that caste and class are the same, since commentators note caste as blurring class divisions as often as they express them. Rather it tells us that class and caste are not 'inimical' or antithetical" (Sharma 1999, 68).

Third, Beals showed that middle-ranking jatis in Gopalpur in the 1960s were willing to use violence to block the upward economic mobility of members of a low-ranking jati. Similar behavior was reported in the work of other anthropologists, like Gerald Berreman, who did fieldwork in the late 1950s in the peasant village of Sirkanda in the lower Himalayas of north India. Berreman observed that low-caste people in Sirkanda "do not share, or are not heavily committed to, the 'common official values' which high-caste people affect before outsiders. . . . Low-caste people resent their inferior position and the disadvantages which inhere in it" while "high castes rely heavily on threats of economic and physical sanctions to keep their subordinates in line," such that when low-caste people do publicly endorse "common official values," they do so only out of fear of these sanctions (1962, 15–16).

In recent years, a number of low-caste groups in urban India have undertaken collective efforts to lift themselves off the bottom of society, either by imitating the ritual practices of higher castes (a process called "Sanskritization") or by converting to a non-Hindu religion (e.g., Buddhism or Christianity) in which caste plays no role. According to Dipankar Gupta, this should not surprise us. His research has shown that "castes are, first and foremost, discrete entities with deep pockets of ideological heritage" and that "the element of caste competition is, therefore, a characteristic of the caste order and not a later addition. . . . This implies that the caste system, as a system, worked primarily because it was enforced by power and not by ideological acquiescence" (2005, 412–13). These challenges have had no effect on changing the negative stereotypes of so-called untouchables held by the so-called clean castes. However, the constitution of India prohibits the practice of untouchability, and the national government has acted to improve the lot of the low castes by passing legislation designed to improve their economic and educational opportunities. In some cases, these measures seem to have succeeded, but violent reprisals have been common. In rural areas, many disputes continue to be over land, as in Gopalpur. However, even worse violence has been seen in urban India, as in 1990, when unrest was triggered by publication of a report recommending increases in the numbers of government jobs and reserved college places set aside for members of low castes. At the end of the twentieth century, relations between low-caste and in some localities" with "caste violence . . . recognized as a serious problem in contemporary India" (Sharma 1999, 67).

A key element recognized by all anthropologists who use the concept of "caste" is the endogamy that is enforced, at least in theory, on the members of each ranked group. As van den Berghe put it, membership in such groups is "determined by birth and for life" (1970, 351). Sharma notes the significance of this link between descent and caste, observing that "in societies where descent is regarded as a crucial and persistent principle (however reckoned, and whatever ideological value it is given) almost any social cleavage can become stabilized in a caste-like form" (1999, 85). She suggests the term *castification* to describe a political process by which ethnic or other groups become part of a ranked social order of some kind, probably managed from the top, but which need not develop into a caste system (92–93).

But the principle of descent has also played a central role in the identification and persistence of race, ethnicity, and nation. As noted above, these three categories are all closely bound up with historical developments over the past 500 years that built the modern world. Indeed, these categories are particularly significant in nation-states, and many contemporary nation-states are of very recent, postcolonial origin. Clearly, to make sense of contemporary postcolonial forms of social stratification, we also need to look more closely at the categories of race, ethnicity, and nation.

Race

As we saw in Chapters 1 and 3, the concept of "**race**" developed in the context of European exploration and conquest, beginning in the fifteenth century. Europeans conquered indigenous peoples in the Americas and established colonial political economies that soon depended on the labor of Africans imported as slaves. By the end of the nineteenth century, light-skinned Europeans had established colonial rule over large territories inhabited by darker-skinned peoples, marking the beginnings of a global racial order (see Smedley 1995, 1998; Harrison 1995; Sanjek 1994; Trouillot 1994; Köhler 1978). Some European intellectuals argued at that time that the human species was subdivided into "natural kinds" of human beings called "races" that could be sharply distinguished from one another on the basis of outward phenotypic appearance. All individuals assigned to the same race were assumed to share many other common features, such as language or intelligence, of which phenotype was only the outward index. *Race* was used both to explain human diversity and to justify the domination of indigenous peoples and the enslavement of Africans.

European thinkers, including many early anthropologists, devised schemes for ranking the "races of mankind" from lowest to highest. Not surprisingly, the "white" northern Europeans at the apex of imperial power were placed at the top of this global hierarchy. Darker-skinned peoples, like the indigenous inhabitants of the Americas or of Asia, were ranked somewhere in the middle. But Africans, whom Europeans had bought and sold as slaves and whose homelands in Africa were later conquered and incorporated into European empires, ranked lowest of all. In this way, the identification of races was transformed into **racism**: the systematic oppression of one or more socially defined "races" by another socially defined "race" that is justified in terms of the supposedly inherent biological superiority of the rulers and the supposed inherent biological inferiority of those they rule. It is important to emphasize once again that all the so-called races of human beings are *imagined communities*. As we emphasized in Chapter 3, there are *no* major biological discontinuities within the

---

race A human population category whose boundaries allegedly correspond to distinct sets of biological attributes.

racism The systematic oppression of one or more socially defined "races" by another socially defined "race" that is justified in terms of the supposedly inherent biological superiority of the rulers and the supposed inherent biological inferiority of those they rule.

human species that correspond to the supposed racial boundaries that nineteenth-century European observers thought they had discovered. This means that the traditional concept of biological "race" in Western society is incoherent and biologically meaningless.

Nevertheless, racial thinking persists at the beginning of the twenty-first century, suggesting that racial categories have their origins not in biology but in society. And as we saw in earlier chapters, anthropologists have long argued that race is a culturally constructed social category whose members are identified on the basis of certain selected phenotypic features (e.g., skin color) that all are said to share. The end result is a highly distorted but more or less coherent set of criteria that members of a society can use to assign people they see to one or another culturally defined racial category. Once these criteria exist, members of society can treat racial categories *as if* they reflect biological reality, using them to build institutions that include or exclude particular culturally defined races. In this way, race can become "real" in its consequences, even if it has no reality in biology.

The social category of "race" is a relatively recent invention. Audrey Smedley reminds us that in the worlds of European classical antiquity and through the Middle Ages, "no structuring of equality . . . was associated with people *because of their skin color*" (1998, 693; emphasis in original), and Faye Harrison points out that "phenotype prejudice was not institutionalized before the sixteenth century" (1995, 51). By the nineteenth century, European thinkers (some early anthropologists among them) were attempting to classify all humans in the world into a few, mutually exclusive racial categories. Significantly, from that time until this, as Harrison emphasizes, "blackness has come to symbolize the social bottom" (1998, 612; see also Smedley 1998, 694–95).

White domination of European American racial hierarchies has been a constant, but some anthropologists who study the cultural construction of whiteness point out that even in the United States "whiteness" is not monolithic and that the cultural attributes supposedly shared by "white people" have varied in different times and places. Some members of white ruling groups in the southern United States, for example, have traditionally distanced themselves from lower-class whites, whom they call "white trash"; and the meaning of whiteness in South Africa has been complicated by differences of class and culture separating British South Africans from Afrikaners (Hartigan 1997). For that matter, "blackness"

is not monolithic, either. In Haiti, for example, white French colonists were expelled at independence in 1804, but an internal racial divide has persisted since then between the mass of black Haitians descended from freed slaves and a minority of wealthy, well-educated "mulattos" who originally comprised the offspring of white French fathers and black slave mothers. Throughout Haitian history, this mulatto elite has struggled to distinguish itself from the black majority, in the face of outsiders who have steadfastly refused to recognize any difference between the two groups. At times of unrest, however, the U.S. government has regularly supported members of this elite, who have defended their interests by ruthlessly dominating other Haitians, especially the poor (Schiller and Fouron 2001). In the United States, the sharp "caste-like" racial divide between blacks and whites is currently being complicated by new immigrants identified with so-called brown/Hispanic and yellow/Asian racial categories. Harrison and others recognize that racial categorization and repression take different forms in different places.

Colorism in Nicaragua

Anthropologist Roger Lancaster argues that in Nicaragua racism exists but that it is "not as absolute and encompassing a racism as that which one encounters in the United States" even though it remains, in his opinion, "a significant social problem" (1992, 215). One dimension of Nicaraguan racism contrasts the Spanish-speaking *mestizo* (or "mixed" European and indigenous) majority of the highlands with the indigenous Miskitos and African Caribbeans along the Atlantic coast. The highland mestizos Lancaster knew tended to regard these coastal groups as backward, inferior, and dangerous. These notions were overlaid with political suspicions deriving from the fact that Lancaster's informants were Sandinistas and that some Miskito factions had fought with the Contras against the Sandinistas after the Sandinistas deposed the dictator Anastasio Somoza in 1979.

But Lancaster came to see racism toward the coastal peoples as simply an extension of the pattern of race relations internal to highland mestizo culture that he calls **colorism**: a system of color identities negotiated situationally along a continuum between white and black (Figure 14.6). In colorism, no fixed race boundaries exist. Instead, individuals negotiate their color identity anew in every social situation they enter, with the result that the color they might claim or be accorded changes from situation to situation.

Lancaster's informants used three different systems of color classification. The first, or "phenotypic" system, has three categories—*blanco* (white), *moreno* (brown),

---

colorism A system of social identities negotiated situationally along a continuum of skin colors between white and black.

In Their Own Words

On the Butt Size of Barbie and Shani

Dolls and Race in the United States

Anthropologist Elizabeth Chin writes about race and Barbie dolls, based on some hands-on research.

The Shani line of dolls introduced by Mattel in 1991 reduces race to a simulacrum consisting of phenotypical features: skin color, hair, and butt. Ann DuCille . . . has discussed much of their complex and contradictory nature, highlighting two central issues: derriere and hair. According to DuCille's interviews with Shani designers, the dolls have been remanufactured to give the illusion of a higher, rounder butt than other Barbies. This has been accomplished, they told her, by pitching Shani's back at a different angle and changing some of the proportions of her hips. I had heard these and other rumors from students at the college where I teach: "Shani's butt is bigger than the other Barbies' butts," "Shani dolls have bigger breasts than Barbie," "Shani dolls have bigger thighs than Barbie." DuCille rightly wonders why a bigger butt is necessarily an attribute of blackness, tying this obsession to turn-of-the-century strains of scientific racism.

Deciding I had to see for myself, I pulled my Shani doll off my office bookshelf, stripped her naked, and placed her on my desk next to a naked Barbie doll that had been cruelly mutilated by a colleague's dog (her arms were chewed off and her head had puncture wounds, but the rest was unharmed). Try as I might, manipulating the dolls in ways both painful and obscene, I could find no difference between them, even after prying their legs off and smashing their bodies apart. As far as I have been able to determine, Shani's bigger butt is an illusion (see photo). The faces of Shani and Barbie dolls are more visibly different than their behinds, yet still, why these differences could be considered natural indicators of race is perplexing. As a friend of mine remarked acidly, "They still look like they've had plastic surgery." The most telling difference between Shani and Barbie is at the base of the cranium, where Shani bears a raised mark similar to a branding iron scar: © 1990 MATTEL INC. Barbie's head reads simply © MATTEL INC. Despite claims of redesign, both Barbie and Shani's torsos bear a 1966 copyright, and although DuCille asserts that Shani's

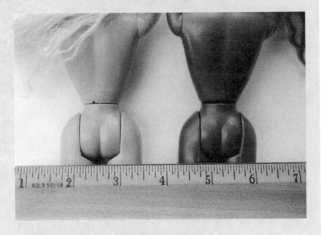

Barbie and Shani from behind.

legs are shaped differently than Barbie's, their legs are imprinted with the same part numbers. This all strongly suggests that despite claims and rumors to the contrary, Shani and Barbie are the same from the neck down.

These ethnically correct dolls demonstrate one of the abiding aspects of racism: that a stolid belief in racial difference can shape people's perceptions so profoundly that they will find difference and make something of it, no matter how imperceptible or irrelevant its physical manifestation might be. If I had to smash two dolls to bits in order to see if their butts were different sizes, the differences must be small indeed: holding them next to each other revealed no difference whatsoever—except color—regardless of the positioning (crack to crack or cheek to cheek). With the butt index so excruciatingly small, its meaning as a racial signifier becomes frighteningly problematic. Like the notion of race itself, Shani's derriere has a social meaning that is out of all proportion to its scientific measurement.

Source: Chin 1999, 311–13.

and *negro* (black)—that people use to describe the various skin tones that can be seen among Nicaraguan mestizos: "Nicaraguan national culture is mestizo; people's physical characteristics are primarily indigenous; and in the terms of this phenotypic system, most people are moreno. In this system, *negro* can denote either persons

of African ancestry or sometimes persons of purely indigenous appearance, whether they are culturally classified as Indio or mestizo" (1992, 217).

Lancaster calls the second system Nicaraguans use the "polite" system, in which all the colors in the phenotypic system are "inflated." That is, Europeans are

Figure 14.6 This photograph of Brazilian children shows a range of skin tones. In some parts of Latin America, such as Nicaragua and Brazil, such variation is used to create a system of classification based on lightness or darkness of skin tone that assigns people with relatively lighter skin to higher status, a phenomenon that anthropologist Roger Lancaster calls colorism.

called *chele* (a Mayan word meaning "blue," referring to the stereotypically blue eyes of people of European ancestry), morenos are called blanco, and negros are called moreno. Polite terms are used in the presence of the person about whom one is speaking, and Lancaster was told that it was "a grave and violent offence to refer to a black-skinned person as *negro*" (1992, 217). In rural areas, for similar reasons, Indians are called *mestizos* rather than *Indios*.

Lancaster calls the third system of color terms the "pejorative and/or affectionate" system. This system has only two terms, *chele* (fairer skin and lighter hair) and *negro* (darker skin, darker hair). For example, when the less powerful man in an interaction feels he is being imposed upon by the more powerful man, the former might express his displeasure by addressing the latter as *chele* or *negro*, both of which would be seen as insulting. Paradoxically, members of families call one another *negro* or *negrito mio* as affectionate and intimate terms of address, perhaps precisely because these terms are "informal" and violate the rules of polite discourse (1992, 218).

Lancaster discovered that "Whiteness is a desired quality, and polite discourse inflates its descriptions of people" (1992, 219). People compete in different settings to claim whiteness. In some settings, individuals may be addressed as *blanco* if everyone else has darker

skin; but in other settings, they may have to yield the claim of whiteness to someone else with lighter skin than theirs and accept classification as *moreno*.

Because it allows people some freedom of maneuver in claiming higher-status color for themselves, Nicaraguan colorism may seem less repressive than the rigid black–white racial dichotomy traditional in the United States. Lancaster points out, however, that all three systems of colorist usage presuppose white superiority and black inferiority. "Africanos, Indios, and lower-class mestizos have been lumped together under a single term—*negro*—that signifies defeat" (1992, 223). Lancaster is not optimistic about the possibilities of successfully overturning this system any time soon in Nicaragua. Similarly, Harrison argues that racial solidarity and rebellion are hard to achieve or sustain in societies like Nicaragua, and she is not optimistic that adoption of a similar system in the United States would improve race relations. On the contrary, she fears that a "more multishaded discourse" would be more likely to contribute to "an enduring stigmatization of blackness" than to "democratization and the dismantling of race" (1998, 618–19).

Ethnicity

ethnicity A principle of social classification used to create groups based on selected cultural features such as language, religion, or dress. Ethnicity emerges from historical processes that incorporate distinct social groups into a single political structure under conditions of inequality.

For anthropologists, ethnic groups are social groups whose members distinguish themselves (and/or are distinguished by others) in terms of **ethnicity**—that is, in terms of distinctive cultural features, such as language, religion, or dress. Ethnicity, like race, is a culturally

In Their Own Words

The Politics of Ethnicity

Stanley Tambiah reflects on the late twentieth-century upsurge in ethnic conflict that few people predicted because many assumed that ethnic particularisms would disappear within modern nation-states.

The late-twentieth-century reality is evidenced by the fact that ethnic groups, rather than being mostly minority or marginal subgroups at the edges of society, expected in due course to assimilate or weaken, have figured as major "political" elements and major political collective actors in several societies. Moreover, if in the past we typically viewed an ethnic group as a subgroup of a larger society, today we are also faced with instances of majority ethnic groups within a polity or nation exercising preferential or "affirmative" policies on the basis of that majority status.

The first consideration that confirms ethnic conflict as a major reality of our time is not simply its ubiquity alone, but also its cumulative increase in frequency and intensity of occurrence. Consider these conflicts, by no means an exhaustive listing, that have occurred since the sixties (some of them have a longer history, of course): conflicts between anglophone and francophone in Canada; Catholic and Protestant in Northern Ireland; Walloon and Fleming in Belgium; Chinese and Malay in Malaysia; Greek and Turk in Cyprus; Jews and other minorities on the one hand and Great Russians on the other in the Soviet Union; and Ibo and Hausa and Yoruba in Nigeria; the East Indians and Creoles in Guyana. Add, to these instances, upheavals that became climactic in recent years: the Sinhala–Tamil war in Sri Lanka, the Sikh–Hindu, and Muslim–Hindu, confrontations in India, the Chackma–Muslim turmoil in Bangladesh, the actions of the Fijians against Indians in Fiji, the Pathan–Bihari clashes in Pakistan, and last, but not least, the inferno in Lebanon, and the serious erosion of human rights currently manifest in Israeli actions in Gaza and the West Bank. That there is possibly no end to these eruptions, and that they are worldwide has been forcibly brought to our attention by a century-old difference that exploded in March 1988 between Christian Armenians and Muslim Azerbaijanis in the former U.S.S.R.

Most of these conflicts have involved force and violence, homicide, arson, and destruction of property. Civilian riots have evoked action by security forces: sometimes as counteraction to quell them, sometimes in collusion with the civilian aggressors, sometimes both kinds of action in sequence. Events of this nature have happened in Sri Lanka, Malaysia, India, Zaire, Guyana, and Nigeria. Mass killings of civilians by armed forces have occurred in Uganda and in Guatemala, and large losses of civilian lives have been recorded in Indonesia, Pakistan, India, and Sri Lanka.

The escalation of ethnic conflicts has been considerably aided by the amoral business of gunrunning and free trade in the technology of violence, which enable not only dissident groups to successfully resist the armed forces of the state, but also civilians to battle with each other with lethal weapons. The classical definition of the state as the authority invested with the monopoly of force has become a sick joke. After so many successful liberations and resistance movements in many parts of the globe, the techniques of guerrilla resistance now constitute a systematized and exportable knowledge. Furthermore, the easy access to the technology of warfare by groups in countries that are otherwise deemed low in literacy and in economic development—we have seen what Afghan resistance can do with American guns—is paralleled by another kind of international fraternization among resistance groups who have little in common save their resistance to the status quo in their own countries, and who exchange knowledge of guerrilla tactics and the art of resistance. Militant groups in Japan, Germany, Lebanon, Libya, Sri Lanka, and India have international networks of collaboration, not unlike—perhaps more solidary than—the diplomatic channels that exist between mutually wary sovereign countries and the great powers. The end result is that the professionalized killing is no longer the monopoly of state armies and police forces. The internationalization of the technology of destruction, evidenced in the form of terrorism and counterterrorism, has shown a face of free-market capitalism in action unsuspected by Adam Smith and by Immanuel Wallerstein.

Source: Tambiah 1989, 431–32.

constructed concept. Many anthropologists today would agree with John and Jean Comaroff that ethnicity is created by historical processes that incorporate distinct social groups into a single political structure under conditions of inequality (1992, 55–57; see also Williams 1989, Alonso 1994). The Comaroffs recognize that ethnic consciousness existed in precolonial and precapitalist societies; however, they and most contemporary anthropologists have been more interested in forms of ethnic consciousness that were generated under capitalist colonial domination.

Ethnicity develops as members of different groups try to make sense of the material constraints they experience within the single political structure that confines them. This is sometimes described as a struggle between *self-ascription* (i.e., insiders' efforts to define their own identity) and *other-ascription* (i.e., outsiders' efforts to define the identities of other groups). In the Comaroffs' view, furthermore, the ruling group turns both itself and the subordinated groups into *classes* because all subordinated social groupings lose independent control "over the means of production and/or reproduction" (1992, 56).

One outcome of this struggle is the appearance of new **ethnic groups** and identities that are not continuous with any single earlier cultural group (Comaroff and Comaroff 1992, 56). In northern Cameroon, for example, successive German, French, and British colonial officials relied on local Muslim chiefs to identify for them significant local social divisions and adopted the Muslim practice of lumping together all the myriad non-Muslim peoples of the hills and plains and calling them *Haabe* or *Kirdi*—that is, "pagans." To the extent, therefore, that Guidar, Daba, Fali, Ndjegn, or Guiziga were treated alike by colonial authorities and came to share a common situation and set of interests, they developed a new, more inclusive level of ethnic identity, like the young man we met in Guider who introduced himself to us as "just a Kirdi boy." This new, postcolonial "Kirdi" identity, like many others, cannot be linked to any single precolonial cultural reality but has been constructed out of cultural materials borrowed from a variety of non-Muslim indigenous groups who were incorporated as "Pagans" within the colonial political order (see Figure 14.7 and EthnoProfile 14.3: Guider).

The Comaroffs argue that a particular structure of nesting opposed identities was quite common throughout European colonies in Africa. The lowest and least inclusive consisted of local groups, often called "tribes,"

EthnoProfile 14.3

Guider

Region: Western Africa

Nation: Cameroon

Population: 18,000 (1976)

Environment: Savanna

Livelihood: Farming, commerce, civil service, cattle raising

Political organization:
Traditionally, an emirate; today, part of a modern nation-state

For more information:
Schultz, Emily. 1984. From Pagan to Pullo: Ethnic identity change in northern cameroon. *Africa* 54(1): 46–64.

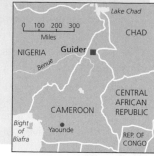

who struggled to dominate one another within separate colonial states. The middle levels consisted of a variety of entities that crossed local boundaries, sometimes called "supertribes" or "nations." For example, the British administered the settler colony of southern Rhodesia (later to become Zimbabwe) according to the policy of "indirect rule," which used indigenous "tribal" authorities to maintain order on the local level. The effect of indirect rule was thus both to reinforce "tribal" identities where they already existed and to create them where they had been absent in precolonial times. Two such tribal identities, those of the Shona and Ndebele, became preeminent; and each gave rise to its own "(supratribal) nationalist movement."

Both movements joined together in a "patriotic front" to win a war of independence fought against white settlers. This confrontation took place at the highest level of the ethnic hierarchy, which the Comaroffs call "race." At this level, "Europeans" and "Africans" opposed one another, and each group developed its own encompassing ethnic identity. For example, Africans dealing regularly with Europeans began to conceive of such a thing as "African culture" (as opposed to European culture) and "pan-African solidarity" (to counter the hegemony of the European colonizers). Conversely, in the British settler colonies of southern and eastern Africa, European immigrants defined themselves in opposition to Africans by developing their own "settler-colonial order" based on a caricature of aristocratic Victorian English society (Comaroff and Comaroff 1992, 58).

---

ethnic groups Social groups that are distinguished from one another on the basis of ethnicity.

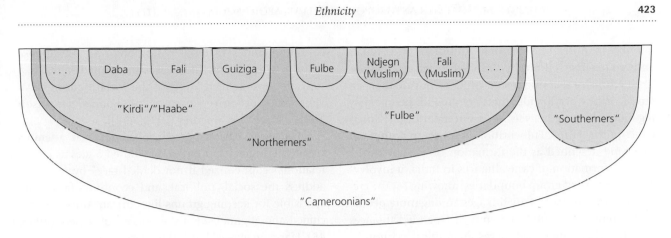

Figure 14.7 Nesting identities in northern Cameroon (1976).

Because ethnic groups are incorporated into the colony on unequal terms (and, if we follow the Comaroffs, in different class positions), it is not surprising to discover that many individuals in colonies attempted to achieve upward mobility by manipulating their ethnicity. Anthropological studies of such attempts at ethnic mobility constitute, as the Comaroffs put it, "the very stuff of the ethnography of urban Africa" (1992, 63); and one of us (E. A. S.) investigated ethnic mobility in the northern Cameroonian town of Guider.

Guider began as a small settlement of non-Muslim Guidar. In 1830 it was brought into the Muslim Fulbe empire of Yola and remained a Fulbe stronghold under subsequent colonial rule. The Fulbe remained numerically dominant in town until after World War II; by 1958, however, individuals from over a dozen non-Fulbe groups had migrated to town, primarily from the surrounding countryside. By 1976, 83 percent of household heads in town were recent migrants, and 74 percent did not claim Fulbe origins.

In the Comaroffs' terms, all these groups, including the Fulbe, had lost political and economic independence with the coming of colonial rule and, under conditions of inequality, were incorporated by the colonizers as ethnic groups into first the German and later the French colony of Cameroon. The Europeans uniformly admired the political, cultural, and religious accomplishments of the Muslim Fulbe. In their own version of indirect rule, they allowed Fulbe chiefs to administer territories they had controlled prior to colonization and, in some cases, handed over to them additional territories whose residents had successfully resisted Fulbe domination in precolonial times.

In 1976, the local ethnic hierarchy in Guider placed Fulbe at the top and recent non-Muslim, non-Fulfulde-speaking migrants from rural areas at the bottom. But in the middle were numerous individuals and families of Fulfulde-speaking Muslims who could claim, and in some cases be accorded, recognition as Fulbe by others in the town. For example, two young men whom I hired as field assistants first described themselves to me as "100 percent Fulbe." As I got to know them better, however, I learned that the family of one was Ndjegn and the family of the other was Fali. Neither young man saw anything contradictory about being both Fulbe and Ndjegn or Fulbe and Fali. In fact, each ethnic identity was emphasized in different situations. Ndjegn and Fali ethnicity mattered to them in the domain of family and kinship; these ethnic identities nested within the broader Fulbe ethnicity that mattered in urban public settings, especially high-status ones associated with education and cash salaries.

Indeed, by 1976, Fulbe identity had become an achieved status; it was the ethnicity claimed by the upwardly mobile in Guider. It was therefore possible for people born outside the dominant Fulbe ethnic group to achieve Fulbe status in their lifetimes (Schultz 1984). To do this, they had to be successful at three tasks: they had to adopt the Fulbe language (Fulfulde), the Fulbe religion (Islam), and the Fulbe "way of life," which was identified with urban customs and the traditional Muslim high culture of the western Sudan. Many Fulbe claimed that descent from one or another Fulbe lineage was needed in order to claim Fulbe identity. Nevertheless, they seemed willing to accept "Fulbeized Pagans" as Fulbe (e.g., by giving their daughters to them as brides) because those people were committed defenders of the urban Fulbe way of life. Those who were "Fulbeizing," however, came from societies in which descent had never been an important criterion of group membership. For these people, ethnic identity depended on the territorial affiliation of the group to which they were currently committed. From their perspective, in becoming Fulbe, they had simply chosen to commit themselves to Fulfulde, Islam, and life in "Fulbe territory," the town.

This example illustrates some of the key attributes often associated with ethnicity: it is fluid, malleable, something that can be voluntarily embraced or successfully ignored in different situations. Ambitious individuals and groups in an ethnically stratified society can manipulate ethnicity as a resource in order to pursue their interests. When nesting identities are present, people may regularly alternate between different identities in different contexts. Ethnic Fulbeization in northern Cameroon might be described as the formation of a "supertribe." Like the formation of caste alliances in India, it involves the expansion of group boundaries, allowing for the creation of stronger solidarity linkages among more people of different backgrounds. When such expanded alliances actually achieve increased success in political, economic, and social struggles, they may affect the very structures that gave rise to them (as the Shona-Ndebele alliance did in Zimbabwe) (Comaroff and Comaroff 1992, 61).

For dominant groups, however, defense of ethnic identity can be a way of defending privilege. Those who dominate may be threatened rather than flattered by subordinate groups who master elite cultural practices. Members of the dominant ethnic group may stress their cultural superiority and question the eligibility (and even the humanity) of subordinate groups who challenge them. It is at this point that anthropologists like Faye Harrison would argue that ethnicity becomes *racialized*. In her view, race differs from ethnicity precisely because it is used to "mark and stigmatize certain peoples as essentially and irreconcilably different, while treating the privileges of others as normative. This quality of difference, whether constructed through a biodeterminist or culturalist idiom, is what constitutes the social category and material phenomenon of 'race'" (Harrison 1998, 613). Racialization in Western societies would thus bear a family resemblance to castification in South Asian societies.

Harrison argues that by the middle of the nineteenth century white northern Europeans, connecting their growing colonial power with their whiteness, began to racialize ethnic, religious, or class stereotypes associated with other Europeans (e.g., Irish, Jews, Italians, Poles, Slavs), viewing them as less human or, at any rate, differently human from themselves and attributing this difference to biologically inherited factors (1995, 52). Conversely, some racialized ethnic groups, such as the Irish, were able to reverse this process once they moved to the United States, shedding their stigma and *ethnicizing* into just another "ordinary" American ethnic group. Some social scientists might argue, or at any rate hope, that all racialized groups should be able to ethnicize sooner or later. But such a perspective risks ignoring the plight of racialized groups whose status never seems to change. Historians argue, for example, that the Irish were able to ethnicize precisely because they accepted the racialization of African Americans (Allen 1997). Indeed,

operating under material conditions that presuppose white privilege, nonwhite races in the United States "historically have defined layers of the social bottom vis-à-vis several successive waves of immigrants" (Harrison 1995, 49; see also Smedley, 1998, 690).

For these reasons, Harrison argues that attempts to interpret race relations in the United States as ethnic relations "euphemized if not denied race" by failing to address the social, political, and economic factors responsible for keeping groups like African Americans excluded and stigmatized at the bottom of society (1995, 48). Harrison agrees that African Americans do engage in "ethnicizing practices emphasizing cultural heritage," but in her view such practices have never been able to overcome the "caste-like assumptions of the most systematically oppressive racial orders" like that of the United States (1998, 613; 1995, 54; see also Sharma 1999, 91).

As we have seen, anthropologists have argued about which technical terms ought to be used to describe which forms of identity under which circumstances. We agree with Ursula Sharma that social scientists should use a particular term only if it highlights a dimension of social relationships that would otherwise go unnoticed (1999, 93). Thus, ethnicity probably needs to be supplemented by the notion of race in order to distinguish the dehumanizing confinement of certain social groups to the bottom layers of society, and caste's emphasis on endogamy and hierarchical ranking highlights features of social organization that elude the usual scope of race, class, or ethnicity. Anthropologist Pnina Werbner (1997) further builds on these distinctions when she argues that in order to make progress in analyzing ethnic violence as a social force, practices of "everyday" ethnic identification need to be distinguished from racism.

Based on her research on multicultural social relations in Britain, Werbner distinguishes two different social processes, objectification and reification. *Objectification* simply refers to the intentional construction of a collective public identity; it is the process that produces "everyday" or "normal" ethnicity. Ethnic identities are distinguished by the fact that they are "evoked situationally . . . highlighted pragmatically, and objectified relationally and contingently" and by the fact that they focus on two key issues, "a demand for ethnic rights, including religious rights, and a demand for protection against racism" (1997, 241). Social relations between objectified ethnic groups are based on a "rightful performance" of multiple, shifting, highly valued forms of collective identification, based on religion, dress, food, language, and politics. Interaction between groups that differentiate themselves along such lines ordinarily does not lead to violent confrontations (229). *Reification*, by contrast, is a form of negative racial or ethnic absolutism that encourages the violent elimination of targeted groups and is central to the practice of racism. Reification "distorts and silences"; it is "essentialist in the pernicious sense" (229). It is violence that differentiates racism from everyday ethnicity; and if ethnic confrontation becomes violent, then it turns into a form of racism (234–35). For Werbner, making this distinction is crucial in multiethnic situations because when people fail to distinguish nonviolent forms of everyday ethnicity from racism, they are, in effect, criminalizing valid ethnic sentiments and letting racists off the hook (233).

Nation and Nationalism

As we saw earlier, state societies are not new social forms. Nation-states, however, are a far more recent invention. Prior to the French Revolution, European states were ruled by kings and emperors whose access to the throne was officially believed to have been ordained by God. After the French Revolution in 1789, which thoroughly discredited the divine right of kings, rulers needed to find a new basis on which to found legitimate state authority. The solution that was eventually adopted rooted political authority in **nations**: groups of people believed to share the same history, culture, language, and even the same physical substance. Nations were associated with territories, as were states, and a **nation-state** came to be viewed as an ideal political unit in which national identity and political territory coincided.

The building of the first nation-states is closely associated with the rise and spread of capitalism and its related cultural institutions during the nineteenth century. Following the demise of European colonial empires and the end of the Cold War, the final decades of the twentieth century witnessed a scramble in which former colonies or newly independent states struggled to turn themselves into nation-states capable of competing successfully in what anthropologist Liisa Malkki has called a "transnational culture of nationalism" (1992).

On the one hand, the ideology of the nation-state implies that every nation is entitled to its own state. On the other hand, it also suggests that a state containing heterogeneous populations *might be made into a nation* if all peoples within its borders could somehow be made to adopt a common **nationality**: a sense of identification with and loyalty to the nation-state. The attempt made by government officials and state institutions to instill into the citizens of a state this sense of nationality has been called **nation building**, or **nationalism**.

As we learned in our discussion of ethnicity, states are the very political structures that generate ethnic identities among the various cultural groupings that are incorporated within them on unequal terms. Thus, anthropologists studying state formation often find themselves studying ethnicity as well as nationalism (Alonso 1994). However, groups with different forms of identity that continue to persist within the boundaries of the nation-state often are viewed as obstacles to nationalism. If such groups successfully resist assimilation into the nationality that the state is supposed to represent, their very existence calls into question the legitimacy of the state. Indeed, if their numbers are sufficient, they might well claim that they are a separate nation, entitled to a state of their own!

To head off this possibility, nationalist ideologies typically include some cultural features of subordinate cultural groups. Thus, although nationalist traditions are invented, they are not created out of thin air. The prototype of national identity is usually based on attributes of the dominant group, into which are integrated specially chosen elements of the cultural practices of other, subordinated groups. That is, those who control the nation-state will try to define nationality in ways that "identify and ensure loyalty among citizens . . . the goal is to create criteria of inclusion and exclusion to control and delimit the group" (Williams 1989, 407). The hope seems to be that if at least some aspects of their ways of life are acknowledged as essential to national identity subordinated groups will identify with and be loyal to the nation. Following Gramsci, Brackette Williams calls this process a **transformist hegemony** in which nationalist ideologues are attempting to "create purity out of impurity" (1989, 429, 435).

National leaders will measure the trustworthiness and loyalty of citizens by how closely they copy (or refuse to copy) the cultural practices that define national identity (Williams 1989, 407). Unfortunately, the practices of subordinated groups that are not incorporated into nationalist ideology are regularly marginalized and devalued. Continued adherence to such practices may be viewed as subversive, and practitioners may suffer

---

nation A group of people believed to share the same history, culture, language, and even physical substance.

nation-state An ideal political unit in which national identity and political territory coincide.

nationality A sense of identification with and loyalty to a nation-state.

nation building (or nationalism) The attempt made by government officials to instill into the citizens of a state a sense of nationality.

transformist hegemony A nationalist program to define nationality in a way that preserves the cultural domination of the ruling group while including enough cultural features from subordinated groups to ensure their loyalty.

Anthropology in Everyday Life

Anthropology and Democracy

There is a trend among anthropologists to engage in policy work as partners with other groups. Their support and expertise can enable the people most affected by government policies to become effective advocates for their own causes. Even beyond ethnography, an anthropologist may act as advocate, observer, and witness in the cause of democracy and human rights. For example, anthropologists have been drawn into a growing debate about what democracy has been and can be. In particular, their work has helped to show that formal Western electoral politics may produce less democratic outcomes than other, traditional institutions.

Anthropologist Serge Tcherkézoff (1998) followed policy debates about the shape democracy ought to take in the independent nation of Samoa (see EthnoProfile 14.4: Samoa). Traditionally, Samoa had been a land of villages, each of which was governed by a council of *matai*, or "sacred chiefs." This system survived Christian missionaries, German colonization, and the effects of 42 years as a protectorate of New Zealand. A referendum sponsored by the United Nations in 1962 led to independence, and the people of what was called Western Samoa until 1997 voted to set up a parliamentary system of national government (Figure 14.8). However, their constitution specified that only matai could vote and run for office. In 1990, the law was changed to allow all citizens to vote, but matai were still the only ones allowed to run for office.

Does this hybrid of Western parliamentary system and the Samoan *faamatoi*, or "chief-system," represent an undemocratic attempt by chiefly "aristocrats" to maintain power within formally democratic political institutions? In Tcherkézoff's opinion, the question is deeply misleading, because it rests on a fundamental misunderstanding of how the Samoan chief-system functions. He points out that if outsiders insist on thinking of matai as aristocrats, then there are no families in Samoa who are not aristocratic. This is because each matai or chief is actually the head of an extended family. Each extended family is held together by kinship connections, joint ownership of land, and joint participation in rituals directed to their founding ancestor.

Matai, in fact, means "the one who bears the family name," and members of each extended family choose the person who will be ritually invested with this title. It is the job of each matai to serve his family and his matai name by leading worship directed to the ancestor and engaging in other activities designed to elevate the reputation of his extended family. If a matai fails to live up to these expectations, his extended family can strip him of his title and give it to someone else. Every family has a matai, which is why Tcherkézoff says that there are no families that are not chiefly families; and

EthnoProfile 14.4

Samoa

Region: Oceania

Nation: Western Samoa

Population: 182,000

Environment: Tropical island

Livelihood: Horticulture, fishing, wage labor in capital

Political organization: Ranked, with linguistic markers for high- and low-status people; now part of a modern nation-state

For more information: Duranti, Alessandro. 1994. *From grammar to politics, Linguistic anthropology in a western Samoan village.* Berkeley: University of California Press.

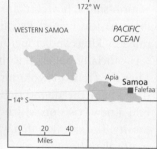

matais serve at the will of the kin who choose them, which is why, he tells us, that "when Samoans heard about 'democracy,' they said that they 'already have it'" (1998, 423).

So why are Samoans arguing about the connection between the Matai system and democracy? As Tcherkézoff explains, this debate involves a variety of different ideas about what democracy means and which kinds of institutional arrangements are most likely to ensure it. Those who want universal suffrage favor a view of democracy in which the emphasis is on individual freedom: anyone can run for office, and anyone can vote. They point out, for example, that traditionally nobody becomes a matai until he has served his family for many years and his predecessor has died, which limits the field of possible parliamentary candidates to one (relatively) old man per extended family. How can it be democratic to restrict the opportunities of younger people to run for office? These sorts of arguments fit well with traditional Western arguments that speak of democracy in connection with individual freedom from arbitrary restrictions.

But those Samoans who want the matai system to continue stress that it is more democratic than universal suffrage. It creates representatives who can never forget that they are responsible to those who elected them—the other members of their extended family. In thinking about democracy in this

Figure 14.8 The parliament building in Samoa. Samoans today are taking part in a debate that involves a variety of ideas about what democracy means and what kinds of institutional arrangements are most likely to ensure it.

way, these Samoans are refusing to reduce democratic citizenship to the right to vote. Rather, they take the view that democracy obligates those who make political decisions for others to remain accountable and accessible to those whom they represent (O'Donnell and Schmitter 1986; Rubin 1997). Thus, the matai system ensures that every extended family will be represented in some form in the electoral process, and any matais elected to parliament will not be able to ignore the wishes of those who put them in office.

Politics in Samoa also has a regional dimension. Tcherkézoff points out that Samoa primarily has been a nation of villages but that the capital city has been growing in size in recent years. Many of those who live in the growing urban area depend more on wage labor and less on agriculture and fishing, the activities central to village life where matais traditionally exercised their authority. Thus, those who want to preserve the matai system also defend it as a way of maintaining equality between those who live in the city and those who still live in rural areas. They fear that if parliamentary elections were to operate in terms of universal suffrage,

Samoa would be fractured into two societies: an urban sector with a Western political system and no way to hold their parliamentary representatives accountable and a rural sector in which matais still exist but have become powerless guardians of local folklore. Should this happen, "then some Samoans say that 'democracy' will not be achieved and will even go backwards" (1998, 427).

As Tcherkézoff makes clear, the policy debate about democracy in Samoa is complex and subtle: Samoans have a sophisticated understanding of the advantages and drawbacks of different democratic political forms, some of which are indigenous to Samoa and some of which came there from elsewhere. "The problem is that Samoa has the chance to build its future on ideas and experiences that come both from the faamatai tradition and from the Western tradition of democracy and to maybe create a new synthesis where the advent of democracy will not just be the replacement of hierarchy (in the faamatai) by inequality (in the Western-style politics). There lies the real question of the future of the country" (1998, 430).

persecution and even extermination. Other groups, by contrast, may be totally ignored. Alonso points out, for example, that Mexican nationalism is "mestizo nationalism" rooted in the official doctrine that the Mexican people are a hybrid of European whites and the indigenous people they conquered. African slaves were also a part of early colonial Mexican society, but nationalist ideology erases their presence entirely (1994, 396).

Australian Nationalism

Australia began its existence as a settler colony of Great Britain. Over the past 200 years, the prototype of Australian national identity was based on the racial and cultural features of the settler population. The phenotypically distinct indigenous people, called "Aborigines" by the settlers, were completely excluded from citizenship. Settlers' claims to land and other resources rested on the doctrine of *terra nullius*: the idea that, before their arrival, the land had been owned by nobody. In European capitalist terms, "ownership" meant permanent settlement and "improvement" of the land by clearing it and planting crops or grazing animals. Since the Aborigines living on the continent of Australia were foraging peoples who did not depend on domesticated plants or animals, European settlers felt justified in displacing them and "improving" the land as they saw fit. Aborigines were viewed as a "dying race," and white settler domination was taken as a foregone conclusion.

But times change, and currently Australians are seriously rethinking the nature of Australian national identity. Indeed, according to Robert Tonkinson (1998), two kinds of nation building are going on at the same time. First, an intense national debate has developed in recent years that would favor creating a new Australian republic whose constitution would affirm the existence and rights of the country's indigenous peoples. For that to happen, however, "the nation as a whole must reimagine itself via a myth-making process, in which the search for distinctively Australian national symbols may well include elements drawn from indigenous cultures" (287–88).

And this will not be easy because such a myth-making process (or transformist hegemony) immediately runs up against the second, alternative myth-making process generated by Australia's indigenous minorities, who have for decades struggled to construct for themselves a sense of "pan-Aboriginal" identity. Since the 1970s, a central theme in this struggle has been the demand for land rights, which was given an enormous boost by the decision handed down by the High Court of Australia in 1992 in the case of Eddie Mabo and others versus the State of Queensland. The so-called Mabo decision rejected the doctrine of terra nullius. It proclaimed that the right of Australia's indigenous peoples to ownership of their original lands was protected by Australian common law.

The symbolic significance of the Mabo decision has been enormous. For those Australians who want to remake Australian nationalism, Mabo clears ground for constructing a multicultural national identity. The Australian federal government has therefore made reconciliation with indigenous minorities a major policy goal, well aware that "unless Australia achieves a formal and lasting reconciliation with its indigenous people, its self-image as a fair and just land will continue to be mocked by the history of its oppression of them" (Tonkinson 1998, 291). Many white Australians and the national government are seeking ways of incorporating Aboriginality into Australian national identity. A measure of success is indicated by increasing interest on the national level in the artistic, literary, and athletic accomplishments of Aboriginal people. As a popular reconciliation slogan puts it, "White Australia has a Black History" (Figure 14.9).

While all this might augur favorably for a reconstructed Australian national identity that includes Aboriginal people, many problems remain. Some come from white Australians who reject a multicultural national identity or who see their economic interests threatened by the Mabo decision. But even Aboriginal people whom it is supposed to help criticize the Mabo decision because of its limitations and unresolved complexities. For example, the only lands eligible for indigenous claims turn out to be those that have demonstrable historical connection to contemporary Aboriginal groups who continue to practice "traditional" Aboriginal customs. This not only exempts most of Australia from indigenous land claims but also means that most of Australia's quarter of a million Aboriginal people will

Figure 14.9 Australian Aboriginal people marching in protest over the Australian Bicentennial celebrations that, they argued, did not pay appropriate attention to them.

be barred from making land claims because they live in Australia's large towns and cities and have for generations been separated from the lands of their ancestors.

Following the Mabo decision, expressions of Aboriginality seemed to be moving toward "a more culture-centered—and to non-Aboriginal Australians more easily accommodated—emphasis on Aboriginal commonalities, continuity, and survival" (Tonkinson 1998, 289). The Mabo decision had ratified the legitimacy and revival of not only Aboriginal land rights but also Aboriginal customs. This stimulated an explosion of Aboriginal cultural expression that white Australians came to appreciate, as well as numerous programs that have brought urban Aboriginals into remote areas to work, to learn about rural Aboriginal traditions, and to contribute to the growth of biculturalism among rural Aboriginal people.

Writing in 1998, Tonkinson was hopeful that, "despite the limitations of Mabo . . . its symbolic force is such that it may provide the basis for reconciliation between indigenous and other Australians" (1998, 300). Over a decade later, those hopes have experienced a setback. When John Howard became Liberal Prime Minister in 1996, he entered office with a record of opposition to the recognition of native title, to the unique status of Aboriginal people, and to the Aboriginal and Torres Strait Islander Commission (ATSIC), established in 1990 as a political structure through which indigenous Australians might participate in self-government (Dodson 2007). One of Howard's first acts as prime minister was to slash the ATSIC budget and to introduce legislation to abolish it, which passed in 2005.

The Howard government was also responsible, in 2007, for the highly controversial Northern Territory National Emergency Response. The Australian government justified this intervention by citing a report titled *Little Children Are Sacred*, which documented widespread child sexual abuse and neglect in Aboriginal communities in the Northern Territory. For several reasons, however, many Aboriginal activists and their allies have found this justification for the intervention unpersuasive (Behrendt 2007). First, the kinds of problems the intervention was intended to address were not new; some Aborigines initially thought the intervention was a belated attempt to reverse decades of government neglect. Second, the actions taken during the intervention ignored virtually all the recommendations made by the *Little Children Are Sacred* report, emphasizing instead unilateral changes in welfare and land tenure policies that were implemented without using evidence-based research and without consulting Aboriginal communities. Finally, the Australian government suspended its own *Racial Discrimination Act* in order to implement some of these policies.

As John Sanderson observed, "It is true that only about 20 percent of Indigenous people now live on the land that is the source of their Dreaming . . . But . . . respect for the relationship with the land and the culture that sustained Aboriginal people . . . remains the source of their well-being" (2007, 35). Melinda Hinkson concluded that the intervention "is aimed at nothing short of the production of a newly oriented, 'normalised' Aboriginal population, one whose concerns with custom, kin and land will give way to the individualistic aspirations of private home ownership, career and self-improvement" (2007, 6).

When a new Labor government took power in 2007, many Aborigines and their allies hoped that the intervention would be reversed. For example, the new Prime Minister, Kevin Rudd, and both houses of the Australian parliament offered a formal apology in 2008 for the "stolen generations" of Aboriginal children forcibly removed from their homes in the nineteenth and twentieth centuries as a consequence of government policy. Still, indigenous Australians complained to the United Nations about the provisions of the Northern Territory intervention, and the United Nations communicated with the Rudd government in March 2009, pointing out that suspension of the *Racial Discrimination Act* put Australia in violation of two international human rights conventions that it had signed. In April 2009, Rudd endorsed the United Nations *Declaration on the Rights of Indigenous Peoples*; in November 2009, the Rudd government introduced a bill in Parliament to reinstate the *Racial Discrimination Act*. The bill passed in June 2010.

Naturalizing Discourses

We have emphasized more than once in this chapter that all the social categories under discussion—class, caste, race, ethnicity, and nation—are culturally created and cannot be justified with reference to biology or nature. At the same time, many members of the societies anthropologists study argue just the opposite, employing what some anthropologists call **naturalizing discourses**. That is, they regularly represent particular identities as if they were rooted in biology or nature, rather than in history and culture, thereby making them appear eternal and unchanging.

Naturalizing discourses rely on the imaginary reduction, or *conflation*, of identities to achieve persuasive

---

naturalizing discourses The deliberate representation of particular identities (e.g., caste, class, race, ethnicity, and nation) as if they were a result of biology or nature, rather than history or culture, making them appear eternal and unchanging.

power (Williams 1989). For example, every one of the forms of identity we have discussed in this chapter has been described or justified by someone at some time in terms of *shared bodily substance*. Thus, living within the same borders is conflated with having the same ancestors and inheriting the same culture, which is conflated with sharing the same blood or the same genes. Culture is reduced to blood, and "the magic of forgetfulness and selectivity, both deliberate and inadvertent, allows the once recognizably arbitrary classifications of one generation to become the given inherent properties of reality several generations later" (Williams 1989, 431).

Nation-states frequently use trees as national symbols, rooting the nation in the soil of its territory (Figure 14.10). Sometimes they use kinship imagery, referring to the nation-state as a "motherland" or "fatherland"; sometimes the territory of a nation-state itself can be a unifying image, especially when portrayed on a map (Alonso 1994). The case of Australia shows, however, that doctrines like terra nullius enable newcomers to deny the "natural" links to the land of indigenous inhabitants while specifying how newcomers may proceed to establish their own "natural" links to the land through "improvement."

Figure 14.10   Nation–states frequently use trees as national symbols, rooting the nation in the soil of its territory. The treelike symbol at the center of the Mexican national seal (the cactus on which an eagle perches holding a snake in its beak) is a pre-Conquest Aztec symbol. Other versions of the image are encircled by the Spanish words *Estados Unidos Mexicanos* (United Mexican States). These combined elements stand for the officially mixed—*mestizo*—Mexican people the state is supposed to represent, the offspring of Spanish conquerors.

The Paradox of Essentialized Identities

The struggle of Aboriginal people to defend themselves and claim their rights after centuries of exploitation and neglect was extraordinarily important in making the Mabo decision possible. In response to dominant groups that attempted to conflate their humanity with a narrow, unflattering stereotype, they chose to accept the racial designation but to view it as a positive *essence*, an "inner something or distinctive 'spirituality' possessed by everyone who is Aboriginal" (Tonkinson 1998, 294–95). Similar kinds of essentialist rhetoric have helped many stigmatized groups build a positive self-image and unite politically.

Many anthropologists and other observers would argue that the essentialist rhetoric of Aboriginal activists does not, in fact, reflect their beliefs about Aboriginality at all. They would describe what the activists are promoting as *strategic essentialism*: that is, essentialist rhetoric is being used as a conscious political strategy. Many activists are perfectly aware that essentialized racial or ethnic identities have no biological validity. Nevertheless, they press their claims, hoping that by stressing their difference they may be able to extract concessions that the national government cannot refuse without violating its own laws and sense of justice. The concessions may be substantial, as in the case of the Mabo decision. At the same time, strategic essentialism is troubling to

many observers and participants in these struggles, for those who promote it as a political strategy risk "reproducing the same logic that once oppressed them" (Hale 1997, 567); and, rather than bringing about a more just society, it may simply "serve to perpetuate an ethnically ordered world" (Comaroff and Comaroff 1992, 62).

Nation Building in a Postcolonial World: The Example of Fiji

Nation building involves constructing a shared public identity, but it also involves establishing concrete legal mechanisms for taking group action to influence the state. That is, as John Kelly and Martha Kaplan (2001) argue, nation-states are more than imagined communities; they are also *represented* communities. For this reason, nation building involves more than constructing an image of national unity; it also requires institutions of political representation that channel the efforts of citizens into effective support for the state. But what happens when citizens of a nation-state do not agree about exactly what nation they are building or what kinds of legal and political structures are necessary to bring it about? One answer to these questions can be see in the South Pacific island nation of Fiji, which became independent from Britain in 1970 and has experienced two political coups since 1987(see EthnoProfile 14.5: Fiji).

EthnoProfile 14.5

Fiji

Region: Oceania

Nation: Fiji

Population: 905,000

Environment: Tropical marine climate; volcanic mountains

Livelihood: Natural resource export, especially sugar; subsistence agriculture; tourism

Political organization: Multiparty nation-state

For more information: Kelly, John D., and Martha Kaplan. 2001. *Represented communities: Fiji and world decolonization.* Chicago: University of Chicago Press.

At independence, the image of the Fijian nation was that of a "three-legged stool," each "leg" being a separate category of voters: "general electors" (a minority of the population including Europeans), "Fijians" (ethnic Fijians, descended from the original inhabitants of the island), and "Indians" (or Indo-Fijians, descendants of indentured laborers brought to Fiji by the British from Bombay and Calcutta in the nineteenth century). Kelly and Kaplan (2001) show that these three categories have deep roots in the colonial period, where they were said to correspond to separate "races." In the British Empire, race was an accepted way to categorize subordinated peoples, even though in many cases—as in the case of the Indo-Fijians—the people so labeled had shared no common identity prior to their arrival in Fiji.

These racial distinctions were concretized in colonial law, and the legal status of the ethnic Fijians was different from the legal status of Indo-Fijians. The status of ethnic Fijians was determined by the Deed of Cession, a document signed by some Fijian chiefs with the British in 1874, which linked ethnic Fijians to the colonial government through their hierarchy of chiefs. The status of Indo-Fijians, by contrast, was determined by the contracts of indenture (*girmit*) which each individual laborer had signed in order to come to Fiji. Thus, ethnic Fijians were accorded a hierarchical, collective legal identity, whereas the Indo-Fijians had the status of legal individuals, with no legally recognized ties to any collectivity.

Inspired by the Freedom Movement in India in the early twentieth century, Indo-Fijians began to resist racial oppression and struggle for equal rights in Fiji; but their efforts were repeatedly quashed by the British. When it became possible for them to vote after 1929, for example, Indo-Fijians lobbied for equal citizenship and the abolition of separate racial voting rolls, and they lost: the voting rolls were divided by race in order to limit representation for Indo-Fijians in government. At the time of World War II, Indo-Fijians agreed to serve in the armed forces but only if they were treated as equals with white soldiers, and their efforts were resisted: they spent the war serving in a labor battalion for very low wages, while ethnic Fijians joined the Fijian Defense Force. It was primarily Indo-Fijians who pushed for independence in the late 1960s, and once again they engaged in difficult negotiations for equal citizenship and a common voting roll but finally consented to separate race-based voting rolls in 1969 in order to obtain independence.

Thus, when Fiji's independence became real in 1970, the constitution insisted that races still existed in Fiji and that they had to vote separately. Since then, political parties have generally and increasingly followed racial lines and the army has remained an enclave of indigenous Fijians. When political parties backed mostly by Indo-Fijian voters won Fiji's 1987 election, the army staged a coup and took over the country after only a month. The constitution that was then installed in 1990 returned to even more naked discrimination against Indo-Fijians with regard to voting rights (Kelly and Kaplan 2001, 77).

The constitution was revised yet again, in a manner that favored ethnic Fijian chiefly interests and seemed guaranteed to prevent parties backed by Indo-Fijian voters from winning control of the government in the 1999 election. To everyone's surprise, parties backing ethnic Fijians lost again. On May 19, 2000, came a second coup. Finally, after new elections in 2001, ethnic Fijians won control of the government (Figure 14.11).

The new government lasted until a December 2006 military takeover. One of the military's demands was an end to the "race-based" voting system, to be replaced by a new "one citizen-one vote" system. However, there has been no election since the coup. In fact, in April 2009, the president suspended the constitution and appointed himself head of state. In September 2009, the British Commonwealth expelled Fiji for its failure to schedule democratic elections by 2010.

What lessons does this history suggest about nation building in postcolonial states? The issues are many and complex. But one key factor emphasized by Kelly and Kaplan is that the image of a united Fijian nation, projected at independence, was severely undermined by legal mechanisms of political representation carried over from the colonial period, particularly the race-based voting rolls. What became apparent in the years after

Figure 14.11   A Fijian citizen reads a newspaper on the day of the military coup in May 2000.

independence was the fact that Indo-Fijians and ethnic Fijians had imagined very different national communities. Indo-Fijians had supported the image of a nation in which all citizens, Indo-Fijian and ethnic Fijian and "general elector," would have equal status, voting on a single roll, working together to build a constitutional democracy. However, "few among the ethnic Fijians have yet come to see themselves as partners with immigrants" (2001, 41). Ever since independence, and particularly after each coup, ethnic Fijians worked to construct an image of the nation based solely on chiefly traditions in which Indo-Fijians had no meaningful place. Thus, Kelly and Kaplan conclude, in Fiji (and in many other parts of the world) "'the nation' is a contested idea, not an experienced reality" (142).

Nationalism and Its Dangers

The most horrifying consequence of nation building movements in the twentieth century has been the discovery of just how far the ruling groups of some nation-states are willing to go in order to enforce their version of national identity.

After World War II, the world was shocked to learn about Nazi programs to "liquidate" Jews, Gypsies, and other groups that failed to conform to Nazi ideals of Aryan purity (Linke 1997). Many people hoped that the Nazi Holocaust was exceptional, but subsequent developments suggest that it may have been only the most dramatic example of an exterminationist temptation that accompanies all drives to nationalism. Sociologist Zygmunt Bauman argued in his book *Modernity and the Holocaust* (1989) that modern nation-states

Figure 14.12   Relatives of 8,000 Muslim men and boys slaughtered in the 1995 Srebrenica massacre walk between rows of coffins next to freshly dug graves, looking for those belonging to their relatives, in a field in the town, March 31, 2003.

with rationalized bureaucracies and industrial technology were the first societies in history to make efficient mass extermination of deviants technically possible. In a transnational culture of nationalism, not to belong to a nation-state made up of loyal, ambitious, like-minded citizens is a severe, possibly fatal handicap. Using violence against all citizens who undermine claims of national homogeneity and common purpose may thus be a peculiarly modern way for insecure rulers of embattled nation-states to try to bring about solidarity and stability. In the late twentieth century, warring nationalities in the former Yugoslavia deployed selective assassinations and forced migration to rid their fledgling nation-states of unwanted others, a policy known as *ethnic cleansing*. Thus, rather than relics of a barbarian past, ethnic cleansing, *ethnocide* (the destruction of a culture), and *genocide* (the extermination of an entire people) may constitute a series of related practices that are all signs of things to come. All are measures of the high stakes for which rulers of these nation-states see themselves competing (Figure 14.12).

Inevitably, such policies create populations of immigrants and refugees whose social status is anomalous and ambiguous in a world of nation-states and whose presence as new pockets of heterogeneity in a different nation-state sets the stage for new rounds of social struggle that may lead to violence. As we will see in the next chapter, the economic, political, and cultural processes that made this possible have undergone important shifts in the last few years.

Chapter Summary

1. All people in the world today, even refugees, must deal with the authority of one or another nation-state, each of which contains multiple and sometimes contradictory hierarchies of stratification. Every one of these hierarchies is a cultural invention designed to create boundaries around different kinds of imagined communities. Some patterns of stratification may reach back thousands of years, but others are closely associated with the rise of European capitalism and colonialism.

2. Gender stratification draws on sexual imagery to create and rank categories of people. Stratification by gender regularly subordinates phenotypic females to phenotypic males, but it is often applied more widely to other categories of people, artifacts, or events: to structure relations between different categories of men, for example, or between different ethnic groups or "races."

3. The concept of "class" in anthropology has a double heritage: Europeans tended to view class boundaries as closed and rigid, whereas North Americans tended to view them as open and permeable. Class solidarity may be undercut by clientage relations that bind individuals to one another across class boundaries.

4. The stratification system of India has been taken as the prototype of caste stratification, although anthropologists also have applied the concept to social hierarchies encountered elsewhere in the world. Local caste divisions (*jatis*) in village India adhere to rules of purity and pollution defined in terms of the occupations their members perform and the foods they eat and which govern whom they may marry. Members of jatis of similar rank do not observe most of these distinctions with one another, especially in urban settings. Caste associations in large cities of India use jati ties to promote their members' economic well-being. The use of violence by higher-ranking jatis to block the advance of lower-ranking jatis has also increased in recent years. Contemporary anthropologists reject views of caste in India that portray it as internally harmonious and uncontested by those at the bottom of the hierarchy, pointing to the rise in caste violence in recent years.

5. The contemporary concept of "race" developed in the context of European exploration and conquest beginning in the fifteenth century as light-skinned Europeans came to rule over darker-skinned peoples in different parts of the world. The so-called races whose boundaries were forged during the nineteenth century are imagined communities; human biological variation does not naturally clump into separate populations with stable boundaries. Despite variations in opinions and practices regarding race over the centuries, a global hierarchy persists in which whiteness symbolizes high status and blackness symbolizes the social bottom.

(continued on next page)

Chapter Summary (continued)

6. Although ethnic consciousness existed in precolonial and precapitalist societies, contemporary anthropologists have been most interested in forms of ethnicity that were generated under capitalist colonial domination, when different groups were subordinated within a single political structure under conditions of inequality. This process can produce ethnic groups not continuous with any single earlier group and is often characterized by nesting, opposed identities that individuals often manipulate in order to achieve upward mobility. When dominant ethnic groups feel threatened, they may attempt to stigmatize subordinate groups by "racializing" them.

7. Nation-states were invented in nineteenth-century Europe, but they have spread throughout the world along with capitalism, colonialism, and eventual political decolonization. Nationalist thinking aims to create a political unit in which national identity and political territory coincide, and this has led to various practices designed to force subordinate social groups to adopt a national identity defined primarily in terms of the culture of the dominant group. When subordinate groups resist, they may become the victims of genocide or ethnic cleansing. Alternatively, the dominant group may try to recast its understanding of national identity in a way that acknowledges and incorporates cultural elements belonging to subordinate groups. If the creation of such an imagined hybrid identity is not accompanied by legal and political changes that support it, however, the end result may be political turmoil, as shown in the recent history of Fiji.

8. Because membership in social categories such as gender, class, caste, race, ethnicity, and nation can determine enormous differences in peoples' life chances, much is at stake in defending these categories and all may be described as if they were rooted in biology or nature, rather than culture and history. Conceptualizing these forms of identity as essences can be a way of stereotyping and excluding, but it has also been used by many stigmatized groups to build a positive self-image and as a strategic concept in struggles with dominant groups. Although strategic essentialism may be successful in such struggles, it also risks repeating the same logic that justifies oppression.

For Review

1. Explain structural violence, using the example of Haiti.
2. What are the key points in the discussion of gender in this chapter?
3. Summarize the key points in the text's discussion of class.
4. How does caste differ from class?
5. Based on the Gopalpur case study, discuss how caste worked in village India.
6. Describe some of the caste struggles occurring in contemporary India.
7. What is race?
8. Summarize the key arguments in the discussion of race in the textbook.
9. What are the key points in the discussion of colorism in Nicaragua?
10. Summarize the main arguments in the discussion of ethnicity in this chapter.
11. How are ethnicity and race related?
12. What is a nation? Discuss the relationship between nation-states and nation building or nationalism.
13. Summarize the key arguments in the discussion of Australian nationalism.
14. What are naturalizing discourses?
15. Explain strategic essentialism.
16. What are the dangers of nationalism, according to the textbook?

Key Terms

caste 411
class 410
clientage 410
colorism 418
ethnic groups 422

ethnicity 420
nation 425
nation building (or
    nationalism) 425
nationality 425

nation-state 425
naturalizing
    discourses 429
race 417

racism 417
structural violence 406
transformist
    hegemony 425

Suggested Readings

American Anthropological Association. 1998. Statement on race, http://www.aaanet.org/stmts/racepp.htm.

Anderson, Benedict. 1991. *Imagined communities,* rev. ed. London: Verso. *The classic discussion of the cultural processes that create community ties between people—such as citizens of a nation-state—who have never seen one another, producing the personal and cultural feeling of belonging to a nation.*

Farmer, Paul. 2003. *Pathologies of power: Health, human rights and the new war on the poor.* Berkeley: University of California Press. *Paul Farmer, a physician and anthropologist, uses his experiences in several different parts of the world to show how patterns of disease and suffering are shaped by social and political policies that violate human rights, creating landscapes of "structural violence."*

Hinton, Alexander Laban. 2002. *Annihilating difference: The anthropology of genocide.* Berkeley: University of California Press. *A recent collection of articles probing the ways in which anthropology can help explain and perhaps contribute to the prevention of genocide. Case studies include Nazi Germany, Cambodia under the Khmer Rouge, Rwanda, Guatemala, and the former Yugoslavia.*

Kidder, Tracy. 2003. *Mountains beyond mountains.* New York: Random House. *A very readable book about Paul Farmer, the work he does, and the values he holds. Journalist Tracy Kidder travels with Farmer to many of the sites where he works in Haiti, Peru, Cuba, and Russia.*

Malkki, Liisa. 1995. *Purity and exile: Memory and national cosmology among Hutu refugees in Tanzania.* Chicago:

University of Chicago Press. *This ethnography chronicles a recent example in Africa of the bloody consequences of nationalist politics and explores the connections between the conditions of refugee resettlement and the development of refugee identities.*

Nash, Manning. 1989. *The cauldron of ethnicity in the modern world.* Chicago: University of Chicago Press. *Nash looks at ethnicity in the postcolonial world and sees more of a seething cauldron than a melting pot. He examines the relations between Ladinos and Maya in Guatemala, Chinese and Malays in Malaysia, and Jews and non-Jews in the United States.*

Sharma, Ursula. 1999. *Caste.* Philadelphia: Open University Press. *A brief, up-to-date survey of recent anthropological scholarship dealing with caste in south Asia.*

Smedley, Audrey. 1998. *Race in North America: Origin and evolution of a worldview,* 2nd ed. Boulder, CO: Westview Press. *This book offers a comprehensive historical overview of the development of the concept of race in North America, beginning in the late eighteenth century. The second edition includes additional coverage of developments in the nineteenth and twentieth centuries. Smedley shows how the concept of "race" is a cultural construct that over time has been used in different ways, for different purposes.*

Strathern, Marilyn. 1988. *The gender of the gift.* Berkeley: University of California Press. *This is a challenging volume but a classic. Strathern expands the notion of "gender" beyond the traditional bounds of feminist anthropology in order to make sense of the complexities of Melanesian cultural practices.*

What Can Anthropology Tell Us about Globalization?

15

A very popular term these days is "globalization." But what does it mean? In this chapter, we will look at how anthropologists study globalization by following global flows of information, people, and commodities. You will learn how anthropologists approach debates about such contemporary matters as international migration, multiculturalism, and human rights. We will also show how cultural anthropology's traditional ethnographic focus can make unique contributions to our understanding of globalization.

Chapter Outline

◀ *Khao San Road in Bangkok, Thailand.*

In this chapter, we take up again the story of relations between the West and the rest of the world, how those relations have changed over the last 50 years, and with what consequences. We look at ourselves as much as we look at the traditional subjects of anthropological research (Figure 15.1).

What Happened to the Global Economy after the Cold War?

In 1989, the Cold War came to an end. The Soviet Union and its satellite states collapsed, and China began to encourage some capitalist economic practices. These radical changes in the global political economy left no part of the world unaffected. For some, this period of uncertainty offered a chance to challenge long-unquestioned truths about development and underdevelopment that had guided government policies throughout the Cold War. From new social movements such as the *rondas campesinas* of Peru to squatter movements in cities to movements defending the rights of women and homosexuals and movements to preserve rain forests, people attempted to construct entirely new social institutions that often bypassed national governments or development agencies (see Figure 15.2). Anthropologist Arturo Escobar (1992) argued that the new social movements

in Latin America were struggles over meanings as well as over material conditions.

This work promoted the hope that new social movements might succeed in promoting less exploitative forms of society in generations to come. But the world toward which such arguments were aimed was already disappearing. The breakdown of communism led to a crisis of confidence among many who had been inspired by key tenets of marxian thought. At the same time, the apparent triumph of capitalism reanimated the former proponents of a Cold War theory called "modernization," which held that there were a series of stages of economic growth that successful countries like Britain or the United States had gone through and that should be followed by new, "underdeveloped" nations if they, too, wished to be stable and prosperous. These scholars and political figures now defended a new view called "neoliberalism." Under neoliberalism, no nation-state would be expected to rely on itself to achieve prosperity and avoid communist revolution. Instead, states would be encouraged by international institutions like the World Bank and the International Monetary Fund to seek prosperity by finding a niche in the growing global capitalist market. Market discipline would force state bureaucrats to support economic enterprises that would earn them income in the market and to eliminate expensive state institutions and subsidies that had provided a safety net for the poor. Western leaders embraced with enthusiasm the beckoning opportunity to bring the entire world within the compass of the capitalist economy.

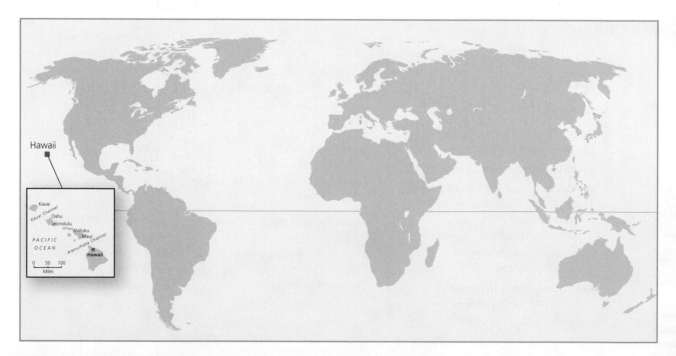

Figure 15.1 Location of society whose EthnoProfile appears in Chapter 15.

Figure 15.2 Beginning in the mid-1970s, peasants in the highlands of northern Peru developed rural justice groups, called *rondas campesinas* ("peasant rounds"). These were armed groups of peasants who walked the paths around their villages at night, keeping an eye out for animal rustlers. During the 1980s, they spread throughout the north and became an alternative justice system, with assemblies to resolve problems ranging from wife-beating to land disputes. This social movement, concludes anthropologist Orin Starn (1999), gave Peruvian peasants the vision of an alternative modernity and renewed among them a powerful sense of independent identity. Here a group of ronderos pose with a stolen donkey recovered from rustlers in 1986.

Less enthusiastic observers began to suspect that forces unleashed at the end of the Cold War were remaking the global political economy in unprecedented new ways, with outcomes that no one could predict or control.

Cultural Processes in a Global World

Cold War–era economic and political theories presupposed a world in which geographic and cultural boundaries were relatively clear-cut: only if this is the case does it make sense to distinguish developed from underdeveloped nations, cores from peripheries, or local cultures from global social processes. The worldwide political, economic, and technological changes of recent decades, however, have challenged the utility of these distinctions. The cybernetics revolution led to advances in manufacturing, transportation, and communications technology that removed the seemingly unbreakable barriers to long-distance communication and contact, a phenomenon called "space–time compression" (Harvey 1990). These changes made it easier, cheaper, and faster to move people and things around the world than ever

before; they also made it possible to stretch social relationships of all kinds over huge distances that previously would have been unbridgeable (Giddens 1990). And with the end of the Cold War, no part of the globe was blocked from the effects of these changes. The outcome has been the widely recognized phenomenon of **globalization**: the reshaping of local conditions by powerful global forces on an ever-intensifying scale. Globalization suggests a "world full of movement and mixture, contacts and linkages, and persistent cultural interaction and exchange" (Inda and Rosaldo 2002, 2).

Globalization is understood and evaluated differently by different observers. Anthropologists ordinarily approach globalization from the perspective of those among whom they do their research. From this point of view, it has been apparent for some time that the effects of globalization are *uneven*: "large expanses of the planet are only tangentially tied to the webs of interconnection that encompass the globe" (Inda and Rosaldo 2002, 4). As a result, global processes are interpreted and

---

globalization Reshaping of local conditions by powerful global forces on an ever-intensifying scale.

experienced in contradictory ways by different groups and actors.

Faye Ginsburg and Rayna Rapp, for example, describe a global process they call "stratified reproduction," in which some categories of people are empowered to nurture and reproduce while others are not: "Low-income African American mothers, for example, often are stereotyped as undisciplined 'breeders' who sap the resources of the state through incessant demands on welfare. But historically and in the present, they were 'good enough' nurturers to work as childcare providers for other, more privileged class and ethnic groups" (1995, 3). Globalization has created new opportunities for some groups, like the Kayapó of Brazil and other indigenous peoples, to build worldwide organizations to defend their interests (Kearney 1995, 560) (Figure 15.3). At the same time, global forces can also reinforce old constraints. Evaluating the record of new social movements in Latin America, for example, John Gledhill writes that "to date the challenge that popular forces have been able to mount to the remorseless progress of the neoliberal, neomodernization agenda, has remained limited" (1994, 198).

It would be difficult to find any research project in contemporary cultural anthropology that does not in some way acknowledge the ways in which global forces affect the local societies in which anthropologists work. In this respect, globalization studies emphasize the ways in which *the global articulates with the local*: anthropological studies of globalization aim to show "how globalizing processes exist in the context of, and must come to terms with, the realities of particular societies" (Inda and Rosaldo 2002, 4). In other words, "while everyone might continue to live local lives, their phenomenal worlds have to some extent become global" (9).

Globalization is seen in the growth of transnational corporations that relocate their manufacturing operations from core to periphery or that appropriate local cultural forms and turn them into images and commodities to be marketed throughout the world (Figure 15.4). It is seen in tourism, which has grown into the world's largest industry, and in migration from periphery to the core on such a massive scale that observers now speak of the "deterritorialization" of peoples and cultures that, in the past, were presumed to be firmly attached to specific geographic locations. Not only that: deterritorialized people always "reterritorialize" in a new location. Such reterritorialization regularly sparks social conflicts and generates new forms of cultural identity, as nation-states try to retain control over citizens who have migrated beyond their borders and as relocated populations struggle both for recognition in their new homes and for influence in their places of origin. Globalization has drawn the attention of many anthropologists to regions such as the borderland between northern Mexico and the southwestern United States, where struggles with contradictory social practices and ambiguous identities have long been the rule, rather than the exception. Such contexts exhibit a "diffusion of culture traits gone wild, far beyond that imagined by the Boasians" (Kearney 1995, 557). In other words, borderland conditions are now becoming worldwide, and they undermine views of culture that depend upon settled peoples with distinct cultural attributes.

Figure 15.3 To publicize their opposition to a proposed hydroelectric dam complex that threatened to flood their traditional territories, indigenous Amazonian peoples, under the leadership of the Kayapó, engaged in a variety of activities. Here, Kayapó chief Paiakan (left) and British rock star Sting hold a press conference.

Figure 15.4 One dimension of globalization involves the appropriation of local cultural forms and their use in a variety of widely sold commodities. For example, the image of "Kokopelli," taken from ancient rock art of the southwestern United States, has been reproduced on many items with no connection to its region or culture of origin, including this mailbox flag from Albuquerque, New Mexico. Such items are readily available on the Internet.

In Their Own Words

Slumdog Tourism

This and the following In Their Own Words *boxes offer two different understandings of tourism from the perspectives of the people whom the tourists go to see. In August 2010, the* New York Times *published an op-ed essay by Kennedy Odade, then a junior at Wesleyan University and the executive director of Shining Hope for Communities, a social services organization that he cofounded to work in the Kibera slum. Shining Hope for Communities can be found at www.hopetoshine.org.*

Slum tourism has a long history—during the late 1800s, lines of wealthy New Yorkers snaked along the Bowery and through the Lower East Side to see "how the other half lives."

But with urban populations in the developing world expanding rapidly, the opportunities and demands to observe poverty firsthand have never been greater. The hot spots are Rio de Janeiro, Mumbai—thanks to *Slumdog Millionaire*, the film that started a thousand tours—and my home, Kibera, a Nairobi slum that is perhaps the largest in Africa.

Slum tourism has its advocates, who say it promotes social awareness. And it's good money, which helps the local economy.

But it's not worth it. Slum tourism turns poverty into entertainment, something that can be momentarily experienced and then escaped from. People think they've really "seen" something—and then go back to their lives and leave me, my family, and my community right where we were before.

I was 16 when I first saw a slum tour. I was outside my 100-square-foot house washing dishes, looking at the utensils with longing because I hadn't eaten in 2 days. Suddenly a white woman was taking my picture. I felt like a tiger in a cage. Before I could say anything, she had moved on.

When I was 18, I founded an organization that provides education, health, and economic services for Kibera residents. A documentary filmmaker from Greece was interviewing me about my work. As we made our way through the streets, we passed an old man defecating in public. The woman took out her video camera and said to her assistant, "Oh, look at that."

For a moment I saw my home through her eyes: feces, rats, starvation, houses so close together that no one can breathe. I realized I didn't want her to see it, didn't want to give her the opportunity to judge my community for its poverty—a condition that few tourists, no matter how well intentioned, could ever understand.

Other Kibera residents have taken a different path. A former schoolmate of mine started a tourism business. I once saw him take a group into the home of a

Tourists walk through Dharavi, a slum neighborhood of Mumbai, India, in June 2008.

young woman giving birth. They stood and watched as she screamed. Eventually the group continued on its tour, cameras loaded with images of a woman in pain. What did they learn? And did the woman gain anything from the experience?

To be fair, many foreigners come to the slums wanting to understand poverty, and they leave with what they believe is a better grasp of our desperately poor conditions. The expectation, among the visitors and the tour organizers, is that the experience may lead the tourists to action once they get home.

But it's just as likely that a tour will come to nothing. After all, looking at conditions like those in Kibera is overwhelming, and I imagine many visitors think that merely bearing witness to such poverty is enough.

Nor do the visitors really interact with us. Aside from the occasional comment, there is no dialogue established, no conversation begun. Slum tourism is a one-way street: they get photos; we lose a piece of our dignity.

Slums will not go away because a few dozen Americans or Europeans spent a morning walking around them. There are solutions to our problems—but they won't come about through tours.

Source: Odade 2010

Such heterogeneous and unstable cultural spaces also call into question views like Wallerstein's (1974) that portray global processes as part of a coherent world system. Anthropologist Arjun Appadurai (1990) claims, to the contrary, that ever-intensifying global flows of people, technology, wealth, images, and ideologies are highly contradictory, generating global processes that are fundamentally disorganized and unpredictable. Jonathan Friedman (1994), by contrast, argues that the disorder may be real but that it is also a predictable consequence of the breakdown of Western global hegemony, with the dissolution of European colonial empires and the decentralization of capitalist economic accumulation from Europe and North America to parts of the world such as the Pacific Rim. In his view, these developments exemplify a pattern of global commercial expansion and contraction that began at least 5,000 years ago with the rise of the first commercial civilizations—world systems in Wallerstein's sense—each of which was characterized by its own form of "modernity." Recognition of this pattern makes Friedman even more pessimistic than Wallerstein about possibilities for the future.

Not all anthropologists accept Friedman's conclusions. But even if Friedman's overall schema of civilizational cycles seems plausible, it cannot by itself account for the "local structures" and "autonomous cultural schemes" that appear at any point in the cycle. It is this historically specific local detail—what Inda and Rosaldo (2002, 27) call "the conjunctural and situated character of globalization"—that anthropologists aim to document and analyze. In the rest of this chapter, we examine three important areas of study in the anthropology of globalization: the effect of global forces on nation-states, human rights as the emerging discourse of globalization, and debates about cultural hybridization and cosmopolitanism.

Globalization and the Nation-State

Are Global Flows Undermining Nation-States?

In the second half of the twentieth century, one of the fundamental suppositions about global social organization was that it consisted of an international order of independent nation-states. This assumption has roots that can be traced back to nineteenth-century nationalist struggles in Europe, but it seems to have come fully into its own after World War II, with the final dissolution of European empires, as former colonies achieved independence. The

Figure 15.5 Queen Elizabeth II at Nigerian independence ceremonies, January 1956.

United Nations (UN), created in 1945, presupposed a world of nation-states (Figure 15.5).

The flow of wealth, images, people, things, and ideologies unleashed by globalization, however, has undermined the ability of nation-states to police their boundaries effectively and has seemed to suggest that the conventional ideas about nation-states require revision. Many observers have suggested that globalization inevitably undermines the power and sovereignty of nation-states. National governments are virtually powerless to control what their citizens read or watch in the media: satellite services, telecommunications, and the Internet elude state-ordered censorship. Nation-states allow migrants, students, and tourists to cross their borders because they need their labor, tuition, or vacation expenditures; but in so doing, states must contend with the political values, religious commitments, or families that these outsiders bring with them. Some people have argued that to weaken boundaries between states is a good thing since border restrictions and censorship need to be overcome. Since 1989, however, as we witness the ways that forces of globalization have made weakened states vulnerable to chaos and violence, the ability of the nation-state to protect its citizens from such destruction has led some to ask whether stronger nation-states might not have at least some points in their favor.

Massive global displacements of people have characterized Western modernity, starting with the slave trade and the movement of indentured labor to the colonies. In the nineteenth century, as developing capitalist markets pushed and pulled waves of European and Asian emigrants out of their homelands and installed them in different parts of the globe, colonial authorities revived the institution of indentured labor to rearrange

In Their Own Words

Cofan

Story of the Forest People and the Outsiders

Randy Borman is president of the Centro Cofan Zabalo. He was born to missionary parents and grew up in Cofan culture in the Ecuadorian Amazon. Borman briefly attended school in North America and then returned to Ecuador to become a leader in the Cofan fight for economic and cultural survival. He has written in Cultural Survival Quarterly *about the development of ecotourism in the Cofan area of Ecuador. The results of tourism elsewhere in the world are not always as positive as they have been for the Cofan people, in part because tourism is often imposed from the outside. To find out more about the Cofan people, visit www.cofan.org.*

I had the fortune to grow up as a forest person, enjoying the clean rivers and unlimited forests, learning the arts and skills of living comfortably in a wonderland of the marvelous, beautiful, and deadly. I experienced firsthand both the good and the bad of a world which will never again be possible, at least in the foreseeable future. And I also experienced the crushing physical, psychological, and spiritual impact of the invasion of the outside that erased our world.

In 1955, the Cofan people were the sole inhabitants of more than 1,000,000 hectares of pristine forest in northeastern Ecuador. By 1965, oil exploration and exploitation had begun. And by 1975, the forest was fast disappearing before a massive mestizo colonization, which was brought in by roads created to access vast quantities of oil. The rivers were fouled with chemicals and raw crude; the animals disappeared; boom towns sprung up all over; and the Cofan struggled to survive on less than 15,000 hectares of badly degraded forest. The old life was gone forever, and my companions and I faced the numbing prospect of discarding our culture and way of life, and becoming peasant farmers like so many others, trying to eke out a living from crops and animals which were never meant to grow in this environment. We had been powerless to maintain our forests in the face of outsider pressures to make every given piece of land profitable. If we were to save anything from the wreckage we needed alternatives, and quickly. . . .

[As the only member of his community with an outsider education, Borman worked with the community in trying to develop strategies for community survival, including those associated with marketing forest products. These strategies did not work.]

As we were wrestling with these possible alternatives, we were also acting as boatmen for the slowly increasing economy on the river. Several of us had managed to buy outboard motors with carefully saved returns from corn fields, animal skins, and short stints as trail makers with the oil companies. We had a long tradition of carving dugouts, and soon our canoes were traveling up and down the rivers with loads of lumber, corn, and coffee; occasional trips carrying cattle provided excitement and variety. This was not an alternative for the entire community, and it was only viable until roads were built, but it worked as a stop-gap measure for some of us. And unexpectedly, it led us directly into the alternative, which we have adopted as our own in the years since.

Travelers were coming to our region. The roads made it easier than at any previous time, and people from First World countries—the USA, Canada, England, Germany, Israel, Italy—began to come, searching for the vanishing rain forest. Most of them were primarily interested in seeing wildlife. This fit with our view of the situation precisely. We had our motorboats. There was still a lot of good forest out there, but it was hard to access with regular paddling and poling expeditions. So when these travelers arrived and wanted to go to "wild jungle," we were delighted to take them. They paid the transportation cost, and we took our shotguns and spears along to go hunting. Our attitude was that if the traveler wanted to go along with us, and didn't mind that we were hunting, why, we were happy to have them along to help carry the game home! From such a pragmatic beginning, we slowly developed our concept of tourism.

There were changes. We soon learned that the traveler had a lot more fun if we modified our normal hunting pattern a bit, and we even got paid extra for it. We found out that the average tourist didn't mind if we shot birds that looked like chickens, even if they were rare. But if we shot a toucan they were outraged, despite the fact that toucans are very common. Tourists preferred a board to a stick as a seat in the canoe, and a pad made them even happier. Tourists' food needed to be somewhat recognizable, such as rice, rather than the lumpy, thick manioc beer we normally eat and drink. But the community as a whole decided early that our role would be that of guides and service providers for tourists interested in the forest. We would not dress up and do dances, or stage fake

(continued on next page)

In Their Own Words *(continued)*

Cofan

Story of the Forest People and the Outsiders

festivals, or in any way try to sell our traditions and dress. We would not accept becoming the objects of tourism— rather, we would provide the skills and knowledge for the tourist to understand our environment. We would sell our education, at a price that was in line with the importance to the outsiders who wanted to buy it, such as lawyers, biologists, doctors, teachers, and other professionals the world over do.

Being guides for the tourism experience, not the objects of it, has provided both a very real economic alternative and a very solid incentive for the younger generation to learn the vast body of traditional knowledge, which lies at the heart of our culture. A deep conservation ethic—the roots of which lie at the hearts of most cultures who maintain a viable relation with their environments—has helped the Cofan community to create a number of projects which combine outsider science with our traditional knowledge. Interestingly enough, this has also turned out to be an economic success, as many of our projects began to receive funding in recognition of their innovation and replicability in other communities throughout Amazonia. . . .

Tourism is not for everyone. Some of our experiences have been negative. One of our biggest and most constant headaches is effective commercialization. To operate a community-based tourism business while maintaining our cultural heritage is not possible using the outsider formula of a tour operator. The implied hierarchy of manager, finance department, buyers, transport specialists, etc., all

working eight hours a day, five days a week, with an office and a fax machine is clearly not applicable. Instead, we rely on teams, which rotate in their work, leaving time for farms, family duties, crafts, fishing, hunting and the garden. But the lack of a full-time office makes it difficult to commercialize effectively, and we walk the precarious line between too much tourism (no time left over to live a normal life, and possible loss of our cultural way of life) and too little (not enough jobs, not enough income, lack of attraction for a forest-based life and education for our young people). If we commercialize effectively, we run the risk of the operation snowballing, with more and more tourists arriving, and eventually, we are all wealthy in outsider goods and income but without our culture's wealth of time and interpersonal relationships that we all value so much now. If we don't commercialize effectively, we will wake up tomorrow back at the beginning, with the need to destroy our forest for short-term survival.

But in the overall scheme of things, our experiment with tourism has been overwhelmingly positive. Contact with people who wish to know what we can teach, who value our forests and are willing to pay to help us maintain them has been very important. Our increased awareness of the conservation imperatives facing us has led to many changes in our way of life, all aimed at preserving core values for future generations.

Source: Borman 1999, 48–50.

populations within their dominions. A hundred years ago, when volumes of immigration were lower and moved at a slower pace and jobs were plentiful, assimilation into the society of reterritorialization was often possible. Today, however, desperate economic and political situations in migrants' home territories plus ease of transportation have increased the volume and speed of migration, while market crises in the countries where migrants have settled have sharply reduced the economic opportunities available to them once they arrive.

Migrants often find themselves caught. On the one hand, they now form sizeable minority populations in the countries of settlement, which still offer them better opportunities for economic survival and political security than the nations from which they came, factors that encourage them to stay where they are. On the

other hand, local economic crises and their visibility in enclaves of settlement, often in the poorer areas of cities, increases the hostility and sometimes violence directed against them by locals whenever there is an economic downturn. Many migrants thus conclude that the possibility of permanent assimilation is unrealistic, which encourages them to maintain ties to the homeland or to other communities of migrants located elsewhere.

Migration, Transborder Identities, and Long-Distance Nationalism

The term *diaspora* is commonly used to refer to migrant populations with a shared identity who live in a variety of different places around the world, but Nina Glick Schiller and Georges Fouron point out that not all such populations see themselves in the same way. Schiller and Fouron describe different types of "transborder identities" that characterize different groups of migrants. They prefer to use the term **diaspora** to identify a form of transborder identity that does not focus on nation building. Should members of a diaspora begin to organize in support of nationalist struggles in their homeland or to agitate for a state of their own, they become **long-distance nationalists** (Schiller and Fouron 2002, 360–61). "Long-distance nationalism" was coined by political scientist Benedict Anderson to describe the efforts of émigrés to offer moral, economic, and political support to the nationalist struggles of their countries of origin. In his original discussion, Anderson emphasized the dangerous irresponsibility of the "citizenshipless participation" of the long-distance nationalist: "while technically a citizen of the state in which he comfortably lives, but to which he may feel little attachment, he finds it tempting to play identity politics by participating (via propaganda, money, weapons, any way but voting) in the conflicts of his imagined *Heimat* [homeland]" (2002, 269–70). Schiller and Fouron argue, however, that the conditions of globalization have led to new forms of long-distance nationalism that do not correspond to Anderson's original description but that have led to the emergence of the **transborder state**: a form of state "claiming that its emigrants and their descendants remain an integral and intimate part of their ancestral homeland, even if they are legal citizens of another state" (Schiller and Fouron 2002, 357).

The idea of a transborder state did not characterize earlier periods of mass emigration in the nineteenth and twentieth centuries. At that time, nations sending emigrants abroad regarded permanent settlement of emigrants elsewhere as national betrayal and encouraged them to think of migration as temporary, expecting them eventually to return home with new wealth and skills to build the nation. But in today's global world, political leaders of many states sending emigrants not only accept the likelihood that those emigrants will settle permanently elsewhere but also insist that such permanently settled émigrés retain full membership in the nation-state from which they came. This form of long-distance nationalism creates what Schiller and Fouron call a **transborder citizenry**: "Citizens residing within the territorial homeland and new emigrants and their descendants are part of the nation, whatever legal citizenship the émigrés may have" (2002, 358).

Transborder states and transborder citizenries are more than symbolic identities: they have become concretized in law. For example, several Latin American countries, including Mexico, Colombia, the Dominican Republic, Ecuador, and Brazil, permit emigrants who

Figure 15.6 The Dominican Republic permits emigrants who have become naturalized citizens of the United States to vote in Dominican elections. Here, a Dominican woman in New York campaigns in 2004 for a second term for President Hipólito Mejía.

have become naturalized citizens in countries such as the United States to retain dual nationality and even voting rights in their country of origin (Figure 15.6). Special government ministries are set up to address the needs of citizens living abroad. This is very different from Anderson's notion of "citizenless participation." Schiller and Fouron stress that transborder states and citizenries spring "from the life experiences of migrants of different classes" and are "rooted in the day to day efforts of people in the homeland to live lives of dignity and self-respect that compel them to include those who have migrated (2002, 359).

But some transborder citizenries face difficulties. First, their efforts at nation building are sometimes blocked by political forces in the homeland that do not welcome their contributions. This has been the case for Haitians living abroad while Haiti was ruled by the Duvalier family dictatorship and for Cubans living abroad whose efforts are blocked by the Castro revolutionary

diaspora Migrant populations with a shared identity who live in a variety of different locales around the world; a form of transborder identity that does not focus on nation building.

long-distance nationalists Members of a diaspora organized in support of nationalist struggles in their homeland or to agitate for a state of their own.

transborder state A form of state in which it is claimed that those people who left the country and their descendants remain part of their ancestral state, even if they are citizens of another state.

transborder citizenry A group made up of citizens of a country who continue to live in their homeland plus the people who have emigrated from the country and their descendants, regardless of their current citizenship.

government. Second, the states in which immigrants have settled may not welcome the continued involvement of transborder citizens in the affairs of another state. Such involvement has often been seen as even more threatening since terrorists destroyed the World Trade Center and attacked the Pentagon on September 11, 2001. Yet, in an era of globalization, attempts to control migration threaten to block the flows of people that keep the global economy going. Moreover, the vulnerability of transborder citizens in these circumstances often increases the appeal of long-distance nationalism (Schiller and Fouron 2002, 359–360)

The globalizing forces that produce long-distance nationalism and transborder states and citizens have undermined previous understandings of what a world made up of nation-states should look like. In addition, unacknowledged contradictions and weaknesses of actual nation-states are revealed. For example, the existence and strength of transborder states and citizenries show that some nation-states—especially those sending migrants—are actually what Schiller and Fouron call "apparent states": they have all the outward attributes of nation-states (government bureaucracies, armies, a seat in the UN), but in fact they are unable to meet the needs of their people (2002, 363). The strength of long-distance nationalism and transborder citizenries also exposes inconsistencies and paradoxes in the meaning of citizenship in the nation-states where migrants settle.

Schiller and Fouron contrast legal citizenship with what they call "substantive citizenship" and point out that, for transborder citizens, the two often do not coincide. As we saw, **legal citizenship** is accorded by state laws and can be difficult for migrants to obtain. But even those transborder citizens who obtain legal citizenship often experience a gap between what the legal citizenship promises and the way they are treated by the state. For example, people of color and women who are U.S. citizens are not treated by the state the same way white male citizens are treated. By contrast, **substantive citizenship** is defined by the actions people take, regardless

of their legal citizenship status, to assert their membership in a state and to bring about political changes that will improve their lives. Some transborder citizenries call for the establishment of full-fledged **transnational nation-states**. That is, "they challenge the notion that relationships between citizens and their state are confined within that territory" and work for the recognition of a new political form that contradicts the understandings of political theory but reflects the realities of their experiences of national identity (Schiller and Fouron 2002, 359).

How Can Citizenship Be Flexible?

Schiller and Fouron's observations about the way globalization has undermined the stability of conventional nation-states expose contradictory and ambiguous practices associated with such basic concepts as "national identity" and "citizenship." Their contrast between formal and substantive citizenship suggests that conventional notions of citizenship that previously seemed straightforward begin to break down in the context of globalization. Another way of speaking about these contradictions and ambiguities is suggested by anthropologist Aihwa Ong, who speaks of **flexible citizenship**: "the strategies and effects of mobile managers, technocrats, and professionals seeking both to circumvent *and* benefit from different nation-state regimes by selecting different sites for investment, work, and family relocation" (2002, 174). As we saw in Chapter 12, Ong's research concerns diaspora communities of elite Chinese families who have played key roles in the economic successes of the Pacific Rim in recent years. Although their success is often attributed by outsiders to "Chinese culture," Ong's research calls this simplistic explanation into question. Ong documents the ways in which Chinese families have responded creatively to opportunities and challenges they have encountered since the end of the nineteenth century as they found ways to evade or exploit the governmentality of three different kinds of institutions: Chinese kinship and family, the nation-state, and the marketplace.

The break from mainland Chinese ideas of kinship and Confucian filial piety came when Chinese first moved into the capitalist commercial circuits of European empires. Money could be made in these settings, but success required Chinese merchant families to cut themselves off from ties to mainland China and to reinforce bonds among family members and business partners in terms of *guanxi* ("relationships of social connections built primarily upon shared identities such as native place, kinship or attending the same school" [Smart 1999, 120]). The family discipline of overseas Chinese enabled them

---

legal citizenship The rights and obligations of citizenship accorded by the laws of a state.

substantive citizenship The actions people take, regardless of their legal citizenship status, to assert their membership in a state and to bring about political changes that will improve their lives.

transnational nation-state A nation-state in which the relationships between citizens and the state extend to wherever citizens reside.

flexible citizenship The strategies and effects employed by managers, technocrats, and professionals who move regularly across state boundaries and seek both to circumvent and to benefit from different nation-state regimes.

to become wealthy and provided the resources to subvert the governmentality of the nation-state. The orientation of these wealthy families toward national identity and citizenship, Ong explains, is "market-driven." In Hong Kong, for example, in the years leading up to its return to mainland China in 1997, many wealthy Chinese thought of citizenship "not as the right to demand full democratic representation, but as the right to promote familial interests apart from the well-being of society" (2002, 178). None of the overseas Chinese she knew expressed any commitment to nationalism, either local or long-distance. This understanding of citizenship could not be more different from the committed transborder citizenship of long-distance nationalists described by Schiller and Fouron.

Quite the contrary. Relying on family discipline and loyalty and buttressed by considerable wealth and strong interpersonal ties, they actively worked to evade the governmentality of nation-states. For example, Chinese from Hong Kong who wanted to migrate to Britain in the 1960s were able to evade racial barriers that blocked other "colored" immigrants because of their experience with capitalism and their reputation for peaceful acquiescence to British rule. When the British decided to award citizenship to some Hong Kong residents in the 1990s, they used a point system that favored applicants with education, fluency in English, and training in professions of value to the economy, such as accountancy and law. These attributes fitted well the criteria for citizenship valued under the government of Margaret Thatcher, while other applicants for citizenship who lacked such attributes were excluded. Citizenship, or at least a passport, could be purchased by those who had the money:

"well-off families accumulated passports not only from Canada, Australia, Singapore and the United States but also from revenue poor Fiji, the Philippines, Panama and Tonga (which required in return for a passport a down payment of U.S. $200,000 and an equal amount in installments)" (Ong 2002, 183) (Figure 15.7).

Although wealthy overseas Chinese families had thus managed to evade or subvert both the governmentality of Chinese kinship and of nation-states, they remained vulnerable to the discipline of the capitalist market. To be sure, market discipline under globalization was very different from the market discipline typical in the 1950s and 1960s. Making money in the context of globalization required the flexibility to take advantage of economic opportunities wherever and whenever they appeared. Ong describes one family in which the eldest son remained in Hong Kong to run part of the family hotel chain located in the Pacific region while his brother lived in San Francisco and managed the hotels located in North America and Europe. Children can be separated from their parents when they are, for example, installed in one country to be educated while their parents manage businesses in other countries on different continents.

These flexible business arrangements are not without costs. "Familial regimes of dispersal and localization . . . discipline family members to make do with very little emotional support; disrupted parental responsibility, strained marital relations, and abandoned children are such common circumstances that they have special terms." At the same time, individual family members truly do seem to live comfortably as citizens of the world. A Chinese banker in San Francisco told Ong that he could live in Asia, Canada, or Europe:

Figure 15.7 Overseas Chinese in Tahiti. Overseas Chinese are to be found in many parts of the world. They are not always millionaire businesspeople, but are shopkeepers and small businesspeople as well.

"I can live anywhere in the world, but it must be near an airport"(2002, 190).

The values and practices to which overseas Chinese adhere and which seem to be responsible for their tremendous achievements in a globalized capitalist economy suggest to Ong that, for these elite Chinese, the concept of nationalism has lost its meaning. Instead, she says, they seem to subscribe to a **postnational ethos** in which they submit to the governmentality of the capitalist market while trying to evade the governmentality of nation-states, ultimately because their only true loyalty is to the family business (2002, 190). Ong notes, however, that flexible citizenship informed by a postnational ethos is not an option for non-elite migrants: "whereas for bankers, boundaries are always flexible, for migrant workers, boat people, persecuted intellectuals and artists, and other kinds of less well-heeled refugees, this . . . is a harder act to follow" (190).

She points out that, on the way to their success, contemporary Chinese merchants "have also revived premodern forms of child, gender, and class oppression, as well as strengthened authoritarianist regimes in Asia" (2002, 190). Yet, neither the positives nor the negatives should, she insists, be attributed to any "Chinese" essence; instead, she thinks these strategies are better understood as "the expressions of a habitus that is finely tuned to the turbulence of late capitalism" (191).

Are Human Rights Universal?

Globalization has stimulated discussions about **human rights**: powers, privileges, or material resources to which people everywhere, by virtue of being human, are justly entitled. Rapidly circulating capital, images, people, things, and ideologies juxtapose different understandings about what it means to be human or what kinds of rights people may be entitled to. The context within which human-rights discourse becomes relevant is often described as **multiculturalism**: living permanently in

---

postnational ethos An attitude toward the world in which people submit to the governmentality of the capitalist market while trying to evade the governmentality of nation-states.

human rights Powers, privileges, or material resources to which people everywhere, by virtue of being human, are justly entitled.

multiculturalism Living permanently in settings surrounded by people with cultural backgrounds different from one's own and struggling to define with them the degree to which the cultural beliefs and practices of different groups should or should not be accorded respect and recognition by the wider society.

---

settings surrounded by people with cultural backgrounds different from your own and struggling to define with them the degree to which the wider society should accord respect and recognition to the cultural beliefs and practices of different groups. It is precisely in multicultural settings—found everywhere in today's globalized world—that questions of rights become salient and different cultural understandings of what it means to be human, and what rights humans are entitled to, become the focus of contention.

Human–Rights Discourse as the Global Language of Social Justice

Discourses about human rights have proliferated in recent decades, stimulated by the original UN Universal Declaration on Human Rights in 1948 and followed by numerous subsequent declarations. For example, in 1992, the Committee for the Elimination of Discrimination against Women (CEDAW) declared that violence against women was a form of gender discrimination that violated the human rights of women. This declaration was adopted by the UN General Assembly in 1993 and became part of the rights platform at the Fourth World Conference on Women in Beijing, China, in 1995 (Figure 15.8). Anthropologist Sally Merry observes that this declaration "dramatically demonstrates the creation of new rights—rights which depend on the state's failure to protect women rather than its active violation of rights" and that "the emergence of violence against women as a distinct human rights violation depends on redefining the family so that it is no longer shielded from legal scrutiny" (2001, 36–37).

Although CEDAW has proved particularly contentious, other human-rights documents have been signed without controversy by many national governments. Signing a human-rights declaration supposedly binds governments to take official action to implement changes in local practices that might be seen to violate the rights asserted in the declaration. Human-rights discourses are common currency in all societies, at all levels.

Because of the wide adoption of human-rights discourses throughout the world, some people have come to speak of an emerging "culture of human rights" which has now become "the preeminent global language of social justice" (Merry 2001, 38). As Jane Cowan, Marie Bénédicte Dembour, and Richard Wilson write, it is "no use imagining a 'primitive' tribe which has not yet heard of human rights . . . what it means to be 'indigenous' is itself transformed through interaction with human-rights discourses and institutions" (2001, 5). These developments mean that anthropologists need to take note of the important influence this human-rights

Figure 15.8 Women marching against violence at the Fourth World Conference on Women in Beijing, 1995.

discourse is having in the various settings where they do their research.

What counts as "human rights" has changed over time, due not only to the action of international bodies like the UN but also to the efforts of an increasing number of nongovernmental organizations (NGOs) that have become involved in various countries of the world, many of them deeply committed to projects designed to improve people's lives and protect their rights (Figure 15.9). As Merry says, these developments "have created a new legal order" that has given birth to new possibilities throughout the world for the elaboration and discussion of what human rights are all about (2001, 35).

In addition, because the "culture of human rights" is increasingly regarded, in one way or another, as the "culture of globalization," it would seem to be a topic

Figure 15.9 Women's shelters run by NGOs in Afghanistan provide a variety of services. Classmates applaud a fellow student after she stood up to read in a literacy class at one such shelter.

well-suited to anthropological analysis in itself. This is because, as we shall see, human-rights discourse is not as straightforward as it seems. On the face of things, defending human rights for all people would seem unproblematic. Few people who are aware of the devastation wrought by colonial exploitation, for example, would want to suggest that the victims of that exploitation did not have rights that needed to be protected at all costs. Yet, when we look closely at particular disputes about human rights, the concept no longer seems so simple.

Cowan and her colleagues have noted that there are two major arguments that have developed for talking about the way human rights and culture are related. The first involves the idea that *human rights are opposed to culture* and that the two cannot be reconciled. The second involves the idea that a key universal human right is precisely one's *right to culture*. We will consider each in turn.

Rights versus Culture?

Arguments that pit human rights against culture depend upon the assumption that "cultures" are homogeneous, bounded, and unchanging sets of ideas and practices and that each society has only one culture, which its members are obligated to follow. As we saw in Chapter 8, this view of culture has been severely criticized by cultural anthropologists. But it is a view of culture that is very much alive in many human-rights disputes. For if people have no choice but to follow the rules of the culture into which they were born, international interference with customs said to violate human rights would seem itself to constitute a human-rights violation. Outsiders would be disrupting a supposedly harmonious way of life and preventing those who are committed to such a way of life from observing their own culturally specific understandings about rights. Thus, it is concluded, cultures should be allowed to enjoy absolute, inviolable protection from interference by outsiders. This has been the position adopted, for example, by some national governments that have refused to sign the CEDAW declaration that violence against women violates women's human rights. "Many states have opposed this conception of human rights on cultural or religious grounds, and have refused to ratify treaties." (Merry 2001, 37). Nevertheless, by 2009, 186 countries had ratified CEDAW (http://www.unifem.org/cedaw30/).

Sometimes representatives of non-Western nation-states may feel free to dismiss rights talk as an unwelcome colonial imposition of ideas that, far from being universal, reflect ethnocentric European preoccupations. But such a dismissal of human-rights discourse needs to be closely examined. In the case of the right of women to protection from violence, for example, Merry points out that although some forms of violence against women may be culturally sanctioned in some societies, there are many forms that violence against women can take even in those societies and not all of these are accorded the same amount of cultural support. As we saw in Chapter 8, practices such as female genital cutting could be justified in the past in some circumstances as an appropriate cultural action, but it is now being questioned and even outlawed in the societies where it was traditional. This suggests that "culture values" cannot be held responsible for everything that people do in any society and that members of the same society can disagree about these matters and sometimes change their minds.

As talk about human rights has become incorporated into local cultural discussions in recent decades, anthropologists are not surprised to discover that the notion undergoes transformation as people try to make sense of what it means in their own local contexts (Cowan et al. 2001, 8). Being forced to choose between rights and culture, however, seems increasingly unviable in a globalizing, multicultural world. In their own anthropological work on these matters, Cowan and her colleagues are convinced that the rights-versus-culture debate exaggerates cultural differences. Like many cultural anthropologists today, they find that "it is more illuminating to think of culture as a field of creative interchange and contestation" (2001, 4) Such a view of culture makes it possible to find points of connection between the defense of certain human rights and the defense of particular cultural values.

Finally, it is worth asking if "culture" is sometimes used as a scapegoat to mask the unwillingness of a government to extend certain rights to its citizens for reasons that have nothing to do with culture. Cowan and colleagues observe that states like Indonesia and Singapore, which position themselves as stout defenders of "Asian values," have welcomed Western industrial capitalism. To reject human-rights discourse because it contradicts "Asian values" would, at the very least, suggest "an inconsistent attitude toward westernization," which in turn feeds suspicions that the defense of "Asian values" may be a political tactic designed "to bolster state sovereignty and resist international denunciations of internal repression and political dissent" (2001, 6–7).

Rights to Culture?

A second popular argument about the relationship between rights and culture begins from very different premises. This argument does not view universal "human rights" as alien and opposed to "cultures." Instead, it says that all peoples have a universal human right to maintain their own distinct cultures. The *right to culture* has already been explicit in a number of international rights documents.

This argument is interesting because it seems to concede that such things as universal human rights do exist after all. The list of universal rights is simply amended to include the right to one's culture. It draws strength from the idea that cultural diversity is intrinsically valuable and that people should be able to observe their own cultural practices free from outside interference. However, it calls into question the common understanding that people frequently cannot enjoy their full human rights until they are *freed* from the constraints of local cultures. A right to culture, therefore, shows how the very idea of rights and culture is transformed and contested by globalization.

One key issue in the struggle to protect the right to culture is shared by *any* claim to human rights. It concerns the kinds of legal mechanisms needed to ensure protection. The great promise of international documents like the UN Declaration on Human Rights seems to be that people are now free to bring allegations of human-rights abuses to an international forum to seek redress. But in fact this is not the case. As human-rights activists have discovered, human rights are legally interpreted as *individual* rights, not group rights. This means that people must demand that the *governments of the nation-states in which they are citizens* recognize and enforce the individual rights defended in international documents. International institutions like the UN have been unwilling to challenge the sovereignty of individual nation-states.

The defense of all human rights, including a right to culture, thus depends on the policies of national governments. Some activists see this as a serious contradiction in human-rights discourse that undermines its effectiveness. Talal Asad recounts, for example, how Malcolm X argued in the 1960s that African Americans who wanted redress for abuses of their human rights should go directly to the UN and press their case against the government of the United States: "When you expand the civil-rights struggle to the level of human rights, you can then take the case of the black man in this country before the nations in the UN" (quoted in Asad 2003, 141).

In fact, however, this is not the way the system was intended to work. Asad reminds us that

> *The Universal Declaration of Human Rights* begins by asserting 'the inherent dignity' and the 'equal and inalienable rights of all members of *the human family*,' and then turns immediately to the state. In doing so, it implicitly accepts the fact that the universal character of the rights-bearing person is made the responsibility of sovereign states (137).

In this legal universe, African Americans (and similarly situated groups in other nation-states) occupied an anomalous position: "they were neither the bearers of national rights nor of human rights" (144). The recognition of the human rights of African Americans thus depended on persuading the *U.S. government* to recognize those rights; the UN might use its persuasive power to urge such changes, but it had no coercive power to force the United States—or any other national government —to come into compliance.

Martin Luther King's strategy, Asad points out, took a very different tack, using arguments drawn from prophetic religious discourse and the discourse of American liberalism. His movement aimed at "mobilizing American public opinion for change," and it was effective at pressing for progressive social change in a way that, among other things, was compatible with the division of labor set forth by the UN Declaration of Human Rights (2003, 146). In a globalizing world, however, this division of human-rights labor—international bodies propose, but nation-states implement—is being challenged. For example, transborder citizenries lack any forum in which their status and their demands are clearly accorded legitimacy. The right-to-culture movement has succeeded in recent years in highlighting such anomalies and eroding the traditionally recognized right of nation-states to determine the kinds of rights their citizens will be accorded (Cowan et al. 2001, 8–9). As in the case of the rights-versus-culture argument, however, the right-

to-culture argument can be "called upon to legitimate reactionary projects as easily as progressive ones . . . the uses to which culture can be put in relation to rights are evidently multiple" (10).

Anthropological disciplinary commitments have allowed anthropologists to approach debates about rights and culture in ways that contribute something new to the discussion. These anthropological contributions can be seen in two ways. First, anthropologists have addressed the ways in which human-rights discourse can itself be seen as culture. Second, their own struggles with the concept of "culture" allow them to mount a critique of some of the ways that this concept has been mobilized in discussions of human rights.

Are Rights Part of Culture?

Anthropological approaches are well suited for investigating the so-called culture of human rights that appears to have emerged in recent years. As in the cultures traditionally studied by anthropologists, the culture of human rights is based on certain ideas about human beings, their needs, and their ability to exercise agency, as well as the kinds of social connections between human beings that are considered legitimate and illegitimate. The entire question of "legitimacy" in human-rights discourse points to the central role played by *law*, both as a way of articulating specific human rights and as a tool for defending those rights. Cowan and colleagues (2001) have drawn on earlier anthropological work in which systems of law were analyzed as cultural systems.

One important source has been the "law and culture" framework developed by anthropologists Clifford Geertz, Laura Nader, and Lawrence Rosen and nonanthropologists like Boaventura de Sousa Santos. In this framework, "law is conceived as a worldview or structuring discourse . . . 'Facts' . . . are socially constructed through rules of evidence, legal conventions, and the rhetoric of legal actors" (Cowan et al. 2001, 11). Analysts who talk about a "culture of human rights" as the new culture of a globalizing world point out that the key features of the human-rights worldview clearly indicate its origins in Western secular discourse. That is, it focuses on the rights of individuals, it proposes to relieve human suffering through technical rather than ethical solutions, and it emphasizes rights over duties or needs (2001, 11–12).

In the meantime most anthropologists would probably agree that anthropology can clarify the idea of a "culture of human rights" (Cowan et al. 2001, 13). An understanding of culture as open, heterogeneous, and supple could be effective in helping us understand how human-rights processes work.

Anthropology and Indigenous Rights

Anthropologists are increasingly participating in organizations for the defense of human rights. In particular, they have contributed to the recognition by human-rights legal advocates that the collective rights of groups (such as indigenous peoples) deserve as much attention as the rights of individuals. For example, one of the foremost anthropologically oriented organizations involved with human rights is Cultural Survival, founded in 1972 by anthropologists Pia Maybury-Lewis and David Maybury-Lewis (Figure 15.10) and dedicated to helping indigenous people and ethnic minorities deal as equals in their encounters with industrial society, and this includes struggles for indigenous rights (E. Lutz 2006).

Settings in which indigenous rights are debated and policies are formulated have become sites for ethnographic research, much of it multisited. For example, anthropologist Ronald Niezen began his career in the time-honored fashion of carrying out single-sited research on Islamic reform in Mali. Later he undertook community-based research with the eastern James Bay Crees in northern Quebec, Canada. Nevertheless, he writes, "the James Bay Crees also introduced me to international politics." In 1994, he traveled as an observer delegate with the Grand Council of the Crees to a meeting of the Working Group on Indigenous Populations at the United Nations in Geneva, Switzerland. People on the reservation were also learning via the Internet about the struggles of other indigenous communities for rights and were starting to "see

themselves as leading a cause for justice directly analogous to (and without distinguishing among) a variety of liberation movements, including the American civil rights movement and resistance to South African apartheid" (Niezen 2003, xiii).

As his involvement with the James Bay Crees increased, Niezen found that the Crees valued his ability to provide a link between their own aboriginal government and the government of Canada. He was called on to perform many roles in addition to that of participant-observer: during the first two years he found himself acting "as an observer, witness, advocate, author—roles that were pretty much informally developed as needs became felt" (xiv). As he moved back and forth from reservation to government meetings, he came to realize that a global movement of indigenous peoples had come into existence and was getting noticed at places such as the United Nations. His earlier research in Mali also became relevant in a new way when, during one of his trips to Geneva, he encountered delegates from West Africa who were coming to identify themselves as indigenous peoples and who were working "to develop human rights standards appropriate to their concerns" (xiv).

Indigeneity is supposed to refer to a primordial identity that preceded the establishment of colonial states. Yet the very possibility that groups from West Africa, Latin America, and North America might come together as indigenous peoples "is predicated upon global sameness of experience, and is expressed through the mechanisms of law and bureaucracy"

Figure 15.10 Anthropologists have become increasingly involved in the defense of human rights. David Maybury-Lewis (pictured here with Xavante informants in Brazil) and Pia Maybury-Lewis founded Cultural Survival, an organization dedicated to helping indigenous peoples and ethnic minorities deal as equals in their encounters with industrial society.

(Niezen 2003, 2–3). "Indigenous peoples" is not just a badge of identity, but also a legal term that has been included in international conventions issued by the International Labor Organization.

According to Niezen, it is important to distinguish what he calls *ethnonationalism* from *indigenism*. Ethnonationalism, he believes, describes a movement of people who "have defined their collective identities with clear cultural and linguistic contours and who express their goals of autonomy from the state with the greatest conviction and zeal, sometimes with hatreds spilling over into violence." For example, in Canada the advocates of sovereignty for Quebec have pushed for an independent French-speaking nation-state (8). Indigenism, by contrast, "is not a particularized identity but a global one, . . . grounded in international networks" (9). What connects specific groups to this identity, whether they live in dictatorships or democratic states, "is a sense of illegitimate, meaningless, and dishonorable suffering" (13; Figure 15.11).

Unlike ethnonationalists, indigenous-rights activists do not seek to form breakaway states of their own. Their approach is entirely different: indigenous representatives lobby for their rights before international bodies such as the United Nations, attempting to hold states accountable for abusing their indigenous citizens. In Niezen's opinion, the strategy "shows some indigenous leaders to be, despite their limited power and resources, some of the most effective political strategists on the contemporary national and international scenes" (2003, 16). Their goal is to get nation-states to live up to their responsibilities and promises to indigenous people, which are often explicitly stated in treaties. Thus, they seek affirmation of their rights to land and compensation for past losses and suffering; they seek cultural self-determination and political sovereignty. The goal of indigenous liberation thus involves the recognition of *collective rights*.

While Niezen urges us to acknowledge the daring and effectiveness of the indigenous movement, he also warns against romanticizing it: "Significant obstacles remain to be overcome before a new order of relations between indigenous peoples and the state can be said to have truly arrived" (2003, 23). For example, the United Nations has been less responsive than many indigenous delegates might have hoped, because some of its member states continue to equate the movement for indigenous sovereignty with ethnonationalism. Hence the UN Permanent Forum on Indigenous Issues is not called the UN Permanent Forum on Indigenous *Peoples* (160–164).

Some liberal human-rights theorists are also concerned that the recognition of collective rights would serve as a green light to despotic governments, who could use the rights of distinct cultures as an excuse for repression. Niezen concluded that

> if indigenous claims to self-determination are to avoid playing into the hands of despotic governments, they must have individual rights built into them. . . . Human rights do not offer protection of cultural practices that themselves violate individual rights. The concept of "indigenous peoples" developed principally within Western traditions of scholarship and legal reform . . . has transcended its symbolic use by acquiring legal authority. . . . It has been taken control of by its living subjects—reverse-engineered, rearticulated, and put to use as a tool of liberation. (219–221)

Figure 15.11 Sidney Hill, Tadodaho Chief of the Haudenosaunee, speaking at the United Nations Permanent Forum on Indigenous Issues.

How Can Culture Help In Thinking about Rights?

To use the culture concept as a tool for analyzing human-rights processes means looking for "patterns and relationships of meaning and practice between different domains of social life" that are characteristic of the culture of human rights (Cowan et al. 2001, 13). Since human rights are articulated in legal documents and litigated in courts, one of the most important patterns that become visible in the culture of human rights is the way they are shaped to accommodate the law. Groups and individuals who assert that their human rights have been violated regularly take their cases to courts of law. But this means that in order to get the courts to take them seriously, they need to understand how the law operates. A key feature of this understanding involves a realistic awareness of the kinds of claims that the law pays attention to and the kinds of claims that it dismisses.

Looking at human-rights law as culture reveals that only certain kinds of claims are admissible. As we saw above, the culture of human rights as currently constituted is best suited to redress the grievances of individuals, not groups. It also provides technical, not ethical, remedies, and it emphasizes rights over duties or needs. Plaintiffs are therefore likely to have a difficult time if they want to claim that their group rights have been violated, that they want the violator exposed and punished, or that the state itself has failed to fulfill its responsibilities toward them. Part of the human-rights process therefore involves learning how to craft cases that will fit the laws. This can be tricky if the categories and identities recognized in human-rights law do not correspond to categories and identities that are meaningful to the plaintiffs.

Anthropologists have worked with many social groups struggling with national governments to practice their culture freely. These political struggles regularly include claims about distinct and unchanging values and practices. As we saw in Chapter 14, these kinds of arguments for a right to culture are often cases of "strategic essentialism." That is, the unity and unchanging homogeneity of a particular "culture" is deliberately constructed in order to build group solidarity and to engage the state in a focused and disciplined way. But the "essentialism" that often comes to dominate discussions of group rights is not due entirely to the strategies of activists. Once they choose to make their case in a court of law, they become subject to the "essentializing proclivities of the law" (Cowan et al. 2001, 11). Because human-rights law recognizes only certain kinds of violations, groups with grievances must tailor those grievances to fit.

According to Merry, for example, groups like the Hawaiian Sovereignty Movement have successfully achieved some of their political goals by making claims based on the requirements of their "traditional culture." But this is because they live in a society that is "willing to recognize claims on the basis of cultural authenticity and tradition but not reparations based on acts of conquest and violation" (Merry 2001, 42–43). Outside the courtroom, many members of indigenous groups think of their culture the way contemporary anthropologists think about culture: there are some common patterns but culture is basically unbounded, heterogeneous, and open to change. The conflict between these two understandings of culture has the potential to reshape their ideas about what their culture is. Groups that enter into the human rights process, thus, are entering into ethically ambiguous territory that is "both enabling and constraining" (Cowan et al. 2001, 11).

Human Rights in Hawaii: Violence against Women

Merry has studied how changing legal regimes in Hawaii over nearly two centuries have reshaped local understandings of Hawaiian culture (see EthnoProfile 15.1: Hawaii). Part of her work has addressed the ways "local human rights activists are struggling to create a new space which incorporates both cultural differences and transnational conceptions of human rights" (2001, 32). Hawaii is a particularly interesting setting for such a study, since for much of the nineteenth century it was located "at the crossroads of a dizzying array of peoples and at the center of a set of competing cultural logics" (44)—in a setting, that is very much like the globalized, multicultural settings that are increasingly common today. Over the course of the century, Hawaiian law went through two important periods of "legal transplantation:" the first, 1820–1844, involved the adoption of a Christianized Hawaiian law; and the second, 1845–1852, involved the adoption of a secularized Western law. Although these legal transformations involved colonial imposition, they also depended upon active collaboration by Hawaiian elites (43–44). Indeed, Merry says that these legal changes are best understood as a process of *transculturation* in which subjugated Hawaiians received and adopted forms of self-understanding imposed by the Christian West, even as the Christian West was modified in response to this reception and adoption. Because the Hawaiians were not passive in this process and tried to make use of Christianity and Western ideas for purposes of their own, the process, Merry argues, was fraught with frustration and failure. Missionaries and rulers who wanted to turn Hawaii into a "civilized" place were forced to try to impose their will in stages, rather than all at once, and the end result still bore many Hawaiian traces that, to their dismay, seemed to evade the civilizing process (Figure 15.12).

This process of cultural appropriation is uncertain: change comes in fits and starts, constantly requiring adjustment as circumstances vary. Merry argues that human-rights discourse is being appropriated by contemporary Hawaiians in much the same way (2001, 46–47). For the past decade, she has studied a feminist program in Hilo, Hawaii, that "endeavors to support women victims of violence and retrain male batterers" (48). This program is based on one originally created in Duluth, Minnesota, and it works closely with the courts. In 1985, the courts adopted the language of rights in dealing with violence against women. This means that the law supports the notion of gender equality and, when husbands are found guilty of battering their wives, calls for separation of the couple. By contrast, Hawaiian couples who participate in the program are often conservative Christians who do not believe in divorce. It might seem that this is a classic example of the conflict between "rights" and "culture," but in fact "local adaptations of the rights model do take place" (47). This was done by tailoring the program's curriculum to local circumstances using Hawaiian images and examples. Particularly interesting was the way the part of the program designed to teach anger management to batterers was made locally relevant by combining Christian ideas with ideas from Hawaiian activists that

EthnoProfile 15.1

Hawaii

Region: Polynesia

Nation: United States

Population: 1,244,000 (2002 census)

Environment: Tropical Pacific island

Livelihood: Agriculture, industry, tourism, service, state and local government

Political organization: Modern state within United States

For more information: Merry, Sally Engle. 1999. *Colonizing Hawai'i.* Princeton: Princeton University Press.

Figure 15.12 The Hawaiian Sovereignty Movement has emphasized traditional culture and has taken action more broadly. Here members lead a march protesting the Asian Development Bank.

connected male anger to the losses they have suffered as a consequence of conquest. Merry visited a similar kind of program in New Zealand based on the same Minnesota model, which had been locally modified for Maori men in a way that linked their anger to Maori experiences of racism and loss. "Although all of these programmes share a similar commitment to a rights-based approach that works in conjunction with the criminal justice system, each has developed a local accommodation of the curriculum, a reframing which takes into account local problems and cultural practices" (49).

These examples suggest two important conclusions: first, it is possible to find ways of accommodating the universal discourse of human rights to the particularities of local conditions; second, no single model of the relationship between rights and culture will fit all cases. Moreover, as the culture of human rights becomes better established, it increasingly becomes enmeshed in political and legal institutions that go beyond the local level. As activists become more experienced operating in globalized circumstances, moreover, they are likely to become more sophisticated about making use of these different settings as they plan their human-rights strategies (Cowan et al. 2001, 21). Struggles over human rights are hardly likely to go away; indeed, along with struggles over global citizenship, they can be seen as the prime struggles of our time (Mignolo 2002). Anthropologists are well positioned to help make sense of these complex developments as they unfold.

Cultural Imperialism or Cultural Hybridity?

The impact of the global spread of images, ideas, people, things, and ideologies in local social settings has clearly been profound, as illustrated by the preceding examples. But how should anthropologists characterize the processes by which these changes have come about?

What Is Cultural Imperialism?

One explanation, formulated during the Cold War was called **cultural imperialism**. Cultural imperialism is based on two notions. First is the idea that some cultures dominate other cultures. In recent history, it is the

culture(s) of Europe, or the United States or "the West," that are seen to have come to dominate all other cultures of the world, due to the spread of colonialism and capitalism. Second, domination by one culture is said to lead inevitably to the destruction of subordinated cultures and their replacement by the culture of those in power. Thus, Western cultural imperialism is seen as responsible for destroying, for example, local music, technology, dress, and food traditions and replacing them with rock and roll, radios, flashlights, cell phones, T-shirts, blue jeans, McDonald's hamburgers, and Coca-Cola (Figure 15.13). The inevitable outcome of Western cultural imperialism is seen to be "the cultural homogenization of the world," with the unwelcome consequence of "dooming the world to uniformity" (Inda and Rosaldo 2002, 13–14).

The idea of cultural imperialism developed primarily outside anthropology, but anthropologists could not ignore it because it claimed to describe what was happening to the people they studied. Anthropologists, too, were aware that Western music, fashion, food, and technology had spread among those they worked with. But cultural imperialism did not seem to be a satisfactory explanation for this spread, for at least three reasons (Inda

Figure 15.13 People line up outside McDonald's in Cairo, Egypt.

---

cultural imperialism The idea that some cultures dominate others and that domination by one culture leads inevitably to the destruction of subordinated cultures and their replacement by the culture of those in power.

and Rosaldo 2002, 22–24). First, as we saw in Chapter 12, the discourse of cultural imperialism denies *agency* to non-Western peoples who make use of Western cultural forms. It assumes that they are passive and without the resources to resist anything of Western origin that is marketed to them. Second, cultural imperialism assumes that non-Western cultural forms never move "from the rest to the West." But this is clearly false. Non-Western music, food, and material culture have large and eager followings in western Europe and the United States. Third, cultural imperialism ignores that cultural forms and practices sometimes move from one part of the non-Western world to other parts of the non-Western world, bypassing the West entirely. For example, movies made in India have been popular for decades in northern Nigeria (Larkin 2002), Mexican soap operas have large followings in the Philippines, and karaoke is popular all over the world.

Cultural Hybridity

Dissatisfied with the discourse of cultural imperialism, anthropologists began to search for alternative ways of understanding global cultural flows. From the days of Franz Boas and his students, anthropologists had recognized the significance of cultural borrowing. They had also emphasized that borrowing cultural forms or practices from elsewhere always involves *borrowing-with-modification*. That is, people never adopt blindly but always adapt what they borrow for local purposes. Put another way, people rarely accepted ideas or practices or objects from elsewhere without *domesticating* or *indigenizing* them—that is, finding a way of reconciling them with local practices in order to serve local purposes.

In the 1980s, for example, weavers in Otavalo, Ecuador, were making a lot of money selling textiles to tourists. They could then organize small production firms and purchase television sets to entertain their employees while they worked at their looms. In addition, some men had so much business that they encouraged their wives to take up weaving, even though women were not traditionally weavers. In order to spend more time weaving, women started to use indoor cookstoves, which relieved them from the time-consuming labor of traditional meal preparation over an open fire (Colloredo-Mansfeld 1999). From the perspective of anthropologist Rudi Colloredo-Mansfeld, these uses of Western technology could not be understood as the consequences of Western cultural imperialism because they clearly had nothing to do with trying to imitate a Western lifestyle. It made more sense to interpret these changes as Otavalan domestication or indigenization of televisions and cookstoves, since these items from elsewhere

were adopted precisely in order to promote indigenous Otavalan weaving. Put yet another way, borrowing-with-modification always involves customizing that which is borrowed to meet the purposes of the borrowers, which may be quite remote from the purposes of those among whom the form or practice originated (Inda and Rosaldo 2002, 16). This form of cultural change is very different from having something from elsewhere forced on you against your will (Figure 15.14).

At the same time, the consequences of borrowing-with-modification can never be fully controlled. Thus, Otavalan weavers may start watching television because local reruns of old American television series relieve the tedium of weaving. However, once television watching becomes a habitual practice, it also exposes them to advertising and news broadcasts, which may stimulate other local changes that nobody can predict. The domestication or indigenization of cultural forms from

Figure 15.14 Musical performance has become an important part of the Otavalo Indian economy as musicians from Otavalo travel throughout the world performing and selling woven goods. They have domesticated CD production as well, and have been quite successful at selling CDs of their music to tourists in Otavalo and listeners abroad.

In Their Own Words

How Sushi Went Global

Talk of "global flows" can seem abstract and divorced from everyday life, but one of the strengths of anthropology is its ability to capture the articulation of the local with the global. As sushi has swept the United States, anthropologist Theodore Bestor looked at the trade in tuna.

A 40-minute drive from Bath, Maine, down a winding two-lane highway, the last mile on a dirt road, a ramshackle wooden fish pier stands beside an empty parking lot. At 6:00 p.m. nothing much is happening. Three bluefin tuna sit in a huge tub of ice on the loading dock.

Between 6:45 and 7:00, the parking lot fills up with cars and trucks with license plates from New Jersey, New York, Massachusetts, New Hampshire, and Maine. Twenty tuna buyers clamber out, half of them Japanese. The three bluefin, ranging from 270 to 610 pounds, are winched out of the tub, and buyers crowd around them, extracting tiny core samples to examine their color, fingering the flesh to assess the fat content, sizing up the curve of the body.

After about 20 minutes of eyeing the goods, many of the buyers return to their trucks to call Japan by cellphone and get the morning prices from Tokyo's Tsukiji market—the fishing industry's answer to Wall Street where the daily tuna auctions have just concluded. The buyers look over the tuna one last time and give written bids to the dock manager, who passes the top bid for each fish to the crew that landed it.

The auction bids are secret. Each bid is examined anxiously by a cluster of young men, some with a father or uncle looking on to give advice, others with a young woman and a couple of toddlers trying to see Daddy's fish. Fragments of concerned conversation float above the parking lot: "That's all?" "Couldn't we do better if we shipped it ourselves?" "Yeah, but my pickup needs a new transmission now!" After a few minutes, deals are closed and the fish are quickly loaded onto the backs of trucks in crates of crushed ice, known in the trade as "tuna coffins." As rapidly as they arrived, the flotilla of buyers sails out of the parking lot—three bound for New York's John F. Kennedy Airport, where their tuna will be airfreighted to Tokyo for sale the day after next.

Bluefin tuna may seem at first an unlikely case study in globalization. But as the world rearranges itself—around silicon chips, Starbucks coffee, or sashimi-grade tuna—new channels for global flows of capital and commodities link far-flung individuals and communities in unexpected new relationships. The tuna trade is a prime example of the globalization of a regional industry, with intense international competition and thorny environmental regulations; centuries-old practices combined with high technology; realignments of labor and capital in response to international regulation; shifting markets; and the diffusion of culinary culture as tastes for sushi, and bluefin tuna, spread worldwide. . . .

Culture Splash

Just because sushi is available, in some form or another, in exclusive Fifth Avenue restaurants, in baseball stadiums in Los Angeles, at airport snack carts in Amsterdam, at an apartment in Madrid (delivered by motorcycle), or in Buenos Aires, Tel Aviv, or Moscow, doesn't mean that sushi has lost its status as Japanese cultural property. Globalization doesn't necessarily homogenize cultural differences nor erase the salience of cultural labels. Quite the contrary, it grows the franchise. In the global economy of consumption, the brand equity of sushi as Japanese cultural property adds to the cachet of both the country and the cuisine. A Texan Chinese-American restauranteur told me, for example, that he had converted his chain of restaurants from Chinese to Japanese cuisine because the prestige factor of the latter meant he could charge a premium; his clients couldn't distinguish between Chinese and Japanese employees (and often failed to notice that some of the chefs behind his sushi bars were Latinos).

The brand equity is sustained by complicated flows of labor and ethnic biases. Outside of Japan, having Japanese hands (or a reasonable facsimile) is sufficient warrant for sushi competence. Guidebooks for the current generation of Japanese global *wandervogel* sometimes advise young Japanese looking for a job in a distant city to work as a sushi chef; U.S. consular offices in Japan grant more than 1,000 visas a year to sushi chefs, tuna buyers, and other workers in the global sushi business. A trade school in Tokyo, operating under the name Sushi Daigaku (Sushi University), offers short courses in sushi preparation so "students" can impress prospective employers with an imposing certificate. Even without papers, however, sushi remains firmly linked in the minds of Japanese and foreigners alike with Japanese cultural identity. Throughout the world, sushi restaurants operated by Koreans, Chinese, or Vietnamese maintain Japanese identities. In sushi bars from Boston to Valencia, a customer's simple greeting in Japanese can throw chefs into a panic (or drive them to the far end of the counter).

In Their Own Words

On the docks, too, Japanese cultural control of sushi remains unquestioned. Japanese buyers and "tuna techs" sent from Tsukiji to work seasonally on the docks of New England laboriously instruct foreign fishers on the proper techniques for catching, handling, and packing tuna for export. A bluefin tuna must approximate the appropriate *kata*, or "ideal form," of color, texture, fat content, body shape, and so forth, all prescribed by Japanese specifications. Processing requires proper attention as well. Special paper is sent from Japan for wrapping the fish before burying them in crushed ice. Despite high shipping costs and the fact that 50 percent of the gross weight of a tuna is unusable, tuna is sent to Japan whole, not sliced into salable portions. Spoilage is one reason for this, but form is another. Everyone in the trade agrees that Japanese workers are much more skilled in cutting and trimming tuna than Americans, and no one would want to risk sending botched cuts to Japan.

Not to impugn the quality of the fish sold in the United States, but on the New England docks, the first determination of tuna buyers is whether they are looking at a "domestic" fish or an "export" fish. On that judgment hangs several dollars a pound for the fisher, and the supply of sashimi-grade tuna for fishmongers, sushi bars, and seafood restaurants up and down the Eastern seaboard. Some of the best tuna from New England may make it to New York or Los Angeles, but by way of Tokyo—validated as top quality (and top price) by the decision to ship it to Japan by air for sale at Tsukiji, where it may be purchased by one of the handful of Tsukiji sushi exporters who supply premier expatriate sushi chefs in the world's leading cities.

Source: Bestor 2000.

elsewhere *both* makes it possible to do old things in new ways *and* leaves open the possibility of doing new things as well. Put another way, cultural borrowing is double-edged; borrowed cultural practices are both amenable to domestication and yet able to escape it. No wonder that cultural borrowing is often viewed with ambivalence.

The challenges are particularly acute in globalizing conditions, colonial or postcolonial, where borrowed ideas, objects, or practices remain entangled in relationships with donors even as they are made to serve new goals by recipients (Thomas 1991). People in multicultural settings must deal on a daily basis with tempting cultural alternatives emanating from more powerful groups. It is therefore not suprising that they regularly struggle to control processes of cultural borrowing and to contain domesticated cultural practices within certain contexts or in the hands of certain people only.

Many social scientists have borrowed a metaphor from biology to describe this complex process of globalized cultural exchange and speak of **cultural hybridization** or **hybridity**. Both these concepts were meant to highlight forms of cultural borrowing that produced something new that could not be collapsed or subsumed, either within the culture of the donor or within the culture of the recipient. In addition, they stressed the positive side of cultural mixing: rather than indicating a regrettable loss of original purity, hybridity and creolization draw attention to positive processes of cultural creativity.

Furthermore, if cultural hybridization is a normal part of all human social experience, then the idea that "authentic" traditions never change can legitimately be challenged. For members of a social group who wish to revise or discard cultural practices that they find outmoded or oppressive, hybridity talk is liberating. Choosing to revise or discard, borrow or invent *on terms of one's own choosing* also means that one possesses *agency*, the capacity to exercise at least some control over one's life. And exercising agency calls into question charges that one is succumbing to cultural imperialism or losing one's cultural "authenticity."

The Limits of Cultural Hybridity

However, as anthropologist Nicholas Thomas puts it, "hybridity is almost a good idea, but not quite" (1996, 9). Close examination of talk about cultural hybridization reveals at least three problems. First, it is not clear that this concept actually frees anthropologists from the modernist commitment to the existence of bounded,

---

cultural hybridization (or hybridity) Cultural mixing.

homogeneous, unchanging "cultures." That is, the idea of cultural hybridity is based on the notion of cultural mixing. But what is it that is mixed? Two or more non-hybridized, original, "pure," cultures! But such "pure" homogeneous, bounded, unchanging cultures are not supposed to exist. Thus, we are caught in a paradox. For this reason, Jonathan Friedman, among others, is highly critical of discussions of cultural hybridity; in his view, cultures have *always* been hybrid and it is the existence of *boundaries*, not cultural borrowing, that anthropologists need to explain. Besides, hybrid cultural mixtures often get transformed into new, unitary cultural identities. This process can be seen, he argues, in the way in which the "mixed race" category in the United States has been transformed into a "new, unitary group of mixtures for those who feel 'disenfranchised' by the current single-race categories"(1997, 83). Friedman also points out that hybrid identities are not liberating when they are thrust upon people rather than being adopted freely. He draws attention to cases in Latin America where the "mestizo" identity has been used "as a middle-/upper-class tool" against indigenous groups. "We are all part-Indian, say members of the elite who have much to lose in the face of minority claims" (1997, 81–82).

These examples highlight a second difficulty with hybridity talk: those who celebrate cultural hybridization often ignore the fact that its effects are experienced differently by those with power and those without power. As Friedman says, "the question of class becomes crucial" (1997, 81). The complexity of this issue appears in many popular discussions of "multiculturalism" that celebrate cultural hybridization and turn hybridity into a marketable commodity. The commodification of hybridity is problematic because it smooths over differences in the experience of cultural hybridization, offering multiculturalism as an array of tempting consumables for outsiders. "Multiculturalism is aimed at nourishing and perpetuating the kind of differences which do not [threaten]," writes Nira Yuval-Davis (1997, 197). International folk festivals, festivals of nations, and the like—events that emphasize costume, cuisine, music, and dance—spring to mind. But the troubling fact is that cultural hybridity is experienced as both nonthreatening and very threatening, depending on the terms on which it is available.

Because of power differences among groups challenged by cultural hybridization, any globalized "multicultural" setting reveals active cultural hybridization *together with* active *resistance* to cultural hybridization (Werbner 1997, 3). Werbner observes that cultural hybridization is unobjectionable when actors perceive it to be under their own control but resisted when it is "perceived by actors themselves to be potentially threatening to their sense of moral integrity" (1997, 12). The threat of cultural hybridization is greatest for those with the least power, who feel unable to control forms of hybridity that threaten the fragile survival structures on which they depend in an unwelcoming multicultural setting.

And this leads to a third problem with the concept of cultural hybridization. Fashionable hybridity talk hides the differences between elite and nonelite experiences of multiculturalism. Anthropologist John Hutnyk, for example, deplores the way "world music" is marketed to middle-class consumers because such sales strategies divert attention "from the urgency of anti-racist politics" (1997, 122). That is, when cultural hybridization becomes fashionable, it easily turns the experiences of hybridized elites into a hegemonic standard, suggesting that class exploitation and racial oppression are easily overcome or no longer exist. But to dismiss or ignore continuing nonelite struggles with cultural hybridization can spark dangerous confrontations that can quickly spiral out of control.

Anthropologist Peter van der Veer argues that such a dynamic ignited the furor in Britain that followed the publication of Salman Rushdie's novel *The Satanic Verses*. Rushdie is an elite, highly educated South Asian migrant to Britain who experienced cultural hybridity as a form of emancipation from oppressive religious and cultural restrictions. His novel contained passages describing Islam and the Prophet Muhammad that, from this elite point of view, embodied a liberating form of cultural "transgression." But migrants from South Asia in Britain are not all members of the elite. Most South Asian Muslim immigrants in Britain are workers, and they saw *The Satanic Verses* not as a work of artistic liberation but as a deliberate attempt to mock their beliefs and practices. "These immigrants, who are already socially and culturally marginalized, are thus double marginalized in the name of an attack on 'purity' and Islamic 'fundamentalism'" (1997, 101–102).

Even more important, however, may be the way popular interpretations of their objections in the press and among Western intellectuals ignored these immigrants' own, very different but very real, nonelite experiences of cultural hybridization. Put simply, elites experience globalization and cultural hybridization in ways that are often very different from the way nonelites experience cultural hybridization. To ignore this difference is not only politically short-sighted but also bad social science.

Can We Be at Home in a Global World?

The era of globalization in which we live is one of uncertainty and insecurity. Possibilities for emancipatory new ways of living are undercut by sharpening economic and political differences and the looming threat of violence. Is it possible, in the midst of all this confusion and conflict, to devise ways of coping with our circumstances that would provide guidance in the confusion, moderation to the conflict? No one expects such efforts to be easy. But anthropologists and other concerned scholars are currently struggling to come up with concepts and practices that might be helpful.

Cosmopolitanism

Our era is not the first to have faced such challenges. Walter Mignolo argues that multiculturalism was born in the sixteenth century when Iberian conquest in the New World first raised troubling issues among Western thinkers about the kinds of relationships that were possible and desirable between the conquerors and the indigenous peoples whom they conquered. During the ensuing centuries, the challenges posed by a multicultural world did not disappear. In the context of eighteenth-century Enlightenment promises of human emancipation based on the "rights of man and the citizen," philosopher Immanuel Kant concluded that the achievements of the Enlightenment offered individuals new opportunities for developing ways of being at home in the world wherever they were.

To identify this orientation, he revived a concept that was first coined by the Stoic philosophers of ancient Rome: **cosmopolitanism** (Mignolo 2002). Historically, cosmopolitanism "by and large meant being versed in Western ways and the vision of 'one world' culture was only a sometimes unconscious, sometimes unconscionable, euphemism for 'First World' culture" (Abbas 2002, 210).

But is it possible to rework our understandings of cultural hybridity to stretch the notion of cosmopolitanism beyond its traditional association with privileged Western elites? Many anthropologists have become comfortable talking about "alternative" or "minority" modernities that depart from the Western European norm. In a similar fashion, any new anthropological understanding of cosmopolitanism would have to be plural, not singular, and would have to include nonelite experiences of cultural hybridization.

What Is Friction?

Anthropologist Anna Lowenhaupt Tsing has worked in Indonesia for many years, investigating what she calls **friction**, "the awkward, unequal, unstable aspects of interconnection across difference" (2005, 4). Tsing seeks to understand how capitalist interests brought about the destruction of the Indonesian rain forests in the

1980s and 1990s as well as how environmental movements emerged to defend the forests and the people who live in them. Discussions of cultural imperialism assume that processes of global change will be smooth and unstoppable, that "globalization can be predicted in advance" (2005, 3). After the Cold War, for example, a number of politicians and social theorists predicted "an inevitable, peaceful transition" to global integration of the capitalist market (2005, 11). On the contrary, her research showed that the encounters between Japanese lumber traders and Indonesia government officials that turned Indonesia into the world's largest tropical lumber producer by 1973 were "messy and surprising" (2005, 3). She points out that "Indonesian tropical rain forests were not harvested as industrial timber until the 1970s" because "large-scale loggers prefer forests in which one valuable species predominates; tropical rain forests are just too biologically diverse" (2005, 14). However, in the 1970s the Japanese trading companies that began negotiations with the Indonesian New Order regime of President Suharto did not want access to valuable hardwoods; instead, they wanted "large quantities of cheaply produced logs," which they intended to turn into plywood.

The Japanese traders did not get what they wanted right away, however. Rather, as Tsing points out, this could not happen until three specific transformations had occurred. First, the forest had to be "simplified." Japanese lumber traders and Indonesian officials ignored species diversity, recognizing as valuable only those species that could be turned into plywood and regarding everything else—"the rest of the trees, fungi, and fauna . . . the fruit orchards, rattans, and other human-tended plants of forest dwellers"—as waste (2005, 16). Second, to make such forest simplification politically palatable, forests were reconfigured as a "sustainable resource" that could be replaced later by industrial tree plantations. However, once the Japanese traders were successful, Indonesian businessmen built their own plywood industry, based on the Japanese model. This led to the development of links between destruction of the forest and nation-building, as the state came to depend on income from selling forest concessions to favored political cronies. Once this alliance was forged, legal and illegal forms of forest exploitation could no longer be distinguished from one another, and it became impossible for forest dwellers

---

cosmopolitanism Being at ease in more than one cultural setting.

friction The awkward, unequal, unstable aspects of interconnection across difference.

to defend their own, preexisting property rights. "Either official or unofficial alone could be challenged, but together they overwhelmed local residents. . . . Together they transform the countryside into a free-for-all frontier" (2005, 17). But the production of such a frontier was not inevitable. It was the outcome of contingent encounters that people reworked in order to produce desired outcomes, along with additional, unintended consequences.

In response to rain forest destruction, a strong Indonesian environmental movement came into existence (Figure 15.15). Once again, however, this cannot be understood as a simple, predictable extension of Western environmentalist practices into Indonesia. On the contrary, "the movement was an amalgam of odd parts: engineers, nature lovers, reformers, technocrats" (2005, 17). In fact, activists who were dissatisfied with other features of President Suharto's New Order regime decided to focus on environmental issues, because these seemed to be issues less likely to trigger government censorship and repression. In any case, as Tsing says, "the movement was organized around difference" (2005, 17). It was not centralized, but "imagined itself as coordinating already existing but scattered and disorganized rural complaints. Activists' jobs, as they imagined it, involved translating subaltern demands into the languages of the powerful" and "translating back to let people know their rights" (2005, 18). It was messy, but this did not deter activists. "Within the links of awkwardly transcended difference, the environmental movement has tried to offer an alternative to forest destruction and the erosion of indigenous rights."

Like the alliance between businessmen and New Order government officials, the environmental movement emerged out of relationships forged by unlikely parties who struggled to find ways of working together to achieve overlapping but nonidentical goals. Thus, friction in the struggle to bridge differences makes new things possible: "Rubbing two sticks together produces heat and light; one stick alone is just a stick. As a metaphorical image, friction reminds us that heterogeneous and unequal encounters can lead to new arrangements of culture and power" (2005, 3–5). And these arrangements, while potentially dangerous, may also be seen as a source of hope: "Just as the encounter of Japanese trading companies and Indonesian politicians produced simplified dipterocarp forests, these activist-inspired encounters may yet produce different kinds of forests" (2005, 18).

What Is Border Thinking?

Tsing's understanding of "friction" as an unavoidable and productive feature of the process of cultural hybridization has much in common with what Walter Mignolo calls "border thinking." For Mignolo, in a globalized world, concepts like "democracy" and "justice" can no longer be defined within a single Western logic—or, for that matter, from the perspective of the political left or the political right. Border thinking involves detaching these concepts from their hegemonic "Western" meanings and practices and using them as *connectors*, tools for imagining and negotiating new, cosmopolitan forms of democracy or justice informed by the ethical and political judgments of nonelites (Mignolo 2002, 179, 181).

Figure 15.15 Heavy logging activity has led to destruction of the rain forest in Kalimantan and to the emergence of a strong Indonesian environmental movement.

Finally, in reimagining what cosmopolitanism might mean, it is important to go beyond not only Kantian limitations but also standard anthropological orientations to other ways of life. The hope is that border thinking can produce a *critical cosmopolitanism* capable of negotiating new understandings of human rights and global citizenship in ways that can dismantle the barriers of gender and race that are the historical legacies of colonialism (Mignolo 2002, 161, 180; Figure 15.16). In many cases, attempts to overcome power differentials and threats to moral integrity experienced by nonelites may lead to serious revision of Western modernist ideas and practices. But because cosmopolitanism involves border thinking, ideals and practices with Enlightenment credentials may also turn out to be valuable counterweights to extremism and violence. For example, relationships between Hindus and Muslims in India took a severe turn for the worse after Hindu vandals destroyed a mosque in the city of Ayodhya in 1992. Arjun Appadurai, who followed these developments closely, noted that the brutal Hindutva movement pushing to turn India into a Hindu state "violates the ideals of secularism and interreligious harmony enshrined in the constitution" (Appadurai 2002, 273–74). Appadurai writes of Indian citizens of Mumbai (formerly Bombay), India, from many walks of life, rich and poor, Muslim and Hindu, who have shown "extraordinary displays of courage and critical imagination in Mumbai," who have "held up powerful images of a cosmopolitan, secular, multicultural Bombay." Their "radical moderation" in resisting violent religious polarization is, he argues, neither naive nor nostalgic: "These utopian visions and critical practices are resolutely modernist in their visions of equity, justice, and cultural cosmopolitanism" (Appadurai 2002, 279). Secularism, of course, is a notion with impeccable European Enlightenment credentials. As anthropologist Talal Asad explains, the concept of "secular citizenship" developed in Europe following the post-Reformation wars of religion and aimed to "transcend the different identities built on class, gender, and religion, replacing conflicting perspectives by unifying experience. In a sense, this transcendent mediation *is* secularism" (2003, 5). Secularism arrived in India with British colonialism. Yet, it has become, over time, a "situated secularism"—indigenized, customized, domesticated, *Indian* secularism, opposed to *Indian* interreligious violence. Appadurai and many other Indian citizens see Indian secularism as a key element of Indian cosmopolitanism that has been effective in preventing religious strife in the past and may be able to do so again.

Many of the cases in this chapter demonstrate the human ability to cope creatively with changed life circumstances. They remind us that human beings are not passive in the face of the new, that they actively and resiliently respond to life's challenges. Nevertheless, successful outcomes are never ensured. Modes of livelihood that may benefit some human groups can overwhelm and destroy others. Western capitalism and modern technology have exploded into a vortex of global forces that resist control. A critical cosmopolitanism involving concerted practical action to lessen violence and exploitation has perhaps never been more necessary.

Figure 15.16 Cosmopolitanism is no longer only for Western elites. Otavalo Indian tourist José María Cotachaci, visiting the San Francisco Bay Area, November 2000. Otavalos have created their own form of modernity.

In Their Own Words

The Anthropological Voice

Anthropologist Annette Weiner traces the history of anthropological challenges to colonialism and Western capitalism, pointing out why the perspective of anthropologists has so often been ignored.

Colonialism brought foreign governments, missionaries, explorers, and exploiters face-to-face with cultures whose values and beliefs were vastly different. As the harbingers of Western progress, their actions were couched in the rhetoric of doing something to and for "the natives"—giving them souls, clothes, law—whatever was necessary to lift them out of their "primitive" ways. Anthropologists were also part of the colonial scene, but what they came to "do" made them different from those who were carrying out the expectations of missions, overseas trade, and government protectorates. Anthropologists arrived in the field determined to understand the cultural realities of an unfamiliar world. The knowledge of these worlds was to serve as a warning to those in positions of colonial power by charging that villagers' lives were not to be tampered with arbitrarily and that changing the lives of powerless people was insensitive and inhumane, unless one understood and took seriously the cultural meanings inherent in, for example, traditional land ownership, the technologies and rituals surrounding food cultivation, myths, magic, and gender relations.

All too often, however, the anthropologist's voice went unnoticed by those in power, for it remained a voice committed to illuminating the cultural biases under which colonialists operated. Only recently have we witnessed the final demise of colonial governments and the rise of independent countries. Economically, however, independence has not brought these countries the freedom to pursue their own course of development. In many parts of the world, Western multinational corporations, often playing a role not too dissimilar from colonial enterprises, now determine the course of that freedom, changing people's lives in a way that all too often is harmful or destructive. At the same time, we know that the world's natural resources and human productive capabilities can no longer remain isolates. Developed and developing countries are now more dependent on one another than ever before in human history. Yet this interdependency, which should give protection to indigenous peoples, is often worked out for political ends that ignore the moral issues. Racism and the practice of discrimination are difficult to destroy, as evidenced by the United States today, where we still are not completely emancipated from assumptions that relegate blacks, women, Asians, Hispanics, and other minorities to second-class status. If we cannot bridge these cultural differences intellectually within our own borders, then how can we begin to deal politically with Third World countries—those who were called "primitives" less than a century ago—in a fair, sensitive, and meaningful way?

This is the legacy of anthropology that we must never forget. Because the work of anthropology takes us to the neighborhoods, villages, and campsites—the local level—we can ourselves experience the results of how the world's economic and political systems affect those who have no voice. Yet once again our voices too are seldom heard by those who make such decisions. Anthropologists are often prevented from participating in the forums of economic and government planning. Unlike economists, political scientists, or engineers, we must stand on the periphery of such decision making, primarily because our understanding of cultural patterns and beliefs forces on others an awareness that ultimately makes such decisions more formidable.

At the beginning of the twentieth century, anthropologists spoke out strongly against those who claimed that "savage" societies represented a lower level of biological and social development. Now, as we face the next century, the anthropological approach to human nature and human societies is as vital to communicate as ever. We face a difficult, potentially dangerous, and therefore complex future. A fundamental key to our future is to make certain that the dynamic qualities of human beings in all parts of the world are recognized and that the true value of cultural complexities is not ignored. There is much important anthropology to be done.

Source: Weiner 1990, 392–93.

Why Study Anthropology?

Anthropology can have a direct effect on people who never take another course in it.

Studying anthropology brings students into contact with different ways of life. It makes them aware of just how arbitrary their own understanding of the world is as they learn how other people have developed satisfying but different ways of living. In addition, if they are from Western countries that were responsible for colonialism and its consequences, it makes them painfully aware of just how much their own tradition has to answer for in the modern world.

Knowing and experiencing cultural variety gives rise, perhaps inevitably, to doubt. We come to doubt the ultimate validity of the central truths of our own cultural tradition, which have been ratified and sanctified by the generations who preceded us. We doubt because a familiarity with alternative ways of living makes the ultimate meaning of any action, of any object, a highly ambiguous matter. Ambiguity is part of the human condition. Human beings have always coped with ambiguity by using culture, which places objects and actions in contexts and thereby makes their meanings plain. This doubt can lead to anxiety, but it can also be liberating.

All human beings, ourselves included, live in culturally shaped worlds, enmeshed in webs of interpretation and meaning that we have spun. It has been the particular task of anthropology and its practitioners to go out into the world to bear witness to and record the vast creative diversity in world-making that has been the history of our species. In our lifetimes, we will witness the end of many of those ways of life—and if we are not careful, of all ways of life. This loss is tragic, for as these worlds disappear, so too does something special about humanity: variety, creativity, and awareness of alternatives.

Our survival as a species and our viability as individuals depend on the possibility of choice, of perceiving and being able to act on alternatives in the various situations we encounter during our lives. If, as a colleague has suggested, human life is a minefield, then the more paths we can see and imagine through that minefield, the more likely we are to make it through—or at least to have an interesting time trying. As alternatives are destroyed, wantonly smashed, or thoughtlessly crushed, our own human possibilities are reduced. A small group of men and women have for the last century labored in corners of the world, both remote and nearby, to write the record of human accomplishment and bring it back and teach it to others.

Surely our greatest human accomplishment is the creation of the sometimes austerely beautiful worlds in which we all live. Anthropologists have rarely given in to the romantic notion that these other worlds are all good, all life-enhancing, all fine or beautiful. They are not. Ambiguity and ambivalence are, as we have seen, hallmarks of the human experience. There are no guarantees that human cultures will be compassionate rather than cruel or that people will agree they are one or the other. There are not even any guarantees that our species will survive. But all anthropologists have believed that these are human worlds that have given those who have lived in them the ability to make sense out of their experiences and to derive meaning for their lives, that we are a species at once bound by our culture and free to change it.

This is a perilous and fearsome freedom, a difficult freedom to grasp and to wield. Nevertheless, the freedom is there, and in this tension of freedom and constraint lies our future. It is up to us to create it.

Chapter Summary

1. Globalization is understood and evaluated differently by different observers, but most anthropologists agree that the effects of globalization are uneven. In a globalizing world, wealth, images, people, things, and ideologies are deterritorialized. Some groups in some parts of the world benefit from global flows, contacts, and exchanges, whereas others are bypassed entirely. Anthropologists disagree about whether global processes are or are not systemic and whether they are only the latest in a series of expansions and contractions that can be traced back to the rise of the first commercial civilizations several thousand years ago. But none of these overall schemas can by itself account for the historically specific local details of the effects of global forces in local settings, which is what most anthropologists aim to document and analyze.

2. The flows unleashed by globalization have undermined the ability of nation-states to police their boundaries effectively, suggesting that conventional

(continued on next page)

Chapter Summary (continued)

ideas about nation-states require revision. Contemporary migrants across national borders have developed a variety of transborder identities. Some become involved in long-distance nationalism that leads to the emergence of transborder states claiming emigrants as transborder citizens of their ancestral homelands even if they are legal citizens of another state. Some transborder citizenries call for the establishment of full-fledged transnational nation-states. Struggles of these kinds can be found all over the globe, including in the contemporary states of the European Union.

3. The contrasts between formal and substantive citizenship suggest that conventional notions of citizenship are breaking down in the context of globalization. Diaspora communities of elite Chinese families have developed a strategy of flexible citizenship that allows them to both circumvent and benefit from different nation-state regimes by investing, working, and settling their families in different sites. For these elite Chinese, the concept of nationalism has lost its meaning, and they seem to subscribe instead to a postnational ethos in which their only true loyalty is to the family business.

4. Discussions of human rights have intensified as global flows juxtapose and at least implicitly challenge different understandings of what it means to be human or what kinds of rights people may be entitled to under radically changed conditions of everyday life. But different participants in this discourse have different ideas about the relationship between human rights and culture. As talk about human rights becomes incorporated into local cultural discussions, the notion is transformed to make sense in local contexts. Sometimes, "culture" may be used as a scapegoat for a government unwilling to extend certain rights to its citizens.

5. Some arguments about human rights include the right to one's culture. One of the key issues involved concerns the kinds of legal mechanisms needed to insure such protection. But most international human-rights documents protect only individual human rights, not group rights. And even those who seek to protect their individual rights are supposed to appeal to the governments of their own nation-states to enforce rights defended in international documents. Many activists and others view this factor as a serious contradiction in human-rights discourse that undermines its effectiveness.

6. Some anthropologists argue that a "culture of human rights" has emerged in recent years that is based on certain ideas about human beings, their needs, and their abilities that originated in the West. Some consider this culture of human rights to be the culture of a globalizing world that emphasizes individual rights over duties or needs and that proposes only technical rather than ethical solutions to human suffering. Anthropologists disagree about the value of such a culture of human rights in contemporary circumstances.

7. Groups and individuals who assert that their human rights have been violated regularly take their cases to courts of law. But because human-rights law recognizes only certain kinds of rights violations, groups with grievances must tailor those grievances to fit the violations that human-rights law recognizes. Groups that enter into the human-rights process are entering into ethically ambiguous territory that is both enabling and constraining. Debates about women's rights in Hawaii show both that it is possible to accommodate the universal discourse of human rights to local conditions and that no single model of the relationship between rights and culture will fit all cases.

8. The discourse of cultural imperialism, which developed primarily outside anthropology, tried to explain the spread of Western cultural forms outside the West. But anthropologists reject cultural imperialism as an explanation because it denies agency to non-Western peoples, because it assumes that cultural forms never move "from the rest to the West," and because it ignores flows of cultural forms that bypass the West entirely.

9. Anthropologists have developed alternatives to the discourse of cultural imperialism. They speak about borrowing-with-modification, domestication, indigenization, or customization of practices or objects imported from elsewhere. Many anthropologists describe these processes as examples of cultural hybridization or hybridity. Talk of cultural hybridization has been criticized because the very attempt to talk about cultural mixtures assumes that "pure" cultures existed prior to mixing. Others object to discussions of cultural hybridization that fail to recognize that its effects are experienced differently by those with power and those without power. Cultural hybridization is unobjectionable when actors perceive it to be under their own control but resisted when they see it threatening their moral integrity.

10. Some anthropologists would like to revive the notion of "cosmopolitanism" originally associated with Western elite forms of cultural hybridization and rework it in order to be able to speak about alternative or discrepant cosmopolitanisms that reflect the experiences of those who have been the victims of modernity. The ideal end result would be a critical cosmopolitanism capable of negotiating new understandings of human rights and global citizenship in ways that can dismantle barriers of gender and race that are the historical legacies of colonialism.

For Review

1. How is globalization defined in the textbook? What are the key features of the anthropological approach to the study of globalization?
2. Discuss the effects of migration on the nation-state.
3. What does it mean to talk about a transborder citizenry?
4. What is "flexible citizenship" and how is it used to describe Chinese diaspora communities?
5. How do anthropologists study human rights?
6. What is the "rights versus culture" debate?
7. What does it meant to defend "rights to culture"?
8. Explain how the anthropological concept of culture can help clarify issues in discussions of human rights.
9. What are the key points in the case study of violence against women in Hawaii? Describe how programs to deal with violence against women in Hawaii and elsewhere in the world are connected to globalization.
10. What is cultural imperialism? What are the three difficulties that anthropologists have found with this concept?
11. Discuss cultural hybridity, paying particular attention to the idea of borrowing-with-modification.
12. What are the difficulties associated with the concept of cultural hybridity?
13. What does it mean to be cosmopolitan?
14. Summarize Anna Tsing's discussion of "friction."
15. Describe border thinking.

Key Terms

cosmopolitanism   461
cultural hybridization
   (or hybridity)   459
cultural imperialism   456
diaspora   445
flexible citizenship   446

friction   461
globalization   439
human rights   448
legal citizenship   446
long-distance
   nationalists   445

multiculturalism   448
postnational ethos   448
right to culture   450
substantive
   citizenship   446

transborder citizenry   445
transborder state   445
transnational
   nation-state   446

Suggested Readings

Goodale Mark, ed. 2009. *Human rights: An anthropological reader.* Malden, MA: Wiley-Blackwell. *An excellent collection of historical and contemporary readings about human rights.*

Hobart, Mark, ed. 1993. *An anthropological critique of development.* London: Routledge. *Anthropologists from Britain, Holland, and Germany challenge the notion that Western approaches to development have been successful. They use ethnographic case studies to demonstrate how Western experts who disregard indigenous knowledge contribute to the growth of ignorance.*

Inda, Jonathan Xavier, and Renato Rosaldo, eds. 2007. *The anthropology of globalization: A reader,* 2nd ed. Malden, MA: Blackwell. *A recent, comprehensive collection of articles by anthropologists who address the process of globalization from varied points of view and different ethnographic situations.*

Lewellen, Ted. 2002. Westport, CT: Bergin & Garvey. *The anthropology of globalization: Cultural anthropology enters the twenty-first century. An introduction to key issues in the anthropology of globalization, situating it historically in terms of earlier views of the global political economy, such as modernization theory and dependency theory.*

Tsing, Anna Lowenhaupt. 2005. *Friction: An ethnography of global connection.* Princeton, NJ: Princeton University Press. *An innovative multisited ethnography illustrating how a global environmental movement formed across different kinds of boundaries, for different reasons, and prevented rain forest destruction in one region of Indonesia for a number of years in the 1980s.*

Glossary

acclimatization: A change in the way the body functions in response to physical stress.

Acheulean tradition: A Lower Paleolithic stone-tool tradition associated with *Homo erectus* and characterized by stone bifaces, or "hand axes."

achieved statuses: Social positions people may attain later in life, often as the result of their own (or other people's) effort.

adaptation: (1) The mutual shaping of organisms and their environments; (2) The shaping of useful features of an organism by natural selection for the function they now perform.

adoption: Kinship relationships based on nurturance, often in the absence of other connections based on mating or birth.

affinal relationships: Kinship connections through marriage, or affinity.

affinity: Connection through marriage.

affluence: The condition of having more than enough of whatever is required to satisfy consumption needs.

agriculture: The systematic modification of the environments of plants and animals to increase their productivity and usefulness.

agroecology: The systematically modified environment (or constructed niche) which becomes the only environment within which domesticated plants can flourish.

alleles: All the different forms that a particular gene might take.

anagenesis: The slow, gradual transformation of a single species over time.

analogy: Convergent, or parallel, evolution, as when two species with very different evolutionary histories develop similar physical features as a result of adapting to a similar environment.

anatomically modern human beings: Hominin fossils assigned to the species *H. sapiens* with anatomical features similar to those of living human populations: short and round skulls, small brow ridges and faces, prominent chins, and light skeletal build.

anthropology: The study of human nature, human society, and the human past.

anthropomorphism: The attribution of human characteristics to nonhuman animals.

applied anthropologists: Specialists who use information gathered from the other anthropological specialties to solve practical cross-cultural problems.

aptation: The shaping of any useful feature of an organism, regardless of its origin.

archaeological record: All material objects constructed by humans or near-humans revealed by archaeology.

archaeology: A cultural anthropology of the human past involving the analysis of material remains left behind by earlier societies.

archaic *Homo sapiens*: Hominins dating from 500,000 to 200,000 years ago that possessed morphological features found in both *Homo erectus* and *Homo sapiens*.

art: Play with form producing some aesthetically successful transformation-representation.

artifacts: Objects that have been deliberately and intelligently shaped by human or near-human activity.

ascribed statuses: Social positions people are assigned at birth.

assemblage: Artifacts and structures from a particular time and place in an archaeological site.

assumptions: Basic, unquestioned understandings about the way the world works.

avunculocal residence: A postmarital residence pattern in which a married couple lives with (or near) the husband's mother's brother (from avuncular, "of uncles").

band: The characteristic form of social organization found among foragers. Bands are small, usually no more than 50 people, and labor is divided ordinarily on the basis of age and sex. All adults in band societies have roughly equal access to whatever material or social valuables are locally available.

bifurcation: A criterion employed in the analysis of kinship terminologies in which kinship terms referring to the mother's side of the family are distinguished from those referring to the father's side.

bilateral descent: The principle that a descent group is formed by people who believe they are related to each other by connections made through their mothers and fathers equally (sometimes called *cognatic descent*).

biocultural organisms: Organisms (in this case, human beings) whose defining features are codetermined by biological and cultural factors.

biological anthropology (or **physical anthropology**): The specialty of anthropology that looks at human beings as biological organisms and tries to discover what characteristics make them different from other organisms and what characteristics they share.

biopower: Forms of power preoccupied with bodies, both the bodies of citizens and the social body of the state itself.

biostratigraphic dating: A relative dating method that relies on patterns of fossil distribution in different rock layers.

bipedalism: Walking on two feet rather than four.

blades: Stone tools that are at least twice as long as they are wide.

blended family: A family created when previously divorced or widowed people marry, bringing with them children from their previous families.

bloodwealth: Material goods paid by perpetrators to compensate their victims for their loss.

bridewealth: The transfer of certain symbolically important goods from the family of the groom to the family of the bride on the occasion of their marriage. It represents compensation to the wife's lineage for the loss of her labor and childbearing capacities.

broad-spectrum foraging: A subsistence strategy based on collecting a wide range of plants and animals by hunting, fishing, and gathering.

capitalism: An economic system dominated by the supply-demand-price mechanism called the "market"; an entire way of life that grew in response to and in service of that market.

caste: A ranked group within a hierarchically stratified society that is closed, prohibiting individuals to move from one caste to another.

catastrophism: The notion that natural disasters, such as floods, are responsible for the extinction of species, which are then replaced by new species.

chiefdom: A form of social organization in which a leader (the chief) and close relatives are set apart from the rest of the society and allowed privileged access to wealth, power, and prestige.

chromosomes: Sets of paired bodies in the nucleus of cells that are made of DNA and contain the hereditary genetic information that organisms pass on to their offspring.

cladogenesis: The birth of a variety of descendant species from a single ancestral species.

clan: A descent group formed by members who believe they have a common (sometimes mythical) ancestor, even if they cannot specify the genealogical links.

classes: Ranked group within a hierarchically stratified society whose membership is defined primarily in terms of wealth, occupation, or other economic criteria.

clientage: The institution linking individuals from upper and lower levels in a stratified society.

cline: The gradual intergradation of genetic variation from population to population.

coevolution: The dialectical relationship between biological processes and symbolic cultural processes, in which each makes up an important part of the environment to which the other must adapt.

cognition: (1) The mental process by which human beings gain knowledge. (2) A tangle of connections between the mind at work and the world in which it works.

collaterality: A criterion employed in the analysis of kinship terminologies in which a distinction is made between kin who are believed to be in a direct line and those who are "off to one side," linked to the speaker by a lineal relative.

colorism: A system of social identities negotiated situationally along a continuum of skin colors between white and black.

commodity exchanges: Impersonal economic exchanges typical of the capitalist market in which goods are exchanged for cash and exchange partners need have nothing further to do with one another.

common origin: Darwin's claim that similar living species must all have had a common ancestor.

communicative competence: A term coined by anthropological linguist Dell Hymes to refer to the mastery of adult rules for socially and culturally appropriate speech.

communitas: An unstructured or minimally structured community of equal individuals found frequently in rites of passage.

comparison: A characteristic of the anthropological perspective that requires anthropologists to consider similarities and differences in as wide a range of human societies as possible before generalizing about human nature, human society, or the human past.

complex societies: Societies with large populations, an extensive division of labor, and occupational specialization.

composite tools: Tools such as bows and arrows in which several different materials are combined (e.g., stone, wood, bone, ivory, antler) to produce the final working implement.

concentrations of particular artifacts: Sets of artifacts indicating that particular social activities took place at a particular area in an archaeological site when that site was inhabited in the past.

conjugal family: A family based on marriage; at a minimum, a husband and wife (a spousal pair) and their children.

consanguineal relationships: Kinship connections based on descent.

consumption: The using up of material goods necessary for human survival.

continuous variation: A pattern of variation involving polygeny in which phenotypic traits grade imperceptibly from one member of the population to another without sharp breaks.

cosmopolitanism: Being at ease in more than one cultural setting.

cranial capacity: The size of the braincase.

cranium: The bones of the head, excluding the jaw.

cross cousins: The children of a person's parents' opposite-gender siblings (a father's sister's children or a mother's brother's children).

crossing over: The phenomenon that occurs when part of one chromosome breaks off and reattaches itself to a different chromosome during meiosis; also called *incomplete linkage*.

cultural anthropology: The specialty of anthropology that shows how variation in the beliefs and behaviors of members of different human groups is shaped by sets of learned behaviors and ideas that human beings acquire as members of society—that is, by culture.

cultural hybridization (or **hybridity**): Cultural mixing.

cultural imperialism: The idea that some cultures dominate others and that domination by one culture leads inevitably to the destruction of subordinated cultures and their replacement by the culture of those in power.

cultural relativism: Understanding another culture in its own terms sympathetically enough so that the culture appears to be a coherent and meaningful design for living.

culture: Sets of learned behavior and ideas that human beings acquire as members of society. Human beings use culture to adapt to and to transform the world in which they live.

culture shock: The feeling, akin to panic, that develops in people living in an unfamiliar society when they cannot understand what is happening around them.

dentition: The sizes, shapes, and number of an animal's teeth.

descent: The principle based on culturally recognized parent–child connections that define the social categories to which people belong.

dialectic of fieldwork: The process of building a bridge of understanding between anthropologists and informants so that each can begin to understand the other.

diaspora: Migrant populations with a shared identity who live in a variety of different locales around the world; a form of transborder identity that does not focus on nation building.

discontinuous variation: A pattern of phenotypic variation in which the phenotype (e.g., flower color) exhibits sharp breaks from one member of the population to the next.

discourse: A stretch of speech longer than a sentence united by a common theme.

diurnal: Describes animals that are active during the day.

DNA (deoxyribonucleic acid): The structure that carries the genetic heritage of an organism as a kind of blueprint for the organism's construction and development.

domestication: Human interference with the reproduction of another species, with the result that specific plants and animals become more useful to people and dependent on them.

domination: Coercive rule.

dowry: The wealth transferred, usually from parents to their daughter, at the time of her marriage.

Early Stone Age (ESA): The name given to the period of Oldowan and Acheulean stone-tool traditions in Africa.

ecological niche: Any species' way of life; what it eats and how it finds mates, raises its young, relates to companions, and protects itself from predators.

economic anthropology: The part of the discipline of anthropology that debates issues of human nature that relate directly to the decisions of daily life and making a living.

egalitarian social relations: Social relations in which no great differences in wealth, power, or prestige divide members from one another.

endogamy: Marriage within a defined social group.

essentialism: The belief, derived from Plato, in fixed ideas, or "forms," that exist perfect and unchanging in eternity. Actual objects in the temporal world, such as cows or horses, are seen as imperfect material realizations of the ideal form that defines their kind.

ethnic groups: Social groups that are distinguished from one another on the basis of ethnicity.

ethnicity: A principle of social classification used to create groups based on selected cultural features such as language, religion, or dress. Ethnicity emerges from historical processes that incorporate distinct social groups into a single political structure under conditions of inequality.

ethnoarchaelogy: The study of the way present-day societies use artifacts and structures and how these objects become part of the archaeological record.

ethnocentrism: The opinion that one's own way of life is natural or correct and, indeed, the only true way of being fully human.

ethnography: An anthropologist's written or filmed description of a particular culture.

ethnology: The comparative study of two or more cultures.

ethnopragmatics: The study of language use that relies on ethnography to illuminate the ways in which speech is both constituted by and constitutive of social interaction.

evidence: What is seen when a particular part of the world is examined with great care. Scientists use two different kinds of evidence: material and inferred.

evolution: The process of change over time.

evolutionary niche: Sum of all the natural selection pressures to which a population is exposed.

evolutionary theory: The set of testable hypotheses that assert that living organisms can change over time and give rise to new kinds of organisms, with the result that all organisms ultimately share a common ancestry.

exaptation: The shaping of a useful feature of an organism by natural selection to perform one function and the later reshaping of it by different selection pressures to perform a new function.

excavation: The systematic uncovering of archaeological remains through removal of the deposits of soil and other material covering them and accompanying them.

exogamy: Marriage outside a defined social group.

extended family: A family pattern made up of three generations living together: parents, married children, and grandchildren.

fact: A widely accepted observation, a taken-for-granted item of common knowledge. Facts do not speak for themselves but only when they are interpreted and placed in a context of meaning that makes them intelligible.

family: Minimally, a woman and her dependent children.

features: Nonportable remnants from the past, such as house walls or ditches.

feminist archaeology: A research approach that explores why women's contributions have been systematically written out of the archaeological record and suggests new approaches to the human past that include such contributions.

fieldwork: An extended period of close involvement with the people in whose language or way of life anthropologists are interested, during which anthropologists ordinarily collect most of their data.

fitness: A measure of an organism's ability to compete in the struggle for existence. Those individuals whose variant traits better equip them to compete with other members of their species for limited resources are more likely to survive and reproduce than individuals who lack such traits.

flexible citizenship: The strategies and effects employed by managers, technocrats, and professionals who move regularly across state boundaries and seek both to circumvent and to benefit from different nation-state regimes.

formal models: Mathematical formulas used to predict outcomes of particular kinds of human interactions under different hypothesized conditions.

framing: A cognitive boundary that marks certain behaviors as "play" or as "ordinary life."

free agency: The freedom of self-contained individuals to pursue their own interests above everything else and to challenge one another for dominance.

friendship: The relatively "unofficial" bonds that people construct with one another that tend to be personal, affective, and often a matter of choice.

friction: The awkward, unequal, unstable aspects of interconnection across difference.

gender: The cultural construction of beliefs and behaviors considered appropriate for each sex.

gender archaeology: Archaeological research that draws on insights from contemporary gender studies to investigate how people come to recognize themselves as different from others, how people represent these differences, and how others react to these claims.

gene: Portion or portions of the DNA molecule that code for proteins that shape biological traits.

gene flow: The exchange of genes that occurs when a given population experiences a sudden expansion due to in-migration of outsiders from another population of the species.

gene frequency: The frequency of occurrence of the variants of particular genes (i.e., of alleles) within the gene pool.

gene pool: All the genes in the bodies of all members of a given species (or a population of a species).

genetic drift: Random changes in gene frequencies from one generation to the next due to a sudden reduction in population size as a result of disaster, disease, or the out-migration of a small subgroup from a larger population.

genetics: The scientific study of biological heredity.

genome: The sum total of all the genetic information about an organism, carried on the chromosomes in the cell nucleus.

genotype: The genetic information about particular biological traits encoded in an organism's DNA.

genus: The level of the Linnaean taxonomy in which different species are grouped together on the basis of their similarities to one another.

gift exchanges: Noncapitalist forms of economic exchange that are deeply embedded in social relations and always require a return gift.

globalization: Reshaping of local conditions by powerful global forces on an ever-intensifying scale.

governmentality: The art of governing appropriately to promote the welfare of populations within a state.

grammar: A set of rules that aim to describe fully the patterns of linguistic usage observed by speakers of a particular language.

grave goods: Objects buried with a corpse.

Great Chain of Being: A comprehensive framework for interpreting the world, based on Aristotelian principles and elaborated during the Middle Ages, in which every kind of living organism was linked to every other kind in an enormous, divinely created chain. An organism differed from the kinds immediately above it and below it on the chain by the least possible degree.

hegemony: The persuasion of subordinates to accept the ideology of the dominant group by mutual accommodations that nevertheless preserve the rulers' privileged position.

heterozygous: Describes a fertilized egg that receives a different particle (or allele) from each parent for the same trait.

historical archaeology: The study of archaeological sites associated with written records; frequently the study of post-European contact sites in the world.

holism: A characteristic of the anthropological perspective that describes, at the highest and most inclusive level, how anthropology tries to integrate all that is known about human beings and their activities.

hominins: Humans and their immediate ancestors.

Homo erectus: The species of large-brained, robust hominins that lived between 1.8 mya and 0.4 mya.

Homo habilis: The species of large-brained, gracile hominins 2 million years old and younger.

homology: Genetic inheritance due to common ancestry.

homozygous: Describes a fertilized egg that receives the same particle (or allele) from each parent for a particular trait.

human agency: The way people struggle, often against great odds, to exercise some control over their lives.

human rights: Powers, privileges, or material resources to which people everywhere, by virtue of being human, are justly entitled.

hypotheses: Statements that assert a particular connection between fact and interpretation.

ideology: A worldview that justifies the social arrangements under which people live.

informants: People in a particular culture who work with anthropologists and provide them with insights about their way of life. Also called respondents, teachers, or friends.

institutions: Complex, variable, and enduring forms of cultural practices that organize social life.

intrusions: Artifacts made by more recent populations that find their way into more ancient strata as the result of natural forces.

isotopic dating: Dating methods based on scientific knowledge about the rate at which various radioactive isotopes of naturally occurring elements transform themselves into other elements by losing subatomic particles.

joint family: A family pattern made up of brothers and their wives or sisters and their husbands (along with their children) living together.

kinship systems: Social relationships that are prototypically derived from the universal human experiences of mating, birth, and nurturance.

labor: The activity linking human social groups to the material world around them; from the point of view of Karl Marx, labor is therefore always social labor.

language: The system of arbitrary vocal symbols used to encode one's experience of the world and of others.

language ideology: A marker of struggles between social groups with different interests, revealed in what people say and how they say it.

law of crosscutting relationships: A principle of geological interpretation stating that where old rocks are crosscut by other geological features, the intruding features must be younger than the layers of rock they cut across.

law of superposition: A principle of geological interpretation stating that layers lower down in a sequence of strata must be older than the layers above them and, therefore, that objects embedded in lower layers must be older than objects embedded in upper layers.

legal citizenship: The rights and obligations of citizenship accorded by the laws of a state.

liminality: The ambiguous transitional state in a rite of passage in which the person or persons undergoing the ritual are outside their ordinary social positions.

lineages: The consanguineal members of descent groups who believe they can trace their descent from known ancestors.

linguistic anthropology: The specialty of anthropology concerned with the study of human languages.

linguistic competence: A term coined by linguist Noam Chomsky to refer to the mastery of adult grammar.

linguistic relativity principle: A position, associated with Edward Sapir and Benjamin Whorf, that asserts that language has the power to shape the way people see the world.

linguistics: The scientific study of language.

linkage: An inheritance pattern in which unrelated phenotypic traits regularly occur together because the genes responsible for those co-occurring traits are passed on together on the same chromosome.

locus: A portion of the DNA strand responsible for encoding specific parts of an organism's biological makeup.

long-distance nationalism: Members of a diaspora organized in support of nationalist struggles in their homeland or to agitate for a state of their own.

macroevolution: A subfield of evolutionary studies that focuses on long-term evolutionary changes, especially the origins of new species and their diversification across space and over millions of years of geological time.

magic: A set of beliefs and practices designed to control the visible or invisible world for specific purposes.

mandible: The lower jaw.

market exchange: The exchange of goods (trade) calculated in terms of a multipurpose medium of exchange and standard of value (money) and carried out by means of a supply-demand-price mechanism (the market).

marriage: An institution that transforms the status of the participants, carries implications about permitted sexual access, perpetuates social patterns through the birth of offspring, creates relationships between the kin of partners, and is symbolically marked.

matrilineage: A social group formed by people connected by mother-child links.

matrilocal residence: A postmarital residence pattern in which a married couple lives with (or near) the wife's mother.

means of production: The tools, skills, organization, and knowledge used to extract energy from nature.

medical anthropology: The specialty of anthropology that concerns itself with human health—the factors that contribute to disease or illness and the ways that human populations deal with disease or illness.

meiosis: The way sex cells make copies of themselves, which begins like mitosis, with chromosome duplication and the formation of two daughter cells. However, each daughter cell then divides again without chromosome duplication and, as a result, contains only a single set of chromosomes rather than the paired set typical of body cells.

Mendelian inheritance: The view that heredity is based on nonblending, single-particle genetic inheritance.

metacommunication: Communication about the process of communication itself.

metaphor: A form of figurative or nonliteral language that violates the formal rules of denotation by linking expressions from unrelated semantic domains.

microevolution: A subfield of evolutionary studies that devotes attention to short-term evolutionary changes that occur within a given species over relatively few generations of ecological time.

Middle Stone Age (MSA): The name given to the period of Mousterian stone-tool tradition in Africa, 200,000 to 40,000 years ago.

mitosis: The way body cells make copies of themselves. The pairs of chromosomes in the nucleus of the cell duplicate and line up along the center of the cell. The cell then divides, each daughter cell taking one full set of paired chromosomes.

mode of production: A specific, historically occurring set of social relations through which labor is deployed to wrest energy from nature by means of tools, skills, organization, and knowledge.

modes of exchange: Patterns according to which distribution takes place: reciprocity, redistribution, and market exchange.

monogamy: A marriage pattern in which a person may be married to only one spouse at a time.

monumental architecture: Architectural constructions of a greater-than-human scale, such as pyramids, temples, and tombs.

morphology: (1) The physical shape and size of an organism or its body parts; (2) In linguistics, the study of the minimal units of meaning in a language.

mosaic evolution: A phenotypic pattern that shows how different traits of an organism, responding to different selection pressures, may evolve at different rates.

Mousterian tradition: A Middle Paleolithic stone-tool tradition associated with Neandertals in Europe and southwestern Asia and with anatomically modern human beings in Africa.

multiculturalism: Living permanently in settings surrounded by people with cultural backgrounds different from one's own and struggling to define with them the degree to which the cultural beliefs and practices of different groups should or should not be accorded respect and recognition by the wider society.

multisited fieldwork: Ethnographic research on cultural processes that are not contained by social, ethical, or national boundaries, in which the ethnographer follows the process from site to site, often doing fieldwork at sites and with persons who traditionally were never subjected to ethnographic analysis.

mutation: The creation of a new allele for a gene when the portion of the DNA molecule to which it corresponds is suddenly altered.

myths: Stories that recount how various aspects of the world came to be the way they are. The power of myths comes from their ability to make life meaningful for those who accept them. The truth of myths seems self-evident because they effectively integrate personal experiences with a wider set of assumptions about the way society, or the world in general, must operate.

nation: A group of people believed to share the same history, culture, language, and even physical substance.

nationality: A sense of identification with and loyalty to a nation-state.

nation building (or **nationalism**): The attempt made by government officials to instill into the citizens of a state a sense of nationality.

nation-state: An ideal political unit in which national identity and political territory coincide.

nativism: A return to the old ways; a movement whose members expect a messiah or prophet who will bring back a lost golden age of peace, prosperity, and harmony.

naturalizing discourses: The deliberate representation of particular identities (e.g., caste, class, race, ethnicity, and nation) as if they were a result of biology or nature, rather than history or culture, making them appear eternal and unchanging.

natural selection: A two-step, mechanistic explanation of how descent with modification takes place: (1) every generation, variant individuals are generated within a species due to genetic mutation, and (2) those variant individuals best suited to the current environment survive and produce more offspring than other variants.

Neandertals: An archaic species of *Homo* that lived in Europe and western Asia from 130,000 to 35,000 years ago.

neoclassical economic theory: A formal attempt to explain the workings of capitalist enterprise, with particular attention to distribution.

Neolithic: The "New Stone Age," which began with the domestication of plants 10,300 years ago.

neolocal residence: A postmarital residence pattern in which a married couple sets up an independent household at a place of their own choosing.

niche construction: When an organism actively perturbs the environment or when it actively moves into a different environment, thereby modifying the selection pressures it is subject to.

nocturnal: Describes animals that are active during the night.

nonconjugal family: A woman and her children; the husband/father may be occasionally present or completely absent.

nonisotopic dating methods: Dating methods that assign age in years to material evidence but not by using rates of nuclear decay.

norm of reaction: A table or graph that displays the possible range of phenotypic outcomes for a given genotype in different environments.

nuclear family: A family pattern made up of two generations: the parents and their unmarried children.

numerical dating: Dating methods based on laboratory techniques that assign age in years to material evidence.

objectivity: The separation of observation and reporting from the researcher's wishes.

occupational specialization: Specialization in various occupations (e.g., weaving or pot making) or in new social roles (e.g., king or priest) that is found in socially complex societies.

Oldowan tradition: A stone-tool tradition named after the Olduvai Gorge (Tanzania), where the first specimens of the oldest human tools (2–2.5 mya) were found.

omnivorous: Eating a wide range of plant and animal foods.

oracles: Invisible forces to which people address questions and whose responses they believe to be truthful.

orthodoxy: "Correct doctrine"; the prohibition of deviation from approved mythic texts.

orthopraxy: "Correct practice"; the prohibition of deviation from approved forms of ritual behavior.

paleoanthropology: The search for fossilized remains of humanity's earliest ancestors.

pangenesis: A theory of heredity suggesting that an organism's physical traits are passed on from one generation to the next in the form of multiple distinct particles given off by all parts of an organism, different proportions of which get passed on to offspring via sperm or egg.

parallel cousins: The children of a person's parents' same-gender siblings (a father's brother's children or a mother's sister's children).

participant-observation: The method anthropologists use to gather information by living as closely as possible to the people whose culture they are studying while participating in their lives as much as possible.

patrilineage: A social group formed by people connected by father-child links.

patrilocal residence: A postmarital residence pattern in which a married couple lives with (or near) the husband's father.

perception: The processes by which people organize and experience information that is primarily of sensory origin.

personality: The relative integration of an individual's perceptions, motives, cognitions, and behavior within a sociocultural matrix.

phenotype: The observable, measurable overt characteristics of an organism.

phonology: The study of the sounds of language.

phyletic gradualism: A theory arguing that one species gradually transforms itself into a new species over time, yet the actual boundary between species can never be detected and can only be drawn arbitrarily.

pidgin: A language with no native speakers that develops in a single generation between members of communities that possess distinct native languages.

plasticity: Physiological flexibility that allows organisms to respond to environmental stresses, such as temperature changes.

play: A framing (or orienting context) that is (1) consciously adopted by the players, (2) somehow pleasurable, and (3) systemically related to what is nonplay by alluding to the nonplay world and by transforming the objects, roles, actions, and relations of ends and means characteristic of the nonplay world.

pleiotropy: The phenomenon whereby a single gene may affect more than one phenotypic trait.

political anthropology: The study of social power in human society.

polyandry: A marriage pattern in which a woman may be married to more than one husband at a time.

polygamy: A marriage pattern in which a person may be married to more than one spouse at a time.

polygeny: The phenomenon whereby many genes are responsible for producing a phenotypic trait, such as skin color.

polygyny: A marriage pattern in which a man may be married to more than one wife at a time.

polymorphous: Describes alleles that come in a range of different forms.

population genetics: A field that uses statistical analysis to study short-term evolutionary change in large populations.

postcranial skeleton: The bones of the body, excluding those of the head.

postnational ethos: An attitude toward the world in which people submit to the governmentality of the capitalist market while trying to evade the governmentality of nation-states.

power: Transformative capacity; the ability to transform a given situation.

pragmatics: The study of language in the context of its use.

prehensile: The ability to grasp, with fingers, toes, or tail.

priest: A religious practitioner skilled in the practice of religious rituals, which he or she carries out for the benefit of the group.

primatology: The study of nonhuman primates, the closest living relatives of human beings.

principle of independent assortment: A principle of Mendelian inheritance in which each pair of particles (genes) separates independently of every other pair when germ cells (egg and sperm) are formed.

principle of segregation: A principle of Mendelian inheritance in which an individual gets one particle (gene) for each trait (i.e. one-half of the required pair) from each parent.

prototypes: Examples of a typical instance, element, relation, or experience within a culturally relevant semantic domain.

punctuated equilibrium: A theory claiming that most of evolutionary history has been characterized by relatively stable species coexisting in an equilibrium that is occasionally punctuated by sudden bursts of speciation, when extinctions are widespread and many new species appear.

races: Social groupings that allegedly reflect biological differences.

racism: The systematic oppression of one or more socially defined "races" by another socially defined "race" that is justified in terms of the supposed inherent biological superiority of the rulers and the supposed inherent biological inferiority of those they rule.

reciprocity: The exchange of goods and services of equal value. Anthropologists distinguish three forms of reciprocity: *generalized,* in which neither the time nor the value of the return is specified; *balanced,* in which a return of equal value is expected within a specified time limit; and *negative,* in which parties to the exchange hope to get something for nothing.

redistribution: A mode of exchange that requires some form of centralized social organization to receive economic contributions from all members of the group and to redistribute them in such a way as to provide for every group member.

reflexivity: Critically thinking about the way one thinks, reflecting on one's own experience.

regional continuity model: The hypothesis that evolution from *Homo erectus* to *Homo sapiens* occurred gradually throughout the entire traditional range of *H. erectus.*

relatedness: The socially recognized ties that connect people in a variety of different ways.

relations of production: The social relations linking the people who use a given means of production within a particular mode of production.

relative dating: Dating methods that arrange material evidence in a linear sequence, each object in the sequence being identified as older or younger than another object.

religion: "ideas and practices that postulate reality beyond that which is immediately available to the senses." (Bowen 2008)

replacement model: The hypothesis that only one subpopulation of *Homo erectus,* probably located in Africa, underwent a rapid spurt of evolution to produce *Homo sapiens* 200,000 to 100,000 years ago. After that time, *H. sapiens* would itself have multiplied and moved out of Africa, gradually populating the globe and eventually replacing any remaining populations of *H. erectus* or their descendants.

revitalization: A conscious, deliberate, and organized attempt by some members of a society to create a more satisfying culture in a time of crisis.

rite of passage: A ritual that serves to mark the movement and transformation of an individual from one social position to another.

ritual: A repetitive social practice composed of a sequence of symbolic activities in the form of dance, song, speech, gestures, or the manipulation of objects, adhering to a culturally defined ritual schema; and closely connected to a specific set of ideas that are often encoded in myth.

schemas: Patterned, repetitive experiences.

science: The invention of explanations about what things are, how they work, and how they came to be that can be tested against evidence in the world itself.

scientific theory: A coherently organized series of testable hypotheses used to explain a body of material evidence.

sedentism: The process of increasingly permanent human habitation in one place.

segmentary opposition: A mode of hierarchical social organization in which groups beyond the most basic emerge only in opposition to other groups on the same hierarchical level.

self: The result of the process of socialization/enculturation for an individual.

semantics: The study of meaning.

seriation: A relative dating method based on the assumption that artifacts that look alike must have been made at the same time.

sex: Observable physical characteristics that distinguish two kinds of humans, females and males, needed for biological reproduction.

sexual dimorphism: The observable phenotypic differences between males and females of the same species.

sexual practices: Emotional or affectional relationships between sexual partners and the physical activities they engage in with one another.

shaman: A part-time religious practitioner who is believed to have the power to contact supernatural forces directly on behalf of individuals or groups.

sherds: Pieces of broken pots.

site: A precise geographical location of the remains of past human activity.

socialization/enculturation: The learning process by which individuals develop the skills they need to interact successfully with other members of the social groups to which they belong and come to terms with the ways of thinking and feeling that are considered appropriate in their respective cultures.

social organization: The patterning of human interdependence in a given society through the actions and decisions of its members.

social stratification: A form of social organization in which people have unequal access to wealth, power, and prestige.

sodalities: Special purpose groupings that may be organized on the basis of age, sex, economic role, and personal interest.

species: (1) For Linnaeus, a Platonic "natural kind" defined in terms of its essence. (2) For modern biologists, a reproductive community of populations (reproductively isolated from others) that occupies a specific niche in nature.

species selection: A process in which natural selection is seen to operate among variant, related species within a single genus, family, or order.

state: A stratified society that possesses a territory that is defended from outside enemies with an army and from internal disorder with police. A state, which has a separate set of governmental institutions designed to enforce laws and to collect taxes and tribute, is run by an elite that possesses a monopoly on the use of force.

status: A particular social position in a group.

stereoscopic vision: A form of vision in which the visual field of each eye of a two-eyed (binocular) animal overlaps, producing depth perception.

stratum: Layer; in geological terms, a layer of rock and soil.

structural violence: Violence that results from the way that political and economic forces structure risk for various forms of suffering within a population.

subjectivity: "The felt interior experience of the person that includes his or her positions in a field of relational power." (Das and Kleinman 2000)

subsistence strategy: Different ways that people in different societies go about meeting their basic material survival needs.

substantive citizenship: The actions people take, regardless of their legal citizenship status, to assert their membership in a state and to bring about political changes that will improve their lives.

surplus production: The production of amounts of food that exceed the basic subsistence needs of the population.

survey: The physical examination of a geographical region in which promising sites are most likely to be found.

symbol: Something that stands for something else. A symbol signals the presence of an important domain of experience.

syncretism: The synthesis of old religious practices (or an old way of life) with new religious practices (or a new way of life) introduced from outside, often by force.

syntax: The study of sentence structure.

taphonomy: The study of the various processes that objects undergo in the course of becoming part of the fossil and archaeological records.

taxon: Each species, as well as each group of related species, at any level in a taxonomic hierarchy.

taxonomy: A classification; in biology, the classification of various kinds of organisms.

testability: The ability of scientific hypotheses to be matched against nature to see whether they are confirmed or refuted.

transborder citizenry: A group made up of citizens of a country who continue to live in their homeland plus the people who have emigrated from the country and their descendants, regardless of their current citizenship.

transborder state: A form of state in which it is claimed that those people who left the country and their descendants remain part of their ancestral state, even if they are citizens of another state.

transformational evolution: Also called *Lamarckian evolution*, it assumes essentialist species and a uniform environment. Each individual member of a species transforms itself to meet the challenges of a changed environment through the laws of use and disuse and the inheritance of acquired characters.

transformist hegemony: A nationalist program to define nationality in a way that preserves the cultural domination of the ruling group while including enough cultural features from subordinated groups to ensure their loyalty.

transnational nation-state: A nation-state in which the relationships between citizens and the state extend to wherever citizens reside.

tribe: A society that is generally larger than a band, whose members usually farm or herd for a living. Social relations in a tribe are still relatively egalitarian, although there may be a chief who speaks for the group or organizes certain group activities.

uniformitarianism: The notion that an understanding of current processes can be used to reconstruct the past history of the earth, based on the assumption that the same gradual processes of erosion and uplift that change the earth's surface today had also been at work in the past.

Upper Paleolithic/Late Stone Age (LSA): The name given to the period of highly elaborate stone-tool traditions in Europe in which blades were important; 40,000 to 10,300 years ago.

variational evolution: The Darwinian theory of evolution, which assumes that variant members of a species respond differently to environmental challenges. Those variants that are more successful ("fitter") survive and reproduce more offspring, who inherit the traits that made their parents fit.

witchcraft: The performance of evil by human beings believed to possess an innate, nonhuman power to do evil, whether or not it is intentional or self-aware.

worldviews: Encompassing pictures of reality created by the members of societies.

References

Abbas, Akhbar. 2002. Cosmopolitan description: Shanghai and Hong Kong. In *Cosmopolitanism*, ed. Carol Breckenridge, Sheldon Pollock, Homi Bhaba, and Dipeesh Chakrabarty, 209–28. Durham, NC: Duke University Press.

Abu El-Haj, Nadia. 2007. The genetic reinscription of race. *Annual Review of Anthropology* 36:283–300.

Abusharaf, Rogaia Mustafa. 2000. Female circumcision goes beyond feminism. *Anthropology News* 41 (March):17–18.

Abwunza, Judith M. 1997. Women's voices, women's power: Dialogues of resistance from East Africa. Peterborough, ON: Broadview Press.

Adams, Robert. 1981. *Heartland of cities*. Chicago: University of Chicago Press.

Adams, Robert, and Hans Nissen. 1972. *The Uruk countryside*. Chicago: University of Chicago Press.

Adovasio, J. M., J. D. Gunn, J. L. Donahue, and R. Stuckenrath. 1978. Meadowcraft Rockshelter, 1977: An overview. *American Antiquity* 43:632–51.

Advocates for Indigenous California Language Survival. 2010. Master-apprentice program. http://www.aicls.org (accessed April 10, 2010).

Agar, Michael. 1996. *The professional stranger*, 2nd ed. San Diego: Academic Press.

Aiello, Leslie C. 1986. The relationships of the tarisiiformes: A review of the case for the haplorhini. In *Major topics in primate and human evolution*, ed. B. Wood, L. Martin, and P. Andrews, 47–65. Cambridge: Cambridge University Press.

Aiello, Leslie. 1993. The fossil evidence for modern human origins in Africa: A revised view. *American Anthropologist* 95:73–96.

Akmajian, Adrian, Richard A. Demers, Ann K. Farmer, and Robert M. Harnish. 1997. *Linguistics: An introduction to language and communication*, 4th ed. Cambridge, MA: MIT Press.

Alland, Alexander. 1977. *The artistic animal*. New York: Doubleday Anchor.

Allen, Theodore. 1997. *The invention of the white race*. London: Verso.

Alonso, Ana María. 1994. The politics of space, time, and substance: State formation, nationalism, and ethnicity. *Annual Review of Anthropology* 23:379–405.

Alverson, Hoyt. 1977. Peace Corps volunteers in rural Botswana. *Human Organization* 36, (3):274–81.

Alverson, Hoyt. 1990. Guest editorial in *Cultural anthropology: A perspective on the human condition*, by Emily Schultz and Robert Lavenda, 43. 2nd ed. St. Paul: West.

Anderson, Benedict. 2002. The new world disorder. In *The anthropology of politics*, ed. Joan Vincent, 261–70. Malden, MA: Blackwell.

Anderson, Richard L. 1990. *Calliope's sisters: A comparative study of philosophies of art*. Englewood Cliffs, NJ: Prentice Hall.

Appadurai, Arjun. 1990. Disjuncture and difference in the global cultural economy. In *Global culture*, ed. Mike Featherstone, 295–310. London: Sage.

Appadurai, Arjun. 2002. Grassroots globalization and the research imagination. In *The anthropology of politics*, ed. Joan Vincent, 271–84. Malden, MA: Blackwell.

Arensburg, B. 1989. New skeletal evidence concerning the anatomy of Middle Palaeolithic population in the Middle East: The Kebara skeleton. In *The human revolution*, ed. P. Mellars and C. B. Stringer, 165–71. Princeton, NJ: Princeton University Press.

Arnold, Jeanne E. 1995. Social inequality, marginalization, and economic process. In *Foundations of social inequality*, ed. T. Douglas Price and Gary M. Feinman. New York: Plenum.

Arsuaga, Juan-Luis, Ignacio Martinez, Ana Gracia, José-Miguel Carretero, and Eudald Carbonell. 1993. Three new human skulls from the Sima de los Huesos, Middle Pleistocene site in Sierra de Atapuerca, Spain. *Nature* 362(8 April):534–37.

Asad, Talal. 2003. *Formations of the secular: Christianity, Islam, modernity*. Palo Alto, CA: Stanford University Press.

Asfaw, B., T. White, O. Lovejoy, B. Latimer, S. Simpson, and G. Suwa. 1999. *Australopithecus garhi*: A new species of early hominid from Ethiopia. *Science* 284 (5414):629–35.

Asfaw, Berhane, Yonas Beyene, Gen Suwa, Robert C. Walter, Tim D. White, Giday Wolde Gabriel, and Tesfaye Yemane. 1992. The earliest Acheulean from Konso-Gardula. *Nature* 360:732–35.

Aufderheide, Patricia. 1993. Beyond television. *Public Culture* 5:579–92.

Autobiografías campesinas. 1979. Vol. 1. Heredia, Costa Rica: Editorial de la Universidad Nacional.

Baer, Hans, Merrill Singer, and Ida Susser. 2003. *Medical anthropology and the world system*, 2nd ed. Westport, CT: Praeger.

Bailey, W., D. H. A. Fitch, D. A. Tagle, J. Czelusniak, J. L. Slightom, and M. Goodman. 1991. Molecular evolution of the psi-eta-globin gene locus: Gibbon phylogeny and the hominoid slowdown. *Molecular Biology and Evolution* 8:155–84.

Bakhtin, M. M. 1981. *The dialogic imagination: Four essays*, Ed. Michael Holquist, trans. Michael Holquist and Caryl Emerson. Austin: University of Texas Press.

Bar-Yosef, O. 1989. Geochronology of the Levantine Middle Paleolithic. In *The human revolution*, ed. P. A. Mellars and C. Stringer, 586–610. Princeton, NJ: Princeton University Press.

Bar-Yosef, Ofer, and Mordechai Kislev. 1989. Early farming communities in the Jordan Valley. In *Foraging and farming: The evolution of plant exploitation*, ed. David Harris and Gordon Hillman. One World Archaeology, vol. 13:632–42. London: Unwin Hyman.

Bar-Yosef, Ofer, and Steven L. Kuhn. 1999. The big deal about blades: Laminar technologies and human evolution. *American Anthropologist* 101 (2):322–28.

Basham, Richard. 1978. *Urban anthropology*. Palo Alto, CA: Mayfield Publishing.

Bateson, Gregory. 1972. A theory of play and fantasy. In *Steps to an ecology of mind*, ed. Gregory Bateson, 177–93. New York: Ballantine Books.

Beals, Alan. 1962. *Gopalpur, a south Indian village*. New York: Holt, Rinehart and Winston.

Bearder, Simon K. 1987. Lorises, bushbabies, and tarsiers: Diverse societies in solitary foragers. In *Primate societies*, ed. Barbara Smuts, Dorothy Cheney, Robert Seyfarth, Richard Wrangham, and Thomas Struhsaker, 11–24. Chicago: University of Chicago Press.

Behrendt, Larissa. 2007. The emergency we had to have. In *Coercive reconciliation: Stabilise, normalise, exit aboriginal Australia*, eds. Jon Altman and Melinda Hinkson, 15–20. North Carlton, Australia: Arena Publications Association.

Belfer-Cohen, Anna. 1988. The Natufian settlement at Hayonim Cave. Ph.D. diss. Jerusalem: Hebrew University.

Belfer-Cohen, Anna. 1991. The Natufian in the Levant. *Annual Review of Anthropology* 20:167–86.

Bell, Sandra, and Simon Coleman. 1999. The anthropology of friendship: Enduring themes and future possibilities. In *The anthropology of friendship*, ed. Sandra Bell and Simon Coleman, 1–19. Oxford: Berg.

Bender, Barbara. 1977. Gatherer–hunter to farmer: A social perspective. *World Archaeology* 10:204–22.

Benefit, Brenda, and Monte L. McCrossin. 1995. Miocene hominoids and hominid origins. *Annual Review of Anthropology* 24:237–56.

Berger, Richard L. 1988. Unity and heterogeneity within the Chavín Horizon. In *Peruvian prehistory*, ed. R. Keatinge, 99–144. Cambridge: Cambridge University Press.

Berman, Judith C. 1999. Bad hair days in the Paleolithic: Modern (re)constructions of the cave man. *American Anthropologist* 101 (2):288–304.

Bermúdez de Castro, J. M., J. L. Arsuaga, E. Carbonell, A. Rosas, I. Martinez, and M. Mosquera. 1997. A hominid from the Lower Pleistocene of Atapuerca, Spain. *Science* 276 (5317):1392–95.

Bernard, H. R. 2006. *Research methods in anthropology*. 4th ed. Thousand Oaks, CA: Sage Publications.

Berreman, Gerald D. 1962. Behind many masks: Ethnography and impression management in a Himalayan village. Lexington, KY: Society for Applied Anthropology.

Bestor, Theodore C. 2000. How sushi went global. *Foreign Policy* (November-December), 54–63.

Bigenho, Michelle. 2002. *Sounding indigenous: Authenticity in Bolivian music performance*. New York: Palgrave.

Binford, Lewis R., and Chuan Kun Ho. 1985. Taphonomy at a distance: Zhoukoudian, "the cave home of Beijing Man"? *Current Anthropology* 26 (4):413–29.

Blackwood, Evelyn, and Saskia E. Wieringa. 1999. Preface. In *Female desires: Same sex relations and transgender practices across cultures*, ed. Evelyn Blackwood and Saskia E. Wieringa, ix–xiii. New York: Columbia University Press.

Bledsoe, Caroline. 1993. The politics of polygyny in Mende education and child fosterage transactions. In *Sex and gender hierarchies*, ed. Barbara Diane Miller, 170–92. Cambridge: Cambridge University Press.

Boaz, Noel T. 1995. Calibration and extension of the record of Plio-Pleistocene Hominidae. In *Biological anthropology: The state of the science*, ed. Noel T. Boaz and Linda Wolfe, 23–47. Bend, OR: International Institute for Human Evolutionary Research.

Boaz, Noel T., and Linda Wolfe, eds. 1995. *Biological anthropology: The state of the science*. Bend, OR: International Institute for Human Evolutionary Research.

Bock, Philip. 1994. *Rethinking psychological anthropology: Continuity and change in the study of human action*, 2nd ed. Prospect Heights, IL: Waveland.

Boddy, Janice. 1997. Womb as oasis: The symbolic context of Pharaonic circumcision in rural northern Sudan. In *The gender/sexuality reader*, ed. Roger Lancaster and Micaela De Leonardo, 309–24. New York: Routledge.

Boesch Ackermann, H., and C. Boesch. 1994. Hominization in the rainforest: The chimpanzee's piece of the puzzle. *Evolutionary Anthropology* 3 (1):9–16.

Bogin, Barry. 1995. Growth and development: Recent evolutionary and biocultural research. In *Biological anthropology: The state of the science*, ed. Noel T. Boaz and Linda Wolfe. Bend, OR: International Institute for Human Evolutionary Research.

Bökönyi, Sandor. 1989. Definitions of animal domestication. In *The walking larder: Patterns of domestication, pastoralism, and predation*, ed. Juliet Clutton-Brock. One World Archaeology, vol. 14, 22–27. London: Unwin Hyman.

Borman, Randy. 1999. Cofán: Story of the forest people and the outsiders. *Cultural Survival Quarterly* 23(2):48–50.

Bourgois, Philippe. 1995. *In search of respect: Selling crack in El Barrio*. New York: Cambridge University Press.

Bowen, John. 2008. *Religions in practice: An approach to the anthropology of religion*, 4th ed. Needham Heights, MA: Allyn and Bacon.

Bowen, John R. 2010. *Can Islam be French? Pluralism and pragmatism in a secularist state*. Princeton, NJ: Princeton University Press.

Bowie, Fiona. 2006. *The anthropology of religion: An introduction*. 2nd ed. Malden, MA: Blackwell.

Bowie, Katherine. 2008. Standing in the shadows: of matrilocality and the role of women in a village election in northern Thailand. *American Ethnologist*, 35(1), 136–53.

Bradburd, Daniel. 1998. *Being there: The necessity of fieldwork*. Washington DC: Smithsonian Institution Press.

Brain, C. K. 1985. Interpreting early hominid death assemblages: The rise of taphonomy since 1925. In *Hominid evolution: Past, present, and future*, ed. P. V. Tobias, 41–46. New York: Alan R. Liss.

Brain, C. K., and A. Sillen. 1988. Evidence from the Swartkrans Cave for the earliest use of fire. *Nature* 336:464–66.

Brain, Robert. 1976. *Friends and lovers*. New York: Basic Books.

Branam, Kelly M. 2012. *Constitution making: Law, power, and kinship in Crow Country*. Forthcoming. Albany, NY: SUNY Press.

Bräuer, Günter. 1989. The evolution of modern humans: A comparison of the African and non-African evidence. In *The human revolution*, ed. P. A. Mellars and C. Stringer, 123–54. Princeton, NJ: Princeton University Press.

Brenneis, Donald, and Ronald Macaulay, eds. 1996. *The matrix of language: Contemporary linguistic anthropology*. Boulder, CO: Westview Press.

Briggs, A. W., Jeffrey M. Good, Richard E. Green, et al. 2009. Targeted retrieval and analysis of five Neandertal mtDNA genomes. *Science* 325:318–321.

Brooke, James. 2003. Dowry too high: lose bride and go to jail. *New York Times*, May 17.

Brooks, Allison, and J. N. Leith Smith. 1991. Politics and problems: Gorilla and chimp conservation in Africa. *Anthro Notes* 13(1):14.

Brooks, Allison, and John Yellen. 1992. Decoding the Jul/huasi past. *Symbols*, September: 24–31.

Brown, Michael F. 1997. *The channeling zone: American spirituality in an anxious age*. Cambridge, MA: Harvard University Press.

Brown, P., T. Sutinka, M. Morwood, et al. 2004. A new small-bodied hominin from the Late Pleistocene of Flores, Indonesia. *Nature* 431:1055–61.

Browne, Malcolm. 1994. Asian fossil prompts new ideas on evolution. *New York Times*, February 24.

Brunet, M. A. Beauvilain, Y. Coppens, E. Heintz, A. H. E. Moutaye, and D. Pilbeam. 1995. The first australopithecine 2,500 kilometers west of the Rift Valley (Chad). *Nature* 378:273–75.

Brunet M., et al. 2002. A new hominid from the upper Miocene of Chad, central Africa. *Nature* 418: 145–51.

Bruno, Maria C. 2009. Practice and history in the transition to food production. *Current Anthropology* 50(5):703–06.

Burch, Ernest. 1970. Marriage and divorce among the North Alaska Eskimos. In *Divorce and after*, ed. Paul Bohannan, 152–81. Garden City, NY: Doubleday.

Burling, Robbins. 2005. *The talking ape: How language evolved*. New York: Oxford University Press.

Cann, R. L., M. Stoneking, and A.C. Wilson. 1987. Mitchondrial DNA and human evolution. *Nature* 325:31–36.

Carneiro, Robert. 1970. A theory of the origin of the state. *Science* 169:733–38.

Cartmill, M. 1972. Arboreal adaptations and the origin of the order Primates. In *The functional and evolutionary biology of primates*, ed. R. Tuttle, 97–122. Chicago: Aldine Atherton.

Caryl, Christian. 2009. Reality check: Human Terrain Teams. *Foreign Policy*. September 8. http://www.foreignpolicy.com/articles/2009/09/08/reality_check_human_terrain_teams.

Chase, Philip G. 1989. How different was Middle Palaeolithic subsistence? A zooarchaeological perspective on the Middle to Upper Palaeolithic transition. In *The human revolution*, ed. P. A. Mellars and C. Stringer, 321–37. Princeton, NJ: Princeton University Press.

Chauchat, Claude. 1988. Early hunter-gatherers on the Peruvian coast. In *Peruvian prehistory*, ed. R. Keatinge, 41–66. Cambridge: Cambridge University Press.

Cheney, D. L., R. M. Seyfarth, B. B. Smuts, and R. W. Wrangham. 1987. The study of primate societies. In *Primate societies*, ed. Barbara Smuts, Dorothy Cheney, Robert Seyfarth, Richard Wrangham, and Thomas Struhsaker, 1–10. Chicago: University of Chicago Press.

Chin, Elizabeth. 1999. Ethnically correct dolls: Toying with the race industry. *American Anthropologist* 101 (2):305–21.

Chomsky, Noam. 1957. *Syntactic structures*. Cambridge, MA: MIT Press.

Chomsky, Noam. 1965. *Aspects of the theory of syntax*. Cambridge, MA: MIT Press.

Clarke, Ronald J. 1985. *Australopithecus* and early *Homo* in southern Africa. In *Ancestors: The hard evidence*, ed. E. Delson, 171–77. New York: Alan R. Liss.

Cole, Michael, and Sylvia Scribner. 1974. *Culture and thought: A psychological introduction*. New York: Wiley.

Collier, J., M. Z. Rosaldo, and S. Yanagisako. 1997. Is there a family? New anthropological views. In *The Gender/ Sexuality*

Reader, ed. R. Lancaster and M. Di Leonardo, 71-81. New York: Routledge.

Colloredo-Mansfeld, Rudi. 1999. *The native leisure class: Consumption and cultural creativity in the Andes*. Chicago: University of Chicago Press.

Colwell-Chanthaphonh, Chip. 2009. The archaeologist as world citizen: On the morals of heritage preservation and destruction. In *Cosmopolitan archaeologies*, ed. Lynn Meskell, 140-65. Durham, NC: Duke University Press.

Comaroff, Jean, and John Comaroff. 1992. *Ethnography and the historical imagination*. Boulder, CO: Westview.

Comaroff, John, and Jean Comaroff. 1991. *Of revelation and revolution*. Chicago: University of Chicago Press.

Conkey, Margaret W., and Joan M. Gero. 1991. Tensions, pluralities, and engendering archaeology: An introduction to women and prehistory. In *Engendering archaeology*, 3-30. Oxford: Blackwell.

Cords, Marina. 1987. Forest guenons and patas monkeys: Male-male competition in one-male groups. In *Primate societies*, ed. Barbara Smuts, Dorothy Cheney, Robert Seyfarth, Richard Wrangham, and Thomas Struhsaker, 98-111. Chicago: University of Chicago Press.

Counihan, Carole M. 2004. *Around the Tuscan table: Food, family, and gender in twentieth-century Florence*. New York: Routledge.

Cowan, Jane, Marie-Bénédicte Dembour, and Richard A. Wilson. 2001. Introduction. In *Culture and rights: anthropological perspectives*, ed. Jane Cowan, Marie-Bénédicte Dembour, and Richard A. Wilson, 1-26. Cambridge: Cambridge University Press.

Crehan, Kate. 2002. *Gramsci and cultural anthropology*. Berkeley: University of California Press.

Daly, Mary. 1978. *Gyn/Ecology: The metaethics of radical feminism*. Boston: Beacon Press.

D'Andrade, Roy G. 1992. Cognitive anthropology. In *New directions in psychological anthropology*, ed. Theodore Schwartz, Geoffrey M. White, and Catherine A. Lutz, 47-58. Cambridge: Cambridge University Press.

Daniel, E. Valentine. 1997. Suffering nation and alienation. In *Social suffering*, ed. Arthur Kleinman, Veena Das, and Margaret Lock, 309-58. Berkeley: University of California Press.

Daston, Lorraine. 1999. Objectivity and the escape from perspective. In *The science studies reader*, ed. Mario Biagioli, 110-23. New York: Routledge.

Day M. H. 1985. Pliocene hominids. In *Ancestors: The hard evidence*, ed. E. Delson, 91-93. New York: Alan R. Liss.

Day, M. H. 1986. Bipedalism: Pressures, origins, and modes. In *Major topics in primate and human evolution*, ed. B. Wood, L. Martin, and P. Andrews, 188-202. Cambridge: Cambridge University Press.

Deacon, Terrence. 1997. *The symbolic species: The co-evolution of language and the brain*. New York: W. W. Norton.

Deacon, Terrence. 2003. The hierarchic logic of emergence: Untangling the interdependence of evolution and self-organization. In *Evolution and learning: The Baldwin effect reconsidered*, ed. Bruce H. Weber and David J. Depew, 273-308. Cambridge, MA: MIT Press.

Defleur, A., O. Dutour, H. Valladas, and V. Vandermeersch. 1993. Cannibals among the Neanderthals. *Nature* 362:214.

Defleur, A., T. D. White, P. Valensi, L. Slimak, and E. Cregut-Bonnoure. 1999. Neanderthal cannibalism at Moula-Guercy, Ardeche, France. *Science* 286:128-131.

De Heinzelin, J., J. D. Clark, T. White, W. Hart, P. Renne, G. Woldegabriel, Y. Beyene, and E. Vrba. 1999. Environment and behavior of 2.5-million-year-old Bouri hominids. *Science* 284 (5414):625-9.

de Meer, K., R. Bergman, and J. S. Kusner. 1993. Differences in physical growth of Aymara and Quechua children living at high altitude in Peru. *American Journal of Physical Anthropology* 90:59-75.

Department of Communications, Information Technology, and the Arts. 2005. *Return of indigenous cultural property program*. Canberra: Government of Australia. http://www.dcita.gov.au/arts/councils/return_of_indigenous_cultural_property_(ricp)_program.

Depew, David J., and Bruce H. Weber. 1989. The evolution of the Darwinian research tradition. *Systems Research* 6 (3):255-63.

De Vos, George, and Hiroshi Wagatsuma. 1966. *Japan's invisible race*. Berkeley: University of California Press.

De Waal, Frans. 1989. *Peacemaking among primates*. Cambridge, MA: Harvard University Press.

DeWalt, K., and B. DeWalt. 2002. *Participant observation*. Walnut Creek, CA: AltaMira Press.

Diamond, Jared. 1997. *Guns, germs, and steel: The fates of human societies*. New York: Norton.

Diamond, Jared. 2005. *Collapse: How societies choose to fail or succeed*. New York: Viking.

Dibble, Harold L. 1989. The implications of stone tool types for the presence of language during the Lower and Middle Palaeolithic. In *The human revolution*, ed. P. A. Mellars and C. Stringer, 415-32. Princeton, NJ: Princeton University Press.

Dillehay, Thomas D. 2000. *The settlement of the Americas*. New York: Basic Books.

Dodson, Mick. 2007. Bully in the playground: a new stolen generation? In *Coercive reconciliation: stabilise, normalise, exit Aboriginal Australia*, ed. Jon Altman and Melinda Hinkson. North Carlton, Australia: Arena Publications Association.

Dolgin, Janet. 1995. Family law and the facts of family. In *Naturalizing power*, ed. Sylvia Yanagisako and Carol Delaney, 47-67. New York: Routledge.

Doretti, Mercedes and Clyde Snow. 2009. Forensic anthropology and human rights: The Argentine experience. In *Hard evidence: Case studies in forensic anthropology*, 2nd ed., ed. Dawnie Wolfe Steadman, 303-320. Upper Saddle River, N.J.: Prentice Hall.

Douglas, Mary. 1970. Introduction. In *Witchcraft confessions and accusations*, ed. Mary Douglas, vi-xxxviii. London: Tavistock.

Douglas, Mary, and Baron Isherwood. 1979. *The world of goods: Towards an anthropology of consumption*. New York: W. W. Norton.

Drewal, Margaret Thompson. 1992. *Yoruba ritual: Performers, play, agency*. Bloomington: Indiana University Press.

Duranti, Alessandro. 1994. *From grammar to politics: Linguistic anthropology in a western Samoan village*. Berkeley: University of California Press.

Durham, William H. 1991. *Coevolution: Genes, culture, and human diversity*. Stanford: Stanford University Press.

Eldredge, Niles. 1985. *Time frames: The rethinking of Darwinian evolution and the theory of punctuated equilibria*. New York: Simon & Schuster.

Eldredge, Niles, and Ian Tattersall. 1982. *The myths of human evolution*. New York: Columbia University Press.

Elliot, Alison. 1981. *Child language*. Cambridge: Cambridge University Press.

Errington, Shelly. 1998. *The death of authentic primitive art and other tales of progress*. Berkeley: University of California Press.

Escobar, Arturo. 1992. Culture, economics, and politics in Latin American social movements theory and research. In *The making of social movements in Latin America*, ed. Arturo Escobar and Sonia Alvarez, 62-85. Boulder, CO: Westview Press.

Evans-Pritchard, E. 1940. *The Nuer*. Oxford: Oxford University Press.

Evans-Pritchard, E. E. 1951. *Kinship and marriage among the Nuer*. Oxford: Oxford University Press.

Evans-Pritchard, E. E. [1937] 1976. *Witchcraft, oracles, and magic among the Azande*, abridged ed., prepared by Eva Gillies. Oxford: Oxford University Press.

Fagan, Brian. 1990. *The Journey from Eden*. London: Thames & Hudson.

Fagan, Brian, and Christopher DeCorse. 2005. *In the beginning: An introduction to archaeology*, 11th ed. New York: HarperCollins.

Fagen, Robert. 1981. *Animal play behavior*. New York: Oxford University Press.

Fagen, Robert. 1992. Play, fun, and the communication of well-being. *Play and Culture* 5(1):40-58.

Fagen, Robert. 2005. Play, five gates of evolution, and paths to art. In *Play: An interdisciplinary synthesis*, vol. 6, ed. F. F. McMahnon, Donald E. Lytle, and Brian Sutton-Smith. Play and Culture Studies. Lanham, MD: University Press of America.

Falk, D., et al. 2009. LB1's virtual endocast, microcephaly and hominin brain evolution. *Journal of Human Evolution*, 597-607.

Farmer, Paul. 2002. On suffering and structural violence: A view from below. In *The anthropology of politics*, ed. Joan Vincent, 424-37. Malden, MA: Blackwell.

Farmer, Paul. 2003. *Pathologies of power: Health, human rights, and the new war on the poor*. Berkeley: University of California Press.

Fedigan, Linda M. 1986. The changing role of women in models of human evolution. *Annual Review of Anthropology* 15:25-66.

Feibel, Craig S., Neville Agnew, Bruce Latimer, Martha Demas, Fiona Marshall, Simon A. C. Waane, and Peter Schmid. 1995/96. The Laetoli hominid footprints—a preliminary report on the conservation and scientific restudy. *Evolutionary Anthropology* 4 (5):149–54.

Fernandez, James W. 1990. Guest editorial. In *Cultural anthropology: A perspective on the human condition*, 2nd ed., ed. Emily Schultz and Robert Lavenda. St. Paul, MN: West.

Fernandez-Jalvo, Y. J., J. C. Diez, I. Cáceres, and J. Rosell. 1999. Human cannibalism in the Early Pleistocene of Europe (Gran Dolina, Sierra de Atapuerca, Burgos, Spain). *Journal of Human Evolution* 37:407–36.

Field, Les. 2004. Beyond "applied" anthropology. In *A companion to the anthropology of American Indians*, ed. Thomas Biolsi, 472–89. Malden, MA: Blackwell.

Firth, Raymond. [1936] 1984. *We, the Tikopia*. Reprint. Stanford, CA: Stanford University Press.

Fleagle, John. 1995. "Origin and radiation of anthropoid primates. In *Biological anthropology: The state of the science*, ed. Noel T. Boaz and Linda Wolfe, 1–21. Bend, OR: International Institute for Human Evolutionary Research.

Floating on the air, followed by the wind. 1973. Film distributed by Indiana University Instructional Support Services, Gunter Pfaff (cinematographer) and Ronald A. Simons (psychiatric consultant). East Lansing: Michigan State University.

Foley, Douglas. 1989. *Learning capitalist culture: Deep in the heart of Tejas*. Philadelphia: University of Pennsylvania Press.

Foley, Robert. 1995. *Humans before humanity*. Oxford: Blackwell.

Forge, Anthony. 1967. The Abelam artist. In *Social organization: Essays presented to Raymond Firth*, ed. Maurice Freedman, 65–84. London: Cass.

Fortes, Meyer. 1953. The structure of unilineal descent groups. *American Anthropologist* 55:25–39.

Foucault, Michel. 1991. Governmentality. In *The Foucault effect: Studies in governmentality*, ed. Graham Burchell, Colin Gordon, and Peter Miller, 87–104. Chicago: University of Chicago Press.

Frayer, David, Milford Wolpoff, Alan G. Thorne, Fred H. Smith, and Geoffrey G. Pope. 1993. Theories of modern human origins: The paleontological test. *American Anthropologist* 95 (1):14–50.

Freeman, Leslie G. 1981. The fat of the land: Notes on paleolithic diet in Iberia. In *Omnivorous primates*, ed. Robert S.O. Harding and Geza Teleki, 104–65. New York: Columbia University Press.

Fried, M. H. 1967. *The evolution of political society*. New York: Random House.

Friedman, J. 1994. *Cultural identity and global process*. London: Sage.

Friedman, Jonathan. 1997. Global crises, the struggle for cultural identity and intellectual porkbarrelling: Cosmopolitans versus locals. Ethnics and nationals in an era of dehegemonisation. In *Debating cultural hybridity: Multicultural identities and the politics of anti-racism*, ed. Pnina Werbner and Tariq Modood, 70–89. London: Zed Books.

Gallivan, Martin and Danielle Moretti-Langholtz. 2007. Civic engagement at Werowocomoco: Reasserting Native narratives from a Powhatan place of power. In *Archaeology as a Tool of Civic Engagement*, ed. Barbara J. Little and Paul A. Shackel, 47–66. Lanham, MD: AltaMira Press.

Gardner, H. 2000. Intelligence reframed: Multiple intelligences for the 21st century. New York: Basic Books.

Garralda, M. D., and B. Vandermeersch. 2000. Les Néandertaliens de la Grotte de Combe-Grenal (Domme, France). *Paléo* 12:213–259.

Geertz, Clifford. 1973. *The interpretation of cultures*. New York: Basic Books.

Gentner, Dedre, and Susan Goldin-Meadow. 2003. Whither Whorf? In *Language in mind: Advances in the study of language and thought*, ed. Dedre Gentner and Susan Goldin-Meadow, 3–14. Cambridge, MA: MIT Press.

Georges, Eugenia. 1990. *The making of a transnational community: Migration, development, and cultural change in the Dominican Republic*. New York: Columbia University Press.

Gero, Joan M. 1991. Genderlithics: Women's roles in stone tool production. In *Engendering archaeology*, ed. Margaret Conkey and Joan Gero, 163–93. Oxford: Blackwell.

Giddens, Anthony. 1979. *Central problems in social theory*. Berkeley: University of California Press.

Giddens, Anthony. 1990. *The consequences of modernity*. Stanford: Stanford University Press.

Gillman, Neil. 1992. *Sacred fragments: Recovering theology for the modern Jew*. New York: Jewish Publication Society.

Ginsburg, Faye, and Rayna Rapp. 1995. *Conceiving the new world order: The global politics of reproduction*. Berkeley: University of California Press.

Gledhill, John. 1994. *Power and its disguises*. London: Pluto Press.

Goodman, M. 1986. Molecular evidence of the ape subfamily Homininae. In *Evolutionary perspectives and the new genetics*. New York: Alan R. Liss.

Goodman, M., D. A. Tagle, D. H. A. Fitch, W. Bailey, J. Czelusniak, B. F. Koop, P. Benson, and J. L. Slighton. 1990. Primate evolution at the DNA level and a classification of the hominoids. *Journal of Molecular Evolution* 30:260–66.

Goody, Jack, and Stanley Tambiah. 1973. *Bridewealth and dowry*. Cambridge: Cambridge University Press.

Gordon, Colin. 1991. Governmental rationality: An introduction. In *The Foucault effect: Studies in governmentality*, ed. Graham Burchell, Colin Gordon, and Peter Miller, 1–52. Chicago: University of Chicago Press.

Gottlieb, Alma. 1988. American premenstrual syndrome: A mute voice. *Anthropology Today* 4 (6).

Gould, Stephen J. 1987. *Time's arrow, time's cycle*. Cambridge, MA: Harvard University Press.

Gould, Stephen J. 1996. *Full house: The spread of excellence from Plato to Darwin*. New York: Harmony Books.

Gould, S. J. 2002. *The Structure of Evolutionary Theory*. Cambridge, MA: Harvard University Press.

Gould, Stephen J., and N. Eldredge. 1977. Punctuated equilibria: The tempo and mode of evolution reconsidered. *Paleobiology* 3:115–51.

Gould, Stephen J., and Elisabeth Vrba. 1982. Exaptation—A missing term in the science of form. *Palaeobiology* 8:4–15.

Gramsci, Antonio. 1971. *Selections from the prison notebooks*, Trans. Q. Hoare and G. N. Smith. New York: International Publishers.

Green, Richard E., Johannes Krause, Adrian W. Briggs, et al. 2010. A draft sequence of the Neandertal genome. *Science* 328 (5979):710–722.

Greenwood, David, and William Stini. 1977. *Nature, culture, and human history*. New York: Harper and Row.

Gregory, Richard. 1981. *Mind in science: A history of explanations in psychology and physics*. Cambridge: Cambridge University Press.

Greska, L. P. 1990. Developmental responses to high-altitude hypoxia in Bolivian children of European ancestry: A test of the developmental adaptation hypothesis. *American Journal of Human Biology* 2:603–12.

Grinker, Roy Richard. 1994. Houses in the rainforest: Ethnicity and inequality among farmers and foragers in Central Africa. Berkeley: University of California Press.

Guneratne, Arjun. 2002. Caste and state. In *South Asian folklore: An encyclopedia*, ed. Peter Claus and Margaret Mills. New York: Garland.

Gupta, Akhil, and James Ferguson. 1997. Discipline and practice: "The Field" as site, method, and location in anthropology. In *Anthropological locations: Boundaries and grounds of a field science*, ed. Akhil Gupta and James Ferguson, 1–46. Berkeley: University of California Press.

Gupta, Dipankar. 2005. Caste and politics: Identity over system. *Annual Review of Anthropology* 34:409–27.

Hacking, Ian. 1991. How should we do the history of statistics?" In *The Foucault effect: Studies in governmentality*, ed. Graham Burchell, Colin Gordon, and Peter Miller, 181–96. Chicago: University of Chicago Press.

Hager, Lori D., ed. 1997. *Women in human evolution*. London: Routledge.

Haile Selassie, Y. 2001. Late Miocene hominids from Middle Awash. *Nature* 412:178–81.

Haile Selassie, Y., G. Suwa, and T. D. White. 2004. Late Miocene teeth from Middle Awash, Ethiopia, and early hominid dental evolution. *Science* 303:1503–5.

Hale, Charles. 1997. Cultural politics of identity in Latin America. *Annual Review of Anthropology* 26:567–90.

Halperin, Rhoda H. 1994. *Cultural economies: Past and present.* Austin: University of Texas Press.

Handelman, Don. 1977. Play and ritual: Complementary frames of meta-communication. In *It's a funny thing, humour,* ed. A. J. Chapman and H. C. Foot, 185–92. London: Pergamon.

Hanks, William. 1996. *Language and communicative practices.* Boulder, CO: Westview Press.

Hannerz, Ulf. 1996. *Transnational connections: Culture, people, places.* London: Routledge.

Haraway, Donna. 1989. *Primate visions.* New York: Routledge.

Harris, David. 1989. An evolutionary continuum of people-plant interaction. In *Foraging and farming: The evolution of plant exploitation,* ed. David Harris and Gordon Hillman. One World Archaeology, vol. 13, 1–30. London: Unwin Hyman.

Harrison, Faye. 1995. The persistent power of "race" in the cultural and political economy of racism. *Annual Review of Anthropology* 24:47–74.

Harrison, Faye. 1998. Introduction: Expanding the discourse on "race." *American Anthropologist* 100 (3):609–31.

Hartigan, John, Jr. 1997. Establishing the fact of whiteness. *American Anthropologist* 99 (3):495–504.

Harvey, David. 1990. *The condition of postmodernity.* Malden, MA: Blackwell.

Hayden, Brian. 1981. Subsistence and ecological adaptations of modern hunter/gatherers. In *Omnivorous primates,* ed. Robert S. O. Harding and Geza Telecki, 344–421. New York: Columbia University Press.

Heider, Karl. 1979. *Grand Valley Dani.* New York: Holt, Rinehart and Winston, Inc.

Henry, Donald. 1989. From foraging to agriculture: The Levant and the end of the ice age. Philadelphia: University of Pennsylvania Press.

Herdt, Gilbert, ed. 1994. *Third sex, third gender: Beyond sexual dimorphism in culture and history.* New York: Zone Books.

Herrnstein, Richard, and Charles Murray. 1994. *The bell curve.* New York: Free Press.

Herskovits, Melville. 1973. *Cultural relativism.* New York: Vintage Books.

Herzfeld, Michael. 1987. *Anthropology through the looking glass.* Cambridge: Cambridge University Press.

Herzfeld, Michael. 2003. Competing diversities: Ethnography in the heart of Rome. *Plurimundi* 3(5):147–54.

Hess, David J. 1997. *Science studies: An advanced introduction.* New York: New York University Press.

Hill, Jane, and Judith Irvine, eds. 1992. *Responsibility and evidence in oral discourse.* Cambridge: Cambridge University Press.

Hillman, Gordon. 1989. Late Paleolithic plant foods from Wadi Kubbaniya in Upper Egypt: Dietary diversity, infant weaning, and seasonality in a riverine environment. In *Foraging and farming: The evolution of plant exploitation,* ed. David Harris and Gordon Hillman. One World Archaeology, vol. 13, 207–39. London: Unwin Hyman.

Hinkson, Melinda. Introduction: In the name of the child. In *Coercive reconciliation: Stabilise, normalise, exit aboriginal Australia,* ed. Jon Altman and Melinda Hinkson, 1–12. North Carlton, Australia: Arena Publications Association.

Hinton, Leanne. 1998. Language loss and revitalization in California: Overview. In *Making sense of language,* ed. Susan Blum, 216–22. New York: Oxford University Press.

Hockett, C. F. 1966. The problems of universals in language. In *Universals of language,* ed. J. H. Greenberg, 1–29. Cambridge, MA: MIT Press.

Hodder, Ian. 1982. *Symbols in action.* Cambridge: Cambridge University Press.

Hoffman, M. 1991. *Egypt before the pharaohs: The prehistoric foundations of Egyptian civilization,* rev. ed. Austin: University of Texas Press.

Holm, John. 1988. *Pidgins and Creoles.* Theory and Structure, vol. 1. Cambridge: Cambridge University Press.

Holy, Ladislav. 1996. *Anthropological perspectives on kinship.* London: Pluto Press.

Horton, Robin. 1982. Tradition and modernity revisited. In *Rationality and relativism,* ed. M. Hollis and Steven Lukes, 201–60. Cambridge, MA: MIT Press.

Hublin, J., F. Spoor, M. Braun, F. Zonneveld, and S. Condemi. 1996. A late Neandertal associated with Upper Palaeolithic artifacts. *Nature* 381:224–26.

Hudson, R. A. 1980. *Sociolinguistics.* Cambridge: Cambridge University Press.

Hultkrantz, Åke. 1992. *Shamanic healing and ritual drama: Health and medicine in native North American religious traditions.* New York: Crossroads.

Hunter, David, and Phillip Whitten. 1976. *Encyclopedia of anthropology.* New York: Harper and Row.

Hutnyk, John. 1997. Adorno at Womad: South Asian crossovers and the limits of hybridity-talk. In *Debating cultural hybridity: Multicultural identities and the politics of anti-racism,* ed. Pnina Werbner and Tariq Modood, 106–36. London: Zed Books.

Huyghe, Patrick. 1988. Profile of an anthropologist: No bone unturned. *Discover* (December).

Hymes, Dell. 1972. On communicative competence. In *Sociolinguistics: Selected readings,* ed. J. B. Pride and J. Holmes, 269–93. Baltimore: Penguin.

Inda, Jonathan Xavier, and Renato Rosaldo. 2002. Introduction: A world in motion. In *The anthropology of globalization,* ed. Jonathan Xavier Inda and Renato Rosaldo. Malden, MA: Blackwell.

Ingold, Tim. 1983. The significance of storage in hunting societies. *Man* 18:553–71.

Ingold, Tim. 1994. General introduction. In *Companion encyclopedia of anthropology,* ed. Tim Ingold, xiii–xxii. London: Routledge.

Ingold, Tim. 2000. *The perception of the environment: Essays in livelihood, dwelling and skill.* London: Routledge.

Isaac, Glynn L., and Diana C. Crader. 1981. To what extent were early hominids carnivorous? An archaeological perspective. In *Omnivorous primates,* ed. Robert S. O. Harding and Geza Teleki, 37–103. New York: Columbia University Press.

Isbell, William H. 1988. City and state in middle horizon Huari. In *Peruvian prehistory,* ed. R. Keatinge, 164–89. Cambridge: Cambridge University Press.

Jablonski, N. 2004. The evolution of human skin and skin color. *Annual Review of Anthropology* 33: 585–623.

Jablonski, N., and G. Chaplin. 2000. The evolution of skin coloration. *Journal of Human Evolution* 39: 57–106.

Jarman, M. R., G. N. Bailey, and H. N. Jarman, eds. 1982. *Early European agriculture: Its foundations and development.* Cambridge: Cambridge University Press.

Johansen, R. E. 2006. Care for infibulated women giving birth in Norway: An anthropological analysis of health workers' management of a medically and culturally unfamiliar issue. *Medical Anthropology Quarterly* 20(4):516–44.

Johanson, Donald, and Maitland A. Edey. 1981. *Lucy: The beginnings of humankind.* New York: Simon & Schuster.

Johnson, M. 1999. *Archaeological theory: An introduction.* Oxford: Blackwell Publishers.

Jolly, Alison. 1985. *The evolution of primate behavior,* 2nd ed. New York: Macmillan.

Jolly, Alison. 2004. *Lords and lemurs.* Boston: Houghton Mifflin.

Jones, J. S. 1986. The origin of *Homo sapiens:* The genetic evidence. In *Modern trends in primate and human evolution,* ed. B. Wood, L. Martin, and P. Andrews, 317–30. Cambridge: Cambridge University Press.

Jourdan, Christine. 1991. Pidgins and Creoles: The blurring of categories. *Annual Review of Anthropology* 20:187–209.

Joyce, Rosemary A. 2008. *Ancient bodies, ancient lives: Sex, gender, and archaeology.* New York: Thames and Hudson.

Judson, Sheldon, and Marvin E. Kauffman. 1990. *Physical geology.* Englewood Cliffs, NJ: Prentice-Hall.

Kapferer, Bruce. 1983. *A celebration of demons.* Bloomington: Indiana University Press.

Karp, Ivan. 1990. Guest editorial in *Cultural anthropology: A perspective on the human condition,* by Emily Schultz and Robert Lavenda, 74–75. 2nd ed. St. Paul: West.

Karp, Ivan, and Martha B. Kendall. 1982. Reflexivity in field work. In *Explanation in social science,* ed. P. Secord. Los Angeles: Sage.

Kearney, Michael. 1995. The local and the global: The anthropology of globalization and transnationalism. *Annual review of anthropology* 24:547–65.

Keatinge, Richard W. 1988. A summary view of Peruvian prehistory. In *Peruvian prehistory*, ed. R. Keatinge, 303–16. Cambridge: Cambridge University Press.

Keesing, Roger. 1982. *Kwaio religion: The living and the dead in a Solomon Island society*. New York: Columbia University Press.

Keesing, Roger. 1992. *Custom and confrontation: The Kwaio struggle for cultural autonomy*. Chicago: University of Chicago Press.

Kelly, John D., and Martha Kaplan. 2001. *Represented communities: Fiji and world decolonization*. Chicago: University of Chicago Press.

Kelly, Raymond. 1993. *Constructing inequality: The fabrication of a hierarchy of virtue among the Etoro*. Ann Arbor: University of Michigan Press.

Kimbel, William H., Donald C. Johanson, and Yoel Rak. 1994. The first skull and other new discoveries of *Australopithecus afarensis* at Hadar, Ethiopia. *Journal of Human Evolution* 31:549–61.

Kipp, R.S., and E.M. Schortman. 1989. The political impact of trade in chiefdoms. *American Anthropologist* 91:370–85.

Kitcher, P. 1982. *Abusing science*. Cambridge, MA: MIT Press.

Klein, Richard G. 2009. *The human career: Human biological and cultural origins*. 3rd ed. Chicago: University of Chicago Press.

Köhler, G. 1978. *Global apartheid*. New York: Institute for World Order.

Kondo, Dorinne K. 1990. Crafting selves: Power, gender, and discourses of identity in a Japanese workplace. Chicago: University of Chicago Press.

Krause, J., C. Lalueza-Fox, L. Orlando, W. Enard, R. E. Green, H. A. Burbano, J.-J. Hublin, et al. 2007. The derived FOXP2 variant of modern humans was shared with Neandertals. *Current Biology* 17:1–5.

Krings, M., H. Geisart, R. W. Schmitz, H. Krainitzki, and S. Pääbo. 1999. DNA sequence of the mitochondrial hypervariable region II from the Neandertal type specimen. *Proceedings of the National Academy of Sciences* 95:5581–5585.

Krings, M. A. Stone, R. W. Schmitz, H. Krainitzki, and M. Stoneking. 1997. Neandertal DNA sequences and the origin of modern humans. *Cell* 90:19–30.

Kulish, Nicholas. 2009. As economic turmoil mounts, so do attacks on Hungary's Gypsies. *New York Times*, April 26.

Kumar, Nita. 1992. *Friends, brothers, and informants: Fieldwork memories of Banares*. Berkeley: University of California Press, 1992.

Kuper, Adam. 1982. *Wives for cattle: Bridewealth and marriage in southern Africa*. London: Routledge and Kegan Paul.

Labov, William. 1972. *Language in the inner city: Studies in the black English vernacular*. Philadelphia: University of Pennsylvania Press.

Lahr, Marta, and Robert Foley. 1994. Multiple dispersals and modern human origins. *Evolutionary Anthropology* (2): 48–60.

Lahr, M. M., and R. Foley. 2004. Human evolution writ small. *Nature* 431:1043–44.

Lakoff, George, and Mark Johnson. 1980. *Metaphors we live by*. Berkeley: University of California Press.

Lalueza-Fox, C., M. Lourdes Sampietro, D. Caramelli, et al. 2005. Neandertal evolutionary genetics: Mitochondrial DNA data from the Iberian Peninsula. *Molecular Biology and Evolution* 22:1077–1081.

Lalueza-Fox, C., M. Lourdes Sampietro, D. Caramelli, et al. 2007. A Melanocortin 1 Receptor allele suggests varying pigmentation among Neanderthals. *Science* 318:1453–1455.

Lalueza-Fox, Carles, Antonio Rosas, Almudena Estalrrich, et al. 2010. Genetic evidence for patrilocal mating behavior among Neandertal groups *PNAS* 108 (1):250–253; published ahead of print December 20, 2010. doi:10.1073/pnas.1011553108

Lancaster, Roger. 1992. *Life is hard: Machismo, danger, and the intimacy of power in Nicaragua*. Berkeley: University of California Press.

Lancaster, Roger. 2004. Two cheers for gay marriage. *Anthropology News*, 45(6).

Landau, M. 1984. Human evolution as narrative. *American Scientist* 72:262–68.

Larkin, Brian. 2002. Indian films and Nigerian lovers: Media and the creation of parallel modernities. In *The anthropology of globalization*, ed. Jonathan Xavier Inda and Renato Rosaldo, 350–78. Malden, MA: Blackwell.

Lassiter, Luke E., Clyde Ellis, and Ralph Kotay. 2002. *The Jesus road: Kiowas, Christianity, and Indian hymns*. Lincoln: University of Nebraska Press.

Leacock, E. 1983. Interpreting the origins of gender inequality: Conceptual and historical problems. *Dialectical Anthropology* 7(4):263–84.

Leakey, M. G., C. S. Feibel, I. McDougall, and A. C. Walker. 1995. New four-million-year-old hominid species from Kanapoi and Allia Bay, Kenya. *Nature* 376:565–71.

Leakey, M. G., F. Spoor, F. Brown, et al. 2001. New hominin genus from eastern Africa shows diverse Middle Pliocene lineages. *Nature* 410:433–40.

Lederman, Rena. 2005. Unchosen grounds: Cultivating cross-subfield accents for a public voice. In *Unwrapping the sacred bundle*, ed. Daniel Segal and Sylvia Yanigisako, 49–77. Durham, NC: Duke University Press.

Lee, R.B. 1974. Male–female residence arrangements and political power in human hunter-gatherers. *Archaeology of Sexual Behavior* 3:167–73.

Lee, Richard B. 1992. *The Dobe Ju/'hoansi*, 2nd ed. New York: Holt, Rinehart and Winston.

Lee, Richard B., and Irven DeVore, eds. 1968. *Man the hunter*. Chicago: Aldine.

LeGros Clark, W. E. 1963. *The antecedents*, 2nd ed. New York: Harper & Row.

Leighton, Donna Robbins. 1987. Gibbons: Territoriality and monogamy. In *Primate societies*, ed. Barbara Smuts, Dorothy Cheney, Robert Seyfarth, Richard Wrangham, and Thomas Struhsaker, 135–45. Chicago: University of Chicago Press.

Le Mort, F. 1989. Traces de décharnement sur les ossements néandertaliens de Combe-Grenal (Dordogne). *Bulletin de la Société Préhistorique Française* 86:77–97.

Leonard, W. R., R. L. Leatherman, J. W. Carey, and R. B. Thomas. 1990. Contributions of nutrition versus hypoxia to growth in rural Andean populations. *American Journal of Human Biology* 2:612–26.

Lerner, I.M., and W.J. Libby. 1976. *Heredity, evolution, and society*, 2nd ed. San Francisco: W. H. Freeman.

Leslie, Paul W., and Michael Little. 2003. Human biology and ecology: Variation in nature and the nature of variation. *American Anthropologist* 105(1):28–37.

Levine, Nancy. 1980. Nyinba polyandry and the allocation of paternity. *Journal of Comparative Family Studies* 11(3):283–88.

Levine, Nancy. 1988. *The dynamics of polyandry: Kinship, domesticity, and population on the Tibetan border*. Chicago: University of Chicago Press.

Levine, Nancy, and Walter Sangree. 1980. Women with many husbands. *Journal of Comparative Family Studies* 11(3).

Levins, Richard, and Richard Lewontin. 1985. *The dialectical biologist*. Cambridge, Massachusetts: Harvard University Press.

Lévi-Strauss, Claude. 1967. *Structural anthropology*, trans. Claire Jacobson, Brooke Grundfest Schoepf. New York: Doubleday Anchor.

Lewellen, Ted C. 1992. *Political anthropology*, 2nd ed. South Hadley, MA: Bergin and Garvey.

Lewin, Roger. 1989. *Human evolution*, 2nd ed. Boston: Blackwell Scientific Publications.

Lewis, I. M. 1967. *A pastoral democracy: A study of pastoralism and politics among the northern Somali of the Horn of Africa*. Oxford: Oxford University Press.

Lewis, Philip. 1997. Arenas of ethnic negotiations: Cooperation and conflict in Bradford. In *The politics of multiculturalism in the new Europe: Racism, identity, and community*, ed. Tariq Modood and Pnina Werbner, 126–46. London: Zed Books.

Lewis-Williams, J.D. 1984. Ideological continuities in prehistoric southern Africa: The evidence of the rock art. In *Past and present in hunter–gatherer studies*, ed. C. Schrire, 225–52. New York: Academic Press.

Lewontin, Richard. 1982. *Human diversity*. New York: Scientific American Books.

Lewontin, Richard. 1983. Introduction. In *Scientists confront creationism*, ed. Laurie R. Godfrey, xxiii–xxvi. New York: Norton.

Lewontin, R. 1991. *Biology as ideology: The doctrine of DNA*. New York: HarperPerennial.

Lieberman, Daniel E., and Dennis M. Bramble. 2007. The evolution of marathon running. *Sports Medicine* 37(4/5):288–90.

Lienhardt, Godfrey. 1961. *Divinity and experience.* Oxford: Oxford University Press.

Little, Michael. 1995. Adaptation, adaptability, and multidisciplinary research. In *Biological anthropology: The state of the science,* ed. Noel T. Boaz and Linda Wolfe. Bend, OR: International Institute for Human Evolutionary Research.

Livingstone, F. B. 1958. Anthropological implications of sickle cell gene distribution in West Africa. *American Anthropologist* 60:533–62.

Livingstone, F. B. 1964. On the nonexistence of human races. In *The concept of race,* ed. M. F. Ashley-Montagu, 46–60. New York: Collier.

Longino, Helen E. 1990. *Science as social knowlege.* Princeton, NJ: Princeton University Press.

Lovejoy, A.O. [1936] 1960. *The Great Chain of Being.* New York: Harper Torchbooks.

Lutz, Ellen. 2006. Fighting for the right rights. *Cultural Survival Quarterly* 30(4):3–4.

Malinowski, Bronislaw. 1944. *A scientific theory of culture and other essays.* Oxford: Oxford University Press.

Malinowski, Bronislaw. [1926] 1948. *Magic, science, and religion, and other essays.* New York: Doubleday Anchor.

Malkki, Liisa. 1992. National geographic: the rooting of peoples and the territorialization of national identity among scholars and refugees. *Cultural Anthropology* 7(1):24–44.

Mann, Alan E. 1981. Diet and human evolution. In *Omnivorous primates,* ed. Robert S.O. Harding and Geza Teleki, 10–36. New York: Columbia University Press.

Maquet, Jacques. 1970. Rwanda castes. In *Social stratification in Africa,* ed. Arthur Tuden and Leonard Plotnikov. New York: Free Press.

Marcus, George. 1995. Ethnography in/of the world system: The emergence of multi-sited Ethnography. *Annual Review of Anthropology* 24:95–117.

Marks, Jonathan. 1995. *Human biodiversity.* New York: Aldine.

Marks, Jonathan. 2011. *The alternative introduction to biological anthropology.* New York and Oxford: Oxford University Press.

Martin, R.D. 1986. Primates: A definition. In *Major topics in primate and human evolution,* ed, B. Wood, L. Martin, and P. Andrews, 1–31. Cambridge: Cambridge University Press.

Martin, R. D. 1993. Primate origins: Plugging the gaps. *Nature* 363(20 May):223–34.

Marx, Karl. 1963. *The 18th brumaire of Louis Bonaparte.* New York: International Publishers.

Mauss, Marcel. 2000. *The gift: The form and reason for exchange in archaic societies.* New York: W. W. Norton.

Mayer, Ernst. 1982. *The growth of biological thought.* Cambridge, MA: Harvard University Press.

McAnany, Patricia A., and Norman Yoffee, eds. 2010. *Questioning collapse: Human resilience, ecological vulnerability, and the aftermath of empire.* Cambridge, New York: Cambridge University Press.

McCoid, Catherine Hidge, and LeRoy D. McDermott. 1996. Toward decolonizing gender: Female vision in the Upper Paleolithic. *American Anthropologist* 98(2):319–326.

McCorriston, Joy, and Frank Hole. 1991. The ecology of seasonal stress and the origins of agriculture in the Near East. *American Anthropologist* 93:46–69.

McDermott, F., R. Grun, C. B. Stringer, and C. J. Hawkesworth. 1993. Mass-spectrometric U-series dates for Israeli Neanderthal/early modern hominid sites. *Nature* 363(20 May):252–56.

McHenry, Henry. 1985. Implications of postcanine megadontia for the origin of *Homo.* In *Ancestors: The hard evidence,* ed. E. Delson, 178–83. New York: Alan R. Liss.

McHenry, Henry, and L. R. Berger. 1998. Body proportions in *Australopithecus afarensis* and *A. africanus* and the origin of the genus *Homo. Journal of Human Evolution* 35:1–22.

McKinnon, S., and S. Silverman, eds. 2005. *Complexities: Beyond Nature and Nurture.* Chicago: University of Chicago Press.

Mead, George Herbert. 1934. *Mind, self, and society.* Chicago: University of Chicago Press.

Meadow, Richard H. 1989. Osteological evidence for the process of animal domestication. In *The walking larder: Patterns of*

domestication, pastoralism, and predation, *ed. Juliet Clutton-Brock, 80–90. London: Unwin Hyman.*

Mellars, Paul. 1996. *The Neandertal legacy.* Princeton, NJ: Princeton University Press.

Mellars, Paul, and Christopher Stringer. 1989. Introduction. In *The human revolution,* ed. P.A. Mellars and C. Stringer, 1–14. Princeton: Princeton University Press.

Melotti, Umberto. 1997. International migration in Europe: Social projects and political cultures. In *The politics of multiculturalism in the new Europe: Racism, identity and community,* ed. Tariq Modood and Pnina Werbner, 73–92. London: Zed Books.

Merry, Sally Engle. 2001. Changing rights, changing culture. In *Culture and rights: Anthropological perspectives,* ed. Jane Cowan, Marie-Bénédicte Dembour, and Richard A. Wilson, 31–55. Cambridge: Cambridge University Press.

Merry, Sally. 2003. Human-Rights Law and the Demonization of Culture. *Anthropology Newsletter,* 44(2), Feb.

Meskell, Lynn, ed. 2009. *Cosmopolitan archaeologies.* Durham, NC: Duke University Press.

Meunier, Jacques, and A. M. Savarin. 1994. *The Amazon chronicles.* Translated by Carol Christensen. San Francisco: Mercury House.

Mielke, James H., Lyle W. Konigsberg, and John H. Relethford. 2011. *Human biological variation.* New York and Oxford: Oxford University Press.

Mignolo, Walter D. 2002. The many faces of cosmo-polis: Border thinking and critical cosmopolitanism. In *Cosmopolitanism,* ed. Carol Breckenridge, Sheldon Pollock, Homi Bhaba, and Dipeesh Chakrabarty, 157–87. Durham, NC: Duke University Press.

Miller, Barbara Diane. 1993. The anthropology of sex and gender hierarchies. In *Sex and gender hierarchies,* ed. Barbara Diane Miller, 3–31. Cambridge: Cambridge University Press.

Miller, Daniel. 1995. Consumption and commodities. *Annual Review of Anthropology* 24:141–61.

Miller, Daniel. 1998. Coca-Cola: A black sweet drink from Trinidad. In *Material cultures: Why some things matter,* ed. Daniel Miller, 169–88. Chicago: University of Chicago Press.

Miller, Daniel, and Don Slater. 2000. *The Internet: An ethnographic approach.* Oxford: Berg.

Milton, Katherine. 1993. Diet and primate evolution. *Scientific American* 269(2):86–93.

Miracle, Andrew. 1991. Aymara joking behavior. *Play and Culture* 4(2): 144–52.

Mitchell-Kernan, Claudia. 1972. On the status of black English for native speakers: An assessment of attitudes and values. In *Functions of language in the classroom,* ed. C. Cazden, V. John, and D. Hymes, 195–210. New York: Teachers College Press.

Mitra, Subrata. 1994. Caste, democracy and the politics of community formation in India. In *Contextualizing caste: Post-Dumontian approaches,* ed. Mary Searle-Chatterjee and Ursula Sharma, 49–71. Oxford: Blackwell Publishers/Sociological Review.

Miyamoto, M. M., and M. Goodman. 1990. DNA systematics and evolution of primates. *Annual Review of Ecology and Systematics* 2:197–220.

Modood, Tariq. 1997. Introduction: The politics of multiculturalism in the new Europe. In *The politics of multiculturalism in the new Europe: Racism, identity, and community,* ed. Tariq Modood and Pnina Werbner, 1–25. London: Zed Books.

Molnar, S. 1992. *Human variation: Races, types, and ethnic groups,* 3rd ed. Englewood Cliffs, NJ: Prentice Hall.

Molnar, Stephen. 2001. *Human variation.* New York: Prentice-Hall.

Moore, Sally Falk. 2005. Comparisons: Possible and impossible. *Annual Review of Anthropology* 34:1–11.

Morbeck, Mary Ellen. 1997. Life history, the individual and evolution. In *The evolutionary female: A life-history perspective,* ed. Mary Ellene Morbeck, Alison Galloway, and Adrienne Zihlman, 3–14. Princeton, NJ: Princeton University Press.

Morgan, Lewis Henry. [1877] 1963. *Ancient society.* Cleveland, OH: Meridian Books.

Morgan, Marcyliena. 1995. Theories and politics in African American English. *Annual Review of Anthropology* 23:325–45.

Morgan, Marcyliena. 1997. Commentary on Ebonics. *Anthropology Newsletter* 38(3):8.

Morgan, Marcyliena. 2002. *Language, discourse, and power in African American culture.* Cambridge: Cambridge University Press.

Morris, Craig. 1988. Progress and prospect in the archaeology of the Inca. In *Peruvian prehistory*, ed. R. Keatinge, 233–56. Cambridge: Cambridge University Press.

Morwood M., et al. 2004. Archaeology and age of a new hominin from Flores in eastern Indonesia. *Nature* 431: 1087–91.

Nanda, Serena. 1994. An alternative sex and gender role. In *Third sex, third gender*, ed. Gilbert Herdt, 373–417. New York: Zone Books.

Niezen, Ronald. 2003. *The origins of indigenism: Human rights and the politics of identity.* Berkeley: University of California Press.

Nishida, Toshisada, and Mariko Hiraiwa-Hasegawa. 1987. Chimpanzees and bonobos: Cooperative relationships among males. In *Primate societies*, ed. Barbara Smuts, Dorothy Cheney, Robert Seyfarth, Richard Wrangham, and Thomas Struhsaker, 165–77. Chicago: University of Chicago Press.

Nissen, H. 1988. *The early history of the ancient Near East, 9000–2000 B.C.* Chicago: University of Chicago Press.

Nixon, Ron. 2007. DNA tests find branches but few roots. *New York Times*, November 25.

Nordstrom, Carolyn. 1993. Treating the wounds of war. *Cultural Survival Quarterly* 17 (2):28–30.

Ochs, Elinor. 1986. Introduction. In *Language socialization across cultures*, ed. Bambi Schieffelin and Elinor Ochs, 1–13. Cambridge: Cambridge University Press.

Odade, Kennedy. 2010. Slumdog tourism. *New York Times*, August 2010, A25.

Odling-Smee, F. J. 1994. Niche construction, evolution and culture. In *Companion encyclopedia of anthropology: Humanity, culture, and social life*, ed. Tim Ingold. London: Routledge.

Odling-Smee, F. John, Kevin L. Laland, and Marcus W. Feldman. 2003. *Niche construction: The neglected process in evolution.* Princeton, NJ: Princeton University Press.

O'Donnell, Guillermo, and Philippe Schmitter. 1986. *Tentative conclusions about uncertain democracies.* Baltimore, MD: Johns Hopkins University Press.

Omohundro, John. 2000. *Careers in anthropology.* New York: McGraw-Hill.

Ong, Aihwa. 2002. The Pacific shuttle: Family, citizenship, and capital circuits. In *The anthropology of globalization*, ed. Jonathan Xavier Inda and Renato Rosaldo, 172–97. Malden, MA: Blackwell.

Ortner, Sherry. 1973. On key symbols. *American Anthropologist* 75(5):1338–46.

Ortner, S. 1974. Is female to male as nature is to culture? In *Woman, culture, and society*, ed. M. Z. Rosaldo and L. Lamphere. Stanford, CA: Stanford University Press.

Ortony, Andrew. 1979. Metaphor: A multidimensional problem. In *Metaphor and thought*, ed. Andrew Ortony, 1–18. Cambridge: Cambridge University Press.

Oyama, S., P. Griffiths, and R. Gray, eds. 2001. *Cycles of contingency: Developmental systems and evolution.* Cambridge, MA: MIT Press.

Oxnard C., P. J. Obendorf, and B. J. Kefford. 2010. Post-cranial skeletons of hypothyroid cretins show a similar anatomical mosaic as *Homo floresiensis*. *PLoS ONE* 5(9):e13018. doi:10.1371/journal.pone.0013018

Pagels, Hans. 1985. *Perfect symmetry.* New York: Simon & Schuster, Inc.

Parkin, David. 1990. Guest editorial in *Cultural anthropology: A perspective on the human condition*, by Emily Schultz and Robert Lavenda, 90–91. 2d ed. St. Paul: West.

Parsons, Jeffrey R., and Charles M. Hastings. 1988. The late intermediate period. In *Peruvian prehistory*, ed. R. Keatinge, 190–229. Cambridge: Cambridge University Press.

Pennington, Renee. 1992. Did food increase fertility: Evaluation of !Kung and Herero history. *Human Biology* 64:497–501.

Pineda, Rosa Fung. 1988. The late preceramic and initial period. In *Peruvian Prehistory*, ed. R. Keatinge, 67–96. Cambridge: Cambridge University Press.

Plotkin, Henry. 2003. *The imagined world made real.* New Brunswick, NJ: Rutgers University Press.

Polanyi, Karl. 1977. *The livelihood of man.* New York: Academic Press.

Potts, Richard. 1993. Archaeological interpretations of early hominid behavior and ecology. In *The origin and evolution of humans and humanness*, ed. D. Tab Rasmussen, 49–74. Boston: Jones and Bartlett.

Potts, Rick. 1996. *Humanity's descent.* New York: William Morrow.

Price, T. Douglas. 1995. Social inequality at the origins of agriculture. In *Foundations of social inequality*, ed. T. Douglas Price and Gary M. Feinman. New York: Plenum Press.

Price, T. Douglas, and Anne Birgitte Gebauer, eds. 1995. *Last hunters, first farmers.* Santa Fe, NM: SAR Press.

Rabinow, Paul. 1977. *Reflections on fieldwork in Morocco.* Berkeley: University of California Press.

Raymond, J. Scott. 1988. A view from the tropical forest. In *Peruvian prehistory*, ed. R. Keatinge, 279–300. Cambridge: Cambridge University Press.

Redford, Kent H. 1993. The ecologically noble savage. In *Talking about people*, ed. W. A. Haviland and R. J. Gordon, 11–13. Mountain View, CA: Mayfield.

Reeves, Edward, Billie DeWalt, and Kathleen DeWalt. 1987. The International Sorghum/Millet Research Project. In *Anthropological praxis*, ed. Robert Wolfe and Shirley Fiske, 72–83. Boulder, CO: Westview Press.

Reeves-Ellington, Richard H. 1993. Using cultural skills for cooperative advantage in Japan. *Human Organization* 52(2):203–16.

Reich, David, Richard E. Green, Martin Kircher, et al. 2010. Genetic history of an archaic hominin group from Denisova Cave in Siberia. *Nature* 468:1053–1060.

Reichel-Dolmatoff, Gerardo. 1971. *Amazonian cosmos: The sexual and religious symbolism of the Tukano indians.* Chicago: University of Chicago Press.

Relethford, John. 2001. *Genetics and the search for modern human origins.* New York: Wiley.

Renfrew, Colin, and Paul Bahn. 2008. *Archaeology: Theories, methods and practice.* 5th ed. London: Thames and Hudson.

Rezende, Claudia Barcellos. 1999. Building affinity through friendship. In *The anthropology of friendship*, ed. Sandra Bell and Simon Coleman, 79–97. Oxford: Berg.

Rice, Dan Stephen, and Prudence M. Rice. 1993. Lessons from the Maya. In *Talking about people*, ed. William Haviland and Robert J. Gordon, 81–91. Mountain View, CA: Mayfield. First published in *Latin American Research Review* 19(3, 1984):7–34.

Richerson, Peter, and Robert Boyd. 2005. *Not by genes alone: How culture transformed human evolution.* Chicago: University of Chicago Press.

Richerson, Peter, Robert Boyd, and Joseph Henrich. 2003. Cultural evolution of human cooperation. In *Genetic and cultural evolution of cooperation*, ed. Peter Hammerstein, 357–88. Cambridge, MA: MIT Press.

Rick, John W. 1988. The character and context of highland preceramic society. In *Peruvian prehistory*, ed. R. Keatinge, 3–40. Cambridge: Cambridge University Press.

Rightmire, G. Philip. 1990. *The Evolution of Homo erectus.* Cambridge: Cambridge University Press.

Rightmire, G. Philip. 1995. Diversity within the genus *Homo*. In *Paleoclimate and evolution, with emphasis on human origins*, ed. Elisabeth Vrba, George Denton, Timothy Partridge, and Lloyd Burckle. 483–92. New Haven, CT: Yale University Press.

Rindos, David. 1984. *The origins of agriculture: An evolutionary perspective.* New York: Academic Press.

Ringrose, Katheryn. 1994. Living in the shadows: Eunuchs and gender in Byzantium. In *Third sex, third gender*, ed. Gilbert Herdt, 85–109. New York: Zone Books.

Roberts, D.F. 1968. Genetic effects of population size reduction. *Nature* 220:1084–88.

Rodriguez, Clara. 1994. Challenging racial hegemony: Puerto Ricans in the United States. In *Race*, ed. Stephen Gregory and Roger Sanjek, 131–45. New Brunswick, NJ: Rutgers University Press.

Rogers, A. R., D. Iltis, and S. Wooding. 2004. Genetic variation at the MCIR locus and the time since loss of human body hair. *Current Anthropology* 45:105–7.

Romero, Simon. 2009. Protestors gird for long fight over opening Peru's Amazon. *New York Times*, June 12.

Rosas, A., C. Martinez-Maza, M. Bastir, et al. 2006. Paleobiology and comparative morphology of a late Neandertal simple from El Sidron, Asturias, Spain. *Proceedings of the National Academy of Sciences* 103:15266–15271.

Roscoe, Will. 1994. How to become a berdache: Toward a unified analysis of gender diversity. In *Third sex, third gender*, ed. Gilbert Herdt, 329–72. New York: Zone Books.

Rose, Kenneth. 1994. The earliest primates. *Evolutionary anthropology*, 3(5):159–73.

Rothwell, Norman V. 1977. *Human Genetics*. Englewood Cliffs, NJ: Prentice-Hall.

Rouhani, Shahin. 1989. Molecular genetics and the pattern of human evolution: Plausible and implausible models. In *The human revolution*, ed. Robert S.O. Mellars and C. Stringer, 47–61. Princeton, NJ: Princeton University Press.

Rubin, Jeffrey W. 1997. *Decentering the regime: Ethnicity, radicalism, and democracy in Juchitán, Mexico*. Durham, NC: Duke University Press.

Ruvolo, Maryellen, and David Pilbeam. 1986. Hominoid evolution: molecular and palaeontological patterns. In *Major topics in primate and human evolution*, ed. B. Wood, L. Martin, and P. Andrews, 157–60. Cambridge: Cambridge University Press.

SAGA (Support for African/Asian Great Apes). 2005. http://www.saga-jp.org (accessed August 24, 2006).

Sahlins, Marshall. 1972. *Stone Age economics*. Chicago: Aldine.

Sahlins, Marshall. 1976. *Culture and practical reason*. Chicago: University of Chicago Press.

Sanderson, John. 2007. Reconciliation and the failure of neo-liberal globalisation. In *Coercive reconciliation: stabilise, normalise, exit Aboriginal Australia*, ed. Jon Altman and Melinda Hinkson. North Carlton, Australia: Arena Publications Association.

Sanjek, Roger. 1994. The enduring inequalities of race. In *Race*, ed. Stephen Gregory and Roger Sanjek, 1–17. New Brunswick, NJ: Rutgers University Press.

Sapir, Edward. 1921. *Language*. New York, NY: Harvest/HBJ.

Sapir, Edward. [1933] 1966. *Culture, language, and personality*, ed. David Mandelbaum. Berkeley: University of California Press.

Scheper-Hughes, Nancy. 1994. Embodied knowledge: Thinking with the body in critical medical anthropology. In *Assessing cultural anthropology*, ed. Robert Borofsky, 229–42. New York: McGraw-Hill.

Schiffauer, Werner. 1997. Islam as a civil religion: Political culture and the organisation of diversity in Germany. In *The politics of multiculturalism in the new Europe: Racism, identity, and community*, ed. Tariq Modood and Pnina Werbner, 147–66. London: Zed Books.

Schiller, Nina Glick, and Georges Fouron. 2001. *Georges woke up laughing: Long-distance nationalism and the search for home*. Durham, NC: Duke University Press.

Schiller, Nina Glick, and Georges Fouron. 2002. Long-distance nationalism defined. In *The anthropology of politics*, ed. Joan Vincent, 356–65. Malden, MA: Blackwell.

Schneider, David. 1968. *American kinship: A cultural account*. Englewood Cliffs, NJ: Prentice-Hall.

Schultz, Emily. 1984. From pagan to Pullo: Ethnic identity change in northern Cameroon. *Africa* 54(1):46–64.

Schultz, Emily. 1990. *Dialogue at the margins: Whorf, Bakhtin, and linguistic relativity*. New Directions in Anthropological Writing. Madison: University of Wisconsin Press.

Schultz, Emily. 2009. Resolving the anti-antievolutionism dilemma: A brief for relational evolutionary thinking in anthropology. *American Anthropologist* 111(2):224–37.

Schwartzman, Helen. 1978. *Transformations: The anthropology of children's play*. New York: Plenum Press.

Scott, James. 1987. *Weapons of the weak*. New Haven, CT: Yale University Press.

Scott, James C. 1990. *Domination and the arts of resistance*. New Haven, CT: Yale University Press.

Semaw, S., J. Renne, J. W. K. Harris, et al. 1997. 2.5-million-year-old stone tools from Gona, Ethiopia. *Nature* 385:333–36.

Senut B., et al. 2001. First hominid from the Miocene (Lukeino Formation, Kenya). *Comptes Rendus Des Seances de l'Academie Des Sciences* 332:137–44.

Serre, D., A. Langaney, M. Chech, et al. 2004. No evidence of Neandertal mtDNA contribution to early modern humans. *PLoS Biol.* 2:313–317.

Service, Elman. 1962. *Primitive social organization*. New York: Random House.

Shanks, Michael, and Christopher Tilley. 1987. *Social theory and archaeology* Oxford: Polity Press.

Sharma, Ursula. 1999. *Caste*. Buckingham, UK: Open University Press.

Sharp, Lesley. 2006. *Strange harvest: Organ transplants, denatured bodies, and the transformed self*. Berkeley: University of California Press.

Sheehan, Elizabeth A. 1997. Victorian clitoridectomy: Isaac Baker Brown and his harmless operative procedure. In *The gender/sexuality reader*, ed. Roger Lancaster and Micaela De Leonardo, 324–34. New York: Routledge.

Shepherd, Gil. 1987. Rank, gender, and homosexuality: Mombasa as a key to understanding sexual options. In *The cultural construction of sexuality*, ed. Pat Caplan, 240–70. London: Tavistock.

Shipman, Pat. 1984. Scavenger hunt. *Natural History* (April):22–27.

Shostak, Marjorie. 1981. *Nisa: The life and words of a !Kung woman*. New York: Vintage.

Silk, Joan. 2003. Cooperation without counting: The puzzle of friendship. In *Genetic and cultural evolution of cooperation*, ed. Peter Hammerstein, 37–54. Cambridge, MA: MIT Press.

Silverstein, Michael. 1976. Shifters, linguistic categories, and cultural description. In *Meaning in anthropology*, ed. Keith Basso and Henry Selby, 11–55. Albuquerque: University of New Mexico Press.

Silverstein, Michael. 1985. The functional stratification of language and ontogenesis. In *Culture, communication, and cognition: Vygotskian perspectives*, ed. James Wertsch, 205–35. Cambridge: Cambridge University Press.

Simons, Elwyn L. 1985. Origins and characteristics of the first hominids. In *Ancestors: The hard evidence*, ed. E. Delson, 37–41. New York: Alan R. Liss.

Simons, Elwyn, and D. Tab Rasmussen. 1994. A whole new world of ancestors: Eocene australopithecines from Africa. *Evolutionary Anthropology* 3(4):129–39.

Singer, Merrill. 1998. The development of critical medical anthropology: Implications for biological anthropology. In *Building a new biocultural synthesis*, ed. Alan H. Goodman and Thomas L. Leatherman, 93–123. Ann Arbor: University of Michigan Press.

Singer, Natasha. 2007. Is looking your age now taboo? *New York Times*, 1 March, E1, E3.

Sjovold, Torstein. 1993. Frost and found. *Natural History* 4:60–64.

Slobin, Dan. 1987. Thinking for speaking. *Proceedings of the Berkeley Linguistics Society* 13:435–44.

Slobin, Dan. 2003. Language and thought online: Cognitive consequences of linguistic relativity. In *Language in mind: Advances in the study of language and thought*, ed. Dedre Gentner and Susan Goldin-Meadow, 157–91. Cambridge, MA: MIT Press.

Smart, Alan. 1999. Expressions of interest: Friendship and *Guanzi* in Chinese societies. In *The anthropology of friendship*, ed. Sandra Bell and Simon Coleman, 119–36. Oxford: Berg.

Smedley, Audrey. 1995. *Race in North America: Origin and evolution of a worldview*. Boulder, CO: Westview Press.

Smedley, Audrey. 1998. "Race" and the construction of human identity. *American Anthropologist* 100(3):690–702.

Smith, Andrea. 1994. For all those who were Indian in a former life. *Cultural Survival Quarterly* (Winter):71.

Smith, Bruce. 1995. *The emergence of agriculture*. New York: Scientific American Library.

Smith, Bruce. 1995. The origins of agriculture in the Americas. *Evolutionary Anthropology* (5):174–84.

Smith, Gavin A., and R. Brooke Thomas. 1998. What could be: Biocultural anthropology for the next generation. In *Building a new biocultural synthesis*, ed. Alan H. Goodman and Thomas L. Leatherman, 451–73. Ann Arbor: University of Michigan Press.

Smith, M. G. [1954] 1981. Introduction. In *Baba of Karo*, by Mary Smith. New Haven, CT: Yale University Press.

Smith, Wilfred Cantwell. 1982. *Towards a world theology*. Philadelphia: Westminster.

Spector, Janet D. 1993. *What this awl means*. St. Paul: Minnesota Historical Society Press.

Spencer, Jonathan. 2000. On not becoming a "Terrorist": Problems of memory, agency, and community in the Sri Lankan conflict. In *Violence and subjectivity*, ed. Veena Das, Arthur

Kleinman, Mamphela Ramphele, and Pamela Reynolds, 120–40. Berkeley: University of California Press.

Spiro, Melford. 1977. *Kinship and marriage in Burma: A cultural and psychodynamic account.* Berkeley: University of California Press.

Stammbach, Eduard. 1987. Desert, forest and montane baboons: Multilevel societies. In *Primate societies,* ed. Barbara Smuts, Dorothy Cheney, Robert Seyfarth, Richard Wrangham, and Thomas Struhsaker, 112–20. Chicago: University of Chicago Press.

Stang, John. 2009. Kennewick Man's secrets still mostly secret. *Seattle Post Intelligencer,* July 19.

Stanley, Steven M. 1981. *The new evolutionary timetable.* New York: Basic Books.

Starn, Orin. 1999. *Nightwatch: The making of a movement in the Peruvian Andes.* Durham, NC: Duke University Press.

Steiner, Christopher. 1994. *African art in transit.* Cambridge: Cambridge University Press.

Stewart, Charles, and Rosalind Shaw. 1994. *Syncretism/antisyncretism.* London: Routledge.

Stewart, Kelly J, and Alexander H. Harcourt. 1987. Gorillas: Variation in female relationships. In *Primate Societies,* ed. Barbara Smuts, Dorothy Cheney, Robert Seyfarth, Richard Wrangham, and Thomas Struhsaker, 155–64. Chicago: University of Chicago Press.

Stocks, Anthony. 2005. Too much for too few: Problems of indigenous land rights in America. *Annual Review of Anthropology* 34:85–104.

Strathern, Marilyn. 1988. *The gender of the gift.* Berkeley: University of California Press.

Strathern, Marilyn. 1992. *Reproducing the future: Anthropology, kinship, and the new reproductive technologies.* New York: Routledge.

Strier, Karen. 1997. An American primatologist abroad in Brazil. In *Primate encounters: Models of science, gender, and society,* ed. Shirley Strum and Linda Fedigan, 194–207. Chicago: University of Chicago Press.

Stringer, Chris, and Peter Andrews. 2005. *The complete world of human evolution.* London, New York: Thames and Hudson.

Struhsaker, T., and L. Leland. 1987. Colobines: Infanticide by adult males. In *Primate Societies,* ed. Barbara Smuts, Dorothy Cheney, Robert Seyfarth, Richard Wrangham, and Thomas Struhsaker, 83–97. Chicago: University of Chicago Press.

Strum, Shirley, Donald G. Lindburg, and David Hamburg, eds. 1999. *The new physical anthropology: Science, humanism, and critical reflection.* Upper Saddle River, NJ: Prentice Hall.

Suplee, Curt. 1997. Find may rewrite America's prehistory. *Washington Post,* February 11, A2.

Susman, Randall L., Jack T. Stern, Jr., and William L. Jungers. 1985. Locomotor adaptations in the Hadar hominids. In *Ancestors: The hard evidence,* ed. E. Delson, 184–92. New York: Alan R. Liss.

Sussman, Robert. 1991. Primate origins and the evolution of angiosperms. *American Journal of Physical Anthropology* 23:209–23.

Tamari, Tal. 1991. The development of caste systems in West Africa. *Journal of African History* 32:221–50.

Tambiah, Stanley J. 1989. The politics of ethnicity. *American Ethnologist* 16(2):335–49.

Tattersall, Ian. 1998. *Becoming human: Evolution and human uniqueness.* San Diego: Harcourt, Brace.

Tattersall, Ian. 2009. *The fossil trail.* 2nd ed. New York: Oxford University Press.

Taylor, Julie. 1987. Tango. *Cultural Anthropology* 2(4):481–93.

Tcherkézoff, Serge. 1998. Is aristocracy good for democracy? A contemporary debate in Western Samoa. In *Pacific answers to Western hegemony: Cultural practices of identity construction,* ed. Jürg Wassmann, 417–34. Oxford: Berg.

Templeton, Alan R. 1993. The "Eve" hypothesis: A genetic critique and reanalysis. *American Anthropologist* 95:51–72.

Thomas, Nicholas. 1991. *Entangled objects.* Cambridge, MA: Harvard University Press.

Thomas, Nicholas. 1996. Cold fusion. *American Anthropologist* 98:9–25.

Thorne, Alan G., and Milford H. Wolpoff. 1992. The multiregional evolution of humans. *Scientific American* (April):76–83.

Tonkinson, Robert. 1998. National identity: Australia after Mabo. In *Pacific answers to Western hegemony: Cultural practices of identity construction,* ed. Jürg Wassmann, 287–310. Oxford: Berg.

Trigger, Bruce. 1993. *Early civilizations: Ancient Egypt in context.* Cairo: American University in Cairo Press.

Trinkaus, Erik. 1984. Neanderthal public morphology and gestation length. *Current Anthropology* 25:508–14.

Trotter, Robert. 1987. A case of lead poisoning from folk remedies in Mexican American communities. In *Anthropological praxis,* ed. Robert Wolfe and Shirley Fiske, 146–59. Boulder, CO: Westview Press.

Trouillot, Michel-Rolph. 1991. Anthropology and the savage slot: The poetics and politics of otherness. In *Recapturing anthropology,* ed. Richard Fox, 17–44. Santa Fe, NM: SAR Press.

Trouillot, Michel-Rolph. 1994. Culture, color and politics in Haiti. In *Race,* ed. Stephen Gregory and Roger Sanjek, 146–74. New Brunswick, NJ: Rutgers University Press.

Tsing, Anna Lowenhaupt. 2005. *Friction: An ethnography of global connection.* Princeton, NJ: Princeton University Press.

Turnbull, Colin. 1961. *The forest people.* New York: Simon & Schuster.

Turner, Victor. 1969. *The ritual process.* Chicago: Aldine.

Tylor, E. B. [1871] 1958. *Primitive culture.* New York: Harper and Row.

Underwood, J.H. 1979. *Human variation and human microevolution.* Englewood Cliffs, NJ: Prentice-Hall.

Valentine, Bettylou. 1978. *Hustling and other hard work.* New York: Free Press.

Valentine, Charles. 1978. Introduction. In *Hustling and other hard work,* by Bettylou Valentine, 1–10. New York: Free Press.

van den Berghe, Pierre. 1970. Race, class, and ethnicity in South Africa. In *Social stratification in Africa,* ed. Arthur Tuden and Leonard Plotnikov, 345–71. New York: Free Press.

van der Veer. 1997. "The enigma of arrival": Hybridity and authenticity in the global space. In *Debating cultural hybridity: Multicultural identities and the politics of anti-racism,* ed. Pnina Werbner and Tariq Modood, 90–105. London: Zed Books.

Van Gennep, Arnold. 1960. *The rites of passage.* Chicago: University of Chicago Press.

van Willigen, John, and V. C. Channa. 1991. Law, custom, and crimes against women. *Human Organization* 50(4):369–77.

Vaughan, James. 1970. Caste systems in the western Sudan. In *Social stratification in Africa,* ed. Arthur Tuden and Leonard Plotnikov, 59–92. New York: Free Press.

Vaughan, James. 1973. Engkyagu as artists in Marghi society. In *The traditional artist in African societies,* ed. Warren d'Azevedo, 162–93. Bloomington: Indiana University Press.

Vincent, Joan. 2002. Introduction. In *The anthropology of politics,* ed. Joan Vincent, 1–13. Malden, MA: Blackwell.

Voloshinov, V. N. [1926] 1987. Discourse in life and discourse in art. In *Freudianism,* ed. and trans. I. R. Titunik, in collaboration with Neil H. Bruss, 93–116. Bloomington: Indiana University Press.

Vygotsky, Lev. 1978. *Mind in society: The development of higher psychological processes.* Cambridge, MA: Harvard University Press.

Walker, Alan. 1993. The origin of the genus *Homo.* In *The origin and evolution of humans and humanness,* ed. D. Tab Rasmussen. Sudbury, MA: Jones and Bartlett.

Wallace, Anthony F. C. 1966. *Religion: An anthropological view.* New York: Random House.

Wallace, A. F. C. 1972. *The death and rebirth of the Seneca.* New York: Vintage.

Wallerstein, Immanuel. 1974. *The modern-world system: Capitalist agriculture and the origins of the European world-economy in the sixteenth century.* New York: Academic Press.

Wallmann, Joel. 1992. *Aping language.* Cambridge, Cambridge University Press.

Warner, W. Lloyd. 1936. American caste and class. *American Sociological Review* 42(2):237–57.

Washburn, Sherwood, and C.S. Lancaster. 1968. The evolution of hunting. In *Man the hunter,* ed. R. Lee and I. DeVore, 293–303. Chicago: Aldine.

Waters, Michael, R., Steven L. Forman, Thomas A. Jennings, et al. 2011. The Buttermilk Creek Complex and the origins of Clovis at the Debra L. Friedkin Site, Texas. *Science* 331:1599–1603.

Weatherford, Jack. 1988. *Indian givers: How the Indians of the Americas transformed the world.* New York: Fawcett.

Webster, D. 1975. Warfare and the evolution of the state: A reconsideration. *American Antiquity* 40:471–75.

Weiner, Annette. 1980. Stability in banana leaves: Colonization and women in Kiriwina, Trobriand Islands. In *Women and colonization: Anthropological perspectives*, ed. Mona Etienne and Eleanor Leacock, 270–93. New York: Praeger.

Weiner, Annette. 1988. *The Trobrianders of Papua New Guinea*. New York: Holt, Rinehart, and Winston.

Weiner, Annette. 1990. Guest editorial in *Cultural anthropology: A perspective on the human condition*, by Emily Schultz and Robert Lavenda, 392–93. 2nd ed. St. Paul: West.

Weinker, Curtis. 1995. Biological anthropology: The current state of the discipline. In *Biological anthropology: The state of the science*, Noel T. Boaz and Linda Wolfe. Bend, OR: International Institute for Human Evolutionary Research.

Weismantel, Mary. 1995. Making kin: Kinship theory and Zumbagua adoptions. *American Ethnologist* 22(4):685–709.

Wenke, Robert J. 1999. *Patterns in prehistory*, 4th ed. Oxford: Oxford University Press.

Wenke, Robert J., and Deborah I. Olszewski. 2007. *Patterns in prehistory: Humankind's first three million years*, 5th ed. New York: Oxford University Press.

Werbner, Pnina. 1997. Introduction: The Dialectics of Cultural Hybridity. In *Debating cultural hybridity: multi-cultural identities and the politics of anti-racism*, ed. Pnina Werbner and Tariq Modood. London: Zed Books.

West-Eberhard, Mary Jane. 2003. *Developmental plasticity and evolution*. Oxford: Oxford University Press.

Weston, Kath. 1991. *Families we choose: Lesbians, gays, kinship*. New York: Columbia University Press.

Weston, Kath. 1995. Forever is a long time: Romancing the real in gay kinship ideologies. In *Naturalizing power*, ed. Sylvia Yanagisako and Carol Delaney, 87–110. New York: Routledge.

White, Leslie. 1949. *The science of culture*. New York: Grove Press.

White, T. D., B. Asfaw, Y. Beyene, Y. Haile-Selassie, C. O. Lovejoy, G. Suwa, and G. Wolde-Gabriel. 2009. *Ardipithecus ramidus* and the paleobiology of early hominids. *Science* 326:64, 75–86.

White, T. D., G. Suwa, and B. Asfaw. 1994. *Australopithecus ramidus*, a new species of early hominid from Aramis, Ethiopia. *Nature* 371:306–12.

White, Tim D., Gen Suwa, William K. Hart, Robert C. Walter, Giday WoldeGabriel, Jean de Heinzelin, J. Desmond Clark, Berhane Asfaw, and Elisabeth Vrba. 1993. New discoveries of *Australopithecus* at Maka in Ethiopia. *Nature* 366 (18 November):261–65.

Whitten, Patricia L. 1987. Infants and adult males. In *Primate societies*, ed. Barbara Smuts, Dorothy Cheney, Robert Seyfarth, Richard Wrangham, and Thomas Struhsaker, 343–57. Chicago: University of Chicago Press.

Whorf, Benjamin Lee. 1956. *Language, thought, and reality*. Cambridge, MA: M.I.T. Press.

Wieringa, Saskia, and Evelyn Blackwood. 1999. Introduction. In *Female desires: Same sex relations and transgender practices across cultures*, ed. Evelyn Blackwood and Saska Wieringa, 1–38. New York: Columbia University Press.

Wilford, John Noble. 1996. In Australia, signs of artists who predate *Homo sapiens*. *New York Times*, September 21.

Wilk, Richard. 1996. *Economies and cultures: Foundations of economic anthropology*. Boulder, CO: Westview Press.

Williams, Brackette F. 1989. A class act: Anthropology and the race to nation across ethnic terrain. *Annual Review of Anthropology* 18:401–44.

Williams, Brett. 1984. Why migrant women feed their husbands tamales: Foodways as a basis for a revisionist view of Tejano family life. In *Ethnic and regional foodways in the United States*, ed. Linda Keller Brown and Kay Mussell. Knoxville: University of Tennessee Press.

Wilson, Allan C., and Rebecca L. Cann. 1992. The recent African genesis of humans. *Scientific American* (April):68–73.

Wimsatt, William C., and J. C. Schank. 1988. Two constraints on the evolution of complex adaptations and the means for their avoidance. In *Evolutionary progress*, ed. M. Nitecki, 231–73. Chicago: University of Chicago Press.

Witherspoon, Gary. 1975. *Navajo kinship and marriage*. Chicago: University of Chicago Press.

Wittfogel, Karl. 1957. *Oriental despotism: A comparative study of total power*. New Haven, CT: Yale University Press.

Wolcott, Harry F. 1999. *Ethnography: A way of seeing*. Walnut Creek, CA: AltaMira Press.

Wolf, Eric. 1982. *Europe and the people without history*. Berkeley: University of California Press.

Wolf, Eric. 1994. Facing power: Old insights, new questions. In *Assessing cultural anthropology*, ed. Robert Borofsky, 218–28. New York: McGraw-Hill.

Wolfe, Linda. 1995. Current research in field primatology. In *Biological anthropology: The state of the science*, Noel T. Boaz and Linda Wolfe, 149–67. Bend, OR: International Institute for Human Evolutionary Research.

Wolpoff, Milford H. 1985. Human evolution at the peripheries: The pattern at the eastern edge. In *Hominid evolution: Past, present and future*, ed. P. V. Tobias, 355–65. New York: Alan R. Liss.

Wolpoff, Milford H. 1989. Multiregional evolution: The fossil alternative to Eden. In *The human revolution*, ed. P. A. Mellars and C. Stringer, 62–108. Princeton, NJ: Princeton University Press.

Woodward, V. 1992. *Human heredity and society*. St. Paul, MN: West.

Woolard, Kathryn A. 1998. Introduction: Language ideology as a field of inquiry. In *Language ideologies: Practice and theory*, ed. Bambi Schieffelin, Kathryn Woolard, and Paul V. Kroskrity, 3–47. New York: Oxford University Press.

Woost, Michael D. 1993. Nationalizing the local past in Sri Lanka: Histories of nation and development in a Sinhalese village. *American Ethnologist* 20(3):502–21.

Wrangham, Richard. 2009. *Catching fire: How cooking made us human*. New York: Basic Books.

Yuval-Davis, Nira. 1997. Ethnicity, gender relations, and multiculturalism. In *Debating cultural hybridity: Multicultural identities and the politics of anti-racism*, ed. Pnina Werbner and Tariq Modood, 193–208. London: Zed Books.

Zeder, Melinda A., and Bruce D. Smith. 2009. A conversation on agricultural origins. *Current Anthropology* 50(5):681–91.

Credits

Index